WORLD TRADE ORGANIZATION

Dispute Settlement Reports

2005
Volume VI

Pages 2293-2746

CAMBRIDGE
UNIVERSITY PRESS

TABLE OF CONTENTS

Page

TABLE OF ANNEXES

ANNEX J

ANSWERS OF THIRD PARTIES TO THE QUESTIONS FROM THE PANEL AND FROM OTHER THIRD PARTIES', AND COMMENTS THERETO

Contents		Page

ANNEX K

COMMUNICATIONS FROM PARTIES AND THIRD PARTIES

ANNEX L

COMMUNICATIONS FROM THE PANEL

ANNEX M

WORKING PROCEDURES AND TIMETABLE OF THE PANEL

[1] Communications included as L-1.4, -1.7, -1.11, -1.12, -1.13 and -1.14 were also sent to 3rd parties.

ANNEX N

REQUEST FOR CONSULTATIONS AND REQUEST FOR THE ESTABLISHMENT OF A PANEL

ANNEX O

LIST OF EXHIBITS

ANNEX J-1

REPLIES BY ARGENTINA TO QUESTIONS POSED BY THE PANEL TO THE THIRD PARTIES FIRST SESSION OF THE FIRST SUBSTANTIVE MEETING OF THE PANEL

11 August 2003

Article 13 of the Agreement on Agriculture

1. Australia has argued that Article 13 of the *Agreement on Agriculture* is an affirmative defence. How do you reconcile this with your view that the conditions in Article 13 are a "prerequisite" to the availability of a right or privilege? Australia Would other third parties have any comments on Australia's assertion? 3rd parties, in particular Argentina, Benin, China, Chinese Taipei

Argentina agrees with Australia that Article 13 of the Agreement on Agriculture is an affirmative defence and that in these proceedings the United States therefore carries the burden of proof on the question of whether its subsidies conform with the terms of Article 13.

According to the Appellate Body in *US-Shirts and Blouses*:

> *" ... the burden of proof rests upon the party, whether complaining or defending, who asserts the affirmative of a particular claim or defence. If that party adduces evidence sufficient to raise a presumption that what is claimed is true, the burden then shifts to the other party, who will fail unless it adduces sufficient evidence to rebut the presumption".*[2]

As stated by Brazil in Paragraph 112 of its first written submission, in the case of claims of violation of the positive obligations of the WTO Agreement, it is the complaining party that has the burden of providing a prima facie case of violation. However, in the case of affirmative defences, such as Articles XX and XI:2(c)(i), the Appellate Body itself established that it is only reasonable that the burden of establishing such a defence should rest upon the party asserting it.[3]

According to the standards established by the Appellate Body,[4] Article 13 of the Agreement on Agriculture is a provision in the nature of an affirmative defence. As such, it does not create new obligations for Members, but limits the scope of certain provisions of the SCM Agreement and the GATT 1994 subject to certain conditions. Nor does it alter the legal nature of Members' measures, but simply permits Members to maintain those measures exempt from actions, if the measures meet the conditions specified in Article 13(a), (b) or (c). As Argentina stated in its Third Party Initial Brief:[5]

---

2 Appellate Body Report, *US – Shirts and Blouses,* WT/DS33/AB/R, p. 14, text at note 16.
3 *Ibid.,* p. 16, text preceding note 23.
4 See paras. 113 to 116 of Brazil's First Written Submission.
5 Argentina's Third Party Initial Brief, para. 14.

"Argentina considers that the provisions contained in Article 13 of the AoA have an exceptional nature. This would imply that the Member who alleges to be protected by the Peace Clause has the burden of proving the fulfilment of its legal requirements. As long as the US does not demonstrate prima facie that it fulfils all the conditions that would allow a protection against a claim by virtue of Article 13 of the AoA, the Panel should consider as appropriate the claims under Article XVI of GATT 1994 or Articles 3, 5 and 6 of the SCM Agreement".

The exceptional nature of Article 13 of the Agreement on Agriculture (AoA) cannot change merely because the conditions justifying it include conformity with rules that create positive obligations for Members (e.g. Article 6 of the AoA). This legal nature comes out clearly in the chapeau of Article 13 of the AoA which begins with the words "*Notwithstanding the provisions of GATT 1994 and the Agreement on Subsidies and Countervailing Measures ...*", providing guidance to the effect that the purpose of the entire Article 13 is to create exceptions, subject to certain conditions, to the provisions of the GATT 1994 and the SCM Agreement.

For example the party claiming defence under Article 13 of the AoA clearly must prove, inter alia, that the domestic support measures which it claims should be exempt from actions based on Articles 5 and 6 of the SCM Agreement and Article XVI of the GATT 1994 do not grant support to a specific commodity in excess of that decided during the 1992 marketing year.

If Article 13 of the AoA did not exist, any domestic support measure would unquestionably be subject to actions based on Articles 5 and 6 of the SCM Agreement and Article XVI of the GATT 1994. The temporary defence accorded by Article 13 is an exception to that situation, and it is therefore up to the claimant to demonstrate that the conditions permitting such defence have been fulfilled.

Mere reference, as one of the conditions justifying the measure, to conformity with a positive obligation of the AoA, cannot alter the exceptional nature that informs all of Article 13.

Article 13(b) of the *Agreement on Agriculture*: Domestic Support Measures

2. Please explain the difference, if any, between the meaning of "defined" and the meaning of "fixed" in the phrase "a defined and fixed base period" in paragraph 6(a) of Annex 2 of the *Agreement on Agriculture*. 3rd parties, in particular Australia, Argentina, Canada, EC, NZ

Argentina considers that while the term "defined" refers to the need for the base period to be clearly determined in the order authorising the payments, the term "fixed" refers to the need for the base period to be identified in terms which prevent it from *being shifted or modified a posteriori*. The term "fixed" indicates that the payments made in accordance with the criteria stipulated in paragraph 6(a) must always rely on the same base period, and no change is possible.

3. Please explain the meaning of "a" in "a defined and fixed base period" in paragraph 6(a) of Annex 2 of the *Agreement on Agriculture*, the meaning of "the" in "the base period" in paragraphs 6(b), (c) and (d), and the difference between these and the phrase "based on the years 1986-88" in Annex 3. 3rd parties, in particular Australia, Argentina, Canada, EC, NZ

The purpose of the term "a" in paragraph 6(a) of Annex 2 of the Agreement on Agriculture is to establish the obligation for Members to identify a single period, which may cover two, three or more years depending on the Member. For example the base periods established by the EU, the United States and Argentina are different with respect to the payments referred to in paragraph 6(a) of Annex 2. However, although different for each Member – the identification of the period is up to the Members in that it is not specified in the text of the Agreement *per se* – the period must be identified by the Member concerned and must remain constant. Otherwise, the choice of the word "a" in this provision would be difficult to explain. If the negotiators of the AoA had not wanted the period to maintain an identity over time, they would have so indicated by using a different preposition, for example, "some" period, indicating that the period could be subject to a certain mobility.

In the case at issue, the United States identified, for the purposes of paragraph 6(a) of Annex 2, the period running from 1986 to 1988, as shown in document G/AG/AGST/USA on pages 1-7, referred to in Part IV of the United States' Schedule of Commitments – Schedule XX.

In paragraph 6(b), (c) and (d), Argentina understands the term "*the* base period" to refer to the base period 1986-1988, the only base period identified in the AoA for domestic support (Annex 3).

"The" base period refers to the base period 1986-1988, since there is no other period for domestic support. Indeed, Article 1(a)(i) also refers to "the" base period, which is none other than the period specified in Annex 3 of the AoA. Article 1(d)(i) and Article 1(h)(i) also mention "the" base period.

In other words, "a" base period is different from "the" base period. Moreover, the second sentence of paragraph 5 of Annex 2 of the AoA requires the adoption of "the" base period established in paragraphs 6(b), (c) and (d), clearly reflecting this difference with paragraph 6(a).

In the case of payments by the United States under paragraph 6 of Annex 2 of the AoA, this distinction is irrelevant since "a" base period in the context of paragraph 6(a) and "the" base period of paragraphs 6(b), (c) and (e) are the same - 1986-1988 - having been so defined by the United States in its Schedule of Commitments.

4. How often can a Member define and fix a base period in accordance with paragraph 6 of Annex 2 of the *Agreement on Agriculture*? 3rd parties, in particular Australia, Argentina, Canada, China, EC, NZ

It is Argentina's understanding that under paragraph 6 of Annex 2 of the Agreement on Agriculture, for each programme a Member may only define and establish a base period once. Otherwise, the term "fixed" would lose all of its relevance.

5. Do you agree that a payment penalty based on crops produced is "related to type of production"? EC

6. Please explain the meaning of the word "criteria" in Article 6.1 and 7.1. What effect, if any, does the use of the word "Accordingly" in paragraph 1 of Annex 2 of the *Agreement on Agriculture* have on the meaning of the preceding sentence? 3rd parties, in particular Australia, Argentina, Canada, EC, NZ

The word "criteria" in Article 6.1 and 7.1 signifies the parameters, rules or precepts which serve to distinguish the domestic support measures that are not subject to reduction.

In relation to the preceding sentence, the use of the word "accordingly" in paragraph 1 of Annex 2 of the Agreement on Agriculture indicates that the basic criteria listed thereafter are a corollary to the "fundamental principle" set forth in the preceding sentence. However, this does *not* imply that the preceding sentence does not contain "stand-alone" obligations.

On the contrary, the domestic support measures for which exemption from the reduction commitments is sought must conform to the two basic criteria (set forth in paragraph 1(a) and (b)), plus the policy-specific criteria and conditions set out in the subsequent paragraphs of Annex 2, in addition to which they must meet "the *fundamental requirement* that they have no, or at most minimal, trade-distorting effects or effects on production". A measure which meets the two criteria set forth in paragraph 1(a) and (b) plus the policy-specific criteria and conditions set out in the subsequent paragraphs of Annex 2 may also violate the general principle. Any other interpretation would deprive of any meaning the first sentence of paragraph 1 of Annex 2, which the text itself qualifies as a "fundamental requirement".

7. Please explain the meaning of the words "the fundamental requirement" as used in paragraph 1 of Annex 2 of the *Agreement on Agriculture*. 3rd parties, in particular Australia, Argentina, Canada, EC, NZ

In Argentina's view, the words "the fundamental requirement" as used in paragraph 1 of Annex 2 signify the establishment of a general mandatory condition governing the establishment and application of any measure whose inclusion in the "Green Box" is claimed.

8. In your oral statement, you emphasize the use of the word "criteria" in other parts of the *Agreement on Agriculture*, as distinct from the reference to "fundamental requirement" in the first sentence of paragraph 1 of Annex 2. Is it the case that sub-paragraphs (a) and (b) of paragraph 1 of Annex 2 are also "criteria"? EC

9. If the first sentence of paragraph 1 of Annex 2 is a stand-alone obligation, does this allow effects-based claims of non-compliance with Annex 2? If so, how does this affect the purpose of Article 13(b)? 3rd parties, in particular Australia, Argentina, Canada, EC, NZ

The first sentence of paragraph 1 of Annex 2 of the AoA contains a stand-alone obligation.

Since the first sentence of paragraph 1 of Annex 2 imposes an obligation by requiring that the measures for which exemption from a reduction commitment is claimed must, as a primary or essential condition, be such that they do not artificially alter trade or production, it permits claims of non-compliance with Annex 2 based on the effects of the domestic support measures, regardless of whether they meet the basic criteria set out in the second sentence of paragraph 1 and with the policy-specific criteria and conditions set out in the rest of Annex 2.

Otherwise, we would be exempting from the reduction commitments measures that might be complying with the two basic criteria set forth in paragraph 1(a) and (b) of Annex 2 plus the policy-specific criteria and conditions set out in the subsequent paragraphs of Annex 2 while at the same time violating the general principle of meeting "the fundamental requirement that they have no, or at most minimal, trade-distorting effects or effects on production."

It might then be possible to evade conformity with the provisions of Article 6 of the AoA or with the level of support to a specific commodity decided during the 1992 marketing year.

The result could be to undermine the purpose of Article 13(b) of exempting from countervailing duties or actions based on Article XVI.I or Articles 5 and 6 of the SCM Agreement only those measures which comply with the conditions set forth therein.

10. If the first sentence of paragraph 1 of Annex 2 is not a stand-alone obligation, then must new, non- or minimally trade-distorting measures that do not conform to the criteria listed in Annex 2 be classified as non-Green Box? 3rd parties, in particular Australia, Argentina, Canada. EC, NZ

Yes. Argentina considers that non- or minimally trade-distorting measures that do not conform to the criteria listed in Annex 2 must be excluded from the Green Box. In other words, the measures which satisfy the fundamental requirement of having no, or at most minimal, trade-distorting effects or effects on production, but which do not meet the criteria established in paragraph 1(a) and (b) of Annex 2 and the policy-specific criteria and conditions set out in the subsequent paragraphs of Annex 2, cannot be exempted from reduction commitments.

11. If the first sentence of paragraph 1 of Annex 2 expresses a general principle which informs the interpretation of the criteria in Annex 2, please explain how this affects the assessment of the direct payments programme's compliance with paragraph 6 of Annex 2. 3rd parties, in particular, Australia, Argentina, Canada, EC, NZ

Argentina considers that there is a clear hierarchy between the two provisions, in which the principal obligation for Members is to ensure that their support programmes, even if they could qualify as decoupled support programmes under paragraph 6 of Annex 2, do not have trade-distorting effects or effects on production, as stipulated in paragraph 1 of the same Annex.

Consequently, even if the Direct Payments programme complies with the requirements of the second sentence of paragraph 1 of Annex 2, if it does not comply with the fundamental requirement laid down in the first sentence, it cannot be considered a Green Box programme.

Argentina agrees with Brazil's statement in paragraphs 183-191 of its first written submission with respect to the strong production and trade-distorting effects of the Direct Payments programme.

12. Where does Article 13(b) require a year-on-year comparison? 3rd parties, in particular Australia, Argentina, Canada, China, EC, NZ

As stated in paragraph 21 of its oral submission, Argentina maintains that the domestic support measures granted during any one of the marketing years of the period covered between the entry into force of the AoA in 1995 and the expiry of Article 13 on 31 December 2003 are relevant for the purpose of determining conformity with Article 13(b), the text of which does not explicitly establish the requirement of a year-on-year comparison.

Thus, the excess support granted during any one of the years of the period of implementation suffices to cancel the protection provided by the Peace Clause.

Nor can a year-on-year comparison be inferred from Article 13 or from its context. Otherwise, at the beginning of each marketing year the Member that had exceeded the level of support in the previous year would be covered by the Peace Clause once again and exempt from any claims.

In practical terms, this interpretation would turn Article 13 protection into an absolute defence, given the difficulty of challenging the level of support granted during the current marketing year at the time of the complaint. If it were only possible to challenge the support granted during a past marketing year independently of the support granted during the current year, what would be the use of any successful claim under Articles 5 and 6 of the SCM Agreement? How would it be possible, in that case, to eliminate the adverse effects of a subsidy already granted?

13. Does a failure by a Member to comply in a given year with either the chapeau of Article 13(b) or the proviso in subparagraph (ii) of Article 13(b) impact its entitlement to benefit in an earlier or a later year from the exemption from action provided by Article 13(b)? 3rd parties, in particular Australia, Argentina, Canada, China, EC, NZ

In Argentina's view, the failure by a Member to comply in a given year with either the *chapeau* of Article 13(b) or the proviso in sub paragraph (ii) of Article 13(b) results in the loss of the protection granted by the Peace Clause.

Regarding the "*chapeau*" of Article 13(b): domestic support that does not conform to the provisions of Article 6.1, for example distorting support in excess of the reduction commitment in violation of Article 3.2 of the AoA, is outside the scope of Article 13(b). Indeed, that Article refers to "domestic support measures that conform fully to the provisions of Article 6 … ". Consequently, domestic support of the kind referred to in Article 13(b) that does not conform to

Article 6 does not bear any relation to Article 13(b)(ii). Such support is prohibited and does not enjoy the protection of the Peace Clause.

Regarding failure to comply with the proviso in Article 13(b)(ii): any failure to comply in whatever year implies exclusion from the scope of Article 13(b) for all of the distorting domestic support measures concerning the specific commodity in question.

14. Does a failure of a Member to comply with Article 13(b) in respect of a *specific commodity* impact its entitlement to benefit in respect of other agricultural products from the exemption from action provided by Article 13(b)? 3rd parties, in particular Australia, Argentina, Canada, China, EC, NZ

In Argentina's view, failure by a Member to comply with Article 13(b)(i) and (ii) in respect of a specific commodity does not impact its entitlement to benefit in respect of other agricultural products from the exemption action provided by Article 13(b).

However, failure to comply with the conditions laid down in the *chapeau* of Article 13(b) i.e. failure of the domestic support to conform with the provisions of Article 6 of the AoA, could result in exclusion from the protection offered by Article 13(b) in respect of domestic support granted to all products, for example, if the domestic support measure exceeds the level of the commitment in the schedule of the Member concerned.

15. Is there any basis on which counter-cyclical payments could be considered product-specific? 3rd parties, in particular Australia, Argentina, Canada, China, EC, NZ

As stated in paragraph 8 of its Oral Submission, Argentina considers that "*support to a specific commodity*" in Article 13(b)(ii) includes any domestic support measure that is not a Green Box measure and that provides any identifiable support to a commodity in particular, regardless of whether the measure may provide support to a greater number of commodities.[6] In this respect, counter-cyclical payments explicitly provide support to cotton (upland) as can be seen in the text of the United States Farm Act of 2002 (2002 Farm Security and Rural Investment Act, Title I, Subtitle A, Exhibit US-1).

16. If the word "specific" were deleted from Article 13(b)(ii), would this change the meaning of the subparagraph? 3rd parties, in particular Australia, Argentina, Benin, Canada, China, EC, NZ

The word "specific" is an adjective qualifying the noun "commodity". The adjective "specific" does not qualify the support (the calculation of which may or may not be product-specific, as stated in paragraph 1 of Annex 3 of the AoA).

If the word "specific" qualifying the noun "commodity" were not there, the text would no longer have the precision that it currently has, although this does not mean that even then it could not be interpreted as referring to any type

---

6 In this respect, Argentina agrees with New Zealand: " ... *New Zealand sees no basis on which to suggest that support to a specific commodity should be excluded simply because other commodities may receive similar support*". Third Party Submission of New Zealand, 15 July 2003, para. 2.23.

of domestic support (regardless of whether it is categorized as product-specific or non-specific under Annex 3 of the AoA).

17. What is the relevance, if any, of the concept of "specificity" in Article 2 of the *SCM Agreement* and references to a "product" or "subsidized product" in certain provisions of the SCM Agreement to the meaning of "support to a specific commodity" in Article 13(b)(ii) *Agreement on Agriculture*? 3rd parties, in particular Australia, Argentina, Canada, China, EC, NZ

In Argentina's view the concept of specificity in Article 2 of the SCM Agreement is not linked to the term "*specific* commodity" in Article 13(b)(ii) of the AoA. In Article 2 of the SCM Agreement, the specificity is a characteristic *of the subsidies* (prohibited or actionable) covered by the current SCM Agreement, while the specificity referred to in the phrase "specific commodity" is characteristic of the commodity and not of the subsidy granted. The phrase "support to a *specific* commodity" cannot be identified with "*specific support* to a commodity".

The concept of "specificity" in Article 2 of the SCM Agreement is what indicates whether a subsidy is subject to the provisions of Part II or to the provisions of Parts III or V of that Agreement.

18. Benin's oral statement considers the phrase "support to a specific commodity" in Article 13(b)(ii) of the *Agreement on Agriculture*. How does Benin believe that phrase is best interpreted? Please substantiate your response, commenting on other submissions by parties and third parties as you believe appropriate. Benin

19. Where does Article 13(b)(ii) require a year-on-year comparison? 3rd parties, in particular Australia, Argentina, Canada, EC, NZ

Argentina submits that the domestic support measures granted in any of the marketing years of the period covered between 1995 and 2003 are relevant for the purposes of determining conformity with Article 13(b)(ii), which does not explicitly require a year-on-year comparison.

20. Does Article 13(b)(ii) require a comparison of support granted with support decided? How could such a comparison be made?

In Argentina's view Article 13(b)(ii) requires a comparison of support granted with support decided. Such a comparison is possible by making a calculation in terms of budgetary outlays in each one of the periods in question (support granted in the implementation period as compared to support decided during the 1992 marketing year).

21. Please comment on Brazil's assertion that the terms "grant" and "decided" in Article 13(b)(ii) have broadly the same meaning. If so, why did the drafters not use the same term? 3rd parties, in particular, Australia, Argentina, Canada, China, EC, NZ

According to the text of Article 13(b)(ii) the word "*decided*" signifies the decision to provide payments for a specific commodity (including the revenue foregone under Article 1(c) of the AoA), whether those payments are classified as product-specific or non-specific, as well as other forms of domestic support in monetary terms as set forth in Annex 3 of the AoA.

The phrase "*support decided during the 1992 marketing year*" is necessarily linked to the phrase "grant support" - indeed, there would be no basis for comparison if in one case the support was granted, while in the other case, the support was only planned. In other words, as indicated in the reply to the preceding question, the Article 13(b)(ii) requirement necessarily involves a comparison of domestic support measured in the same manner in each one of the periods in question, i.e. a "comparison of the comparable".

In principle, the comparison must be made between the support granted in any year of the implementation period and the support "decided" during 1992. The support "decided during the 1992 marketing year" refers to a legislative or administrative decision by a Member during the 1992 marketing year on the domestic support to be granted during the implementation period in terms of budgetary outlays.

Where no "decision" has been taken in terms of budgetary outlays during 1992, Argentina understands that the only support that can be considered as "decided" during that marketing year is the support granted during that year.

22. What is the meaning of "support" in *Agreement on Agriculture* 13(b)(ii)? Why would it be used differently from Annexe 3, where it refers to total outlays? 3rd parties, in particular, Australia, Argentina, Canada, China, EC, NZ

The "support granted" in each marketing year of the implementation period must necessarily be linked to the budgetary outlays for those years.

The term "support" used in Article 13(b)(ii) of the AoA refers to budgetary outlays for any kind of support that is not Green Box. For example, the term "support" could include assistance granted by the State by foregoing tax revenue or writing off producers' debts.

23. Should support be compared under Article 13(b)(ii) in terms of unit of production or total volume of support or both? 3rd parties, in particular, Australia, Argentina, Canada, China, EC, NZ

Support should be compared under Article 13(b)(ii) in total monetary terms. In paragraph 16 of its oral submission, Argentina submits that the term "decided" in Article 13(b)(ii) should not be interpreted as meaning that the rate per unit of production is the factor to be considered in determining the amount of support granted. If the argument put forward by the United States were accepted, this would enable an unlimited amount of domestic support to be granted for each product provided the total AMS is not exceeded, since it would be covered by Article 13. Thus, the amount of the AMS could be granted to one or several products, provided its maximum bound level is not exceeded.

The comparison must be made in terms of total value of support for a specific product, comparing the levels for each marketing year subsequent to 1992 and up to 31 December 2003 with the levels of support decided during the 1992 marketing year.

24. Please provide any written drafting history which could shed light on why the proviso was added to what is now Article 13(b)(ii) of the *Agreement on Agriculture* and, in particular, why the words "grant" and "decided" were used. EC

25. Please comment on an interpretation of the words "decided during" in Article 13(b)(ii) that would read them as synonymous with the words "authorized during". 3rd parties, in particular Australia, Argentina, Canada, China, EC, NZ

The term "decided during" in Article 13(b)(ii) refers to a decision made by the Member granting the support during the 1992 marketing year with respect to the budgetary outlays that would be made for domestic support, excluding Green Box.

If there was no decision during the 1992 marketing year, the budgetary outlays effectively made during that marketing year must be considered to constitute the support "decided during" the 1992 marketing year (i.e. if there is no express decision in this respect, we must fall back on what was effectively disbursed which also, implicitly, represents a "decision").

26. Under Article 13(b)(ii), a comparison is required between support at different times. One of the issues which is contested between the parties is whether the only later period that the Panel can consider is the present one (i.e. the period underway at the time of the request for establishment of the Panel). This argument is based on the present tense of the words "do not grant" in the English text. The Panel asks whether there is any difference in the verb tense as used in the Spanish-language text, or any other difference which might aid the Panel in interpreting these words? Argentina, EC, Paraguay, Venezuela

While it is true that in the English version of the Agreement on Agriculture, the verb tense used in Article 13(b)(ii) is the present tense, as stated by the United States in paragraph 90 of its first written submission (… the proviso is written in the present tense …), it should be stressed that in the Spanish text, the present tense is clearly used in the subjunctive mode ("*a condición de que* ***no otorguen*** *ayuda …* ")

The expression "*a condición de que*" uses the subjunctive mode to indicate the conditional or possible nature and expresses syntactic subordination.

The use of the subjunctive mode in Article 13(b)(ii) is important, because in Spanish it is used to express and form sentences in which the action remains in doubt, as opposed to the indicative mode where the tenses always indicate that the action, concretely, is taking place, has taken place, or will be taking place.

The Spanish text coincides with the verbal tense used in the French version ("*à condition que ces mesures n'accordent pas*"), in which the present subjunctive is also used.

Consequently, Argentina does not agree with the United States' contention that the present tense criterion in Article 13(b)(ii) implies that the only support the Panel may consider is current support.

27. If the 1992 "decision" led to or was the funding source for the money provided in 1992 and later years, is it the full amount of all that funding that constitutes the "support" decided in 1992? If the answer to this question is that it is the full amount of all the support provided pursuant to the "decision" that must be taken into account, must this be compared with the total amount of support that will or might flow from the decision made in the more recent period for the purposes of the comparison required under Article 13(b)(ii)? If a Member did not make a "decision" (however that may be interpreted) in 1992 about "support", is it the case that the Member has a zero base for the purposes of the comparison required under Article 13(b)(ii)? EC

28. In paragraph 13 of Australia's oral statement, you state that a "question" is: "could conditions of price competition for the purposes of a non-violation or impairment claim be assessed solely on the basis of budgetary outlay figures, as argued by Brazil, or on the basis of a rate of payment, as argued by the United States? In Australia's view, both factors put forward by Brazil and the United States would properly form a part of that assessment, but not the whole." Could you please clarify this statement (indicating other elements which would complete the "whole" and explain its relevance for the purposes of our consideration of Article 13 of the *Agreement on Agriculture*?) Australia, EC

Export Credit Guarantee Programme

29 (a) Is an export credit guarantee a financial contribution in the form of a "potential direct transfer of funds or liabilities (e.g. loan guarantee)" within the meaning of Article 1.1(a)(1)(i) of the *SCM Agreement*? Why or why not? 3rd parties, in particular, Argentina, Canada, EC, NZ

An export credit guarantee is a "financial contribution" in the form of a "potential direct transfer of funds or liabilities" within the meaning of Article 1.1(a)(1)(i) of the SCM Agreement when it involves the granting of a financial credit in conditions more favourable than those that can normally be found on the market. Those conditions may contain all or some of the following elements: lower interest rates, longer repayment terms for loans, lower down-payment requirement, reduced frequency of payments per year and/or total or partial exemption from any fee or premium to provide the US Government with adequate protection against potential flaws in its export credit guarantee portfolio. This is confirmed in practice by the fact that no company on the market is prepared to provide coverage equivalent to the coverage accorded with the credit guarantees of the Commodity Credit Corporation of the United States.

Moreover, items (j) and (k) of the Illustrative List in (Annex 1) of the SCM Agreement set out the circumstances in which this type of operation should be considered an export subsidy.

29. (b) How, if at all, would this be relevant to the claims of Brazil? 3rd parties, in particular, Argentina, Canada, EC, NZ

It is relevant to the claims of Brazil in that the fact of being a "financial contribution" is the first element of a prohibited export subsidy claim.

30. The Panel could arguably take the view that Articles 1 and 3 of the *SCM Agreement* were relevant in assessing the WTO-consistency of United States export credit guarantees. The Panel would therefore appreciate third party views on this situation, including with respect to the viability of an *a contrario* interpretation of item (j) of the Illustrative List (as addressed in paragraphs 180-183 of the United States' first written submission). 3rd parties, in particular, Argentina, Canada, EC, NZ

As stated by the Appellate Body in *US - FSC* and in *Canada - Dairy Products*, the AoA does not contain its own definition of a subsidy, and hence we must turn to the SCM Agreement for the context. The Appellate Body has also established (FSC case) that export subsidies under Article 3.1(a) of the SCM Agreement constitute export subsidies under the AoA.

The relevance of Articles 1 and 3 of the SCM Agreement is therefore unquestionable when it comes to evaluating the consistency of the export credit guarantees with WTO rules.

Moreover, Annex I of the *SCM Agreement* identifies export subsidies by providing an illustrative list thereof. In other words, a measure which constitutes an export subsidy classified in the Illustrative List is *per se* a prohibited subsidy under Article 3.1(a) of the *SCM Agreement*. Obviously, the "Illustrative" List in no way covers all measures that could qualify as an export subsidy under Article 3.1(a) of the SCM Agreement. As its name indicates, it is only an "illustrative" list and not an exhaustive one.

Now, footnote 5 in Article 3.1(a) of the SCM Agreement states that "*measures referred to*" in Annex I as not constituting export subsidies shall not be prohibited.

There are two paragraphs in this Annex that refer to credit, guarantee or insurance programmes: (j) and (k). There is a fundamental difference between the two. Item (k) explicitly recognises that a measure, in the circumstances set forth in its second paragraph, shall not be considered an export subsidy (see the last sentence of the second paragraph), fulfilling the requirement set forth in footnote 5 to the SCM Agreement:

> (k) The grant by governments (or special institutions controlled by and/or acting under the authority of governments) of export credits at rates below those which they actually have to pay for the funds so employed (or would have to pay if they borrowed on international capital markets in order to obtain funds of the same maturity and other credit terms and denominated in the same currency as the export credit), or the payment by them of all or part of the costs incurred by exporters or financial institutions in obtaining credits, in so far as they are used to secure a material advantage in the field of export credit terms.
>
> Provided, however, that if a Member is a party to an international undertaking on official export credits to which at least twelve original Members

to this Agreement are parties as of 1 January 1979 (or a successor undertaking which has been adopted by those original Members), or if in practice a Member applies the interest rates provisions of the relevant undertaking, an export credit practice which is in conformity with those provisions shall not be considered an export subsidy prohibited by this Agreement. (Emphasis added)

Argentina does not agree with the *a contrario* interpretation provided by the United States in paragraphs 180 to 183 of its submission, either with respect to the first paragraph of item (k) or with respect to item (j) of Annex I to the *SCM Agreement*, because unlike the final sentence of the second paragraph of item (k), the text does not explicitly recognize that the measure will not be an export subsidy, and an *a contrario* interpretation that circumvents the test of Article of 3.1(a) of the *SCM Agreement* is not possible.

That is to say, even if a given credit, guarantee or insurance programme includes:

- either, in relation to item (j), premium rates which are adequate to cover the long-term operating costs and losses of the programmes;
- or, in relation to the first paragraph of item (k), interest rates below the cost of funds that are not used to secure a material advantage in the field of export credit terms,$

none of this in any way enables us to infer that because they display either or both of these characteristics, they should not be considered to be export subsidies if they meet the conditions set forth in Articles 1 and 3.1(a) of the *SCM Agreement.*

For the situation put forward by the United States to be possible, there would have to be a text similar to the final sentence of the second paragraph of item (k) which explicitly states that a given measure is not considered to be an export subsidy. Only then would footnote 5 of the *SCM Agreement* become operational.

Now, even if the appropriate language had been included in item (j) and the first paragraph of the item (k) of Annex I of the SCM Agreement and footnote 5 were operational, an *a contrario* interpretation would still be unacceptable because, in addition to the test of Article 3.1(a) of the *SCM Agreement*, Members using such programmes must also comply with the AoA obligations, in particular Articles 8, 10.1 and 10.3, without prejudice to the application of Article 3 of the *SCM Agreement* to agricultural subsidies after the expiry of the Peace Clause in Article 13 of the AoA. In other words, the absence in Article 1(e) of the AoA of a footnote such as footnote 5 of the SCM Agreement precludes any *a contrario* interpretation in favour of users of export credits for agricultural products. Furthermore, Article 10.3 of the SCM Agreement itself places on the user Member the entire burden of proof that such programmes are not export subsidies.

31. If the Panel decides to refer to provisions of the *SCM Agreement* for contextual guidance in the interpretation of the terms in Article 10 *Agree-*

***ment on Agriculture*, should the Panel refer to item (j) or Articles 1 and 3 of the *SCM Agreement* or both?** 3rd parties, in particular, Argentina, Canada, EC, NZ

If the Panel decides to refer to provisions of the *SCM Agreement* for contextual guidance, as established by the Appellate Body, in the interpretation of the terms of Article 10 of the *Agreement on Agriculture* (Prevention of Circumvention of Export Subsidy Commitments), the Panel should refer to *both*: first of all to item (j) of Annex I (*Illustrative List of Export Subsidies*) of the *SCM Agreement*, and subsidiarily to Articles 1 and 3 of the *SCM Agreement*. Naturally, if the Panel should conclude that the challenged credit guarantees come under indent (j) of Annex I, it would have to conclude that they violate Articles 1 and 3.1(a) of the *SCM Agreement per se*.

32. The Panel's attention has been drawn to Article 14(c) of the *SCM Agreement* (see third party submission of Canada) and to the panel report in DS 222 *Canada - Export Credits and Loan Guarantees*. How and to what extent are Article 14(c) of the *SCM Agreement*, and the cited panel report, relevant to the issue of whether or not the United States export credit guarantee programmes confer a "benefit"? What would the appropriate market benchmark be to use for any comparison? Please cite any other relevant material. 3rd parties, in particular, Argentina, Canada, EC, NZ

Argentina agrees with Canada's interpretation in paragraphs 41 to 48 of its written submission to the effect that Article 14(c) of the SCM Agreement and the Panel and Appellate Body reports in WT/DS70, as well as the Panel report in WT/DS222, are relevant to the issue of whether the export credit guarantee programmes of the United States confer a "benefit". The standard established therein for the determination of the existence of a "benefit" constitutes the appropriate legal framework for the interpretation of the facts in the present case.

According to the last part of paragraph 157 of the report of the Appellate Body in WT/DS70, *" ... the marketplace provides an appropriate basis for comparison in determining whether a 'benefit' has been 'conferred', because the trade-distorting potential of a 'financial contribution' can be identified by determining whether the recipient has received a 'financial contribution' on terms more favourable than those available to the recipient in the market."*

33. What is the relevance (if any) of Brazil's statement that: " ... export credit guarantees for exports of agricultural exports [sic] are not available on the marketplace by commercial lenders". 3rd parties, in particular, Argentina, Canada, EC, NZ

The relevance of Brazil's statement lies in the fact that if the marketplace is unable to provide export credit guarantees for agricultural products, the mere granting of such guarantees by the Government of the United States would constitute an export subsidy. It would demonstrate that the market was unable to equal the conditions offered by the challenged programmes.

34. Comment on the United States' view of the meaning of "long term operating costs and losses" in item (j) of the Illustrative List of Export Subsidies in Annex I of the *SCM Agreement* as meaning "claims paid" under the

export credit guarantee programmes. Does the United States' interpretation give meaning to both "costs" and "losses"? Do claims paid represent "losses"? 3rd parties, in particular, Argentina, Canada, EC, NZ

35. Did the drafters of the *Agreement on Agriculture* include export credit guarantees in Article 9.1 of the *Agreement on Agriculture*? Why or why not? 3rd parties, in particular, Argentina, Canada, EC, NZ

Article 9.1 of the Agreement on Agriculture is a list of export subsidies that are subject to reduction commitments. As such, it does not include export credit guarantees. However, there are other export subsidies, as emerges the actual text of Article 10.1, which are also subject to disciplines.

In this respect, Argentina agrees with Canada's statement in paragraph 32 of its Written Submission that:

> *"Article 9 of the Agriculture Agreement lists and describes certain export subsidies that are subject to reduction commitments. All other export subsidies fall within the scope of Article 10.1 ... "*

36. Please explain any possible significance the following statements may have in respect of Brazil's claims about GSM102 and 103 (7 CFR 1493.10(a)(2), Exhibit BRA-38). 3rd parties, in particular, Argentina, Canada, EC, NZ

(a) "The programmes operate in cases where credit is necessary to increase or maintain US exports to a foreign market and where U.S. financial institutions would be unwilling to provide financing without CCC's guarantee. (7 CFR 1493.10(a)(2) Exhibit BRA-38)

The fact that the programmes operate in cases where credit is necessary to increase or maintain exports and where US private financial institutions would be unwilling to provide financing without the CCC's guarantee is relevant to Brazil's claims about the GSM 102 and GSM 103 programmes in that it implies a recognition of the impact and trade-distorting effect of the export credit guarantees.

(b) "The programmes are operated in a manner intended not to interfere with markets for cash sales. The programmes are targeted toward those countries where the guarantee is necessary to secure financing of the exports but which have sufficient financial strength so that foreign exchange will be available for scheduled payments." (7 CFR 1493.10(a)(2) Exhibit BRA-38)

This is another recognition of the fact that without such measures, there would be no exports, or there would be fewer exports from the United States.

(c) "In providing this credit guarantee facility, CCC seeks to expand market opportunities for US agricultural exporters and assist long-term market development for US agricultural commodities." (7 CFR 1493.10(a)(2) Exhibit BRA-38)

The fact that in providing this credit guarantee facility, the CCC seeks to expand market opportunities for US agricultural exporters and assist long-term market development for US agricultural commodities once again reinforces the negative impact and distortion caused by the export credit guarantees to world trade.

37. The United States seems to argue that, at present, by virtue of Article 10.2 of the *Agreement on Agriculture*, there are no disciplines on agricultural export credit guarantees under the *Agreement on Agriculture* (or the SCM Agreement).

(a) Comment on the following proposition: a WTO Member may therefore extend agricultural export credit guarantees without charging a premium, and for an indefinite period, in addition to any other terms and conditions it may wish? How would this reconcile with the title of Article 10 of the Agreement on Agriculture ("Prevention of Circumvention on Export Subsidy Commitments"), and with other commitments contained in the *Agreement on Agriculture*? Please cite any relevant material, including any past WTO dispute settlement cases. 3rd parties, in particular, Argentina, Canada, EC, NZ

It is wrong to state that there are no disciplines on export credits and export credit guarantees. Article 10.2 must be analysed together with Article 10.1, in that when the export guarantee and credit programmes contain a subsidy component and are therefore genuine export subsidies, they must automatically comply with the requirement of not circumventing export subsidy commitments.

The export credits and export credit guarantees granted by the United States constitute export subsidies for the reasons set forth in the replies to questions 29 and 36 above. They do not comply with Articles 3, 8 and 10.1 of the AoA.

Regarding the first question of the Panel in (a) above, the answer is no. The granting of export credit guarantees under conditions in which no consideration is required, in this case a premium charged by the granting institution, is tantamount to the transfer of funds to the beneficiary. The beneficiary, in the absence of an adequate premium, transfers all of the credit and commercial risk of the operation to the institution granting the guarantee without any cost to itself. In other words, we are speaking of a subsidy.

(b) If, as the United States argues, there are no disciplines on export credit guarantees in the *Agreement on Agriculture*, how could export credit guarantees "conform fully to the provisions of Part V" of the *Agreement on Agriculture* within the meaning of Article 13 (how can you assess "conformity" or non-conformity with non- existent disciplines)? 3rd parties, in particular, Argentina, Canada, EC, NZ

In Argentina's view, the United States' interpretation of Article 10.2 is entirely at odds with the context of the provision and the object and purpose of Article 10 of the AoA, since it would contribute to the circumvention of export subsidy commitments by excluding an entire category of export subsidies from the general disciplines in that area.

Article 1(e) of the AoA clearly defines export subsidies without excluding those that are not listed in Article 9.1 of the Agreement.

At the same time, Article 13(c) of the AoA stipulates that in order to be exempted, export subsides must conform fully to the provisions of Part V of the AoA, and not to a particular article. Article 10, which forms part of Part V of the AoA, stipulates in paragraph 1 that: " ... *export subsidies not listed in paragraph 1 of Article 9 shall not be applied in a manner which results in, or which threatens to lead to, circumvention of export subsidy commitments ...* ".

Thus, the lack of disciplines specifically developed for export credit guarantees does not necessarily imply the absence or shortage of criteria that would make it possible to establish objectively whether these instruments *"conform fully to the provisions of Part V of this Agreement"* as stipulated in the chapeau of Article 13(c).

STEP 2 PAYMENTS

38. Please comment on the statement in note 119 of the United States' first written submission that "...to the extent a consumer that had intended to export instead opens the bale, then that consumer could still obtain the Step 2 payment upon submission of the requisite documentation". The Panel notes that Step 2 payments all involve upland cotton produced in the United States. What are the two distinct factual situations that Step 2 payments involve? Other than the panel report in Canada-Dairy and the findings of the Appellate Body in US-FSC (21.5)[7], do any other dispute settlement reports offer guidance on this issue? For example, how, if at all is the Appellate Body's report in Canada-Aircraft relevant here?[8] 3rd parties, in particular, Australia, Argentina, NZ, Paraguay

As stated by Argentina in paragraphs 80-85 of its written submission, both the corresponding section of the 2002 SFRI Act and the provisions of the Section 1427.100ff. of the Code of Federal Regulations clearly establish that the

---

[7] "We recall that the ETI measure grants a tax exemption in two different sets of circumstances: (a) where property is produced *within* the United States and held for use *outside* the United States; and (b) where property is produced *outside* the United States and held for use outside the United States. Our conclusion that the ETI measure grants subsidies that are export contingent in the first set of circumstances is not affected by the fact that the subsidy can also be obtained in the second set of circumstances. The fact that the subsidies granted in the second set of circumstances *might* not be export contingent does not dissolve the export contingency arising in the first set of circumstances. Conversely, the export contingency arising in these circumstances has no bearing on whether there is an export contingent subsidy in the second set of circumstances. Where a United States taxpayer is simultaneously producing property within and outside the United States, for direct use outside the United States, subsidies may be granted under the ETI measure in respect of both sets of property. The subsidy granted with respect to the property produced within the United States, and exported from there, is export contingent within the meaning of Article 3.1(a) of the *SCM Agreement*, irrespective of whether the subsidy given in respect of property produced outside the United States is also export contingent."

[8] There, the Appellate Body stated that,

> "the fact that some of TPC's contributions, in some industry sectors, are *not* contingent upon export performance, does not necessarily mean that the same is true for all of TPC's contributions. It is enough to show that one or some of TPC's contributions do constitute subsidies "contingent ... in fact ... upon export performance".[8]

Commodity Credit Corporation (CCC) must issue marketing certificates or cash payments to exporters and/or users of US (upland) cotton.

Given that the purpose of the programme is to provide a direct incentive for US cotton exports and consists of a direct payment to exporters based on the difference between the US domestic cotton price and the world market price, there can be no doubt that whenever the former is higher than the latter, an export subsidy is present inasmuch as the existence of these payments enables the US product to compete artificially with the lower-cost products of more efficient producers.

It should be noted that the programme known as *Step 2* establishes the right of exporters to receive a subsidy for shipments made in connection with foreign sale operations, while establishing an obligation upon the CCC to grant that subsidy once the particular requirements are satisfied.

We stress that the payment is the difference between the domestic market and the international market because that would be the most relevant evidence that the subsidy seeks to ensure that the product can be exported at prices lower than the domestic price.

39. Please comment on the United States assertions at paragraph 129 of its first written submission, that "[t]he program is indifferent to whether recipients of the benefit of this programme are exporters or parties that open bales for the processing of manufacturing raw cotton into cotton products in the United States." 3rd parties, in particular, Australia, Argentina, NZ, Paraguay

The fact that the Step 2 programme is indifferent to whether the recipients are exporters or users of cotton in the United States does not alter its inconsistency, since the United States has not specified upland cotton in its schedule of commitments and this type of subsidy under the Step 2 programme is granted for cotton. Consequently, any provision in the legal texts with respect to the granting of such a subsidy makes it inconsistent per se with Articles 3.3 and 8 of the AoA, while for the same reason any sum distributed, budgeted or provided for under the programme constitutes a prohibited subsidy within the meaning of Article 3 of the SCM Agreement.

40. With respect to paragraph 32 of the oral statement of the EC, are subsidies contingent on the use of domestic goods consistent with the AoA? Does the phrase "provide support in favour of domestic producers" refer to, and/or permit such subsidies? What is the meaning and relevance of this (if any) to Brazil's claims under Article 3 of the *SCM Agreement* and Article III:4 of the GATT 1994. 3rd parties, in particular, Australia, Argentina, EC, NZ, Paraguay

Are subsidies contingent on the use of domestic goods, because they are prohibited under Article 3.1(b) of the SCM Agreement, also prohibited under the AoA given that there is no specific provision in the AoA that is explicitly mentioned in the introductory sentence of Article 3 of the SCM Agreement? Indeed, Article 3 of the SCM Agreement reads "except as provided in the Agreement on

Agriculture ... ". The AoA does not contain any provision which explicitly *permits such subsidies*.

"Except as provided in the Agreement on Agriculture ..." also means that Article 3 of the SCM Agreement applies to agricultural subsidies to the extent that they are not in conflict with the AoA. In this connection, no provision can be found in the AoA that is in conflict with Article 3.1(b) of the SCM Agreement, permitting the granting of "subsidies contingent, whether solely or as one of several other conditions, upon the use of domestic over imported goods." Consequently, Argentina considers that subsidies contingent upon the use of domestic over imported goods are prohibited under the AoA.

Regarding the EC's argument in which it tries to distinguish between the terms "to" and "in favour" with respect to support for agricultural producers, this difference does not tally with the Spanish text, and "in favour", "to" and "benefit" are synonyms.

Article from the Agreement on Agriculture	Spanish	English
1.a	a	in favour
1.d	a	to
1.h	a	in favour
3.2.	a	in favour
6.1.	en favor	in favour
6.2.	a	to
6.3.	a	in favour
7.1.	en favor	in favour
7.2.a	en favor	in favour
7.2.b	a	to
9.1.a	a	to
Annex 2	a	to (in different paragraphs throughout the annex)
Annex 3.7	beneficio a	benefit
Annex 4.4	beneficio a	benefit

In other words, the text does not contain the difference that the EC is attempting to expose, nor can a phrase such as "in favour" be interpreted as the waiver of a prohibition under Article 3.1(b) of the SCM Agreement, since such a waiver does not appear in the text.

Regarding the second sentence of paragraph 7 of Annex 3 of the AoA concerning "measures directed at agricultural processors", it makes no reference whatsoever to the "subsidies contingent ... upon the use of domestic over imported goods" mentioned in Article 3.1(b) of the SCM Agreement. Obviously, these are two different matters. Moreover, paragraph 7 of Annex 3 contains no mention of the SCM Agreement. If the intention had been to exempt these measures from the prohibition contained in Article 3.1(b) of the SCM Agreement, this would have been expressly stated, specifically mentioning the provision of the SCM Agreement, i.e. Article 3.1(b).

As regards the second question, for the reasons provided above, the phrase "provide support in favour of domestic producers" neither refers to the subsidies in Article 3.1(b) of the SCM Agreement, nor permits them.

With respect to the third question, Article III:4 of the GATT 1994 prohibits discrimination against imported products, so that this article is also applicable, as well as Article 2.1 of the Agreement on Trade-Related Investment Measures. Moreover, the TRIMs Agreement does not make the slightest reference to the Agreement on Agriculture.

ETI Act

41. Concerning its claims on the ETI Act, Brazil relies on the US – FSC case. However, it appears that the United States did not raise the issue of the Peace Clause in that case, nor did the US appear to invoke Article 6 of the *Agreement on Agriculture*. If the Panel's understanding is correct, how, if at all, are these differences relevant here? Argentina, China, EC, NZ

42. How do you view the reference in paragraph 43 of the EC's third party oral statement with respect to the relevance of Article 17.14 of the DSU, and, in particular, the phrase "a final resolution to *that* dispute" (emphasis added)? Please explain the use, and relevance (if any) of the term "disputes" in Articles 9.3 and 12 and Appendix 3 of the DSU, and please cite any other provisions you consider relevant. Argentina, China, EC, NZ

ANNEX J-2

ANSWERS BY AUSTRALIA TO THE QUESTIONS FROM THE PANEL

11 August 2003

ARTICLE 13 OF THE AGREEMENT ON AGRICULTURE

1. Australia has argued that Article 13 of the *Agreement on Agriculture* is an affirmative defence. How do you reconcile this with your view that the conditions in Article 13 are a "prerequisite" to the availability of a right or privilege? Australia Would other third parties have any comments on Australia's assertion? 3RD parties, in particular Argentina, Benin, China, Chinese Taipei

Reply

Australia does not see any inconsistency in its views. In Australia's view, the potential availability of an affirmative defence in the general sense is in the nature of a right or privilege. Australia wishes to clarify, however, that it considers Article 13 in the specific sense to be a right available when the conditions prescribed therein are met, rather than a privilege.

ARTICLE 13(B) OF THE *AGREEMENT ON AGRICULTURE*: DOMESTIC SUPPORT MEASURES

2. Please explain the difference, if any, between the meaning of "defined" and the meaning of "fixed" in the phrase "a defined and fixed base period" in paragraph 6(a) of Annex 2 of the Agreement on Agriculture. 3rd parties, in particular Australia, Argentina, Canada, EC, NZ

Reply

In Australia's view, having regard to their ordinary meanings in their context of the object and purpose of the *Agreement on Agriculture*, the words "defined" and "fixed" have distinct meanings.[1] The word "defined" refers to the period of time stipulated for the purposes of determining initial eligibility for a particular decoupled income support payment. The word "fixed" establishes that once it has been "defined", that period of time is unchangeable for that payment.

---

[1] *The New Shorter Oxford English Dictionary*, Ed. Lesley Brown, Clarendon Press, Oxford, Volume 1 provides the following potentially relevant definitions of the words:
"defined": "having a definite or specified outline or form; clearly marked, definite" (page 618);
"fixed": "**1** Definitely and permanently placed or assigned; stationary or unchanging in relative position; definite, permanent, lasting. **2a** Directed steadily or intently towards an object. **b** ... **3** Placed or attached firmly; made firm or stable in position. ...

3. Please explain the meaning of "a" in "a defined and fixed base period" in paragraph 6(a) of Annex 2 of the Agreement on Agriculture, the meaning of "the" in "the base period" in paragraphs 6(b), (c) and (d), and the difference between these and the phrase "based on the years 1986-88" in Annex 3. 3rd parties, in particular Australia, Argentina, Canada, EC, NZ

Reply

In Australia's view, "a" is used in the phrase "a defined and fixed base period" in paragraph 6(a) of Annex 2 to the *Agreement on Agriculture* as an indefinite article, and is defined as meaning "one, some, any"[2]. Thus, having regard to the ordinary meaning of the words in their context and in the light of the object and purpose of the Agreement on Agriculture, "a defined and fixed base period" is the base period selected *by an individual WTO Member* for the purposes of determining initial eligibility for a particular decoupled income support payment. Once that base period is selected, it is fixed, that is, it is unchangeable.

"The" is defined as "designating one or more ... things already mentioned or known, particularized by context or circumstances, inherently unique, familiar, or otherwise sufficiently identified".[3] Thus, the use of "the" as a definite article in the phrase "after the base period" in paragraphs 6(b), (c) and (d) of Annex 2 establishes a relationship to the base period already identified, that is, to the base period selected by an individual WTO Member for the purposes of determining initial eligibility for a particular decoupled income support payment in accordance with paragraph 6(a) and which, once fixed, is unchangeable.

Australia does not consider that there is any relationship between any base period defined and fixed for a support programme for the purposes of paragraph 6 of Annex 2 and the use of the years 1986-88 as a base period under Annex 3, nor was there intended to be. Annex 3 relates to the calculation of a Member's AMS for the purposes of implementing its reduction commitments in relation to production and trade-distorting domestic support measures, consistent with the object and purpose of the Agreement on Agriculture. By definition in the first sentence of paragraph 1, Annex 2 domestic support measures may not, or may only minimally, distort production and trade. Thus, there is no logical or other basis for there to be any relationship.

Australia notes too that Article 7.2(a) of the *Agreement on Agriculture* specifically envisages the introduction of domestic support measures after entry into force of the *WTO Agreement* by providing for "any [domestic support] measure that is subsequently introduced that cannot be shown to satisfy the criteria in Annex 2 to this Agreement". Australia considers that, had the negotiators intended that the 1986-88 period be required to be used as the base period for the purposes of making decoupled income support payments – or indeed for any other purpose envisaged in Annex 2 – paragraph 6(a) would have expressly provided for this rather than for "a defined and fixed base period".

---

2 *The New Shorter Oxford English Dictionary*, Volume 1, page 1.

3 *The New Shorter Oxford English Dictionary*, Volume 2, page 3269.

4. How often can a Member define and fix a base period in accordance with paragraph 6 of Annex 2 of the Agreement on Agriculture? 3rd parties, in particular Australia, Argentina, Canada, China, EC, NZ

Reply

In Australia's view, and consistent with the use of the word "a" in the phrase "a defined and fixed base period", a Member may only define and fix a base period once for the purposes of a particular decoupled income support payment. Once that base period is defined and fixed, it is unchangeable.

5. Do you agree that a payment penalty based on crops produced is "related to type of production"? EC

6. Please explain the meaning of the word "criteria" in Article 6.1 and 7.1. What effect, if any, does the use of the word "Accordingly" in paragraph 1 of Annex 2 of the Agreement on Agriculture have on the meaning of the preceding sentence? 3rd parties, in particular Australia, Argentina, Canada, EC, NZ

Reply

The ordinary meaning of "criteria", as the plural of "criterion", is "principle[s], standard[s], or test[s] by which a thing is judged, assessed, or identified"[4]. Thus, the "criteria" in Articles 6.1 and 7.1 as these relate to Annex 2 of the *Agreement on Agriculture* encompasses *all* of the relevant principles, standards or tests established in Annex 2 against which domestic support measures for which exemption from reduction commitments is claimed are to be judged, assessed and/or identified.

As Australia said in its Oral Statement,[5] the word "accordingly" has several, equally valid meanings that are potentially applicable in the context: "harmoniously", "agreeably", "in accordance with the logical premises" and "correspondingly"[6]. A further definition is "in conformity with a given set of circumstances".[7]

In Australia's view, having regard to its ordinary meanings in its context and in light of the object and purpose of the A*greement on Agriculture*, including to "[correct] and [prevent] ... distortions in world agricultural markets",[8] the word "accordingly" can and should properly be interpreted in the sense of "consistent with" or "in conformity with" the fundamental requirement established in the first sentence. Consistent with that interpretation, the obligation that "green box" measures "meet the fundamental requirement ..." is cumulative with the additional basic criteria established in paragraph 1 and the policy specific criteria established in paragraphs 2-13 of Annex 2. To interpret the word "accor-

[4] *The New Shorter Oxford English Dictionary*, Volume 1, page 551.

[5] Oral Statement by Australia, paras. 35-36.

[6] *The New Shorter Oxford English Dictionary*, Volume 1, page 15.

[7] *Webster's Third New International Dictionary*, Ed. Philip Babcock Gove, Merriam-Webster Inc, Springfield, Massachusetts, 1993, page 12.

[8] Third preambular paragraph of the *Agreement on Agriculture*.

dingly" otherwise would be to negate the plain and unambiguous obligation established in the first sentence of paragraph 1 of Annex 2 that "[d]omestic support measures for which exemption from the reduction commitments is claimed shall meet the fundamental requirement that they have no, or at most minimal, trade-distorting effects or effects on production".

7. Please explain the meaning of the words "the fundamental requirement" as used in paragraph 1 of Annex 2 of the Agreement on Agriculture. 3rd parties, in particular Australia, Argentina, Canada, EC, NZ

Reply

The word "fundamental" has a number of meanings[9] which can be summarised as "primary" or "essential". The word "requirement" too has a number of meanings[10] which can be summarised as a "condition". Thus, a "fundamental requirement" is a primary or essential condition. [11] It is an overarching, freestanding obligation that applies to all "green box" measures cumulatively with the additional basic criteria established in paragraph 1 and the policy specific criteria established in paragraphs 2-13 of Annex 2. To interpret a "fundamental requirement" otherwise than as a primary or essential condition would not give the words their ordinary meaning in their context and in light of the object and purpose of the *Agreement on Agriculture*.

8. In your oral statement, you emphasize the use of the word "criteria" in other parts of the Agreement on Agriculture, as distinct from the reference to "fundamental requirement" in the first sentence of paragraph 1 of Annex 2. Is it the case that sub-paragraphs (a) and (b) of paragraph 1 of Annex 2 are also "criteria"? EC

9. If the first sentence of paragraph 1 of Annex 2 is a stand-alone obligation, does this allow effects-based claims of non-compliance with Annex 2? If so, how does this affect the purpose of Article 13(b)? 3rd parties' in particular Australia, Argentina, Canada, EC, NZ

Reply

It is not clear to Australia what is meant by "effects-based claims" in the context of this question. In Australia's view, a claim of non-compliance with the first sentence of paragraph 1 of Annex 2 would require an assessment of whether a domestic support measure meets the primary or essential condition that such measures have no, or at most minimal, trade-distorting effects or effects on pro-

---

9 *The New Shorter Oxford English Dictionary*, Volume 1, page 1042, provides relevant definitions of "fundamental" as "**1** Of or pertaining to the basis or groundwork; going to the root of the matter. **2** Serving as the base or foundation; essential or indispensable. Also, primary, original; from which others are derived."

10 *The New Shorter Oxford English Dictionary*, Volume 1, page 2557, provides definitions of "requirement" as "**1** The action of requiring something; a request. **2** A thing required or needed, a want, a need. Also the action or an instance of needing or wanting something. **3** Something called for or demanded; a condition which must be complied with."

11 Third Party Submission of Australia, para. 31, and Oral Statement by Australia, para. 33.

duction, that is, that such measures not, or only negligibly, bias or unnaturally alter trade or production.

10. If the first sentence of paragraph 1 of Annex 2 is not a stand-alone obligation, then must new, non- or minimally trade-distorting measures that do not conform to the criteria listed in Annex 2 be classified as non-Green Box? 3rd parties, in particular Australia, Argentina, Canada, EC, NZ

Reply

Yes.

11. If the first sentence of paragraph 1 of Annex 2 expresses a general principle which informs the interpretation of the criteria in Annex 2, please explain how this affects the assessment of the direct payments programme's compliance with paragraph 6 of Annex 2. 3rd parties, in particular, Australia, Argentina, Canada, EC, NZ

Reply

Australia assumes that the "direct payments programme" referred to in this question is the Direct Payments programme of the United States at issue in this dispute.

Even if the first sentence of paragraph 1 of Annex 2 were to express only a general principle which informs the interpretation of the other criteria in Annex 2, the US Direct Payments programme would still be non-compliant with paragraph 6(b) of Annex 2 because it:

- penalises producers based on the type of production undertaken after the base period, and
- because it allowed producers to update their base acreage and base yield(s) after the base period,

contrary to the express requirement of paragraph 6(b) that the amount of decoupled income support payments not be related to, or based on the type and/or volume of production undertaken by the producer in any year after the base period.

12. Where does Article 13(b) require a year-on-year comparison? 3RD parties, in particular Australia, Argentina, Canada, China, EC, NZ

Reply

In Australia's view, a requirement for a temporal comparison of measures granting support to a specific commodity is an implicit and integral component of the requirement in Article 13(b)(ii) that such measures not be "in excess of" that decided during the 1992 marketing year. "In excess of" is defined as "more than"[12] and "to an amount or degree beyond"[13].

See question 28 below.

---

12 *The New Shorter Oxford English Dictionary*, Volume 1, page 873.
13 *Webster's Third New International Dictionary*, page 792.

13. Does a failure by a Member to comply in a given year with either the chapeau of Article 13(b) or the proviso in subparagraph (ii) of Article 13(b) impact its entitlement to benefit in an earlier or a later year from the exemption from action provided by Article 13(b)? 3RD parties, in particular Australia, Argentina, Canada, China, EC, NZ

Reply

It is Australia's view that there is no obligation with which a Member is required to comply in either the chapeau of Article 13(b), or the proviso of Article 13(b)(ii).

See question 28 below.

14. Does a failure of a Member to comply with Article 13(b) in respect of a specific commodity impact its entitlement to benefit in respect of other agricultural products from the exemption from action provided by Article 13(b)? 3RD parties, in particular Australia, Argentina, Canada, China, EC, NZ

Reply

Yes. In Australia's view, there is no requirement that the application of the proviso be considered only in relation to a specific commodity at issue in a dispute. The failure of a Member to comply with Article 13(b)(ii) and (iii) in respect of one specific commodity affects its right to exemption from actions under Article 13(b)(ii) and (iii) in respect of all commodities.

Australia notes that the basic text of both Article 13(b)(ii) and (iii) reads as follows:

> During the implementation period, ... domestic support measures that conform fully to the provisions of Article 6 ... shall be ... exempt from actions based on [*the specified provisions*], provided that such measures do not grant support to a specific commodity in excess of that decided during the 1992 marketing year.

The phrase "such measures" in the proviso refers to "domestic support measures that conform fully to the provisions of Article 6 ...". Thus, the proviso states "provided that [*domestic support measures that conform fully to the provisions of Article 6*] do not grant support to *a* specific commodity in excess of that decided during the 1992 marketing year".

Similarly to its use in the context of question 3 above, "a" is used in the phrase "support to a specific commodity" as an indefinite article, and is defined as meaning "one, some, any"[14]. Having regard to the ordinary meaning of the word in its context and in light of the object and purpose of the *Agreement on Agriculture*, "support to a specific commodity" means support to any one commodity.

[14] *The New Shorter Oxford English Dictionary*, Volume 1, page 1.

Further, Australia considers that this interpretation is consistent with the object and purpose of the *Agreement on Agriculture*, including as expressed in the preambular clauses to that Agreement, for example, "to provide for substantial progressive reductions in agricultural support and protection sustained over an agreed period of time, resulting in correcting and preventing restrictions and distortions in world agricultural markets". The *Agreement on Agriculture* resulted from lengthy and complex negotiations and provided a finely balanced set of rights and obligations aimed at reducing the unnatural distortions of global agricultural production and trade. During an agreed transition period, so long as a Member adheres to its obligations intended to achieve that objective and does not introduce domestic support measures which result in new or additional distortions in trade and production, it would enjoy, as a right, protection for actions that would otherwise be WTO-inconsistent. On the other hand, if a Member did not observe the obligations that form part of the negotiated outcome, it would lose its generic right to the protection that constituted an essential element of that outcome. See also question 28 below.

15. Is there any basis on which counter-cyclical payments could be considered product-specific? 3RD parties, in particular Australia, Argentina, Canada, China, EC, NZ

Reply

In this question, Australia understands that the panel uses the term "product-specific" in the sense of "product-specific" support as argued by the United States in its First Written Submission.[15]

Australia notes that counter-cyclical payments (CCPs) are expressly differentiated by product.[16] Even though the CCP programme applies to more than one commodity and there is no requirement for a producer to grow any of those commodities, actual payments are made by product. Further, notwithstanding that there is no requirement for a producer to grow upland cotton to receive the CCP for upland cotton, it is not possible for a producer to receive the CCP for upland cotton if that producer has never actually produced upland cotton. Similarly, a producer could not receive the CCP for another eligible commodity under the program, e.g., corn, if that producer has never grown corn. Thus, CCPs for eligible commodities, in this case upland cotton, are effectively product-specific.

Australia notes too that CCPs for upland cotton are product-specific if there is a correlation between enrolled acreage for the purposes of the CCP (and Direct Payments) programme and the acreage actually used to grow upland cotton. However, there is insufficient current information available to Australia to assess whether CCPs can be considered to be product-specific on this basis.

That said, Australia re-iterates its strong view that "support to a specific commodity" within the meaning of subparagraph (ii) (and (iii)) of Article 13(b) does not equate to product-specific support and that "support to a specific com-

15 First Written Submission of the United States, paras. 77-81.

16 Section 1104, 2002 Farm Security and Rural Investment Act, Exhibit Bra-29.

modity" includes that portion of non-product specific support that benefits the commodity at issue, in this case upland cotton.[17] Had the authors of Article 13 intended that "support to a specific commodity" not include non-product specific support, Australia believes that they would have said so, consistent with the usage of such terminology elsewhere in the *Agreement on Agriculture*, for example, in Articles 1(a), 4(a) and paragraph 1 of Annex 3.

Further, "such measures" in the proviso of Article 13(b)(ii) and (iii) refers to "domestic support measures that conform fully to the provisions of Article 6" in the chapeau of Article 13(b), which include non-product specific support measures other than "green box" support measures. In Australia's view, to exclude non-product specific domestic support measures from the assessment of "support [*granted by such measures*] to a specific commodity" would be contrary to the express meaning of the text.

See also question 28 below.

16. If the word "specific" were deleted from Article 13(b)(ii), would this change the meaning of the subparagraph? 3RD parties, in particular Australia, Argentina, Benin Canada, China, EC, NZ

Reply

No. See also questions 14 and 28.

17. What is the relevance, if any, of the concept of "specificity" in Article 2 of the *SCM Agreement* and references to "a product" or "subsidized product" in certain provisions of the SCM Agreement to the meaning of "support to a specific commodity" in Article 13(b)(ii) Agreement on Agriculture? 3RD parties, in particular Australia, Argentina, Canada, China, EC, NZ

Reply

Australia does not consider that the concept of "specificity" in SCM Article 2, or references to "a product" or "subsidized product" in certain provisions of the *SCM Agreement*, have any express textual relationship to the meaning of "support to a specific commodity" in Article 13(b)(ii).

However, Australia notes that a subsidy does not need to be enterprise or industry-specific to be "specific" within the meaning of SCM Article 2. SCM Article 2.1(c) expressly provides that a subsidy can be specific notwithstanding an appearance of non-specificity if a subsidy programme is in fact directed at certain enterprises or industries. SCM Article 2 could therefore be considered to provide broad contextual support for Australia's view that CCPs for upland cotton are product-specific .

18. Benin's oral statement considers the phrase "support to a specific commodity" in Article 13(b)(ii) of the Agreement on Agriculture. How does Benin believe that phrase is best interpreted. Please substantiate your res-

17 Oral Statement by Australia, paras. 20-25.

ponse, commenting on other submissions by parties and third parties as you believe appropriate. Benin

19. Where does Article 13(b)(ii) require a year-on-year comparison? 3rd parties, in particular Australia, Argentina, Canada, EC, NZ

Reply

See questions 12 above and 28 below.

20. Does Article 13(b)(ii) require a comparison of support granted with support decided? How could such a comparison be made?

Reply

See question 28 below.

21. Please comment on Brazil's assertion that the terms "grant" and "decided" in Article 13(b)(ii) have broadly the same meaning. If so, why did the drafters not use the same term? 3rd parties, in particular, Australia, Argentina, Canada, China, EC, NZ

Reply

See question 28 below.

22. What is the meaning of "support" in Agreement on Agriculture 13(b)(ii) ? Why would it be used differently from Annex 3, where it refers to total outlays? 3rd parties, in particular, Australia, Argentina, Canada, China, EC, NZ

Reply

Australia believes it is significant that the proviso of Article 13(b)(ii) and (iii) uses "support" rather than "AMS" , "support as calculated in Annex 3", or a similar term and that it bears out Australia's view that the use of the term "support" in the proviso was not intended to have the same meaning.

See question 28 below.

23. Should support be compared under Article 13(b)(ii) in terms of unit of production or total volume of support or both? 3rd parties, in particular, Australia, Argentina, Canada, China, EC, NZ

Reply

See question 28 below.

24. Please provide any written drafting history which could shed light on why the proviso was added to what is now Article 13(b)(ii) of the Agreement on Agriculture and, in particular, why the words "grant" and "decided" were used. EC

25. Please comment on an interpretation of the words "decided during" in Article 13(b)(ii) that would read them as synonymous with the words "authorized during". 3rd parties, in particular Australia, Argentina, Canada, China, EC, NZ

Reply

Australia is concerned that use of the phrase "authorised during" may be considered to imply a relationship with budgetary approval and expenditure processes and that this would not necessarily be a correct interpretation. As an alternative, Australia suggests "committed to during" could be an appropriate interpretation of the phrase "decided during". See question 28 below.

26. Under Article 13(b)(ii), a comparison is required between support at different times. One of the issues which is contested between the parties is whether the only later period that the Panel can consider is the present one (i.e. the period underway at the time of the request for establishment of the Panel). This argument is based on the present tense of the words "do not grant" in the English text. The Panel asks whether there is any difference in the verb tense as used in the Spanish-language text, or any other difference which might aid the Panel in interpreting these words? Argentina, EC, Paraguay, Venezuela

27. If the 1992 "decision" led to or was the funding source for the money provided in 1992 and later years, is it the full amount of all that funding that constitutes the "support" decided in 1992? If the answer to this question is that it is the full amount of all the support provided pursuant to the "decision" that must be taken into account, must this be compared with the total amount of support that will or might flow from the decision made in the more recent period for the purposes of the comparison required under Article 13(b)(ii)? If a Member did not make a "decision" (however that may be interpreted) in 1992 about "support", is it the case that the Member has a zero base for the purposes of the comparison required under Article 13(b)(ii)? EC

28. In paragraph 13 of Australia's oral statement, you state that a "question" is: "could conditions of price competition for the purposes of a non-violation or impairment claim be assessed solely on the basis of budgetary outlay figures, as argued by Brazil, or on the basis of a rate of payment, as argued by the United States? In Australia's view, both factors put forward by Brazil and the United States would properly form a part of that assessment, but not the whole." Could you please clarify this statement (indicating other elements which would complete the "whole" and explain its relevance for the purposes of our consideration of Article 13 of the Agreement on Agriculture? Australia, EC

Reply

The proviso "provided that such measures do not grant support to a specific commodity in excess of that decided during the 1992 marketing year" appears in both subparagraphs (ii) and (iii) of Article 13(b). In both cases, the basic textual provision is the same:

> During the implementation period … domestic support measures that conform fully to the provisions of Article 6 … shall be … exempt from actions based on [*the specified provisions*], provided

> that such measures do not grant support to a specific commodity in excess of that decided during the 1992 marketing year.

Yet Article 13(b)(ii) deals with situations of violation nullification or impairment complaints in relation to actionable subsidies, and Article 13(b)(iii) deals with situations of non-violation nullification or impairment complaints in relation to tariff concessions. It does not seem to Australia to be feasible that the authors of the text of Article 13 of the *Agreement on Agriculture* would have intended exactly the same language within the same Article to have distinct meanings. Indeed, Australia believes it must be assumed that, had the authors intended that the proviso be interpreted and applied differently in the context of violation and non-violation complaints, they would have used different texts, consistent with the normal rules of treaty interpretation. In Australia's view, therefore, it must be assumed that the authors of Article 13 intended that the proviso have the same meaning in the context of both violation and non-violation complaints, and the proviso must be interpreted in such a way as to be capable of being applied in relation to both situations. To this end, it would be a proper exercise of the Panel's discretionary powers to consider also the nature of a non-violation complaint to determine the proviso's meaning.

Australia recalls that the text of the proviso, as well as the draft text of what became Article 13 of the *Agreement on Agriculture* first appeared in the "Blair House Accord" and that the Accord also included provisions concerning the *EEC – Oilseeds* dispute.[18] In Australia's view, that dispute is crucially relevant to the proper interpretation of Article 13(b)(ii) and (iii).[19]

The panel in *EEC – Oilseeds* described the purpose of GATT Article XXIII:1(b) in the following terms:

> … The Panel noted that these provisions, as conceived by the drafters and applied by the contracting parties, serve mainly to protect the value of tariff concessions.[...] The idea underlying them is that the improved competitive opportunities that can legitimately be expected from a tariff concession can be frustrated not only by measures proscribed by the General Agreement but also by measures consistent with that Agreement. …[20]

The *EEC – Oilseeds* panel went on to say:

> The Panel carefully analysed the price mechanism established in the framework of the Community's market organization for oilseeds and found that the production subsidy schemes of the Community protect Community producers completely from the move-

[18] *European Economic Community – Payments and Subsidies Paid to Processors and Producers of Oilseeds and Related Animal-Feed Proteins ("EEC – Oilseeds")*, Report of the Panel, adopted 25 January 1990, BISD 37S/86.

[19] Australia notes that the report of the *EEC – Oilseeds* panel has been cited with approval in subsequent WTO jurisprudence, for example, *Japan – Measures Affecting Consumer Photographic Film and Paper*, Report of the Panel, WT/DS44/R, para. 10.35, and *EC – Measures Affecting Asbestos and Asbestos-Containing Products*, Report of the Appellate Body, WT/DS135/AB/R, para. 185.

[20] *EEC – Oilseeds*, para. 144.

> ment of prices for imports and hence prevent the lowering of import duties from having any impact on the competitive relationship between domestic and imported oilseeds. ...[21]

The *EEC – Oilseeds* panel also said:

> ... The Panel considered that the main value of a tariff concession is that it provides an assurance of better market access through improved price competition. Contracting parties negotiate tariff concessions primarily to obtain that advantage. They must therefore be assumed to base their tariff negotiations on the expectation that the price effect of the tariff concessions will not be systematically offset. ... The Panel does not share the view of the Community that the recognition of the legitimacy of such expectations would amount to a re-writing of the rules of the General Agreement. ... The recognition of the legitimacy of an expectation relating to the use of production subsidies therefore in no way prevents a contracting party from using production subsidies consistently with the General Agreement; it merely delineates the scope of the protection of a negotiated balance of concessions. For these reasons the Panel found that the United States may be assumed not to have anticipated the introduction of subsidies which protect Community producers completely from the movement of prices for imports and thereby prevent tariff concessions from having any impact on the competitive relationship between domestic and imported oilseeds, and which have as one consequence that all domestically-produced oilseeds are disposed of in the internal market notwithstanding the availability of imports.[22]

In summary, the *EEC – Oilseeds* panel considered that the basis for assessing whether the benefits of tariff concessions are being nullified or impaired in a non-violation complaint is the legitimate expectations of the "conditions of price competition" for a product. In assessing those conditions, matters to be considered included market prices and the applicable tariff concession(s) as well as any other relevant measures, including measures that were not inconsistent with GATT 1947. Further, that assessment involved a temporal comparison between the "conditions of price competition" that could legitimately have been expected at the time a tariff concession was negotiated and the conditions that actually prevailed at a later point of time.

Accordingly, to enable its application in a situation of non-violation nullification or impairment of the benefits of tariff concessions accruing to another Member, the proviso of Article 13(b)(iii) must be interpreted in a manner capable of:

- establishing other Members' legitimate expectations of the "conditions of price competition";

---

[21] *EEC – Oilseeds*, para. 147.
[22] *EEC – Oilseeds*, para. 148.

- taking account of factors such as the applicable tariff concession(s), market prices and domestic support measures that conform fully to the provisions of Article 6 of the *Agreement on Agriculture*; and
- allowing a comparison between two different points in time.

In Australia's view, interpreting the phrase "grant support" in a manner that limits the factors to be considered to domestic support measures that conform fully to the provisions of Article 6 as measured by budgetary outlays, as argued by Brazil, or the rate of payment, as argued by the United States, could not lead to a proper application of the proviso of Article 13(b)(iii) in the context of a non-violation dispute. Such an interpretation cannot establish other Members' legitimate expectations of "conditions of price competition" as these have been understood in GATT and WTO jurisprudence, as it cannot capture issues relating to tariff concessions and market prices that are integral to a non-violation complaint of nullification or impairment of the benefits of tariff concessions accruing to another Member. The only essential element that such an interpretation is capable of capturing is the basic point in time for the purposes of comparison: instead of being the time at which a tariff concession was negotiated, it is the 1992 marketing year.

It would not be possible for the interpretations of the proviso offered by Brazil and the United States to apply in the context of a non-violation dispute. Thus, Australia believes it is incumbent upon the Panel to consider whether it is possible to apply in the context of an actionable subsidy complaint the proviso in the sense of legitimate expectations of the "conditions of price competition" as this applies to a non-violation nullification or impairment complaint. That application would need to take account as appropriate of tariff concessions, market prices and domestic support measures that conform fully to the provisions of Article 6.

Australia considers that such a "conditions of price competition" test is capable of being applied in the context of a violation complaint covered by Article 13(b)(ii) and was in fact intended by the authors of the text of Article 13. In Australia's view, a "conditions of price competition" test as this was interpreted and applied in *EEC – Oilseeds*, allowing as appropriate tariff concessions, market prices and domestic support measures that conform fully to the provisions of Article 6, forms "the whole".

Further, such an interpretation overcomes the many interpretive questions raised by the arguments put forward by the parties to the dispute. Notwithstanding that legitimate expectations of "conditions of price competition" are not normally applicable in the context of a violation complaint, Australia cannot identify any provision of the *Agreement on Agriculture*, or indeed any other of the covered agreements, that would preclude the application of such a test in the context of Article 13(b)(ii).

The use of such a test would explain why the phrase "grant support" was used without further elaboration, such as "support as measured by AMS", "support as calculated in Annex 3" or similar wording. "Support" in the context of subparagraphs (ii) and (iii) of Article 13(b) was purposefully intended to mean all non-"green box" domestic support measures, whether specific or not, which benefit a specific commodity in the sense of a "conditions of price competition" test. In this context, Australia notes that paragraph 8 of Annex 3 expressly excludes from the calculation of AMS some forms of "support" within the meaning of subparagraphs (ii) and (iii) of Article 13(b).

The proviso establishes "support ... decided during the 1992 marketing year" as the basis for comparison. In other words, the basis for comparison is the legitimate expectations of other Members of the "conditions of price competition" having regard to the applicable tariff measures and non-"green box" domestic support measures as these were committed to by a Member during the 1992 marketing year, vis-à-vis market prices. It requires a comparison of the legitimate expectations of other Members of the "conditions of price competition" to apply in future on the basis of decisions made by a Member during the 1992 marketing year with the actual "conditions of price competition" at a future point in time. Thus, question concerning whether a year-on-year comparison is required or whether a failure by a Member to comply in a given year affects that Member's entitlement to invoke Article 13(b) in other years become moot. So long as a Member's non-"green box" domestic support measures that conform fully to the provisions of Article 6 "grant support to a specific commodity" in the sense of a "conditions of price competition" test "in excess of that decided during the 1992 marketing year", Article 13(b)(ii) and (iii) does not provide an exemption from actions based on the specified provisions. Conversely, once a Member's non-"green box" domestic support measures no longer grant support in excess of that decided during the 1992 marketing year, the Member re-acquires the right to invoke Article 13(b)(ii) and (iii).

In Australia's view, interpreting the proviso of Article 13(b)(ii) as requiring the application of a "conditions of price competition" test is consistent with the ordinary meaning of the words in their context:

> provided that [*domestic support measures that conform fully to the provisions of Article 6*] do not grant [agree to, bestow or confer][23] support [*assistance or backing*][24] to a specific commodity in excess of [*more than*][25] that decided [*determined or resolved,*[26]*, i.e., committed to*] during the 1992 marketing year.

Moreover, interpreted in the sense of legitimate expectations of "conditions of price competition" in respect of both Article 13(b)(ii) and (iii), the proviso is consistent with the object and purpose of the *Agreement on Agriculture*, including as expressed in the preamble of the Agreement "to establish a fair and *market*-oriented agricultural trading system and that a reform process should be initiated through the negotiation of commitments on support and protection and through the establishment of strengthened and more operationally effective ... rules and disciplines" and "to provide for substantial progressive reductions in

[23] *The New Shorter Oxford English Dictionary*, Volume 1, page 1131.
[24] *The New Shorter Oxford English Dictionary*, Volume 2, pages 3152-3153.
[25] *The New Shorter Oxford English Dictionary*, Volume 1, page 873.
[26] *The New Shorter Oxford English Dictionary*, Volume 1, 607.

agricultural support and protection sustained over an agreed period of time, resulting in correcting and preventing restrictions and distortions in world agricultural markets". The provisos of Article 13(b)(ii) and (iii) establish the outer limits within which the market distorting support that continues to be permitted under the *Agreement on Agriculture* must remain during the implementation period if a Member is to benefit from the protection against actionable subsidy claims offered by Article 13(b) during that time. In other words, a Member's domestic support measures may not create a more market distorting situation in respect of any one commodity than could reasonably have been anticipated on the basis of that Member's decisions made known during the 1992 marketing year for that product.

However, should the Panel consider that another interpretation of the proviso of Article 13(b)(ii) was intended by the authors of the text of Article 13, Australia believes it incumbent upon the Panel to test its interpretation in the context of a non-violation complaint covered by Article 13(b)(iii).

EXPORT CREDIT GUARANTEE PROGRAMMES

29. (a) Is an export credit guarantee a financial contribution in the form of a "potential direct transfer of funds or liabilities (e.g. loan guarantee)" within the meaning of Article 1.1(a)(1)(i) of the SCM Agreement? Why or why not? 3rd parties, in particular, Argentina, Canada, EC, NZ

(b) How, if at all, would this be relevant to the claims of Brazil? 3rd parties, in particular, Argentina, Canada, EC, NZ

30. The Panel could arguably take the view that Articles 1 and 3 of the SCM Agreement were relevant in assessing the WTO-consistency of United States export credit guarantees. The Panel would therefore appreciate third party views on this situation, including with respect to the viability of an a contrario interpretation of item (j) of the Illustrative List (as addressed in paragraphs 180-183 of the United States' first written submission). 3rd parties, in particular, Argentina, Canada, EC, NZ

31. If the Panel decides to refer to provisions of the SCM Agreement for contextual guidance in the interpretation of the terms in Article 10 Agreement on Agriculture, should the Panel refer to item (j) or Articles 1 and 3 of the SCM Agreement or both? 3rd parties, in particular, Argentina, Canada, EC, NZ

32. The Panel's attention has been drawn to Article 14(c) of the SCM Agreement (see third party submission of Canada) and to the panel report in DS 222 Canada- Export Credits and Loan Guarantees. How and to what extent are Article 14(c) of the SCM Agreement, and the cited panel report, relevant to the issue of whether or not the United States export credit guarantee programmes confer a "benefit"? What would the appropriate market benchmark be to use for any comparison? Please cite any other relevant material. 3rd parties, in particular, Argentina, Canada, EC, NZ

33. What is the relevance (if any) of Brazil's statement that : "...export credit guarantees for exports of agricultural exports [sic] are not available on the marketplace by commercial lenders". 3rd parties, in particular, Argentina, Canada, EC, NZ

34. Comment on the United States' view of the meaning of "long term operating costs and losses" in item (j) of the Illustrative List of Export Subsidies in Annex I of the SCM Agreement as meaning "claims paid" under the export credit guarantee programmes. Does the United States' interpretation give meaning to both "costs" and "losses"? Do claims paid represent "losses"? 3rd parties, in particular, Argentina, Canada, EC, NZ

35. Did the drafters of the Agreement on Agriculture include export credit guarantees in Article 9.1 of the Agreement on Agriculture? Why or why not? 3rd parties, in particular, Argentina, Canada, EC, NZ

36. Please explain any possible significance the following statements may have in respect of Brazil's claims about GSM102 and 103 (7 CFR 1493.10(a)(2), Exhibit BRA-38) 3rd parties, in particular, Argentina, Canada, EC, NZ

(a) "The programmes operate in cases where credit is necessary to increase or maintain US exports to a foreign market and where US financial institutions would be unwilling to provide financing without CCC's guarantee. (7 CFR 1493.10(a)(2) Exhibit BRA-38)

(b) "The programmes are operated in a manner intended not to interfere with markets for cash sales. The programmes are targeted toward those countries where the guarantee is necessary to secure financing of the exports but which have sufficient financial strength so that foreign exchange will be available for scheduled payments." (7 CFR 1493.10(a)(2) Exhibit BRA-38)

(c) "In providing this credit guarantee facility, CCC seeks to expand market opportunities for US agricultural exporters and assist long-term market development for US agricultural commodities." (7 CFR 1493.10(a)(2) Exhibit BRA-38)

37. The United States seems to argue that, at present, by virtue of Article 10.2 of the Agreement on Agriculture, there are no disciplines on agricultural export credit guarantees under the Agreement on Agriculture (or the SCM Agreement).

(a) Comment on the following proposition: a WTO Member may therefore extend agricultural export credit guarantees without charging a premium, and for an indefinite period, in addition to any other terms and conditions it may wish? How would this reconcile with the title of Article 10 of the Agreement on Agriculture ("Prevention of Circumvention on Export Subsidy Commitments"), and with other commitments contained in the

Agreement on Agriculture? Please cite any relevant material, including any past WTO dispute settlement cases. 3rd parties, in particular, Argentina, Canada, EC, NZ

(b) **If, as the United States argues, there are no disciplines on export credit guarantees in the Agreement on Agriculture, how could export credit guarantees "conform fully to the provisions of Part V" of the Agreement on Agriculture within the meaning of Article 13 (how can you assess "conformity" or non-conformity with non- existent disciplines)? 3rd parties, in particular, Argentina, Canada, EC, NZ**

STEP 2 PAYMENTS

38. Please comment on the statement in note 119 of the United States' first written submission that "...to the extent a consumer that had intended to export instead opens the bale, then that consumer could still obtain the Step 2 payment upon submission of the requisite documentation". The Panel notes that Step 2 payments all involve upland cotton produced in the United States. What are the two distinct factual situations that Step 2 payments involve? Other than the panel report in Canada-Dairy and the findings of the Appellate Body in US-FSC (21.5)[27], do any other dispute settlement reports offer guidance on this issue? For example, how, if at all is the Appellate Body's report in Canada-Aircraft relevant here?[28] 3rd parties, in particular, Australia, Argentina, NZ, Paraguay

39. Please comment on the United States assertions at paragraph 129 of its first written submission, that "[t]he programme is indifferent to whether recipients of the benefit of this programme are exporters or parties that open bales for the processing of manufacturing raw cotton into cotton pro-

---

[27] "We recall that the ETI measure grants a tax exemption in two different sets of circumstances: (a) where property is produced *within* the United States and held for use *outside* the United States; and (b) where property is produced *outside* the United States and held for use outside the United States. Our conclusion that the ETI measure grants subsidies that are export contingent in the first set of circumstances is not affected by the fact that the subsidy can also be obtained in the second set of circumstances. The fact that the subsidies granted in the second set of circumstances *might* not be export contingent does not dissolve the export contingency arising in the first set of circumstances.[27] Conversely, the export contingency arising in these circumstances has no bearing on whether there is an export contingent subsidy in the second set of circumstances. Where a United States taxpayer is simultaneously producing property within and outside the United States, for direct use outside the United States, subsidies may be granted under the ETI measure in respect of both sets of property. The subsidy granted with respect to the property produced within the United States, and exported from there, is export contingent within the meaning of Article 3.1(a) of the *SCM Agreement*, irrespective of whether the subsidy given in respect of property produced outside the United States is also export contingent."

[28] There, the Appellate Body stated that,

> "the fact that some of TPC's contributions, in some industry sectors, are *not* contingent upon export performance, does not necessarily mean that the same is true for all of TPC's contributions. It is enough to show that one or some of TPC's contributions do constitute subsidies "contingent ... in fact ... upon export performance".[28]

ducts in the United States". 3rd parties, in particular, Australia, Argentina, NZ, Paraguay

Reply

This comment responds to both questions 38 and 39.

Australia provided detailed comment on the "Step 2" payment programme having regard to the Appellate Body's findings in *US – FSC (21.5)* at paragraphs 49-69 of its Third Party Submission. Australia does not dispute that "Step 2" payments may be made on either export or domestic use of a bale of cotton, or that the "intent" with which a buyer purchased a bale of cotton has no effect on an entitlement to a "Step 2" payment in respect of that particular bale. However, these arguments by the United States are not determinative of the issue.

To qualify for a "Step 2" payment, a bale of cotton must be either exported or consumed by a domestic user. These are the two distinct factual situations covered by the "Step 2" payment programme: by definition, a particular bale of cotton cannot be both exported and consumed by a domestic user.

The Appellate Body's findings in *Canada – Aircraft*[29] provide further support for the view that "Step 2" payments are export or local content subsidies. In each of the distinct factual situations of export or domestic use, "Step 2" payments are contingent upon export performance or contingent upon the use of domestic over imported goods respectively.

40. With respect to paragraph 32 of the oral statement of the EC, are subsidies contingent on the use of domestic goods consistent with the AoA? Does the phrase "provide support in favour of domestic producers" refer to, and/or permit such subsidies? What is the meaning and relevance of this (if any) to Brazil's claims under Article 3 of the SCM Agreement and Article III:4 of the GATT 1994. 3rd parties, in particular, Australia, Argentina, EC, NZ, Paraguay

Reply

Australia does not consider that the phrase "provide support in favour of domestic producers" in Article 3.2 of the *Agreement on Agriculture* permits subsidies contingent upon the use of domestic goods.

In Australia's view, the legal issue in question relates to the *condition* attached to the grant of a subsidy, not the grant of a subsidy *per se* or who might benefit from the subsidy. The fact that a measure may benefit an agricultural producer ("support in favour of domestic producers") does not serve to override measures otherwise prohibited.

Article 21.1 of the *Agreement on Agriculture* provides that "[t]he provisions of GATT 1994 and of other Multilateral Trade Agreements in Annex 1A to the WTO Agreement shall apply subject to the provisions of this Agreement". Article 3.1 of the *SCM Agreement* applies "[e]xcept as provided in the Agree-

[29] *Canada – Measures Affecting the Export of Civilian Aircraft*, Report of the Appellate Body, WT/DS70/AB/R, para. 179.

ment on Agriculture". The General Interpretive Note to Annex 1A of the *Marrakesh Agreement Establishing the World Trade Organization* also provides contextual guidance. Pursuant to that Note, the *Agreement on Agriculture* would prevail to the extent of any conflict with GATT 1994.

However, in the case of subsidies contingent upon the use of domestic goods, there is no conflict between either the *Agreement on Agriculture*, which inter alia disciplines the amounts of domestic support in favour of domestic producers which distorts trade and production, and the *SCM Agreement* or GATT 1994, which discipline or prohibit certain conditions attached to subsidies, including subsidies in favour of agricultural producers (subject only to the provisions of Article III:8(b) of GATT 1994). There is no provision in the *Agreement on Agriculture* which provides for an exception to, or cover for, local content conditions attached to the grant of a subsidy.

Australia has already noted[30] that Article 13(b)(ii) does not exempt non-"green box" domestic support measures from actions based on Article 3 of the *SCM Agreement*. Neither does Article 13 anywhere refer to GATT Article III:4. Nor with regard to these Articles is there any provision comparable to Articles 5 and 12 of the *Agreement on Agriculture*. As stated in the preambular clauses of the *Agreement on Agriculture*, the "long-term objective is to provide for substantial progressive reductions in agricultural support and protection": it is not intended to provide for a weakening of disciplines, particularly when such disciplines are not specifically mentioned.

Australia also notes that the domestic support provisions of the *Agreement on Agriculture* provide for a strengthening and elaboration of the provisions of Article XVI of GATT 1994. They are not directed towards a diminution of basic GATT obligations. National treatment is central to the multilateral trading system. It is inconceivable to Australia that the negotiators of the Agreement on Agriculture would, as part of a reform programme designed to strengthen disciplines, agree to weaken national treatment disciplines.

However, in the event the Panel were to consider that the phrase "provide support in favour of domestic producers" refers to and/or permits subsidies contingent upon the use of domestic goods, Australia notes that such support could be permitted only to the extent that the support was actually passed through to the producers of the basic agricultural product.

ETI ACT

41. Concerning its claims on the ETI Act, Brazil relies on the US – FSC case. However, it appears that the United States did not raise the issue of the Peace Clause in that case, nor did the US appear to invoke Article 6 of the Agreement on Agriculture. If the Panel's understanding is correct, how, if at all, are these differences relevant here? Argentina, China, EC, NZ

42. How do you view the reference in paragraph 43 of the EC's third party oral statement with respect to the relevance of Article 17.14 of the DSU,

[30] Oral Statement by Australia, paras. 29-30.

and, in particular, the phrase "a final resolution to that dispute" (emphasis added)? Please explain the use, and relevance (if any) of the term "disputes" in Articles 9.3 and 12 and Appendix 3 of the DSU, and please cite any other provisions you consider relevant. Argentina, China, EC, NZ

ANNEX J-3

ANSWERS OF BENIN TO THE PANEL'S QUESTIONS OF 25 JULY 2003

11 August 2003

Benin offers the following responses to the 25 July questions of the Panel, as they pertain to the scope of Benin's Third Party Submission or Oral Statement:

1. Australia has argued that Article 13 of the *Agreement on Agriculture* is an affirmative defence. How do you reconcile this with your view that the conditions of Article 13 are a "prerequisite" to the availability of a right or privilege? Australia. Would other third parties have any comments on Australia's assertion? 3rd parties, in particular Argentina, Benin, China, Chinese Taipei

Reply

Benin agrees with the basic assertion of Australia that Article 13 of the *Agreement on Agriculture* is an affirmative defence.

In Benin's view, the notion of Article 13 as an affirmative defence is easily reconciled with the view that the conditions set out in Article 13 are a prerequisite to its availability. As Benin argued in its Third Party submission, the language used in Article 13 shows the clear intent of its drafters that the Member seeking to invoke the peace clause defence must bear the burden of demonstrating full compliance with all of the preconditions set out in this provision. As noted by Benin, this intent is demonstrated, *inter alia*, by the use of the proviso "provided that." In the *Quantitative Restrictions* case, also referred to in Benin's Third Party submission, the Appellate Body considered similar language in GATT Article XVIII:11, and found that the burden lay on the Member seeking to invoke the proviso.

While Benin and Australia thus share the same view on the nature of Article 13, Benin would not find it necessary to refer to the invocation of Article 13 as a "privilege." In Benin's view, a Member that has met the burden of demonstrating full compliance with all of the preconditions set out in Article 13 could invoke this defence as a right. However, the United States has clearly not met this burden in the present case.

16. If the word "specific" were deleted from Article 13(b)(ii), would this change the meaning of the subparagraph? 3rd parties, in particular Australia, Argentina, Benin, Canada, China, EC, NZ

Reply

Please see Benin's answer to Question 18, which also addresses the issue raised in Question 16.

18. Benin's oral statement considers the phrase "support to a specific commodity" in Article 13(b)(ii) of the *Agreement on Agriculture*. How does Benin believe that phrase is best interpreted? Please substantiate your response, commenting on other submissions by parties and third parties you believe appropriate. Benin

Reply

In Benin's view, the phrase "support to a specific commodity" in Article 13(b)(ii) means any support, other than green box support, provided to a particular, identifiable agricultural commodity. Such support can be provided through either a product-specific or non product-specific programme.

The United States argues that "the phrase 'support to a specific commodity' should be understood to mean 'product-specific support'". This position is supported by the European Communities, which suggests that the word "specific" was inserted in Article 13 as "a qualifier to the word 'support'".

As noted by Benin in its oral statement of July 24, if the drafters of the Agreement on Agriculture had wanted to use the term "product-specific support" in Article 13(b)(ii), they obviously could have done so, as they did elsewhere in Agreement, such as in Article 6(4), or in Annex 3.

The interpretation proposed by the United States and the European Communities is contrary to the language actually used in Article 13(b)(ii), which refers to support to a "specific commodity" and not "specific support" to a commodity, or "product-specific support." The treaty interpreter must give meaning to the words actually used by the drafters of this provision.

As noted by New Zealand in its Third Party submission, the use of the term "specific commodity" in Article 13(b)(ii) was used to distinguish the "peace clause" from general domestic support commitments, which are determined on the basis of total "Aggregate Measure of Support". As stated by New Zealand, without such wording, "peace clause" protection could be lost for any agricultural product if total AMS increased, even if support to a specific product had not increased.

Moreover, to re-iterate another point raised by Benin in its oral statement, acceptance of the US interpretation would clearly elevate form over substance. Benin agrees with Brazil that the US interpretation "would carve out a category of non-'green box' subsidies simply because the measures distort trade in *multiple* commodities...This interpretation would permit Members to insulate their trade-distorting non-'green box' measures from challenge by manipulating the *form* of the support so that it does not mandate the production of a specific commodity in order to receive the subsidy, or by providing such support through a non-'product-specific' measure."

Benin also notes that the Appellate Body has made clear that the WTO-consistency of subsidies must be determined by their *substance*, and not by their *form*.[1]

Therefore, support provided to any specific or identifiable commodity, regardless of the nature of that support, must be included in the analysis required by Article 13(b)(ii). In Benin's view, this interpretation would remain the same if the word "specific" were deleted from Article 13(b)(ii), an issue raised in Question 16. Such a deletion, in Benin's view, would reinforce the view that support provided to "a commodity", regardless of the form of that support, would come under this provision.

In any event, whether the drafters chose the term "support to a specific commodity" or "support to a commodity", the result would be the same. The most important point is that the drafters of the Agreement could have used "product-specific support", a term of art found elsewhere in the Agreement, but did not.

In addition, Benin would offer the following views on the ETI Act:

41. Concerning its claims on the ETI Act, Brazil relies on the *US – FSC* case. However, it appears that the United States did not raise the issue of the Peace Clause in that case, nor did the US appear to invoke Article 6 of the *Agreement on Agriculture*. If the Panel's understanding is correct, how, if at all, are these differences relevant here? Argentina, China, EC, NZ

Reply

Brazil has asked the Panel to find that "the ETI Act constitutes an export subsidy violating AoA Articles 10.1 and 8 and ASCM Article 3.1(a)." [Paragraph 330 of Brazil's First Submission.]

As is well-known, the Appellate Body has found that the ETI measure is inconsistent, *inter alia*, with the same provisions cited by Brazil: Articles 10.1 and 8 of the *Agreement on Agriculture*, and Article 3.1(a) of the SCM Agreement.[2]

---

[1] In Benin's view, it is useful to recall how the Appellate Body interpreted the export subsidy commitments of the *Agreement on Agriculture* in the *Canada Dairy* dispute, where the tribunal emphatically rejected an interpretation that would have elevated form over substance. The Appellate Body refused to read the word "payments" in Article 9.1(c) narrowly, i.e. to mean monetary payments only, but not payments-in-kind:

> "...if a restrictive reading of the words "payments" were adopted, such that "payments" under Article 9.1(c) had to be monetary, no account could be taken, under Article 9.1(c), of "revenue foregone". This would, we believe, prevent a proper assessment of the commitments made by WTO Members under Article 9.2, as envisaged by Article 1(c) of the *Agreement on Agriculture*. We, therefore, prefer a reading of Article 9.1(c) that allows full account to be taken of "revenue foregone". The contrary view would, in our opinion, *elevate form over substance and permit Members to circumvent the subsidy disciplines* set forth in Article 9 of the *Agreement on Agriculture*." [emphasis added]

Appellate Body Report, Canada – Measures Affecting the Importation of Milk and the Exportation of Dairy Products, WT/DS103/AB/R, WT/DS113/AB/R, para. 110.

[2] Appellate Body report, *United States – Tax Treatment for 'Foreign Sales Corporations': Recourse to Article 21.5 of the DSU by the European Communities*. WT/DS108/AB/RW.

The Appellate Body report was adopted by the DSB on January 29, 2002, and the ETI has remained unamended since that time.

Before responding directly to Question 41, Benin would offer some preliminary observations on the relevance of earlier Panel and Appellate Body reports.

In Benin's view, prior adopted Panel or Appellate Body reports are not technically binding on subsequent Panels. As the Appellate Body stated in *Japan Alcohol*, adopted panel reports "are not binding, except with respect to resolving the particular dispute between the parties to that dispute." [3] Thus, the adopted Appellate Body decision in the FSC/ETI dispute is binding only on the parties to that dispute, the United States and the EC.

However, the Appellate Body in *Japan Alcohol* also made clear that prior panel decisions "create legitimate expectations among WTO Members, and, therefore, should be taken into account where they are relevant to any dispute."[4]

A similar approach was taken by the Panel in the *India – Patent Protection* case. The Panel, established at the request of the EC, had to determine what weight to give to the adopted Panel and Appellate Body reports on the same subject matter in an earlier case brought by the United States. The Panel stated that:

> "It can thus be concluded that panels are not *bound* by previous decisions of panels or the Appellate Body even if the subject-matter is the same. In examining dispute WT/DS79 [the EC complaint] we are not legally bound by the conclusions of the Panel in dispute WT/DS50 [the prior US complaint] as modified by the Appellate Body report. However, in the course of "normal dispute settlement procedures" required under Article 10.4 of the DSU, we will take into account the conclusions and reasoning in the Panel and Appellate Body reports in WT/DS50. Moreover, in our examination, we believe that we should give significant weight to both Article 3.2 of the DSU, which stresses the role of the WTO dispute settlement system in providing security and predictability to the multilateral trading system, and to the need to avoid inconsistent rulings (which concern has been referred to by both parties). In our view, these considerations form the basis of the requirement of the referral to the "original panel" wherever possible under Article 10.4 of the DSU."[5] [original emphasis]

---

[3] Appellate Body report, *Japan - Taxes on Alcoholic Beverages*. WT/DS8/AB/R, WT/DS10/AB/R, WT/DS11/AB/R. Page 14.

[4] Appellate Body report, *Japan - Taxes on Alcoholic Beverages*. *Ibid.*, page 14. In the *Shrimp-Turtle* compliance panel appeal, the Appellate Body added that: "This reasoning applies to adopted Appellate Body Reports as well." Appellate Body report, *United States – Import Prohibition of Certain Shrimp and Shrimp Products: Recourse to Article 21.5 of the DSU by Malaysia*. WT/DS58/AB/RW, para. 109.

[5] Panel report, India - Patent Protection for Pharmaceutical and Agricultural Chemical Products, WT/DS79/R, para. 7.30.

It is also highly instructive to recall the position taken by the United States as a third party to the EC complaint, since there are direct parallels to the current situation in *Cotton*. The US position, as summarized by the Panel, included the following:

> "The United States argued in its third party submission that the precise measures and provisions of the WTO Agreement at issue in this dispute had been the subject of a previous WTO dispute settlement proceeding....*[T]he Appellate Body had thoroughly analyzed the legal issues in the case and it was neither necessary nor appropriate for the Panel to repeat that work.* The Panel should consider the arguments of the parties, but be guided by the Appellate Body's recent interpretation of the obligations at issue....
>
> The United States supported the view of the EC that *it was not necessary or appropriate to repeat all of the legal arguments made in the earlier dispute* (WT/DS50) in the context of the present proceedings....India appeared to seek an entirely redundant proceeding. Despite India's obligation under Article 17.14 of the DSU to accept the Appellate Body's report in the earlier case unconditionally, India's submission gratuitously disparaged the work of the Appellate Body....
>
> The United States added that, moreover, India did not argue that it had modified its patent regime since the Appellate Body's ruling and that, in that situation, the Panel should be guided by the Appellate Body's decision, not by allegedly new arguments about the same patent regime.
>
> India should not be permitted to reopen legal issues that had been conclusively determined by a panel and the Appellate Body. Such a result would invite repetitive litigation....The drafters had wanted to avoid giving complainants or defendants an incentive to relitigate disputes to see if different panels would produce different results. If such "panel shopping" did produce different results, the effect on the dispute settlement system would be profoundly destabilizing.
>
> The WTO dispute settlement system could not function effectively without consistent panel judgments....Without consistent judgments, WTO Members would find little guidance in the legal interpretations developed by dispute settlement panels and the Appellate Body. The role of the dispute settlement system [would be] greatly diminished and the system could not fulfill its purpose: to serve as a "central element in providing security and *predictability* to the multilateral trading system." [emphasis added]

The parallels between *India – Patent Protection* and *Cotton* are striking, and the US submission in the former case provide clear guidance as to how the *Cotton* panel should examine Brazil's current ETI claims.

As was the case in *Patent Protection*, the Appellate Body has "thoroughly analyzed the legal issues in the [FSC/ETI] case" and it is "neither necessary nor appropriate" for the *Cotton* Panel to "repeat that work." The *Cotton* Panel should consider the arguments of the parties, but "be guided by the Appellate Body's recent interpretation of the obligations at issue." The United States should not be permitted to "reopen legal issues [related to the ETI] that had been conclusively determined by a panel and the Appellate Body." Benin shares the US concern that "such a result would invite repetitive litigation", would promote "panel shopping", and that different results could be "profoundly destabilizing."

Thus, in Benin's view, the *Cotton* panel should be guided by the Appellate Body's interpretation of the US ETI measure.

Turning to the specific question raised by the Panel: as noted above, Benin agrees with the position advanced by the United States in *Patent Protection* that a responding party in a subsequent case dealing with the same measure should not be permitted to reopen issues "that had been conclusively determined by a panel and the Appellate Body." However, in *Cotton*, the United States would have the right to advance specific new defences that were not considered by the Panel or the Appellate Body in the FSC/ETI dispute (e.g. that the United States is entitled to the protection of Article 13 because its export subsidies for cotton "conform fully" to the provisions of Part V of the *Agreement on Agriculture*).

Thus, as a procedural matter, the *Cotton* Panel could consider such US arguments. However, as a substantive matter, Benin would note that the relevant obligations in Part V of the *Agreement on Agriculture* are Articles 8 and 10.1. As stated above, the Appellate Body has already determined that the ETI involves export subsidies inconsistent with US obligations under both these provisions. Therefore, in Benin's view, US export subsidies for cotton do not "conform fully to the provisions of Part V." Accordingly, the ETI is not exempt from action by virtue of the Peace Clause.

42. How do you view the reference in paragraph 43 of the EC's third party oral statement with respect to the relevance of Article 17.14 of the *DSU*, and, in particular, the phrase "a final resolution to *that* dispute" (emphasis added)? Please explain the use, and relevance (if any) of the term "disputes" in Articles 9.3 and 12 and Appendix 3 of the *DSU*, and please cite any other provisions you consider relevant. Argentina, China, EC, NZ

Reply

As noted in the footnote to paragraph 43 of the EC statement, the reference to adopted Appellate Body reports providing "a final resolution to the dispute" was taken from the decision of the Appellate Body in the *Shrimp-Turtle* compliance panel appeal.[6] However, the context of that case was slightly different from the present dispute. The Appellate Body decision in the Article 21.5

[6] Appellate Body report, United States – Import Prohibition of Certain Shrimp and Shrimp Products: Recourse to Article 21.5 of the DSU by Malaysia. Op. Cit.

proceeding in *Shrimp Turtle* involved the same dispute as had been litigated earlier between Malaysia and the United States, although it had by then moved to the compliance panel stage.[7] By contrast, *Cotton* is a new dispute, albeit one that includes the same measure that had been found to be WTO-inconsistent in the earlier EC-US *FSC* dispute.

Thus, in the present context, the reference to "the dispute" in DSU Article 17.14 would refer to the EC-US dispute in FSC/ETI, since that is the "dispute" which has resulted in an adopted Appellate Body report. The "dispute" referred to in Article 12 and Appendix 3 would be the *Cotton* dispute, as these proceedings are now underway. Article 9.3 provides that if more than one panel is established to examine the complaints related to the same matter, to the greatest extent possible, the same persons shall serve as panelists on each of the separate panels, and the timetables shall be harmonized. While this provision might have had some potential relevance if the *Cotton* and *FSC* cases had been running concurrently, given the partial overlap of claims, it seems of little relevance now to the Panel as it assesses the weight to ascribe to prior rulings on the FSC/ETI.

In any event, Benin would strongly re-iterate its position, as set out above, that the *Cotton* panel should be guided by the Appellate Body's interpretation of the ETI, particularly since the measure has not been amended since the DSB adopted the Appellate Body's report.

---

7 Similar kinds of issues are raised in European Communities – Antidumping Duties on Imports of Cotton-Type Bed Linen from India: Recourse to Article 21.5 of the DSU by India. Report of the Appellate Body. WT/DS141/AB/RW.

ANNEX J-4

CANADA'S RESPONSES TO PANEL QUESTIONS TO THIRD PARTIES AT THE FIRST SUBSTANTIVE MEETING OF THE PANEL WITH THE PARTIES (FIRST SESSION)

11 August 2003

Canada sets out responses to the questions of the Panel in which Canada has a systemic interest:

2. Please explain the difference, if any, between the meaning of "defined" and the meaning of "fixed" in the phrase "a defined and fixed base period" in paragraph 6(a) of Annex 2 of the *Agreement on Agriculture.*

Reply

1. The meaning of the term "defined" is "having a definite or specified outline or form; clearly marked, definite".[1] The term "fixed" is defined as "definitely and permanently placed or assigned; stationary or unchanging in relative position; definite, permanent, lasting".[2] Based on the ordinary meaning of these terms, the base period for US direct payments must be clearly set out and remain unchanged. Because the structure of direct payment programme and the parameters for direct payments are essentially the same as those regarding PFC payments, the Panel should find that the applicable base period for direct payments is the base period for PFC payments. By allowing base acreage for direct payments to be updated, the United States acts inconsistently with paragraph 6(a) of Annex 2 because the base period is not "fixed". Canada refers the Panel to paragraphs 4-6 of its third party oral statement.

3. Please explain the meaning of "a" in "a defined and fixed base period" in paragraph 6(a) of Annex 2 of the *Agreement on Agriculture*, the meaning of "the" in "the base period" in paragraphs 6(b), (c) and (d), and the difference between these and the phrase "based on the years 1986-88" in Annex 3.

Reply

2. Paragraph 6(a) of Annex 2 of the *Agriculture Agreement* requires eligibility for decoupled income support payments to be determined by "clearly-defined criteria such as... production level in a defined and fixed based period". Use of the indefinite article "a" in this provision means that no base period is specified. To the contrary, paragraph 11 of Annex 3 specifies a base period.

3. Use of the definite article "the" in paragraphs 6(b), (c) and (d) of Annex 2 creates a reference to the base period established pursuant to paragraph 6(a).

---

1 *New Shorter Oxford English Dictionary*, p. 618 ("defined") [Exhibit CDA-4].

2 *New Shorter Oxford English Dictionary*, p. 962 ("fixed") [Exhibit CDA-5].

4. How often can a Member define and fix a base period in accordance with paragraph 6 of Annex 2 of the *Agreement on Agriculture*?

Reply

4. A Member may define and fix a base period only once for any given type of decoupled income support payment.

16. If the word "specific" were deleted from Article 13(b)(ii), would this change the meaning of the subparagraph?

Reply

5. The Appellate Body explained in *United States – Reformulated Gasoline* that "[o]ne of the corollaries of the 'general rule of interpretation' in the *Vienna Convention* is that interpretation must give meaning and effect to all the terms of a treaty".[3] The term "specific commodity" means a commodity that is clearly and explicitly defined.[4] Deletion of the word "specific" would imply an examination of support benefiting a potentially broader product class, a result that is not supported by the text of Article 13(b)(ii) of the *Agriculture Agreement.*

17. What is the relevance, if any, of the concept of "specificity" in Article 2 of the *SCM Agreement* and references to "a product" or "subsidized product" in certain provisions of the *SCM Agreement* to the meaning of "support to a specific commodity" in Article 13(b)(ii) *Agreement on Agriculture*?

Reply

6. Article 2 of the *SCM Agreement* sets out principles that apply to determine whether a subsidy "is specific to [certain enterprises]". In the context of Article 2, the phrase "is specific to" means that a government restricts the availability of a subsidy to certain enterprises.[5] In the context of Article 13(b)(ii) of the *Agriculture Agreement*, the term "specific commodity" means a commodity that is clearly and explicitly defined.[6] Article 13(b)(ii) requires an examination of all support that is not exempt under Annex 2 and that benefits a "precise", "exact", or "defined" commodity. Such support may be provided either through product-specific or non-product-specific support programmes.

29. (a) Is an export credit guarantee a financial contribution in the form of a "potential direct transfer of funds or liabilities (e.g. loan guarantee)" within the meaning of Article 1.1(a)(1)(i) of the *SCM Agreement* ? Why or why not?

---

[3] *United States – Standards for Reformulated and Conventional Gasoline*, Report of the Appellate Body, WT/DS2/AB/R, adopted 20 May 1996, p. 23.

[4] US First Written Submission, para. 77, fn 66. ("Clearly or explicitly defined; precise, exact, definite.")

[5] US First Written Submission, para. 77. ("'Specific' means '[s]pecially or peculiarly pertaining to a particular thing or person, or a class of these; peculiar (to)'.")

[6] US First Written Submission, para. 77, fn 66. ("Clearly or explicitly defined; precise, exact, definite.")

Reply

7. Yes, an export credit guarantee is a potential direct transfer of funds under Article 1.1(a)(1)(i) of the *SCM Agreement*. The GSM programmes "underwrite credit extended by the private banking sector in the United States (or, less commonly, by the US exporter) to approved foreign banks using dollar-denominated, irrevocable letters of credit to pay for food and agricultural products sold to foreign buyers."[7] Under the SCGP, "CCC guarantees a portion of payments due from importers under short-term financing (up to 180 days) that exporters have extended directly to the importers for the purchase of US agricultural products."[8] Where a foreign bank or foreign importer defaults under the terms of the credit/financing that has been extended, the CCC will transfer funds to the US bank or US exporter directly.

(b) How, if at all, would this be relevant to the claims of Brazil?

Reply

8. Where the guarantees provided under the US programmes confer a "benefit", a "subsidy" exists within the meaning of Article 1.1 of the *SCM Agreement*. Whether a "subsidy" exists under Article 1.1 of the *SCM Agreement* is relevant to determining whether the US programmes grant export subsidies within the meaning of Article 1(e) of the *Agriculture Agreement*. Panels and the Appellate Body have relied upon the definition of a "subsidy" in Article 1.1 of the *SCM Agreement* as context to determining whether an "export subsidy" exists under Article 1(e) of the *Agriculture Agreement*. This Panel should do the same.

9. Were the Panel to find that these programmes provide export subsidies within the meaning of Article 1(e) of the *Agriculture Agreement* (a likely result in this case), then it would also find that the United States has violated Articles 8 and 10.1 at the very least in respect of exports of upland cotton because it is an unscheduled product and the US quantitative export subsidy reduction commitment level for that commodity is therefore zero.

30. The Panel could arguably take the view that Articles 1 and 3 of the *SCM Agreement* were relevant in assessing the WTO-consistency of United States export credit guarantees. The Panel would therefore appreciate third party views on this situation, including with respect to the viability of an *a contrario* interpretation of item (j) of the Illustrative List (as addressed in paragraphs 180-183 of the United States' first written submission).

Reply

10. Whether an export subsidy exists under Articles 1 and 3 of the *SCM Agreement* is relevant to determining whether the US programmes grant export subsidies within the meaning of Article 1(e) of the *Agriculture Agreement*. Item (j) of the Illustrative List may not be interpreted *a contrario* to deem US export

---

[7] See Exhibit BRA-71 ("Fact Sheet: CCC Export Credit Guarantee Programmes (GSM-102/103)").

[8] See Exhibit BRA-72 ("Fact Sheet: CCC Supplier Credit Guarantee Programme").

credit guarantee practices as not providing export subsidies under Article 10.1 of the *Agriculture Agreement*. Where US programmes may not be deemed to provide export subsidies because they do not meet the requirements of item (j), Articles 10.1 and 10.3 of the *Agriculture Agreement* nevertheless require the United States to demonstrate that it has not granted export subsidies within the meaning of Articles 1 and 3 of the *SCM Agreement* in respect of the relevant quantity of exports. Canada refers the Panel to paragraphs 49-50 of its written third party submission and paragraphs 12-14 of its third party oral statement.

31. If the Panel decides to refer to provisions of the *SCM Agreement* for contextual guidance in the interpretation of the terms in Article 10 *Agreement on Agriculture*, should the Panel refer to item (j) or Articles 1 and 3 of the *SCM Agreement* or both?

Reply

11. The Panel should refer to both. Item (j) of the Illustrative List in Annex I of the *SCM Agreement* allows the Panel to determine whether the United States provides "export credit guarantee... programmes" such that guaranteed export credit transactions guaranteed under those programmes are subsidized *per se*. Articles 1 and 3 of the *SCM Agreement* allow the Panel to determine, on a transaction-by-transaction basis, whether given quantities of US exports are subsidized.

32. The Panel's attention has been drawn to Article 14(c) of the *SCM Agreement* (see third party submission of Canada) and to the panel report in DS 222 *Canada - Export Credits and Loan Guarantees*. How and to what extent are Article 14(c) of the *SCM Agreement*, and the cited panel report, relevant to the issue of whether or not the United States export credit guarantee programmes confer a "benefit"? What would the appropriate market benchmark be to use for any comparison? Please cite any other relevant material.

Reply

12. Canada refers the Panel to paragraphs 41-48 of its written third party submission with respect to how and to what extent Article 14(c) of the *SCM Agreement* and the cited panel report are relevant.

13. Whether a benefit is conferred under Article 1.1(b) of the *SCM Agreement* is a question of fact, to be assessed in the light of all the relevant financial considerations of a given export credit transaction. The Panel's findings in this respect will depend on an examination of: 1) the terms of credit transactions that are guaranteed by the CCC, including the length of the repayment period and any fees charged for the guarantee, and 2) credit transactions with similar terms that are occurring in the market without a CCC guarantee.

33. What is the relevance (if any) of Brazil's statement that : "...export credit guarantees for exports of agricultural exports [sic] are not available on the marketplace by commercial lenders."

Reply

14. Were the Panel to find that support for exports of agricultural products such as export credit guarantees are not available on the marketplace from commercial lenders, this would suggest that a benefit under Article 1.1(b) of the *SCM Agreement* exists because the provision of such support in the market would otherwise require uneconomical terms and conditions (based on factors such as a lack of security provided by the product and a lack of lender confidence in sales of the product).

34. Comment on the United States' view of the meaning of "long term operating costs and losses" in item (j) of the Illustrative List of Export Subsidies in Annex I of the *SCM Agreement* as meaning "claims paid" under the export credit guarantee programmes. Does the United States' interpretation give meaning to both "costs" and "losses"? Do claims paid represent "losses"?

Reply

15. The term "costs" must be distinct in meaning from the term "losses", otherwise the coordinating conjunction "and" is rendered meaningless. This is confirmed by the French version of the phrase ("*les frais et les pertes*"). In Canada's view, any "claims paid" may yield "losses" when they are added to any other "operating costs" incurred under the programme. Such losses would be required to be covered over the long term by the premiums charged to avoid a finding that transactions guaranteed under the programme are subsidized *per se*.

35. Did the drafters of the *Agreement on Agriculture* include export credit guarantees in Article 9.1 of the *Agreement on Agriculture*? Why or why not?

Reply

16. Export credit guarantees were not included in Article 9.1 of the *Agreement on Agriculture* because Members could not agree on specific language. Article 10.1 therefore covers any export subsidies granted by such guarantees.

36. Please explain any possible significance the following statements may have in respect of Brazil's claims about GSM102 and 103 (7 CFR 1493.10(a)(2), Exhibit BRA-38)

> **(a) "The programmes operate in cases where credit is necessary to increase or maintain US exports to a foreign market and where US financial institutions would be unwilling to provide financing without CCC's guarantee. (7 CFR 1493.10(a)(2) Exhibit BRA-38)**

Reply

17. This statement suggests that similar credit transactions that are not guaranteed by the CCC would involve uneconomical terms and conditions. Therefore, it suggests that a "benefit" exists within the meaning of Article 1 of the *SCM Agreement*. The statement also confirms that the US programmes are

contingent upon export performance within the meaning of Article 1(e) of the *Agriculture Agreement*.

(b) **"The programmes are operated in a manner intended not to interfere with markets for cash sales. The programmes are targeted toward those countries where the guarantee is necessary to secure financing of the exports but which have sufficient financial strength so that foreign exchange will be available for scheduled payments." (7 CFR 1493.10(a)(2) Exhibit BRA-38)**

Reply

18. This statement also suggests that a "benefit" exists within the meaning of Article 1 of the *SCM Agreement*, and confirms that the US programmes are contingent upon export performance within the meaning of Article 1(e) of the *Agriculture Agreement*.

(c) **"In providing this credit guarantee facility, CCC seeks to expand market opportunities for US agricultural exporters and assist long-term market development for US agricultural commodities." (7 CFR 1493.10(a)(2) Exhibit BRA-38)**

Reply

19. This statement confirms that the US programmes are contingent upon export performance within the meaning of Article 1(e) of the *Agriculture Agreement*.

37. The United States seems to argue that, at present, by virtue of Article 10.2 of the *Agreement on Agriculture*, there are no disciplines on agricultural export credit guarantees under the *Agreement on Agriculture* (or the *SCM Agreement*).

(a) **Comment on the following proposition: a WTO Member may therefore extend agricultural export credit guarantees without charging a premium, and for an indefinite period, in addition to any other terms and conditions it may wish? How would this reconcile with the title of Article 10 of the *Agreement on Agriculture* ("Prevention of Circumvention on Export Subsidy Commitments"), and with other commitments contained in the *Agreement on Agriculture*? Please cite any relevant material, including any past WTO dispute settlement cases.**

Reply

20. Were the Panel to find that US export credit guarantee programmes provide export subsidies within the meaning of Article 1(e) of the *Agriculture Agreement*, then it would also find that the United States has violated its export subsidy commitments under the *Agriculture Agreement* at the very least in respect of exports of upland cotton. In this respect, Canada refers the Panel to para-

graphs 51-54 of its written third party submission, paragraphs 15-16 of its third party oral statement, and paragraphs 133-153 of the Appellate Body's original report in *US – FSC*.[9]

(b) If, as the United States argues, there are no disciplines on export credit guarantees in the *Agreement on Agriculture*, how could export credit guarantees "conform fully to the provisions of Part V" of the *Agreement on Agriculture* within the meaning of Article 13 (how can you assess "conformity" or non-conformity with non- existent disciplines)?

Reply

21. For export credit guarantees to be exempt from the obligations set out in the *Agriculture Agreement*, the Agreement would have to expressly provide for the exemption. No provision of the *Agriculture Agreement* exempts export credit guarantees from any obligation under the Agreement. The US guarantees will therefore "conform fully to the provision of Part V" only if they do not confer export subsidies within the meaning of Articles 1(e) of the *Agriculture Agreement* "in a manner which results in, or which threatens to lead to, circumvention of [US] export subsidy commitments" under Article 10.1.

[9] *United States – Tax Treatment for "Foreign Sales Corporations"*, Report of the Appellate Body, WT/DS108/AB/R, adopted March 20, 2000.

ANNEX J-5

RESPONSE BY CHINA TO THE PANEL'S QUESTIONS TO THIRD PARTIES

11 August 2003

1. China appreciates this opportunity to present its views to the Panel in relation to the Panel's questions posed to third parties on July 28, 2003. While it was specifically asked to address Questions 1, 4, 12, 13, 14, 15, 16, 17, 21, 22, 23, 25, 41 and 42, China notes the Panel in the fax cover page granted freedom to third parties "to respond to or comment on questions posed to the other third parties". Given the short period within which third parties are required to submit their views, China therefore responds to and comments on the following underlined questions.

ARTICLE 13 OF THE AGREEMENT ON AGRICULTURE

2. **Question 1. Australia has argued that Article 13 of the *Agreement on Agriculture* is an affirmative defence. How do you [Australia] reconcile this with your [Australian] view that the conditions in Article 13 are a "prerequisite" to the availability of a right or privilege? Would other third parties have any comments on Australia's assertion?**

Reply

3. China agrees with the interpretation of Article 13 of the *Agreement on Agriculture* (the "Peace Clause") put forward by Australia. As explained in its written submission, China believes that the Peace Clause does not impose positive obligations; it only stands to provide limited exemptions from actions to measures that may otherwise be subject to actions based on GATT 1994 and the Agreement on Subsidies and Countervailing Measures (the "*Subsidies Agreement*"). As wording of the Peace Clause indicates, such exemptions are not automatically available or granted upon a simple allegation by a Member that it is protected; certain conditions built into the Peace Clause must be met before such a Member can enjoy entitlement to Peace Clause exemption.

4. The United States alleged that if conditions do have to be met for availability of Peace Clause protection, it is upon the complaining party to prove that the US measures do not meet such conditions, and hence do not enjoy Peace Clause protection. In support of its reasoning, it asserts that the Peace Clause imposes positive obligations by its built-in reference to Annex 2 to and Article 6 of the *Agreement on Agriculture*[1]. China disagrees on that point. In its written submission, China stated that when Annex 2 and Article 6 are brought under the Peace Clause as conditions, they lose any positive obligation nature, if any, in

[1] Para. 43, US First Written Submission, United States – Subsidies on Upland Cotton, WT/DS267, 11 July 2003.

their original places; they have come to form conditions precedent for entitlement to Peace Clause exemption. Since the Peace Clause contains limited exemptions from actions based on GATT and the *Subsidies Agreement*, it is affirmative defence in nature, and the party claiming its entitlement bears the burden of proving that it is so entitled.

5. China sees no need to "reconcile" the affirmative defence nature with the conditions that must be met to enjoy that defence. The latter is simply required to happen prior to availability of affirmative defence. The two elements, i.e. conditions to be met and availability of exemptions, form an organic whole of the Peace Clause. To China's understanding, parties to this dispute share greater disagreement on who should bear the burden of proof under the Peace Clause than whether conditions under the Peace Clause are pre-requisites to availability of Peace Clause exemption.

ARTICLE 13(B) OF THE AGREEMENT ON AGRICULTURE: DOMESTIC SUPPORT MEASURES

6. Question 4, How often can a Member define and fix a base period in accordance with paragraph 6 of Annex 2 of the *Agreement on Agriculture*?

Reply

7. In relation to US direct payments under the 2002 FRSI Act, the European Communities ("EC") in its oral statement took a unique stance different from those of all other parties. Noting the United States argument that updating of base periods was necessary in order to bring support for oilseeds production under the direct payment scheme, the EC argued that "it must be possible to have different reference periods while eligibility is based on previous eligibility for production distorting subsidies" "to ensure the progressive movement of production distorting subsidies to decoupled subsidies"; on the other hand, the EC also expressed concern that "continued updating of reference periods in respect of the same already decoupled support, creating an expectation that production of certain crops will be rewarded with a greater entitlement to supposedly decoupled payments, tends to undermine the decoupled nature of such payments"[2]. Such a line of reasoning may have given rise to the question raised by the Panel.

8. While sharing the same concern with the EC, China does not see eye to eye with the EC on the proposed allowance for an initial jump of the reference period over the transition from production distorting subsidies to "decoupled subsidies", even if the latter are found to be decoupled. In China's opinion, the issue is not about frequency of reference period updating; the issue is whether Para. 6 of Annex 2 to the *Agreement on Agriculture* allows updating of the reference period at all.

9. Specifically, the Panel in this case is faced with a direct payment programme that was initiated by a Member several years prior to the coming into effect of the *Agreement on Agriculture*, but was over the years, maintained in the

[2] Para. 30, Oral Statement by the European Communities, United States – Subsidies on Upland Cotton, WT/DS267, 24 July 2003.

Member country by successor legislations with slight variations. While Para. 6 of Annex 2 to the *Agreement on Agriculture* does not specify when "a fixed and defined base period" falls, it certainly does not provide a window of opportunity for an existing production distorting support measure to transform into a kind of payment with an increased production factor (acreage) in a new up-to-date period. Such an interpretation would grant a bonus not intended by the drafters. The requirement by Para. 6 for a "base" period reflects the drafters' intention to freeze any "Green Box" programme at its initial support level, as opposed to a period selected by a Member. If a Member wishes to carry out a transformation, it should certainly follow the spirit of Para. 6 and use the base period that is already fixed and defined by the predecessor legislation.

10. Therefore, with respect to the interpretation Para. 6 of Annex 2 to the *Agreement on Agriculture* as applied to a direct payment programme that is a direct descendent of predecessor programmes, China is of the view that no updating shall be allowed at all.

11. Question 12. Where does Article 13(b) require a year-on-year comparison?

Reply

12. Main elements of Article 13(b)(ii) and (iii) read: "domestic support measures that fully conform to ... shall be exempt from actions ... , provided that such measures do not grant support to a specific commodity *in excess of that* decided *during the 1992 marketing year*" (emphasis added). The full conformity chapeau and the proviso are two conditions to the availability of exemption granted by this Article.

13. The Panel's question relates to interpretation of the proviso. Key to the interpretation are the words "that", "during the 1992 marketing year" and "in excess of". The word "that" is inserted in the second portion of the proviso to refer back to what was described in the previous portion, i.e. "support to a specific commodity". The phrase "in excess of" requires a comparison. The phrase "during the 1992 marketing year" indicates a requisite element of comparison, a common denominator in time frame without which a comparison is impossible. The combination of these three elements requires a comparison of support levels between a given year at issue and 1992 marketing year, i.e. a year-on-year comparison.

14. Obviously, the proviso does not contemplate the comparison of the sum of support levels for more than one year with that of 1992 marketing year. Such a comparison would be one between two grossly unequal numbers, resulting in no statistical significance and would destroy the purpose of the proviso being a condition precedent to the availability of a protection.

15. In addition, the proviso, properly interpreted, cannot be limited to a comparison only of measures currently in effect against those during the 1992 marketing year, as the US argues. The US based its argument on the present tense of the proviso, arguing that such a tense only calls for determination of the support that challenged measures currently grant. With respect, China disagrees. While it

is indeed written in the present tense, the sentence is led by the key word "provided" in a strong limitation and demand style. As such, the present tense serves the purpose. The intention of such tense is to ensure that support levels beyond those in 1992 are not to be protected by the Peace Clause. Further, the US argument fails to recognize that the present tense is "present" only in respect of 1995, when the *Agreement on Agriculture* came into effect. It seeks to govern then "future" measures. Using the time of panel dispute resolution as the vantage point, as the United States argues, seriously limits the proviso's scope to examining only measures current as of the time of dispute. Thirdly, the US interpretation that a comparison is only limited to the measures currently in effect drives a significant loophole into the treaty language, and seeks to remove the proviso requirement for measures that are not current during the year of dispute resolution. Such an interpretation would also be tantamount to placing a period of limitation within which a complaining member must seek dispute settlement against dispute-current measures only. Neither the loophole nor the period of limitation can be intended by the drafters. It follows therefore, while Article 13(b) requires a year-on-year comparison, that comparison is not limited to measure currently in effect. The issue of what measures are before this Panel are set out in the terms reference for this Panel.

16. Question 13. Does a failure by a Member to comply in a given *year* with either the chapeau of Article 13(b) or the proviso in subparagraph (ii) of Article 13(b) impact its entitlement to benefit in an earlier or a later year from the exemption from action provided by Article 13(b)?

Reply

17. China proposes to address this question in two parts: one, does a failure by a Member to comply in a given year with the chapeau of Article 13(b) impact its entitlement to benefit in an earlier or a later year from the exemption from action provided by Article 13(b)? Two, does a failure by a Member to comply in a given year with the proviso in subparagraph (ii) of Article 13(b) impact its entitlement to benefit in an earlier or a later year from the exemption from action provided by Article 13(b)? In this respect, it is again useful to turn back to the elements in Article 13(b)(ii) and (iii), which read: "domestic support measures that fully conform to ... shall be exempt from actions ... , provided that such measures do not grant support to a specific commodity in excess of that decided during the 1992 marketing year". As discussed in China's answers to Question 12, both the chapeau and the proviso are two co-existing conditions, and breach of either will lead to loss of the exemption granted by these Articles.

18. For the first part, a failure by a Member to comply in a given year with the chapeau of Article 13(b) will not impact its entitlement to benefit in an earlier or a later year from the exemption from action. The chapeau requires that domestic support measures conform fully to provisions of Article 6. Articles 6.1 and 6.3 in turn provide that all non-green box domestic support measures of a Member are considered to be in compliance with Article 6 if the Member's "*Current Total AMS* does not *exceed* the *corresponding annual* or final bound commitment level specified in Part IV of the Member's Schedule" (emphasis added).

The word "exceed" requires a comparison. The words "current", "corresponding" and "annual" indicate that the comparison is to be made on an annual basis between the level of support actually provided in a given year and annual bound commitment level in the same year as indicated in the Member's Schedule. A Member's actual level of support varies from year to year, so does a Member's annual bound commitment level. Therefore a factual comparison between the two in a given year shall not have any bearing on a comparison of different support levels in an earlier or later year.

19. In respect of the second part of the question, China would like to reiterate its answer to Question 12 that Article 13 (b) requires a year-on-year comparison between the annual level of support at issue and the level of support in 1992 marketing year. Whether domestic support measures in a given marketing year exceeds same in 1992 marketing year is a matter of fact. The level of support in each given year challenged shall be compared separately to same in the 1992 marketing year. A factual conclusion on the "excess" issue for measures in one year certainly shall not preclude an examination of a different set of facts in another year.

20. Question 14. Does a failure of a Member to comply with Article 13(b) in respect of a *specific commodity* impact its entitlement to benefit in respect of other agricultural products from the exemption from action provided by Article 13(b)?

Reply

21. The chapeau of Article 13(b) requires compliance with Article 6 for the purpose of determining whether Peace Clause protection is available. As discussed in China's answers to Question 13, Article 6 provides that a Member's Current Total AMS in any year shall not exceed the corresponding annual or final bound commitment level specified in Part IV of the Member's Schedule. In other words, in considering the "exceed" issue, Current Total AMS, being the monetary sum value of all measures provided by a Member in a given year shall be compared against the corresponding annual bound commitment committed by the Member in its Schedule. Such a comparison disregards the issue of support to a specific commodity. Furthermore, the phrase "support to a specific commodity" only appears in the proviso of Article 13(b), but not in the chapeau. Therefore support to a specific commodity is not an issue under consideration by the chapeau of Article 13(b).

22. In respect of the proviso of Article 13(b), China believes a failure of a Member to comply thereof in respect of *a specific commodity* does not impact its entitlement to benefit in respect of other agriculture products from the exemption from action provided by Article 13(b).

23. For the purpose of this discussion, support measures can be classified into two categories: support measures provided exclusively to one specified product or those generally available to a number of specified products.

24. Where a programme is designed to provide support exclusively to one product, e.g. upland cotton for the purpose of this case, other products are not

brought under its coverage. Failure by the Member's upland cotton-specific programme (if there is any in this case) to comply with Article 13(b)'s proviso would only take the exclusively cotton support programme at issue out of the protection of exemption by Article 13(b). Whether that Member's other support programmes are protected under Article 13(b)'s protection against actions is a matter not related to the cotton support measures at issue.

25. Where support measures are generally available to a number of products including upland cotton, the term "specific commodity" requires break up and attribution of the general budgetary outlay to each specific product for comparison under the proviso. For the purpose of this case, only the portion of outlay that was used for upland cotton is relevant for that comparison. Outlays broken up for other products covered by the same programme is not at issue before this Panel. In addition, terms of reference governing this Panel procedure does not require the Panel to review measures involving other products.

26. Question 16. If the word "specific" were deleted from Article 13(b)(ii), would this change the meaning of the subparagraph?

Reply

27. China believes that a hypothetical deletion suggested would not change the fundamental meaning of Article 13(b)(ii).

28. China understands that the word "specific" is inserted to avoid a lump-sum treatment of measures generally applicable to a number of commodities. It is to emphasize that when calculating the amount of support granted to one commodity, the portion that is delivered to that specific commodity at issue shall be singled out and counted as part of the amount of all support granted to that specific commodity. Doing the comparison otherwise would render the requisite comparison as part of the proviso meaningless.

29. If the word "specific" were to be deleted, the proviso would read:

> ..., provided that such measures do not grant support to *a* commodity in excess of that decided during the 1992 marketing year. (emphasis added)

With "specific" deleted, while the emphasis effect may be diminished, the word "a" remains and the fundamental meaning of this proviso will not change. A comparison is still required for the support levels that are directly applicable and those attributable to upland cotton.

30. The above interpretation accords with the views of New Zealand and Australia that the term "support to a specific commodity" is not synonymous with the term "product-specific support"[3]. The term "product-specific support" focuses on "product-specific", pointing to a support programme designed for and provided exclusively to a specified product. On the other hand, the term "support to a specific commodity" is used to incorporate a level of support delivered to a

[3] Paras. 23 – 24, Oral Statement by Australia, *United States – Subsidies on Upland Cotton*, WT/DS267, 24 July 2003; para. 9, New Zealand's Oral Statement, *United States – Subsidies on Upland Cotton*, WT/DS267, 24 July 2003.

specific commodity, combining both product specific support and the attributed portion of a much larger programme generally available to a number of products including upland cotton.

31. Question 17. What is the relevance, if any, of the concept of "specificity" in Article 2 of the *SCM Agreement* and references to "a product" or "subsidized product" in certain provisions of the *SCM Agreement* to the meaning of "support to a specific commodity" in Article 13(b)(ii) *Agreement on Agriculture*?

32. China believes that the concept of "specificity" in Article 2 of the *Subsidies Agreement* is used in a sense and for purposes different from that used in the proviso of Article 13(b)(ii) of the *Agreement on Agriculture*. References to "a product" or "subsidized product" in certain provisions of the *Subsidies Agreement* is not relevant at all to the meaning of "support to a specific commodity".

33. Pursuant to Article 1.2 of the *Subsidies Agreement*, a subsidy shall be subject to WTO disciplines only if its availability is restricted to specified recipients, i.e. to a *specific enterprise or industry or a group of enterprises or industries*. (emphasis added) The word defines what falls under WTO discipline over subsidies. In contrast, the word "specific" used in the phrase "support to a specific commodity" of the Peace Clause proviso, as China explains in its answers to Question 16, is an emphasis for calculating year on year support levels on a product basis. The latter is only an indicator for a method of calculation and comparison. The same word in the two different places carry with them separate meanings and purposes.

34. Question 21. Please comment on Brazil's assertion that "grant" and "decided" in Article 13(b)(ii) have broadly the same meaning. If so, why did the drafters not use the same term?

35. Debate among the parties revolves around the word "decided" in the proviso of Article 13(b)(ii). The United States argued that its domestic support measures "did not decide on an outlay or expenditure amount in favor of upland cotton"; rather, it argued that "US measures 'determined'" a per pound rate of support during 1992 marketing year while actual outlays or expenditures were known or completed after the marketing year's end. As the actual outlay would come to its knowledge upon final accounting of the world prices, no amount of outlay was "decided" during the 1992 marketing year[4].

36. In China's opinion, the above US interpretation does not lend any utility to interpreting the proviso in Article 13(b)(ii). The proviso, of which "decided" is an element, serves, together with the chapeau, as a qualifier to the entitlement to exemption from actions. Were the US interpretation to prevail, no measure involving year end accounting for the calculation of expenditure would exceed "that decided during the 1992 marketing year", as the former is not capable of measuring up to the 1992 level.

37. In support of the US reading, EC argued that Brazil's the use of "decided" as opposed to "granted" is indication that use of budgetary outlays shall be ruled

4 Para. 94, *First Written Submission of the US*, 11 July 2003.

out; that "decided" implies one-off determination, not involving "deciding" countless applications for support under a particular programme; and that use of the word "during" in the same sentence means that "decided" may also cover future periods.[5] However, the EC in its arguments fails to point out expressly what should constitute the 1992 benchmark[6].

38. Interpretation of the word "decided" shall be carried out "in accordance with the ordinary meaning to be given to the terms of the treaty in their context and in the light of its object and purpose"[7]. Drafters of this Article must be understood to have used the word to carry out the Article's object and purpose, being a 1992 benchmark against which to measure whether certain supports are entitled to exemption. Measures involving agricultural support above that benchmark must risk challenges on the basis of Article XVI:1 of the GATT and Articles 5 and 6 of the *Subsidies Agreement*. As such, the 1992 benchmark must be established for the purpose of comparison.

39. Preference of the word "decided" over "granted" by drafters of the Article may be a result of numerous possibilities. Choosing "decided" to imply a "fixed determination" can be reflective of an intention to exclude expenditures that cannot be precisely allocated to a specific marketing year; certain support payments may be granted by an administration, but may not have reached its beneficiaries in 1992; it may well be an indication of the drafters' intention to cover the exact scenario described by the US, i.e. granted in 1992 but decided in 1993. However, such choice of the word shall not push aside the core intention, which is to choose the year 1992 for establishing that benchmark support level.

40. Again, the issue of burden of proof comes up. If a subsidizing Member wishes to avail itself of the protection of Article 13(b)(ii), it is obligated to prove that the measures being challenged do not exceed the 1992 benchmark. Subsequent to the coming effect of GATT 1994, there exists a reasonable expectation that all subsidizing Members should have notified the WTO Committee on Agriculture their respective level of support in 1992 to allow a workable comparison. In the absence of such notice, evidence of a 1992 benchmark level can only be established by the complaining party, in the form of actual budgetary outlays by the subsidizing Member. Such is the best information available for a proper comparison.

41. Question 22, What is the meaning of "support" in *Agreement on Agriculture* 13(b)(ii)? Why would it be used differently from Annex 3, where it refers to total outlays? Question 23, Should support be compared under Article 13(b)(ii) in terms of unit of production or total volume of support or both?

42. Annex 3 of the *Agreement on Agriculture* is an aid to calculating AMS, which is required not to exceed the corresponding annual or final bound commitment level specified in a Member's domestic support reduction commitments

---

5 Paras. 14 - 17, *Oral Statement by the European Communities*, 24 July 2003.

6 Para. 19, *Ibid.*

7 Article 31.1, *Vienna Convention on the Law of Treaties*.

in the Member's schedule under Article 6 of the *Agreement on Agriculture*. In other words, the support calculated on the basis of outlays is part of the concept of replacing commitments to reduce domestic support on a product by product basis with a commitment to reduce overall support to the agricultural sector, a breakthrough in the Agreement's negotiations effected by the Blair House accord.

43. Insertion of the Peace Clause into the *Agreement on Agriculture* is again a part of the Blair House accord. Budgetary outlay, as exemplified by the calculation method in Annex 3, is the approach adopted to ensure that levels of support to upland cotton, whether generally available to a number of products including the product at issue, or product specific, do not overstep the 1992 marketing year level if it is to be protected by the Peace Clause exemption.

44. The United States argued that the comparison required should be between the "per pound rates" of product specific supports[8]. With respect, such an approach fails to recognize the thrust of the Blair House accord. In addition, while domestic support programmes may have specific designs, e.g. paid on per unit basis, such designs shall not guide how Article 13(b)(ii) should be interpreted. The Article has no reference at all to per unit calculation for the purpose of comparison.

45. If unit of production is to be accepted as an method for comparison in addition to absolution support level comparison, under Article 13(b)(ii), four possibilities exists. A decision as to whether a Member asserting affirmative defence is entitled to Peace Clause protection is possible only when both the absolute support level and the per unit support level are higher or lower than those during the 1992 marketing year. A decision on whether Peace Clause shields the measures at issue may have to be made taking into account extraneous factors if one method yields a plus and another minus. Those factors are, however, nowhere to be found under Article 13(b)(ii) and thus the inclusion of product unit comparison is certainly not contemplated by the drafters.

ETI ACT

46. Question 41. Concerning its claims on the ETI Act, Brazil relies on the *US – FSC* case. However, it appears that the United States did not raise the issue of the Peace Clause in that case, nor did the US appear to invoke Article 6 of the *Agreement on Agriculture*. If the Panel's understanding is correct, how, if at all, are these differences relevant here?

47. China believes that it is not necessary for the Panel to consider the issue of the Peace Clause or Article 6 of the *Agreement on Agriculture* regarding Brazil's claims on the ETI Act.

48. The issue is dealt with by Article 7.2 of the *DSU*, which provides:

> Panels shall address the relevant provisions in any covered agreement or agreements *cited by the parties* to the dispute." (emphasis added)

[8] Paras. 82 – 87, US First Written Submission, *United States – Subsidies on Upland Cotton*, WT/DS267, 11 July 2003.

In effect, under this article, a Panel is required to consider and address relevant provisions *cited by the parties* only. Since the US in this case has not claimed defence for its ETI Act, there is no need for this Panel to consider same.

49. Question 42. How do you view the reference in paragraph 43 of the EC's third party oral statement with respect to the relevance of Article 17.14 of the *DSU*, and, in particular, the phrase "a final resolution to *that* dispute" (emphasis added)? Please explain the use, and relevance (if any) of the term "disputes" in Articles 9.3 and 12 and Appendix 3 of the *DSU*, and please cite any other provisions you consider relevant.

50. The phrase "a final resolution to that dispute" cited by the EC in its third party oral statement comes from the Appellate Body Report in *US-Shrimp (21.5)* case, in which the Appellate Body stated,

> [I]t must also be kept in mind that Article 17.14 of the DSU provides not only that Reports of the Appellate Body 'shall be' adopted by the DSB, by consensus, but also that such Reports 'shall be unconditionally accepted by the parties to the dispute.' Thus, Appellate Body Reports that are adopted by the DSB are, as Article 17.14 provides, 'unconditionally accepted by the parties to the dispute', and, therefore, *must be treated by the parties to a particular dispute as a final resolution to that dispute.* In this regard, we recall, too, that Article 3.3 of the DSU states that the 'prompt settlement' of disputes 'is essential to the effective functioning of the WTO'. (emphasis added)

51. The word "that" appears to limit the binding force of Appellate Body report only to the parties in the case on which the Appellate Body's report is made. Panels in other cases are not bound by any precedential effect of an earlier Appellate Body report, because the facts, parties and other circumstances of claim may be entirely different. Generally speaking, such an interpretation is widely accepted by commentators[9].

52. Be that as it may, the ETI Act in this current case is the very same one challenged by the EC, and found to violate the *Agreement on Agriculture* and the *Subsidies Agreement* by both the panel[10] and the Appellate Body[11] in *US – FSC (21.5)*, whose reports were adopted on 29 January 2002 by the DSB. While in *that* case, the complaint was the EC, and in *this* case, the complaint was Brazil, the measures being challenged were the same, and the Member whose measures were challenged were the same. Countermeasures against the same measures were authorized by the DSB. While both the panel and the Appellate Body reports must be treated by EC and the US as final resolution to that dispute, the US is the party whose measures were found to be non-WTO compliant, and the same

[9] John H. Jackson, "The Legal Meaning of a GATT Dispute Settlement Report: Some Reflections", Towards More Effective Supervision by International Organization: Essays in Honour of Henry G. Schermers (Martinus Nijhoff Publishers, Dordrecht, Boston and London, 1994).

[10] Panel Report, *US - FSC (21.5),* WT/DS108/RW, adopted on 29 January, 2002.

[11] Appellate Body Report in *US - FSC (21.5)*, AB-2002-1, WT/DS108/AB/RW,adopted on 29 January 2002.

measures, since not having been withdrawn, is brought to this dispute. Brazil, as a Member of the WTO system, indeed with other Members of the WTO, has reasonable expectations for the US to withdraw the measures after the DSB authorization. In respect of ETI Act, there is no difference between *that* case, being *US – FSC (21.5)* and *this* case, *US – Subsidies to Upland Cotton*. Under the circumstances, there is no reason why "final resolution to that dispute" as reflected in *US – FSC (21.5)* should not be considered and taken by this Panel.

53. In respect of the term "disputes" under Article 12 and Appendix 3 of the *DSU*, it is simply used in the general context of limiting participation to only parties to a dispute for the purpose of assisting panels in organizing their respective working procedures. Meaning and interpretation of the term "dispute" lends no support to interpretation of the Appellate Body's exclamation in *US-Shrimp (21.5)* that its report in a specific case "must be treated by the parties to a particular dispute as a final resolution to that dispute". Therefore, China believes that the term "dispute(s)" used in Article 12 and Appendix 3 of the *DSU* is not helpful for interpretation of the Appellate Body's statement.

54. Article 9.3 of the *DSU*, on the other hand, is part of *DSU* Article 9 which deals with procedures for multiple complainants. It is an attempt to consolidate panel proceedings while the matter at issue has been challenged by more than one Member. Specifically, Article 9.3 reads:

> If more than one panel is established to examine the complaints related to the same matter, to the greatest extent possible the same persons shall serve as panelists on each of the separate panels and the timetable for the panel process in such disputes shall be harmonized.

The Article seeks, to the extent possible, uniformity and consistency in panel reasoning and conclusions, in the event that more than one panel is established, by having the same jurists sitting on separate panels. The requirement for having the same panelists and harmonization of panel processes, on the other hand, is only capable of being carried out if the first panel's proceedings were on-going.

55. For the current case, direct application of Article 9.3 is practically impossible. While complaints raised by Brazil in this case do cover the same ETI Act of the United States which was the subject matter of *US – FSC (21.5)*, the panel in the latter case completed its proceedings as early as 29 January 2002. In addition, the complaint by Brazil involves a whole plethora of US measures, of which the US ETI Act was only one. The majority of the measures challenged by Brazil were not dealt with by the panel in *US – FSC (21.5)*.

56. Having said that, China believes that the spirit of Article 9.3 is still of guidance value. Since the ETI Act challenged by Brazil in this case is exactly the same challenged by the EU in *US – FSC (21.5)*, and that the panel proceedings have long progressed beyond the panelist selection stage, the only way to ensure uniformity and consistency in panel reasoning and conclusions is to have this Panel consider and adopt the reasoning and conclusion of the panel and the Appellate Body *US – FSC (21.5)* in respect of the US ETI Act.

57. China thanks this Panel for granting this opportunity to present its views on issues related to this proceeding, and hopes that this Panel will finds the above points helpful.

ANNEX J-6

RESPONSES TO THE PANEL'S QUESTIONS AND THE QUESTIONS OF CERTAIN THIRD PARTIES SUBMITTED BY THE EUROPEAN COMMUNITIES

11 August 2003

TABLE OF CONTENTS

I. ARTICLE 13 OF THE AGREEMENT ON AGRICULTURE

Q1. Australia has argued that Article 13 of the *Agreement on Agriculture* is an affirmative defence. How do you reconcile this with your view that the conditions in Article 13 are a "prerequisite" to the availability of a right or privilege? Australia Would other third parties have any comments on Australia's assertion? 3RD parties, in particular Argentina, Benin, China, Chinese Taipei

Answer

1. Australia's views cannot be reconciled. Australia is correct in noting that the conditions in Article 13 can be considered a prerequisite for taking action under the *SCM Agreement*.[1] In using the term "prerequisite", Australia essentially recognises that, in respect of measures covered by Article 13, a complainant can only invoke the relevant provisions of the *SCM Agreement* if it proves that the threshold requirements or prerequisites referred to in Article 13 have been satisfied. As the European Communities has pointed out, such a situation is very different from the situation where, in the event of a violation of a WTO Agreement, a WTO Member pleads a defence which potentially exculpates it from this

[1] Australia's Oral Statement, para. 18.

violation (e.g. Article XX GATT) in respect of which it bears the burden of proof.

2. Comparing Article 13 with Article 3.3 of the *SPS Agreement* shows that Australia's views are irreconcilable. This provision permits WTO Members not to base SPS measures on international standards but to impose higher standards where there is a scientific justification or an appropriate risk assessment has been carried out. This provision has some similarities with Article 13 of the *Agreement on Agriculture* since it sets a threshold which must be met before a Member can act. However, Article 3.3 may be seen as going further than Article 13 since it provides a derogation from the central discipline of the *SPS Agreement* ; the obligation to base SPS measures on international standards. On the other hand, Article 13 is simply one element regulating the interface between the *Agreement on Agriculture* and the other Annex I Agreements and cannot be seen as a derogation therefrom. Despite the extent to which Article 3.3 could be thought of as a derogation from the *SPS Agreement*, the Appellate Body ruled in *EC Hormones* that it could not be considered an affirmative defence, and that the burden of proof did not, therefore lie with the defendant.[2] In particular, the Appellate Body noted that the situation in Article 3.3 of the SPS Agreement is "qualitatively different" from the relationship between for instance, Article 1 and XX GATT.[3]

3. Consequently, Australia is correct to consider that Article 13 is a prerequisite or a threshold condition before the other Annex I Agreements may become applicable but is incorrect to consider that Article 13 can be considered an affirmative defence.

II. ARTICLE 13(B) OF THE *AGREEMENT ON AGRICULTURE*: DOMESTIC SUPPORT MEASURES

Q2. Please explain the difference, if any, between the meaning of "defined" and the meaning of "fixed" in the phrase "a defined and fixed base period" in paragraph 6(a) of Annex 2 of the *Agreement on Agriculture*. 3rd parties, in particular Australia, Argentina, Canada, EC, NZ

Answer

4. The two words have slightly different meanings, as is suggested by the use of the conjunctive "and". "Defined" means "having a definite or specified outline, or form; clearly marked, definite"[4] and thus implies, in terms of interpretation of paragraph 6, that the base period for any measure which is claimed to be green box must be set down in the measure itself. "Fixed" is defined as "definite-

---

2 Appellate Body Report, *EC Measures Concerning Meat and Meat Products (Hormones) ("European Communities – Hormones")*, WT/DS26/AB/R, WT/DS48/AB/R, adopted 13 February 1998, para. 109.

3 Appellate Body Report, *EC Measures Concerning Meat and Meat Products (Hormones) ("European Communities – Hormones")*, WT/DS26/AB/R, WT/DS48/AB/R, adopted 13 February 1998, para. 105.

4 The New Shorter Oxford English Dictionary, 1993.

ly and permanently placed or assigned, stationary or unchanged in relative position, definite, permanent lasting"[5] and suggests that the base period for a particular measure cannot be changed at a later date. In other words, a Member may define a base period by means of a formula whereas a fixed base period implies that the years chosen for the base period do not change.

5. Decoupled support within a WTO Member need not take the form of a single measure, but may involve several measures. The first sentence of Paragraph 1 of Annex 2 refers to "domestic support measures". Different measures may have different base periods, and a single measure may have several different base periods.[6] Each measure will, or course, have to be judged against the basic and policy specific criteria set down in Annex 2. However, it would defeat the objective of Annex 2 paragraph 6 if a Member could adopt repeated, practically identical measures, in respect of which farmers are aware that they may update the base period. If a farmer knows that a base period is going to be updated, and knows the type of production that will qualify for payments, a WTO Member inevitably encourages the growth of a particular crop, cannot be considered to have decoupled support from production and inevitably creates trade or production distorting effects.

6. The European Communities also refers the Panel to its response to question 11.

Q3. Please explain the meaning of "a" in "a defined and fixed base period" in paragraph 6(a) of Annex 2 of the *Agreement on Agriculture*, the meaning of "the" in "the base period" in paragraphs 6(b), (c) and (d), and the difference between these and the phrase "based on the years 1986-88" in Annex 3. 3rd parties, in particular Australia, Argentina, Canada, EC, NZ

Answer

7. In the view of the European Communities, the word "a" indicates that it is for the Member concerned to choose a base period, rather than the base period be fixed for all WTO Members.

8. "The" in paragraphs 6(b),(c) and (d) refers to the base period or periods established for eligibility for payments in paragraph 6(a).

9. There are notable differences between these phrases and the phrase "based on the years 1986 to 1988" in Annex 3. First, Annex 3 refers to an already defined and fixed period. Second, the reference period 1986-1988 refers to all measures taken by all Members, and not to specific measures which are intended to conform to Annex 2 taken by specific Members.

---

5 *Ibid.*

6 For instance, in the experience of the European Communities, where decoupled payments are based on past payments of production aids, and not all production aids are brought under a decoupled scheme, it must be envisioned that new products could be brought into the decoupled payment scheme, with the possibility that such payments are based on a different base period.

Q4. How often can a Member define and fix a base period in accordance with paragraph 6 of Annex 2 of the *Agreement on Agriculture*? 3rd parties, in particular Australia, Argentina, Canada, China, EC, NZ

Answer

10. As explained in question 2 above, a Member may provide decoupled support through several measures which may have different base periods. However, a Member may not renew a measure, with essentially the same characteristics as previous measures, where, as a matter of fact, farmers are aware that they will have the possibility to update their base periods and thus have an interest in producing certain crops.

11. We also refer the Panel to our response to question 11.

Q5. Do you agree that a payment penalty based on crops produced is "related to type of production"? EC

Answer

12. The European Communities believes that an examination of the conformity of a decoupled scheme with the criteria set out in Annex 2 must involve an examination of the scheme as a whole. In that light, the European Communities is not convinced that where, as part of a scheme where no production is required to receive payments, and that the production of any type of crop is permitted, reducing payments where certain crops are produced can be such as to make the scheme, when taken as a whole, related to a type of production. Consequently, the reduction of payment linked to the production of fruit and vegetables must be seen as part of a scheme which permits a farmer to grow any type of crop, or even not to produce at all. Such a scheme, it is submitted, taken as a whole, meets the criteria that payments are not related to a type of production. To find otherwise would not permit a WTO Member wishing to introduce decoupled payments to take account of important elements of internal competition, in an historical perspective, and avoid those farmers receiving decoupled payments from enjoying both the decoupled payments and a privileged position vis-à-vis farmers who are not entitled to such payments. Moreover, as the European Communities has explained, such a finding would require a Member to increase its subsidy programmes in order to prevent internal distortions of competition, running directly contrary to the process of reform instituted by the *Agreement on Agriculture*.

13. We also refer the Panel to our response to question 11.

Q6. Please explain the meaning of the word "criteria" in Article 6.1 and 7.1. What effect, if any, does the use of the word "Accordingly" in paragraph 1 of Annex 2 of the *Agreement on Agriculture* have on the meaning of the preceding sentence? 3rd parties, in particular Australia, Argentina, Canada, EC, NZ

Answer

14. Both Article 6.1 and 7.1 refer to the "criteria set out in [..] Annex 2". When one considers Annex 2, there are two sets of "criteria". The first is the "basic criteria" set out in subparagraphs (a) and (b) of paragraph 1, and the second is the "policy-specific criteria" set out in paragraphs 2 to 13. This understanding is confirmed by the text of paragraph 5 of Annex 2, which refers to the "basic criteria" and the "specific criteria". Thus, Articles 6.1 and 7.1 of the *Agreement on Agriculture* refer to the basic and policy specific criteria set out in Annex 2.

15. The European Communities has already set out its understanding of the term "accordingly" in its Third Party Written Submission.[7] In the European Communities view, the term "accordingly" is intended to link the purposive language of the first sentence, with the "basic criteria" set out in the second sentence. In its Third Party Submission the EC offered a dictionary definition, "in accordance with the logical premises" which showed that the word "accordingly" operates as a linkage between the premise or understanding set out in the first sentence and the operative language in the second sentence. Australia offers the Panel another definition: "harmoniously" or "agreeably", but fails to note that that the Oxford English Dictionary considers this usage of the word "accordingly" obsolete.[8]

16. The European Communities would point out that both the French and Spanish text support the view that the use of the word "accordingly" links the general statement in the first sentence with the specific obligations of the second sentence. The French text uses the term "en conséquence" and the Spanish the term "por consiguiente". Both of these terms show that the criteria in the second sentence are intended to express the principle set out in the first sentence. Moreover, had the negotiators intended that the first sentence be a self-standing obligation, rather than use the term "accordingly" they would have used the term "additionally" or "in addition", or a synonymous term.

17. Further support for this view can be found in the frequent use of the term "accordingly" in the WTO Agreement. A survey of the term's use suggests that it links a general statement, often recognising that a particular situation causes specific effects, with a right or obligation to take some type of action set out in an ancillary sentence.[9] These general statements are not such as to impose specific obligations. The Appellate Body had occasion to consider the relationship bet-

[7] First Third Party Submission of the European Communities, 15 July 2003, para. 20. The European Communities recall, in this context, the opinion of Professor Desta set out in footnote 19 to para. 20.

[8] Australia's Oral Statement, para 35. Oxford English Dictionary, p. 15. Australia refers to the first sense of the word "accordingly" which is preceded by the symbol "" which indicates that a particular usage is obsolete (see Abbreviations and Symbols, page xxvi).

[9] See Articles II.6(a), III.9, XII.3(d), XVI.3, XVIIII.5, XXIV.5 GATT 1994, together with Ad Article III and Ad Article XXVIII.4 to GATT 1994, Articles 2.1 and 11 of the Dispute Settlement Understanding, Article A(i) of the Trade Policy Review Mechanism, Article 12.8 of the Agreement on Technical Barriers to Trade, Article 1 of the GATS Annex on Telecommunications and Article 5.1 of the Agreement on Textiles and Clothes.

ween such provisions in the *Turkey-Textiles* dispute (Articles XXIV.4 and XXIV.5 GATT). It concluded:

> The chapeau of paragraph 5 of Article XXIV begins with the word "accordingly", which can only be read to refer to paragraph 4 of Article XXIV, which immediately precedes the chapeau.
>
> [..]
>
> 57. According to paragraph 4, the purpose of a customs union is "to facilitate trade" between the constituent members and "not to raise barriers to the trade" with third countries. This objective demands that a balance be struck by the constituent members of a customs union. A customs union should facilitate trade within the customs union, but it should *not* do so in a way that raises barriers to trade with third countries. [..] *Paragraph 4 contains purposive, and not operative, language. It does not set forth a separate obligation itself but, rather, sets forth the overriding and pervasive purpose for Article XXIV which is manifested in operative language in the specific obligations that are found elsewhere in Article XXIV.* Thus, the purpose set forth in paragraph 4 informs the other relevant paragraphs of Article XXIV, including the chapeau of paragraph 5. For this reason, the chapeau of paragraph 5, and the conditions set forth therein for establishing the availability of a defence under Article XXIV, must be interpreted in the light of the purpose of customs unions set forth in paragraph 4. The chapeau cannot be interpreted correctly without constant reference to this purpose.[10] (emphasis added)

18. The Appellate Body has, consequently, recognised the linking function of the word "accordingly", and the fact that provisions which may be linked to later provisions through the use of the word "accordingly" may not impose separate obligations.

19. The European Communities would also point out that the Appellate Body has found that other provisions (e.g. Article III.1 GATT) which contain general principles are set up as "a guide to understanding and interpreting the specific obligations contained" in other provisions (e.g. Article III.2 and the other paragraphs of Article III).[11] Such provisions do not, however, impose additional obligations supplemental to the specific obligations, unless expressly stated.[12]

---

[10] Appellate Body Report, *Turkey – Restrictions on Imports of Textile and Clothing Products ("Turkey – Textiles")*, WT/DS34/AB/R, adopted 19 November 1999, paras. 56 and 57 (emphasis added). Note that the Panel also found that Article XXIV.4 was "not expressed as an obligation" (Panel Report, *Turkey – Restrictions on Imports of Textile and Clothing Products ("Turkey – Textiles")*, WT/DS34/R, adopted 19 November 1999, as modified by the Appellate Body Report, WT/DS34/AB/R, para. 9.126).

[11] Appellate Body Report, *Japan – Taxes on Alcoholic Beverages ("Japan – Alcoholic Beverages")*, WT/DS8/AB/R, WT/DS10/AB/R, WT/DS11/AB/R, adopted 1 November 1996, p. 17.

[12] See Appellate Body Report, *European Communities - Regime for the Importation, Sale and Distribution of Bananas ("European Communities – Bananas")*, WT/DS27/AB/R, adopted 25 Sep-

20. The Panel may find it useful to refer to the European Communities' response to a question posed by Australia (see question no. 44 in this document). In its response, the European Communities deals with Australia's unfounded assertion that the European Communities' reading of the first sentence of paragraph 1 would render that provision ineffective.

Q7 Please explain the meaning of the words "the fundamental requirement" as used in paragraph 1 of Annex 2 of the *Agreement on Agriculture*. 3rd parties, in particular Australia, Argentina, Canada, EC, NZ

Answer

21. The phrase "the fundamental requirement" signals the negotiators intent to treat differently measures which are less or not at all distortive to trade or production and sets forth the general purpose of Annex 2; a purpose which permeates the rest of Annex 2. Considering the term in the abstract does not answer the question whether a panel must examine the effects of measures for which green box status is claimed in addition to examining whether such measures respect the basic and policy-specific criteria set out in Annex 2, or whether respecting the basic and policy-specific criteria is such that a measure is deemed not to have the effects mentioned in the first sentence. As the European Communities has explained, there are compelling textual and purpose based arguments which support the latter interpretation.

Q8. In your oral statement, you emphasize the use of the word "criteria" in other parts of the *Agreement on Agriculture*, as distinct from the reference to "fundamental requirement" in the first sentence of paragraph 1 of Annex 2. Is it the case that sub-paragraphs (a) and (b) of paragraph 1 of Annex 2 are also "criteria"? EC

Answer

22. Yes. The second sentence of paragraph 1 refers to sub-paragraphs (a) and (b) as "basic criteria". Paragraph 5 refers to the same "basic criteria". The European Communities considers that the "criteria" referred to in Articles 6.1 and 7.1 of the *Agreement on Agriculture* (mentioned in question 6 above) refer to both the basic criteria set out in the second sentence of paragraph 1 and the policy-specific criteria set out in paragraphs 2 to 13 of Annex 2.

Q9. If the first sentence of paragraph 1 of Annex 2 is a stand-alone obligation, does this allow effects-based claims of non-compliance with Annex 2? If so, how does this affect the purpose of Article 13(b)? 3rd parties ' in particular Australia, Argentina, Canada, EC, NZ

tember 1997, paras. 214-216 holding that the absence of a specific reference to Article III.1 GATT in Article III.4 GATT meant that an examination of the consistency of a measure with Article III.4 GATT did not require, in addition, an examination of the consistency of the measure with Article III.1 GATT.

Answer

23. The implication of finding that the first sentence of paragraph 1 is a stand-alone obligation is that an effects test would become applicable to assessing compliance with Annex 2. The result of such an interpretation is two fold. First, as the Panel implies, another WTO Member could bring a WTO dispute alleging that because of its effects a measure does not comply with Annex 2. Second, WTO Members, when designing measures intended to conform to Annex 2, will be required to attempt to identify the effects of such measures. Such a task is often only feasible on an *ex post facto* basis. The correct classification of measures is a vital element for a Member to ensure that it respects it domestic support ceilings. Requiring a Member to measure effects diminishes the ability of a Member to ensure correct classification. Such an interpretation should, therefore, be avoided.[13]

24. It is rather remarkable, had the drafters intended that the first sentence of paragraph 1 be a self-standing obligation, that no indication of how such effects are to be measured was included in the *Agreement on Agriculture*. It is far from obvious how the effects of a measure on production and/or trade is to be measured. Nor is it clear how it can be decided that a particular effect can be considered as going beyond "minimal". This can be contrasted with Article 6.3 of the *SCM Agreement* where the negotiators set out with some precision certain criteria deemed to cause serious prejudice to the interests of another Member. This leads to the inevitable conclusion that the criteria by which a Member or a panel is required to determine whether a measure has more than minimal trade or production distorting effects are the basic and policy specific criteria set out in Annex 2.

25. Article 13(b) is one element of a complex series of arrangements intended to provide legal security and certainty to Members who have embarked on a process of agricultural reform. It is designed to ensure that a Member may design its domestic support measures in such a way as to ensure that they do not provide support in excess of that decided in 1992 in order that it be exempted from the actions listed in Article 13(b). This requires a Member to be able to classify its measures as green box, other exempt policies, or as amber box. Only by being sure of its classification can a Member ensure that it maintains the protection provided by Article 13(b). This is one reason why the criteria for treatment as green box, or as another exempt measure, are so precisely defined. (Other exempt measures are precisely defined in Articles 6.4 and 6.4 of the *Agreement on Agriculture*). Consequently, bringing an effects test into an analysis of green box compatibility would make it very difficult for a Member to be sure that it remains within the level of support decided in 1992 and would therefore render nugatory the security and predictability necessary to permit the process of agricultural reform initiated by the Agreement on Agriculture.

Q10. If the first sentence of paragraph 1 of Annex 2 is not a stand-alone obligation, then must new, non- or minimally trade-distorting measures that

---

[13] See, in this sense, First Third Party Submission of the European Communities, para. 24.

do not conform to the criteria listed in Annex 2 be classified as non-Green Box? 3rd parties, in particular Australia, Argentina, Canada, EC, NZ

Answer

26. The European Communities is not convinced that "non- or minimally trade-distorting measures" might exist which would not be covered by Annex 2. Annex 2 has at least two paragraphs which are designed as "catch–all" provisions. Paragraph 2 of Annex 2 acts as a "catch-all" for general service programmes not involving direct payments to producers or processors.[14] Paragraph 5 acts as a "catch-all" for all direct payments.[15] Moreover, Annex 2 is designed to cover all domestic support measures which are deemed to have no or at least minimal trade-distorting effects. Consequently, it would seem surprising if a non- or minimally trade-distortive measure would not meet the criteria of Annex 2.

27. In the hypothesis that a measure which had no or minimal trade-distorting effects did not conform to the criteria in Annex 2 the European Communities would conclude that it could not be considered as Green Box support. As the European Communities explained in its Third Party Submission, rather than defining those domestic support measures which were to be subject to reduction commitments, the negotiators of the *Agreement on Agriculture* chose to define all those measures which were not to be subject to reduction commitments – hence Annex 2.[16] Such a result does not run counter to the objectives of the *Agreement on Agriculture* since it ensures the security and predictability of the reform process.

Q11 If the first sentence of paragraph 1 of Annex 2 expresses a general principle which informs the interpretation of the criteria in Annex 2, please explain how this affects the assessment of the direct payments programme's compliance with paragraph 6 of Annex 2. 3rd parties, in particular, Australia, Argentina, Canada, EC, NZ

Answer

28. The European Communities considers that the first sentence of paragraph 1 of Annex 2 sets out the general purpose of Annex 2 and therefore informs the interpretation of the criteria in Annex 2. It is relevant to the interpretation of paragraph 6 in that it should be considered to be part of the context of paragraph 6. Nevertheless, while the first paragraph informs the interpretation of paragraph 6

[14] The third sentence of paragraph 2 reads "[S]uch programmes, which include but are not restricted to the following list, shall meet the general criteria in paragraph 1 above and policy-specific conditions where set out below [..]".

[15] The second sentence of paragraph 5 reads "[w]here exemption from reduction is claimed for any existing or new type of direct payment other than those specified in paragraphs 6 through 13, it shall conform to criteria (b) through (e) in paragraph 6, in addition to the general criteria set out in paragraph 1."

[16] First Third party Submission, paras. 19 & 20. Obviously, some other exempted support measures are defined in Article 6 of the *Agreement on Agriculture*.

it cannot detract from the words actually used in paragraph 6.[17] As the Panel considers its interpretation of the words used in paragraph 6, it can take account of the purposive language of the first sentence of paragraph 1.

29. There are two issues which the Panel must resolve with respect to direct payments – the reduction of payments where certain crops are grown and the updating of base periods.

30. With respect to the former, the European Communities has already explained why it considers that reducing payments upon growing certain crops cannot be considered to base payments on a type of production (see also the EC's response to Panel question 5 above). The European Communities position is supported not only by the text of paragraph 6(b) but also by an interpretation informed by the first sentence of paragraph 1. Permitting such a reduction of payments does not distort trade – it minimises any distortion which may be caused by any decoupled payments in markets which were historically undistorted by subsidies. It ensures that the equilibrium established by the market in the relevant product is maintained. To the extent decoupled support can be seen as having an effect on trade or production by providing support to farmers who produce some crops, the reduction in payment prevents subsidised farmers from potentially upsetting the market equilibrium, and thus serves to prevent effects on trade or production in the market for crops for which payment is reduced. Seen the other way, not ensuring such a reduction would allow subsidised farmers to grow the relevant crops and thus upset the historical market equilibrium with potential effects on trade and production. In the light of the first sentence of paragraph 1, the only possible application of Article 6(b) to payment reductions imposed where certain crops are grown is to find that such reductions are not such as to make the payment based on a type of production.

31. The situation is rather different with respect to the updating of base periods. The European Communities considers that where farmers know that base periods will be updated, and that the production of certain crops will give them a greater entitlement to support in a later period, there will be a production distorting effect. Such updating is clearly inconsistent with notions set out in the first sentence of paragraph 1 since knowledge of such updating will incite farmers to produce more of certain crops which qualify for support and thus will have effects on production.

Q12. Where does Article 13(b) require a year-on-year comparison? 3RD parties, in particular Australia, Argentina, Canada, China, EC, NZ

Answer

32. The European Communities does not consider that Article 13(b) *requires* a year-on-year comparison. It permits such a year-on-year comparison and given that support is generally expressed in annual amounts, appears a reasonable basis for making such a comparison. In considering this issue, the Panel must compare

---

17 Appellate Body Report, *Japan – Taxes on Alcoholic Beverages ("Japan – Alcoholic Beverages")*, WT/DS8/AB/R, WT/DS10/AB/R, WT/DS11/AB/R, adopted 1 November 1996, p.17.

two elements. The first is the domestic support measure challenged. The second is, at least for Article 13(b)(ii), support "decided" in an earlier period.

33. We examine first the domestic support measure challenged. In order to benefit from the protection of Article 13 a measure must conform to the provisions of Article 6 and must "not grant support" in excess of that decided in during the 1992 marketing year. The European Communities interprets the present tense of "not grant support" as requiring the Panel to determine the support at the time the measure is challenged when Panel is asked to determine whether Article 13 is applicable. Inevitably, such a determination requires that the Panel consider a specific period, which is comparable with an earlier period. The European Communities considers that the Panel has some discretion in choosing a specific period, although it is clear it must be as close as possible to the time of the dispute. However, since the Panel must consider the support *granted* it must choose a period for which data is complete. Given Article 1(i) of the *Agreement on Agriculture*, the period chosen may well be based on the calendar, financial or marketing year of the Member complained against.

34. In respect of support "decided", the Panel must consider the nature of the support decided during the 1992 marketing year. As the European Communities has explained at length elsewhere, the relevant element for comparison is not the support actually granted for the 1992 marketing year – rather it is the support decided. Consequently, in each case, the element for comparison must depend on the decision made during the 1992 marketing year. As a function of that decision, the Panel will have to choose a period which is comparable with the most recent period. This may well be a marketing year, but need not be so.

Q13. Does a failure by a Member to comply in a given *year* with either the chapeau of Article 13(b) or the proviso in subparagraph (ii) of Article 13(b) impact its entitlement to benefit in an earlier or a later year from the exemption from action provided by Article 13(b)? 3RD parties, in particular Australia, Argentina, Canada, China, EC, NZ

Answer

35. Failure to comply with Article 6 of the *Agreement on Agriculture* or granting support in excess of that decided in 1992 in a given year does not impact a Member's entitlement to benefit from the protection of Article 13(b) in a later (or earlier) year, provided that the Member concerned complies with Article 6 of the *Agreement on Agriculture* and does not grant support at present in excess of that decided during marketing year 1992. This is clear from the present tense of "do not grant support" which makes it clear that the comparison must be with the support granted in the most recent period.

Q14. Does a failure of a Member to comply with Article 13(b) in respect of a *specific commodity* impact its entitlement to benefit in respect of other agricultural products from the exemption from action provided by Article 13(b)? 3RD parties, in particular Australia, Argentina, Canada, China, EC, NZ

Answer

36. No. A failure to maintain support granted within the level decided during marketing year 1992 in respect of a specific commodity would not affect the availability of Article 13(b) in respect of other commodities, provided that support granted to that specific commodity was not in excess of that decided during 1992.

Q15. Is there any basis on which counter-cyclical payments could be considered product-specific? 3RD parties, in particular Australia, Argentina, Canada, China, EC, NZ

Answer

37. The European Communities considers that, since counter-cyclical payments are paid as a function of fluctuations in the price of different commodities with respect to target prices also specified by commodity, they should be considered product specific.

Q16. If the word "specific" were deleted from Article 13(b)(ii), would this change the meaning of the subparagraph? 3RD parties, in particular Australia, Argentina, Benin Canada, China, EC, NZ

Answer

38. Yes. Article 13(b)(ii) refers to product specific support. It does not refer to all support which may be attributed to a product. The use of the word "specific" has meaning, because it makes it clear that the support in question is that granted or decided in respect of a specific product, rather than that granted or decided in respect of all products and which could arguably be attributed to a product.

Q17. What is the relevance, if any, of the concept of "specificity" in Article 2 of the *SCM Agreement* and references to "a product" or "subsidized product" in certain provisions of the *SCM Agreement* to the meaning of "support to a specific commodity" in Article 13(b)(ii) *Agreement on Agriculture*? 3RD parties, in particular Australia, Argentina, Canada, China, EC, NZ

Answer

39. The European Communities is not convinced that the drafters of the *Agreement on Agriculture* had Article 2 of the *SCM Agreement* in mind when drafting Article 13(b) of the *Agreement on Agriculture*. It may comment further depending on the views of the other third parties on this issue.

40. The European Communities has already referred to the relevance of the references to " a product" and a "subsidised product" in its Oral Statement.[18]

Q18. Benin's oral statement considers the phrase "support to a specific commodity" in Article 13(b)(ii) of the *Agreement on Agriculture*. How does Benin believe that phrase is best interpreted. Please substantiate your res-

[18] EC Oral Statement, 24 July 2003, para. 23.

ponse, commenting on other submissions by parties and third parties as you believe appropriate. Benin

Answer

41. The European Communities may comment, as necessary, on Benin's response.

Q19. Where does Article 13(b)(ii) require a year-on-year comparison? 3rd parties, in particular Australia, Argentina, Canada, EC, NZ

Answer

42. See the answer to question 12 above.

Q20. Does Article 13(b)(ii) require a comparison of support granted with support decided? How could such a comparison be made?

Answer

43. Yes. See the answer to question 22 below.

Q21. Please comment on Brazil's assertion that the terms "grant" and "decided" in Article 13(b)(ii) have broadly the same meaning. If so, why did the drafters not use the same term? 3rd parties, in particular, Australia, Argentina, Canada, China, EC, NZ

Answer

44. As the European Communities has explained elsewhere, the use of the term "decided" is crucial to an understanding of Article 13(b). It is now established that a panel is obliged to use the normal rules of interpretation of international law as codified in the Vienna Convention on the Law of Treaties. This requires it to look, in the first place, to the ordinary meaning of the words. "Granted" does not mean the same as "decided".

45. Granted is the past tense of the verb "grant" which means "to give or confer, (a possession, a right etc) formally; transfer (property) legally".[19] "Decided" is the past tense of the verb "decide" which means "come to a determination or resolution *that, to do, whether*".[20] Thus, in this context, "granted" refers to support which has been provided, to which a farmer (or all eligible farmers in a Member) has obtained a right. "Decided" implies that a political authority (be it a legislature or a government department or agency) has determined that a particular crop is to be entitled to a particular type of assistance.

46. The European Communities believes that the use of the term "decided", as opposed to "granted" and "provided" (which are used elsewhere in the *Agreement on Agriculture*) is very deliberate. Article 13(b) is designed to protect support which was "decided" during 1992. It was negotiated in November 1992 as

19 The New Shorter Oxford English Dictionary, 1993, p. 1131.
20 The New Shorter Oxford English Dictionary, 1993, p. 607. Italics in the original.

part of the first Blair House Agreement and later multilateralised.[21] In November 1992, the negotiators could not have known the support granted for the marketing year 1992, which was of course running during that period. They did not, therefore, intend to refer to the support granted when using the term "decided". Rather, they were referring to decisions taken during 1992 in respect of support which WTO Members intended to grant – not that actually granted.

Q22. What is the meaning of "support" in *Agreement on Agriculture* 13(b)(ii) ? Why would it be used differently from Annex 3, where it refers to total outlays? 3rd parties, in particular, Australia, Argentina, Canada, China, EC, NZ

Answer

47. With respect, the European Communities does not consider that support is equated in Annex 3 to total outlays. Annex 3 provides methodologies for calculating the Aggregate Measure of Support (AMS). Article 1(a) defines the AMS as "the annual level of support, expressed in monetary terms [...]". However, AMS is not necessarily calculated in terms of budgetary outlays. For instance, market price support is calculated "using the gap between a fixed external reference price and the applied administered price multiplied by the quantity of production eligible to receive the applied administered price. Budgetary payments made to maintain this gap [...] shall not be included in the AMS." (Annex 3, para. 8) Similarly, non-exempt payments dependent on a price gap are to be calculated "either using the gap between the fixed reference price and the applied administered price multiplied by the quantity of production eligible to receive the administered price, or using budgetary outlays" (Annex 3, para. 10). This makes it clear that AMS need not be calculated in terms of total outlays.

48. The European Communities considers the term "support" in Article 13(b)(ii) must be considered from several perspectives. First, it is clear that the word "support" refers to the support *granted* in a recent period. Second, and at the same time, the word "that" used in the phrase "that decided" is also a reference to the word "support". However, as already noted, there is crucial distinction in this comparison between the "support decided" and the "support granted". The support decided does not equal the support actually granted during marketing year 1992. For the later period, there is no reason that the support granted should not be calculated on the basis of the AMS methodology set out in Annex 3. Indeed, Article 1(a) of the *Agreement on Agriculture* refers to AMS as "the annual level of *support*" (emphasis added).

49. For the support decided AMS-like criteria should be used. This would take into account the reference to AMS as the annual level of *support*, but would also recognise that Article 13(b)(ii) refers to the support "decided" rather than granted. Crucially, the support decided must be considered as that which it was decided to provide during the 1992 marketing year. This must be determined on

[21] The main change made in the second Blair House Agreement, in respect of Article 13(b) was the extension of the implementation period for the purposes of the Article 13(b).

a case-by-case basis. It should be determined on the basis of the information available to the decision makers. It may be that only a certain amount of production would be eligible,[22] or that the decision makers had production estimates at their disposal, and thus knew the extent of the support that was being decided. Alternatively, the amount of support decided could also be determined from budgetary acts, preparing expenditure for future years, in which the decision making authorities would have knowledge of the support they wished to grant, and the quantity of production which would likely enjoy such support. Using such a basis, it would be possible to use AMS-like criteria. AMS-like criteria can be used because it will often be possible to establish, for certain measures, a gap between the applied administered price and the internal or external fixed reference price[23] and establish, on the basis of information available to the decision makers, the amount of production which was eligible, or which was estimated. For other measures, it may also be possible to use appropriation or budgetary decisions.

Q23. Should support be compared under Article 13(b)(ii) in terms of unit of production or total volume of support or both? 3rd parties, in particular, Australia, Argentina, Canada, China, EC, NZ

Answer

50. The European Communities considers that the Panel should use AMS for the most recent period, and an AMS - like calculation for calculating the support decided during the 1992 marketing year, as explained in our response to question 22.

Q24. Please provide any written drafting history which could shed light on why the proviso was added to what is now Article 13(b)(ii) of the *Agreement on Agriculture* and, in particular, why the words "grant" and "decided" were used. EC

Answer

51. As the European Communities has noted above, the current text of Article 13(b)(ii) formed part of the first Blair House Agreement of November 1992. We have annexed the text which resulted from these negotiations[24], together with the relevant sections of the "Dunkel Draft", which were replaced by Article 13(b)(ii).[25]

52. The European Communities also considers that it may assist the Panel to have a copy of some of the key decisions reforming the EC's Common Agricultural Policy adopted during 1992. Thus, we have annexed Council Regulation (EC) No. 1766/92 on the common organisation of the market in cereals and

22 For instance, because of quotas on eligible production or definitive budgetary ceilings.
23 See para. 9 & 11 of Annex 3.
24 Exhibit EC-1.
25 Exhibit EC-2.

Council Regulation (EC) No. 1765/92 establishing a system of compensatory payments.[26]

Q25. Please comment on an interpretation of the words "decided during" in Article 13(b)(ii) that would read them as synonymous with the words "authorized during". 3rd parties, in particular Australia, Argentina, Canada, China, EC, NZ

Answer

53. The European Communities finds some merit in such an interpretation. It would be consistent with the careful choice of the negotiators to use the word "decided" rather than the term "granted" or "provided". The European Communities is concerned, however, that the term "authorised" is more restrictive than the term "decided". For that reason, while the European Communities sees support for the interpretation that "decided during" is synonymous with "authorised during", it is not clear to the European Communities that "authorised" has exactly the same meaning as "decided".

Q26. Under Article 13(b)(ii), a comparison is required between support at different times. One of the issues which is contested between the parties is whether the only later period that the Panel can consider is the present one (i.e. the period underway at the time of the request for establishment of the Panel). This argument is based on the present tense of the words "do not grant" in the English text. The Panel asks whether there is any difference in the verb tense as used in the Spanish-language text, or any other difference which might aid the Panel in interpreting these words? Argentina, EC, Paraguay, Venezuela

Answer

54. The European Communities notes that both the French and Spanish text also use the present tense.

Q27. If the 1992 "decision" led to or was the funding source for the money provided in 1992 and later years, is it the full amount of all that funding that constitutes the "support" decided in 1992? If the answer to this question is that it is the full amount of all the support provided pursuant to the "decision" that must be taken into account, must this be compared with the total amount of support that will or might flow from the decision made in the more recent period for the purposes of the comparison required under Article 13(b)(ii)? If a Member did not make a "decision" (however that may be interpreted) in 1992 about "support", is it the case that the Member has a zero base for the purposes of the comparison required under Article 13(b)(ii)? EC

---

[26] Council Regulation (EC) No. 1766/92 on the common organisation of the market in cereals (Exhibit EC-3) and Council Regulation (EC) No. 1765/92 (Exhibit EC-4).

Answer

55. The European Communities does not consider that it is the full amount of support decided in 1992 for later years that should be taken into account. Such an approach might not be feasible where the decision taken in 1992 was an open-ended one. This approach also sits uneasily with the practice in the *Agreement on Agriculture* of expressing support on an annual basis. Since the regulation of agricultural production takes place on a yearly basis, it seems unlikely that a decision would be taken setting a maximum amount for a number of years without regulating how such support would be allocated between specific years.

56. The European Communities considers that the Panel should use a level of support readily comparable with the support currently granted. This may well be the support decided for a particular marketing year. If a decision was made in 1992 for future years, it would be to ignore the drafters intent to rule out the possibility that the support decided for later years is the relevant support.

57. The European Communities does not consider that it will ever be the case that a Member which provides subsidies can be said never to have made a decision in 1992 which would qualify under Article 13(b). At the very least, a Member would have decided, on the basis of its subsidy programmes, and the amount of eligible production and/or estimated production, to set aside a specific amount of budgetary appropriations for future years. If, however, a Member decided not to provide support to a specific commodity, the level of support for purposes of the comparison would be zero.

Q28. In paragraph 13 of Australia's oral statement, you state that a "question" is: "could conditions of price competition for the purposes of a non-violation or impairment claim be assessed solely on the basis of budgetary outlay figures, as argued by Brazil, or on the basis of a rate of payment, as argued by the United States? In Australia's view, both factors put forward by Brazil and the United States would properly form a part of that assessment, but not the whole." Could you please clarify this statement (indicating other elements which would complete the "whole" and explain its relevance for the purposes of our consideration of Article 13 of the *Agreement on Agriculture*? Australia, EC

Answer

58. The European Communities would prefer to let Australia clarify its statement. The European Communities will comment upon Australia's clarification in its comments on the responses of the other third parties.

III. EXPORT CREDIT GUARANTEE PROGRAMMES

Q29. (a) Is an export credit guarantee a financial contribution in the form of a "potential direct transfer of funds or liabilities (e.g. loan guarantee)" within the meaning of Article 1.1(a)(1)(i) of

the *SCM Agreement*? Why or why not? 3rd parties, in particular, Argentina, Canada, EC, NZ

Answer

59. Export credits may involve the provision of "loans". Export credit guarantees, like other types of guarantees, normally involve an obligation to cover losses resulting from defaults on guaranteed loans. If provided by a government, they may involve a "financial contribution" within the meaning of Article 1.1(a)(1)(i) of the *SCM Agreement.*

(b) How, if at all, would this be relevant to the claims of Brazil? 3rd parties, in particular, Argentina, Canada, EC, NZ

Answer

60. Whether or not export credit guarantees are "financial contributions" is directly relevant to Brazil's claim that GSM 102, GSM 103 and SCGP constitute "export subsidies" within the meaning of Article 3.1 (a) of the *SCM Agreement.*

61. It is also relevant, by way of context, for Brazil's claim that those programmes are "export subsidies" for the purposes of Article 10.1 of the *Agreement on Agriculture.*

Q30. The Panel could arguably take the view that Articles 1 and 3 of the *SCM Agreement* were relevant in assessing the WTO-consistency of United States export credit guarantees. The Panel would therefore appreciate third party views on this situation, including with respect to the viability of an *a contrario* interpretation of item (j) of the Illustrative List (as addressed in paragraphs 180-183 of the United States' first written submission). 3rd parties, in particular, Argentina, Canada, EC, NZ

Answer

62. The relationship between the Illustrative List and Article 3.1(a) is addressed specifically by footnote 5, which provides that

> Measures referred to in Annex I as not constituting export subsides shall not be prohibited under this or any other provision of the Agreement.

63. In this regard, the European Communities recalls the reasoning followed by the panels in *Brazil –Aircraft (21.5) I* and *II*[27], which concluded that the first paragraph of item (k) of the Illustrative List does not provide *a contrario* an "affirmative defence".

64. As noted by the panel in *Brazil –Aircraft (21.5) – II*, the Appellate Body's statement relied upon by the United States "does not form part of the legal basis

[27] Panel report, *Brazil – Export Financing Programme for Aircraft – Recourse by Canada to Article 21.5 of the DSU*, WT/DS64/RW, ("Brazil – Aircraft (21.5) – I"), paras. 6.24-6.67; Panel report, *Brazil – Export Financing Programme for Aircraft – Second Recourse by Canada to Article 21.5 of the DSU*, WT/DS46/RW/2, (Brazil – Aircraft (21.5) - II, paras5.269-5.275.

for its disposition of the appeal, nor did the Appellate Body explain its statement".[28]

65. Item (j) of the illustrative list describes circumstances in which, *inter alia,* export credit guarantee programmes may constitute export subsidies. In certain circumstances (e.g. where the Government is the only provider), it may be that the requirement set out in item (j) – that export credit guarantees must not be provided at premium rates which are inadequate to cover the long-term operating costs and losses of the programme – represents the appropriate benchmark for determining that an export subsidy does not exist.

Q31. If the Panel decides to refer to provisions of the *SCM Agreement* for contextual guidance in the interpretation of the terms in Article 10 *Agreement on Agriculture*, should the Panel refer to item (j) or Articles 1 and 3 of the *SCM Agreement* or both? . 3rd parties, in particular, Argentina, Canada, EC, NZ

Answer

66. Both.

Q32. The Panel's attention has been drawn to Article 14(c) of the *SCM Agreement* (see third party submission of Canada) and to the panel report in DS 222 *Canada- Export Credits and Loan Guarantees.* How and to what extent are Article 14(c) of the *SCM Agreement*, and the cited panel report, relevant to the issue of whether or not the United States export credit guarantee programmes confer a "benefit"? What would the appropriate market benchmark be to use for any comparison? Please cite any other relevant material. . 3rd parties, in particular, Argentina, Canada, EC, NZ

Answer

67. The European Communities agrees that Article 14(c) may be relevant context for the interpretation of Article 1.1(b) of the *SCM Agreement*, where the subsidy consists of a loan guarantee. However, Article 14(c) may not be applicable if the government is the only supplier of a certain type of service and no comparable type is provided by other suppliers. In that case it may be necessary to resort to alternative benchmarks, such as the one set out in item (j) of the Illustrative List. This would depend on the particular circumstances of the case.

Q33 What is the relevance (if any) of Brazil's statement that : "...export credit guarantees for exports of agricultural exports [*sic*] are not available on the marketplace by commercial lenders." . 3rd parties, in particular, Argentina, Canada, EC, NZ

Answer

68. The European Communities does not agree with the proposition that the provision by a government of finance not available from other suppliers confers

[28] Panel report, *Brazil –Aircraft (21.5) – II*, footnote 214.

per se a benefit. The European Communities recalls that the Panel in *Canada – Export Credits and Loan Guarantees* left open this issue.[29]

Q34. Comment on the United States' view of the meaning of "long term operating costs and losses" in item (j) of the Illustrative List of Export Subsidies in Annex I of the *SCM Agreement* as meaning "claims paid" under the export credit guarantee programmes. Does the United States' interpretation give meaning to both "costs" and "losses"? Do claims paid represent "losses"? 3rd parties, in particular, Argentina, Canada, EC, NZ

Answer

69. The European Communities does not express an opinion on this question at this time.

Q35. Did the drafters of the *Agreement on Agriculture* include export credit guarantees in Article 9.1 of the *Agreement on Agriculture*? Why or why not? 3rd parties, in particular, Argentina, Canada, EC, NZ

Answer

70. Export credit guarantees are not included in Article 9.1. Article 9.1 represents a list of export subsidies which were permitted to be maintained, but which were made subject to reduction commitments. Article 9.1 is a list of permitted export subsidies negotiated by the drafters of the *Agreement on Agriculture*. All other export subsides are regulated by Article 10.1.

Q36. Please explain any possible significance the following statements may have in respect of Brazil's claims about GSM102 and 103 (7 CFR 1493.10(a)(2), Exhibit BRA-38) 3rd parties, in particular, Argentina, Canada, EC, NZ

(a) "The programmes operate in cases where credit is necessary to increase or maintain US exports to a foreign market and where US financial institutions would be unwilling to provide financing without CCC's guarantee. (7 CFR 1493.10(a)(2) Exhibit BRA-38)

(b) "The programmes are operated in a manner intended not to interfere with markets for cash sales. The programmes are targeted toward those countries where the guarantee is necessary to secure financing of the exports but which have sufficient financial strength so that foreign exchange will be available for scheduled payments." (7 CFR 1493.10(a)(2) Exhibit BRA-38)

(c) "In providing this credit guarantee facility, CCC seeks to expand market opportunities for US agricultural exporters and

---

29 Panel report, *Canada – Export Credits and Loan Guarantees for Regional Aircraft*, WT/DS222/R, para. 7.341.

assist long-term market development for US agricultural commodities." (7 CFR 1493.10(a)(2) Exhibit BRA-38)

Answer

71. At this stage, the European Communities does not comment on the factual aspects of this claim.

Q37. The United States seems to argue that, at present, by virtue of Article 10.2 of the *Agreement on Agriculture*, there are *no* disciplines on agricultural export credit guarantees under the *Agreement on Agriculture* (or the *SCM Agreement)*.

(a) Comment on the following proposition: a WTO Member may therefore extend agricultural export credit guarantees without charging a premium, and for an indefinite period, in addition to any other terms and conditions it may wish? How would this reconcile with the title of Article 10 of the *Agreement on Agriculture* ("Prevention of Circumvention on Export Subsidy Commitments"), and with other commitments contained in the *Agreement on Agriculture*? Please cite any relevant material, including any past WTO dispute settlement cases. 3rd parties, in particular, Argentina, Canada, EC, NZ

Answer

72. The European Communities considers that it is only the operation of export credit guarantees as export subsidies which is regulated by the *Agreement on Agriculture*. Other elements of the provision of export credit guarantees are not regulated by the *Agreement on Agriculture*. To the extent that the scenario developed by the Panel would lead to the provision of export subsidies which circumvent, or which threaten to circumvent, a Member's export subsidy commitments the European Communities considers that it cannot be reconciled with Article 10.1 of the *Agreement on Agriculture*.

(b) If, as the United States argues, there are no disciplines on export credit guarantees in the *Agreement on Agriculture*, how could export credit guarantees "conform fully to the provisions of Part V" of the *Agreement on Agriculture* within the meaning of Article 13 (how can you assess "conformity" or non-conformity with non- existent disciplines)? 3rd parties, in particular, Argentina, Canada, EC, NZ

Answer

73. The European Communities disagrees with the US argument that there are no disciplines on export credit guarantees. The discipline applying to export credit guarantees, where they operate as export subsidies, is that they should not be provided in a manner inconsistent with Article 10.1. If they are provided inconsistently with Article 10.1 then they are not protected by Article 13

IV. STEP 2 PAYMENTS

Q38. Please comment on the statement in note 119 of the United States' first written submission that "...to the extent a consumer that had intended to export instead opens the bale, then that consumer could still obtain the Step 2 payment upon submission of the requisite documentation". The Panel notes that Step 2 payments all involve upland cotton produced in the United States. What are the two distinct factual situations that Step 2 payments involve? Other than the panel report in *Canada-Dairy* and the findings of the Appellate Body in *US-FSC (21.5)*[30], do any other dispute settlement reports offer guidance on this issue? For example, how, if at all is the Appellate Body's report in *Canada-Aircraft* relevant here?[31] . 3rd parties, in particular, Australia, Argentina, NZ, Paraguay

Answer

74. This is a question of fact on which the European Communities takes no position. It will comment, as necessary, on the replies of the other third parties.

Q39. Please comment on the United States assertions at paragraph 129 of its first written submission, that "[t]he programme is indifferent to whether recipients of the benefit of this programme are exporters or parties that open bales for the processing of manufacturing raw cotton into cotton products in the United States." . 3rd parties, in particular, Australia, Argentina, NZ, Paraguay

Answer

75. This is a statement of fact on which the European Communities offers no comment at present. The European Communities will comment further depending on the replies of other third parties.

---

[30] [Original footnote to question] "We recall that the ETI measure grants a tax exemption in two different sets of circumstances: (a) where property is produced *within* the United States and held for use *outside* the United States; and (b) where property is produced *outside* the United States and held for use outside the United States. Our conclusion that the ETI measure grants subsidies that are export contingent in the first set of circumstances is not affected by the fact that the subsidy can also be obtained in the second set of circumstances. The fact that the subsidies granted in the second set of circumstances *might* not be export contingent does not dissolve the export contingency arising in the first set of circumstances.[30] Conversely, the export contingency arising in these circumstances has no bearing on whether there is an export contingent subsidy in the second set of circumstances. Where a United States taxpayer is simultaneously producing property within and outside the United States, for direct use outside the United States, subsidies may be granted under the ETI measure in respect of both sets of property. The subsidy granted with respect to the property produced within the United States, and exported from there, is export contingent within the meaning of Article 3.1(a) of the *SCM Agreement*, irrespective of whether the subsidy given in respect of property produced outside the United States is also export contingent."

[31] There, the Appellate Body stated that,

> "the fact that some of TPC's contributions, in some industry sectors, are *not* contingent upon export performance, does not necessarily mean that the same is true for all of TPC's contributions. It is enough to show that one or some of TPC's contributions do constitute subsidies contingent ... in fact ... upon export performance".[31]

Q40. With respect to paragraph 32 of the oral statement of the EC, are subsidies contingent on the use of domestic goods consistent with the *AoA*? Does the phrase "provide support in favour of domestic producers" refer to, and/or permit such subsidies? What is the meaning and relevance of this (if any) to Brazil's claims under Article 3 of the *SCM Agreement* and Article III:4 of the GATT 1994.. 3rd parties, in particular, Australia, Argentina, EC, NZ, Paraguay

Answer

76. The Panel's question involves two elements. First, is a Member entitled to provide domestic content subsidies under the *Agreement on Agriculture*? Second, if such subsidies are permitted, what is the relevance of such a rule to Brazil's claims under Article 3 of the *SCM Agreement* and Article III.4 GATT. The European Communities has already provided elements of a response in its oral statement.[32] These are expanded upon below.

77. First, a Member is entitled to provide domestic content subsidies under the *Agreement on Agriculture* provided such subsidies are provided consistently with the Member's domestic support commitment levels. This conclusion flows from a number of factors. First, the *Agreement on Agriculture* disciplines domestic support. Article 6.1 refers to "domestic support reduction commitments". Article 3.1 refers to "domestic support [..] commitments [...] constitut[ing] commitments limiting subsidization" and Article 3.2 obliges Members "not [to] provide support in favour of domestic producers in excess of the [domestic] support commitment levels". Despite these clear rules on domestic support, the *Agreement on Agriculture* does not define "domestic support".

78. AMS is the measurement of domestic support. AMS is defined as "the annual level of support, expressed in monetary terms, provided for an agricultural product in favour of the producers of the basic agricultural product or non-product-specific support provided in favour of agricultural producers in general, other than [that exempted etc]." This is very general – it covers all support in favour of agricultural producers. This broad scope of domestic support measures which can be maintained consistently with the *Agreement on Agriculture* is confirmed by Article 6.1 which states that the domestic support reduction commitments "shall apply to all of its [i.e. the Member's] domestic support measures in favour of agricultural producers [...]". Paragraph 1 of Annex 3 on the calculation of the AMS refers to AMS being calculated "on a product specific-basis for each basic agricultural product receiving market prices support, non-exempt direct payments, *or any other subsidy* not exempted from the reduction commitment". (emphasis added)

79. Consequently, the range of domestic support measures which a Member may maintain (consistent with reduction commitments) is very broad and is only limited by the condition that such support must be in favour of agricultural pro-

32 Paras. 34 to 38 of the EC's Oral Statement (as delivered). The Panel's reference to para. 32 corresponds to the text provided at the third party session.

ducers. As the European Communities has noted, paragraph 7 of Annex 3 explicitly states that "measures directed at agricultural processors shall be included to the extent that such measures benefit the producers of the basic agricultural products".[33] The European Communities considers that the term "benefit" used here must be regarded as being synonymous with "favour" in the sense of "in favour of agricultural producers". Moreover, it is clear that by "measures directed at agricultural processors" the negotiators intended subsidies which were paid to processors, where the benefit went to the agricultural producer. Consequently, in light of the broad definition of "domestic support" and the specific reference to domestic content subsidies in paragraph 7 of Annex 3, the European Communities considers that a Member is entitled to maintain domestic content subsidies consistently with the *Agreement on Agriculture*.

80. Second, in response to the Panel's question, the effect of finding that domestic content subsidies are provided consistently with the *Agreement on Agriculture* would be that they cannot be found inconsistent with either Article 3.1(b) of the *SCM Agreement* or Article III.4 GATT 1994. Article 21.1 of the *Agreement on Agriculture* states that "the provisions of GATT 1994 and of other Multilateral Trade Agreements in Annex 1A to the WTO Agreement shall apply subject to the provisions of this Agreement." As the European Communities pointed out in its oral statement, this means that provisions of the other Annex 1A Agreements are "subordinated" to the *Agreement on Agriculture.*[34]

81. To find that such subsidies were inconsistent with either Article 3.1(b) of the *SCM Agreement* or Article III.4 GATT would be to subordinate the right to provide such domestic content subsidies under the *Agreement on Agriculture* to the *SCM Agreement* or GATT 1994. Such an interpretation directly contradicts Article 21.1 of the *Agreement on Agriculture*.

82. Indeed, it can be pointed out that applying Article 3.1(b) of the *SCM Agreement* and Article III.4 GATT to domestic content subsidies provided consistently with the *Agreement on Agriculture* would lead to stricter disciplines being applied to domestic subsidies for agriculture than are applicable to domestic subsidies for industrial goods. If Article 3.1(b) and Article III.4 were to apply, domestic subsidies for agricultural products would be subject to reduction commitments and Article 3.1(b) *SCM Agreement* and Article III.4 GATT. However, domestic subsidies for industrial products are not subject to reduction commitments. Since the *Agreement on Agriculture* establishes "a basis for initiating a process of reform of trade in agriculture", it would seem contradictory to find that domestic support for agriculture is in fact subject to stricter obligations than

---

33 In terms of negotiating background, it may be useful to the Panel to note that paragraph 7 of Annex 3 was subject to negotiation during the period in which a Panel had ruled that the EC's payments to oilseed processors was not covered by Article III.8(b) GATT 1947 and were consequently inconsistent with Article III.4 GATT 1947 (*European Economic Community – Payments and Subsidies Paid to Processors and Producers of Oilseeds and Related Animal-Feed Proteins* Report of the Panel (L/6627 BISD 37S/86) adopted on 25 January 1990. That the negotiators retained this text must therefore be considered as a clear sign that they intended to permit Members to maintain such subsidies, subject to reduction commitments, in the *Agreement on Agriculture*.

34 Oral Statement, para. 38.

domestic support for other industries. This explains the "subject to" language of Article 21.1 of the *Agreement on Agriculture*. Article 21.1 and the *Agreement on Agriculture* more generally can also be compared with the other sectoral agreement included in Annex 1A of the WTO Agreement. The *Agreement on Textiles and Clothing* explicitly provides, in its Article 9, that the textiles and clothing sector is to be fully integrated into the GATT 1994. The *Agreement on Agriculture* has no such language, and Article 21.1 runs directly counter to this notion. It cannot be lightly assumed that the negotiators, while providing for the possibility to maintain domestic content subsidies, intended that such subsidies also be subject to rules which effectively makes it impossible to maintain such subsidies.[35]

83. The Panel should therefore reject Brazil's arguments that domestic content subsidies granted in favour of agricultural producers can be found to be inconsistent with Article 3.1(b) of the *SCM Agreement* and Article III.4 GATT 1994.

V. ETI ACT

Q41. Concerning its claims on the ETI Act, Brazil relies on the *US – FSC* case. However, it appears that the United States did not raise the issue of the Peace Clause in that case, nor did the US appear to invoke Article 6 of the *Agreement on Agriculture*. If the Panel's understanding is correct, how, if at all, are these differences relevant here? Argentina, China, EC, NZ

Answer

84. The European Communities does not consider that either the Peace Clause or Article 6 of the *Agreement on Agriculture* is relevant. The ETI Act provides export subsidies.[36] Article 6 of the *Agreement on Agriculture* does not apply to export subsidies, and therefore the US would not have been in a position to invoke it.

85. The Peace Clause will only apply in respect of export subsidies which "conform fully to the provisions of Part V" of the *Agreement on Agriculture* (Article 13(c)). The Appellate Body upheld the panel's findings that the ETI Act provided export subsidies in violation of Article 10.1 of the *Agreement on Agriculture*.[37] Consequently, the US could not have legitimately maintained that it was entitled to peace clause protection.

---

[35] See, in a similar sense, Appellate Body Report, *EC Measures Concerning Meat and Meat Products (Hormones) ("European Communities – Hormones")*, WT/DS26/AB/R, WT/DS48/AB/R, adopted 13 February 1998, para. 165.

[36] The Appellate Body confirmed the panel's findings of a violation of Article 3.1(a) of the SCM Agreement see Article 231.5 Appellate Body Report, *United States – Tax Treatment for "Foreign Sales Corporations"* ("United States – FSC (21.5)"), WT/DS108/AB/RW, adopted 29 January 2002, para. 120.

[37] Appellate Body Report, *United States – Tax Treatment for "Foreign Sales Corporations"* ("United States – FSC (21.5)"), WT/DS108/AB/RW, adopted 29 January 2002, para. 196.

Q42. How do you view the reference in paragraph 43 of the EC's third party oral statement with respect to the relevance of Article 17.14 of the *DSU*, and, in particular, the phrase "a final resolution to *that* dispute" (emphasis added)? Please explain the use, and relevance (if any) of the term "disputes" in Articles 9.3 and 12 and Appendix 3 of the *DSU*, and please cite any other provisions you consider relevant. Argentina, China, EC, NZ

Answer

86. Article 17.14 DSU states that an Appellate Body Report shall be "adopted by the DSB and unconditionally accepted by the parties to the dispute". The reference in the EC's oral statement to the phrase "a final resolution to *that* dispute" (emphasis from the Panel) is from the Appellate Body in *United States – Shrimp (21.5)*.[38]

87. In the present case the Panel must decide a preliminary question. It must determine whether the claims brought by Brazil against the ETI Act are in any way different from those which the panel and Appellate Body upheld against the ETI Act in the EC's Recourse to Article 21.5. If Brazil's claims are identical to those upheld against the ETI Act, the European Communities considers that the United States must be considered to have unconditionally accepted the Appellate Body's findings as adopted by the DSB.

88. The Panel may find some assistance in the Appellate Body's findings in *United States – Shrimp (21.5)*. In that recourse to Article 21.5, Malaysia attempted to challenge certain aspects of the revised US measure at issue which were identical in the measure which was subject to the original challenge.[39] These aspects had been found by the panel and the Appellate Body to be consistent with the United States' WTO obligations. The Appellate Body found that there was no need for the panel, having determined that this aspect of the measure had not changed, to re-examine the consistency of the measure with the US' WTO obligations.[40]

89. The situation before the Panel is the inverse. Here, the US measure was found to be inconsistent with US' WTO obligations. The European Communities understands that the measure before the Panel in this case and before the panel and the Appellate Body in *United States – FSC (21.5)* is identical. On the assumption that the claims are identical, applying Article 17.14 DSU and the Appellate Body's findings in *United States – Shrimp (21.5)* the United States must be assumed to have unconditionally accepted the findings against the ETI Act.

---

[38] Para. 97, Article 21.5 Appellate Body Report, *United States – Import Prohibition of Certain Shrimp and Shrimp Products – Recourse to Article 21.-5 of the DSU by Malaysia* ("United States – Shrimp (21.5)"), WT/DS58/AB/RW, adopted 21 November 2001.

[39] United States – Shrimp (21.5), para. 96.

[40] The Appellate Body made a similar finding with respect to a claim not pursued before a panel. See, Report of the Appellate Body in *European Communities – Anti-Dumping Duties on Imports of Cotton-Type Bed Linen from India – Recourse to Article 21.5 of the DSU by* India, WT/DS141/AB/RW, adopted on 24 April 2003.

90. The European Communities does not consider it material that the present case concerns a party (Brazil) which was not party to the FSC dispute. Article 17.14 states that a "party to the dispute" must unconditionally accept the findings of the Appellate Body adopted by the DSB. Of the parties before the Panel, the United States is a party to the FSC dispute, and must, therefore, unconditionally accept the Appellate Body's findings in that dispute. This is further reinforced by Articles 3.2 and 3.3 DSU which state that the dispute settlement system must provide security and predictability and promote prompt settlement of disputes. Consequently, given the United States is required to unconditionally accept the findings in the Article 21.5 procedure, the European Communities believes that Brazil, by adopting the EC' claims and the Appellate Body's findings in the FSC dispute, would make a sufficient case to compel the Panel to find that the ETI Act is inconsistent with the US' WTO obligations in this dispute.

VI. QUESTIONS FROM OTHER THIRD PARTIES ADDRESSED TO THE EUROPEAN COMMUNITIES

Questions from Australia to the European Communities

Q43. Would the European Communities please explain why, in its view, the ordinary meaning of the phrase "shall meet the fundamental requirement" as it appears in the first sentence of paragraph 1 of Annex 2 to the *Agreement on Agriculture* does not give meaning and effect to all provisions of that agreement.[41]

Answer

91. The European Communities did not state that the phrase "shall meet the fundamental requirement" does not give meaning and effect to all provisions of that agreement. The question appears to be based on an erroneous characterisation of the EC's position. In paragraph 17 of its First Written Submission the European Communities stated that the first sentence of Annex 2 did not create a free-standing obligation. This view is compelling when an interpreter considers the ordinary meaning of the terms, in their context, and in light of the object and purpose of the provision. The European Communities has explained this in some detail in its answers to the Panel's questions 6-11 and in its previous submissions to the Panel.

Q44. The European Communities argues that, under the "accepted canons of interpretation of international law", "context and objective" require that the first sentence of paragraph 1 of Annex 2 to the *Agreement on Agriculture* be considered to set out an objective.[42] Would the European Communities please explain the legal authorities for its argument, having regard to rele-

[41] [Original footnote to question] First Third Party Submission by the European Communities, para. 17.

[42] [Original footnote to question] Oral Statement by the European Communities, para. 25.

vant statements by the Appellate Body, particularly those in *Japan – Alcohol Taxes.*[43]

Answer

92. European Communities understands from Australia's question that Australia considers that the European Communities' interpretation of the first sentence of Paragraph 1 of Annex 2 would deprive the first sentence of effect.

93. Australia's implication is quite erroneous, and built upon an incomplete, examination of the Appellate Body's rulings. The European Communities interpretation does not deprive the first sentence of effect. Stating that the first sentence does not impose a self-standing obligation is not the same as stating that it is deprived of effect. Indeed, the Appellate Body has arrived at exactly the same conclusion with respect to other provisions containing purposive language, similar to that contained in the first sentence of paragraph 1. In *Japan – Alcoholic Beverages* the Appellate Body found:

> Article III:1 articulates a general principle that internal measures should not be applied so as to afford protection to domestic production. This general principle informs the rest of Article III. The purpose of Article III:1 is to establish this general principle as a guide to understanding and interpreting the specific obligations contained in Article III:2 and in the other paragraphs of Article III, while respecting, and not diminishing in any way, the meaning of the words actually used in the texts of those other paragraphs. In short, Article III:1 constitutes part of the context of Article III:2, in the same way that it constitutes part of the context of each of the other paragraphs in Article III. *Any other reading of Article III would have the effect of rendering the words of Article III:1 meaningless, thereby violating the fundamental principle of effectiveness in treaty interpretation.* Consistent with this principle of effectiveness, and with the textual differences in the two sentences, we believe that Article III:1 informs the first sentence and the se-

---

43 [Original footnote to question] In *Japan – Taxes on Alcoholic Beverages*, Report of the Appellate Body, WT/DS8/AB/R, WT/DS10/AB/R, WT/DS11/AB/R, pages 11-12, the Appellate Body said:

> Article 31 of the *Vienna Convention* provides that the words of the treaty form the foundation for the interpretive process: "interpretation must be based above all upon the text of the treaty".[...] The provisions of the treaty are to be given their ordinary meaning in their context.[...] The object and purpose of the treaty are also to be taken into account in determining the meaning of its provisions.[20] A fundamental tenet of treaty interpretation flowing from the general rule of interpretation set out in Article 31 is the principle of effectiveness ...[...] In *[US – Gasoline]*, we noted that "[o]ne of the corollaries of the 'general rule of interpretation' in the *Vienna Convention* is that interpretation must give meaning and effect to all the terms of the treaty. An interpreter is not free to adopt a reading that would result in reducing whole clauses or paragraphs of a treaty to redundancy or inutility".[...]
>
> ---
>
> *Footnote 20:* That is, the treaty's "object and purpose" is to be referred to in determining the meaning of the "terms of the treaty" and not as an independent basis for interpretation: ...

cond sentence of Article III:2 in different ways.[44] (emphasis added)

94. Moreover, the Appellate Body has also found that Article XXIV.4 GATT, which the Appellate Body qualified as "purposive language", was relevant for the interpretation of Article XXIV.5.[45] Clearly this gave a provision which had no operational effects, an effect, within the meaning of the Appellate Body's statements in *United States – Gasoline*.[46] Similarly, the European Communities has argued that while the first sentence of paragraph 1 does not impose a self standing obligation, it does set out the purpose of Annex 2 which informs the interpretation of other elements of Annex 2. (See the European Communities response to question 11 from the Panel).

Q45. The European Communities argues that the omission of a reference to the "fundamental requirement" as set out in the first sentence of paragraph 1 of Annex 2 to the *Agreement on Agriculture* in paragraphs 5, 6 and 7 of that Annex provides "contextual support" to its argument that the first sentence sets out an objective.[47] Would the European Communities please explain the legal authorities for its argument, having regard to its arguments and the Appellate Body's findings in *Argentina – Footwear Safeguard*.[48]

Answer

95. We refer Australia in part to the European Communities' answer to the previous question where the European Communities has explained that its interpretation of the first sentence of Paragraph 1 does not deprive the provision of effect. Second, the issue in *Argentina – Footwear Safeguards* was whether the panel had given any effect to Article XIX GATT.[49] The panel in that case erroneously concluded that because of the omission of a reference to unforeseen developments in the *Agreement on Safeguards* it need not give effect to this requirement set out in Article XIX GATT. As the European Communities has explai-

---

[44] Appellate Body Report, *Japan – Taxes on Alcoholic Beverages ("Japan – Alcoholic Beverages")*, WT/DS8/AB/R, WT/DS10/AB/R, WT/DS11/AB/R, adopted 1 November 1996, page 18.

[45] Appellate Body Report, *Turkey – Restrictions on Imports of Textile and Clothing Products* ("Turkey – Textiles"), WT/DS34/AB/R, adopted 19 November 1999, para. 57.

[46] Appellate Body Report, *United States - Standards for Reformulated and Conventional Gasoline* ("United States – Gasoline"), WT/DS2/AB/R, adopted 20 May 1996, page 23.

[47] [Original footnote to question] First Third Party Submission by the European Communities, para. 21.

[48] [Original footnote to question] In *Argentina – Safeguard Measures on Imports of Footwear*, Report of the Appellate Body, WT/DS121/AB/R, the European Communities argued (paras. 38-44) on appeal, and the Appellate Body found (para. 88), that the Panel erred by:

> fail[ing] to give meaning and legal effect to *all* the relevant terms of the *WTO Agreement*, contrary to the principle of effectiveness ... in the interpretations of treaties. [...] The Panel states that the '*express omission* of the criterion of unforeseen developments' in Article XIX:1(a) from the *Agreement on Safeguards* 'must, in our view, have meaning'. [...] On the contrary, in our view, if they had intended to *expressly omit* this clause, the Uruguay Round negotiations would and could have said so in the *Agreement on Safeguards*. They did not.

[49] Appellate Body Report, *Argentina – Safeguard Measures on Imports of Footwear* ("Argentina – Footwear Safeguards"), WT/DS121/AB/R, adopted 12 January 2000.

ned, by interpreting the first sentence of paragraph 1 as setting an objective informing the rest of Annex 2, the Panel would be giving effect to the first sentence.

Questions from Argentina to the European Communities

Q46. In paragraph 18 of its Oral Statement, the European Communities state that Article 13 (b)(ii) and (iii) of the Agreement on Agriculture are clearly "not intended to set up a comparison between domestic support granted in 1992 and domestic support granted in a more recent period" and request the Panel to reject the equation of the term "decided" with the term "granted".

What would be, in the opinion of the EC, the appropriate benchmark in a hypothetical case in which a subsidizing Member has taken no decision on internal support during 1992 ?

Answer

96. We refer Argentina to the European Communities' response to question 27.

ANNEX J-7

NEW ZEALAND ANSWERS TO QUESTIONS FROM THE PANEL TO THIRD PARTIES

11 August 2003[1]

Article 13(b) of the *Agreement on Agriculture*: Domestic support measures

Q2. Please explain the difference, if any, between the meaning of "defined" and the meaning of "fixed" in the phrase "a defined and fixed base period" in paragraph 6(a) of Annex 2 of the Agreement on Agriculture. 3rd parties, in particular Australia, Argentina, Canada, EC, NZ

Reply

"Defined" and "fixed" mean two different things and impose two distinct and different requirements for a base period under paragraph 6(a) of Annex 2. "Defined" means "having a definite or specified outline or form".[2] "Fixed" means "definitely and permanently placed or assigned; stationary or unchanging in relative position; definite, permanent, lasting".[3] Accordingly a base period must have a definite and specified form that is permanent.

Q3. Please explain the meaning of "a" in "a defined and fixed base period" in paragraph 6(a) of Annex 2 of the Agreement on Agriculture, the meaning of "the" in "the base period" in paragraphs 6(b), (c) and (d), and the difference between these and the phrase "based on the years 1986-88" in Annex 3. 3rd parties, in particular Australia, Argentina, Canada, EC, NZ

Reply

"A" in the context of paragraph 6(a) refers to one single defined and fixed base period. "The" in "the base period" in the context of subsequent sub-paragraphs refers to the single base period required under paragraph 6(a). Paragraph 6(a), however, does not specify a particular base period – only that once it is determined it is fixed. On the other hand, Annex 3 specifies that the "fixed" base period in that instance must be the 1986-88 period.

Q4. How often can a Member define and fix a base period in accordance with paragraph 6 of Annex 2 of the Agreement on Agriculture? 3rd parties, in particular Australia, Argentina, Canada, China, EC, NZ

Reply

Once, when a programme is first established. Thereafter, so long as the programme retains fundamentally the same elements, it should be considered to be the same programme and apply the same base periods.

---

1 New Zealand has not responded to questions not directed specifically to New Zealand.

2 *The New Shorter Oxford English Dictionary*, Vol 1, Clarendon Press, Oxford (1993), page 618.

3 *Ibid.*, page 962.

Q6. Please explain the meaning of the word "criteria" in Article 6.1 and 7.1. What effect, if any, does the use of the word "Accordingly" in paragraph 1 of Annex 2 of the Agreement on Agriculture have on the meaning of the preceding sentence? 3rd parties, in particular Australia, Argentina, Canada, EC, NZ

Reply

"Criteria" are the standards by which a thing is assessed. In this case they are the standards by which domestic support measures must be assessed in order to qualify for exemption from reduction commitments. These criteria are set out in Article 6 and Annex 2 of the *Agreement on Agriculture*, and include: the "fundamental requirement" in Annex 2 paragraph 1 that measures have at most minimal trade-distorting effects; the "basic criteria" in paragraph 1(a) and (b); and the "policy-specific criteria and conditions" set out elsewhere in Annex 2. The use of the word "accordingly" signifies that the intention of the drafters was to indicate that in order to meet the first criterion – the "fundamental requirement" that they be at most minimally trade-distorting – measures would at the very least have to meet the subsequent basic and policy-specific criteria.

Q7. Please explain the meaning of the words "the fundamental requirement" as used in paragraph 1 of Annex 2 of the Agreement on Agriculture. 3rd parties, in particular Australia, Argentina, Canada, EC, NZ

Reply

"The fundamental requirement" as used in paragraph 1 of Annex 2 refers to a characteristic which, if not present, excludes a measure from a claim of exemption from reduction commitments. In this case that characteristic is that the measure has "no, or at most minimal, trade-distorting effects or effects on production." Paragraph 1 specifies that measures for which exemption is claimed "shall meet" this fundamental requirement. Had the drafters intended to make only a general statement of principle they would not have referred to a "requirement" that "shall be met". The use of the term "fundamental" only serves to underline the importance placed on all measures meeting this requirement in order to be exempt.

Q9. If the first sentence of paragraph 1 of Annex 2 is a stand-alone obligation, does this allow effects-based claims of non-compliance with Annex 2? If so, how does this affect the purpose of Article 13(b)? 3rd parties' in particular Australia, Argentina, Canada, EC, NZ

Reply

If the first sentence of paragraph 1 of Annex 2 is a stand-alone obligation it would allow effects-based claims of non-compliance with Annex 2. This is consistent with Article 13(b) because it means that the measures excluded from Annex 2 have a more than minimal distorting effect on trade or production, and as such they could potentially give rise to the kind of adverse effects to the interests of other Members that the *GATT 1994* and the *SCM Agreement* establish a right to address. As such those measures should not be exempt from reduction commitments and should be required to meet the requirements of Article 13(b) in order to be exempt from actions under the *Agreement on Subsidies and Countervailing Measures* (the "*SCM Agreement*") and *General Agreement on Tariffs and Trade 1994* (the "*GATT 1994*").

Q10. If the first sentence of paragraph 1 of Annex 2 is not a stand-alone obligation, then must new, non- or minimally trade-distorting measures that do not conform to the criteria listed in Annex 2 be classified as non-Green Box? 3rd parties, in particular Australia, Argentina, Canada, EC, NZ

Reply

Yes.

Q11. If the first sentence of paragraph 1 of Annex 2 expresses a general principle which informs the interpretation of the criteria in Annex 2, please explain how this affects the assessment of the direct payments programme's compliance with paragraph 6 of Annex 2. 3rd parties, in particular, Australia, Argentina, Canada, EC, NZ

Reply

If the first sentence of paragraph 1 of Annex 2 expresses a general principle then the criteria in paragraph 6 of Annex 2 must be strictly applied to ensure that only genuinely decoupled income support that had at most minimal impacts on trade and/or production qualified for exemption from reduction commitments.

Irrespective of whether the first sentence of paragraph 1 of Annex 2 is to be considered a general principle or a stand-alone obligation, the requirement that there be only one defined and fixed base period in paragraph 6 is unambiguous. In New Zealand's view the updating of base acreage under the Direct Payments programme alone is sufficient to exclude it from the scope of permitted green box measures set out in paragraph 6 of Annex 2, as outlined in paragraph 2.29 of New Zealand's Third Party Submission.[4]

Q12. Where does Article 13(b) require a year-on-year comparison? 3RD parties, in particular Australia, Argentina, Canada, China, EC, NZ

Reply

Article 13(b)(ii) and 13(b)(iii) require a comparison with 1992 of any year in which injury, nullification or impairment or serious prejudice is alleged to have occurred.

Q13. Does a failure by a Member to comply in a given year with either the chapeau of Article 13(b) or the proviso in subparagraph (ii) of Article 13(b) impact its entitlement to benefit in an earlier or a later year from the exemption from action provided by Article 13(b)? 3RD parties, in particular Australia, Argentina, Canada, China, EC, NZ

---

4 Third Party Submission of New Zealand, 15 July 2003.

Reply

The nature of the non-compliance at issue may be such that it does impact on a Member's entitlement to benefit in an earlier or later year from the exemption from action provided by Article 13(b). Whether or not that is so must be assessed on a case-by-case basis.

Q14. Does a failure of a Member to comply with Article 13(b) in respect of a specific commodity impact its entitlement to benefit in respect of other agricultural products from the exemption from action provided by Article 13(b)? 3RD parties, in particular Australia, Argentina, Canada, China, EC, NZ

Reply

No. The language of Article 13(b) makes it clear that the exemption from action applies to a "specific commodity", which means that the eligibility for such exemption must be assessed on a product-by-product basis.

Q15. Is there any basis on which counter-cyclical payments could be considered product-specific? 3RD parties, in particular Australia, Argentina, Canada, China, EC, NZ

Reply

Yes. The basis upon which counter-cyclical payments should be considered product-specific have been outlined in the First Written Submission of Brazil,[5] and highlighted in New Zealand's Third Party Submission.[6]

Q16. If the word "specific" were deleted from Article 13(b)(ii), would this change the meaning of the subparagraph? 3RD parties, in particular Australia, Argentina, Benin Canada, China, EC, NZ

Reply

Not necessarily. The application of the rules of treaty interpretation to the provision, taking into account its object and purpose, would still support a conclusion that the relevant support was that granted to an individual commodity. The use of the word "specific" simply reinforces that interpretation.

Q17. What is the relevance, if any, of the concept of "specificity" in Article 2 of the SCM Agreement and references to "a product" or "subsidized product" in certain provisions of the SCM Agreement to the meaning of "support to a specific commodity" in Article 13(b)(ii) Agreement on Agriculture? 3RD parties, in particular Australia, Argentina, Canada, China, EC, NZ

5 Brazil's First Submission to the Panel Regarding the "Peace Clause" and Non-"Peace Clause" Related Claims, 24 June 2003 ("First Written Submission of Brazil"), paras. 199-202 and 207-213.

6 Paras. 2.17-2.13.

Reply

The *SCM Agreement* provisions cited would seem to shed little light on the meaning of "support to a specific commodity" in Article 13(b)(ii). Article 2 of the *SCM Agreement* sets out principles for determining whether a subsidy is specific to an enterprise or industry or group of enterprises or industries. Article 13(b)(ii) of the *Agreement on Agriculture* is concerned with the support granted to a specific commodity. The two assessments are unrelated. In relation to the second part of the question, the references to "a product" or "subsidised product" seem fully consistent with interpreting "support to a specific commodity" referred to in Article 13(b)(ii) as meaning support to a particular product.

Q19. Where does Article 13(b)(ii) require a year-on-year comparison? 3rd parties, in particular Australia, Argentina, Canada, EC, NZ

Reply

See New Zealand's answer to question 12 above.

Q20. Does Article 13(b)(ii) require a comparison of support granted with support decided? How could such a comparison be made?

Reply

Such a comparison could be made by interpreting these terms logically as requiring a comparison between the total volume of support to a specific commodity in 1992 and in any other year in respect of which claims under the *SCM Agreement* and *GATT 1994* are made.

Q21. Please comment on Brazil's assertion that the terms "grant" and "decided" in Article 13(b)(ii) have broadly the same meaning. If so, why did the drafters not use the same term? 3rd parties, in particular, Australia, Argentina, Canada, China, EC, NZ

Reply

Article 13(b)(ii) would be devoid of meaning if it were to be interpreted as requiring a comparison between two things that were not like ie if "support granted" was somehow different from "support decided". Therefore the issue is not the difference in wording used, but substantively, what comparison meets the object and purpose of the provision. In New Zealand's view that is a comparison between the total volume of support to a specific commodity in 1992 and in any other year in respect of which claims under the *SCM Agreement* and *GATT 1994* are made.

Q22. What is the meaning of "support" in Agreement on Agriculture 13(b)(ii) ? Why would it be used differently from Annex 3, where it refers to total outlays? 3rd parties, in particular, Australia, Argentina, Canada, China, EC, NZ

Reply

Annex 3 refers to budgetary outlays as a component of the Aggregate Measurement of Support ("AMS") calculation. There is nothing to suggest that budgetary outlays should not also be a component of the calculation of "support" in the context of Article 13(b)(ii).

Q23. Should support be compared under Article 13(b)(ii) in terms of unit of production or total volume of support or both? 3rd parties, in particular, Australia, Argentina, Canada, China, EC, NZ

Reply

The rationale behind the comparison required by Article 13(b)(ii) is to create an upper limit to the level of trade and production distortion resulting from Members' domestic support programmes. Therefore the appropriate comparison is with the total volume of support because that provides the truest indication of the real effects of the support programmes on trade and production. Support in terms of unit of production may well be a relevant factor in that calculation but it will not be the only one.

Q25. Please comment on an interpretation of the words "decided during" in Article 13(b)(ii) that would read them as synonymous with the words "authorized during". 3rd parties, in particular Australia, Argentina, Canada, China, EC, NZ

Reply

New Zealand is not sure what "authorised" in such a context would mean. Presumably it requires evidence of some kind of formal "authorisation". What support was formally authorised, by legislation or regulation, might provide some insight into what level of support was received for specific commodities, but it cannot provide the full picture. It therefore makes no sense to interpret "decided" in such a limited way.

Export credit guarantee programmes

Q29. (a) Is an export credit guarantee a financial contribution in the form of a "potential direct transfer of funds or liabilities (e.g. loan guarantee)" within the meaning of Article 1.1(a)(1)(i) of the SCM Agreement? Why or why not? 3rd parties, in particular, Argentina, Canada, EC, NZ

Reply

An export credit guarantee is a "financial contribution" under Article 1.1(a)(1) because it is a "loan guarantee".

Q29. (b) How, if at all, would this be relevant to the claims of Brazil? 3rd parties, in particular, Argentina, Canada, EC, NZ

Reply

It is relevant because a financial contribution is a necessary element of a "subsidy" under Article 1.1(a)(1)(i) of the *SCM Agreement*. Brazil has presented arguments to support a finding that the US export credit guarantee programmes are subsidies as defined in Article 1.1(a)(1)(i), that are contingent upon export according to the terms of Article 3.1(a). The *SCM Agreement* has been found to provide useful context for determining what constitutes an export subsidy for the purposes of Article 10.1 of the *Agreement on Agriculture*. Brazil has demonstrated that, in the terms of Article 10.1, the United States export credit guarantee programmes are applied so as to result in, or threaten to lead to, circumvention of the United States export subsidy commitments.

Brazil has therefore demonstrated that the United States export credit guarantee programmes do not conform fully to the provisions of Part V of the *Agreement on Agriculture* and therefore cannot be exempt from actions based on Article XVI of *GATT 1994* or Articles 3, 5 and 6 of the *SCM Agreement* by the terms of Article 13(c)(ii) of the *Agreement on Agriculture*.

Q30. The Panel could arguably take the view that Articles 1 and 3 of the SCM Agreement were relevant in assessing the WTO-consistency of United States export credit guarantees. The Panel would therefore appreciate third party views on this situation, including with respect to the viability of an a contrario interpretation of item (j) of the Illustrative List (as addressed in paragraphs 180-183 of the United States' first written submission). 3rd parties, in particular, Argentina, Canada, EC, NZ

Reply

New Zealand notes that the Illustrative List simply lists measures that constitute export subsidies under Article 3.1(a) of the *SCM Agreement*. As stated by the Panel in Canada – Export Credits, "item (j) sets out the circumstances in which the grant of loan guarantees is *per se* deemed to be an export subsidy (i.e. when the "premium rates ... are inadequate to cover the long-term operating costs and losses" of the loan guarantee)."[7]

Q31. If the Panel decides to refer to provisions of the SCM Agreement for contextual guidance in the interpretation of the terms in Article 10 Agreement on Agriculture, should the Panel refer to item (j) or Articles 1 and 3 of the SCM Agreement or both? 3rd parties, in particular, Argentina, Canada, EC, NZ

Reply

The Panel should refer to both. The *SCM Agreement* provides both a general definition of an "export subsidy" (specifically the definition of a "subsidy" in the terms of Article 1 and the requirement of contingency upon export in the terms of Article 3) and an Illustrative List containing specific examples of export

[7] Report of the Panel, *Canada – Export Credits and Loan Guarantees for Regional Aircraft*, WT/DS/222, para. 7.395.

subsidies. Therefore Articles 1 and 3 and item (j) of the Illustrative List provide contextual guidance for the interpretation of the terms in Article 10.

Q32. The Panel's attention has been drawn to Article 14(c) of the SCM Agreement (see third party submission of Canada) and to the panel report in DS 222 Canada- Export Credits and Loan Guarantees. How and to what extent are Article 14(c) of the SCM Agreement, and the cited panel report, relevant to the issue of whether or not the United States export credit guarantee programmes confer a "benefit"? What would the appropriate market benchmark be to use for any comparison? Please cite any other relevant material. . 3rd parties, in particular, Argentina, Canada, EC, NZ

Reply

The Panel in Canada – Export Credits and Loan Guarantees[8] considered that Article 14(c) of the *SCM Agreement* provided contextual guidance for interpreting 'benefit' in relation to loan guarantees. In that case it was determined that the relevant benchmark for determining whether a loan guarantee conferred a "benefit" was whether there was "a difference between the amount that the firm receiving the guarantee pays on a loan guaranteed ... and the amount that the firm would pay on a comparable commercial loan absent the ... guarantee." This confirms that the appropriate point of reference for determining whether a "benefit" has been conferred is the marketplace, in this case the extent to which the premium rates charged on current export credit guarantees are lower than the corresponding financing rates that a commercial bank would normally require given a similar level of risk.

Q33. What is the relevance (if any) of Brazil's statement that : "...export credit guarantees for exports of agricultural exports [sic] are not available on the marketplace by commercial lenders." . 3rd parties, in particular, Argentina, Canada, EC, NZ

Reply

Brazil's statement goes toward a conclusion that a "benefit" is conferred in the terms of Article 1.1(b) of the *SCM Agreement*. It is significant because it indicates that either commercial lenders are not prepared to accept the risks associated with such guarantees or that the United States export credit programme is so big that it has forced any competition from commercial programmes out of the marketplace. For whatever reason, the United States export credit guarantee programmes provide the recipient with export credit guarantees not available in, and therefore on terms more favourable than, the marketplace, and thus confers a "benefit" in the terms of Article 1.1(b).

Q34. Comment on the United States' view of the meaning of "long term operating costs and losses" in item (j) of the Illustrative List of Export Subsidies in Annex I of the SCM Agreement as meaning "claims paid" under the export credit guarantee programmes. Does the United States' interpre-

---

[8] *Ibid.*, para. 7.397.

tation give meaning to both "costs" and "losses"? Do claims paid represent "losses"? 3rd parties, in particular, Argentina, Canada, EC, NZ

Reply

"Claims paid" is one element of the calculation of the costs and losses of an export credit guarantee programme. Other elements to be taken into account would include, for example, costs and losses associated with reinsurance costs, administration costs and the costs of refinancing (i.e. the rescheduling (not the full amount, but the net present value of the losses)).

Q35. Did the drafters of the Agreement on Agriculture include export credit guarantees in Article 9.1 of the Agreement on Agriculture? Why or why not? 3rd parties, in particular, Argentina, Canada, EC, NZ

Reply

The drafters of the *Agreement on Agriculture* did not include export credit guarantees in Article 9.1 of the *Agreement* because export credit guarantees are not, *per se*, export subsidies. They may involve export subsidies, but this depends on whether they provide a benefit in relation to the marketplace.

Q36. Please explain any possible significance the following statements may have in respect of Brazil's claims about GSM102 and 103 (7 CFR 1493.10(a)(2), Exhibit BRA-38) 3rd parties, in particular, Argentina, Canada, EC, NZ

"The programs operate in cases where credit is necessary to increase or maintain U.S. exports to a foreign market and where U.S. financial institutions would be unwilling to provide financing without CCC's guarantee. (7 CFR 1493.10(a)(2) Exhibit BRA-38)

Reply

See New Zealand's answer to Question 33 above.

"The programs are operated in a manner intended not to interfere with markets for cash sales. The programs are targeted toward those countries where the guarantee is necessary to secure financing of the exports but which have sufficient financial strength so that foreign exchange will be available for scheduled payments." (7 CFR 1493.10(a)(2) Exhibit BRA-38)

Reply

This statement simply supports Brazil's analysis in relation to the "benefit" and "export contingency" elements of the export credit guarantee programme.

"In providing this credit guarantee facility, CCC seeks to expand market opportunities for US agricultural exporters and assist long-term market development for U.S. agricultural commodities." (7 CFR 1493.10(a)(2) Exhibit BRA-38)

Reply

This statement reinforces the obvious export contingency of the export credit guarantee programme and through the reference to expand[ing] opportunities and assist[ing] long-term market development makes it clear that the intention of the programme is to provide a benefit to US exporters.

Reply

Q37. The United States seems to argue that, at present, by virtue of Article 10.2 of the Agreement on Agriculture, there are no disciplines on agricultural export credit guarantees under the Agreement on Agriculture (or the SCM Agreement).

(a) Comment on the following proposition: a WTO Member may therefore extend agricultural export credit guarantees without charging a premium, and for an indefinite period, in addition to any other terms and conditions it may wish? How would this reconcile with the title of Article 10 of the Agreement on Agriculture ("Prevention of Circumvention on Export Subsidy Commitments"), and with other commitments contained in the Agreement on Agriculture? Please cite any relevant material, including any past WTO dispute settlement cases. 3rd parties, in particular, Argentina, Canada, EC, NZ

Reply

The proposition is not reconcilable with the title of Article 10 of the *Agreement on Agriculture* as such an export credit guarantee would clearly provide an export subsidy and thus potentially circumvent export subsidy commitments. It also ignores the findings of the Panel in US-FSC Article 21.5[9], affirmed by the Appellate Body,[10] that the threat of circumvention of export subsidy reduction commitments in the terms of Article 10.1 exists in relation to both unscheduled and scheduled agricultural products when the amount of a subsidy is unqualified or unlimited, as implied in the proposition above.

(b) If, as the United States argues, there are no disciplines on export credit guarantees in the Agreement on Agriculture, how could export credit guarantees "conform fully to the provisions of Part V" of the Agreement on Agriculture within the meaning of Article 13 (how can you assess "conformity" or non-conformity with non- existent disciplines)? 3rd parties, in particular, Argentina, Canada, EC, NZ

9 Report of the Panel, *United States – Tax Treatment for "Foreign Sales Corporations", Recourse to Article 21.5 of the DSU by the European Communities* (WT/DS108/RW), paras. 8.118 and 8.119.

10 Report of the Appellate Body, *United States – Tax Treatment for "Foreign Sales Corporations", Recourse to Article 21.5 of the DSU by the European Communities* (WT/DS108AB/RW).

Reply

The United States interpretation would render the phrase "conforming fully to the provisions of Part V" meaningless in respect of export credit guarantees and it therefore cannot be sustained.

Step 2 payments

Q38. Please comment on the statement in note 119 of the United States' first written submission that "...to the extent a consumer that had intended to export instead opens the bale, then that consumer could still obtain the Step 2 payment upon submission of the requisite documentation". The Panel notes that Step 2 payments all involve upland cotton produced in the United States. What are the two distinct factual situations that Step 2 payments involve? Other than the panel report in Canada-Dairy and the findings of the Appellate Body in US-FSC (21.5), do any other dispute settlement reports offer guidance on this issue? For example, how, if at all is the Appellate Body's report in Canada-Aircraft relevant here? 3rd parties, in particular, Australia, Argentina, NZ, Paraguay

Reply

The two distinct factual situations involved are 1) where cotton is exported, and 2) where cotton is used domestically. The notional consumer referred to by the United States cannot be both an exporter and domestic user of the same bale of cotton.

Even if the Panel were to find that there are not two distinct factual situations involved, ie that there was only one 'Step 2 payment' programme as alleged by the United States, the findings of the Appellate Body in Canada-Aircraft[11] referred to in the question above make it clear that the fact that some of the payments made under that programme are *not* contingent upon export performance, does not necessarily mean that the same is true for all of the payments under the programme. To paraphrase the Appellate Body, it is enough to show that one or some of the Step 2 payments do constitute subsidies "contingent ... in fact ... upon export performance." Those payments made upon production of proof of export clearly meet the export contingency requirement.

Q39. Please comment on the United States assertions at paragraph 129 of its first written submission, that "[t]he program is indifferent to whether recipients of the benefit of this programme are exporters or parties that open bales for the processing of manufacturing raw cotton into cotton products in the United States." . 3rd parties, in particular, Australia, Argentina, NZ, Paraguay

[11] Report of the Appellate Body, *Canada - Measures Affecting the Export of Civilian Aircraft*, WT/DS70/AB/R , para. 179.

Reply

The fact that an applicant is required to identify themselves as either an exporter or domestic user and an exporter is required to provide proof of export in order to receive the payment would seem to suggest that the programme is not, in fact, so 'indifferent'.

Q40. With respect to paragraph 32 of the oral statement of the EC, are subsidies contingent on the use of domestic goods consistent with the AoA? Does the phrase "provide support in favour of domestic producers" refer to, and/or permit such subsidies? What is the meaning and relevance of this (if any) to Brazil's claims under Article 3 of the SCM Agreement and Article III:4 of the GATT 1994.. 3rd parties, in particular, Australia, Argentina, EC, NZ, Paraguay

Reply

New Zealand does not agree that a right to provide subsidies contingent upon the use of domestic products contrary to Article 3 of the *SCM Agreement* can be found in the requirement that subsidies "directed at agricultural producers ... to the extent that they benefit producers of the basic agricultural product" be included in the calculation of AMS. There is no basis for reading such a right into the *Agreement on Agriculture*. To do so would allow the possibility for exemption from action under the *SCM Agreement* to exist other than by virtue of the peace clause. The peace clause explicitly does not provide such exemption from action under Article 3 of the *SCM Agreement* when it quite clearly could have done so. In New Zealand's view that indicates that there was no intention on the part of the drafters that domestic support measures, whether they conform with Article 6 of the *Agreement on Agriculture* or not, should be so exempt. The same is true in respect of *GATT 1994* Article III:4 claims.

ETI Act

Q41. Concerning its claims on the ETI Act, Brazil relies on the US – FSC case. However, it appears that the United States did not raise the issue of the Peace Clause in that case, nor did the US appear to invoke Article 6 of the Agreement on Agriculture. If the Panel's understanding is correct, how, if at all, are these differences relevant here? Argentina, China, EC, NZ

Reply

While it is open to the United States to claim exemption from action for such measures under the peace clause, the United States has no reduction commitments in respect of upland cotton and it cannot therefore provide export subsidies to upland cotton in a WTO-consistent manner.

Q42. How do you view the reference in paragraph 43 of the EC's third party oral statement with respect to the relevance of Article 17.14 of the DSU, and, in particular, the phrase "a final resolution to that dispute" (emphasis added)? Please explain the use, and relevance (if any) of the term "disputes"

in Articles 9.3 and 12 and Appendix 3 of the DSU, and please cite any other provisions you consider relevant. Argentina, China, EC, NZ

Reply

References to "disputes" in the Dispute Settlement Understanding must be interpreted in context. Article 17.14 requires that parties to a dispute unconditionally accept the report of the Appellate Body once adopted by the Dispute Settlement Body ("DSB"). That acceptance is in the context of that particular dispute between those particular parties. However that does not preclude a Panel from finding that a *prima facie* case of WTO-inconsistency has been made out where a Member makes a complaint in relation to a measure that has previously been ruled to be WTO-inconsistent where that ruling has been adopted by the DSB and where the measure remains unchanged.

ANNEX J-8

PARAGUAY'S REPLY AS THIRD PARTY TO THE FOLLOWING QUESTION

11 August 2003

ARTICLE 13 OF THE AGREEMENT ON AGRICULTURE

26. Under Article 13(b)(ii), a comparison is required between support at different times. One of the issues which is contested between the parties is whether the only later period that the Panel can consider is the present one (i.e. the period underway at the time of the request for establishment of the Panel). This argument is based on the present tense of the words "do not grant" in the English text.

The Panel asks whether there is any difference in the verb tense as used in the Spanish-language text, or any other difference which might aid the Panel in interpreting these words?

Reply

In its analysis of the question raised by the Panel as to the period to be considered and the verb tense used, Paraguay is expressing a view based on both versions:

> *"(ii) exempt from actions based on paragraph 1 of Article XVI of GATT 1994 or Articles 5 and 6 of the Subsidies Agreement, **provided** that such measures **do not grant support** to a specific commodity in excess of that decided during the 1992 marketing year; and ...."*

> *"ii) estarán exentas de medidas basadas en el párrafo 1 del artículo XVI del GATT de 1994 o en los artículos 5 y 6 del Acuerdo sobre Subvenciones, **a condición de que no otorguen** ayuda a un producto básico específico por encima de la decidida durante la campaña de comercialización de 1992; y ..."*

As regards the verb tense used, the English version clearly calls for a present tense interpretation, as the Panel rightly points out.

It clearly reads "**provided** that such measures do not grant support". If we take the word "provided" as indicating the occurrence of an event (**"in the event"**), we must bear in mind that this would introduce conditionality.

The Spanish text expresses the conditionality in even clearer terms through the words **"a condición de que no otorguen"**, a conditionality which introduces a notion of facts.

In Spanish, the verb is used in the present **subjunctive mode**, which according to the ***Larousse Dictionary***, *is the mode used to express possibility, as opposed to the indicative mode, which is the reality mode.*

Although we consider that both versions indicate the present, it appears to us that the Spanish version of the sentence stresses conditionality, which must be given considerable weight in order to arrive at a correct interpretation.

In the case at issue, *the condition under which the measures shall be exempt from actions based on paragraph 1 of Article XVI of GATT 1994 or Articles 5 and 6 of the Subsidies Agreement* is that support should not be granted to a specific commodity in excess of that decided during the 1992 marketing year.

The 1992 marketing year provides the standard needed to carry out a proper comparison between support at different times, so that in our view, we should be considering the entire spectrum and taking a comprehensive view of the background information.

Paraguay concludes that it is the Panel's task to consider the period it deems suitable for determining the effects of this type of measure on world trade.

ANNEX J-9

COMMENTS BY ARGENTINA ON THE REPLY BY THE EUROPEAN COMMUNITIES TO QUESTION 40 FROM THE PANEL

22 August 2003

Argentina would like to make the following comments on the reply by the European Communities to question 40 from the Panel.

Argentina does not share the EC's assertion that Members are entitled to provide domestic content subsidies under the Agreement on Agriculture (AoA) provided such subsidies are provided consistently with the Member's domestic support commitment levels.

It is our view that the rules of the AoA, on the one hand, and of the GATT 1994 and the Agreement on Subsidies and Countervailing Measures (ASCM), on the other, contain disciplines that apply independently unless there is a "conflict" between the provisions, in which case the rules of the AoA apply as a result of Article 21.1 of this Agreement.

Article 21.1 of the AoA states that *"The provisions of GATT 1994 and of other Multilateral Trade Agreements in Annex 1A to the WTO Agreement shall apply subject to* ("a reserva de" in the Spanish text) *the provisions of this Agreement."*

The words "subject to" or "a reserva de" indicate dependency or a condition[1]. Such dependency or condition does not, however, mean that all the disciplines in the GATT 1994 and the Agreements in Annex 1A automatically cease to apply in the case of the AoA. On the contrary, these disciplines "shall apply" unless there is a discrepancy or conflict between a rule in the AoA and the rules in the GATT 1994 or the Agreements in Annex 1A. This conclusion also receives contextual support in the General interpretative note to Annex 1A.

The conditions for the existence for a conflict between two rules was clarified by the Appellate Body in the *Guatemala – Cement case*[2], where it is determined that there is a conflict between two provisions if adherence to one provision leads to a violation of the other. In the case before us, in order to determine whether a rule in the GATT 1994 or in an Agreement in Annex 1A (Article 3.1(b) of the ASCM in this particular case) does not apply, it must first be determined whether there is an inconsistency or discrepancy with a provision of the AoA. In other words, these rules must be applied *together*.

In this connection, Argentina considers that compliance with the obligations laid down in Articles 6.1 and 3.2 of the AoA, and with paragraph 7 of An-

1 The New Oxford Dictionary of English: "subject to: ... 2 dependent or conditionally upon".

2 WT/DS60/AB/R, para. 65.

nex 3, does not allow any inconsistency with Article 3.1(b) of the ASCM to be detected.

Regarding Articles 6.1 and 3.2 of the AoA, nothing in these provisions indicates that it is not possible to apply them together with the prohibition on granting subsidies contingent on the use of domestic rather than imported products. The fact that the term "domestic support" is not defined in the AoA or that the AMS is broadly defined, as indicated by the EC[3], does not imply that the prohibition laid down in Article 3.1(b) of the ASCM is not valid in relation to the AoA. In this connection, the AoA does not contain any reference to possible exclusion.

Regarding paragraph 7 of Annex 3, the statement that "Measures directed at agricultural processors shall be excluded to the extent that such measures benefit the producers of the basic agricultural products" does not mean that such benefits cover measures made subject to the use of national rather than imported products. Producers of the basic agricultural products are allowed the benefits without making the measure contingent on the use of domestic products.

Lastly, with regard to the EC's reference to the preamble to the AoA ("*Having decided* to establish a basis for initiating a process of reform of trade in agriculture ..."), it should be noted that this process could very well envisage stricter obligations concerning certain types of measure that particularly distort international agricultural trade. On the contrary, it appears contradictory to assume that an agricultural trade reform process envisages the weakening of disciplines that could be applied in another way.

For the foregoing reasons, Argentina considers that subsidies that are granted to agricultural producers contingent on the use of domestic rather than imported products, either as a sole requirement or as one of several requirements, are inconsistent with Article 3.1(b) of the ASCM and Article III.4 of the GATT 1994.

3 Replies by the EC to question 40, para. 77.

ANNEX J-10

COMMENTS BY AUSTRALIA ON THE RESPONSES OF THE EUROPEAN COMMUNITIES TO QUESTIONS FROM THE PANEL AFTER THE FIRST SESSION OF THE FIRST SUBSTANTIVE PANEL MEETING

22 August 2003

These comments by Australia are offered in response to some of the answers submitted by the EC to the questions from the Panel after the first session of the first substantive Panel meeting. It is not Australia's intention to comment on all of the answers submitted by the EC, as most issues have already been addressed in Australia's written Third Party Submission, Australia's Oral Statement and Australia's responses to questions from the Panel after the first session of the first substantive Panel meeting.

Panel question no. 6 and Australian question no. 2

The EC refers to the findings of the Appellate Body in the *Turkey – Textiles* dispute concerning the interpretation of the word "accordingly" at the beginning of Article XXIV:5 of GATT 1994 to support its view that the first sentence of paragraph 1 of Annex 2 to the *Agreement on Agriculture* does not establish a freestanding obligation. However, as EC recognises, the Appellate Body expressly found in that dispute that the text of GATT Article XXIV:4 does not contain any operative language, that is, that GATT Article XXIV:4 "does not set forth a separate obligation itself". Nor do any of the other provisions cited by the EC in its footnote 9 contain operative language in the sense of setting forth a separate obligation.

The words "shall meet the fundamental requirement" establish a clear and unambiguous obligation that Annex 2 measures must conform to or satisfy the primary or essential condition that such measures have no, or at most minimal, trade-distorting effects or effects on production. "Shall", when used in the present tense as an auxiliary verb followed by an infinitive as in the first sentence of paragraph 1 of Annex 2, is defined as: "must according to a command or instruction".[1] "Meet" has a number of meanings, including "come into conformity with (a person, a person's wishes or opinion)" and "satisfy (a demand or need); satisfy the requirements of (a particular case); be able or sufficient to discharge (a financial obligation)". The words "shall meet" in context mean that Annex 2 measures must conform to or satisfy an express stipulation. Australia has previously explained that a "fundamental requirement" is a primary or essential condition.[2] When used as a definite article as in the clause "shall meet the fundamental re-

[1] *The New Shorter Oxford English Dictionary*, Volume 2, page 2808.

[2] Australian response to Question no. 7 from the Panel.

quirement", the word "the" establishes the "fundamental requirement" as the express stipulation that Annex 2 measures must conform to or satisfy.[3]

In Australia's view, the normal rules of treaty interpretation do not permit the word "accordingly" to be interpreted so as to obviate a clear and unambiguous obligation. Australia agrees that the Appellate Body found in the *Turkey – Textiles* dispute, in the particular circumstances of GATT Article XXIV, that the word "accordingly" linked the purposive language of Article XXIV:4 to operative language in the specific obligations found elsewhere in Article XXIV. However, the first sentence of paragraph 1 of Annex 2 to the *Agreement on Agriculture* cannot be characterised as purposive. The Appellate Body's finding in the *Turkey – Textiles* dispute is not, and cannot be, a valid interpretative basis to say that because the word "accordingly" has a particular meaning in the context of GATT Article XXIV, that same meaning must apply wherever else the word "accordingly" appears.[4]

Panel question no. 9

It remains unclear to Australia what is meant by "effects-based claims" in the context of the Panel's question.

However, Australia notes that under the EC's interpretation there would be no limits to the amounts that a WTO Member could provide as Annex 2 support, even if such support had profound trade-distorting effects or effects on production. For example, the EC's interpretation would allow a Member to pay "decoupled income support" of such a magnitude that the support would provide the means for that Member's domestic producers to switch from dryland to irrigation production with resulting substantial increases in production and trade-distorting effects. Thus, even if the first sentence of paragraph 1 of Annex 2 of the *Agreement on Agriculture* were considered to express an objective, such an outcome would nevertheless be directly contrary to that objective. At the very least, the magnitude of Annex 2 payments must be able to be a factor in assessing whether Annex 2 domestic support measures "meet the fundamental requirement that they have no, or at most minimal, trade-distorting effects or effects on production".

Further, the EC's argument that identifying the effects of such measures is often only feasible on an *ex post facto* basis is not convincing. First, even the EC argument concedes that in many, if not most, cases, it is feasible to identify the effects of such measures in advance. Secondly, even if the precise effects of such measures cannot be identified in advance, policy makers could draw on past experience and econometric analyses to determine whether certain types of payments would likely be distorting.

---

[3] Australia addressed the meaning of "the" in more detail in its response to question 3 from the Panel.

[4] Australia considers that the Appellate Body's discussion of the meaning of "like products" in *European Communities – Measures Affecting Asbestos and Asbestos-Containing Products* , WTO DS135/AB/R, paras. 87-100, confirms this view.

Finally, Australia considers that the "problems" pointed to by the EC that would be engendered by interpreting the first sentence of paragraph 1 as a frees-tanding obligation are no different to other situations, including under the *Agreement on Agriculture*. If another Member were to argue successfully in a dispute that a measure at issue was indeed an export subsidy, the responding Member could well be required to show "after the fact" that it is in compliance with its export subsidy reduction commitments under the *Agreement on Agriculture*.[5]

[5] See, for example, *United States – Tax Treatment of "Foreign Sales Corporations"*, WT/DS108.

ANNEX J-11

COMMENTS BY THE EUROPEAN COMMUNITIES ON RESPONSES TO THE QUESTIONS OF THE PANEL SUBMITTED BY OTHER THIRD PARTIES

22 August 2003

TABLE OF CONTENTS

I. INTRODUCTION

1. The European Communities has sought to comment on some of the responses to the Panel's questions submitted by other third parties. It has not been possible to do this in an exhaustive manner. Rather, the European Communities has made comments on certain responses which in its view merited further discussion. Evidently, where the European Communities has not commented on a particular argument, this does not imply that we support it.

2. For the Panel's ease of reference, we have retained in this document the Panel's original questions and the responses of the European Communities. Where the European Communities has decided to comment on a particular argument of another third party, we have inserted *verbatim* the text of the other party's arguments. We have deleted all questions which we have decided not to make comments on.

II. ARTICLE 13 OF THE AGREEMENT ON AGRICULTURE

Question

1. Australia has argued that Article 13 of the *Agreement on Agriculture* is an affirmative defence. How do you reconcile this with your view that the conditions in Article 13 are a "prerequisite" to the availability of a right or privilege? *Australia* Would other third parties have any comments on Australia's assertion? *3rd parties, in particular Argentina, Benin, China, Chinese Taipei*

Answer

3. Australia's views cannot be reconciled. Australia is correct in noting that the conditions in Article 13 can be considered a prerequisite for taking action under the *SCM Agreement*.[1] In using the term "prerequisite", Australia essentially recognises that, in respect of measures covered by Article 13, a complainant can only invoke the relevant provisions of the *SCM Agreement* if it proves that the threshold requirements or prerequisites referred to in Article 13 have been satisfied. As the European Communities has pointed out, such a situation is very different from the situation where, in the event of a violation of a WTO Agreement, a WTO Member pleads a defence which potentially exculpates it from this violation (e.g. Article XX GATT) in respect of which it bears the burden of proof.

4. Comparing Article 13 with Article 3.3 of the *SPS Agreement* shows that Australia's views are irreconcilable. This provision permits WTO Members not to base SPS measures on international standards but to impose higher standards where there is a scientific justification or an appropriate risk assessment has been carried out. This provision has some similarities with Article 13 of the *Agreement on Agriculture* since it sets a threshold which must be met before a Member can act. However, Article 3.3 may be seen as going further than Article 13 since it provides a derogation from the central discipline of the *SPS Agreement* ; the obligation to base SPS measures on international standards. On the other hand, Article 13 is simply one element regulating the interface between the *Agreement on Agriculture* and the other Annex I Agreements and cannot be seen as a derogation therefrom. Despite the extent to which Article 3.3 could be thought of as a derogation from the *SPS Agreement*, the Appellate Body ruled in *EC Hormones* that it could not be considered an affirmative defence, and that the burden of proof did not, therefore lie with the defendant.[2] In particular, the Appellate Body noted that the situation in Article 3.3 of the SPS Agreement is "qualitatively different" from the relationship between for instance, Article 1 and XX GATT.[3]

5. Consequently, Australia is correct to consider that Article 13 is a prerequisite or a threshold condition before the other Annex I Agreements may become applicable but is incorrect to consider that Article 13 can be considered an affirmative defence.

Response of Australia

Australia does not see any inconsistency in its views. In Australia's view, the potential availability of an affirmative defence in the general sense is in the nature of a right or privilege. Australia wishes to clarify, however,

---

[1] Australia's Oral Statement, para. 18.

[2] Appellate Body Report, *EC Measures Concerning Meat and Meat Products (Hormones) ("European Communities – Hormones")*, WT/DS26/AB/R, WT/DS48/AB/R, adopted 13 February 1998, para. 109.

[3] Appellate Body Report, *EC Measures Concerning Meat and Meat Products (Hormones) ("European Communities – Hormones")*, WT/DS26/AB/R, WT/DS48/AB/R, adopted 13 February 1998, para. 105.

that it considers Article 13 in the specific sense to be a right available when the conditions prescribed therein are met, rather than a privilege.

EC Comment

6. The European Communities fails to see how Australia can reasonably assert that there is no "inconsistency in its views". If Article 13 *Agreement on Agriculture* is a "prerequisite" for a complainant to bring an action under the *SCM Agreement* it cannot be at the same time a defence. A defence applies when a breach of a WTO Agreement arises, and the defending Member relies on another provision of a WTO Agreement in order to exculpate itself. Article XX GATT is the best example. In such a case, the burden of proof shifts to the Member invoking a defence. A prerequisite is entirely different. It implies that before a Member can undertake a particular action, it must take another action. In this context, a complaining Member must prove that Article 13 *Agreement on Agriculture* does not apply, before proving that the relevant provisions of the *SCM Agreement* apply.

7. Australia's bald assertion, glossing over its previous use of the word "prerequisite", does not adequately explain how its views can be reconciled.

III. ARTICLE 13(B) OF THE *AGREEMENT ON AGRICULTURE*: DOMESTIC SUPPORT MEASURES

Questions 2 - 5

8. The European Communities would only note that the changes presented by Australia to questions 2 and 3 on 15 August 2003 as "corrigenda" altered substantively the meaning of Australia's original response. The change from "program" to "payment" is a substantial change, and not a mere typographical error.

Question

6. Please explain the meaning of the word "criteria" in Article 6.1 and 7.1. What effect, if any, does the use of the word "Accordingly" in paragraph 1 of Annex 2 of the *Agreement on Agriculture* have on the meaning of the preceding sentence? *3rd parties, in particular Australia, Argentina, Canada, EC, NZ*

Answer

9. Both Article 6.1 and 7.1 refer to the "criteria set out in [..] Annex 2". When one considers Annex 2, there are two sets of "criteria". The first is the "basic criteria" set out in subparagraphs (a) and (b) of paragraph 1, and the second is the "policy-specific criteria" set out in paragraphs 2 to 13. This understanding is confirmed by the text of paragraph 5 of Annex 2, which refers to the "basic criteria" and the "specific criteria". Thus, Articles 6.1 and 7.1 of the *Agreement on Agriculture* refer to the basic and policy specific criteria set out in Annex 2.

10. The European Communities has already set out its understanding of the term "accordingly" in its Third Party Written Submission.[4] In the European Communities view, the term "accordingly" is intended to link the purposive language of the first sentence, with the "basic criteria" set out in the second sentence. In its Third Party Submission the EC offered a dictionary definition, "in accordance with the logical premises" which showed that the word "accordingly" operates as a linkage between the premise or understanding set out in the first sentence and the operative language in the second sentence. Australia offers the Panel another definition: "harmoniously" or "agreeably", but fails to note that that the Oxford English Dictionary considers this usage of the word "accordingly" obsolete.[5]

11. The European Communities would point out that both the French and Spanish text support the view that the use of the word "accordingly" links the general statement in the first sentence with the specific obligations of the second sentence. The French text uses the term "en conséquence" and the Spanish the term "por consiguiente". Both of these terms show that the criteria in the second sentence are intended to express the principle set out in the first sentence. Moreover, had the negotiators intended that the first sentence be a self-standing obligation, rather than use the term "accordingly" they would have used the term "additionally" or "in addition", or a synonymous term.

12. Further support for this view can be found in the frequent use of the term "accordingly" in the WTO Agreement. A survey of the term's use suggests that it links a general statement, often recognising that a particular situation causes specific effects, with a right or obligation to take some type of action set out in an ancillary sentence.[6] These general statements are not such as to impose specific obligations. The Appellate Body had occasion to consider the relationship between such provisions in the *Turkey-Textiles* dispute (Articles XXIV.4 and XXIV.5 GATT). It concluded:

> The chapeau of paragraph 5 of Article XXIV begins with the word "accordingly", which can only be read to refer to paragraph 4 of Article XXIV, which immediately precedes the chapeau.
>
> [..]
>
> 57. According to paragraph 4, the purpose of a customs union is "to facilitate trade" between the constituent members and "not to

---

4 First Third Party Submission of the European Communities, 15 July 2003, para. 20. The European Communities recall, in this context, the opinion of Professor Desta set out in footnote 19 to para. 20.

5 Australia's Oral Statement, para 35. Oxford English Dictionary, p. 15. Australia refers to the first sense of the word "accordingly" which is preceded by the symbol " " which indicates that a particular usage is obsolete (see Abbreviations and Symbols, page xxvi).

6 See Articles II.6(a), III.9, XII.3(d), XVI.3, XVIIII.5, XXIV.5 GATT 1994, together with Ad Article III and Ad Article XXVIII.4 to GATT 1994, Articles 2.1 and 11 of the Dispute Settlement Understanding, Article A(i) of the Trade Policy Review Mechanism, Article 12.8 of the Agreement on Technical Barriers to Trade, Article 1 of the GATS Annex on Telecommunications and Article 5.1 of the Agreement on Textiles and Clothes.

> raise barriers to the trade" with third countries. This objective demands that a balance be struck by the constituent members of a customs union. A customs union should facilitate trade within the customs union, but it should *not* do so in a way that raises barriers to trade with third countries. [..] *Paragraph 4 contains purposive, and not operative, language. It does not set forth a separate obligation itself but, rather, sets forth the overriding and pervasive purpose for Article XXIV which is manifested in operative language in the specific obligations that are found elsewhere in Article XXIV.* Thus, the purpose set forth in paragraph 4 informs the other relevant paragraphs of Article XXIV, including the chapeau of paragraph 5. For this reason, the chapeau of paragraph 5, and the conditions set forth therein for establishing the availability of a defence under Article XXIV, must be interpreted in the light of the purpose of customs unions set forth in paragraph 4. The chapeau cannot be interpreted correctly without constant reference to this purpose.[7] (emphasis added)

13. The Appellate Body has, consequently, recognised the linking function of the word "accordingly", and the fact that provisions which may be linked to later provisions through the use of the word "accordingly" may not impose separate obligations.

14. The European Communities would also point out that the Appellate Body has found that other provisions (e.g. Article III.1 GATT) which contain general principles are set up as "a guide to understanding and interpreting the specific obligations contained" in other provisions (e.g. Article III.2 and the other paragraphs of Article III).[8] Such provisions do not, however, impose additional obligations supplemental to the specific obligations, unless expressly stated.[9]

15. The Panel may find it useful to refer to the European Communities' response to a question posed by Australia (see question no. 44 in this document). In its response, the European Communities deals with Australia's unfounded assertion that the European Communities' reading of the first sentence of paragraph 1 would render that provision ineffective.

---

[7] Appellate Body Report, *Turkey – Restrictions on Imports of Textile and Clothing Products ("Turkey – Textiles")*, WT/DS34/AB/R, adopted 19 November 1999, paras. 56 and 57 (emphasis added). Note that the Panel also found that Article XXIV.4 was "not expressed as an obligation" (Panel Report, *Turkey – Restrictions on Imports of Textile and Clothing Products ("Turkey – Textiles")*, WT/DS34/R, adopted 19 November 1999, as modified by the Appellate Body Report, WT/DS34/AB/R, para. 9.126).

[8] Appellate Body Report, *Japan – Taxes on Alcoholic Beverages ("Japan – Alcoholic Beverages")*, WT/DS8/AB/R, WT/DS10/AB/R, WT/DS11/AB/R, adopted 1 November 1996, p. 17.

[9] See Appellate Body Report, *European Communities - Regime for the Importation, Sale and Distribution of Bananas ("European Communities – Bananas")*, WT/DS27/AB/R, adopted 25 September 1997, paras. 214-216 holding that the absence of a specific reference to Article III.1 GATT in Article III.4 GATT meant that an examination of the consistency of a measure with Article III.4 GATT did not require, in addition, an examination of the consistency of the measure with Article III.1 GATT.

Response of Australia

The ordinary meaning of "criteria", as the plural of "criterion", is "principle[s], standard[s], or test[s] by which a thing is judged, assessed, or identified"[10]. Thus, the "criteria" in Articles 6.1 and 7.1 as these relate to Annex 2 of the *Agreement on Agriculture* encompasses *all* of the relevant principles, standards or tests established in Annex 2 against which domestic support measures for which exemption from reduction commitments is claimed are to be judged, assessed and/or identified.

As Australia said in its Oral Statement[11], the word "accordingly" has several, equally valid meanings that are potentially applicable in the context: "harmoniously", "agreeably", "in accordance with the logical premises" and "correspondingly".[12] A further definition is "in conformity with a given set of circumstances".[13]

In Australia's view, having regard to its ordinary meanings in its context and in light of the object and purpose of the *Agreement on Agriculture*, including to "[correct] and [prevent] ... distortions in world agricultural markets",[14] the word "accordingly" can and should properly be interpreted in the sense of "consistent with" or "in conformity with" the fundamental requirement established in the first sentence. Consistent with that interpretation, the obligation that "green box" measures "meet the fundamental requirement ..." is cumulative with the additional basic criteria established in paragraph 1 and the policy specific criteria established in paragraphs 2-13 of Annex 2. To interpret the word "accordingly" otherwise would be to negate the plain and unambiguous obligation established in the first sentence of paragraph 1 of Annex 2 that "[d]omestic support measures for which exemption from the reduction commitments is claimed shall meet the fundamental requirement that they have no, or at most minimal, trade-distorting effects or effects on production".

Response of New Zealand

"Criteria" are the standards by which a thing is assessed. In this case they are the standards by which domestic support measures must be assessed in order to qualify for exemption from reduction commitments. These criteria are set out in Article 6 and Annex 2 of the *Agreement on Agriculture*, and include: the "fundamental requirement" in Annex 2 paragraph 1 that measures have at most minimal trade-distorting effects; the "basic criteria" in paragraph 1(a) and (b); and the "policy-specific criteria and conditions" set out elsewhere in Annex 2. The use of the word "accordingly" signifies that the intention of the drafters was to indicate that

---

10 *The New Shorter Oxford English Dictionary*, Volume 1, page 551.
11 Oral Statement by Australia, paras. 35-36.
12 *The New Shorter Oxford English Dictionary*, Volume 1, page 15.
13 *Webster's Third New International Dictionary*, Ed. Philip Babcock Gove, Merriam-Webster Inc, Springfield, Massachusetts, 1993, page 12.
14 Third preambular paragraph of the *Agreement on Agriculture*.

> in order to meet the first criterion – the "fundamental requirement" that they be at most minimally trade-distorting – measures would at the very least have to meet the subsequent basic and policy-specific criteria.

EC Comment

16. Neither Australia nor New Zealand examine the use of the word "criteria" in Annex 2 where it means something different from the fundamental requirement. The second sentence of the first paragraph of Annex 2 clearly distinguishes the "fundamental requirement" from the general and policy-specific "criteria". Paragraph 5 of Annex 2 is even more explicit in this regard. It would seem odd that Article 6.1 and 7.1 would use criteria to mean both the basic and policy specific criteria and the requirement, while Annex 2 itself operates a distinction between the criteria and the requirement. Thus, while it is the case that the dictionary definition of "criteria" could arguably, in the abstract, cover a "fundamental requirement" in this particular case there are compelling arguments that the use of the word "criteria" in Articles 6.1 and 7.1 does not.

17. The European Communities has already explained why Australia's interpretation of "accordingly" is incorrect. It is quite clear that "accordingly" establishes a relationship between the purposive language of the first sentence of para. 1 of Annex 2 and the operational language of the other parts of Annex 2. Synonyms of "accordingly" include "as a result, consequently, ergo, thus, therefore".[15] To read the term as meaning that the first sentence and the rest of the paragraph applied as cumulative and separate conditions (as suggested by Australia) would deprive the word "accordingly" of effect. Reading the first sentence of paragraph 1 as relevant to the interpretation of the rest of Annex 2, but not as a separate condition would, contrary to Australia's assertion, give the first sentence meaning.

18. New Zealand points out that:

> "the use of the word "accordingly" signifies that the intention of the drafters was to indicate that in order to meet the first criterion – the "fundamental requirement" [...]measures would at the very least have to meet the subsequent basic and policy-specific criteria"

19. New Zealand does not explain how the first sentence can set a self-standing criterion if respecting that so-called criterion depends on satisfying other criteria. What then is the content of the separate "criterion" in the first sentence, if it is already defined in the second sentence of the first paragraph and the rest of Annex 2 ? Moreover, how, given the alleged existence of two sets of self-standing criteria, can it be sufficient to satisfy only one set of criteria and at the same time satisfy the other set (or "at the very least" satisfy the other set) as the final sentence of New Zealand's response implies. Even on its own terms, New Zealand's position that the first sentence of paragraph 1 is a self standing obligation, but that it can be satisfied by meeting the criteria set out in the rest of An-

[15] Chamber's Thesaurus, 1986.

nex 2, is internally inconsistent. This illustrates very well the European Communities' point that the proposition that the first sentence imposes a self-standing obligation cannot be squared with any reasonable interpretation of "accordingly".

Question

7. Please explain the meaning of the words "the fundamental requirement" as used in paragraph 1 of Annex 2 of the *Agreement on Agriculture.* *3rd parties, in particular Australia, Argentina, Canada, EC, NZ*

Answer

20. The phrase "the fundamental requirement" signals the negotiators intent to treat differently measures which are less or not at all distortive to trade or production and sets forth the general purpose of Annex 2; a purpose which permeates the rest of Annex 2. Considering the term in the abstract does not answer the question whether a panel must examine the effects of measures for which green box status is claimed in addition to examining whether such measures respect the basic and policy-specific criteria set out in Annex 2, or whether respecting the basic and policy-specific criteria is such that a measure is deemed not to have the effects mentioned in the first sentence. As the European Communities has explained, there are compelling textual and purpose based arguments which support the latter interpretation.

Response of Australia

> The word "fundamental" has a number of meanings[16] which can be summarised as "primary" or "essential". The word "requirement" too has a number of meanings[17] which can be summarised as a "condition". Thus, a "fundamental requirement" is a primary or essential condition. [18] It is an overarching, freestanding obligation that applies to all "green box" measures cumulatively with the additional basic criteria established in paragraph 1 and the policy specific criteria established in paragraphs 2-13 of Annex 2. To interpret a "fundamental requirement" otherwise than as a primary or essential condition would not give the words their ordinary meaning in their context and in light of the object and purpose of the *Agreement on Agriculture*.

---

[16] *The New Shorter Oxford English Dictionary*, Volume 1, page 1042, provides relevant definitions of "fundamental" as "**1** Of or pertaining to the basis or groundwork; going to the root of the matter. **2** Serving as the base or foundation; essential or indispensable. Also, primary, original; from which others are derived."

[17] *The New Shorter Oxford English Dictionary*, Volume 1, page 2557, provides definitions of "requirement" as "**1** The action of requiring something; a request. **2** A thing required or needed, a want, a need. Also the action or an instance of needing or wanting something. **3** Something called for or demanded; a condition which must be complied with."

[18] Third Party Submission of Australia, para. 31, and Oral Statement by Australia, para. 33.

EC Response

21. Australia executes a logical leap in the fourth sentence of its response. It arrives at the conclusion that the "fundamental requirement" is a "freestanding obligation" that applies "cumulatively" with the other criteria. However, this assertion is without foundation, and is directly contradicted by the use of the word "accordingly" at the beginning of the next sentence.

Question

2. In paragraph 13 of Australia's oral statement, you state that a "question" is: "could conditions of price competition for the purposes of a non-violation or impairment claim be assessed solely on the basis of budgetary outlay figures, as argued by Brazil, or on the basis of a rate of payment, as argued by the United States? In Australia's view, both factors put forward by Brazil and the United States would properly form a part of that assessment, but not the whole." Could you please clarify this statement (indicating other elements which would complete the "whole" and explain its relevance for the purposes of our consideration of Article 13 of the *Agreement on Agriculture*? *Australia, EC*

Answer

22. The European Communities would prefer to let Australia clarify its statement. The European Communities will comment upon Australia's clarification in its comments on the responses of the other third parties.

Australia's Response

Given the length of Australia's response, the European Communities has not reproduced it here.

EC Comment

23. The European Communities is unconvinced of Australia's argument. There is nothing in the text of Article 13 to suggest that in order to determine "support" under Article 13 it is necessary to consider all the factors which are relevant to examining a non-violation case. Moreover, the European Communities notes that Article 13(b)(ii) provides that Articles 5 and 6 of the *SCM Agreement* may be applicable under certain conditions. However, an assessment of whether a measure is inconsistent with Articles 5 and 6 of the *SCM Agreement* is not based on the same criteria as would be applicable in assessing a non-violation complaint. Indeed, such criteria may have nothing to do with the domestic market of the Member which is providing a subsidy. Australia does not explain why the type of criteria relevant to non-violation complaints would also be relevant in assessing a complaint under Articles 5 and 6 of the *SCM Agreement*. Nor does it explain why it is necessary to import notions from the assessment of non-violation complaints, but not notions from Articles 5 and 6 *SCM Agreement* into an assessment of support for the purposes of Article 13 *Agreement on Agriculture*.

24. In short, the European Communities sees no foundation for Australia's assertions.

IV. STEP 2 PAYMENTS

Question

40 With respect to paragraph 32 of the oral statement of the EC, are subsidies contingent on the use of domestic goods consistent with the *AoA*? Does the phrase "provide support in favour of domestic producers" refer to, and/or permit such subsidies? What is the meaning and relevance of this (if any) to Brazil's claims under Article 3 of the *SCM Agreement* and Article III:4 of the GATT 1994.. *3rd parties, in particular, Australia, Argentina, EC, NZ, Paraguay*

Answer

25. The Panel's question involves two elements. First, is a Member entitled to provide domestic content subsidies under the *Agreement on Agriculture*? Second, if such subsidies are permitted, what is the relevance of such a rule to Brazil's claims under Article 3 of the *SCM Agreement* and Article III.4 GATT. The European Communities has already provided elements of a response in its oral statement.[19] These are expanded upon below.

26. First, a Member is entitled to provide domestic content subsidies under the *Agreement on Agriculture* provided such subsidies are provided consistently with the Member's domestic support commitment levels. This conclusion flows from a number of factors. First, the *Agreement on Agriculture* disciplines domestic support. Article 6.1 refers to "domestic support reduction commitments". Article 3.1 refers to "domestic support [..] commitments [...] constitut[ing] commitments limiting subsidization" and Article 3.2 obliges Members "not [to] provide support in favour of domestic producers in excess of the [domestic] support commitment levels". Despite these clear rules on domestic support, the *Agreement on Agriculture* does not define "domestic support".

27. AMS is the measurement of domestic support. AMS is defined as "the annual level of support, expressed in monetary terms, provided for an agricultural product in favour of the producers of the basic agricultural product or non-product-specific support provided in favour of agricultural producers in general, other than [that exempted etc]." This is very general – it covers all support in favour of agricultural producers. This broad scope of domestic support measures which can be maintained consistently with the *Agreement on Agriculture* is confirmed by Article 6.1 which states that the domestic support reduction commitments "shall apply to all of its [i.e. the Member's] domestic support measures in favour of agricultural producers [...]". Paragraph 1 of Annex 3 on the calcula-

19 Paras. 34 to 38 of the EC's Oral Statement (as delivered). The Panel's reference to para. 32 corresponds to the text provided at the third party session.

tion of the AMS refers to AMS being calculated "on a product specific-basis for each basic agricultural product receiving market prices support, non-exempt direct payments, *or any other subsidy* not exempted from the reduction commitment". (emphasis added)

28. Consequently, the range of domestic support measures which a Member may maintain (consistent with reduction commitments) is very broad and is only limited by the condition that such support must be in favour of agricultural producers. As the European Communities has noted, paragraph 7 of Annex 3 explicitly states that "measures directed at agricultural processors shall be included to the extent that such measures benefit the producers of the basic agricultural products".[20] The European Communities considers that the term "benefit" used here must be regarded as being synonymous with "favour" in the sense of "in favour of agricultural producers". Moreover, it is clear that by "measures directed at agricultural processors" the negotiators intended subsidies which were paid to processors, where the benefit went to the agricultural producer. Consequently, in light of the broad definition of "domestic support" and the specific reference to domestic content subsidies in paragraph 7 of Annex 3, the European Communities considers that a Member is entitled to maintain domestic content subsidies consistently with the *Agreement on Agriculture*.

29. Second, in response to the Panel's question, the effect of finding that domestic content subsidies are provided consistently with the *Agreement on Agriculture* would be that they cannot be found inconsistent with either Article 3.1(b) of the *SCM Agreement* or Article III.4 GATT 1994. Article 21.1 of the *Agreement on Agriculture* states that "the provisions of GATT 1994 and of other Multilateral Trade Agreements in Annex 1A to the WTO Agreement shall apply subject to the provisions of this Agreement." As the European Communities pointed out in its oral statement, this means that provisions of the other Annex 1A Agreements are "subordinated" to the *Agreement on Agriculture*.[21]

30. To find that such subsidies were inconsistent with either Article 3.1(b) of the *SCM Agreement* or Article III.4 GATT would be to subordinate the right to provide such domestic content subsidies under the *Agreement on Agriculture* to the *SCM Agreement* or GATT 1994. Such an interpretation directly contradicts Article 21.1 of the *Agreement on Agriculture*.

31. Indeed, it can be pointed out that applying Article 3.1(b) of the *SCM Agreement* and Article III.4 GATT to domestic content subsidies provided consistently with the *Agreement on Agriculture* would lead to stricter disciplines being applied to domestic subsidies for agriculture than are applicable to domes-

---

[20] In terms of negotiating background, it may be useful to the Panel to note that paragraph 7 of Annex 3 was subject to negotiation during the period in which a Panel had ruled that the EC's payments to oilseed processors was not covered by Article III.8(b) GATT 1947 and were consequently inconsistent with Article III.4 GATT 1947 (*European Economic Community – Payments and Subsidies Paid to Processors and Producers of Oilseeds and Related Animal-Feed Proteins* Report of the Panel (L/6627 BISD 37S/86) adopted on 25 January 1990. That the negotiators retained this text must therefore be considered as a clear sign that they intended to permit Members to maintain such subsidies, subject to reduction commitments, in the *Agreement on Agriculture*.

[21] Oral Statement, para. 38.

tic subsidies for industrial goods. If Article 3.1(b) and Article III.4 were to apply, domestic subsidies for agricultural products would be subject to reduction commitments and Article 3.1(b) *SCM Agreement* and Article III.4 GATT. However, domestic subsidies for industrial products are not subject to reduction commitments. Since the *Agreement on Agriculture* establishes "a basis for initiating a process of reform of trade in agriculture", it would seem contradictory to find that domestic support for agriculture is in fact subject to stricter obligations than domestic support for other industries. This explains the "subject to" language of Article 21.1 of the *Agreement on Agriculture*. Article 21.1 and the *Agreement on Agriculture* more generally can also be compared with the other sectoral agreement included in Annex 1A of the WTO Agreement. The *Agreement on Textiles and Clothing* explicitly provides, in its Article 9, that the textiles and clothing sector is to be fully integrated into the GATT 1994. The *Agreement on Agriculture* has no such language, and Article 21.1 runs directly counter to this notion. It cannot be lightly assumed that the negotiators, while providing for the possibility to maintain domestic content subsidies, intended that such subsidies also be subject to rules which effectively makes it impossible to maintain such subsidies.[22]

32. The Panel should therefore reject Brazil's arguments that domestic content subsidies granted in favour of agricultural producers can be found to be inconsistent with Article 3.1(b) of the *SCM Agreement* and Article III.4 GATT 1994.

Australia's response

Australia does not consider that the phrase "provide support in favour of domestic producers" in Article 3.2 of the *Agreement on Agriculture* permits subsidies contingent upon the use of domestic goods.

In Australia's view, the legal issue in question relates to the *condition* attached to the grant of a subsidy, not the grant of a subsidy *per se* or who might benefit from the subsidy. The fact that a measure may benefit an agricultural producer ("support in favour of domestic producers") does not serve to override measures otherwise prohibited.

Article 21.1 of the *Agreement on Agriculture* provides that "[t]he provisions of GATT 1994 and of other Multilateral Trade Agreements in Annex 1A to the WTO Agreement shall apply subject to the provisions of this Agreement". Article 3.1 of the *SCM Agreement* applies "[e]xcept as provided in the Agreement on Agriculture". The General Interpretive Note to Annex 1A of the *Marrakesh Agreement Establishing the World Trade Organization* also provides contextual guidance. Pursuant to that Note, the *Agreement on Agriculture* would prevail to the extent of any conflict with GATT 1994.

[22] See, in a similar sense, Appellate Body Report, *EC Measures Concerning Meat and Meat Products (Hormones) ("European Communities – Hormones")*, WT/DS26/AB/R, WT/DS48/AB/R, adopted 13 February 1998, para. 165.

However, in the case of subsidies contingent upon the use of domestic goods, there is no conflict between either the *Agreement on Agriculture*, which *inter alia* disciplines the amounts of domestic support in favour of domestic producers which distorts trade and production, and the *SCM Agreement* or GATT 1994, which discipline or prohibit certain conditions attached to subsidies, including subsidies in favour of agricultural producers (subject only to the provisions of Article III:8(b) of GATT 1994). There is no provision in the *Agreement on Agriculture* which provides for an exception to, or cover for, local content conditions attached to the grant of a subsidy.

Australia has already noted[23] that Article 13(b)(ii) does not exempt non-"green box" domestic support measures from actions based on Article 3 of the *SCM Agreement*. Neither does Article 13 anywhere refer to GATT Article III:4. Nor with regard to these Articles is there any provision comparable to Articles 5 and 12 of the *Agreement on Agriculture*. As stated in the preambular clauses of the *Agreement on Agriculture*, the "long-term objective is to provide for substantial progressive reductions in agricultural support and protection": it is not intended to provide for a weakening of disciplines, particularly when such disciplines are not specifically mentioned.

Australia also notes that the domestic support provisions of the *Agreement on Agriculture* provide for a strengthening and elaboration of the provisions of Article XVI of GATT 1994. They are not directed towards a diminution of basic GATT obligations. National treatment is central to the multilateral trading system. It is inconceivable to Australia that the negotiators of the *Agreement on Agriculture* would, as part of a reform program designed to strengthen disciplines, agree to weaken national treatment disciplines.

However, in the event the Panel were to consider that the phrase "provide support in favour of domestic producers" refers to and/or permits subsidies contingent upon the use of domestic goods, Australia notes that such support could be permitted only to the extent that the support was actually passed through to the producers of the basic agricultural product.

New Zealand's Response

New Zealand does not agree that a right to provide subsidies contingent upon the use of domestic products contrary to Article 3 of the *SCM Agreement* can be found in the requirement that subsidies "directed at agricultural producers ... to the extent that they benefit producers of the basic agricultural product" be included in the calculation of AMS. There is no basis for reading such a right into the *Agreement on Agriculture*. To do so would allow the possibility for exemption from action under the *SCM Agreement* to exist other than by virtue of the peace clause. The

---

[23] Oral Statement by Australia, paras. 29-30.

peace clause explicitly does not provide such exemption from action under Article 3 of the *SCM Agreement* when it quite clearly could have done so. In New Zealand's view that indicates that there was no intention on the part of the drafters that domestic support measures, whether they conform with Article 6 of the *Agreement on Agriculture* or not, should be so exempt. The same is true in respect of *GATT 1994* Article III:4 claims.

EC Comments

33. Australia confuses legal issues. Article 3.1(b) of the *SCM Agreement* and Article III.4 GATT concern *inter alia* the conditions under which subsidies may be granted. The *Agreement on Agriculture* provides a right, up to a specified limit, to provide support to domestic producers, irrespective of the manner in which such support is provided. That is, a Member is entitled to provide support up to the limits and to do so in any form. Paragraph 3.7 of Annex 3 makes it clear that a Member is entitled to include in its support subsidies granted to processors which benefit agricultural producers. A Member thus has a right to provide support in the form of payments to its agricultural producers. This right conflicts with the prohibition in Article 3.1(b) of the *SCM Agreement* and Article III.4 GATT.

34. The European Communities fails to see the relevance of Article XVI GATT to this issue. Moreover, it is inaccurate of Australia to suggest that interpreting the *Agreement on Agriculture* in this manner would result in a weakening of obligations. Australia conveniently ignores that, in placing absolute limits on the amount of domestic support which a Member may provide, WTO Members agreed to impose stricter disciplines on domestic support for agriculture than that applicable to domestic subsidies for industrial products.

35. New Zealand's argument rests on the conception that it is only Article 13 (the peace clause) which regulates the interface between the *Agreement on Agriculture* and the other Annex 1A Agreements. As Australia points out, Article 21.1 *Agreement on Agriculture* is clearly relevant, as is the General Interpretative Note to Annex 1A. New Zealand's unsubstantiated argument does not stand.

ANNEX J-12

REPLIES FROM ARGENTINA TO PANEL'S QUESTIONS
27 October 2003

A. QUESTIONS TO INDIVIDUAL THIRD PARTIES

Q43. Please elaborate, citing figures, on your statement that polyester fibre prices actually follow cotton prices. Argentina

1. Argentina submits that the explosion in the production of synthetic fibres played no part in the fall in international cotton prices; in fact, the contrary appears to have occurred.[1]

2. The "Fibre Prices" table in paragraph 23 of the Further Submission of the United States shows that polyester prices have always been lower than cotton prices (see the columns "US mill" and "US spot" as compared to "Asia poly") and, moreover, they appear to follow cotton prices. Thus, for example, in 1995, when cotton prices reached their record level for the series, polyester prices happened to follow the same trend, precisely at a time when the price of oil was practically at its lowest for the period under consideration.

3. Another example is the period from 2000 to 2002: while the price of oil was at its highest, the price of polyester reached its low point for the period under consideration, having "accompanied" the very low cotton prices.

4. Attached hereto as Annex ARG-1 is a graph comparing the evolution of cotton prices (US mill and US spot) with that of polyester fibre prices (Asian poly)[2] and with the price of oil per barrel (West Texas)[3], clearly reflecting a very close correlation between cotton and polyester prices.

5. On the other hand, the last few years do not show any correlation between the price per barrel of oil and the price of polyester fibres, which shows that polyester has had to adapt to cotton prices in order to remain competitive, and not the reverse as the United States claims.

B. QUESTIONS TO ALL THIRD PARTIES

Q49. What is the meaning and effect of the introductory phrase of Article 3 of the SCM Agreement ("Except as provided in the *Agreement on Agriculture* ...")?

6. The introductory phrase of Article 3 of the SCM Agreement ("*Except as provided in the Agreement on Agriculture* ...") means that the provisions of that Article apply to agricultural subsidies *to the extent that they do not conflict with*

---

1 Second oral third party submission by Argentina, 8 October 2003, paras. 15-17.

2 Source: Further submission of the United States, "Fibre Prices" table, para. 23.

3 Source: Argentine Oil and Gas Institute (IAPG).

the Agreement on Agriculture (AoA). The phrase "*except as provided* ..." does not necessarily imply that there is a conflict between the two Agreements.

7. In this connection, Argentina replied to question 40 of the Panel to the third parties, stating that no provision could be found in the AoA that conflicted with Article 3.1(b) of the SCM Agreement. Indeed, the AoA does not contain any provision which explicitly permits the granting of "subsidies contingent, whether solely or as one of several other conditions, on the use of domestic over imported products."

8. It is therefore Argentina's understanding that since they are prohibited under Article 3.1(b) of the SCM Agreement, and since there is no specific provision in the AoA that is explicitly mentioned in the introductory phrase of Article 3 of the SCM Agreement, subsidies contingent on the use of domestic over imported goods are also prohibited under the AoA.

9. Likewise, Argentina pointed out in its comments on the reply by the European Communities to question 40 from the Panel that the rules of the AoA, on the one hand, and of the GATT 1994 and the SCM Agreement, on the other, contained disciplines that were applied together, unless there was a discrepancy or "conflict" between the different provisions.[4]

Q50. According to its revised timetable, the Panel will issue its report to the parties after the end of the 2003 calendar year. Does this have any impact on "exempt[ion] from actions" under Article 13(b)(ii) and 13(c)(ii) of the *Agreement on Agriculture*?

10. The impact will depend on the Panel's finding on the preliminary issue raised with respect to the Peace Clause. If the Panel finds, as Argentina maintains, that the United States does not qualify for protection under Article 13 of the AoA, the expiry date of the Peace Clause will be entirely irrelevant.

11. If after 31 December 2003 the Panel should decide not to rule on the substantive claims, this would affect Brazil's right to due process by depriving it, on the basis of rules which are no longer in force, of the right to a finding that would settle of the dispute as to whether or not the subsidies were consistent. Thus, Brazil would be deprived of a positive settlement of the dispute.

Q51. How should the concept of specificity - and, in particular, the concept of specificity to "an enterprise or industry or group of enterprises or industries" - in Article 2 of the *SCM Agreement* apply to subsidies in respect of agricultural commodities? Please answer the following questions citing the principles in Article 2 of the *SCM Agreement*:

---

4 As already stated, "[t]he conditions for the existence for a conflict between two rules was clarified by the Appellate Body in the *Guatemala – Cement case* (WT/DS60/AB/R, para. 65), where it is determined that there is a conflict between two provisions if adherence to one provision leads to a violation of the other. In the case before us, in order to determine whether a rule in the GATT 1994 or in an Agreement in Annex 1A (Article 3.1(b) of the ASCM in this particular case) does not apply, it must first be determined whether there is an inconsistency or discrepancy with a provision of the AoA. In other words, these rules must be applied *together*." (Comments by Argentina on the reply by the European Communities to question 40 from the Panel to the third parties).

(a) Is a subsidy in respect of all agricultural, but not other, products specific?

12. Yes.

(b) Is a subsidy in respect of all agricultural crops (i.e. but not to other agricultural commodities, such as livestock) specific?

13. Yes.

(c) Is a subsidy in respect of certain identified agricultural products specific?

14. Yes.

(d) Is a subsidy in respect of upland cotton, but not other products, specific?

15. Yes.

(e) Is a subsidy in respect of certain proportion of the value of total US commodities (or total US agricultural commodities) specific?

16. Yes.

(f) Is a subsidy in respect of certain proportion of total US farmland specific?

17. Yes.

18. Argentina stresses that the concept of "specificity" in Article 2 of the SCM Agreement is very broad, since it refers to the subsidies for an enterprise or an industry or group of enterprises or industries.

19. From the standpoint of the SCM Agreement, agricultural subsidies are specific within the meaning of Article 2, since they are not available for all products. The mere fact that they are "agricultural" precludes any interpretation that they are not specific.

20. As regards the principle of Article 2.1, agricultural subsidies comply with the requirements of each one of its indents:

- Indent (a), because not all of the enterprises of a Member have access to subsidies under the AoA;
- indent (b), because there is no automatic eligibility for the subsidies under the AoA, nor are they based on objective criteria such as those listed in footnote 2 to Article 2, since they benefit the producers of certain products – in the case in point, those included in Annex I of the AoA;
- indent (c), because a subsidy for an agricultural product complies with all of the requirements of the first sentence thereof. As regards the second sentence of indent (c), there is no evidence for including an agricultural subsidy under any of these factors.

As to the specific case of export subsidies, Article 2.3 reaffirms their specificity. Having already pointed out that specificity is established under Article 2.1 and 2.3, there is no need to address the principle in Article 2.2.

21. Generally speaking, it should be borne in mind that in addition to the principles laid down in indents (a) and (b) of Article 2.1 for determining whether a subsidy is specific, indent (c) stipulates that in case of doubt as to the specificity of a subsidy, a number of other factors should be considered. In Argentina's view, this implies that the intention of the drafters of the Agreement was that the concept of "specificity" should be as comprehensive as possible.

Q52. The Panel notes that different remedies are available in respect of prohibited and actionable subsidies under Article 4.7 and 7.8 of the *SCM Agreement.* If the Panel were to conclude that a subsidy was prohibited and were to make a recommendation under Article 4.7 of the *SCM Agreement* to withdraw the subsidy without delay, can the Panel:

(a) Also conclude that the same subsidy had resulted in adverse effects to the interests of another Member? If so, what would be the value of such a conclusion in terms of the settlement of the matter before the Panel?

22. In Argentina's view, if the Panel were to conclude that a subsidy was prohibited and to make a recommendation – under Article 4.7 of the SCM Agreement – to withdraw the subsidy without delay, it could nevertheless also conclude that the same subsidy had resulted in adverse effects to the interests of another Member and make the same recommendation to withdraw the subsidy under Article 7.8 of the SCM Agreement.

23. Indeed, bearing in mind that we are speaking of two different claims, the value of such a conclusion would be to have made *"an objective assessment of the matter before it, including an objective assessment of the facts of the case and the applicability of and conformity with the relevant covered agreements, and ... such other findings as will assist the DSB in making recommendations or in giving the rulings provided for in the covered agreements"*, in conformity with Article 11 of the DSU.

24. For the reasons set forth above and as stated throughout these proceedings, Argentina requests the Panel to issue the findings and recommendations requested by Brazil, including those related to the Step 2 and GSM 102 programmes which, under Article 4.7 of the SCM Agreement, must be withdrawn without delay. Likewise, the Panel should also make a recommendation that the United States take appropriate steps to remove the adverse effect of those programmes under Article 7.8 of the SCM Agreement.

(b) Take into account the effects of the interaction of those prohibited subsidies with other, allegedly, actionable subsidies? If so, how is this relevant to the issue of causation under Article 5 of the *SCM Agreement*?

25. In Argentina's view, if the Panel concludes that there were prohibited subsidies, it should recommended – under Article 4.7 of the SCM Agreement – that they be withdrawn without delay, without prejudice to taking into account the effects of the interaction of those prohibited subsidies with other actionable subsidies.

26. Taking into account the effects of the said interaction is extremely important to determining causation under Article 5 of the SCM Agreement. Indeed, as already stated[5], Argentina considers that it is the collective impact of all the US subsidies that has effects on the cultivated area, production, exports and prices, notwithstanding the fact that the mere elimination of a prohibited subsidy would not necessarily put an end to the adverse effects of the other actionable subsidies.

Q53. Would a finding of serious prejudice under Article 5(c) of the *SCM Agreement* be determinative for a finding under Article XVI:1 of the GATT 1994? Why or why not? What, if any, is the role of footnote 13 of the *SCM Agreement* in this context?

27. A finding of serious prejudice under Article 5(c) of the SCM Agreement is determinative for a finding under Article XVI:1 of the GATT 1994, since that Article orders the contracting party granting the subsidy to consider the possibility of limiting it "[*i*]*n any case in which it is determined that serious prejudice to the interests of any other contracting party is caused or threatened by such subsidization ...*". In other words, if it is determined that a subsidy causes or threatens to cause serious prejudice under Article 5(c) of the SCM Agreement, it necessarily calls for a finding of violation of Article XVI:1 of the GATT 1994.

28. In this connection, footnote 13 of the SCM Agreement, which states that *"the term 'serious prejudice to the interests of another Member' is used in this Agreement in the same sense as it is used in paragraph 1 of Article XVI of GATT 1994, and includes threat of serious prejudice"*, clearly establishes the link between the two provisions.

Q54. Are US cotton producers able to cover the fixed and variable costs without subsidies? Please provide substantiating evidence. Of what relevance is this, if any, to Brazil's actionable subsidy claims?

29. Argentina has no evidence that US cotton producers are unable to cover their fixed and variable costs without subsidies.

30. What Argentina has repeatedly stated – referring to the evidence submitted by Brazil during these proceedings – is that the US cotton producers cannot bridge the gap between total production costs (i.e. the sum of fixed and variable costs) and market prices for cotton without subsidies.

31. Argentina has pointed out that cotton production costs in the United States are among the highest in the world.[6] According to an ICAC study[7], the cost of production in the United States was US$0.81 per pound of cotton in the marketing year 1999[8], while US producers' market prices fell from US$0.60 to US$0.30 per pound.

---

[5] Second oral third party submission by Argentina, 8 October 2003, para. 33.

[6] Third party submission by Argentina, 15 July 2003, paras. 17 and 18.

[7] Cotton: World Statistics, Bulletin of the International Cotton Advisory Committee, September 2002 (Annex BRA-9).

[8] As stated by Brazil in its first submission to the Panel of 24 June 2003, para. 32, according to the ICAC study the cost of production in Argentina averaged 59 cents per pound of cotton (See Annex BRA-9).

32. Argentina also stated that the only possible explanation how the United States bridged this widening gap between production costs and market prices is subsidies, since without them many US producers would have been compelled to cease production (in spite of the fact that they would eventually have been able to cover their fixed and variable costs).

33. This fact, that without subsidies US cotton producers could not have bridged the gap between their total production costs and market prices, is entirely relevant to Brazil's claims, since it shows that as a result of the subsidies, less efficient US producers are immune to changes in market prices. In other words, without the US subsidies which generate a world market surplus, international cotton prices would have been higher or would not have fallen as much.

34. This confirms both the actual serious prejudice and the threat of serious prejudice caused by the subsidies, in that future subsidies will be as necessary as the current ones for US producers to bridge the gap between market prices and their total production costs.[9] This will enable them to continue competing with more efficient third-country producers, especially considering that the USDA itself forecasts an increase in total production costs.[10]

Q55. In light of the fact that certain third parties have provided submissions about the price effect of claimed US subsidies, which Member or Members is, or are, the "other party" under Article 6.3(c) (*"another Member"*) for the purposes of these proceedings?

35. The concept of "another Member" within the meaning of Article 6.3(c) covers Argentina, which indeed submitted claims relating to the price effect of US subsidies.

36. Notwithstanding, Argentina is aware that in these proceedings, it is Brazil that brought the case and requested consultations and the establishment of this Panel. At the same time, Argentina – which has also suffered serious prejudice – felt that it was appropriate to ask to be joined in the consultations, participated actively in them and raised a number of issues, as well as asking to join as a third party and presenting, in its submissions, arguments relating to price effect.

37. As stated throughout these proceedings, it is in Argentina's interest that the Panel should issue the findings and recommendations requested by Brazil, since this would mean that, in conformity with Article 7.8 of the SCM Agreement, the United States would have to *"take appropriate steps to remove the adverse effects or ... withdraw the subsidy"*.

38. This interest on the part of Argentina is based on the conviction that if the Panel were to issue such findings and recommendations, the elimination of the adverse effects or the withdrawal of the subsidies would have a favourable impact on the international price of cotton – indeed, without the US subsidies which generate a world market surplus, international cotton prices could be hig-

---

9 Second written third party submission by Argentina, 3 October 2003, para. 49.

10 See Annexes BRA-7 (ERS Data: Commodity Costs and Returns); BRA-257 ("Cost of Farm Production Up in 2003", USDA, 6 May 2003) and BRA-82 ("USDA Agricultural Baseline Projections until 2012", USDA, February 2003, p.48).

her or could fall less. Similarly, if its share in the world market were not increased as a result of the subsidies, the international price of cotton would be higher or would not be so low, and as a result, third party producers, including Argentina, would not suffer as much prejudice as a result of artificially depressed prices.[11]

39. As already stated, an increase in the world cotton price would be significant – even if as a result of the subsidies the suppression or depression of international prices amounted to only 1 cent per pound – since it would enable countries like Argentina to recover their competitive position in the world cotton market.[12]

11 Second oral third party submission by Argentina, 8 October 2003, para. 10.

12 Second written third party submission by Argentina, 3 October 2003, paras. 34 to 36, and second oral third party submission by Argentina, 8 October 2003, para. 38.

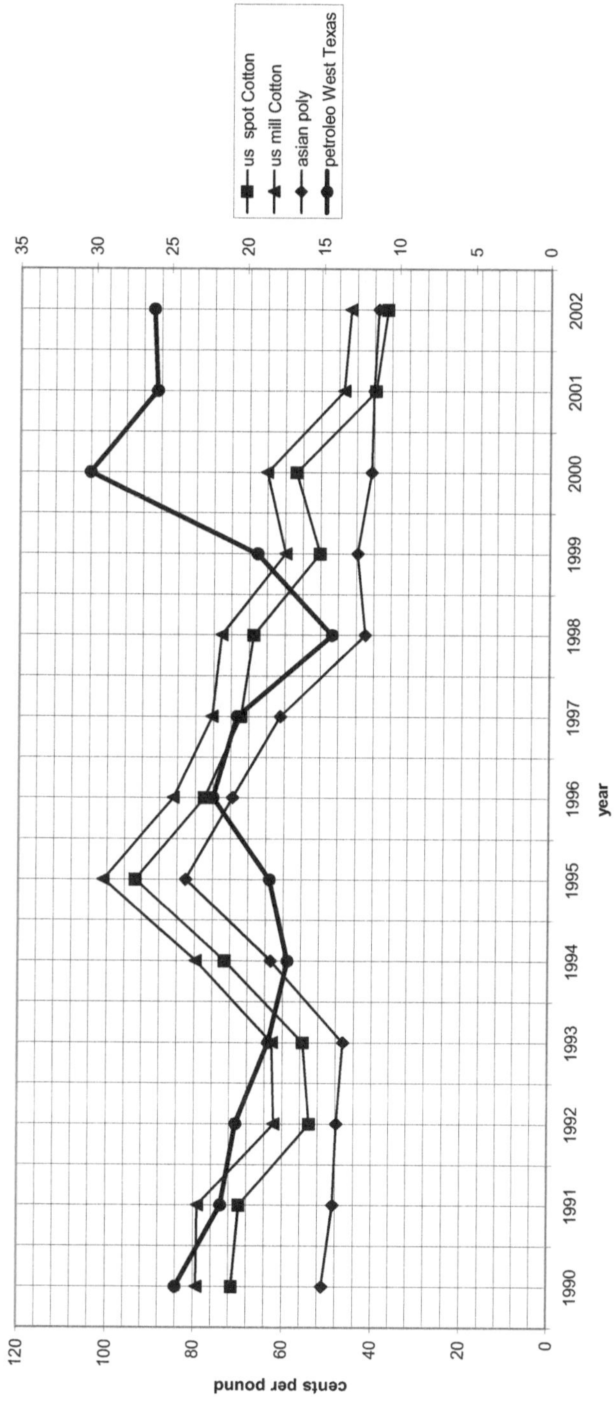
us spot Cotton
us mill Cotton
asian poly
petroleo West Texas
cents per pound
year
0
20
40
60
80
100
120
0
5
10
15
20
25
30
35
1990
1991
1992
1993
1994
1995
1996
1997
1998
1999
2000
2001
2002

ANNEX J-13

RESPONSES BY AUSTRALIA

27 October 2003

A. QUESTIONS TO INDIVIDUAL THIRD PARTIES

43. ...

44. ...

45. ...

46. ...

47. ...

48. ...

B. QUESTIONS TO ALL THIRD PARTIES

Q49. What is the meaning and effect of the introductory phrase of Article 3 of the SCM Agreement ("Except as provided in the Agreement on Agriculture ...")?

Reply

In Australia's view, with regard to subsidies for agricultural products, unless the *Agreement on Agriculture* makes express provision to the contrary, Article 3 of the *SCM Agreement* continues to apply to such subsidies. The simultaneous application of both Agreements to agricultural products is confirmed by Article 21.1 of the *Agreement on Agriculture*.

Australia noted previously in its response to the Panel's earlier question 40 that the legal issue in question concerning the relationship between the *Agreement on Agriculture* and Article 3.1(b) of the *SCM Agreement* derives from the condition attached to the grant of a subsidy, not the grant of a subsidy *per se* or who might benefit from the subsidy. The *Agreement on Agriculture* does not include any provisions concerning the conditionality of domestic support in the sense of SCM Article 3.1(b).

Moreover, the *Agreement on Agriculture* does not confer a right to grant subsidies. Rather, that Agreement establishes disciplines for the use of certain subsidies in relation to agricultural products should a Member choose to provide subsidies for such products. Arguments that the *Agreement on Agriculture* allows local content subsidies based on the phrase "support in favour of domestic producers" and similar phrasing and the provisions of paragraph 7 of Annex 3 of that Agreement are not sustainable. The word "support" is used throughout the *Agreement on Agriculture* in the sense of generic measures providing a calculable financial advantage to agricultural producers, whether price support, direct subsidy payments or any other means not exempted from a Member's commitment to reduce domestic support. Indeed, Annex 3 is headed "Domestic Support: *Calculation* of Aggregate Measurement of Support".

It is inconceivable to Australia that any intended exemption from the very significant and unambiguous local content subsidy disciplines of Article 3.1(b) of the *SCM Agreement* would not have been expressly set out in the *Agreement on Agriculture*. The inclusion of express provisions concerning export subsidies in the *Agreement on Agriculture* indicates that the negotiators of that Agreement were well aware of the need to include express provisions if additional or alternative disciplines concerning subsidies for agricultural products were intended vis-à-vis the disciplines established pursuant to the *SCM Agreement*.

The situation is analogous to that examined by the Panel and the Appellate Body in *EC – Bananas* wherein the Appellate Body upheld the Panel's conclusion that the *Agreement on Agriculture* did not permit the EC to act inconsistently with Article XIII of GATT 1994 in the absence of any provisions dealing specifically with the allocation of tariff quotas on agricultural products.[1] In the absence of provisions dealing specifically with local content subsidies in the *Agreement on Agriculture*, that Agreement does not allow a Member to act inconsistently with the *SCM Agreement*. The fact that the phrase "[e]xcept as provided in the Agreement on Agriculture" in the chapeau of SCM Article 3.1 also applies to paragraph (b) of that Article cannot of itself compel the interpretation that there are provision(s) of the *Agreement on Agriculture* which necessarily apply.

The Panel may not interpret the provisions of the *SCM Agreement* and the *Agreement on Agriculture* so as to diminish or override fundamental WTO obligations in the absence of express provisions to that effect. To do so would constitute, in Australia's view, a misapplication of the customary rules of interpretation of public international law.

Q50. According to its revised timetable, the Panel will issue its report to the parties after the end of the 2003 calendar year. Does this have any impact on "exempt[ion] from actions" under Article 13(b)(ii) and 13(c)(ii) of the Agreement on Agriculture?

Reply

In Australia's view, whether the date the Panel's report will be issued to the parties to the dispute will have any impact on any "exempt[ion] from actions" under Article 13(b)(ii) of the *Agreement on Agriculture* will depend on whether the Panel finds that the United States is granting, through domestic support measures that conform fully to the provisions of Article 6 of that Agreement, support to a specific commodity in excess of that decided during the 1992 marketing year. If the Panel finds that the United States *is* granting support to a specific commodity in excess of that decided during the 1992 marketing year, the United States will have no "exempt[ion] from actions" pursuant to Article 13(b)(ii), ir-

[1] *European Communities – Regime for the Importation, Sale and Distribution of Bananas*, Report of the Appellate Body, WT/DS27/AB/R, paras. 153-158.

respective of when the Panel's report is issued. If the Panel finds that the United States is *not* granting such support to a specific commodity in excess of that decided during the 1992 marketing year, the United States may be "exempt from actions" pursuant to Article 13(b)(ii) until Article 13 expires.

Q51. How should the concept of specificity – and, in particular, the concept of specificity to "an enterprise or industry or group of enterprises or industries" – in Article 2 of the SCM Agreement apply to subsidies in respect of agricultural commodities? Please answer the following questions, citing the principles in Article 2 of the SCM Agreement:

(a) is a subsidy in respect of all agricultural, but not other, products specific?

(b) is a subsidy in respect of all agricultural crops (i.e. but not to other agricultural commodities, such as livestock) specific?

(c) is a subsidy in respect of certain identified agricultural products specific?

(d) is a subsidy in respect of upland cotton, but not other products, specific?

(e) is a subsidy in respect of a certain proportion of the value of total US commodities (or total US agricultural commodities) specific?

Reply

Australia does not wish to comment on this issue.

Q52. The Panel notes that different remedies are available in respect of prohibited and actionable subsidies under Article 4.7 and 7.8 of the SCM Agreement. If the Panel were to conclude that a subsidy was prohibited and were to make a recommendation under Article 4.7 of the SCM Agreement to withdraw the subsidy without delay, can the Panel:

(a) also conclude that the same subsidy had resulted in adverse effects to the interests of another Member? If so, what would be the value of such a conclusion in terms of the settlement of the matter before the Panel?

(b) take into account the effects of the interaction of those prohibited subsidies with other, allegedly, actionable subsidies? If so, how is this relevant to the issue of causation under Article 5 of the SCM Agreement?

Reply

If the Panel were to conclude that a subsidy was prohibited and to make a recommendation under Article 4.7 of the *SCM Agreement* to "withdraw the subsidy without delay", and having regard to the presumption of adverse effects implicit in a finding that a subsidy is prohibited and to the observations of the Appellate Body on the meaning of "withdraw" in SCM Article 4.7[2]:

(a) the Panel could conclude that the same subsidy had also resulted in adverse effects to the interests of another Member under SCM Article 5, particularly if that other Member were a third party to the dispute in light of the provisions of Article 10.1 of the DSU;

(b) the Panel could also consider the interaction of that prohibited subsidy with other, allegedly actionable subsidies. However, the prohibited subsidy would be required to be withdrawn without delay and thus any causative contribution its interaction with other allegedly actionable subsidies may make to the adverse effects of those other actionable subsidies will be removed as a consequence of the withdrawal of the prohibited subsidy.

Q53. Would a finding of serious prejudice under Article 5(c) of the SCM Agreement be determinative for a finding under Article XVI:1 of the GATT 1994? Why or why not? What, if any, is the role of footnote 13 of the SCM Agreement in this context?

Reply

Australia does not wish to comment on this issue.

Q54. Are US cotton producers able to cover the fixed and variable costs without subsidies? Please provide substantiating evidence. Of what relevance is this, if any, to Brazil's actionable subsidy claims?

Reply

Australia does not wish to comment on the facts of US costs of production in relation to upland cotton, but notes the statements of the Appellate Body in relation to the calculation of costs of production in the *Canada – Dairy* dispute.[3]

Q55. In light of the fact that certain third parties have provided submissions about the price effect of claimed US subsidies, which Member or Members is, or are, the "other party" under Article 6.3(c) ("another Member") for the purposes of these proceedings?

Reply

Australia does not wish to comment on this issue.

Q56. Please respond to the following questions concerning the relationship between Article XVI:3 of the GATT 1994, the disciplines on export subsidies and domestic support in the Agreement on Agriculture and the disciplines

---

[2] *Brazil – Export Financing Programme for Aircraft*, Recourse by Canada to Article 21.5 of the DSU, Report of the Appellate Body, WT/DS46/AB/RW, para. 45.

[3] *Canada – Measures Affecting the Importation of Milk and the Exportation of Dairy Products*, Recourse to Article 21.5 of the DSU by New Zealand and the United States, WT/DS103/AB/RW – WT/DS113/AB/RW, paras. 94-96, and Second Recourse to Article 21.5 of the DSU by New Zealand and the United States, WT/DS103/AB/RW2 – WT/DS113/AB/RW2, paras. 91-120.

on prohibited export subsidies and actionable subsidies in Articles 3, 5(c) and 6.3(d) of the SCM Agreement.

(a) **Are agricultural domestic support programmes challengeable under Article XVI:3 of the GATT 1994? How, if at all, is the title of Section B of Article XVI ("Additional provisions on export subsidies" (emphasis added)) relevant? How, if at all, are Articles 13 and 21.1, or any other provisions, of the Agreement on Agriculture, relevant?**

(b) **Are the requirements of Article XVI:3 of the GATT 1994 reflected in, developed by or subsumed by the requirements in Article 6.3(d) of the SCM Agreement, or in any other provisions of the covered agreements? Of what relevance, if any, is the Appellate Body Report in US – FSC, para. 117 here?**

(c) **Of what relevance, if any, is the fact that the definition of "subsidy" in Article 1 of the SCM Agreement and the prohibition on subsidies contingent upon export in Article 3.1(a) were introduced in the Uruguay Round, but did not exist at the time that the GATT 1947 were negotiated?**

Reply

In Australia's view, it is unambiguous that agricultural domestic support programmes are challengeable under Article XVI:3 of GATT 1994.

It is useful to recall to begin with that GATT 1947 did not provide a definition of a "subsidy" or of an "export subsidy" and that the only disciplines on subsidies of any type were the general subsidy disciplines of paragraph 1 of GATT Article XVI. The provisions of Section B of GATT Article XVI, comprising paragraphs 2-5 and headed "Additional Provisions on Export Subsidies", were added at the 1954-55 Review Session and constituted the earliest disciplines directed at "the use of subsidies on the export of primary products". The plurilateral 1979 Tokyo Round Subsidies Code[4] represented a further stage in the elaboration of disciplines on export subsidies and subsidies generally, in particular, Articles 8-11and the Annex. This background is helpful in understanding the evolution of the use of terminology originally found in GATT Article XVI and the relationship between provisions of the covered agreements as they exist today.

In relation to the use of subsidies on the export of primary products, the substantive discipline established by Article XVI:3 of GATT 1994 was that:

> "[i]f a contracting party grants directly or indirectly *any form of subsidy* which operates to increase the export of any primary product from its territory, such subsidy *shall not be applied in a manner which results in that contracting party having more than an equitable share of world export trade in that product*, account being taken of the shares of the contracting parties in such trade in

[4] *Agreement on Interpretation and Application of Articles VI, XVI and XXIII of the General Agreement on Tariffs and Trade*, BISD 26S/56.

> the product during a previous representative period, and any special factors which may have affected or may be affecting such trade in the product".

Thus, the key discipline established by Article XVI:3 of GATT 1994 is that a subsidy that has the effect of increasing a Member's exports of a primary product must not be applied so as to result in that Member having more than an equitable, that is, a "just" or "fair",[5] share of world export trade in that primary product. GATT Article XVI:3 was elaborated by Article 10.1 and 10.2 of the later plurilateral Tokyo Round Subsidies Code, but these provisions were not carried forward to, and incorporated as such, in the *SCM Agreement*.

Notwithstanding the heading of Section B of GATT Article XVI, that discipline is distinct from the export subsidy disciplines later incorporated in Article 3.1(a) of the *SCM Agreement*. In particular, GATT Article XVI:3 is concerned with the effects rather than the conditions of a subsidy's grant.

Moreover, the discipline established by Article XVI:3 of GATT 1994 is distinct from the discipline established by Article 6.3(d) of the *SCM Agreement*, which relates to whether the effect of a subsidy is to increase a Member's world market share compared to the previous three-year average share. At the same time, there may be substantial commonality of facts in demonstrating non-compliance with either provision. Further, both GATT Article XVI:3 and SCM Article 6.3(d) must be applied within the same contextual framework of "serious prejudice" established by GATT Article XVI:1, and SCM Article 5(c) and its footnote.

The GATT Article XVI:3 discipline is also distinct from the disciplines established by other provisions of the covered agreements.

The Appellate Body has previously noted that the *WTO Agreement* was accepted by WTO Members as a "single undertaking".[6] The Appellate Body has also said:

> The relationship between the GATT 1994 and the other goods agreements in Annex 1A is complex and must be examined on a case-by-case basis. Although the provisions of the GATT 1947 were incorporated into, and became a part of the GATT 1994, they are not the sum total of the rights and obligations of WTO Members concerning a particular matter. For example, with respect to subsidies on agricultural products, Articles II, VI and XVI of the GATT 1994 alone do not represent the total rights and obligations of WTO Members. The *Agreement on Agriculture* and the *SCM Agreement* reflect the latest statement of WTO Members as to their rights and obligations concerning agricultural subsidies. The general interpretative note to Annex 1A was added to reflect that the

---

[5] *The New Shorter Oxford English Dictionary*, Ed. Lesley Brown, Clarendon Press, Oxford, 1993, Volume 1, 843.

[6] For example, *Brazil – Measures Affecting Desiccated Coconut*, Report of the Appellate Body, WT/DS22/AB/R, page 13.

other goods agreements in Annex 1A, in many ways, represent a substantial elaboration of the provisions of the GATT 1994, and to the extent that the provisions of the other goods agreements conflict with the provisions of the GATT 1994, the provisions of the other goods agreements prevail. *This does not mean, however, that the other goods agreements in Annex 1A, such as the SCM Agreement, supersede the GATT 1994. ...*"[7] (emphasis added)

In the absence of a conflict between the provisions of Article XVI:3 of GATT 1994 and Article 6.3(d) of the *SCM Agreement* or any other provisions of the covered agreements such that the General Interpretative Note to Annex 1A of the *WTO Agreement* becomes operative, GATT Article XVI:3 continues to apply. In Australia's view, the Appellate Body report in *US – FSC*, paragraph 117, does not affect the interpretation of the relationship between these provisions other than in the sense of confirming that the relationship must be determined on the basis of the texts of the relevant provisions as a whole.

The continued applicability of Article XVI:3 of GATT 1994 is confirmed by Article 13 of the *Agreement on Agriculture*. The exemption from action pursuant to AA Article 13(b)(ii) is only applicable in respect of paragraph 1 of GATT Article XVI, whereas the exemption from action pursuant to AA Article 13(c)(ii) is applicable to the whole of GATT Article XVI. Had the negotiators of the *WTO Agreement* believed that GATT Article XVI:3 had become redundant, they would not have expressly distinguished between the paragraphs of GATT Article XVI in AA Article 13 as they did. Moreover, Australia believes its view is fully consistent with the provisions of Article 21.1 of the *Agreement on Agriculture* and with the nature of the *WTO Agreement* as a whole as a "single undertaking".

Further, the distinction between the provisions of Article XVI of GATT 1994 in Article 13(b)(ii) and 13(c)(ii) of the *Agreement on Agriculture* is entirely consistent with the object and purpose of the *Agreement on Agriculture*, including as expressed in the third preambular paragraph that the "long-term objective is to provide for substantial progressive reductions in agricultural support and protection sustained over an agreed period of time, resulting in correcting and preventing restrictions and distortions in world agricultural markets". It would be directly contrary to that objective if WTO Members were able, albeit otherwise consistently with the domestic support provisions of the *Agreement on Agriculture*, nonetheless to arrange their domestic support payments so as to achieve an inequitable share of the world export market in a particular primary product.

---

[7] *Brazil – Desiccated Coconut*, Report of the Appellate Body, pages 14-15.

ANNEX J-14

RESPONSES OF BENIN AND CHAD TO THE PANEL'S QUESTIONS

27 October 2003

Benin and Chad would offer the following responses to those Panel questions that pertain to the scope of their Third Party Submissions:

"44. Please explain how Articles 5 and 6 of the *SCM Agreement* and Article XVI of the GATT 1994 would permit or require the Panel to take account of any effects of the subsidies in question on the interests of Members other than the complaining party. Benin and Chad."

Brazil is the sole complaining party in this dispute, and ultimately only Brazil would have the right to any remedy provided by the SCM Agreement. However, Benin and Chad submit that the Panel is nevertheless required to take account of the effects of the US subsidies on the interest of Members other than the complaining Member, for the following reasons.

First, the chapeau of Article 5 states that "[n]o Member should cause, through the use of any subsidy referred to in paragraphs 1 and 2 of Article 1, adverse effects to the interests of *other Members*". The drafters of Article 5 referred to "Members" in the plural, connoting an obligation on behalf of the subsidizing Member not to cause adverse effects to the interests of all WTO Members – not just the complaining Member.

Second, when the drafters of the SCM Agreement intended to refer only to the "complaining Member", they used this term specifically, such as in Article 6.7, or in paragraph 2 of Annex V. They could similarly have used the term "complaining Member" elsewhere in Articles 5 and 6, but they did not. Therefore, the term "other Members" cannot be interpreted as synonymous with "complaining Members", just as the term "another Member" cannot be read as limited only to the "complaining Member". The treaty interpreter must give meaning to the terms actually used in the text.[1]

Third, this interpretation is consistent with Article 3.8 of the DSU, which provides as follows:

> In cases where there is an infringement of the obligations assumed under a covered agreement, the action is considered *prima facie* to constitute a case of nullification or impairment. This means that there is normally a presumption that a breach of the rules *has an adverse impact on other Members parties to that covered agreement*, and in such cases, it shall be up to the Member against

[1] The textual analysis set out above applies equally to Article XVI:1 of the GATT 1994, which refers to the "other contracting party." (By virtue of paragraph 2(a) of the *Explanatory Notes to GATT 1994*, the references to "contracting party" are deemed to read "Member.") Article XVI:1 thus refers to the "other Member" and not the "complaining Member."

whom the complaint has been brought to rebut the charge. [emphasis added]

Article 3.8 refers to the "adverse impact" on "other Members" in the plural, referring to all WTO Members. Although the SCM Agreement provides special and additional rules for dispute settlement, these special rules have not ousted the application of DSU Article 3.8. Benin and Chad are "parties to [the] covered agreement", the SCM Agreement, and it can therefore be presumed that the breach of the SCM Agreement by the United States has an adverse impact on these two African countries.

In any event, the Panel need not rely exclusively on the presumption set out DSU Article 3.8, since Benin and Chad have already provided to the Panel detailed evidence about the adverse effects of US subsides on West and Central Africa. Benin and Chad also note the similarities in language between the SCM Agreement ("adverse effects") and DSU Article 3.8 ("adverse impact"). This reinforces the relevance and applicability of the latter provision.

Fourth, DSU Article 10.1, which deals with Third Parties, provides additional support for the position that the Panel should take into account the adverse effects on parties other than just the complaining party:

> The interests of the parties to a dispute and *those of other Members under a covered agreement at issue in the dispute shall be fully taken into account* during the panel process.

DSU Article 10.1 is not limited simply to allowing Third Parties to present their views. That is dealt with elsewhere, including in DSU Article 10.2, which grants to Third Parties the right "to be heard by the Panel". By contrast, DSU Article 10.1 is not limited to providing Third Parties with the right to present views. Instead, it mandates that the "interests" of the third parties shall be "fully taken into account".

Fifth, DSU Article 24.1 provides that "[a]t all stages... of dispute settlement procedures involving a least-developed country Member, particular consideration shall be given to the special situation of least-developed country Members". Benin and Chad are both least-developed countries. The "particular consideration" that must be extended to them goes beyond simply ensuring that their views are heard – as noted above, such procedural protections are provided for elsewhere in the DSU. Instead, Panels must give "particular consideration" to their "special situation". In the context of the present case, the "special situation" of Benin and Chad has been presented in some detail to the panel. Massive US cotton subsidies have had, and continue to have, a devastating impact on the fragile economies of West Africa, pushing hundreds of thousands of people from subsistence farming into absolute poverty. If DSU Article 24.1 has any meaning, this "special situation" of Benin and Chad must be given full, substantive consideration by the Panel.

Finally, Benin and Chad note that the serious prejudice caused to their economies has also been specifically raised before the Panel by one of the disputing parties, Brazil. As the Panel will recall, Part 7 of Brazil's Further Submission of 9 September 2003 is on "Serious Prejudice to the Interests of African Countries by Reason of the US Subsidies on Upland Cotton". This provides addition support for the position that the serious prejudice to Benin and Chad needs to examined by the Panel in assessing the WTO-consistency of the US subsidies.

"55. In light of the fact that certain third parties have provided submissions about the price effect of claimed US subsidies, which Member or Members is, or are, the "other party" under Article 6.3(c) ("another Member") for the purposes of these proceedings? All third parties."

As noted, the drafters of the SCM Agreement used the term "complaining Member" in other provisions of the Agreement. In Article 6.3(c), they chose the term "other Member" rather than "complaining Member." For the reasons set out above, Benin and Chad are of the view that Article 6.3(c) encompasses both the complainant, Brazil, as well as other WTO Members.

The Panel has before it substantial evidence about the effects of the US subsidies, including the significant price undercutting by US cotton compared with the price of the like products of Brazil, Benin and Chad in world markets, as well as significant price suppression and price depression in world cotton markets. In assessing the WTO-consistency of the US subsidies, the Panel is required by the SCM Agreement to take this evidence into account.

ANNEX J-15

CANADA'S RESPONSES TO PANEL QUESTIONS TO THIRD PARTIES FIRST SUBSTANTIVE MEETING OF THE PANEL WITH THE PARTIES (RESUMED FIRST SESSION)

27 October 2003

Canada sets out responses to the questions of the Panel in which Canada has a systemic interest:

49. What is the meaning and effect of the introductory phrase of Article 3 of the *SCM Agreement* ("Except as provided in the *Agreement on Agriculture...*")?

Reply

The meaning and effect of this phrase is that Article 3 of the *SCM Agreement* applies *subject to* the export subsidy disciplines of the *Agreement on Agriculture*, which permit, in some instances and within certain limits, the granting or maintaining of subsidies that would otherwise be prohibited under the *SCM Agreement*.

51. How should the concept of specificity – and, in particular, the concept of specificity to "an enterprise or industry or group of enterprises or industries" – in Article 2 of the *SCM Agreement* apply to subsidies in respect of agricultural commodities? Please answer the following questions, citing the principles in Article 2 of the *SCM Agreement*:

Reply

Canada's answers assume that the phrase "in respect of" has the same meaning as the standard "is specific to" in Article 2.1 of the *SCM Agreement*. Based on the ordinary meaning of the phrase "is specific to", read in context and in light of the object and purpose of Article 2 and of the *SCM Agreement*, the specificity test is concerned with the actual availability of a programme. Analysis on availability may include an assessment of the manner in which a programme is used in the circumstances of a given case. The panel in *US – Softwood Lumber III* recently confirmed: "In our view, Article 2 SCM Agreement is concerned with the distortion created by a subsidy which either in law or in fact is not broadly available."[1] Moreover, a programme may be found either *de jure*

[1] *United States – Final Countervailing Duty Determination with respect to Certain Softwood Lumber from Canada*, Report of the Panel, WT/DS257/R, circulated 29 August 2003, para. 7.116.

or *de facto* specific, and either determination depends on the nature of the evidence relied upon.[2]

(a) is a subsidy in respect of all agricultural, but not other, products specific?

Reply

No. Canada shares the view of the United States in *United States – Continued Dumping and Subsidy Offset Act of 2000*, that, as a general matter, "all agriculture" is too broad to qualify as a "group of enterprises or industries" for specificity purposes.[3]

(b) is a subsidy in respect of all agricultural crops (i.e. but not to other agricultural commodities, such as livestock) specific?

Reply

The answer will depend on the facts of a given case. A panel would have to consider, among other things, the number of enterprises or industries (based on standard industrial classification) within the jurisdiction of the granting authority that are actually eligible to receive the subsidy, and the level of diversification of the "all agricultural crops" universe. Furthermore, the answer would also depend on the nature of the measure in question and whether it excludes enterprises or industries that might otherwise be reasonably or practically included. For example, weather that may cause extensive damage to crops (e.g. hail, frost, excessive moisture, drought) may not cause any damage to livestock. Therefore, it may not be reasonable or practical to include livestock under a crop insurance programme. On the other hand, an income stabilization programme could reasonably or practically include both crops and livestock.

(c) is a subsidy in respect of certain identified agricultural products specific?

Reply

The answer will depend on the facts of a given case, including whether the eligible products involve only "an enterprise or industry or group of enterprises or industries" (based on standard industrial classification) under Article 2.1.

(d) is a subsidy in respect of upland cotton, but not other products, specific?

---

[2] In this respect, a determination under Article 2 is similar to a determination under Article 3. The legal standard expressed by the phrase "is specific to" is the same for both *de jure* or *de facto* determinations; the only difference is the nature of the evidence relied upon. See *Canada – Measures Affecting the Export of Civilian Aircraft*, Report of the Appellate Body, WT/DS70/AB/R, adopted 20 August 1999, para. 167 ("In our view, the legal standard expressed by the word 'contingent' is the same for both *de jure* or *de facto* contingency. There is a difference, however, in what evidence may be employed to prove that a subsidy is export contingent.")

[3] *United States – Continued Dumping and Subsidy Offset Act of 2000*, Report of the Panel, WT/DS217/R, WT/DS234/R, adopted 27 January 2003, at para 4.1146.

Reply

Yes.

(e) is a subsidy in respect of a certain proportion of the value of total US commodities (or total US agricultural commodities) specific?

Reply

Where a programme appears *de jure* non-specific under Articles 2.1(a) and (b), predominant use of a programme by "certain enterprises" (a defined term in Article 2.1) would indicate, in the absence of any other reasonable explanation, that the availability of the subsidy is limited in fact to such enterprises or industries under Article 2.1(c) and 2.4. Likewise, where a programme appears *de jure* non-specific under Articles 2.1(a) and (b), the granting of disproportionately large amounts of subsidy to certain enterprises would indicate, in the absence of any other reasonable explanation, that the availability of the subsidy is limited in fact to such enterprises or industries under Article 2.1(c) and 2.4. In both cases, any predominance or disproportionality should be measured over an appropriate period of time and in relation to the value of production in question as compared to the total value of all agricultural production.

(f) is a subsidy in respect of a certain proportion of total US farmland specific?

Reply

The answer will depend on the facts of a given case, including the proportion of total US farmland involved, whether that proportion involves "an enterprise or industry or group of enterprises or industries", and whether the programme "is specific to" (i.e., available only to) those enterprises or industries.

ANNEX J-16

RESPONSE BY CHINA TO THE PANEL'S QUESTIONS TO THIRD PARTIES

27 October 2003

1. China appreciates this opportunity to present its views again to the Panel in relation to the Panel's questions posed to third parties on October 13, 2003. Given the short period within which third parties are required to submit their views, China responds to and comments on the following underlined questions.

2. Question 49. What is the meaning and effect of the introductory phrase of Article 3 of the *SCM Agreement* ("Except as provided in the *Agreement on Agriculture*...")? All third parties

3. To answer this Panel's question, it is helpful to first look to the relationship between the *Agreement on Agriculture* and the *SCM Agreement*. Art. 21.1 of the *Agreement on Agriculture* provides:

> The provisions of GATT 1994 and of other Multilateral Trade Agreements in Annex 1A to the WTO Agreement shall apply subject to the provisions of this Agreement [on Agriculture].

4. The Appellate Body, in *EC – Bananas III,* further clarified this article by stating that

> the provisions of GATT 1994, [and indeed 'other Multilateral Trade Agreements including the *SCM Agreement*, note added pursuant to Art. 21 of the *Agreement on Agriculture*], ..., apply ..., except to the extent that the *Agreement on Agriculture* contains specific provisions dealing specifically with the same matter".[1]

In other words, Art. 21.1 of the *Agreement on Agriculture*, as interpreted by the Appellate Body, requires that in connection with a specific matter, the *Agreement on Agriculture* prevails over the *SCM Agreement* to the extent that it has more specific provisions over the same matter covered by the *SCM Agreement*.

5. The introductory phrase of Art. 3 of the *SCM Agreement* again, in the matter of prohibited subsidies, grants deference to the *Agreement on Agriculture*. It reads:

> [E]xcept as provided in the *Agreement on Agriculture*, the following subsidies, within the meaning of Article 1, shall be prohibited.

Given that the *SCM Agreement* contains disciplines over all types of subsidies, including agricultural, and the *Agreement on Agriculture* imposes more specific disciplines over subsidies granted to agricultural commodities only, where such

---

[1] Appellate Body Report, *European Communities – Regime for the Importation, Sale and Distribution of Bananas*, WT/DS27/AB/R, DSR 1997:II, para. 155.

specificity of discipline can be established, the *Agreement on Agriculture* shall prevail pursuant to Article 3.1 of the *SCM Agreement*.

6. Therefore, in line with Art. 21.1 of the *Agreement on Agriculture* past Appellate Body interpretation above and Art. 3.1 of the *SCM Agreement*, the *Agreement on Agriculture,* where it is more specific, shall *prevail* over provisions of the *SCM Agreement*.

7. Question 50. According to its revised timetable, the Panel will issue its report to the parties after the end of 2003 calendar year. Does this have any impact on "exempt[ion] from actions" under Article 13(b)(ii) and 13(c)(ii) of the *Agreement on Agriculture*? All third parties

8. China believes Article 13 continues to be applicable to the current case even after it ceases to be in effect.

9. Art. 13 of the *Agreement on Agriculture* protects subsidy measures otherwise prohibited or actionable under the *SCM Agreement* during the nine-year implementation period commencing in 1995. Unless agreed otherwise amongst Members, Article 13 will expire in 2004.

10. Art. 70 of the *Vienna Convention on the Law of Treaties*, in dealing with the consequences of the termination of a treaty, provides to the effect that the termination of a treaty does not affect any right, obligation or legal situation of the parties created through the execution of the treaty prior to its termination. Applied to Art. 13 of the *Agreement on Agriculture*, if a Member's subsidy measures were granted and implemented prior to expiry of the Peace Clause, such Member's possible right to be protected thereunder is not removed by the expiry; neither are obligations on other Members to exercise due restraint. Such rights, obligations and legal situations created through implementation of the Peace Clause for the purpose of these proceedings are allowed by the *Vienna Convention on the Law of Treaties* to be live issues as between parties to a dispute. Even if the Panel were to make its report after the expiry, the rights and obligations and their past interaction are heavily controversial issues the interpretation and resolution of which by this Panel will have bearings on the merits of the case not only between the parties to this dispute, but also to the general WTO membership. Therefore, this Panel, even if it chooses to issue its report after the expiry date of the Peace Clause, is obligated to rule on such rights and obligations during implementation of the Peace Clause.

11. In addition, considering the likelihood of the Peace Clause being extended as reportedly suggested by some Members, however remote, an interpretation of the "exempt from action" requirement and its practical application is of extraordinary value to Members having interests in such an extension proposal; such Members, aided with the Panel's interpretation of the key components of this clause, will have a better basis to form their negotiating policy and stance, not only in terms of the Peace Clause, but also with regard to WTO discipline on agriculture.

12. Question 51. How should the concept of specificity – and, in particular, the concept of specificity to "an enterprise or industry or group of enterprises or industries" - in Article 2 of the *SCM Agreement* apply to subsi-

dies in respect of agricultural commodities? Please answer the following questions, citing the principles in Article 2 of the *SCM Agreement*: All third parties

(a) is a subsidy in respect of all agricultural, but not other, products specific?

(b) is a subsidy in respect of all agricultural crops (i.e. but not to other agricultural commodities, such as livestock) specific?

(c) is a subsidy in respect of certain identified agricultural products specific?

(d) is a subsidy in respect of upland cotton, but not other products, specific?

(e) is a subsidy in respect of a certain proportion of the value of total US commodities (or total US agricultural commodities) specific?

(f) is a subsidy in respect of a certain proportion of total US farmland specific?

13. "Commodity" includes agricultural crops such as upland cotton.[2] While the *Agreement on Agriculture* identifies agricultural products by reference to their respective HS codes[3], in certain places it uses the terms "commodity" and "agricultural product" interchangeably.[4] Hence, in China's opinion, "agricultural commodity" can be understood as equivalent to "agricultural product" under the *Agreement on Agriculture*. Such equivalence is particularly relevant with regard to upland cotton, which being an agricultural product and crop, unquestionably meets the definition of a commodity.

14. On the other hand, "industry" used in the context of Art. 2 of the *SCM Agreement* normally refers to "a particular form or branch of productive labour; a trade, a manufacture"[5], while in the context of trade and commercial policy, "agriculture" means "the science and practice of cultivating the soil and rearing animals; farming".[6] Cultivate, in turn, means "prepare and use soil for crops"[7], i.e. the use of productive labour for soil preparation and use. Hence, agriculture, being the science and practice of using productive labour, meets the definition of "industry". Further, the *Agreement on Agriculture* also treats "agriculture" as an "industry" by extensively using "agricultural producers" and "agricultural production" to refer to the targets of domestic support measures.[8]

---

2 Commodity means "a thing of *use* or value; specially a thing that is an object of trade, especially a raw material or agriculture crop", Lesley Brown (ed.), *The Shorter Oxford English Dictionary*, 5th ed. (Oxford University Press, 2002), p.461.

3 Art. 2, *Agreement on Agriculture*.

4 e.g. under Art. 6, the terms "*product*-specific domestic support" and "*basic agricultural product*" are used in the context of quantifying domestic support commitments, while under Art. 13(b), domestic support measures under Art. 6 that do not grant support to *a specific commodity* in excess of that decided during the 1992 marketing year are required to be exempt from actions as specified therein.

5 *The Shorter Oxford English Dictionary*, p.1363.

6 *Ibid.*, p. 44.

7 *Ibid.*, p. 575.

8 e.g. Art. 6, *Agreement on Agriculture*.

15. Art. 2 of the *SCM Agreement* provides that a subsidy is specific if it is provided to an enterprise or industry or group of enterprises or industries. Based on the analysis in Paras. 12 and 13 above, China believes that any subsidy to agricultural commodities shall be considered as specific for the purpose of Art. 2 of the *SCM Agreement.* By the same token, China believes that:

(a) a subsidy in respect of all agricultural, but not other, product is specific, since agriculture producing all agricultural products is an industry and consists of "group of enterprises" by definition.

(b) Similarly, subsidies in respect of "all agricultural crops (i.e. but not to other agricultural commodities, such as livestock)", "certain identified agricultural products" and "upland cotton, but not other products" should all be deemed as specific since "group of enterprises" producing crops (certain products, upland cotton) are targeted in all the cases.

(c) The use of "a certain proportion of the value of total US commodities" or "a certain proportion of US farmland" will necessarily be equivalent to "an enterprise or industry or group of enterprises or industries" because the "proportion" has to be generated by adding up those data from specific "enterprise or industry or group of enterprises or industries".

16. Question 52, The Panel notes that different remedies are available in respect of prohibited and actionable subsidies under Article 4.7 and 7.8 of the *SCM Agreement.* If the Panel were to conclude that a subsidy was prohibited and were to make a recommendation under Article 4.7 of the *SCM Agreement* to withdraw the subsidy without delay, can the Panel:

(a) also conclude that the same subsidy had resulted in adverse effects to the interests of another Member? If so, what would be the value of such a conclusion in terms of the settlement of the matter before the Panel? All third parties

(b) take into account the effects of the interaction of those prohibited subsidies with other, allegedly, actionable subsidies? If so, how is this relevant to the issue of causation under Article 5 of the *SCM Agreement*? All third parties

17. China believes that if this Panel were to find that a subsidy was prohibited and were to recommend under Article 4.7 of the *SCM Agreement* an immediate withdraw the subsidy, there would be no need for this Panel to dwell on the issue of whether adverse effects have been generated by the same subsidy.

18. The *SCM Agreement* has a primary distinction between prohibited subsidies under Article 3 where effects are presumed and actionable subsidies under Article 5 where the complaining party must demonstrate adverse effects. Amongst differences between prohibited and actionable subsidies, such as degree of proof, dispute settlement procedures, are different remedies under Arts. 4.7 and 7.8.

19. While no panel has dealt squarely with the issued raised by this Panel, the panel on *Australia – Automotive Leather II (Article 21.5 – US)* did touch upon the relationship between Arts. 4.7 and 7.8 briefly.[9]

> As regards the context of Article 4.7, we note that the term "withdraw the subsidy" appears elsewhere in the SCM Agreement. We consider these references to "withdrawal" of subsidies to be relevant for our understanding of the term. In the case of "actionable" subsidies, Members whose trade interests are adversely affected may, under Part III of the SCM Agreement, pursue multilateral dispute settlement in order to establish whether the subsidy in question has resulted in adverse effects to the interests of the complaining Member. If such a finding is made, the subsidizing Member "shall take appropriate steps to remove the adverse effects **or shall withdraw the subsidy**".[10] Alternatively, a Member whose domestic industry is injured by subsidized imports may impose a countervailing measure under Part V of the SCM Agreement, "**unless the subsidy or subsidies are withdrawn**".[11] In both cases, withdrawal of the subsidy is an alternative, available to the subsidizing Member, to some other action. Repayment of the subsidy would certainly effectuate withdrawal of the subsidy by a subsidizing Member so as to allow it to avoid action by the complaining Member.[12]

20. The panel in that case went *on* to elaborate in light of Art. 4.7's object and purpose:

> Turning to the object and purpose of Article 4.7 of the SCM Agreement, we observe that the SCM Agreement as a whole establishes disciplines on subsidies. The SCM Agreement categorizes subsidies as non-actionable, actionable, or prohibited.[13] In the case of non-actionable and actionable subsidies, Members are only allowed to take certain prescribed steps in the event that their trade interests are harmed by another Member's subsidies. Part II of the SCM Agreement, however, establishes an absolute prohibition on certain types of subsidies: Members are obligated, under Article 3.2 of the SCM Agreement, to "neither grant nor maintain" such subsidies. **While the trade effects of prohibited subsidies**

---

[9] Panel Report, *Australia – Subsidies Provided to Producers and Exporters of Automotive Leather – Recourse to Article 21.5 of the DSU by the United States,* WT/DS126/RW and Corr.1, adopted 1 February 2000.

[10] Original note, "*SCM Agreement Article 7.8* (emphasis added)".

[11] Original note, "*SCM Agreement Article 19.1* (emphasis added)".

[12] Panel Report, *Australia – Subsidies Provided to Producers and Exporters of Automotive Leather – Recourse to Article 21.5 of the DSU by the United States,* WT/DS126/RW and Corr.1, adopted 1 February 2000, para. 6.28.

[13] Original note, "[w]e note *that,* pursuant to Article 31 of the SCM Agreement, the provisions of Articles 6.1 (presumption of serious prejudice), and 8 and 9 (non-actionable subsidies) shall apply for five years from the date of entry into force of the WTO Agreement unless extended for a further period."

> **may be countered under Parts III and V of the SCM Agreement, Part II of the SCM Agreement establishes special and additional rules for rapid dispute settlement in cases involving such subsidies. Article 4.7 of the SCM Agreement establishes a specific remedy to be recommended in the case of a violation - withdrawal of the subsidy**. (Original emphasis added)

21. Indeed, the panel considered the Art. 4.7 prescription of withdrawal for subsidies found to be prohibited under to be so "special" that it is "specific remedy" designed to "not merely counteract *adverse* trade effects, but is intended to enforce the absolute prohibition on the grant or maintenance of such subsidies".[14]

22. In other words, such a specific remedy under Art. 4.7 grants the subsidizing Member far less options than Art. 7.8, which allows the subsidizing Member the options of either to "remove the adverse effects" or "withdraw the subsidy".

23. The above interpretation is further supported by the difference in terminology for countermeasures allowed to be taken by a complaining Member in the event that recommendations adopted by the DSB are not followed. The Arbitrators in their Decision on *Brazil – Aircraft (Article 22.6 – Brazil)*[15], stated:

> We also note that, when the negotiators have intended to limit countermeasures to the effect caused by the subsidy on a Member's trade, they have used different terms than 'appropriate countermeasures'. Article 7.9 and 10, which is the provision equivalent for actionable subsidies to Article 4.9 and 10 for prohibited subsidies, uses the terms 'commensurate with the degree and nature of the adverse effects determined to exist'.[16]

while Art. 4.10 only used the term "appropriate countermeasures", without the qualification of commensuration with the degree and nature of adverse effects as required under Arts. 7.9 and 7.10 for actionable subsidies. In deed, the Arbitrators ruled in the arbitration that

> when dealing with a prohibited export subsidy, an amount of countermeasures which corresponds to the total amount of the subsidy is "appropriate"[17] against the Brazilian argument that such an interpretation would be punitive.[18]

24. Hence, past panels and arbitrators have determined that Art. 4.7 remedies are special, specific, and additional to those under Art. 7.8, that when recom-

---

[14] Panel Report, *Australia – Subsidies Provided to Producers and Exporters of Automotive Leather – Recourse to Article 21.5 of the DSU by the United States,* WT/DS126/RW and Corr.1, adopted 1 February 2000, para. 6.34.

[15] Decision by the Arbitrators, *Brazil – Export Financing Programme for Aircraft – Recourse to Arbitration by Brazil under Article 22.6 of the DSU and Article 4.11 of the SCM Agreement,* WT/DS46/ARB, 28 August 2000.

[16] *Ibid.,* para. 3.49.

[17] *Ibid.,* para. 3.60.

[18] *Ibid.,* para. 3.55.

mended by a panel, they more than counteract adverse trade effects. In light of such reasoning, the need for this Panel, after it having established prohibited subsidies, to go an extra step to find adverse effects is superfluous.

25. With respect to this Panel's question as to whether the Panel can "take into account the effects of interaction of those prohibited subsidies with other, allegedly, actionable subsidies" if it were to find prohibited subsidy, China believes the answer is not straight forward.

26. Art. 5 of the *SCM Agreement* makes no express distinction between prohibited and actionable subsidies when discussing adverse effects to the interests of other Members. It simply requires that no Member shall cause adverse effects through the use of any subsidy referred to in Paras. 1 and 2 of Article 1 of the *SCM Agreement*, which covers all types of subsidies that meets the specificity test, i.e. prohibited and actionable.

27. Having said that, the structure of the *SCM Agreement* is such that it sets out highly compartmentalized sections on prohibited, actionable and non-actionable subsides. Analyses of adverse effects are specifically placed under Part III that deals with actionable subsidies only. As discussed above, establishment of a prohibited subsidy does not require any finding of adverse effect, but is contingent upon a finding of a mere existence. In that sense, when this Panel accounts and analyzes adverse effects caused by actionable subsidies, inclusion of adverse effects generated by prohibited subsidies would tend to enlarge adverse effects caused by actionable subsidies, if the former only adds to the latter. In other words, the highly compartmentalized nature of the *SCM Agreement* requires this Panel to form a precise opinion, where partition is possible, on the degree and nature of adverse effects caused by actionable subsidies alone, and such precision is vital for the subsidizing Member to "remove the adverse effects" under Art. 7.8 and for the complaining Member to take commensurate countermeasures under Arts. 7.9 and 7.10. Such a partitioning method is very much relevant to the issue of causation, as in cases where partition is possible, there should be no causal link between prohibited subsidies and adverse effects caused by actionable subsidies.

28. If, however, this Panel finds that a simple partition is not possible to exclude adverse effects generated by prohibited subsidies, due to the fact that such adverse effects compounds or amplifies adverse effects caused by actionable subsidies, the issue is more difficult. Prohibited subsidies may indeed have played a role in causing a compounding or amplification of adverse effects, caused by actionable subsidies in the first place. Such circumstances would necessitate a consideration of the totality of evidence before this Panel and a finding that best reflects a possible attribution of adverse effects to those only caused by actionable subsidies found. Such a finding, China submits, may have to be weighed against the crucial need to discourage the use of multiple types of subsidies that are not WTO compliant to create compounded adverse effects.

29. Question 53. Would a finding of serious prejudice under Article 5(c) of the *SCM Agreement* be determinative for a finding under Article XVI:1 of

the GATT 1994? Why or why not? What, if any, is the role of footnote 13 of the *SCM Agreement* in this context? All third parties

30. China believes that a finding of serious prejudice under Article 5(c) of the *SCM Agreement* would be determinative for a finding under Article XVI:1 of the GATT 1994.

31. Art. 5(c) of the *SCM Agreement* prohibits any Member against using any subsidy to cause serious prejudice to the interests of another Member. Instances of deemed existence and possible occurrence of serious prejudice are further enumerated under Art. 6 of the same agreement. Art. XVI:1 of GATT 1994, on the other hand, requires a subsidizing Member, to discuss, upon request, with the other contracting party or parties concerned, or with the Contracting Parties, the possibility of limiting the subsidization, in the event that its granting of subsidies causes or threatens to cause serious prejudice to the interests of any other contracting party while stopping short of listing those under Art. 6 of the *SCM Agreement.*

32. China believes possible difference, if any, between serious prejudice found under Art. 5(c) of the *SCM Agreement* and serious prejudice found under GATT Art. XVI:1, is effectively removed by footnote 13 of the *SCM Agreement*, which specifically provides:

> The term "serious prejudice to the interests of another Member" is used in this [SCM] Agreement in the same sense as it is used in paragraph 1 of Article XVI of GATT 1994, and includes threat of serious prejudice.

To interpret otherwise would clearly be contrary to the intent of the drafters of this footnote.

33. Question 55. In light of the fact that certain third parties have provided submissions about the price effect of claimed US subsidies, which Member or Members is, or are, the "other party" under Article 6.3(c) ("another Member") for the purposes of these proceedings? All third parties

34. China believes that any Member, the prices of whose like product (upland cotton for these proceedings), as supplied in the same market, at the same level of trade and at comparable times, are capable of being compared to the prices of the subsidized product for the purpose of determining whether significant price undercutting exists under Art. 6.3(c), is *another Member* for the purpose of Art. 6.3(c) of the *SCM Agreement*..

35. First, 6.3(c) of the *SCM Agreement* reads,

> Serious prejudice in the sense of paragraph (c) of Article 5 may arise in any case where one or several of the following apply: …
>
> (c) the effect of the subsidy is a significant price undercutting by the subsidized product as compared with the price of a like product of another Member in the same market or significant price suppression, price depression or lost sales in the same market.

36. Article 6.5 subsequently explains that

> For the purpose of paragraph 3(c), price undercutting shall include any case in which such price undercutting has been demonstrated through a comparison of prices of the subsidized product with prices of a non-subsidized like product supplied to the same market. The comparison shall be made at the same level of trade and at comparable times, due account being taken of any other factor affecting price comparability. However, if such a direct comparison is not possible, the existence of price undercutting may be demonstrated on the basis of export unit values.

37. Essentially, Art. 6.5 requires a comparison between prices of the subsidized product and prices of a *non-subsidized like product supplied to the same market* for the purpose of determining whether significant price undercutting exists under Art. 6.3(c). To ensure fairness and statistical meaningfulness of such a comparison, Art. 6.5 requires it to be made at the same level of trade and at comparable times, as well as any other factor affecting price comparability. No where does Art. 6.5 limit non-subsidized like product to only those from one country, e.g. the complaining party.

38. Second, specific references to the "complaining Member" is made in other paragraphs of this very Article 6. For instance, Article 6.7, reads

> Displacement or impediment resulting in serious prejudice shall not arise under paragraph 3 where any of the following circumstances exist during the relevant period:
>
> (a) prohibition or restriction on exports of the like product from *the complaining Member* (emphasis added) or on imports from the *complaining Member* (emphasis added) into the third country market concerned;...".

39. The same word "complaining Member" is specifically used from Para. (a) through to Para. (e) under Article 6.7. The above reference clearly suggests that for the purpose of these paragraphs, the drafters explicitly distinguished the like product from "the complaining Member" from the like product from other Members. Should the drafters have the same intent to make such a distinction under Article 6.3, they would have done so.

40. Based on the above interpretations, China believes that *another Member* under Art. 6.3 of the *SCM Agreement* shall include any Member, the prices of whose like product, upland cotton for these proceedings, as supplied in the same market, at the same level of trade and at comparable times, is capable of being compared to the prices of the subsidized product for the purpose of determining whether significant price undercutting exists under Art. 6.3(c).

41. Question 56. Please respond to the following questions concerning the relationship between Article XVI:3 of the GATT 1994, the disciplines on export subsidies and domestic support in the *Agreement on Agriculture* and the disciplines on prohibited export subsidies and actionable subsidies in Articles 3, 5(c) and 6.3(d) of the *SCM Agreement*. All third parties

(a) Are agricultural domestic support programmes challengeable under Article XVI:3 of the GATT 1994? How, if at all, is the title of Section B of Article XVI ("Additional provisions on *export subsidies*" (emphasis added)) relevant? How, if at all, are Articles 13 and 21.1, or any other provisions, of the *Agreement on Agriculture,* relevant?

42. In China's opinion, agricultural domestic support programmes are not challengeable under Article XVI:3 of GATT 1994.

43. Negotiating history of the current WTO agreements, being codification of the GATT Uruguay Round, as reported by scholars, indicates that the original Art. XVI of GATT 1947 contained only the first paragraph. Section B of Art. XVI and the interpretive note thereto were added by the *1955 Protocol Amending the Preamble and Part I and II of the Agreement* with an intent to outlaw export subsidies that results in subsidizing Member "having more than equitable share of the world export trade in that product"[19] only.[20] While the added article adopted such vague wordings as "any form of subsidy which operates to increase the export of any product", no where can any express effort to discipline domestic support be found.

44. The addition of Art. 11, entitled "Subsidies other than export subsidies" by the *1979 Agreement on Interpretation and Application of Article VI, XVI and XXIII of the General Agreement* (the "*Subsidies Code*")[21] is further proof that Art. XVI did not contemplate any discipline on domestic support. While not all Contracting Parties of GATT signed the *Subsidies Code*, it does represent the efforts of some GATT Contracting Parties

> [t]o apply fully and to interpret the provisions of Articles VI, XVI and XXIII of the General Agreement on Tariffs and Trade only with respect to subsidies and countervailing measures and to elaborate rules for their application in order to provide greater uniformity and certainty in their implementation.[22]

45. On the issue of subsidies, the *Subsidies Code* is structured to distinguish between export subsidies on certain primary (Art. 10, for the purpose of Art. XVI:3, GATT) and non-primary subsidies (Art. 9 and illustrative Annex) on the one hand, and "[s]ubsidies other than export subsidies" (Art. 11) on the other. Such a distinction represents consensus, at least amongst some GATT Contracting Parties, that GATT Art. XVI:3 only disciplines export subsidies *per se*.

46. In addition, in attempting to develop the "unlawfulness" of these "non-export subsidies", Art. 11(2) of the *Subsidies Code* only specified possible "injury to a domestic industry of another signatory", "serious prejudice to the interests of another signatory", nullification and impairment of "benefits accruing to another signatory under the General Agreement [of Tariffs and Trade] as well as adverse effect on "the conditions of normal competition", to the express exclu-

---

[19] Article XVI:3, GATT 1994.

[20] Terence P. Stewart (ed.), *the GATT Uruguay Round: a Negotiating History* (Kluwer Law and Taxation Publishers, 1993), p. 134.

[21] 26S/56.

[22] Preamble, the *Subsidies Code*.

sion of a GATT Art. XVI:3 action for "more than equitable share of world export trade". The ostensible omission of a GATT XVI:3 challenge against non-export subsides is again indication that GATT XVI:3 did not contemplate a challenge against non-export subsidies, which should include domestic support measures.

47. The *Agreement on Agriculture* of the WTO, while setting out object and quantitative disciplines on agricultural domestic supports, does not engage in a comprehensive and express definition of the term domestic support, except that it is granted in favour of domestic agricultural producers. Yet the agreement does treat domestic support and export subsidies in different sections. Art. 13, in addition, makes a symmetrical reference to the two concepts on equal footing. The polarized treatment lends support to a conclusion that the multilateral trade regime at the Uruguay Round sees a need to discipline agricultural domestic support measures. Given the progression of discipline development for agricultural domestic support and the loss of inequitable world export trade challenge in the *Agreement on Agriculture*, it appears to be a stretching of terms to interpret that Art. XVI:3 of GATT 1947 should contemplate a challenge against agricultural domestic support measures.

48. Language of Article 21.1 of the *Agreement on Agriculture* again supports the above opinion of China. The article governs the relationship of the provisions of GATT 1994 and the Agreement on Agriculture.[23] The Appellate Body, in its *EC – Bananas III* report, stated to the effect that the provisions of GATT 1994 apply to a matter except to the extent that the *Agreement on Agriculture* contains specific provisions dealing specifically with the same matter.[24]

49. Coming back to the text of GATT Art. XVI:3, as well as the general progression of multilateral trade regime on agricultural domestic support measures, specificity on domestic support discipline as provided under the *Agreement on Agriculture* clearly stands out and pales any possible equation of GATT Article XVI:3 to a discipline on agricultural domestic support.

(b) Are the requirements of Article XVI:3 of the GATT 1994 reflected in, developed by or subsumed by the requirements in Article 6.3(d) of the *SCM Agreement*, or in any other provisions of the covered agreements? Of what relevance, if any, is the Appellate Body Report in *US-FSC*, para. 117[25] here?

---

[23] Appellate Body Report, *European Communities – Regime for the Importation, Sale and Distribution of Bananas*, Appellate Body Report, WT/DS27/AB/R, DSR 1997:II, paras. 155-156.

[24] See *Supra*, para. 3.

[25] Original quote from the Appellate Body Report, WT/DS108/AB/R, para. 117:

> "... the provisions of the *SCM Agreement* do not provide explicit assistance as to the relationship between the export subsidy provisions of the *SCM Agreement* and Article XVI:4 of the GATT 1994. In the absence of any such specific textual guidance, we must determine the relationship between Articles 1.1(a)(1) and 3.1(a) of the *SCM Agreement* and Article XVI:4 of the GATT 1994 on the basis of the texts of the relevant provisions as a whole. It is clear from even a cursory examination of Article XVI:4 of the GATT 1994 that it differs very substantially from the subsidy provisions of the *SCM Agreement*, and, in particular, from the export subsidy provisions of both the *SCM Agreement* and the *Agreement on Agriculture*. First of all, the *SCM Agreement* contains an express definition of the term "subsidy" which is not contained in Article XVI:4. In fact, as we have observed previously, the *SCM*

(c) Of what relevance, if any, is the fact that the definition of "subsidy" in Article 1 of the *SCM Agreement* and the prohibition on subsidies contingent upon export in Article 3.1(a) were introduced in the Uruguay Round, but did not exist at the time that the GATT 1947 was negotiated?

50. Art. 6(3)(d), on the other hand, is a natural prolongation of the inequitable world export trade challenge made available by GATT Art. XVI:3 and further developed by the *Subsidies Code*. China believes that requirements of Art. XVI:3 of the GATT 1994 are reflected in and developed by requirements in Article 6.3(d) of the *SCM Agreement*.

51. GATT Art. XVI:3 is the first attempt by the multilateral trade system to seek avoidance of the clinching of "more than equitable share of world export trade in a primary product" by a Member granting "directly or indirectly any form of subsidy which operates to increase the export of any primary product from its territory". The article, led by the word "[a]ccordingly", grants Members the inequitable world export trade challenge to address concerns over possible "harmful effects", "undue disturbance" and hindrance to "the achievement of the objectives" of GATT cause by subsidies to primary products, as enumerated under the preceding article of XVI:2.

52. The *Subsidies Code* further defined "more than an equitable share of world export trade" as including

> any case in which the effect of an export subsidy granted by a signatory is to displace the exports of another signatory bearing in mind the developments on world markets.[26]

In addition to attempting to discipline subsidies to primary products, signatories to the *Subsidies Code* also agreed to a number of general provisions on subsidies, not necessarily limited to primary products. Adverse effects caused by subsidies, exemplified by injury to the domestic industry of another signatory, nullification or impairments to the benefits of another Member and serious prejudice to the

---

Agreement contains a broad package of new export subsidy disciplines that "go well beyond merely applying and interpreting Articles VI, XVI and XXIII of the GATT 1947". Next, Article XVI:4 prohibits export subsidies only when they result in the export sale of a product at a price lower than the "comparable price charged for the like product to buyers in the domestic market". In contrast, the *SCM Agreement* establishes a much broader prohibition against *any* subsidy which is "contingent upon export performance". To say the least, the rule contained in Article 3.1(a) of the *SCM Agreement* that all subsidies which are "contingent upon export performance" are prohibited is significantly different from a rule that prohibits only those subsidies which result in a lower price for the exported product than the comparable price for that product when sold in the domestic market. Thus, whether or not a measure is an export subsidy under Article XVI:4 of the GATT 1947 provides no guidance in determining whether that measure is a prohibited export subsidy under Article 3.1(a) of the *SCM Agreement*. Also, and significantly, Article XVI:4 of the GATT 1994 does not apply to "primary products", which include agricultural products. Unquestionably, the explicit export subsidy disciplines, relating to agricultural products, contained in Articles 3, 8, 9 and 10 of the *Agreement on Agriculture* must clearly take precedence over the *exemption* of primary products from export subsidy disciplines in Article XVI.4 of the GATT 1994."

[26] Para. 10:2(a), the *Subsidies Code*.

interests of another Members, were first introduced under Art. 8 of the *Subsidies Code* as indication of the "unlawfulness" of such subsidies. The very same standards were to be later adopted by Art. 5 of the *SCM Agreement* on actionable subsidies.

53. The concept of inequitable world export share caused by subsidies to primary products, on the other hand, was retained under Art. 6.3(d) of the SCM Agreement, with such changes as "world market share" to replace "share of world export trade" and the addition of a three year period to constitute "representative period" benchmark.

54. While China agrees that the requirements of GATT Art. XVI:3 are reflected in and developed by requirements in Article 6.3(d) of the *SCM Agreement*, prior Appellate Body reports have indicated that to the extent a specific WTO agreement conflict with the provisions of GATT 1994, the former shall prevail. In that respect, it is important to quote the Appellate Body in *Brazil – Desiccated Coconut*:

> The relationship between the GATT 1994 and the other goods agreements in Annex 1A is complex and must be examined on a case-by-case basis. Although the provisions of the GATT 1947 were incorporated into, and became a part of the GATT 1994, they are not the sum total of the rights and obligations of WTO Members concerning a particular matter. For example, with respect to subsidies on agricultural products, Articles II, VI and XVI of the GATT 1994 alone do not represent the total rights and obligations of WTO Members. The *Agreement on Agriculture* and the *SCM Agreement* reflect the latest statement of WTO Members as to their rights and obligations concerning agricultural subsidies. The general interpretative note to Annex 1A was added to reflect that the other goods agreements in Annex 1A, in many ways, represent a substantial elaboration of the provisions of the GATT 1994, and to the extent that the provisions of the other goods agreements conflict with the provisions of the GATT 1994, the provisions of the other goods agreements prevail. This does not mean, however, that the other goods agreements in Annex 1A, such as the *SCM Agreement*, supersede the GATT 1994. As the Panel has said:
>
>> ... the question for consideration is not whether the SCM Agreement supersedes Article VI of GATT 1994. Rather, it is whether Article VI creates rules which are separate and distinct from those of the SCM Agreement, and which can be applied without reference to that Agreement, or whether Article VI of GATT 1994 and the SCM Agreement repre-

> sent an inseparable package of rights and disciplines that must be considered in conjunction.[27]

55. The Appellate Body noted further that "[t]he relationship between the *SCM Agreement* and Article VI of GATT 1994 is set out in Articles 10 and 32.1 of the *SCM Agreement*."[28] Apart from the integrated structure of the *WTO Agreement* and the annexed agreements, the Appellate Body therefore focused on these two provisions of the *SCM Agreement*. The Appellate Body then explicitly agreed with the Panel's statement that:

> Article VI of GATT 1994 and the SCM Agreement represent a new and different package of rights and obligations, as among WTO Members, regarding the use of countervailing duties. Thus, Article VI and the respective SCM Agreements impose obligations on a potential user of countervailing duties, in the form of conditions that have to be fulfilled in order to impose a duty, but they also confer the right to impose a countervailing duty when those conditions are satisfied. The SCM Agreements do not merely impose additional substantive and procedural obligations on a potential user of countervailing measures. Rather, the SCM Agreements and Article VI together define, clarify and in some cases modify the whole package of rights and obligations of a potential user of countervailing measures.[29]

56. The Appellate Body then proceeded to find that:

> [C]ountervailing duties may only be imposed in accordance with Article VI of the GATT 1994 and the *SCM Agreement*. A countervailing duty being a specific action against a subsidy of another WTO Member, pursuant to Article 32.1, it can only be imposed "in accordance with the provisions of GATT 1994, as interpreted by this Agreement". The ordinary meaning of these provisions taken in their context leads us to the conclusion that the negotiators of the *SCM Agreement* clearly intended that, under the integrated *WTO Agreement*, countervailing duties may only be imposed in accordance with the provisions of Part V of the *SCM Agreement* and Article VI of the GATT 1994, taken together. If there is a conflict between the provisions of the *SCM Agreement* and Article VI of the GATT 1994, furthermore, the provisions of the *SCM Agreement* would prevail as a result of the general interpretative note to Annex 1A.
>
> ...

---

[27] Original Appellate Body quote, Panel Report on *Brazil – Desiccated Coconut, Brazil – Measures Affecting Desiccated coconut*, WT/DS22/R, adopted 20 March 1997, para. 227; Appellate Body Report, *Brazil – Measures Affecting Desiccated Coconut*, WT/DS22/AB/R, DSR 1997:I, p. 15.

[28] Appellate Body Report on *Brazil – Desiccated Coconut*, p. 16.

[29] Panel Report, *Brazil - -Desiccated Coconut, Brazil – Measures Affecting Desiccated Coconut*, WT/DS22/R, adopted 20 March 1997, para. 246, as upheld by the Appellate Body Report; Appellate Body Report on *Brazil – Desiccated Coconut*, p. 17.

> The fact that Article VI of the GATT 1947 could be invoked independently of the *Tokyo Round SCM Code* under the previous GATT system does not mean that Article VI of GATT 1994 can be applied independently of the *SCM Agreement* in the context of the WTO. The authors of the new WTO regime intended to put an end to the fragmentation that had characterized the previous system.[30]

57. China takes the above Appellate body statement to mean that Art. 32.1 of the *SCM Agreement*, being the linkage between Art. XVI:3 of GATT 1994 and Art. 6.3(d) of *SCM Agreement* in connection with the inequitable share of world market challenge, requires that the Art. 6.3(d) prevail over GATT Art. XVI:3. In other words, if this Panel were to find that the GATT provision in conflict with the Art. 6.3(d), a claim against agricultural export subsidies cannot be brought under GATT XVI:3, but should be brought as actionable subsidies under Art. 6.3(d) of the *SCM Agreement*; however, if this Panel does not find any conflict, agricultural export subsidies actionable under Art. 6.3(d) of the *SCM Agreement* shall not be precluded from being actionable under GATT XVI:3, which can only be logical interpretation of note 56 to the *SCM Agreement* as it applies to the relationship.

58. Conflicts or differences were obviously found by the Appellate Body in *US-FSC*. It found that Article XVI:4 of GATT 1994

> differs very substantially from the subsidy provisions of the *SCM Agreement*, and, in particular, from the export subsidy provisions of both the *SCM Agreement* and the *Agreement on* Agriculture.

Hence, "[u]nquestionably, the explicit export subsidy disciplines, relating to agricultural products, contained in Articles 3, 8, 9 and 10 of the Agreement on Agriculture must clearly take precedence over … the GATT 1994".

59. Such an interpretation is further supported the general interpretative note to Annex 1A, which provides to the effect that in the event of a conflict between a provision of the GATT 1994 and a provision of another agreement in Annex 1A, the latter shall prevail to the extent of the conflict.

60. This Panel's Question 56(c) is in fact answered by the quoted passage from the Appellate Body in *US-FSC*. When GATT 1947 was negotiated and codified, there was nothing in it that expressly defines the term "subsidy", or the term "export subsidy". Such definitions only came into WTO wording in the Uruguay Round in addition to the new and more comprehensive discipline on "prohibited subsidies" under the *SCM Agreement* and "domestic [agricultural] support" under the *Agreement on Agriculture*. The more explicit disciplines under the *SCM Agreement* and the *Agreement on Agriculture*, as noted by the Appellate Body in the quoted passage, being "the latest statement of WTO Members as to their rights and obligations concerning agricultural subsidies", clearly take precedence over any GATT 1994 provisions to the extent of direct conflict.

---

[30] Appellate Body Report on *Brazil – Desiccated Coconut*, pages 16 and 18.

61. China thanks this Panel for granting this opportunity to present its views on issues related to this proceeding, and hopes that this Panel will finds the above points helpful.

ANNEX J-17

REPLIES OF THE EUROPEAN COMMUNITIES TO THE QUESTIONS FROM THE PANEL

27 October 2003

QUESTIONS TO THE EC

Question 45

In relation to the term "same market" in Article 6.3 (c)of the SCM Agreement states in paragraph 10 of its oral statement that a "world market" cannot exist if there are significant trade barriers between Members. On the other hand, the Panel notes that in relation to cotton, the EC takes the position in paragraph 14 of its further submission that the term "same market" in Article 6.3(c) should be read to include the domestic market of the subsidising Member. In light of the fact that many domestic cotton markets, possibly including that of China, have significant trade barriers, how can the EC reconcile these two positions?

Reply

1. The question does not state correctly the views expressed by the EC. Contrary to what is said in the question, the EC did not state at paragraph 14 of its further submission that "the term '**same market**' in Article 6.3 **(c)** should be read to include the domestic market of the subsidising Member". Rather, the EC said in paragraphs 14-16 of its further submission that the term "**world market share"** in Article 6.3 **(d)** includes also the share of the domestic market of the subsidising Member. This reading of Article 6.3(d) is compatible with the view that the term "same market" in Article 6.3(c) may include the world market, where there is such a world market. On the other hand, there is no reason why Article 6.3(d) should apply only in those cases where it can be established that there is a world market. Rather the term "world market share" should be understood to mean, in that context, the aggregate of the shares in each of the relevant geographical markets.

2. Contrary also to what is stated in the question, the EC has taken no position on the issue of whether, "in relation to cotton", there is a world market for the purposes of Article 6.3 (c). It might well be that, as suggested in the question, there is no world market for cotton, with the consequence that the price effects mentioned in Article 6.3(c) would have to be observed separately within each distinct national or regional market and/or in the residual "rest-of-the world" market. This is a factual matter on which the EC does not wish to express any views.

Question 46

Should the Panel prefer a concept of allocation of the benefit of subsidies to later years, to a concept of fully expensing subsidies to the year in which the benefit was provided?

Reply

3. Whether a subsidy should be "allocated" or "expensed" depends on the nature of the subsidy concerned, having regard to relevant criteria, such as those outlined at paragraph 11 of the EC's further submission.

4. The EC is not expressing any views on the largely factual question of whether the subsidies at issue should be "allocated" or "expensed". The point made by the EC was simply that Brazil cannot have it both ways. If the subsidies are fully expensed to the marketing year where they are granted, as Brazil appears to have done, it is contradictory to claim at the same time that they continue to provide benefits beyond that marketing year.

Question 47

In the EC further submission, it is said that significantly different conditions of competition in regional markets may prevent the Panel from arriving at the conclusion that there is a world market. Is the payment of a subsidy a "condition of competition" and, if so, how should that impact upon the Panel's analysis?

Reply

5. To be precise, the EC's position is that there is no world market for the purposes of Article 6.3 (c) where the existence of trade barriers has the consequence that the conditions of competition, and in particular the price levels prevailing in one geographical area are significantly different from those prevailing in another geographical area.

6. Unlike, for example, import duties, quotas or transport costs, subsidies do not, of themselves, insulate the prices in one geographical area from those in other areas and, therefore, do not lead to existence of separate geographical markets.

QUESTIONS TO ALL THIRD PARTIES

Question 49

What is the meaning and effect of the introductory phrase of Article 3 of the SCM Agreement ("Except as provided in the Agreement on Agriculture...")?

Reply

7. The introductory phrase of Article 3 makes it clear that subsidies which would be inconsistent with Article 3.1, but which are provided consistently with

the export competition provisions of the *Agreement on Agriculture* are not prohibited.

Question 50

According to its revised timetable, the Panel will issue its report to the parties after the end of the 2003 calendar year. Does this have any impact on "exempt[ion] from actions" under Article 13(b)(ii) and 13(c)(ii) of the Agreement on Agriculture?

Reply

8. No.

9. In the first place, and contrary to the Panel's implicit suggestion, it is still an open question, in view of the definition of the terms "implementation period" and "year" in Article 1 (f) and (i), respectively, of the *Agreement on Agriculture*, whether the provisions cited in the question will cease to apply by the end of the 2003 calendar year or at a subsequent date during 2004.

10. In any event, the Panel would be precluded by its terms of reference from taking into account the consequences of the expiry of those provisions. The "matter" before the Panel was defined at the time where the DSB agreed to the establishment of the panel and cannot be modified in the course of the proceedings.[1] In accordance with its terms of reference, the Panel must consider the measures in dispute as they existed when the matter was referred to the DSB, on the basis of the facts existing at that moment and in the light of the WTO provisions that were relevant at that time.

11. Brazil's claim is that the measures at issue were WTO inconsistent at the time when the matter was referred to the DSB. The Panel would go beyond its terms of reference if it were to decide that the measures are WTO inconsistent at a subsequent moment, as a result of the expiry of the peace clause. If, on the other hand, the Panel were to apply WTO provisions that will become relevant only after the expiry of the peace clause to measures and facts as they existed at the time when the matter was referred to the DSB, it would be making an impermissible retroactive application of such provisions.

Question 51

How should the concept of specificity – and, in particular, the concept of specificity to "an enterprise or industry or group of enterprises or industries" - in Article 2 of the SCM Agreement apply to subsidies in respect of agricultural commodities? Please answer the following questions, citing the principles in Article 2 of the SCM Agreement:

(a) is a subsidy in respect of all agricultural, but not other, products specific?

[1] See e.g. Panel report on *India – Measures Affecting the Automotive Sector*, WT/DS1465/R, WT/DS175/R, at para. 7.26.

(b) **is a subsidy in respect of all agricultural crops (i.e. but not to other agricultural commodities, such as livestock) specific?**

(c) **is a subsidy in respect of certain identified agricultural products specific?**

(d) **is a subsidy in respect of upland cotton, but not other products, specific?**

(e) **is a subsidy in respect of a certain proportion of the value of total US commodities (or total US agricultural commodities) specific?**

(f) **is a subsidy in respect of a certain proportion of total US farmland specific?**

Reply

A subsidy granted to an economic operator which does not require any production of agricultural products, and in which the subsidy may be used for any purpose, does not appear, to the EC, to be specific in the sense of Article 2.1(a)

Question 52

The Panel notes that different remedies are available in respect of prohibited and actionable subsidies under Article 4.7 and 7.8 of the SCM Agreement. If the Panel were to conclude that a subsidy was prohibited and were to make a recommendation under Article 4.7 of the SCM Agreement to withdraw the subsidy without delay, can the Panel:

(a) **also conclude that the same subsidy had resulted in adverse effects to the interests of another Member? If so, what would be the value of such a conclusion in terms of the settlement of the matter before the Panel?**

Reply

12. Yes. There is nothing in the *SCM Agreement* which prevents a complaining party from claiming that a subsidy is prohibited under Part II and, in addition, causes "adverse effects" under Part III.

13. A finding that a prohibited subsidy causes "serious prejudice" may still be relevant in so far as at it may be possible for the subsidising Member to withdraw the export or local content condition attached to the subsidy, which causes its prohibition, while maintaining the subsidy and its adverse effects.

(b) **take into account the effects of the interaction of those prohibited subsidies with other, allegedly, actionable subsidies? If so, how is this relevant to the issue of causation under Article 5 of the SCM Agreement?**

14. In a situation where the complaining party has made no claim that a prohibited subsidy causes adverse effects under Part III, it would be necessary to establish the causal link between the actionable subsidies and the adverse effects. However, the EC understands that this situation does not arise in the present dis-

pute, because Brazil claims that all the allegedly prohibited subsidies cause adverse effects.

Question 53

Would a finding of serious prejudice under Article 5(c) of the SCM Agreement be determinative for a finding under Article XVI:1 of the GATT 1994? Why or why not? What, if any, is the role of footnote 13 of the SCM Agreement in this context?

Reply

15. Footnote 13 states that the term "serious prejudice" is used in the *SCM Agreement* in the same sense as in Article XVI:1 of the GATT. Therefore, it seems that a finding that a subsidy causes "serious prejudice" under Article 5(c) of the *SCM Agreement* would have the necessary implication that the same subsidy causes also "serious prejudice" in the sense of Article XVI:1 of the GATT, in so far as that provision can be applied on its own.

Question 54

Are US cotton producers able to cover the fixed and variable costs without subsidies? Please provide substantiating evidence. Of what relevance is this, if any, to Brazil's actionable subsidy claims ?

Reply

16. The EC has not taken any position on the factual issue raised in the question.

17. In principle, whether or not a producer is able to cover all its costs without subsidies is not, as such, directly relevant, let alone determinative of whether the subsidies cause adverse effects.

Question 55

In light of the fact that certain third parties have provided submissions about the price effect of claimed US subsidies, which Member or Members is, or are, the "other party" under Article 6.3(c) ("another Member") for the purposes of these proceedings?

Reply

18. The EC agrees with the United States that, for the purposes of Article 6.3(c), only the price effects on the "products" of Brazil are relevant. (See US Further Submission, para. 86 and the case law cited therein)

Question 56

Please respond to the following questions concerning the relationship between Article XVI:3 of the GATT 1994, the disciplines on export subsidies and domestic support in the Agreement on Agriculture and the disciplines

on prohibited export subsidies and actionable subsidies in Articles 3, 5(c) and 6.3(d) of the SCM Agreement.

(a) Are agricultural domestic support programmes challengeable under Article XVI:3 of the GATT 1994? How, if at all, is the title of Section B of Article XVI ("Additional provisions on export subsidies" (emphasis added)) relevant? How, if at all, are Articles 13 and 21.1, or any other provisions, of the Agreement on Agriculture, relevant?

(b) Are the requirements of Article XVI:3 of the GATT 1994 reflected in, developed by or subsumed by the requirements in Article 6.3(d) of the SCM Agreement, or in any other provisions of the covered agreements? Of what relevance, if any, is the Appellate Body Report in US-FSC, para. 117[2] here?

---

[2] WT/DS108/AB/R, para 117:

> "... the provisions of the *SCM Agreement* do not provide explicit assistance as to the relationship between the export subsidy provisions of the *SCM Agreement* and Article XVI:4 of the GATT 1994. In the absence of any such specific textual guidance, we must determine the relationship between Articles 1.1(a)(1) and 3.1(a) of the *SCM Agreement* and Article XVI:4 of the GATT 1994 on the basis of the texts of the relevant provisions as a whole. It is clear from even a cursory examination of Article XVI:4 of the GATT 1994 that it differs very substantially from the subsidy provisions of the *SCM Agreement*, and, in particular, from the export subsidy provisions of both the *SCM Agreement* and the *Agreement on Agriculture*. First of all, the *SCM Agreement* contains an express definition of the term "subsidy" which is not contained in Article XVI:4. In fact, as we have observed previously, the *SCM Agreement* contains a broad package of new export subsidy disciplines that "go well beyond merely applying and interpreting Articles VI, XVI and XXIII of the GATT 1947". Next, Article XVI:4 prohibits export subsidies only when they result in the export sale of a product at a price lower than the "comparable price charged for the like product to buyers in the domestic market." In contrast, the *SCM Agreement* establishes a much broader prohibition against *any* subsidy which is "contingent upon export performance". To say the least, the rule contained in Article 3.1(a) of the *SCM Agreement* that all subsidies which are "contingent upon export performance" are prohibited is significantly different from a rule that prohibits only those subsidies which result in a lower price for the exported product than the comparable price for that product when sold in the domestic market. Thus, whether or not a measure is an export subsidy under Article XVI:4 of the GATT 1947 provides no guidance in determining whether that measure is a prohibited export subsidy under Article 3.1(a) of the *SCM Agreement*. Also, and significantly, Article XVI:4 of the GATT 1994 does not apply to "primary products", which include agricultural products. Unquestionably, the explicit export subsidy disciplines, relating to agricultural products, contained in Articles 3, 8, 9 and 10 of the *Agreement on Agriculture* must clearly take precedence over the *exemption* of primary products from export subsidy disciplines in Article XVI:4 of the GATT 1994."

(c) Of what relevance, if any, is the fact that the definition of "subsidy" in Article 1 of the SCM Agreement and the prohibition on subsidies contingent upon export in Article 3.1(a) were introduced in the Uruguay Round, but did not exist at the time that the GATT 1947 was negotiated?

Reply

19. Article XVI:3 of the GATT has been elaborated in Article 6.3(d) of the *SCM Agreement*, with the consequence that it cannot be applied independently from Part III of the SCM Agreement, just like Article VI of the GATT cannot be applied independently from Part V of the *SCM Agreement.*[3] Indeed, if Article XVI:3 could be applied on its own, the additional requirements provided for in Article 6.3(d) and related provisions, such as Article 6.7, would be rendered largely redundant.

20. By its own terms, Article XVI:3 is concerned exclusively with "export subsidies". However, as noted by the Appellate Body in the passage of the *FSC* report mentioned in the question, the scope of the notion of export subsidy in Article XVI differs from the scope of the same term in the *SCM Agreement* and in the *Agreement on Agriculture*. It is conceivable, therefore, that one and the same measure may be at the same time an "export subsidy" in the sense of Article XVI:3 and "domestic support" within the meaning of the *Agreement on Agriculture*. This is not saying that the *Agreement on Agriculture* and Article XVI:3 can apply simultaneously to the same measure. Where a measure is subject to the rules on domestic support of the *Agreement on Agriculture*, those rules excludes the application of Article XVI:3 to the same measure, in accordance with Article 21.1 of the *Agreement on Agriculture* (irrespective of whether Article XVI:3 can be applied independently from the *SCM Agreement*.)

21. This interpretation is confirmed by Article 13 of the *Agreement on Agriculture*. It would be odd if the peace clause exempted export subsidies from action under Article XVI:3, but not domestic support, which is assumed to have less pernicious trade effects. Clearly, if the drafters of the peace clause did not deem necessary to exempt domestic support from action under Article XVI:3 it is because they considered that this provision did not apply to domestic support pursuant to Article 21.1 of the *Agreement on Agriculture*.

---

[3] Cf. Panel and Appellate Body reports, *Brazil – Measures Affecting Desiccated Coconuts*, WT/DS22/R and WT/DS22/AB/R.

ANNEX J-18

ANSWER TO PANEL QUESTION TO INDIA
27 October 2003

Question 48

In the further submission of India, it is stated that "there is "no obligation under the *SCM Agreement* to demonstrate serious prejudice separately after establishing that one of the effects of a subsidy listed under Article 6.3 applies, as the effects listed in Article 6.3 themselves equate to serious prejudice". How does this view relate to Article 6.3(d), which appears to contain no element of degree? India

Reply

India presumes that by 'element of degree' the Panel means the 'intensity or amount' of the effects of the subsidy as enumerated in Article 6.3 of the SCM Agreement. India notes that for serious prejudice to arise, in respect of only one out of the four effects of the subsidy in Article 6.3, has the intensity of the effect been specified. This is in respect of the effect of the subsidy in Article 6.3 (c) wherein the 'intensity or amount' of price undercutting, price suppression or price depression has been qualified by 'significant'. Thus, for serious prejudice to arise in case of price undercutting, price suppression or price depression, such effects should be significant. What can constitute 'significant' would vary from case to case. India is of the view that the other cases of effect of the subsidy specified in paragraphs 3 (a), 3(b) and 3 (d) of Article 6 contain no element of degree.

India fails to see how the absence of any element of degree in paragraphs 3 (a), 3(b) and 3 (d) of Article 6 results in the complaining Member being separately required to prove that the prejudice is indeed serious even after having established that one of these effects exists. If the drafters had intended that the complaining Member should separately establish that the prejudice caused by the effects of the subsidy was serious they would have defined the requirements for this purpose. The SCM Agreement contains no such requirement. India is, therefore, of the view that there is no obligation under the *SCM Agreement* to demonstrate serious prejudice separately after establishing that one of the effects of a subsidy listed under Article 6.3 applies.

ANNEX J-19

RESUMED FIRST SESSION OF THE FIRST SUBSTANTIVE MEETING OF THE PANEL NEW ZEALAND ANSWERS TO QUESTIONS FROM THE PANEL TO THIRD PARTIES

14 October 2003

Q49. What is the meaning and effect of the introductory phrase of Article 3 of the SCM Agreement ("Except as provided in the Agreement on Agriculture ...")? All third parties

This phrase refers to provisions in the *Agreement on Agriculture* that provide specific exception from Article 3 of the *SCM Agreement*. New Zealand does not agree that any such exception exists in the *Agreement on Agriculture* that would authorise use of local content subsidies contrary to Article 3.1(b) of the *SCM Agreement,* as argued by the United States.[1] There is no basis upon which to claim that the *Agreement on Agriculture* gives Members a right to use whatever domestic support they wish with complete impunity from action under other WTO Agreements.

Q50. According to its revised timetable, the Panel will issue its report to the parties after the end of the 2003 calendar year. Does this have any impact on "exemp[tion] from actions" under Article 13(b)(ii) and 13(c)(ii) of the Agreement on Agriculture? All third parties

No. Brazil has not claimed that the implementation period in Article 13 has expired. It has claimed that the provision of Articles 13(b) and (c) have not been respected.

Q51. How should the concept of specificity – and, in particular, the concept of specificity to "an enterprise or industry or group of enterprises or industries" – in Article 2 of the SCM Agreement apply to subsidies in respect of agricultural commodities ? Please answer the following questions, citing the principles in Article 2 of the SCM Agreement. All third parties

New Zealand agrees with Brazil that the ordinary meaning, context and object and purpose of Article 2.1(a) of the *SCM Agreement* confirm that subsidies that are available to discrete segments of an economy or to only particular industries are specific. New Zealand considers that Brazil has demonstrated that each of the subsidies provided by the United States to upland cotton are specific within the meaning of Article 2.

Whether or not a subsidy is specific within the terms of Article 2, with the exception of prohibited subsidies which are deemed specific by Article 2.3, requires examination of the particular features of the subsidy at issue, including factual information about the actual usage of the subsidy and not simply its avai-

[1] *United States – Subsidies on Upland Cotton*, Further Submission of the United States, 30 September 2003, para 167.

lability. Thus in relation to the general scenarios outlined below only general responses are possible.

(a) is a subsidy in respect of all agricultural, but not other, products specific?

New Zealand does not consider that this question is relevant to this dispute as none of the subsidies at issue are provided on the same terms to all agricultural products.

(b) is a subsidy in respect of all agricultural crops (ie but not to other agricultural commodities, such as livestock) specific?

Yes such a subsidy would be specific, because access to the subsidy is explicitly limited to certain enterprises within the meaning of Article 2.1(a), specifically to producers of agricultural crops.

(c) is a subsidy in respect of certain identified agricultural products specific?

Yes, because it is specific to producers of certain agricultural products and is thus explicitly limited to certain enterprises within the meaning of Article 2.1(a).

(d) is a subsidy in respect of upland cotton, but not other products, specific?

Yes, because it is specific to producers of one product and is thus explicitly limited to certain enterprises within the meaning of Article 2.1(a).

(e) is a subsidy in respect of a certain proportion of the value of the total US commodities (or total US agricultural commodities) specific?

It is not clear from the question what kind of subsidy is being referred to, and, as noted in New Zealand's general comments on this question, whether or not a subsidy is specific within the terms of Article 2 of the *SCM Agreement* requires examination of the particular features of the subsidy at issue. To the extent that the subsidy referred to in the question is limited to certain enterprises (as suggested by the fact that the subsidy is provided only in respect of a certain proportion of the total value of United States commodities or agricultural commodities) it would be specific within the meaning of Article 2.1(a).

(f) is a subsidy in respect of a certain proportion of total US farmland specific?

See New Zealand's answer to (e) above.

Q52. The Panel notes that different remedies are available in respect of prohibited and actionable subsidies under Article 4.7 and 7.8 of the SCM Agreement. If the Panel were to conclude that a subsidy was prohibited and were to make a recommendation under Article 4.7 of the SCM Agreement to withdraw the subsidy without delay, can the Panel:

(a) also conclude that the same subsidy had resulted in adverse effects to the interests of another Member? If so, what would be the value of

such a conclusion in terms of the settlement of the matter before the Panel? All third parties

A Panel may conclude that a prohibited subsidy had resulted in adverse effects to the interests of another Member. The chapeau of Article 5 of the *SCM Agreement* refers to "any subsidy referred to in paragraphs 1 and 2 of Article 1". Reference is made in paragraph 2 of Article 1 to subsidies being subject to the provisions of Part III only if they are specific in accordance with Article 2. Article 2.3 deems any subsidy falling under the provisions of Article 3, ie prohibited subsidies, to be "specific". Thus a prohibited subsidy may also be subject to the provisions of Part III of the *SCM Agreement*. It is therefore open to a Panel to conclude that a prohibited subsidy resulted in adverse effects to the interests of another Member.

The value of such conclusion in terms of the settlement of the matter before the Panel is to clarify the adverse effects that must be removed by the subsidising Member, albeit that a subsidising Member does not have the option of removing the adverse effects attributable to prohibited subsidies other than by withdrawing the subsidy without delay.

(b) take into account the effects of the interaction of those prohibited subsidies with other, allegedly, actionable subsidies? If so, how is this relevant to the issue of causation under Article 5 of the SCM Agreement? All third parties

A Panel may take into account the effects of the interaction of those prohibited subsidies with other actionable subsidies. For example, actionable subsidies could operate to neutralise the effect of removal of the prohibited subsidy, as would likely be the case in respect of removal of the Step 2 export payments. Removal of this prohibited export subsidy would be likely to lead to a decline in United States exports and thus lower the United States domestic price for upland cotton. However lower prices for upland cotton producers would trigger increased marketing loan deficiency payments that could in turn boost exports and thus maintain the adverse effect of the United States subsidies.

It is therefore important to consider the interaction of the various types of subsidies at issue and look at their collective effect. However no attribution of the effects to either prohibited or actionable subsidies is needed, because there is no conflict between the remedies for prohibited subsidies and actionable subsidies. To the extent that the subsidies causing serious prejudice to the interests of other Members include prohibited subsidies, the subsidising Member must withdraw them without delay, as they do not have the option available in respect of actionable subsidies of maintaining the subsidy so long as the adverse effect is removed.

Q53. Would a finding of serious prejudice under Article 5(c) of the SCM Agreement be determinative for a finding under Article XVI:1 of the GATT 1994? Why or why not? What, if any, is the role of footnote 13 of the SCM Agreement in this context? All third parties

A finding of serious prejudice under Article 5(c) of the *SCM Agreement* would be determinative for a finding under Article XVI:1 of the GATT 1994 because serious prejudice is used in the same sense in Article 5(c) as it is in Article XVI:1. Footnote 13 explicitly clarifies this.

Q54. Are US cotton producers able to cover the fixed and variable costs without subsidies? Please provide substantiating evidence. Of what relevant is this, if any, to Brazil's actionable subsidy claims? All third parties

Without subsidies United States cotton producers would not be covering their full costs of production and so would be making losses over the longer term. Evidence for this has been provided by Brazil in Exhibits Bra-7 and Bra-205. For example in 1999, 2000 and 2001 the USDA estimated that United States cotton producers total costs exceed the value of production by 173, 142 and 259 dollars per planted acre respectively, as shown in "US cotton production costs and returns 1997-2001".[2]

Accordingly the subsidies mean that United States production is higher than it otherwise would be. As Professor Sumner's econometric work shows, without subsidies US production over 1999-2002 would have been an average of 28.7 per cent lower than actual US production[3] and as a consequence United States exports would have declined on average by 41.2 per cent between MY 1999-2002[4] and world prices would have been an average of 12.6 per cent higher. This evidence thus supports Brazil's claim that the United States subsidies have caused serious prejudice to Brazil's interests and threaten to cause serious prejudice to Brazil's interests in the future.

Q55. In light of the fact that certain third parties have provided submissions about the price effect of claimed US subsidies, which Member or Members is, or are, the "other party" under Article 6.3(c) ("another Member") for the purposes of these proceedings? All third parties

Brazil is the "other party" in the context of Article 5(c). But that does not mean that other Members too cannot be suffering the serious prejudice through the use of the subsidies at issue by the United States. Indeed the Oral Statement of Benin to the Panel[5] makes it clear that this is the case.

Q56. Please respond to the following questions concerning the relationship between Article XVI:3 of the GATT 1994, the disciplines on export subsidies and domestic support in the Agreement on Agriculture and the disciplines on prohibited export subsidies and actionable subsidies in Articles 3, 5 and 6.3 (d) of the SCM Agreement. All third parties.

(a) Are agricultural domestic support programmes challengeable under Article XVI:3 of the GATT 1994? How, if at all, is the title of Section B of Article XVI ("Additional provisions on *export subsidies*" (em-

---

2 Exhibit BRA 7.

3 *United States – Subsidies on Upland Cotton,* Brazil's Further Submission to the Panel, 9 September 2003, para 105.

4 *Ibid.*

5 Oral Statement of Benin, 8 October 2003.

phasis added) relevant? How, if at all, are Articles 13 and 21.1, or any other provisions, of the Agreement on Agriculture relevant?

Agricultural domestic support programmes are challengeable under GATT 1994 Article XVI:3 to the extent that they meet the requirements of that Article, including, for example, that they must provide a subsidy that "operates to increase the export of any primary product from its territory".

The title of Section B is relevant in that it reflects the narrower scope of Section B vis-à-vis Section A. Section B addresses "Additional Provisions on Export Subsidies", whereas Section A is broader and addresses "Subsidies in General" – it includes subsidies that operate to reduce imports of any product into the territory of the subsidising Member. The term "export subsidies" in the particular context of GATT Article XVI is not defined, but can be given meaning by the scope of paragraph 3 which applies to "any form of subsidy which operates to increase the export of any primary product" and is thus a broader definition than "contingent ... upon export" found in the *SCM Agreement*.

Article 21.1 of the *Agreement on Agriculture*, which provides that GATT 1994 must be applied subject to the *Agreement*, is relevant in so far as it clarifies that in the event of legal conflict the provisions of the *Agreement on Agriculture* apply. During the implementation period Article 13 of the *Agreement on Agriculture* provides exemption from actions based on specific GATT 1994 provisions, subject to certain criteria being met. Article 13 exempts domestic support measures from action based on Article XVI:1 only if such measures do not grant support in excess of that decided during the 1992 marketing year.

Brazil has brought forward evidence to demonstrate that the subsidies at issue operate to increase United States exports of upland cotton and that they have been applied by the US in a manner that has resulted in the United States having a "more than equitable share of the world export trade" within the meaning of Article XVI:3 and therefore cause serious prejudice within the meaning of Article XVI:1.

(b) Are the requirements of Article XVI:3 of the GATT 1994 reflected in, developed by or subsumed by the requirements in Article 6.3(d) of the SCM Agreement, or in any other provisions of the covered agreements? Of what relevance, if any, is the Appellate Body Report in US-FSC, para 117 here?

Article 6.3(d) of the *SCM Agreement* elaborates on one specific aspect of the disciplines on subsidies in GATT Article XVI:3, and that is in relation to the situation where a subsidy, as defined in the *SCM Agreement*, results in an increase in the world market share of the subsidising Member in the particular subsidised product. However GATT Article XVI:3 addresses a broader situation – where the result of the application of the subsidies is that the subsidising Member has a "more than equitable share" of the world export trade in the product.

A Member challenging a subsidy need not demonstrate that the subsidising Member's share of the world market has necessarily increased. For example, a Member may apply a subsidy that increases its exports of a product in order to simply maintain its market share. "But for" that subsidy, relevant economic factors might have meant that a Member's exports should in fact have declined. Therefore Article 6.3(d) of the *SCM Agreement* covers one specific aspect of how a "more than equitable share" of the world market might manifest itself but not all such situations.

As such the situation is distinguishable from *US-FSC*[6] in relation to GATT Article XVI:4 where the Appellate Body found that the narrow prohibition in Article XVI:4 had been entirely subsumed by Article 3.1(a) of the *SCM Agreement*.

(c) **Of what relevance, if any, is the fact that the definition of "subsidy" in Article 1 of the SCM Agreement and the prohibition on subsidies contingent upon export in Article 3.1(a) were introduced in the Uruguay Round, but did not exist at the time that the GATT 1947 was negotiated?**

See New Zealand's answer to Questions (a) and (b) above.

6 Appellate Body Report, *United States – Tax Treatment for "Foreign Sales Corporation"*, WT/DS108/AB/R, adopted 20 March 2000

ANNEX J-20

RESPONSES TO QUESTIONS FROM THE PANEL FOR THIRD PARTIES THE SEPARATE CUSTOMS TERRITORY OF TAIWAN, PENGHU, KINMEN AND MATSU

27 October 2003

Q49. About the meaning and effect of the introductory phrase of Article 3 of the SCM Agreement.

A: The introductory phrase of Article 3 of the SCM Agreement "Except as provided in the Agreement on Agriculture, the following subsidies, within the meaning of Article 1, shall be prohibited" has the meaning that if there is different provision in the Agreement on Agriculture (AoA) with regard to the subsidies listed in Article 3 of the SCM Agreement, the AoA provision shall prevail. In other words, even if a subsidy is specific within the meaning of Article 1 of the SCM Agreement, and even if it is a subsidy contigent upon export performance or a subsidy contigent upon the use of domestic over imported goods, it is still not within the scope of prohibition under Article 3 of the SCM Agreement. The effect of such agricultural subsidy shall be decided by the AoA.

The critical point here is whether it is "provided in the Agreement on Agriculture". In this regard, Article 8 of the AoA is relevant. Article 8 provides that: "Each Member undertakes not to provide export subsidies otherwise than in conformity with this Agreement and with the commitments as specified in that Member's Schedule." The AoA, at this current stage, only requires reduction of such subsidy, not the elimination of such subsidy. In other words, suppose the subsidy is in conformity with the AoA and with the commitments as specified in the Members' Schedule, it should be allowed by the AoA and thus would not be prohibited under the SCM Agreement according to the introductory phrase of Article 3 of the SCM Agreement.

Q50. About the impact of the revised timetable to issue the Panel report after the end of the 2003 calendar year on the "exempt[ion] from actions" under Articles 13(b)(ii) and 13(c)(ii) of the AoA.

A: We have no comments on this question.

Q51. About the concept of specificity in Article 2 of the SCM Agreement applying to subsidies in respect of agricultural commodities.

A: Article 2.1 of the SCM Agreement provides that "In order to determine whether a subsidy, as defined in paragraph 1 of Article 1, is specific to an enterprise or industry or group of enterprises or industries (referred to in this Agreement as 'certain enterprises') within the jurisdiction of the granting authority, the following principles shall apply:..." Thus, when considering the answers below, the principles set forth in Article 2.1 must also be borne in mind.

Also, the basic reason for excluding "non-specific subsidies" from being prohibited should be that the subsidies are generally available and no competitive advantage is provided to a particular sector or some specific sectors. If there is competitive advantage provided to one or more sectors with the effect of excluding other sectors from receiving the advantages, it should be considered as specific.

Our view is that the concept if specificity applies to the agriculture sector as follows:

(a) *All agricultural products*: not specific. The competitive advantage is provided to all agricultural products. No agricultural products are excluded.

(b) *All agricultural crops*: specific. Although the coverage is broad, some agricultural products are excluded.

(c) *Certain identified agricultural products*: specific. Apparently it excludes a large portion of products.

(d) *Upland cotton*: specific. It excludes all other products and only gives advantage to one product.

(e) *Certain proportion of the value of total US commodities or total US agricultural commodities*: not specific. No commodities or agricultural commodities are excluded.

(f) *Certain proportion of total US farmland*: not specific, as long as farmland is not restricted to that producing certain commodities.

Q52. About different remedies available in respect of prohibited and actionable subsidies.

A(a) The SCM Agreement explicitly divides subsidies into three categories, and Part II and Part III are designed to deal with different categories of subsidies. If a subsidy falls within "Part II Prohibited Subsidies", it would not be falling within "Part III Actionable Subsidies". Thus, it is unthinkable that if the Panel were to conclude, for example, that a subsidy was prohibited and were to make a recommendation under Article 4.7 of the SCM Agreement, it would also have to decide whether the same subsidy had resulted in adverse effects to the interest of another Member.

(b) For the same reason, the Panel should not take into account the interactive effects of those prohibited subsidies with other subsidies.

Q53. About the determinativeness of a finding under the SCM Agreement for a finding under GATT 1994

A: Footnote 13 of the SCM Agreement explains that "The term 'serious prejudice to the interests of another Member' is used in this Agreement in the same sense as it is used in paragraph 1 of Article XVI of GATT 1994, and includes threat of serious prejudice." Although there is no same provision in Article XVI of the GATT 1994, the real intent of the WTO Members should be to harmonize the meaning and concept of the same phrase where it appears in different agreements. It would also be reasonable to interpret the same phrase in the same manner, unless there is strong reason for not doing so. Our view, therefore, would be that if there is a finding of serious prejudice under Article 5(c) of the SCM

Agreement, it should be *de facto* determinative for a finding under Article XVI:1 of the GATT 1994.

Q54. About the evidence of US cotton producers to cover or not to cover the fixed and variable costs without subsidies.

A: We do not have information available on this.

Q55. About "another Member" of Article 6.3(c).

A: We do not claim that we are "another Member" in the sense of Article 6.3(c) of the SCM Agreement.

Q56. About the relationship between Article XVI:3 of the GATT 1994, the disciplines on export subsidies and domestic support in the AoA and the disciplines on prohibited export subsidies and actionable subsidies in Article 3, 5(c) and 6.3(d) of the SCM Agreement.

A(a) Agricultural domestic support should not be challengeable under Article XVI:3 of the GATT 1994. Although the second sentence "grants directly or indirectly any form of subsidy which operates to increase the export of any primary product from its territory" seems to be broad enough to include domestic subsidies, this second sentence still comes after the introductory sentence, which requires Members to avoid the use of subsidies on the export of primary products. Also paragraph 3 of Article XVI of the GATT 1994 is under the title "Section B - Additional Provisions on Export Subsidies". There is no reason why the provisions in paragraph 3 should not be limited to export subsidies. Otherwise, the title would become meaningless and redundant.

(b) Paragraph 117 of the Appellate Body Report in *US-FSC* is an appropriate interpretation of the relationship between the definition of subsidies and export subsidies in Articles 1.1(a)(1) and 3.1(a) of the SCM Agreement on the one hand and export subsidies in Article XVI:4 of the GATT 1994 on the other. However, it does not have relevancy in deciding the relationship between domestic subsidies and export subsidies. The requirements of Article XVI:3 of the GATT 1994 are imposed on export subsidies, as explained above, while Article 6.3(d) of the SCM Agreement is about non-export subsidies. Thus, the requirements of Article XVI:3 of the GATT 1994 are neither reflected in, nor developed by or subsumed by the requirements in Article 6.3(d) of the SCM Agreement.

(c) Under the principle set forth by the above-mentioned Paragraph 117 of the Appellate Body Report in *US-FSC*, if there is conflict between Article XVI of the GATT 1994 and the AoA, the AoA must take precedence over the GATT 1994. Based on the same principle, the SCM Agreement should take precedence over the GATT 1994 to the extent that there is conflict. However, with regard to the definition of subsidy in Article 1 of the SCM Agreement and the prohibition on subsidies contingent upon export in Article 3.1(a), there is no conflict provision in Article XVI of the GATT 1994. Thus, there is no issue here of whether one agreement would take preference over the other. Nevertheless, Article XVI of the GATT

1994 and the SCM Agreement are still the rules under the WTO dealing with the same set of matters. The definition of certain terms in one agreement could serve as a very important source in helping to define the same terms in another agreement. Therefore, unless there is a sound basis for having a different interpretation, we do not see any reason for different meanings of subsidies and export subsidies in Article XVI of the GATT 1994 from those in the SCM Agreement.

ANNEX K

COMMUNICATIONS FROM PARTIES AND THIRD PARTIES

ANNEX K-1

LETTER FROM THE UNITED STATES
21 May 2003

The Panel in this dispute will soon meet with the parties to discuss the Panel's timetable and working procedures. In this regard, we draw to the Panel's attention Brazil's decision to raise claims under the *Agreement on Subsidies and Countervailing Measures* ("Subsidies Agreement") prior to the expiration of the Peace Clause (Article 13 of the *Agreement on Agriculture*) together with its desire to have recourse to the Annex V procedures of the Subsidies Agreement from the outset of this dispute.

Brazil's claims raise procedural and substantive questions that have not previously been faced by a dispute settlement panel. The most fundamental of these is whether Brazil may proceed with claims under the Subsidies Agreement against US support measures, notwithstanding that these claims are barred by the Peace Clause. The United States clearly maintains that Brazil may not.[1] The United States is submitting this letter in advance of the organizational meeting in order to propose a process to resolve these novel issues in an orderly and logical fashion.

Brazil has not contested that, if US support measures conform to the Peace Clause, they are protected from action based on claims of adverse effects or serious prejudice. In fact, Brazil implicitly recognizes that the Peace Clause bars its claims unless Brazil can demonstrate that the US measures are in breach of the Peace Clause – in both its panel request (WT/DS267/7, at 3) and its consultation request (WT/DS267/1, at 3), Brazil asserts that the Peace Clause does not exempt the challenged US measures from action. Thus, Brazil may not maintain this action based on its claims of adverse effects and serious prejudice

---

[1] In this dispute, Brazil is claiming that US support measures for upland cotton have caused adverse effects (including serious prejudice) to Brazil's interests, within the meaning of Articles 5 and 6 of the Subsidies Agreement and GATT 1994 Article XVI. Both the Agriculture Agreement and the Subsidies Agreement make clear that such claims are precluded as long as the measures conform to the Peace Clause. The Peace Clause states that domestic support measures that conform fully to the criteria in Annex 2 of the Agriculture Agreement ("green box" support) "shall be ...exempt from actions based on," *inter alia*, claims of adverse effects, including serious prejudice. Similarly, the Peace Clause states that domestic support measures that conform fully to the criteria in Article 6 of the Agriculture Agreement (for example, "amber box" support) "shall be ...exempt from actions based on," *inter alia*, claims of ad verse effects, including serious prejudice, "provided that such measures do not grant support to a specific commodity in excess of that decided during the 1992 marketing year." The final sentences of both Article 5 (on adverse effects) and Article 6 (further explaining serious prejudice) of the Subsidies Agreement use identical language to recognize the protection afforded by the Peace Clause: "This Article does not apply to subsidies maintained on agricultural products as provided in Article 13 of the Agreement on Agriculture." Thus, domestic support measures that conform to the criteria specified in the Peace Clause are protected against actions claiming adverse effects and serious prejudice.

under the Subsidies Agreement and GATT 1994 Article XVI unless the Panel has found that US support measures for upland cotton do not conform to the Peace Clause.

Accordingly, the United States proposes that the Panel organize its procedures to deal with the threshold Peace Clause issue at the outset of this dispute. We would suggest that the Panel first receive written submissions from both parties on the applicability of the Peace Clause, to be followed by a meeting of the Panel with the parties on this issue, and then rebuttal submissions. The Panel would then make findings on whether any US measure is in breach of the Peace Clause. If the Panel agrees that Brazil has failed to establish that the US measures are inconsistent with the Peace Clause, then that would dispose of those claims. If the Panel finds that the US measures are inconsistent with the Peace Clause, then Brazil could have recourse to the Annex V procedures with respect to its Subsidies Agreement claims on these measures. In either event, briefing and meetings of the Panel with the parties could then proceed on any claims not disposed of by the Peace Clause findings.

This procedure would satisfy the legal requirement that certain claims not be maintained while the Peace Clause is applicable and provide the Panel with a fair and orderly means of addressing the issues in this dispute. The United States notes that the Panel has broad discretion to determine its working procedures under Article 12.1 of the *Understanding on Rules and Procedures Governing the Settlement of Disputes* ("DSU"), and, under DSU Article 12.2, the Panel is charged with establishing panel procedures with "sufficient flexibility so as to ensure high-quality panel reports." Because in this dispute Brazil has made claims under 17 different provisions of the WTO Multilateral Agreements with respect to numerous US programmes under at least 12 US statutes, we believe the Panel's consideration of the critical Peace Clause issue would be aided by briefing and argumentation focused on this threshold issue. Dispute settlement panels have made use of three panel meetings to allow adequate consideration of particular issues. For example, the panel in *Canada – Measures Relating to Exports of Wheat and Treatment of Imported Grain* (DS276) has recently organized its proposed timetable and procedures to provide for the possibility of a panel meeting prior to the first substantive meeting in order to consider any preliminary issues. We also note that three panel meetings have been scheduled in each of the disputes under the *Agreement on the Application of Sanitary and Phytosanitary Measures* to allow a separate meeting of the panel with scientific/technical experts. Similarly, in this dispute, a meeting focused on the Peace Clause issue would assist in considering the complex matter in dispute.

We look forward to discussing this proposal with you in more detail at the organizational meeting. The United States is providing a copy of this letter directly to Brazil.

ANNEX K-2

LETTER FROM BRAZIL
23 May 2003

The Government of Brazil is in receipt of a letter dated 21 May 2003 from the US Mission, proposing that the Panel's working procedures provide for a special advance proceeding to deal with issues relating to Article 13 of the Agreement on Agriculture (AoA), commonly known as the "peace clause". The United States proposes two rounds of submissions by the parties, a meeting of the Panel with the parties, a special "discovery" proceeding and Panel issuance of a separate ruling on these issues. All other work in this dispute would be suspended until after the Panel has issued findings and a preliminary panel report. Brazil opposes these unprecedented and unnecessary procedures, which would impose significant financial and human resource burdens on Brazil and significantly delay this proceeding. Brazil asks that the Panel proceed expeditiously with this case using normal dispute settlement procedures and timeframes, for the reasons set forth below.

Brazil urges the Panel to take full account of Article 3.3 of the Understanding on Rules and Procedures Governing the Settlement of Disputes (DSU), which provides: "The *prompt settlement* of situations in which a Member considers that any benefits accruing to it directly or indirectly under the covered agreements are being impaired by measures taken by another Member is essential to the effective functioning of the WTO and to the maintenance of a proper balance between the rights and obligations of Members." DSU Article 12.9 contemplates that panel proceedings will be completed within six months. DSU Article 12.2 provides that "panel procedures should provide sufficient flexibility so as to ensure high-quality panel reports, *while not unduly delaying the panel process*". The US suggested procedure would unduly delay the panel process to the detriment of Brazil's rights.

The United States has singled out AoA Article 13 as a "special" provision which allegedly requires special and unprecedented procedural treatment. Yet DSU Appendix 2, the closed list of "special and additional" rules and procedures that trump the normal rules of dispute settlement, does not include Article 13 or any other AoA provision, nor does it include the cross-references to the AoA in Articles 3.1 and 7.1 of the Agreement on Subsidies and Countervailing Measures (ASCM). There is no support in the DSU, in the Agreement on Agriculture, or elsewhere in the WTO Agreement for the proposition that a separate "mini-trial" on peace clause issues is required before any claim can be made against subsidies under the Agreement on Agriculture. Acceptance of this proposition would invent a substantial new obstacle to future claims by any government against agricultural subsidy programs, altering the rights of Brazil and many other Members, in contradiction to Article 3.2 of the DSU.

The US notion that two rounds of submissions and a special meeting are required before the parties perform any further work on the case is unprecedented. As the Panel is aware, the concept of preliminary objections is not new. There are many WTO cases in which a defending party has made preliminary objections that a claim or a panel request has not met the requirements of DSU Article 6.2, and has requested an early ruling. Sometimes panels make an early ruling,[1] and sometimes they do not.[2] The decision on how to handle such preliminary objections procedurally is a matter of panel discretion. Where preliminary objections have been resolved in advance of other claims, normally they have been resolved in the panel's first meeting, on the basis of the first round of submissions and oral statements.

The threshold issues posed by AoA Article 13 are no more or less significant than other threshold issues in many WTO Agreements. There are "peace clause"-type provisions in Articles 27.2(b), 27.3, and 27.4 of the ASCM Agreement precluding prohibited subsidy claims against developing country export subsidies under certain conditions. When this provision was invoked by developing countries in prior cases, no special procedures were created by panels and these threshold issues were decided as part of the final panel report.[3] Similarly, no claim may be brought against a measure under the General Agreement on Trade in Services unless the measure falls within the scope of the GATS as defined in GATS Article I. No claim may be brought under Article 2 of the Agreement on Technical Barriers to Trade except in respect of a measure that is a "technical regulation" as defined by that agreement. Claims under the Agreement on Government Procurement may only be brought concerning procurement of an entity covered by Annex I of that agreement. Many more examples exist.

Following the US proposal, panels would be *required* in any case involving such threshold issues to provide for special submissions, special meetings and preliminary panel decisions on admissibility of claims before reaching the substance, adding a month or two to each panel proceeding. The same procedure would be required whenever a defending party makes a preliminary objection under DSU Article 6.2. Resolving such issues, the United States would presumably argue, would be necessary to avoid wasteful litigation of unnecessary claims. But like the Agreement on Agriculture, none of these agreements contain any special procedural provisions for resolution of these threshold issues, and there is no reference to such procedures in Appendix 2 of the DSU. Negotiators could have provided for the type of bifurcated dispute settlement process suggested by the United States for these types of issues. But they did not.

The United States notes that special meetings have been held with experts in cases involving the Agreement on the Application of Sanitary and Phytosani-

---

[1] US – Countervailing Duties on Certain Corrosion-Resistant Carbon Steel Flat Products from Germany, WT/DS213/R, fn. 224.

[2] US – Anti-Dumping Measures on Certain Hot Rolled Steel Products from Japan, WT/DS184/R, fn. 16 to para. 7.1.

[3] Brazil – Export Financing Program for Aircraft, WT/DS46/R (20 August 1999), paras. 7.56-57; Indonesia – Certain Measures Affecting the Automobile Industry, WT/DS54/R (23 July 1998), para. 14.52

tary Measures (SPS). However, these meetings were held pursuant to Article 11.2 of the SPS Agreement that gives the panel the authority to "seek advice from experts chosen by the panel in consultation with the parties to the dispute." With such authority comes an implied need for the Panel to *meet* with the experts. It also creates an expectation of additional delay from the normal panel schedule to accommodate obtaining such advice. Nothing in the AoA contains any similar authority to address peace clause issues.

The peace clause issues in this dispute are not just technical procedural issues (as the US implies in its letter) that can be quickly disposed of without extensive briefing or the presentation of considerable factual evidence and expert econometric testimony. They require careful deliberation by the Panel on the basis of the entire body of evidence submitted by the parties. The peace clause issues are also intertwined with the substance of Brazil's claims regarding prohibited and actionable subsidies under the Agreement on Subsidies and Countervailing Measures. For example:

> Among the issues presented by the peace clause are whether three of the six actionable US domestic support subsidies (Production Flexibility Payment Contract Payments, Direct Payments, and Counter-Cyclical payments) are properly in the "green" or "amber/blue" box of the AoA. To resolve these issues involves, *inter alia*, the presentation of econometric analysis of the trade distorting or production enhancing effects of each of these subsidies to determine whether or not they are properly green box subsidies within Annex 2 AoA. If they are not, then these three subsidies are included in the amount of support in marketing years 1999-2002 for the purpose of comparing against the level of support decided by the United States for marketing year 1992 under Article 13(b)(ii) AoA. However, Brazil's econometric and other extensive documentary evidence regarding the production enhancing effects of such subsidies for the purposes of the peace clause is *exactly* the same evidence Brazil presents for these three referenced subsidies to demonstrate its serious prejudice claims under ASCM Articles 5(c), 6.3(b), 6.3(c), 6.3(d), and Article XVI of GATT 1994.
>
> Brazil has made claims under the AoA and the ASCM regarding prohibited export subsidies under the US Step-2 programme and US export credit guarantee programmes. Brazil will demonstrate in its first submission that these two export subsidies do not "conform fully to the provisions of Part V of this Agreement" in the sense of AoA Article 13(c); obviously, Brazil's evidence and argument regarding the lack of conformity of these two measures with Part V of the AoA largely overlaps with the evidence and argument necessary to demonstrate a violation of ASCM Articles 3.1(a) and (b).

The close relationship between these "threshold" issues and the merits of Brazil's case can be seen by considering the possible outcome of the Panel's preliminary rulings. For instance, if the Panel rules that Brazil may bring its export subsidy claims because the US export subsidies are inconsistent with AoA Part V, it will have decided up front a key issue regarding the merits. But would the United States accept such a ruling and not attempt to re-litigate the same issues raised in the context of the ASCM Agreement? The answer is obvious. It highlights that a preliminary mini-trial of the sort sought by the United States will not save time, expense, and trouble for the Panel or for the parties, and will simply serve to increase the length and expense of this panel proceeding.

The Panel must also consider the position of the 13 interested third parties in this dispute. Many of these third parties may wish to provide their views on the interpretation and application of AoA Article 13 given the implications of any decision for future disputes. If the panel were to decide to request submissions and/or hold a hearing in advance of its first meeting with the parties, third parties will probably claim that they must be accorded the same opportunities for participation as in normal panel proceedings. These opportunities are particularly important since the "mini-trial" called for by the United States would decide key substantive issues relating to the facts and merits of Brazil's complaint.

Brazil would also be prejudiced because the United States proposal would require it to use limited resources to bring its Brazilian counsel and its US econometric experts to Geneva for the proposed special meeting. Further, Brazil would be required to prepare essentially four additional written submissions (a first and rebuttal written submissions, an oral statement submission, and written answers to the Panel's questions) for the proposed special briefing and meeting. The acceptance of the US proposal will create travel, hotel, legal, and human resource expenditures that are particularly burdensome for a developing country with limited financial and human resources such as Brazil. In sum, the US proposal would impair Brazil's rights under WTO rules.

Finally, the United States proposes even more delay in this proceeding with its suggestion in the letter that "Brazil could have recourse to the Annex V procedures with respect to its Subsidies Agreement claims" after the determination by the Panel pursuant to the special procedures. Brazil initiated Annex V procedures on 18 March as the DSB established the panel pursuant to Brazil's request for the establishment of a panel that invoked ASCM Article 7.4. Brazil sought information from third countries and the United States on 1 April 2003 under the provisions of Annex V, paragraphs 2 and 3. Brazil has collected information from a number of third parties pursuant to these requests. The United States on 19 March in WT/DS267/8 informed the DSB that *"any requests for information pursuant to the Annex V procedures may be provided in writing to the US Mission to the World Trade Organization. The United States will gather the information to respond to any such requests and provide the responses through the US Mission"*. Unfortunately, the United States refused to answer Brazil's questions dated 1 April 2003 during the 60-day period of the procedures that ended on 17 May 2003.

Brazil rejects any suggestion by the United States that a new Annex V procedure be conducted during the panel stage of the process to impose even further delays in this proceeding. Instead, Brazil will use the best information available to it when it files its first submission. If appropriate, Brazil will request that the Panel draw adverse inferences from any failure of the United States to provide information requested during the consultation and Annex V process.

In light of the above, Brazil strongly urges the Panel to reject the United States' unprecedented and wasteful procedural proposal. As noted above, much of the evidence involved in demonstrating the absence of peace clause protection *also* is related to Brazil's substantive claims. Given this overlap, the Panel should structure its work so that the peace clause issues and Brazil's claims regarding prohibited subsidies and serious prejudice are dealt with at the same time and in the same two meetings between the Panel and the parties. Use of the normal two meetings and briefing schedule will permit the Panel to have sufficient time to consider the views of Brazil, the United States, and the 13 third parties involved in this dispute. Use of the existing procedures and timeframes will avoid significant prejudice to Brazil by avoiding it having to use its limited resources to litigate the same issues at three, not two meetings. Use of existing procedures will avoid duplication of effort by the Panel and the third parties, and avoid significant delays in the issuance of a final report regarding the subsidies Brazil challenges in this dispute.

Brazil would be pleased to provide the Panel with additional information at the organizational meeting regarding this and any other procedural issues.

ANNEX K-3

LETTER FROM BRAZIL
14 July 2003

Brazil would like to bring to the attention of the Panel in *United States – Subsidies on Upland Cotton* (DS267) the following matter.

The "Working Procedures for the Panel" establish in paragraph 17(b) that,

"the parties and third parties should provide their submissions to the Secretariat by 5:30 pm on the deadline established by the Panel, unless a different time is set by the Panel"

and in paragraph 17(d) that,

"the parties and third parties shall provide electronic copies of all submissions to the Secretariat at the time they provide their submissions [...]".

The electronic version of the US first submission, which was due on Friday, 11 July, 5:30 pm, was delivered after 11 pm, almost 6 hours after the deadline. Brazil had access to the hard copy only on Saturday morning. Because it was a Friday, the failure of the United States to meet the established deadline led to delays in the transmittal and reception of the submission to different Government officials in Brazil and to Brazil's legal advisors. In addition, the delay no doubt caused third parties to have less time to react to the US submission – a not insignificant delay given the fact that third parties had only two working days to respond to the US submission before filing on 15 July. The result was that Brazilian officials were unable to review the submission until Monday, 14 July.

Brazil notes that this delay is not the first in the present case. The US Comments on the initial brief by Brazil, due on 13 July, 5:30 pm, were sent electronically after 8 pm.

Brazil has been faced with extremely short deadlines in this case, including the filing on 24 June its First Submission which required extensive changes to respond to the Panel's determination of 20 June. Nevertheless, Brazil met the deadline and filed the submission prior to 5:30 pm on 24 June. Brazil expects that the United States will, like Brazil, meet its own deadlines in a timely fashion.

Brazil would like the Panel to take note of this delay and to encourage the US to respect the deadlines, with a view to ensuring procedural fairness in these proceedings.

ANNEX K-4

LETTER FROM THE UNITED STATES REQUEST FOR EXTENSION OF DEADLINE FOR RESPONSES TO PANEL QUESTIONS

29 July 2003

In view of the number and the complexity of the questions addressed by the Panel to the United States and Brazil (not counting subparts, it appears that the Panel has asked the United States approximately 95 questions), the United States would like to request an extension of the deadline for the parties' responses until Friday, 15 August 2003. In particular, a number of the questions address new issues and request extensive additional information. Given the issues and volume of information involved, as well as the travel schedules of key members of the US delegation, an extension of the deadline originally proposed by the Panel would assist the parties in providing thorough responses.

While extending the deadline for answers would necessarily shorten the period for commenting on those answers, the parties would still have one week to prepare those comments. The United States considers that both the initial answers and subsequent comments would benefit if proportionately more time were allocated to ensuring that the initial answers are as complete and clear as possible.

ANNEX K-5

LETTER FROM BRAZIL

29 July 2003

Brazil received a letter dated today from the United States requesting until Friday 15 August to provide answers to the Panel's questions. Brazil cannot agree to this request.

Brazil has been working diligently every day since 25 July to comply with the Panel's deadline and is prepared to provide its answers to the Panel's questions by 4 August. A delay until 15 August will prejudice Brazil by not providing it with sufficient time to comment on the US answers or to prepare its Rebuttal Submission.

Brazil also notes that the Panel's questions do not raise new issues. Instead, they address issues either raised to a large extent in the First Written Submissions or that have been dealt with extensively during the first substantive meeting with the parties.

However, in the spirit of cooperation and in recognition of the fact that the Panel did request more questions of the United States than Brazil, Brazil would have no objection if the Panel were to extend the deadline to 7 August for the Parties and the Third Parties to answer the Panel's and each other's questions.

ANNEX K-6

LETTER FROM THE EUROPEAN COMMISSION
31 July 2003

The European Communities would like to thank the Panel for the questions it has posed to the third parties, and for extending the deadlines for responses. In light of the detailed nature of the questions asked and the importance of the issues concerned, the European Communities respectfully makes two requests to the Panel.

First, it would greatly assist the European Communities (and we assume other third parties) in preparing our responses to the Panel's questions to have sight of the oral statements of the main parties to the dispute at the first substantive meeting. So doing would permit third parties to respond to arguments made by the main parties where such a response would be of relevance in answering the Panel's questions. Since the Panel has requested the third parties to answer detailed questions, the European Communities considers that allowing the third parties access to the oral statements would allow the third parties to participate in a "full and meaningful fashion" in the stages of the proceeding where the panel has requested their input.[1] Moreover, the European Communities considers that this would benefit the Panel since the third parties will be able to provide more complete responses to the Panel's questions.

Second, the European Communities welcomes the Panel's decision to allow the third parties to comment on the response of the other third parties. However, it is not clear to the European Communities whether the third parties will also be able to comment upon the responses of the main parties to the Panel's questions, or questions the main parties have asked of each other. Once more, the European Communities considers that the third parties comments will be more full and meaningful, and consequently more beneficial to the Panel, if it is also possible to comment on the responses of the main parties in addition to commenting upon the other third parties responses.

Accordingly, the European Communities requests the Panel to ask the main parties to provide the third parties with copies of their oral statements and copies of their responses to the Panel's questions, when lodged. The European Communities also requests the Panel to invite the third parties to comment upon the responses of the main parties to the Panel's questions, and those posed by the other party.

Finally, the European Communities would also respectfully ask you to clarify the treatment of the Panel's expression of views on Article 13 of the *Agreement on Agriculture* and associated issues, scheduled for 5 September 2003. Given that the Panel's findings on this issue may be considered similar to a

---

[1] Para. 249, Article 21.5 Appellate Body Report, *United States – Tax Treatment for "Foreign Sales Corporations"* ("United States – FSC (21.5)"), WT/DS108/AB/RW, adopted 29 January 2002.

preliminary ruling, and that the third parties will be asked to provide the Panel with further comments on 29 September 2003, the European Communities considers that, in order to protect third parties' due process rights, the Panel's expression of views should be available to the third parties. The European Communities would be obliged if you could confirm this understanding.

A copy of this letter has been provided to the delegations of Brazil and the United States, and to the other third parties.

May I take this opportunity to thank you in advance for your consideration of these issues.

ANNEX K-7

LETTER FROM THE UNITED STATES

1 August 2003

The United States is in receipt of the letter dated 31 July 2003, from the European Communities (EC) relating to third parties' participation in the present dispute. The United States would consent to the Panel's release of its further views on the Peace Clause issue to the third parties as a sensible way forward in this dispute (although we would not necessarily endorse all of the reasoning expressed in the EC letter). Further, the United States has no objection to either party choosing to make its submissions or oral statements public – as the United States and, we understand, Brazil have decided to do. However, we see no basis in the *Understanding on Rules and Procedures Governing the Settlement of Disputes* (DSU) for the additional procedural requirements that the EC is proposing – namely, that the Panel require the parties to make available to the third parties copies of their oral statements and responses to the Panel's questions, and that the third parties comment on the parties' responses to the Panel's questions. The EC proposal appears to erase the distinction between parties and third parties for purposes of dispute settlement.

The United States recalls that in the context of a panel proceeding a third party is welcome to express its interests under any covered agreement at issue in the dispute. Thus, the DSU ensures that third parties may express those interests by providing "an opportunity to be heard by the panel and to make written submissions" (DSU Article 10.2) and the right to "receive the submissions of the parties to the dispute to the first meeting of the panel" (DSU Article 10.3). These requirements have been met in every prior dispute by providing third parties the opportunity to receive the first submissions of the parties, to make one written submission, and to present statements at a third-party session of the first meeting of the panel.

We are aware of no dispute in which third parties have been granted the additional rights now sought by the EC. It would represent a fundamental change in the role of third parties in dispute settlement. Changes of this nature are being discussed in the context of the ongoing negotiations on clarifications and improvements to the DSU, and that is the proper forum for Members to consider these changes.

In addition, on a practical note, if the parties have to deal with the additional work of responding to comments by potentially more than a dozen third parties on (1) each others' answers to the Panel's third-party questions as well as (2) the parties' answers to more than 100 questions from the Panel, the already ambitious timetable established by the Panel will become totally untenable.

Finally, the United States recalls that, like all WTO Members and the public, the EC already has access to US submissions and oral statements on our website. (Indeed, we have already provided a copy of our oral statement directly to the EC at their request.) We also understand that Brazil is making its submissions public within two weeks of filing as contemplated by the parties' agreement and reflected in the Panel's Working Procedures. We would welcome Brazil's making its submissions public upon filing but do not see a basis in the DSU for requiring disclosure of those submissions to the third parties.

The United States is providing a copy of this letter directly to Brazil and the third parties.

ANNEX K-8

LETTER FROM BRAZIL

1 August 2003

Brazil received a letter dated 31 July 2003 from the European Communities requesting the Panel:

(i) to ask the parties to the dispute to provide third parties with copies of their oral statements and copies of their responses to the Panel's questions;

(ii) to invite the third parties to comment upon the responses of the parties to the dispute to the Panel's questions, and those posed by the other party;

(iii) to make the "Panel's expression of views on Article 13 of the *Agreement on Agriculture* and associated issues", scheduled for 5 September 2003, available to the third parties.

2. With respect to the EC's requests, Brazil would like to make the following comments.

3. In light of the Timetable for Panel Proceedings, the Working Procedures for the Panel, and DSU Articles 10.2 and 10.3, Brazil considers that the third parties to the present dispute are entitled to be provided with copies of the parties' First Written Submission and parties' Further Submission only. In Brazil's view, these are the only documents that constitute "submissions of the parties to the dispute to the first meeting of the panel" in accordance with DSU Article 10.3.

4. Brazil further notes that the parties to the dispute did not make any oral statements during the session of the substantive meeting of the Panel set aside for the third parties to present their views (24 July 2003). Thus, there are no oral statements of which the third parties should receive written versions. As a matter of fact, the oral (opening and closing) statements made by Brazil and the US were delivered exclusively at the closed session of the substantive meeting of the Panel which the third parties did not have access to. Again, there would be no reason for providing third parties with copies of those oral statements.

5. As is the case for the oral statements, Brazil submits that third parties need not be given copies of the parties' responses to the Panel's questions. The Panel's questions were put to Brazil and the US in the context of the closed session of the first substantive meeting with the parties, as were the preliminary responses given by both parties to the dispute. Moreover, such responses do not constitute "submissions" within the meaning of DSU Article 10.3.

6. Finally, with regard to the "Panel's views on certain issues", Brazil agrees with the EC that the document should be available also to third parties.

ANNEX K-9

LETTER FROM THE EUROPEAN COMMISSION
4 August 2003

The European Communities refers to its letter to the Panel of 31 July 2003, and the responses of the United States and Brazil of 1 August 2003.

The European Communities would like first to welcome the agreement of both the United States and Brazil that the Panel's views on the Peace Clause and related issues should be communicated to the third parties.

However, in the view of the European Communities, both the United States and Brazil misunderstand the thrust of the EC's letter of 31 July. Both parties enter into a discussion of whether the third parties are entitled to be given access to, and the chance to comment upon, the responses to the Panel's questions of the main parties. Both argue that the documents which the third parties have received are the only documents which the third parties are entitled to. However, these arguments miss the point of the European Communities request.

The European Communities central point was that, given the detailed questions which the third parties have received from the Panel, and given the Panel's decision to permit third parties to comment upon the responses of the other third parties, it would be a reasonable exercise of the Panel's discretion to organise its procedures so as to allow the third parties also to comment upon the responses of the main parties. The European Communities considers that this would be beneficial to the Panel, and would allow the third parties to participate completely, given the extent to which the Panel has already invited the third parties to participate.

The European Communities does not consider that this would set an unfavourable precedent because a panel would always have the discretion, in the light of its own procedures and the dispute before it, to decide whether to grant third parties such possibilities. Moreover, the European Communities sees no possible impairment of the due process rights of the main parties, and indeed neither the United States not Brazil have alleged any such impairment would result from the Panel acceding to the request of the European Communities.

The European Communities is aware of the practical concerns raised by the United States. However, the European Communities notes that a party always has a choice whether to comment upon responses, and that these practical concerns weigh equally on both parties.

Finally, the European Communities is, of course, aware that the United States makes it oral statements public (and is grateful that the US officials involved in this dispute have provided a copy directly to the EC delegation). We also note that the Panel's procedures provide for the submission of non-confidential summaries within 14 days of filing which could be made public.[1] However, the European Communities is not aware, first, whether such summaries shall also be provided to the third parties, and second, whether such summaries can be considered equivalent to the oral statements as delivered. In that light, the European Communities recalls its arguments in favour of provision of the statements as delivered, set out in its letter of 31 July 2003.

A copy of this letter has been provided to the delegations of Brazil and the United States, and to the other third parties.

Thank you in advance for your consideration of these issues.

[1] Para. 3 – Panel's Working Procedures.

ANNEX K-10

LETTER FROM BRAZIL

14 August 2003

Once more, Brazil is faced with the need to detract from its substantive work relating to the dispute *United States – Subsidies on Upland Cotton* (DS267) to bring to the attention of the Panel a new US failure to abide by the "Working Procedures for the Panel" concerning the timing for delivery of documents required by the Panel.

As it had already done on two previous occasions[1], the US did not deliver its answers to the Panel's questions following the first substantive meeting with the parties by the time established in paragraphs 17(b) and (d) of the "Working Procedures".[2] Brazil recalls that the deadline for submitting the parties' answers to the Panel was expressly confirmed by the Panel on its communication dated 30 July 2003 informing about the extension of the deadline for the submission of the parties' responses[3].

As a matter of fact, the electronic version of the US answers, which was due on 11 August, 5:30 pm, was delivered around 11:30 pm, more than 6 hours after the deadline, more than 6 hours after Brazil delivered both its electronic version and hard copies to the Secretariat and the US. Brazil further notes that no hard copy of the US answers was made available either to the Secretariat or to Brazil by the deadline.

Brazil regrets that the US has decided to adopt such a strategy. In this particular case, the US behavior is even more egregious because the deadline – at request of the US and with the good faith and cooperation of Brazil – had been extended by 7 days by the Panel (from 4 August to 11 August).

As stated, the failure of the US to meet the established deadline provided US officials an opportunity to examine Brazil's answers before submitting their own responses more than 6 hours later. Moreover, the US failure led to delays in the transmittal and reception of the US answers to different Government officials in Brazil and to Brazil's legal advisors, diminishing an already short period for Brazil to comment upon the US responses. Due to the 5 hour time zone difference between Brasilia and Geneva, the US delay prevented work by Brazilian officials on the 11th of August. US official, however, had no such impairment

[1] Also the US Comments on the initial brief by Brazil, due on 13 June 2003, and the US First Written Submission, due on 11 July 2003, were delivered after the deadline (see Brazil's letter to the Panel on 14 July 2003).

[2] WP, para. 17(b): "the parties and third parties should provide their submissions to the Secretariat by 5:30 pm on the deadlines established by the Panel, unless a different time is set by the Panel." WP, para. 17(d): "the parties and third parties shall provide electronic copies of all submissions to the Secretariat at the time they provide their submissions [...]".

[3] *"The Panel reminds the parties that paragraph 17(b) of the Panel's working procedures indicates that the responses should be submitted by 17:30 (Geneva time)."*

since the USTR representatives in Geneva had the Brazilian answers to the Panel by 11:30 a.m. Washington D.C. time on that same date.

Needless to repeat that Brazil – a developing country with serious budgetary and human resources constraints – has been faced with extremely short deadlines in this case, including the filing on 24 June of its First Submission which required extensive changes to respond to the Panel's determination of 20 June. However, Brazil has been meeting the deadlines established, and will continue to do so. Although the facts do not recommend Brazil to be very optimistic, Brazil continues to expect that the US will, like Brazil, meet its own deadlines in a timely fashion from now on.

Brazil respectfully asks the Panel to take note of this new delay and to encourage, again, the US to respect the deadlines, with a view to ensuring procedural fairness in these proceedings.

In addition, Brazil would like to bring to the Panel's attention an issue regarding certain of the United States' Answers to the Panel's Questions. In certain answers, the United States has indicated it will provide responsive arguments and information in its rebuttal submission. In other answers, it made allegations without providing any documentary support that would permit Brazil to challenge the accuracy and credibility of allegations. The answers in question are the following:

> Answer to Questions 14 and 26: no detailed information or arguments were provided in the US answers regarding either production flexibility contracts or market loss assistance payments. The last sentence of paragraph 57 of the U.S. answers indicates US will discuss production flexibility contract payments only in the rebuttal submission.
>
> Answer to questions 60 and 66(a): The United States provided no responsive information or calculations to respond to the Panel's questions.
>
> Answer to Questions 66(d): In paragraph 121, the United States indicates that "it will provide a detailed critique of Mr. Sumner's analysis in our rebuttal submission." In paragraph 124 it states: "We will discuss other conceptual errors in Sumner's approach in our rebuttal submission."
>
> Answer to Question 73: Other than an undocumented allegation in US answer to Question 76, the United States provided no information or argument concerning Articles 1 and 3 of the SCM Agreement. Instead, the United States stated in paragraph 140 that it would "review Brazil's submissions, including its responses to these questions, and provide any further response in the US submission".
>
> Answers to Questions 12, 71-88: The United States provided only two exhibits (US-12 and US-20) and no other documentation in support of arguments or allegations.

Brazil recalls that the purpose of scheduling the filing of the answers to the Panel's questions 11 days before the submission of the rebuttal submission was to permit the parties to review each other's answers and supporting documentation and then to comment on those answers in the rebuttal submissions. Brazil cooperated in this process by providing complete and comprehensive answers to all of the Panel's questions together with extensive documentation. As demonstrated above, for certain questions, the United States did not provide complete answers or documentation that would have allowed Brazil the opportunity to comment and rebut in its rebuttal submission.

Brazil will be prejudiced if it does not have the opportunity to comment on information, arguments, and documents the United States makes or provides for the first time in their rebuttal submission that *would have been* responsive to those Panel questions listed above. Accordingly, Brazil requests the right, *only with respect to the questions above*, to comment on any new information, arguments, or documents presented for the first time in the U.S. rebuttal submission.

Providing Brazil with this right is consistent with basic notions of due process. Otherwise, Brazil will not have another opportunity prior to the Panel's 5 September decision on peace clause issues, to comment on any new information, documents, or arguments presented by the United States. The inability or unwillingness of the United States to provide complete answers should not prejudice Brazil. The United States now has the benefit of Brazil's complete answers together with extensive additional documentation to comment on in its rebuttal submission. This is particularly true with respect to issues related to export credit guarantees and issues related to Professor Sumner's analysis. Brazil is entitled the same right.

Brazil requests that it be provided until 28 August to file any such comments. In light of the fact that Brazil provided complete answers to the Panel's questions, there is no basis for the Panel to provide the United States with any corresponding right. Its due process rights have not been adversely impacted.

ANNEX K-11

LETTER FROM THE UNITED STATES
20 August 2003

The United States has received a copy of the letter to the Panel from Brazil of 14 August 2003. We have also received your communication of yesterday, responding to Brazil's requests for additional time to submit its rebuttal. The United States does wish to record its views on Brazil's letter, and my authorities have therefore instructed me to convey their surprise that Brazil would send such a letter and their regret over any burden that it may have placed on the Panel in what is already a very difficult and complicated dispute.

The United States would first like to thank the Panel for agreeing to extend the deadline for the responses to the Panel's questions. The United States appreciates the depth and level of understanding of the issues represented by the Panel's extensive and broad-ranging questions. Without an extension of the deadline, it would have been completely impossible for the United States to have provided responses in a timely manner. Even with the extension, the drafting, compiling, consulting internally with the various relevant officials, and finalizing the responses all required supreme effort and personal sacrifice on the part of the entire US delegation. The United States did provide responses by the August 11 deadline, although it was not possible to accommodate the 5:30 pm filing guideline despite the best efforts of the United States to do so.[1]

The same burden was not placed on Brazil and the outside legal counsel that Brazil has employed for this dispute. As a result, it is not surprising that Brazil found the deadline to be less demanding and resource-intensive. We would note that, if one only counts the main questions and not any of the subquestions, there were 104 questions posed to the United States, but only 63 posed to Brazil.

[2] With all respect, the United States has considerable difficulty with Brazil's complaints about the time within which the United States filed its response in

[1] On the one hand, the United States is flattered that Brazil credits the United States with the ability to finalize its own responses while simultaneously reviewing Brazil's responses filed earlier in the evening. On the other hand, the United States is, to say the least, taken aback that Brazil would suggest that the United States would do so. In any event, the press of finalizing the US responses completely consumed the US delegation and no one was able to spare time to look at Brazil's responses at any point that day, let alone before the US responses were filed.

[2] The difference in the number of questions for each party means that Brazil had nearly 6-1/2 hours to prepare its responses to each question posed to it, whereas the United States had less than four hours per question. (Counting the subquestions would increase the disparity since a preliminary check indicates that there were more subquestions for the United States than for Brazil.) As a result, Brazil had approximately 65 percent more time to prepare its responses. Had the United States taken the same amount of time as Brazil to prepare each response, its responses would have taken 28 days to file (they would have been finished on August 22).

light of the total amount of work required, and effort that the United States expended, to provide its answers to the Panel's questions.[3]

The United States also could not understand how Brazil could ask for an additional opportunity to respond to new material in the rebuttal submissions while at the same time asking that the Panel deny any such opportunity to the United States. (After all, one would expect that Brazil will also provide new material in its rebuttal submission on topics covered in the Panel's questions, and not just repeat material it has already submitted.) Such a one-sided approach would not have achieved the "procedural fairness" that Brazil has said it seeks. In this connection, the United States considers that the approach taken by the Panel in its communication yesterday achieves a fair balance of the parties' interests.

In conclusion, the United States would like to thank the Panel for the approach it has taken on Brazil's request, as well as for its work to date on the many issues presented by this dispute. The United States is also providing a copy of this letter directly to Brazil.

[3] The United States also failed to understand the reference in Brazil's letter to Brazil's "good faith and cooperation" in extending the deadline by seven days. In fact, Brazil did not "cooperate" in the Panel's decision to grant a seven-day extension. Brazil instead objected to any extension beyond three days.

ANNEX K-12

LETTER FROM BRAZIL

23 August 2003

The Government of Brazil is in receipt of the Communication from the Panel dated 19 August 2003. Brazil only received this morning the *Rebuttal Submission of the United States of America*, dated 22 August 2003 ("US Rebuttal Submission"). Brazil notes that consistent with all of its earlier written submissions, the United States filed its Rebuttal Submission 6 hours late. This delay has prejudiced Brazil and prevented it from providing comments responsive to the Panel's 19 August 2003 letter until today. Brazil notes that the United States received its copy of Brazil's Rebuttal Submission, along with Brazil's Comments to the US Answers, consistent with the 5:30 p.m. deadline established in the Panel's Working Procedures.

In accordance with your communication of 19 August 2003, Brazil has reviewed the US Rebuttal Submission to determine "whether there is any specific material on which it has not had an opportunity to comment", and which it would like to address in a 27 August submission. Brazil identifies below the specific US arguments, data and documents on which it would like to comment. Brazil also shows below good cause why it should be granted the opportunity to address each specific argument, data and document.

Brazil recalls that its original 14 August 2003 request to the Panel to afford it this opportunity was triggered by explicit indications by the United States, in its 11 August responses to Panel questions, that it was not providing full responses to the Panel's questions and would instead address a number of issues for the first time in its Rebuttal Submission. Brazil argued that it would be prejudiced by this conduct. The list below is consistent with the spirit of Brazil's 14 August request. Brazil's list only includes specific issues that should have been but were not addressed in the United States' 11 August responses, or specific issues related to new documents relied on by the United States for the first time in its Rebuttal Submission.

There are a number of new arguments or re-packaging of earlier arguments presented by the United States in its Rebuttal Submission. Most of these arguments do not require a further response, since Brazil's various earlier submissions and exhibits addressed or anticipated the new or re-packaged US arguments or issues raised by those arguments. In this regard, Brazil notes that the United States' Rebuttal Submission does not respond to a number of arguments made in earlier submissions by Brazil. Brazil would object to any opportunity given to the United States to provide such a response in its 27 August submission. Brazil is of the view that the purpose of this exercise is not to provide the Parties with a whole-scale opportunity to rebut every point raised in either the United States' or Brazil's Rebuttal Submissions. The Panel should limit the United States to comments on specific issues that should have been but were not addressed in Brazil's 11 August responses, or specific issues related to new documents relied on by Brazil for the first time in its Rebuttal Submission.

Should the Panel grant the United States an opportunity to comment on issues beyond this narrow scope, Brazil reserves its right to revisit the list of material it includes in the list below.

In accordance with the above understanding, Brazil requests leave to comment on the following specific material:

Domestic Support Issues

Para. 43

Subject: US argument regarding the growing of illegal crops, etc.

Good cause: This is a new argument that should have been but was not raised in the United States' 11 August response to questions 25 and 26 from the Panel.

Paras. 96-98

Subject: US argument regarding crop insurance notifications of other Members.

Good cause: This is a new argument referring to new WTO documents not raised in earlier submissions.

Paras. 114-117

Subject: US argument regarding a price gap methodology for marketing loans.

Good cause: This is a new argument that should have been but was not raised in the United States' 11 August response to question 67 from the Panel, and that is directly contradictory to information provided by the United States in paragraphs 128-134 of that response.

Paras. 123-127 and Exhibit US-24

Subject: US new challenge to Professor Dan Sumner's analysis.

Good cause: This is a new argument and exhibit that should have been but was not provided in the United States' 11 August response to question 61(d) from the Panel.

Export Credit Guarantee Issues

Paras. 135-146 and Exhibits US-25 through US-29

Subject: New US arguments concerning the negotiating history of Article 10.2 AoA.

Good cause: These arguments should have been but were not raised in the United States' 11 August response to questions 88(a) and 88(b) from the Panel.

Paras. 147-152

Subject: New US argument that had it intended to subject export credit guarantees to the AoA and the SCM Agreement, it would have included them in the calculation of its reduction commitments.

Good cause: This argument should have been but was not raised in the United States' 11 August response to questions 88(a) and 88(b) from the Panel.

Paras. 156-157, 160-162, and Exhibits US-31 and US-32

Subject: New US arguments and data concerning the FCRA formula and the reestimate process.

Good cause: These arguments and data should have been but were not raised in the United States' 11 August response to questions 81(d)-(g) from the Panel.

Para. 169 and Exhibit US-33

Subject: New US assertion that rescheduled debt is not in arrears.

Good cause: This argument and evidence should have been but was not raised in the United States' 11 August response to question 81(a) from the Panel.

Paras. 172, 174-175:

Subject: US argument that item (j) does not require recovery of long-term losses.

Good cause: This argument should have been but was not raised in response to the United States' 11 August responses to questions 74 and 77 from the Panel.

Paras. 186-191, and Exhibits US-34 through US-37

Subject: US argument that "forfaiting" is analogous to CCC export credit guarantee programs for agricultural commodities.

Good cause: This argument should have been but was not raised in the United States' 11 August response to question 76 from the Panel (as well as questions 71(a) and 73).

Brazil notes that the United States has for the first time addressed Brazil's "threat of circumvention" claims under Article 10.1 AoA (paras. 180-183). In particular, Brazil notes new US arguments contrasting CCC guarantee programs from FSC (and the panel and Appellate Body decisions concerning the *United States – FSC* dispute), asserting that there is no legal entitlement to CCC guarantees, and asserting (*via* new data) compliance with scheduled quantitative reduction commitments. Consistent with the purpose of this exercise – offering an opportunity to comment solely on arguments that should have been addressed in the United States' 11 August responses to questions and to new documents proffered by the United States for the first time in its Rebuttal Submission – Brazil is not asking for an opportunity to address the US "circumvention" arguments in its 27 August submission. Brazil would be pleased, however, to address any questions the Panel has concerning these new US arguments.

Brazil thanks the Panel and the Secretariat for its consideration of this request and for its continuing work on this dispute.

ANNEX K-13

LETTER FROM THE UNITED STATES
25 August 2003

In the Panel's fax dated 19 August 2003, the Panel noted the possibility that a party might lack sufficient opportunity to comment on information, argumentation and documents submitted by the other party in its rebuttal submission, and the Panel invited the parties to request the opportunity to comment on specific material after receiving each other's rebuttal submissions. My authorities have instructed me to submit this letter requesting such an opportunity.

Because of Brazil's tactical decision to defer presenting its entire case with respect to Peace Clause issues, the United States is once again put in the difficult position of attempting to respond to extensive, wholly new evidence and arguments in an extremely compressed time frame. Furthermore, we note the comment of Brazil in its rebuttal submission that it "provides *additional evidence* establishing that under *a variety of interpretations and methodologies* the US level of support granted to upland cotton in MY 1999-2002 was far greater than the support decided in MY 1992".[1]

Under paragraph 13 of the Panel's working procedures, all evidence was supposed to have been submitted no later than during the first substantive meeting, except evidence necessary for purposes of rebuttals or answers to questions. Brazil has not explained why it could not have presented this evidence by the first Panel meeting or why this evidence is necessary for purposes of rebuttal. A quick review of the "additional evidence" appears to indicate that this is all evidence that should have been presented no later than the meeting with the Panel. Accordingly, unless Brazil can show "good cause" for withholding this evidence from the Panel and the parties until now, the United States would respectfully request the Panel to disregard this evidence.

In light of the shortness of time, the United States requests the opportunity to comment with respect to a number of issues raised for the first time in Brazil's rebuttal submission and comments on answers to questions, as listed below. With respect to each such issue, the United States demonstrates that there is good cause to permit such comments. The United States is requesting the opportunity to comment (even though some of this evidence may be disregarded by the Panel in response to the US request) so as to avoid further delay, pending the Panel's finding in response to the request to disregard the evidence.

---

[1] Rebuttal Submission of Brazil, para. 1 (22 August 2003) (emphasis added). We also note that Brazil had indicated in its answers to the Panel's questions that it was deferring presenting its case on several issues pending receipt of the answers to the questions by the United States and in at least one instance by the European Communities (see *e.g.*, para. 80 of Brazil's answers to the Panel questions). Brazil's rebuttal submission for the first time now presents this material.

Rebuttal Submission:

Paras. 4-9: Brazil for the first time responds to the US argument, made in both its opening and closing oral statements at the first panel meeting, that Brazil's interpretation of paragraph 6(b) would create an inconsistency between that provision and the fundamental requirement of the first sentence of Annex 2, paragraph 1. This is a new argument not previously made to the Panel, for example, in either of Brazil's oral statements or in its answers to questions from the Panel.[2]

Paras. 24-26: On the basis of a previously submitted exhibit, Brazil now advances for the first time the argument that production flexibility contract payments may be considered "support to upland cotton" on the basis that such payments were not made "in favour of agricultural producers in general" because payments were linked to acres that produced any of seven crops during a fixed and defined base period.[3] This argument could have been made in Brazil's first submission, either of Brazil's oral statements, or in Brazil's answers to questions from the Panel.[4]

Paras. 29-35: In these paragraphs, Brazil for the first time advances an argument for market loss assistance payments that parallels the argument made for the first time in paragraphs 24-26 with respect to production flexibility contract payments: that market loss assistance payments may be considered "support to upland cotton" on the basis that such payments were not made "in favour of agricultural producers in general" because payments were linked to acres that produced any of seven crops during a fixed and defined base period. In addition, Brazil introduces a raft of assertions, new data, and calculations, including some with respect to crops other than upland cotton, to assert that production flexibility contract payments and market loss assistance payments are support for upland cotton because of costs for upland cotton farmers.[5] Brazil could have presented these data, calculations, and arguments in its previous submissions and statements.

Paras. 36-46: As with production flexibility contract payments and market loss assistance payments, Brazil argues (again for the first time) that direct payments may be considered "support to upland cotton" on the basis that such payments were not made in favor of all agricultural producers, and Brazil introduces a raft of assertions, new data, and calculations, including some with respect to crops other than upland cotton, to assert that direct payments are support

---

[2] *See, e.g.*, Brazil's Answer to Question 27 from the Panel (para. 39 failed to make any such argument in the course of the answer alleging that US decoupled income support has more than a minimal effect on production (and thus is inconsistent with the fundamental requirement of the first sentence of Annex 2, para. 1) because such support "limit[s] payments based on the type of production").

[3] Indeed, none of the citations provided by Brazil in these paragraphs discloses the argument Brazil now advances. *See* Brazil 's Rebuttal Submission, paras. 24-35 fn. 38-44.

[4] *See* Brazil's Answer to Question 23 from the Panel (paras. 25, 27: noting base acreage and addition of crops to base acreage under direct payments program but failing to argue that limitations on base acreage render measure product-specific).

[5] *See, e.g.*, Brazil's Rebuttal Submission, para. 31 fn. 68, 69 (both of these footnotes contain new evidence that should have been presented by the first Panel meeting); *id.*, para. 33 fn. 71 (disclosing new calculation).

for upland cotton because of costs for upland cotton farmers.[6] Brazil could have presented these data, calculations, and arguments in its previous submissions and statements.

Paras. 48-50: Brazil makes a nearly identical argument for counter-cyclical payments as for those indicated above: that is, these payments may be considered "support to upland cotton" on the basis that such payments were not made "in favour of agricultural producers in general" and on the basis of the same or similar assertions, new data, and calculations with respect to costs and subsidies for upland cotton and other crops.[7] Brazil could have presented these data, calculations, and arguments in its previous submissions and statements.

Paras. 55-59: With respect to crop insurance payments, Brazil introduces new evidence (for example, relating to availability of specific policies) and arguments to claim that these payments are product-specific support to cotton.[8] Brazil could have presented this evidence and argument in its previous submissions and statements.

Paras. 73, 75-77: Brazil introduces revised data and calculations relating to alleged budgetary expenditures for upland cotton and an AMS for upland cotton.[9]

Paras. 88, 90-94: Brazil misstates the US position with respect to the Peace Clause analysis for support provided in past marketing years. Brazil also asserts, erroneously, the US Peace Clause interpretation is inconsistent with the position taken by the United States in previous WTO dispute settlement proceedings. These arguments could have been presented by Brazil earlier - for instance, during its first oral statement to the Panel[10] or in its answers to the Panel's questions.[11]

Brazil's Comments on U.S. Answers

Paras. 44-45: Brazil for the first time presents an argument claiming that the US interpretation of paragraph 6(b), made in both its opening and closing oral statements at the first panel meeting, would render paragraph 6(e) a nullity. These arguments could have been presented in Brazil's answers to the Panel's questions. (*See also* paragraphs 4-9 of Brazil's Rebuttal Submission, discussed above.)

Paras. 54-56: In the guise of a "general comment" to questions 47-69, Brazil asserts for the first time that the US argument relating to the level of support decided by US measures does not account for various forms of product-specific support. This erroneous assertion could have been presented as

[6] *See, e.g.*, Brazil's Rebuttal Submission, para. 39 fn. 84 (this footnote contains new evidence that should have been presented by the first Panel meeting), 85.

[7] *See, e.g.*, Brazil's Rebuttal Submission, para. 50 fn. 112, 113, 114 (all of this is new evidence that should have been presented by the first Panel meeting).

[8] *See, e.g.*, Brazil's Rebuttal Submission, para. 56 fn. 131, 132.

[9] *See, e.g.*, para. 73 fn. 172.

[10] *See, e.g.*, Brazil's Oral Statement at First Panel Meeting, paras. 40-43.

[11] *See, e.g.*, Brazil's Answer to Question 15 from the Panel.

early as Brazil's oral statements at the first panel meeting or in its answers to the Panel's questions.

The United States thanks the Panel for its consideration of these requests. In addition, like Brazil, we would of course also welcome the opportunity to respond to any further questions the Panel may have. Moreover, should the Panel consider it useful to hear further argumentation from the Parties, we would of course be pleased to make additional submissions or appear before the Panel on this complicated and sensitive matter.

The United States is providing a copy of this letter directly to Brazil.

ANNEX K-14

LETTER FROM BRAZIL

25 August 2003

The Government of Brazil is in receipt of a letter from the United States dated 25 August. Brazil received that letter at 6 p.m. today. Brazil requests the Panel to take the following action as set forth below.

Rejection of US request as untimely:

Brazil requests that the Panel disregard the United States' request to have the Panel grant it permission to offer rebuttal arguments to Brazil's 22 August rebuttal submission and comments on the US answers. This letter, like *all* prior US submissions to the Panel, was not timely filed. This latest request was made at least 60 hours too late. The Panel's Communication of 19 August 2003 stated:

> when each party receives the other party's rebuttal submission, it is invited, *without delay* to draw the Panel's attention to any specific material on which it has not had an opportunity to comment . . . ."

The Communication further stated that "the Panel is willing to grant such permission on Saturday, 23 August 2003, if necessary."

Brazil interpreted this Communication as requiring it to make the request on Friday evening, 22 August, immediately after reviewing the US Rebuttal Submission. Unfortunately, the US Rebuttal Submission was sent shortly before midnight on Friday, 22 August and could only be accessed by the Brazilian Mission in Geneva at 9:00 a.m. Geneva time on Saturday, 23 August. Brazil informed the Secretariat on Friday evening that it could not make its request that evening since it had not received the US Rebuttal Submission. Brazil further informed the Secretariat on Saturday morning that it would file a request by 2:00 p.m. on Saturday.

By contrast, the United States received Brazil's 22 August Rebuttal Submission and Brazil's 22 August Comments to the US Answers and Brazil's exhibits at 5:30 p.m. Geneva time on Friday, 22 August. Regardless, the United States waited more than 72 hours to file its request that the Panel strike certain information in Brazil's 22 August submissions, and its request for leave to file comments on those Brazilian submissions.

Brazil has endured repeated violations by the United States of the Panel's procedural deadlines over the past three months. If the Panel's procedures are to mean anything, they must be enforced. There is no doubt that this latest request by the United States is well out of time. It was not made "without delay". There is no basis offered by the United States for such delay. There is none. Accordingly, the Panel should reject the United States request as untimely.

Reject US Request to Strike Brazil's Rebuttal Evidence and Argument

The United States also requests the Panel to strike large amounts of Brazil's Rebuttal Submission and Brazil's documents with the argument that Brazil allegedly violated paragraph 13 of the Panel's working procedures. Brazil notes the irony of the United States invoking the Panel's working procedures given their repeated violations of such procedures over the past three months. Nevertheless, the United States ignores the Panel's Determination of 20 June, in which it stated, in paragraph 20, last bullet:

> For the purposes of allowing the Panel to express its views on the exemption conditions of Article 13 of the *Agreement on Agriculture* by 1 September 2003, in relation to those measures which may be affected by Article 13, *full and complete submissions on factual and legal issues related to Article 13 in this dispute will need to be provided, at the latest, in the parties' rebuttal submissions (to be submitted on 22 August 2003).*

Brazil interpreted this ruling as permitting it to provide no later than 22 August all of its evidence and argument that had not already been provided in its earlier submissions. This is the manner in which it treated the new evidence and arguments presented by the United States in its Rebuttal Submissions. Therefore, Brazil did not, in its 23 August letter to the Panel, seek to "strike" new US evidence included in the US 22 August Rebuttal Submission, but simply asked to be provided with an opportunity to respond to that evidence.

Therefore, there is no basis for the US request.

Response to US requests to comment on Brazil's 22 August Submissions

The United States complains at several points in its letter that Brazil is presenting for the first time, in its 22 August Rebuttal Submission, responses to US arguments made in the US opening and closing oral statements at the first panel meeting. Unless particular questions from the Panel offered Brazil the opportunity to respond to arguments made by the United States in the US statements at the first panel meeting, however, Brazil's first opportunity to respond to the US arguments was in Brazil's 22 August Rebuttal Submission.

Brazil has listed below its comments to the requests by the United States:

Brazil's 22 August Rebuttal Submission

Paragraphs 4-9:

These arguments were made by Brazil in rebuttal of US and EC arguments advanced in their first submissions, oral statements and answers to questions, or reflect summaries of earlier arguments made by Brazil. The Panel should, therefore, reject the US request to comment on them.

Paragraphs 24-26:

This evidence and arguments are based on exhibits presented previously and rebut US arguments that PFC payments do not constitute support to upland cotton. Contrary to the US assertion, there is no question by the Panel to which this evidence and arguments would be responsive. Therefore, the US request should be rejected.

Paragraphs 29-35:

This evidence was presented by Brazil in rebuttal to US arguments that market loss assistance payments do not constitute support to upland cotton. The US does not assert that there would have been a question by the Panel to which this evidence and arguments would be responsive. Therefore, the US request should be rejected.

Paragraphs 36-46:

This evidence was presented by Brazil in rebuttal to US arguments that direct payments do not constitute support to upland cotton. The US does not assert that there would have been a question by the Panel to which this evidence and arguments would be responsive. Therefore, the US request should be rejected.

Paragraphs 48-50:

This evidence was presented by Brazil in rebuttal to US arguments that counter-cyclical payments do not constitute support to upland cotton. The US does not assert that there would have been a question by the Panel to which this evidence and arguments would be responsive. Therefore, the US request should be rejected.

Paragraphs 55-59:

This evidence was presented by Brazil in rebuttal to US arguments that crop insurance payments do not constitute support to upland cotton. The US does not assert that there would have been a question by the Panel to which this evidence and arguments would be responsive. Therefore, the US request should be rejected.

Brazil's 22 August Comments on US Answers

Paragraphs 44-45:

These arguments were made in rebuttal of US arguments that the restrictions on planting flexibility contained in the US PFC and direct payment programmes are consistent with Annex 2, paragraph 6. Therefore, the US request should be rejected.

Paragraphs 54-56:

These arguments are a direct reaction and comment to new information provided by the United States in response to Question 67. It is entirely appropriate to react to this information and include it in the peace clause calculation. Therefore, the US request should be rejected.

Brazil would like once more to thank the Panel for the consideration of these requests.

ANNEX K-15

LETTER FROM THE UNITED STATES
27 August 2003

Attached please find the US comments on new material in Brazil's rebuttal filings and answer to the additional question from the Panel in the dispute, *United States – Subsidies on Upland Cotton* (DS267). The United States wishes to take this opportunity to thank the Panel for its rapid consideration of, and response to, the US request to file these comments.

In Brazil's letter to the Panel of 14 August 2003, Brazil raises the concern that "basic notions of due process" require providing parties the opportunity to comment on new material. Brazil's concern and the exchanges with the Panel and the parties over the days since that letter have highlighted a particular aspect of the unique proceedings in this panel process. As a result, my authorities have instructed me to draw another matter to the Panel's attention. The United States notes that the Panel intends to express its views on the issue of the Peace Clause by 5 September 2003. No prior panel nor the Appellate Body has made findings on the Peace Clause. The submissions and material provided to the Panel to date have demonstrated that the issues involved in the Panel's findings on the Peace Clause are fact-intensive, complex and sensitive.

While prior panels have made preliminary rulings on procedural issues, no prior panel has been confronted with the situation presented in this dispute. Here, the Panel will be making substantive findings on key provisions of the covered agreements. In this connection, the United States takes note of the Panel's observation that the fairness of panel proceedings may require ensuring that the parties receive sufficient opportunity to comment on new material.[1] The United States also takes note of the provisions of paragraph 2 of Article 15 of the *Understanding on Rules and Procedures Governing the Settlement of Disputes* in which Members have agreed that parties should have an opportunity to comment on a panel's findings before they are final.

In this dispute, the Panel's findings on the Peace Clause are presumably intended to be dispositive of substantive claims and arguments of the parties for the remainder of the panel proceedings. Because of the substantive nature of those findings, the Panel's findings on 5 September will need to provide the factual basis and basic rationale underlying the findings. Both parties have a significant interest in those findings, in terms not just of the ultimate conclusion reached, but also in terms of the factual findings, rationale underlying those findings, and an understanding of the scope of those findings.[2] Accordingly, in kee-

---

[1] In the Panel's letter of 19 August 2003.

[2] Recent experience in the DSU with panel preliminary rulings has demonstrated the significant effect they can have on the parties and the course of the panel proceedings.

ping with Article 15.2 of the DSU, and in order to be fair to both parties, the United States respectfully requests that the Panel provide Brazil and the United States with the Panel's 5 September Peace Clause findings in an interim form and provide the parties an opportunity to comment on the Panel's findings.[3] The United States suggests that, in keeping with the practice in other panel proceedings and this Panel's timetable for the interim review in this dispute, two weeks should be sufficient time to comment.

The United States would be happy to provide further elaboration or to respond to any questions the Panel may have with respect to this request.

The United States is providing a copy of this submission directly to Brazil.

[3] The United States assumes that the Panel will also include its findings on the Peace Clause in its interim report issued towards the end of the panel proceedings. However, at that point the findings would have already determined the course of the remainder of the panel proceedings and it would be too late for either party to provide comments in a timely manner that would help ensure the accuracy of the facts on which the findings were based or to facilitate a clear understanding of the legal basis for those findings. Accordingly, the opportunity to comment at that stage would be inadequate to preserve the rights of both parties and could instead prejudice those rights. For the same reason, it could be perceived as circumventing the provisions of Article 15.2 of the DSU to issue substantive findings on the claims made (and that have effect on the parties) without an opportunity for the parties to comment prior to the findings having an effect.

ANNEX K-16

LETTER FROM BRAZIL

28 August 2003

The Government of Brazil is in receipt of a letter from the United States dated 27 August. Brazil notes that the US Comments to Brazil's 22 August Rebuttal Submission were filed five hours *after* the deadline of 5:30 p.m. In the covering letter to those Comments, the United States requests that the Panel provide the Parties with an opportunity to comment on an interim form of the Panel's 5 September rulings regarding peace clause-related issues.

Brazil opposes this request for the reasons stated below.

The Panel's ruling of 20 June 2003 revising the timetable for this dispute did so in order to "organize [its] proceedings in an orderly, effective and efficient manner". This 20 June 2003 decision, in the view of Brazil, addressed the concerns of Brazil that the extra briefing and meeting proposed by the United States on peace clause issues would not result in an overly lengthy delay of the resolution of Brazil's serious prejudice claims. To that end, the Panel established the date of September 1 for the Panel's decision and September 4 for Brazil to file its "Further Submission." Those dates were later extended to September 5 and 9 respectively pursuant to a 30 July Panel decision to accommodate a request of the United States for additional time to answer the Panel's questions.

Brazil is ready to file its Further Submission no later than 5:30 p.m. on 9 September. Establishing an unprecedented "interim review" for the peace clause preliminary finding will unquestionably delay Brazil's filing of its Further Submission and the Second meeting of the Panel scheduled for 7-9 October. This request will upset the balance created by the Panel's 20 June proceeding and negatively impact Brazil's rights to a speedy resolution of this dispute pursuant to DSU Article 3.3. The Panel was established more than five months ago and Brazil has yet to file its first submission on many of its claims.

Brazil notes further that DSU Article 15.2 provides an opportunity for the parties to request the panel to review "precise aspects of the interim report prior to the circulation of the final report to the Members". This actual text is contrary to the US statement that Article 15.2 provides Members "an opportunity to comment on a panel's finding before they are final". The parties' rights under Article 15.2 are explicitly recognized and preserved by paragraph 16 of the Panel's Working Procedures.

The US letter argues that the Panel must set forth its complete and full reasoning and factual findings in its 5 September decision. Brazil notes that paragraph 20 of the Panel's 20 June Decision stated that it would "express its views on whether measures raised in this dispute satisfy the conditions in Article 13 of the Agreement on Agriculture" and would "express its views in the form of ruling...". Brazil does not and would not presume or suggest what form the Panel's "ruling" will or should take. However, it is within the Panel's discretion, as with many previous panels, to provide the basic rulings on the preliminary issue and then to further elaborate such rulings in the final determination.

As the United States recognizes, there will be an opportunity for the parties to comment on the interim report that the Panel will issue following the second meeting of the Panel with the Parties. Brazil believes that its procedural rights will be fully protected by the existing procedural safeguards provided by the interim review process. The United States has provided no legitimate reasons why its rights would not also be protected. Both parties will have an equal opportunity to comment on any decision by the Panel regarding the peace clause at that time.

In sum, Brazil requests that the Panel reject the United States request to establish an interim review process to the Panel's 5 September ruling.

ANNEX K-17

LETTER FROM THE UNITED STATES
29 August 2003

By letter of 28 August 2003 Brazil objects to the US request in the dispute *United States – Subsidies on Upland Cotton* (DS267) that the Panel provide Brazil and the United States with the Panel's September 5 Peace Clause findings in an interim form and provide the parties an opportunity to comment on the Panel's findings. My authorities have instructed me to submit this response to Brazil's letter.

The United States has reviewed carefully the concerns raised by Brazil in its letter. Brazil's objection appears solely to be based on the concern that granting this request would mean that the parties would have time to review and provide comments to assist the Panel in finalizing the Panel's findings on this key element of the dispute. Brazil expresses concern that the time for comment may result in some shifting of the schedule for the remainder of the dispute.[1]

Brazil acknowledges that the parties have the right under the DSU to comment on the Panel's Peace Clause findings before they are made final. The only apparent concern for Brazil is when that right to comment can be exercised. For Brazil, the comments should only be provided when they are too late to be effective. According to Brazil's approach, while it is to be expected that the Panel could alter any part of its findings in response to a party's comments, that alteration would come after the Panel's proceedings had already taken place on the basis of the preliminary findings. Any alteration would be unable to affect the past proceedings. The United States is unable to understand how this could possibly mean, as Brazil asserts, that a party's "procedural rights will be fully protected by the existing procedural safeguards provided by the interim review process".

Brazil would compound the problem by suggesting that findings on key substantive claims may be made in just a basic form, with none of the underlying factual basis or legal reasoning. Brazil asserts that would be in keeping "with many previous panels". Brazil's assertion has no foundation. No previous panel has ever been in the current situation, nor has any previous panel made findings part-way through a dispute on the Peace Clause or on any substantive issue, let alone one as factually complex with so many legal questions of first impression. The Panel's situation is unprecedented, thus it is no surprise that there are no precedents on which to draw. However, there *is* the text of the DSU on which to draw. As the United States explained in its 27 August 2003, letter, Article 15.2 of the DSU provides the parties with a right to comment on findings in an inte-

[1] However, granting the request would not appear necessarily to mean any change in the date of circulation of the Panel's final report.

rim form. Brazil argues for an approach that would render that right largely hollow.

The United States has difficulty perceiving the basis for Brazil's objections. As the United States has argued, Brazil is barred by virtue of the Peace Clause from pursuing most of its claims in this dispute. It is strange then that Brazil would not want an opportunity to comment on any finding as to whether the Panel should hear evidence and argument on Brazil's claims.

Brazil has failed to present a basis for denying the parties a timely and effective opportunity to exercise their right to comment on the Panel's findings. Accordingly, the United States respectfully renews its request that the Panel provide Brazil and the United States with the Panel's September 5 Peace Clause findings in an interim form and provide the parties an opportunity to comment on the Panel's findings.

The United States is providing a copy of this submission directly to Brazil.

ANNEX K-18

LETTER FROM BRAZIL

29 August 2003

The Government of Brazil is in receipt of a letter from the United States dated 29 August responding to Brazil's letter of 28 August. Brazil regrets the US continuation of the debate over its unprecedented "interim review" proposal that distracts the Panel and Brazil from substantive work on this dispute. In response, Brazil refers to the arguments set forth in its letter of 28 August that provides the Panel with the basis to reject the US request for a special interim review procedure.

Brazil notes that the United States does not deny that the proposed new interim procedure would result in additional delay. This is apparently not a concern to the United States. But it is a concern to Brazil. The United States ignores the balance in the Panel's June 20 decision that struck the balance protecting Brazil's rights under Article 3.3 of the DSU.

Reviewing the Panel's decision in the Article 15.2 existing procedures will not, as the United States claims, render the parties rights "largely hollow." The practical purpose of the interim review exercise under Article 15.2 is for parties to point out any particular errors of fact or citations that the Panel may wish to correct in the final report. Thus, the "timely and effective right to comment on the Panel's finding" can be accomplished in this case - as Brazil suggests - through the use of the normal Article 15.2 procedures in the normal timeframe for making such comments.

ANNEX K-19

LETTER FROM BRAZIL COMMENTS RE REVISED TIMETABLE

9 September 2003

1. Brazil welcomes the invitation to comment on the draft further revised timetable, as attached to the Panel's communication of 5 September 2003. In this respect, Brazil recognizes that the Panel must be given all the time necessary to make the best and most objective examination of the matter before it in order to provide the Parties to the dispute with a report founded on a sound legal basis and an accurate scrutiny of the facts. Nonetheless, the proposed date for the second substantive meeting with the Parties poses a difficulty for Brazil given commitments previously scheduled by members of the legal team according to the earlier adopted timetables. Indeed, the Brazilian team would face serious difficulties to participate in meetings in Geneva from 12 to 19 November 2003.

2. Brazil would further recall that any adjustments to the draft further revised timetable should take into account the time limits established in DSU Articles 12.8 and 12.9.

3. That said, Brazil would kindly request the Panel to examine the possibility of modifying the date for the second substantive meeting with the Parties. The subsequent deadlines would be adjusted accordingly.

ANNEX K-20

LETTER FROM THE UNITED STATES COMMENTS RE REVISED TIMETABLE

9 September 2003

In the Panel's communication of 5 September 2003, the Panel invited the parties to comment on the draft further revised timetable attached to the communication. My authorities have instructed me to submit the following comments on the draft timetable and, in addition, to request that the further submission of the United States be due on 2 October rather than 23 September.

With respect to the draft timetable, the United States notes that the Panel provides separately for comments on answers to questions, due on 27 October, one week after the rebuttal submissions and answers to questions. The United States appreciates the value of an opportunity for the parties to comment on each others' answers to questions. However, in this case that opportunity comes at the cost of adequate time to prepare the rebuttal submissions and answers to questions themselves. Given the number and complexity of issues in this dispute, and the opportunity available at the second substantive meeting for parties to comment on each other's submissions[1] and responses, it would be best to dispense with the 27 October comments, and instead have 30 October – three weeks after 9 October – as the due date for rebuttal submissions and answers to questions. The first substantive meeting may finish as late as 9 October, leaving less than two weeks for rebuttals and answers to questions[2] if they are due on 22 October. The United States notes that DSU Appendix 3 provides as a guideline for 2-3 weeks between the first substantive meeting and rebuttal submissions. Given the scope and scale of argumentation that has prevailed to date, and that is likely to continue, the United States believes that at least the three week guideline provided for in Appendix 3 is necessary for the parties to have adequate time to prepare their rebuttal submissions and answers.

The United States also wishes to request that it have until 2 October to prepare its further submission. Brazil noted in its submission of 24 June 2003 that its submission due today would include "extensive evidence"[3], and we ex-

---

1 The United States notes as well that comments on rebuttal submissions could be of equal importance or value, and those will be presented at the Panel meeting.

2 The United States assumes that the questions may be at least as comprehensive at this stage as they were in connection with the Peace Clause, and therefore require significant time and care to research, develop and consult on the answers to those questions.

3 Brazil stated in paragraph 18 of its submission of 24 June 2003,

> **Consistent with the Panel's decision of 20 June decision, and because (1) Brazil's claim under GATT Article XVI:3 involves export subsidies conditionally exempt from action and (2) Brazil's actionable subsidy claims under ASCM Articles 5 and 6 involve domestic support and export subsidies conditionally exempt from action, Brazil will only present its extensive evidence in support of those claims in its "further submission".**

pect that it will also include extensive new argumentation. It is therefore likely to require significant effort and time for the preparation of a response. Brazil has had months to prepare this submission, which is a first written submission for purposes of this part of the proceedings. Appendix 3 provides for 2-3 weeks for a first submission of the party complained against[4], and the burdens imposed by this dispute clearly warrant at least a three-week response period.

Preparing the submission in three weeks would likely be extremely challenging under any circumstances. However, the timing for this submission involves unusual circumstances. Many of the US officials involved in this dispute are attending the Fifth Ministerial Conference in Cancun this week and are therefore unavailable to assist with preparation of the submission. At the same time, the head of the US litigation team in this dispute became a father three weeks ahead of schedule. As a result, he will have limited time over the next week (at least) to prepare the US response. For all of these reasons, the United States respectfully requests that its next submission be due no earlier than 2 October.[5]

---

[4] Indeed, in the DSU negotiations many Members have indicated that this is too short a period of time and that the timeframes suggested in Appendix 3 of the DSU for first submissions should be reversed between complaining parties and responding parties.

[5] The United States notes that the third party submissions could then be due on 6 October.

ANNEX K-21

LETTER FROM BRAZIL COMMENTS RE REVISED TIMETABLE

10 September 2003

Brazil is in receipt of a letter dated 9 September 2003 from the United States commenting on the proposed timetable and requesting to be able to file their Further Submission on 2 October.

Brazil opposes the US request that it be granted until 2 October to file its Further Submission for the reasons set out below:

First, the United States has been on notice of Brazil's claims and arguments on the adverse effects portion of this dispute for almost one year when Brazil filed its 27 September 2002 request for consultations (WT/DS 267/1). The Annex to this comprehensive consultation request set forth in detail arguments, facts, and evidence (mostly consisting of US Government documents) that were available to Brazil. The great majority of these arguments and evidence are now found in Brazil's Further Submission. If this information and the three sessions of the consultations discussing these issues were not enough, Brazil's First Submission at paragraphs 1-15 outlined in summary form many of the principle arguments (and evidence) supporting Brazil's adverse effects claims. All of these arguments are again repeated in Brazil's Further Submission. Paragraphs 26-106 of Brazil's First Submission also set out comprehensive facts upon which Brazil relies but not repeated in its Further Submission. Thus, in view of the transparency of Brazil's earlier submissions, the United States' claims concerning the alleged "complexity" of this dispute as justifying more time to prepare is somewhat disingenuous.

Second, Brazil and the Third Parties need sufficient time between the filing of the US Further Submission to prepare their oral statements for the second session of the First Meeting on 7-9 October. Providing the United States until 2 October to file its Further Submission will not provide the Panel, Brazil, or the third parties enough time to prepare for the hearing on 7-9 October. Given the previous practice of the United States to file its submissions six hours late (the equivalent of unilaterally granting itself an additional working day to file each submission, and of giving Brazil one less day to respond), the US request to file on 2 October probably means that Brazil will not be able to review the submission until 3 October.

Third, Brazil (and no doubt some of the third parties) has relied upon the long-standing date of 7-9 October for the resumed session of the First Meeting. Brazil notes that while the United States' letter does not ask to reschedule the date of the resumed Second Session of the First Substantive meeting, the effect of its request to file its Further Submission on 2 October does just that. Brazil strongly opposes any delay in the resumed session of the First Meeting. Brazil intends to present at least three witnesses at the resumed session - Professor Daniel Sumner, Andrew Macdonald, and an upland cotton producer from Brazil. Each of these individuals (as well as the Brazilian delegation travelling from Brasilia) have complicated schedules and they have for some time rearranged their schedules to attend the hearing on 7-9 October.

Fourth, the working procedures of the DSU provide for 2-3 weeks for the Party complained against to file its First Written Submission and 2-3 weeks for the Parties to file their Rebuttal submissions. The United States' request to file on 2 October is beyond that maximum amount of time.

However, in the spirit of compromise, and particularly in view of circumstances set out in the fourth sentence of the last full paragraph of the US letter, Brazil could agree to an extension of time *no later than* Thursday, 25 September 2003 at 5:30 p.m. *Geneva* time. In this regard, Brazil notes that both the United States and Brazil will have, under the revised timetable for Panel proceedings, numerous opportunities to brief the various issues in the adverse effects portion of this dispute and thus to fully articulate, expand, and clarify their arguments and supporting evidence.

The United States also requests that the parties be provided until 30 October to file their rebuttal submissions. Brazil has no objection to this request but believes it is important to keep the 22 October date for answering questions intact. Under Brazil's proposed procedure – which was used in the "peace clause" portion of the proceedings – the parties could use their Rebuttal Submissions as the vehicle for commenting on the Parties' answers to the questions.

ANNEX K-22

LETTER FROM THE UNITED STATES RE DRAFT REVISED TIMETABLE

11 September 2003

My authorities have instructed me to respond to Brazil's letter of 10 September 2003, objecting to the US request for an extension to file its Further Submission.

In this letter, Brazil suggests first that its request for consultations offered sufficient notice of Brazil's arguments that the United States does not now require sufficient time to respond to the Brazilian Further Submission – a submission so extensive that it had to be divided in two for electronic transmission, and which in addition included extensive economic annexes. According to Brazil, the consultation request and additional summaries of Brazil's arguments render the US reference to the complexity of the issues raised by Brazil "disingenuous."

Brazil appears to be making the implausible suggestions that it is possible to respond to arguments that have not yet been written, and that complex issues become less complex if summarized in advance. One need only note again the size of Brazil's submission to conclude that Brazil itself did not consider its previous summaries to adequately present its arguments; yet Brazil considers that those summaries should have provided a sufficient basis for the United States to prepare its response. It is a statement of the obvious that Brazil's 214-page Further Submission represents the first time Brazil has set forth its detailed arguments and evidence (including the lengthy economic analysis found in the annexes). It is this Brazilian submission, and not anticipatory summaries, to which the United States must have the ability to respond. Brazil's suggestion that the United States need not have adequate time to respond to Brazil's massive submission on the basis that Brazil's argumentation cannot, under the circumstances, be considered "complex," strains credulity.

Brazil also objects to the US extension request on the ground that Brazil and third parties need adequate time to prepare for the second session of the first panel meeting. As regards Brazil, this amounts to an argument that while one week is not enough time for it to prepare for the panel meeting, two weeks must be considered sufficient for the US to respond to Brazil's 214-page submission and economic annexes. Apparently, Brazil considers it fair that, after having had months to prepare its Further Submission, the amount of time for the US response (two weeks) should be no greater than that provided to Brazil to prepare for the first panel meeting. While the United States appreciates that the time for third-party submissions will be limited, this is frequently the case in disputes given party and panel schedules. Further, third parties are free to use the third-party session to elaborate on their written statements.

Brazil is correct when it notes that the United States has not asked the Panel to postpone the date of the first panel meeting. However, it errs when it says that the US request would require a change in the date of that meeting. To the contrary, the United States made its requests for modification of the timetable in consideration of the dates of the panel meetings and on the assumption that it might be difficult for the Panel to change that date in light of the panelists' differing schedules. Indeed, but for seeking to accommodate the panelists' schedules by retaining the meeting dates, the United States would have requested a longer response period appropriate to the argumentation and evidence Brazil has submitted.

At the same time, the United States notes that Brazil has asked the Panel to postpone the date of the second meeting. The United States has no objection in principle to this request, but would request that it be consulted on any new dates that might be possible in light of the panelists' schedules. Brazil is not the only one with "complicated schedules."

Brazil also notes that Appendix 3 provides *as a guideline* 2-3 weeks for a responding party's first submission, and states that the US request exceeds that period (by two days). Brazil ignores not only the fact that a panel is free to adjust these time frames, but that a panel is required to adjust these time frames. Article 12.4 of the DSU states that panels must "provide sufficient time for the parties to the dispute to prepare their submissions." Indeed, in the past several disputes in which the United States has been a *complaining* party, panels have on average provided five weeks for the *responding* party to prepare its first written submission, twice the average called for under the DSU.[1] Article 12.4 applies fully to this proceeding, and the time requested by the United States to prepare its submission is more than justified.

In light of the above, and now with confirmation that Brazil's Further Submission does in fact contain "extensive evidence" and "extensive new argumentation", as foreshadowed by the US letter of 9 September, 2003[2], the United States respectfully renews its request that the Panel provide it until 2 October 2003, to submit its Further Submission. We thank the Panel once again for its consideration of this and previous requests.

---

[1] Indeed, of the last 23 panels to which the United States has been a party, the single shortest time period for preparing a responding submission has been the 17 days provided in this proceeding, a marked contrast from the over 35 days provided to responding parties when the United States has been the complaining party.

[2] US letter of September 9, 2003, para. 3.

ANNEX K-23

LETTER FROM BRAZIL

16 September 2003

Brazil thanks the Panel for its "Proposed revision to timetable for Panel Proceedings" of 12 September 2003.

Brazil notices that the second hearing with the parties is scheduled for 2 and 3 December, receipt of answers to Panel's questions for 22 December and receipt of parties' comments on each other's answers for 19 January 2004. Brazil also appreciates that establishing the timetable with the parties, the panelists and the Secretariat requires considerable coordination.

In light of the several changes made to the original schedule and also of the length of time between the second hearing and the answers to questions from the Panel, Brazil would like to suggest that these answers be delivered on 15 December (instead of 22 December) and that the parties' comments on the answers be due on 22 December (instead of 19 January). This would allow for the completion of the parties' main substantive work still in 2003 (the next step would then be the comments on the descriptive part).

Furthermore, Brazil notices that Article 12.9 of the DSU establishes that "in no case should the period from the establishment of the panel to the circulation of the report to the Members exceed nine months". The new proposed timetable of the Panel foresees that circulation of the final report to the WTO Members will take place after 19 May, that is, more than 5 months in excess of the strict time limit set up in DSU Article 12.9. Therefore, Brazil would stress that any changes in the schedule should not postpone the conclusion of the proceedings.

ANNEX K-24

LETTER FROM THE UNITED STATES COMMENTS ON REVISED TIMETABLE

16 September 2003

The United States thanks the Panel for its invitation to comment on the draft further revised timetable attached to its communication of 12 September 2003. My authorities have instructed me to submit the following comments.

The new dates of December 2 and 3 for the second substantive meeting are acceptable to the United States. We note, however, that there is approximately one month between the receipt of the further rebuttals (currently due November 3) and the second substantive meeting. We believe that this one month would be better allocated for the parties to consider and draft responses to the Panel's questions and prepare their rebuttal submissions. Therefore, the United States proposes that the due date for receipt of answers to Panel's questions be changed to Friday, 31 October 2003, and that the due date for the rebuttal submissions be changed to Friday, 21 November 2003. This would leave approximately 10 days before the second Panel meeting (which would be within the DSU guideline of one to two weeks between rebuttal submissions and the second panel meeting).

There also remains some concern with the 3 p.m. deadline for filing the US further submission on 29 September. While we – as always – will try our best to accommodate this deadline, we note that the time difference between Geneva and Washington (opening of business time in Washington would be 3 p.m. Geneva time) may cause additional difficulties with respect to finalizing the US submission in capital. We nonetheless appreciate the Panel's understanding in this regard.

ANNEX K-25

LETTER FROM BRAZIL
17 September 2003

1. The Government of Brazil is in receipt of a letter from the United States dated 16 September commenting on the proposed further revised timetable attached to the Panel's communication of 12 September.

2. Brazil would like to express its opposition to the alterations suggested by the United States. In our view the dates proposed by the Panel on 12 September ensure the parties will have the appropriate amount of time to respond to the Panel's further questions and to elaborate their further rebuttal submissions. Brazil notes, in particular, that between the last day of the resumed second session of the first substantive meeting (9 October) and the deadline for delivering their further rebuttal submissions (3 November), parties will have almost 30 days to prepare such documents. This is more than the amount of time the United States requested on 9 September to elaborate its further submission (previously due on 22 September).

3. Therefore, Brazil submits that parties need not be granted any extension of deadlines as suggested by the United States. Nonetheless, were the Panel inclined to change the timetable to accommodate the US concerns, Brazil would reiterate that any modifications in the schedule should not result in further delays of the proceedings (whose current timetable already exceeds by more than five months the time limit set out in DSU Article 12.9).

ANNEX K-26

LETTER FROM THE UNITED STATES
17 September 2003

My authorities have instructed me to respond to Brazil's letter of 16 September 2003, suggesting that the parties' answers to the Panel's questions related to the second substantive meeting be due 15 December instead of 22 December, and that the comments on these answers be due 22 December instead of 19 January 2004. The United States opposes these suggestions.

As it currently stands, the issues in this dispute are both wide-ranging and complicated. Therefore, it is unrealistic to expect that the parties would need only 10 days to answer the Panel's questions, and only 7 days to comment on each other's answers. Moreover, Brazil's sole justification for its suggestion, *i.e.*, that this "would allow for the completion of the parties' main substantive work still in 2003," is a *non sequitur*, particularly in light of the fact that Brazil does not object to the rest of the Panel's further revised timetable.

ANNEX K-27

LETTER FROM THE UNITED STATES
23 September 2003

As the Panel may be aware, hurricane Isabel hit the mid-Atlantic region of the East Coast of the United States last Thursday and Friday, bringing with it significant flooding, property damage, and extended loss of electricity to hundreds of thousands of homes and businesses. The hurricane forced all US Government offices in the Washington, D.C., area to be closed on Thursday and Friday, 18 and 19 September 2003. Further, several members of the US delegation were without power through the weekend and were unable to access materials for this dispute. During this time the United States delegation was unable to work on the US further submission that is due on 29 September. As result, the United States has been significantly impeded in its preparation of that submission. At the same time, we are mindful of the October 7 through 9 dates for the next meeting with the Panel.

Accordingly, the United States would like to request a modification of the deadline for submitting its further submission so that it would be due on Thursday, 2 October. In order to provide additional time for the Panel and the parties to review the third party further submissions, currently scheduled to be submitted on Friday, October 3, the deadline for these submissions could be changed to the opening of business on Monday, 6 October 2003.

ANNEX K-28

LETTER FROM BRAZIL

23 September 2003

The Government of Brazil is in receipt of a letter from the United States dated 23 September asking for a further extension of time until 2 October 2003 to respond to Brazil's Further Submission. The most recent US request for an extension of time would mean that the Panel, Brazil, and the Third Parties would have only two working days – Friday 3 October and Monday 6 October - to review and draft an oral statement in response to the US Further Submission. Brazil would have no working days to review the numerous third party submissions.

The Panel must balance out the rights of Brazil and the Third Parties with those of the United States. The United States has been in receipt of Brazil's Further Submission for over two weeks. The United States will have a number of opportunities, including in its 7 October Oral Statement and in answering questions posed by the Panel, to clarify and expand on its responses to issues raised in Brazil's Further Submission. Under these circumstances, Brazil requests that the Panel maintain the current schedule requiring the United States to provide its Further Submission on 29 September 2003.

ANNEX K-29

LETTER FROM BRAZIL
2 October 2003

As the Panel may be aware, for the sixth consecutive time in the present proceedings the United States failed to deliver a document by the time expressly determined by the Panel in the Working Procedures and constantly reiterated to the United States in specific communications of the Panel. Instead of abiding by the 5h30 p.m. (Geneva time) deadline, the United States delivered the electronic version of its Further Submission around 11h45 p.m. on 30 September 2003, again more than 6 hours after the deadline. No hard copy of the document, also due on the same day by 5h30 p.m., was available to Brazil before 1 October.

Brazil will not repeat here the whole set of arguments showing the prejudices and obstacles caused by the US tactic to the rights of Brazil. We note however that this sixth delay is particularly egregious given the fact that the Panel provided the United States with two separate extensions of time to prepare its Further Submission. Therefore, Brazil cannot at this time only ask the Panel to take note of the problem and to encourage the United States to respect the deadlines. After six consecutive and totally unjustifiable delays, a more compelling action by the Panel appears to be necessary.

The strict observance of the deadlines is a centerpiece of any procedurally fair proceedings in all legal systems where the due process principle is expected to apply. Consequently, disrespect of the deadlines constitutes a fundamental breach of due process requirements, undermining the procedural fairness in the conduct of the examination of the matter in dispute. In other words, deadlines cannot be taken lightly. This is reinforced by DSU Article 12.5, which states: "Panels should set precise deadlines for written submissions by the parties and the parties should respect those deadlines."

In WTO dispute settlement procedures a Panel, together with the Appellate Body, must act as the guardian of the procedural fairness and, in order to act in this capacity, it is accorded the authority and discretion to establish its own working procedures, in addition to those set out in DSU Appendix 3, as recognized by the Appellate Body.[1] The working procedures are, in effect, the means by which a Panel exercises its authority and discretion to ensure that due process is respected and parties to the dispute have equal opportunities of defense. Brazil is fully aware that the term "working procedures" has been interpreted differently by WTO Members, but it is undeniable that the setting out and enforcement of deadlines is within the boundaries of the Panel's authority to establish its own working procedures.

---

1 See for instance *Australia – Measures Affecting Importation of Salmon* (DS18), Report of the Appellate Body, para. 272.

In view of the fact that Brazil's rights have been systematically impaired by the US contempt of the established rules, and taking into consideration the Panel's authority to set up procedural rules to guarantee the respect for due process requirements, Brazil requests the Panel to determine that in the next steps of the present proceedings any unjustified delay in document delivery by the US results in such document being disregarded by the Panel. In addition, Brazil requests that the Panel reflect each of the violations of the working procedures by the United States in the factual section of its Final Report so that the record of misconduct may be available to the full WTO Membership.

ANNEX K-30

LETTER FROM THE UNITED STATES
6 October 2003

The United States received on Friday, 3 October 2003, a copy of the letter to the Panel from Brazil dated 2 October 2003, and my authorities have instructed me to submit this reply. The United States regrets that Brazil once again distracts the Panel and the United States from the work required to prepare for the second session of the first panel meeting.

The United States takes seriously the time lines established by the Panel and has expended considerable resources and dedicated tremendous personnel time and effort to accommodate each of them.[1] As a result, the United States has filed each of its submissions on the date specified by the Panel. At the same time, the Panel will appreciate that the issues are not only complicated and difficult, but that there are a very large number of them – and that the materials that Brazil has submitted are voluminous.

As the complaining party in this dispute, Brazil has had the advantage of months and months in preparing its case far in advance.[2] Brazil has, however, consistently sought to deny to the United States sufficient time to prepare its own submissions, and Brazil's letter of last week regrettably continues an approach it appears to have adopted at the beginning of this dispute: to employ procedural tactics in an attempt to reduce the material and arguments that the United States could submit to the Panel to respond to Brazil's arguments, to correct factual errors by Brazil, and to explain the legal inaccuracies and omissions committed by Brazil. Those procedural tactics include in particular seeking imbalances between itself and the United States in the time provided to prepare submissions. These imbalances have been manifest from early in this dispute, as Brazil has simultaneously been submitting extraordinarily lengthy and complicated submissions and been resisting every effort of the United States to ensure that, as provided by Article 12.4 of the DSU, "the panel ... provide sufficient time for the parties to the dispute to prepare their submissions."

The United States recalls the very first example of Brazil's approach. During the organizational meeting Brazil objected to the US request that the time for the first US submission be increased beyond the two weeks contemplated in the Panel's draft timetable of 27 May. In that same meeting, however, Brazil ob-

---

[1] The United States also wishes to note that it arranged with the Brazilian Mission in Geneva to transmit a copy of its Further Submission directly to Brasilia upon filing in order to enable the Brazilian authorities to begin reviewing the document as soon as possible. The United States wishes to take this opportunity to express once again its thanks to the Brazilian Mission for its courtesy and cooperation in this connection.

[2] The document "properties" of Brazil's further submission to the Panel suggest quite clearly that Brazil began preparing its submission in April of ***2002*** - i.e., more than a year before filing it.

jected to the suggestion that it have less than two weeks after filing its first submission to submit the executive summary of that submission. As the United States commented at the time, it seemed implausible that the United States could prepare a *substantive response* to a submission in two weeks if Brazil was unable to prepare a *summary* of that submission in less than that time. Brazil's attempt to hold the United States to a two-week period to reply to the first Brazilian submission is particularly telling given that, during that organizational meeting, the Panel had not yet decided to bifurcate the parties' initial submissions. Brazil thus must have hoped to force a response in two weeks to the over 350 pages of material contained in both its first submission (24 June 2003) and in its further written submission (9 September 2003).

The exchange at the organizational meeting was only the first example of a Brazilian approach to this dispute that combines extremely lengthy material with procedural inflexibility. The most recent example was Brazil's unwillingness to contemplate an extension for the filing of the US Further Submission in response to the circumstances in Washington, D.C., brought about by Hurricane Isabel (letter of 23 September 2003).

As the United States noted in its letter of 11 September 2003, the timetable that the Panel has established in this dispute for the filing of the US submissions are much shorter than the amount of time that has been provided to other WTO Members.[3] The length and complexity of Brazil's submissions makes it increasingly difficult to consider that the United States has had sufficient time to prepare its submissions or that the United States does not suffer prejudice in this proceeding as a result.[4]

It is also difficult, in the circumstances of this dispute, to credit the Brazilian suggestion that it is *Brazil* that has suffered an "impairment" of its "rights" when the United States has filed each of its written submissions on the date specified by the Panel. Brazil's sole complaint is with the time, not the date, of filing. There is certainly no basis (and indeed Brazil has not suggested one) for Brazil's astonishing suggestion that the Panel should not consider the views of the United States in the future. Brazil's suggestion is particularly startling in light of the numerous occasions on which Brazil has made extra submissions to the Panel that were nowhere provided for in the Panel's working procedures. Brazil appears to believe that it may ignore the Panel's working procedures at its convenience.[5]

---

[3] The United States noted then that in the most recent 23 panel proceedings to which it had been a party, the single shortest time period for preparing a responding submission has been the 17 days provided in this proceeding - roughly one-half the average time period that respondents had been given when the United States was the complaining party.

[4] The United States would also like to take this opportunity to thank the Panel for agreeing to extend the deadline for the rebuttal submissions; we would hope that this extended time will help in the completion of that submission.

[5] The United States has to date in this dispute deliberately refrained from requesting that the Panel disregard Brazil' s extra-procedural material.

Brazil's suggestion that "the Panel reflect each of the violations of the working procedures by the United States in the factual section of its Final Report" continues Brazil's one-sided approach to presenting material in these proceedings. First, of course, there is no basis for Brazil's characterization of the proceedings to date nor is there any basis for Brazil to seek to use the Panel's report[6] for Brazil's own purposes. Second, the United States notes that Brazil carefully seeks to censor out any reference to Brazil's disregard for the Panel's working procedures. Third, Brazil also would appear to want to avoid any record of the US responses to Brazil's allegations, an approach which would seem to be in keeping with Brazil's attempts throughout this proceeding to limit any material that might refute Brazil's flawed claims.

In conclusion, the United States would like to thank the Panel for its work to date on the many issues presented by this dispute. We look forward to our discussions of the parties' further submissions this week.

The United States is providing a copy of this letter directly to Brazil.

6 The purpose of the Panel's report is supposed to be to help resolve the dispute in accordance with the terms of reference for the Panel, and the content of the report is specified in Articles 12.7 and 19.1 of the DSU. Brazil neglects to refer to these provisions.

ANNEX K-31

LETTER FROM THE UNITED STATES

14 October 2003

As discussed during the second session of the first panel meeting, the United States is providing in the attachment a written description of materials relating to Dr. Sumner's model that Brazil has agreed to provide to the Panel and the United States. The United States looks forward to receiving these materials at Brazil's earliest opportunity, with a view to permitting the United States to undertake its review of these materials in a timely fashion and without delay.

The United States is also providing in the attachment, as agreed, the two remaining exhibits referred to in its opening statement at the second session of the first panel meeting.

ATTACHMENT

Request from the United States to Brazil

Please provide the following information relating to the model used by Dr. Sumner in his analysis presented in Annex I to Brazil's further submission:

(a) Electronic copies of the actual models used for the baseline and each of the seven scenarios described in Annex I.

(b) Printed copies of the exact equation specifications used for the baseline and for each of the seven scenarios described in Annex I, including all parameter estimates. (If no such printed copies currently exist, please develop and provide.)

(c) Documentation of all adaptations to the original FAPRI modelling system made or used by Dr. Sumner for his analysis presented in Annex I. (If no such documentation currently exists, please develop and provide.)

ANNEX K-32

LETTER FROM BRAZIL

5 November 2003

In a letter to the Panel dated 14 October 2003, the United States requested from Brazil electronic and documentary information concerning Professor Sumner's econometric model (items a, b and c of the Annex).

In order to collect and compile that information, Professor Sumner, at the request of Brazil, has been working diligently to provide the United States with the "printed copies" of the exact equation specifications in paragraph (b) of the Annex and the "documentation of all adaptations to the original FAPRI modelling system made or used by Dr. Sumner for his analysis" as requested in paragraph (c). This process is now about to be completed and Brazil expects to provide the United States and the Panel with this information early in the week of 10 November.

As regards the request in paragraph (a) of the Annex for electronic copies of the FAPRI/CARD model used by Professor Sumner, Professor Sumner has contacted Professor Bruce Babcock of the Centre for Agricultural and Rural Development at the Iowa State University, which "owns" the FAPRI model. You will realize by the attached exchange of correspondence between Professor Sumner and Professor Babcock, that "[they] are unable to respond to your request for a simple 'electronic copy' of the FAPRI model used for the baseline and each of the seven scenarios described in Annex I because they literally do not exist".

Brazil notes, however, the last paragraph of Professor Babcock's letter which provides as follows:

> "[W]e would be willing to run USTR-requested scenarios using the FAPRI/CARD modeling system along with the operational additions and adaptations that comprise [Professor Sumner's] model of cotton policy. Our researchers would have to be compensated for the time it would take to run the model and we would have to work out the timing and other logistics of running the model".
>
> It is thus our understanding that this paragraph means that the "electronic version" of the model used by Professor Sumner is presently available for use by the US Government upon coordination with FAPRI staff."

ANNEX K-33

LETTER FROM THE UNITED STATES

11 November 2003

The United States is in receipt of Brazil's letter of 5 November 2003, in which it indicates that it expects to submit during the week of November 10 certain evidence relating to the analysis of Dr. Sumner presented in Annex I to Brazil 's further submission. My authorities have instructed me to submit this response.

The United States is disappointed that Brazil claims not to be able to provide electronic copies of the actual model used in that analysis. In our experience, it is common for electronic copies of econometric models to be disclosed to substantiate claimed model results, even in the context of WTO dispute settlement. Brazil's failure to make electronic copies available will hinder the ability of the Panel and the United States to analyze Dr. Sumner's claimed results.[1]

Brazil states that it will be providing printed copies of the exact equation specifications and documentation of all adaptations to the original FAPRI modelling system. This evidence is expected to be substantial and complex. Brazil has previously stated that its economic model "is built upon hundreds of linear supply, demand and related equations for major commodities - and in particular upland cotton - in the United States" and that "[t]hese equations are linked to a system of equations covering the demand and supply of upland cotton internationally".[2] This substantial new evidence relates to the core of Brazil's case relating to price suppression, as evidenced by the frequent invocation of those results in Brazil's further submission, at the second session of the first panel meeting, and in Brazil's answers to the Panel's further questions.

We note that the Panel and the United States had asked for this evidence during the first panel meeting, nearly five weeks ago. The United States expected this evidence to be submitted by the conclusion of the first panel meeting, or, at the latest, shortly after the United States provided Brazil with a written version of the information requested. Brazil, however, has now indicated that it will submit some of this new evidence mere days before the parties' rebuttal submissions are due.

---

1 The offer by FAPRI to run simulations at the United States request for a fee is not an acceptable substitute. It is unprecedented that a party to a dispute should put another party in the position of not being able to gain access to that party's evidence, and its only recourse is to pay a private entity in order to gain even partial access.

2 *See* Brazil's Further Submission, para. 218 ("The econometric model is built upon *hundreds of linear supply, demand and related equations* for major commodities - and in particular upland cotton - in the United States, but also accounts for regionally varying supply and demand responses in the United States. *These equations are linked to a system of equations* covering the demand and supply of upland cotton internationally.") (emphasis added).

The United States notes that, pursuant to paragraph 13 of the Panel's working procedures, the United States must be provided sufficient time to respond in writing to any new evidence submitted by Brazil. This paragraph reflects the Panel's obligation under Article 12.4 of the *Understanding on Rules and Procedures Governing the Settlement of Disputes* to "provide sufficient time for the parties to the dispute to prepare their submissions." Had Brazil presented that new evidence relating to Dr. Sumner's analysis no later than during the first panel meeting on 7-9 October 2003, as contemplated by the Panel's working procedures, under the current timetable the United States would have been afforded nearly 6 weeks to examine and respond to that evidence.[3]

Given the anticipated complexity of the information and the fact that it will not be provided in electronic form, the United States will need sufficient time to be able to analyze and respond to Brazil's complex and substantial new evidence. To this end, and on the assumption that Brazil meets its expectation of submitting that evidence early this week, the United States would request that the rebuttal submissions be due on 22 December 2003, the current date for answers to panel questions. Remaining items on the timetable set out by the Panel could then be rescheduled accordingly. Adjusting the timetable in light of Brazil's late submission of new evidence is necessary to preserve US rights of defence by providing sufficient opportunity to analyze and critique that new evidence as well as by allowing the United States to present its response to that evidence in its rebuttal submission and at the second panel meeting.[4]

---

[3] Had Brazil presented this evidence as part of Annex I to its further submission of 9 September 2003, moreover, the United States would have been afforded 10 weeks to review and respond to that evidence.

[4] *See* Working Procedures for the Panel, para. 7 ("Formal rebuttals shall be made at a second substantive meeting of the Panel.... . The parties shall submit, prior to that meeting, written rebuttals to the Panel.") (28 May 2003).

ANNEX K-34

LETTER FROM BRAZIL
12 November 2003

The Government of Brazil is in receipt of a letter from the United States dated 11 November requesting yet another lengthy delay in this panel proceeding. Brazil requests the Panel to reject this request and maintain the current schedule including the deadline for rebuttal submissions of 18 November and the second Panel meeting on 2-3 December for the reasons set forth below.

The United States' letter attempts to leave the impression that there will be a tremendous amount of new evidence that will be provided to them in *written* form in response to their request of 14 October. This is incorrect. The bulk of the requested information is in *electronic* form which has been available for the United States to examine, review, and use since 5 November. Attached to this letter are (1) Professor Sumner's *written* adaptations to the FAPRI model for each of the seven scenarios described in Annex I to Brazil's Further Submission (Exhibit Bra-313), and (2) Professor Sumner's summary description of the equations in the FAPRI domestic model and the CARD international cotton model (Exhibit Bra-314). As the Panel can see from Exhibit Bra-313, this document reflecting Professor Sumner's adaptations is not lengthy and does not contain hundreds of equations as the US letter suggests. The "hundreds of equations" referred to in the US letter are those of the *FAPRI/CARD* model used by Professor Sumner and summarized in Exhibit Bra-314. Brazil believes that the US econometric experts who deal with the FAPRI model on a regular basis will not have any difficulty understanding Exhibit Bra-313. Professor Sumner, of course, will be prepared to provide any additional follow-up information and clarifications, as necessary, at the Panel meeting on 2-3 December for which he has made arrangements in his schedule to attend.

Brazil has been informed by Professor Sumner that he is working as quickly and thoroughly as he can in completing this work in addition to his other many responsibilities as the Director of the Agricultural Issues Centre at the University of California at Davis. Professor Sumner indicates he expects to be able to provide the relevant equations for the CARD international cotton model by the close of business on 13 November. This will complete Brazil's response to the US request of 14 October. Because Professor Sumner made no adaptations to the CARD international cotton model, the information to be provided will simply be the equations for a model that is much-used and well-known to USDA economists.

Brazil notes that the United States waited until 14 October to file its request for this information from Brazil. Brazil's letter of 5 November provided the United States with an offer of complete access to the electronic version of the exact same model used by Professor Sumner. The United States then waited almost a week to reply to Brazil's 5 November letter with full knowledge that the date for the Further Rebuttal Submission was 18 November. It appears as if the United States has *not* used the week since 5 November to take advantage of its ability to review and analyze the complete electronic version of everything that Professor Sumner has done in his analysis. As the last paragraph of Professor Babcock's letter of 31 October stated, upon request, the United States will be provided full and immediate access to the FAPRI and CARD models and Professor Sumner's adaptations that are available in electronic form.

Contrary to the US unsupported assertion, Brazil has not "put the United States in the position of not being able to gain access to that party's evidence." Rather, Professor Babcock's offer provides the United States with complete access to the electronic version of *all* of the equations and analysis performed by Professor Sumner and the United States had access to them since 5 November.

Brazil further notes that it was required to use the FAPRI/CARD model for a fee, that neither Brazil nor Professor Sumner owns or can copy this model, and as explained by Professor Babcock, that there is no "written version" of the FAPRI model. The United States can, however, make arrangements with FAPRI officials to use the model and it would certainly not be unprecedented for the United States Government (or other governments or private entities) to compensate FAPRI for the use of the FAPRI model.

Brazil notes that USDA economists and officials use the FAPRI model frequently and are well aware of its parameters (for which the USDA provided it with its highest honorary award in 2002). Therefore, it will not be difficult for the United States to quickly analyze Professor Sumner's limited adaptations to the standard FAPRI/CARD models with which they are familiar. Brazil also notes that the FAPRI project is financed in large part by the US Congress

With respect to the existing schedule, Brazil considers that there is no legal or due process basis for the Panel to again delay the proceedings. Indeed, the existing schedule has considerable flexibility to provide the United States with more than sufficient time to prepare any rebuttal of Professor Sumner's analysis. In order to avoid further delay, Brazil suggests that the United States and Brazil file their rebuttal submissions on 18 November and the Panel hold the second meeting of the Panel with the Parties on 2-3 December as originally scheduled.

If the United States determines that it does not have sufficient time to (a) use the exact same FAPRI/CARD electronic model as adapted by Professor Sumner (as offered by Professor Babcock) and (b) to analyze Professor's Sumner's written equations and explanations of adaptations to the FAPRI model by 18 November, then Brazil would have no objection to the United States providing its rebuttal to Professor Sumner's analysis by 28 November, a few days prior to the Panel meeting on 2-3 December. This rebuttal, however, would be in addition to the 18 November Rebuttal on the multitude of other issues in this proceeding that do not relate in any way to Professor Sumner's analysis.

Brazil notes that the current schedule is also flexible enough to allow for rebuttal and counter-rebuttal by the Parties of the US analysis of Professor Sumner's results, *i.e.,* until the 22 December and 19 January deadlines for answering and then commenting on the Answers to the Panel's Questions. Of course, if the Panel determines that the United States and Brazil need additional time to comment on the econometric models or other issues, then the Panel has the discretion to allow for this for periods after 19 January 2004.

Brazil believes that this proposal will protect the United States' and Brazil's due process rights without yet again delaying this proceeding. It will allow the Panel and the Parties to maintain their current travel and business schedules which have now been in place for some time. Brazil notes that its delegation has scheduled a number of meetings and travel with a view towards the 2-3 December meeting date.

Finally, Brazil stresses that any changes in the schedule must not further delay the date of issuance of the final report to the parties, since the time limits of DSU Articles 12.8 and 12.9 have already been breached.

ANNEX K-35

LETTER FROM THE UNITED STATES

13 November 2003

My authorities have instructed me to respond to Brazil's letter of 12 November 2003, in which Brazil objects to the US request for an extension of time for the filing of rebuttal submissions in this dispute. Brazil ignores the Panel 's working procedures and the arguments in our letter of 11 November 2003, in dismissing the possibility that the United States would be prejudiced if the briefing schedule were not adjusted to take into account Brazil's decision to submit new evidence relating to the analysis of Dr. Sumner nearly five weeks after the conclusion of the first panel meeting. Brazil's 12 November letter cannot change the fact that United States will be prejudiced if it is not given adequate time to analyze the materials Brazil is only now providing.

First, Brazil simply does not discuss either the requirements of DSU Article 12.4, which provides that "[i]n preparing the timetable for the panel process, the panel shall provide sufficient time for the parties to the dispute to prepare their submissions," or the provisions of paragraph 13 of the Panel's working procedures, pursuant to which the United States must be provided sufficient time to respond in writing to any new evidence submitted by Brazil.

Second, Brazil states that it "would have no objection to the United States providing its rebuttal to Professor Sumner's analysis by 28 November, a few days prior to the Panel meeting on 2-3 December" and that "the current schedule is also flexible enough to allow for rebuttal and counter-rebuttal by the Parties of the US analysis of Professor Sumner's results, i.e., until the 22 December and 19 January deadlines for answering and then commenting on the Answers to the Panel's Questions". The United States cannot agree to this proposal. Indeed, this suggestion by Brazil would make it appear that Dr. Sumner's analysis was an issue of secondary importance to Brazil's allegations, such that the US response is not important to the Panel's evaluation. The reality, of course, is that Brazil's main economic conclusions rest on Dr. Sumner's analysis. If not, there would have been no reason for Brazil to reference that analysis repeatedly in its further submission, to attach Dr. Sumner's analysis as a 52-page annex to that submission, to call upon Dr. Sumner to deliver a 16-page statement as part of its opening statement and a four-page statement as part of its closing statement at the second session of the first panel meeting, nor to continue referencing Dr. Sumner's analysis in its answer to the Panel's further questions. It is simply not credible for Brazil to suggest that no prejudice would result to the United States if it were compelled to prepare and file a rebuttal submission without having had sufficient opportunity to examine and critique Brazil's new evidence relating to the very model which allegedly underlies Dr. Sumner's analysis.

Third, Brazil has also indicated that it will file *even more* new evidence on 13 November relating to Dr. Sumner's analysis. In addition to the prejudice that would result from not being able to prepare our rebuttal submission and prepare for the second panel meeting with sufficient time to analyze this new evidence, the United States notes that it has already been prejudiced because preparation of the US rebuttal submission over the last several weeks has been based on the materials which we have had at hand, that is to say, neither the materials included with Brazil 's 12 November letter nor those it says will be forthcoming on 13 November. Elements of the US rebuttal could be superseded or confirmed on the basis of Brazil's new information. Thus, without an extension of time, the United States will be forced either to reply to Dr. Sumner 's analysis in the absence of complete information or to defer responding to the centrepiece of Brazil's case.

Fourth, Brazil is in error when it claims that "the United States waited until 14 October to file its request for this information from Brazil". In fact, both the United States and the Panel Chairman verbally requested access to Brazil' s model on 7 October 2003, at the conclusion of opening statements on the first day of the second session of the first panel meeting. Brazil has provided no explanation for why it should have delayed providing any information in response to that request for nearly five weeks, which merely related to the very model that Dr. Sumner asserts to have employed.

Fifith, Brazil also claims that "Brazil's letter of 5 November provided the United States with an offer of complete access to the electronic version of the exact same model used by Professor Sumner" and "Professor Babcock's offer provides the United States with complete access to the electronic version of all of the equations and analysis performed by Professor Sumner *and the United States had access to them since 5 November*" (italics added). Presumably, Brazil is referring to its suggestion that the United States pay to *run* the model employed by Brazil[1], since FAPRI did not offer to disclose – either to the United States or the Panel – the equations underlying that model, whether for pay or otherwise (and we assume Brazil was also offering to the Panel this opportunity to pay to obtain Brazil's evidence). As stated in the US letter of 11 November, Brazil's suggestion that the responding party (and presumably the Panel) must pay for evidence on which the complaining party so heavily relies is unprecedented.

Sixth, Brazil also claims that "it will not be difficult for the United States to quickly analyze Professor Sumner's limited adaptations to the standard FAPRI/CARD models with which they are familiar." If it is the case that Professor Sumner has made only "limited adaptations to the standard FAPRI/CARD models," a claim we are not in a position to confirm, then again the question arises why Brazil should have delayed five weeks in providing these new materials. Presumably, Professor Sumner knew of and had documented those adaptations

[1] *See* Brazil's Letter of 5 November 2003, p. 2 (quoting FAPRI letter as saying that FAPRI "'would be willing to run USTR-requested scenarios using the FAPRI/CARD modeling system along with the operational additions and adaptations that comprise [Professor Sumner's] model of cotton policy. Our researchers would have to be compensated for the time it would take to run the model and we would have to work out the timing and other logistics of running the model.'").

prior to submitting his analysis to the Panel as part of Brazil' s further submission on 9 September.

The United States respectfully requests the Panel to defer the parties' rebuttal submissions as set out in its letter of 11 November 2003. The United States is providing a copy of this letter directly to Brazil.

ANNEX K-36

LETTER FROM BRAZIL
13 November 2003

Brazil is in receipt of a letter from the United States dated 13 November. Brazil reiterates its request that the Panel adhere to the existing schedule along with the suggested modifications proposed by Brazil in its letter of 12 November. Brazil responds to the numbered paragraphs of the US 13 November letter below using the same paragraph numbers.

First, Brazil notes that with respect to DSU Article 12.4, the normal amount of time for a rebuttal submission set out in Annex 3 of the DSU is 2-3 weeks from the date of the First Substantive meeting. The Panel in this case provided the parties with a period of six weeks to prepare rebuttal submissions. Based on Brazil's suggestion that the United States have until 28 November to prepare a rebuttal on a single aspect of Brazil's evidence, the United States will have had **23 days** (from 5 November or more than three weeks) to examine, use, and analyze the full electronic version of everything that Professor Sumner examined. In addition, the United States would have **16 days** from 12 November to examine Professor Sumner's written adaptations to the FAPRI/CARD model and **15 days** (from November 13) to examine the full CARD international cotton model. All of these time frames either exceed or are within the 2-3 week period for rebuttal submissions set out in Annex 3 to the DSU. Therefore, there is no basis for the United States to claim any violation of either its due process rights or of DSU Article 12.4.

Second, Professor Sumner's analysis is not the "centrepiece" of Brazil's adverse effects case that the United States claims. Brazil has placed an enormous amount of evidence before the Panel that exists independently of Professor Sumner's analysis. Brazil has repeatedly emphasized in this dispute that Professor Sumner's analysis confirms econometrically what common sense and the overwhelming body of other evidence already conclusively demonstrates. The Panel need only examine paragraph 105 of Brazil's Further Submission to appreciate this point. Even Professor Sumner's econometric analysis is only one of many such analyses of the impact of US upland cotton subsidies that is referenced in Brazil's submissions. Professor Sumner has functioned for Brazil in these proceedings as a dual expert – as one who is expert in US subsidy programs and the US agricultural system, as well as an expert in econometric analysis.

Third, Brazil attaches as Exhibit Bra-315 the documentation for the CARD international cotton model.[1] This model is well-known to USDA economists and has not been changed for Professor Sumner's analysis. Therefore, this

---

[1] Brazil is also providing herewith an electronic version of the CARD international cotton model via email.

information will not be "new" to the United States or is something that it could not otherwise have already anticipated in preparing their arguments.

Fourth, the United States did not provide in writing, exactly what evidence it wanted from Professor Sumner until 14 October. Brazil provided access to the complete electronic version of Professor Sumner's analysis – which *only* exists in electronic form – on 5 November. This was not five weeks after receipt of the US request as the US claims. The additional information provided on 12 and 13 November required Professor Sumner to expend considerable amount of time. His busy schedule at the University of California at Davis as well as previous speaking commitments posed additional difficulties in completing this assignment.

Fifth, the United States again demonstrates that it has made no efforts to take advantage of the offer to gain access to *everything* that Professor Sumner did and analyzed, which is contained in the electronic version at the University of Iowa in the care of Professor Babcock. It appears to Brazil that the United States' conduct suggests it may be more interested in delaying this proceeding than in gaining access to Professor Sumner's analysis.

Sixth, the United States claims that it has only a small amount of time to change their rebuttal submission. Brazil notes that on 24 June 2003, it filed a lengthy submission after only being given 4 days notice of what it was required to file. Brazil, at great effort, met that deadline. Further, the additional ten days proposed by Brazil (until 28 November) provide the United States with an opportunity to react to and respond to Professor Sumner's documents delivered on 12 and 13 November. The United States will have additional time to prepare further responses for their oral statement on 2 December. Finally, as Brazil's 12 November letter indicated, both Brazil and the United States will have until 22 December and 19 January to file additional answers to questions and comments relating, *inter alia,* to the econometric models at issue in this dispute.

In conclusion, the Panel has to balance the right of the United States to have sufficient time to prepare a rebuttal to Professor Sumner's analysis with Brazil's right to obtain a timely panel decision. Brazil believes that its suggestion to provide the United States with an additional 10 days to prepare its rebuttal – until 28 November – is an appropriate result which is fair and protects each of the parties' due process rights. However, the request by the United States for another five weeks to prepare their rebuttal and to delay this proceeding by at least as much time, if not more, is grossly out of proportion. Brazil requests the Panel to avoid yet another long delay in these proceedings.

ANNEX K-37

LETTER FROM THE UNITED STATES
18 December 2003

In a communication dated 8 December 2003, the Panel afforded to the United States the opportunity to respond by 18 December 2003, to the request that Brazil had made through the Panel for certain information in Exhibit BRA-369.[1] The United States has completed work on 3 electronic files containing approximately 135 megabytes of requested data related to the production flexibility contract payment era, which are being transmitted with this letter. Work on the data files relating to the direct and counter-cyclical payment era is continuing, and the United States is endeavouring to provide this data by close of business Friday, 19 December.

However, as the United States preliminarily advised Brazil and the Panel at the second panel meeting, the release of planted acreage information associated with a particular farm, county, and state number is confidential information that cannot be released under US domestic law, in particular the Privacy Act of 1974.[2] This is consistent with the position of the United States in Freedom of Information Act[3] appeals raising this issue. One such decision is attached as Exhibit US-104.[4] Although the United States cannot provide planted acreage information associated with an individual farm, in an effort to be as fully responsive as possible, we are providing, for all programme crops and for each marketing year: (1) planted acreage data aggregated for all cotton farms and (2) farm-level planted acreage data without any fields that could identify the particular farm.

The United States is providing all of the pieces of data requested by Brazil in data files organized as follows:[5]

> *First*, a file with aggregate data for yields, bases, cropland, and plantings for all "cotton farms" for all programme crops as defined in the data request, using three categories: (1) farms with "cotton base" but no cotton plantings; (2) farms with cotton plantings but

---

1 *See* Exhibit US-102.

2 *See* 5 USC 552a(b) (Exhibit US-107).

3 Exhibit US-103.

4 We note that no final denial of a release may be made by the US Department of Agriculture without the concurrence of USDA's Office of General Counsel. *See* 7 CFR 1.14 (Exhibit US-105). The attached appeal determination is consistent with USDA's long-standing policy that planted acres will not be released. For example, the policy against release has been stated explicitly since 1997 in FSA's FOIA Handbook. (*See* Exhibit US- 106.)

5 In addition to the data requested by Brazil, the United States has provided total cropland and programme payment units (base acreage x base yield x .85) to allow for more meaningful aggregation.

no "cotton base," and (3) farms with cotton plantings and "cotton base."

Second, a farm-by-farm file (with particular farm identification information) with all of the requested data (plus additional data regarding payment quantities) but not including planted acres and cropland.

Third, farm-by-farm files for planted acres only for all programme crops, but with no other data and with the order of the farms scrambled in order to prevent any matching of farms.

The three files have been copied to a CD. The base and yield data are a text file named "Pfcby.txt." A description of that file and its 118 fields is found at Exhibit US-109. Planted acres are in "Pfcplac.txt". A description of that file is found at Exhibit US-110. Finally, the aggregate data file is named "Pfcsum.xls". That file is an Excel file and the headings within the file should be self- explanatory.

The information that we are providing is also sensitive. We do not consent to release of this information to the public domain and expect that it will be used solely for purposes of this dispute settlement proceeding. Therefore, pursuant to paragraph 3 of the Panel's working procedures, we designate this information as confidential and must exceptionally insist that this information not be disclosed outside of the delegation of the Brazilian Government and the Panel.

During the Panel meeting, Brazil referred to information released by the United States in connection with rice. This release was an error. Apparently, the Kansas City office of the Farm Services Agency (FSA) believed at some point that the Washington FOIA office had approved the release of planted acres so long as names and addresses were left out. FSA Washington personnel were not aware of that misunderstanding. It has been corrected. The farm number is unique and can be linked back to the name and address of persons on the farm using the FSA-supplied Environmental Working Group (EWG) payment and name and address files.[6] The payment files will allow a match by farm number. This leads, by the same file, to the "customer number". That number leads, in the name and address file, to the name and address of the farm owner. At the second Panel meeting, Brazil indicated that the rice request was theirs. We ask accordingly that Brazil and its agents return all copies of the erroneous rice release.[7]

The United States also notes that responding to Brazil's request has not been a simple undertaking. Because of the extensive nature of the request, it was necessary to run through approximately 10 million files to extract the pertinent information. There are approximately 2 million farms involved. For the production flexibility contract ("PFC") payment era under the 1996 Act, there were 7

---

[6] *See* Exhibit US-108 (excerpt of BRA-316).

[7] Regarding that release, the United States notes, too, that no member of the US delegation at the second panel meeting in Geneva was aware of the rice release. On inquiry, no one at FSA in Washington was aware of it either. The rice data was sent to an address in Geneva identified by the requester, a member of the Brazilian delegation, who the Kansas City office was led to understand had "relatives" there.

programme crops. In the direct payment and counter-cyclical ("DCP") payment era under the 2002 Act, there are 10 programme crops (counting "other oilseeds", such as rapeseed, canola, etc., as one "programme crop" only). The PFC file alone, if each field for each farm was considered a cell, contains 25 million cells of information. The task involved is a far bigger, far more complicated task than the erroneous rice release. More than 250,000 farms fit the "cotton farm" definition at work in this exercise. The United States has expended a significant amount of time and resources to respond to this data request.[8]

Per Brazil's request, the United States is providing a copy of this letter, associated exhibits, and three electronic data files relating to the production flexibility contract payment era directly to Brazil through the Brazilian Embassy in Washington, D.C. Because of their size, the electronic data files will be couriered to Geneva for transmission to the Panel.

---

[8] There may well be limitations in the data output since the output depends on the completeness and accuracy of input from the FSA county offices. Moreover, not all farms file crop reports and not all plantings are plantings of programme crops. These are merely some examples.

ANNEX K-38

LETTER FROM THE UNITED STATES

22 December 2003

Further to the letter of the United States to the Panel on 18 December 2003, attached please find a letter from the United States to the Embassy of Brazil in Washington, D.C., dated 19 December 2003, transmitting directly to Brazil the completed electronic data files relating to the direct and counter-cyclical payment era. Please also find attached Exhibits US-111 and US-112. This letter, the electronic data files, and the two exhibits were received by the Embassy of Brazil on 19 December. The electronic data files are presently en route to Geneva, and will be transmitted to the Brazilian Mission to the WTO and to the Panel shortly.

In a letter dated 18 December 2003, to the Chairman of the Panel in the WTO dispute settlement proceeding *United States – Subsidies on Upland Cotton* (DS267), the United States indicated that it would endeavour to provide additional information responding to the request of Brazil conveyed in Exhibit BRA-369 by Friday, 19 December. In particular, we indicated that preparation of certain direct and counter-cyclical payment era electronic files was continuing. Those files have now been completed and are being transmitted with this letter.

There are three direct and counter-cyclical payment era files, containing approximately 85 megabytes of requested data, on the enclosed CD. These three files correspond to the three production flexibility contract payment era files transmitted previously. First, there is a farm-by-farm base and yield data file ("Dcpby.txt"); a description of that file and its 99 fields is found at Exhibit US-111. Second, there is a planted acres file ("Dcpplac.txt"); a description of that file is found at Exhibit US-112. For the reasons set forth in the 18 December letter to the Chairman, we note that the order of the records in the planted acre file is not the same as in the base and yield file. Finally, there is an aggregate data file ("Dcpsum.xls"); that file is an Excel file, and the headings within the file should be self-explanatory.

As indicated in the 18 December letter to the Chairman, the information that we are providing is sensitive. We do not consent to release of this information to the public domain and expect that it will be used solely for purposes of this dispute settlement proceeding. Therefore, pursuant to paragraph 3 of the Panel's working procedures, we designate this information as confidential and must exceptionally insist that this information not be disclosed outside of the delegation of the Brazilian Government and the Panel.

The United States is providing a copy of this letter, associated exhibits, and three electronic data files relating to the direct and counter-cyclical payment era directly to the Panel.

ANNEX K-39

LETTER FROM BRAZIL

23 December 2003

As per its Communication of 8 December 2003, the Panel established 22 December as a deadline for the delivery by Brazil and the United States of the Answers to Questions from the Panel and also for the delivery of the US comments on Brazil's econometric model.

In its Communication of 13 October, the Panel established that "*In accordance with paragraph 17 (b) of the Panel's working procedures, the Panel sets the following time for the provision of submissions by the parties: 11.59 p.m., Geneva time on the dates concerned. This time refers to receipt of submissions by the other party and the Secretariat and not to commencement of transmission. For greater clarity, this time for receipt of submissions also refers to the time of completion of receipt of any Exhibits and service of any Exhibits (if necessary electronically) to the other party and to the Secretariat as envisaged in paragraphs 17 (a)-(d) of the Panel's working procedures. All other provisions of the Working Procedures remain unchanged*".

The "Working Procedures for the Panel" establish in paragraph 17 b that

> *"the parties and third parties should provide their submissions to the Secretariat by 5:30 pm on the deadlines established by the Panel, unless a different time is set by the Panel"*

and in paragraph 17 d that,

> *"the parties and third parties shall provide electronic copies of all submissions to the Secretariat at the time they provide their submissions [...]".*

The US submissions were not delivered within the deadline of 11.59 p.m. provided by the Panel, which is already an exception to the generally observed deadline of 5:30pm. Neither the paper nor the electronic versions of the submissions were delivered on 22 December until 11.59 p.m.. As duly registered at the form provided by the Secretary to the Panel, the US submission had not been delivered until 0.35 a.m. and it was apparently delivered as late as 1.08 a.m.. The electronic version was sent at 0.47 a.m. and received by Brazil at 1.34 a.m.

Brazil notes that, apart of the impairment of Brazil's rights under the DSU, the delay by the US also involves significant administrative constraints for the Brazilian Delegation in Geneva, which maintains human resources active until such a time as the US delivers the documents

This is already the seventh time the United States fails to deliver a document by the time expressly determined by the Panel. This issue has also been addressed during the panel hearing on 7 to 9 October and the Panel has already explicitly requested the United States to respect the deadlines of the dispute – "in order to ensure due process and secure a balance between the two parties" (Panel's Communication of 13 October). In its letter of 2 October, Brazil had requested the Panel to "determine that in the next steps of the present proceedings any unjustified delay in document delivery by the US results in such document being disregarded by the Panel".

Brazil therefore hereby requests that the documents delivered today by the United States, in renewed disrespect of the established deadline, be disregarded by the Panel.

Please accept, Sir, the assurances of my highest consideration.

ANNEX K-40

LETTER FROM BRAZIL

23 December 2003

The Government of Brazil is in receipt of a letter from the Panel dated 23 December enclosing a number of new questions to Brazil (eight) and to the United States (five) with a deadline set for 12 January. These questions address new interpretations by the Appellate Body, are very comprehensive, and in the view of Brazil will require a significant allocation of resources to complete properly.

Brazil notes that in addition to answering these questions, it must also respond to an extensive US critique of Professor Sumner's analysis, as well as provide comments and analysis on the US 18 December 2003 data, by 12 January. Because Brazil was not aware that the Panel would be filing these new questions, its representatives made severely tight travel and professional commitments that try to accommodate the upcoming holidays bearing in mind the original two deadlines for 12 January (Sumner and 18 December rebuttals).

In consideration of the above, Brazil requests that the Panel push the schedule back by only one week. The original 12 January deadline would be moved to 19 January, and the 19 January deadline for comments on the answers to the Parties' questions would be moved to 26 January. Other aspects of the schedule would be adjusted accordingly by the Panel, but with no more than a one week delay for the issuance of the final report, if this should be deemed necessary by the Panel.

Please accept, Sir, the assurances of my highest consideration.

ANNEX K-41

LETTER FROM THE UNITED STATES

23 December 2003

At the Panel's invitation, my authorities have instructed me to provide the following comments on Brazil's letter of 23 December 2003, in which Brazil requests that the upcoming schedule of filings be delayed.

The United States is amenable to Brazil's extension request, with the alternations suggested below, because it is well aware of the burdens that the very tight time frame established in this dispute has imposed on the parties (and the Panel), particularly in light of the complexity of the matter before the Panel and the volume of materials necessary to examine that matter. In fact, the United States has in the past three business days alone:

- Filed via two letters dated 18 and 19 December 2003, approximately two hundred megabytes of data requested by Brazil. Attempting to collect, prepare, and file these data within the time set out by the Panel in its 8 December communication required enormous efforts on the part of the United States, necessarily affecting preparations of the US answers to the Panel's questions and the US comments on Brazil's econometric model.
- Filed answers to approximately 51 questions from the Panel, within the same time that Brazil had to answer approximately 32 questions. (Indeed, given Brazil's comment that the "eight" new questions directed to it "in the view of Brazil will require a significant allocation of resources to complete properly" and therefore justify an extension of time, Brazil should now understand – if it did not before – the significantly greater burdens placed on the United States in responding to approximately 20 more questions than Brazil was asked to respond to.)
- Filed comments on Brazil's econometric model. In making this filing, the United States was faced with examining, and preparing and filing comments on the FAPRI model transmitted to the United States by Dr. Bruce Babcock, per the Panel's communication dated 8 December 2003, within the time originally set out by the Panel only to address Brazil's exhibits and models.

Had the United States focused its energies only on the answers to the Panel's questions and the comments on Brazil's economic modelling, the filing of those documents would not have been delayed, but the United States chose to make best efforts to comply with all of the requests and time frames set by the Panel in this dispute. It is only due to tremendous efforts by US personnel in Washington, Kansas City, and Geneva that Brazil is even in a position to cite the need to respond to the data submitted by the United States as part of the reason a delay in the schedule is needed.

In light of the foregoing, the United States would be willing to agree to an extension of time. However, instead of Brazil 's proposal, the United States would ask that the schedule be altered as follows: First, we would ask that the filing of the parties' responses to the additional questions from the Panel (dated 23 December 2003), as well as Brazil's comments originally scheduled for 12 January 2004, be moved to 21 January (to take into account the fact that 19 January is a US Federal holiday). We would then request that the parties' comments on each other's answers be moved to 2 February. The reason for this latter proposal is because, in addition to filing comments on Brazil's answers to the Panel's additional questions on that date, the United States will also be filing – per the Panel's communication of 8 December 2003 – comments on (1) Brazil's comments on the data provided by the United States on 18 and 19 December 2003, as well as (2) Brazil's comments on the US comments on Brazil's economic model. Given Brazil's confirmation in its letter that its submissions on these matters will require four weeks to prepare, the United States and the Panel can expect that those comments will be extensive. Thus, one week to respond to Brazil 's three submissions would understandably be insufficient; for due process reasons, the United States believes at least two weeks would be needed to respond to Brazil's four weeks worth of comments and answers.

In agreeing to Brazil's extension request, with the above caveats, the United States notes that it is simply seeking to advance the goal of WTO dispute settlement – that is, the effective resolution of disputes, rather than pursuing litigation tactics designed merely to disadvantage the other party procedurally. In this regard, we regret Brazil's second letter of 23 December, requesting that certain US documents "be disregarded by the Panel". The United States has in a communication earlier today expressed its regret for any inconvenience that may have resulted to the Panel and Brazil due to the delay in submitting the US comments and its answers to questions from the Panel, noting largely the same reasons Brazil is now relying on to support its extension request. Indeed, this delay resulted in large measure from the US determination to make best efforts to respond to Brazil's request for certain information while simultaneously preparing its comments and answers. In this connection, we find it interesting that Brazil is seeking to have the Panel "disregard[]" the US answers and comments, but not the extensive data requested by Brazil, which was provided on 19 December, one day after the date set out in the Panel's 8 December communication. The significant burdens on all parties to a WTO dispute, and this dispute in particular, are well-understood. The effective functioning of the dispute settlement system and the resolution of disputes are not served through one-sided approaches that only recognize the burdens place on one party but not the other.

ANNEX K-42

REPLIES OF THE UNITED STATES TO ARTICLE 13 REQUEST
20 January 2004

The United States is in receipt of a request for information from the Panel pursuant to Article 13 of the *Understanding on Rules and Procedures Governing the Settlement of Disputes* transmitted on 12 January 2004. In its request, the Panel "requests the United States to provide the same data that it agreed to provide in its letters dated 18 and 22 December 2003 but in a format which permits matching of farm-specific information on contract payments with farm-specific information on plantings".[1] The Panel's request states that "[d]isclosure is sought to permit an assessment of the total expenditures of PFC, MLA, CCP and direct payments by the US Federal Government to upland cotton producers in the relevant marketing years" and invites the United States to "protect the identity of individual producers by, for example, using substitute farm numbers which still permit data-matching". My authorities have instructed me to submit this response.

With respect to the Panel's explanation that "disclosure is sought to permit an assessment of the total expenditures of PFC, MLA, CCP and direct payments by the US Federal Government to upland cotton producers in the relevant marketing years", the United States notes that it has previously provided data that permits calculation of "total expenditures" for all decoupled payments made to farms planting upland cotton with respect to historical base acres (whether upland cotton base acres or otherwise). In particular, for the production flexibility contract payment era, we provided a farm-by-farm file ("Pfcby.txt") with base acreage and yield data for all programme crops for all "cotton farms" as defined in BRA-369 and data file ("Pfcsum.xls") that aggregated this data for ease of use.[2] The "programme payment units" field allows for easy calculation of "total expenditures" to farms planting upland cotton in any given year by multiplying payment units by the applicable payment rate. Similarly, for the direct and counter-cyclical payment era, the United States provided a farm-by-farm file ("Dcpby.txt") with base acreage and yield data and an aggregate data file ("Dcpsum.xls").[3] Again, the "programme payment units" field allows for easy calculation of total expenditures by multiplying payment units by the applicable

[1] The Panel's request references US letters dated 18 and 22 December 2003, providing certain information from Brazil. The United States understands the latter reference to be to the 19 December letter to Brazil that was transmitted to the Panel and the Brazilian Mission to the WTO on 22 December 2003.

[2] These files were provided, per Brazil's request, to the Brazilian Embassy in Washington, D.C., on 18 December 2003 via CD-ROM. The US letter was filed with the Panel on 18 December, and the CD-ROM was delivered via courier to Geneva and filed with the Panel on 23 December 2003.

[3] These files were provided to the Brazilian Embassy in Washington, D.C., on 19 December 2003 via CD-ROM. The US letter was filed with the Panel on 22 December, and the CD-ROM was delivered via courier to Geneva and filed with the Panel on 23 December 2003.

payment rate. Thus, the data already provided by the United States to Brazil and the Panel would permit an assessment of total expenditures of decoupled payments to farms planting upland cotton.

The United States has studied the Panel's request for certain farm-specific data as well as its suggestions with respect to protecting US producers' privacy interests. The United States thanks the Panel for recognizing the important confidentiality concerns which arise from Brazil's request to receive, by farm number, contract payment and planting information. The Panel will recall that at the second panel meeting the US delegation expressly inquired of the Brazilian delegation whether the United States could provide the requested data in some format that also protected the identity of individual producers. The Brazilian delegation refused to answer and insisted that the requested information be provided with farm numbers, as set out in Exhibit BRA-369. In response to Brazil's request, the United States therefore provided all of the data that it could without violating the privacy interests of US producers, as required under the Privacy Act of 1974.

The United States has studied the Panel's request and has concluded that it is not possible to "protect the identity of individual producers" while providing the requested data in a format that permits data-matching. This results because the United States has already provided, by farm number, farm-specific contract information, including base acreage, base yield, and payment units, for each programme crop for each requested year. For example, for each and every "cotton farm" (as defined in the Brazilian request) identified by its FSA farm number, the United States has provided 96 separate data fields relating to 2002 direct and counter-cyclical contract payments. These 96 fields of contract data form a unique combination, such that – even in the absence of farm numbers – disclosing the farm-specific plantings that correspond to each unique combination of contract data would allow each farm's plantings to be connected to the FSA farm numbers through the farm-by-farm files previously provided. Thus, as a result of Brazil's insistence on receiving data with the FSA farm numbers and refusal to consider any alternative that would respect the privacy interests of US producers, unfortunately there would not appear to be a way to provide the requested data and "protect the identity of individual producers" given the data already provided. Under the Privacy Act of 1974, the United States could not disclose this information without the consent of the submitter.[4] Thus, the existence of confidentiality procedures would still not permit the United States to release each farm's planting information associated with the farm's particular contract payment data (given the previous submission of contract data in association with farm, county, and state numbers).[5]

---

[4] 5 U.S.C. 552a(b) ("No agency shall disclose any record which is contained in a system of records by any means of communication to any person, or to another agency, except pursuant to a written request by, or with the prior written consent of, the individual to whom the record pertains ...").

[5] Moreover, because contract data by farm number may be releasable information – as we have done here with respect to Brazil's specific request – a request to release contract data associated with

With respect to the Panel's reference to the release of certain farm-specific planting data by the Farm Services Agency to a member of the Brazilian delegation, the United States has explained in its December 18 letter to the Panel that this release was in error. We have requested that Brazil assist the United States in curing this breach of confidentiality by returning all copies of the erroneous release but have yet to receive a response.

The Panel makes reference to a weighing of "the public interest in disclosure" against a payment recipient's privacy interests. The question of whether the information could be released – and even whether the "public interest" is a relevant consideration – is a complicated issue under US domestic law. In the first instance, the US Department of Agriculture has determined that it is prohibited under US law from releasing this information without the consent of each submitter. In any event, we note that the Panel states that it requests these data "to permit an assessment of the *total expenditures* of PFC, MLA, CCP and direct payments . . . to upland cotton producers". Thus, the information relevant to the Panel's assessment would not be *farm-specific data* but rather some *aggregation* of data to permit this "assessment of . . . total expenditures". As noted above, the United States has provided both farm-specific and aggregated contract data that would permit an assessment of total expenditures of decoupled payments to farms planting upland cotton.

The United States further notes the Panel's statement that "[a] refusal by the United States to provide the information as requested without an adequate explanation may lead to adverse inferences being drawn". As explained, the United States does not have the authority to provide the farm-specific planting information in the format requested. Further, the United States has provided both farm-specific and aggregated contract data that would permit the Panel to make the assessment it identifies, that is, an assessment of total expenditures of decoupled payments to farms planting upland cotton. The situation here is thus very different from the one in Canada - Aircraft where the Appellate Body first opined that "a panel should be willing expressly to remind parties – during the course of dispute settlement proceedings – that a refusal to provide information requested by the panel may lead to inferences[6] being drawn about the inculpatory character of the information withheld".[7] There is no basis for an "inference" of any kind, adverse or otherwise.[8]

---

a farm's planting information would raise the same privacy concerns because of the potential to link such data back to farm and recipient information that could be separately obtained.

[6] The United States notes that in the same report the Appellate Body was careful to distinguish "adverse" inferences from other "inferences", remarking that: "We note, preliminarily, that the 'adverse inference' that Brazil believes the Panel should have drawn is not appropriately regarded as a punitive inference in the sense of a 'punishment' or 'penalty' for Canada's withholding of information. It is merely an inference which in certain circumstances could be logically or reasonably derived by a panel from the facts before it." *Canada – Measures Affecting the Export of Civilian Aircraft*, WT/DS70/AB/R, adopted 20 August 1999, para. 200 ("*Canada – Aircraft*").

[7] *Canada – Aircraft*, WT/DS70/AB/R, para. 204.

[8] The United States also notes that it is even less appropriate to draw "adverse inferences" in this dispute than in *Canada - Aircraft* in that Annex V, which was referred to by the Appellate Body in *Canada - Aircraft*, was rendered inapplicable by the Peace Clause in this dispute.

Finally, we of course recognize that the Panel has the right to seek information which it deems appropriate pursuant to Article 13.1 of the DSU. We wish to recall, however, that panels must take care not to use the information gathered under this authority to relieve a complaining party from its burden of establishing a *prima facie* case of WTO inconsistency based on specific legal claims asserted by it. In *Japan – Measures Affecting Agricultural Products*, the Appellate Body explained that it is for a complaining party to make arguments supporting its specific legal claims and that the panel had erred in using information it had obtained to make a finding of inconsistency on the basis of an argument and claim not explicitly advanced by the complaining party.[9] In this dispute, Brazil has not advanced legal claims and arguments that decoupled payments should attribute across the total value of the recipients' production, nor has Brazil advanced claims and arguments setting forth any methodology for calculating the total amount of payments it challenges, as reflected in Question 258 from the Panel to Brazil. The Panel may not relieve Brazil of its burden of advancing and establishing claims and arguments relating to the value of decoupled payments benefiting upland cotton, a crucial element in Brazil's *prima facie* case under Articles 5 and 6 of the *Agreement on Subsidies and Countervailing Measures*.

[9] Appellate Body Report, *Japan – Measures Affecting Agricultural Products*, WT/DS76/AB/R, adopted 19 March 1999, paras. 129-30.

ANNEX K-43

LETTER FROM THE UNITED STATES

28 January 2004

Enclosed with this letter the United States is providing a CD containing revised versions of the 6 electronic data files relating to the production flexibility contract era and the direct and counter-cyclical payment era that were transmitted to Brazil on 18 and 19 December 2003, and to the Panel on 18 and 22 December 2003. The enclosed CD contains six revised data files. The file names are identical to those previously submitted but with an "r" preceding the original file name. Thus, the files are now titled "rDcpsum.xls" (aggregate data file), "rDcpby.txt' (farm-by-farm base and yield data file), "rDcpplac.txt" (planted acres file), "rPfcsum.xls" (aggregate data filed), "rPfcby.txt" (base and yield data file), and "rPfcplac.txt" (planted acres file). We have prepared these revised electronic files after becoming aware of certain errors in the original data files submitted.

In the limited time available to reply to Brazil's request for data, certain programming errors appear to have resulted. As indicated in our letter of 18 December to the Panel, responding to the Brazilian request involved extracting pertinent information from approximately 10 million data files; because that request sought information relating to up to 10 programme crops on nearly 250,000 farms, the information provided by the United States ultimately spanned nearly 220 megabytes of data. Because that data was not the product of any established procedure with a protocol for cross-checking and verification, it was perhaps inevitable that certain errors should have occurred.

In preparing comments on Brazil's answer to question 258 from the Panel, the United States became aware that certain fields in the aggregate data files ("Pfcsum.xls" and "Dcpsum.xls") that the United States had prepared to assist the Panel and Brazil in interpreting the voluminous data in the farm-by-farm files contained no data (indicated by a zero ("0") or a dash ("-")). For example, looking at the original summary file for the direct and counter-cyclical payment era ("Dcpsum.xls"), those farms that in marketing year 2002 had upland cotton base acreage (4.7 million acres) but planted no cotton at all (0 acres), are also listed as having planted no acres of wheat, oats, rice, corn, sorghum, barley, flax, sunflower, safflower, soybeans, rapeseed, mustard, canola, crambe, or sesame on 15.9 million acres of cropland.

The United States has now expended significant effort correcting for programming errors and re-running the pertinent search. These efforts revealed that, while the cotton data continues to be correct (that is, farms with 4.7 million base acres of upland cotton planted not a single acre of cotton in marketing year 2002), in fact these farms planted approximately 10.3 million acres of these other crops and not zero as originally reported.

The corrected programming and new search generally corrected for instances in which the original search apparently failed to capture relevant data. The most significant revisions relate to (1) additional planted acres for other crops for those farms with upland cotton base acres that planted no cotton and (2) additional base acres for other crops for those farms without any upland cotton base acres that did plant cotton.

ANNEX K-44

LETTER FROM THE UNITED STATES

30 January 2004

The United States is in receipt of a document filed by Brazil with the Panel on 28 January 2004, providing Brazil's comments regarding data provided by the United States on 18 and 19 December 2003, and related matters. Brazil's filing of these comments was made 8 days after the deadline set by the Panel in communications dated 8 December and 24 December 2003, and on the date that had been established by the Panel for the United States to comment on Brazil's materials. Accordingly, my authorities have instructed me to respectfully request the Panel to specify the new date for the United States to file comments. The United States further suggests that since the Panel had originally provided that the United States would have eight days to provide its comments, the US comments could now be due eight days from the date the Panel establishes the new deadline.

As you know, on 8 December 2003, the Panel communicated to the Parties a revised schedule following the second panel meeting. The second paragraph of that coverfax and timetable reads: "As stated by the Chairman on 3 December, the United States will be given until **18 December** to respond to Brazil's request made in Exhibit BRA-369. Brazil will be given until **12 January 2004**, to comment on the US response." The third paragraph reads: "The parties may submit any further comments on each other's comments by **19 January 2004**."

On 24 December 2003, the Panel amended the timetable, stating that "all submissions originally due 12 January 2004 would now be due **Tuesday, 20 January 2004**" and "all submissions originally due 19 January 2004 would now be due **Wednesday, 28 January 2004**." Thus, Brazil had until 20 January 2004, to file its comments on the US data, and the United States had until 28 January 2004, to file its comments on Brazil's comments.

Brazil did not file its comments on 20 January, nor did it seek an extension of time from the Panel. Instead, Brazil simply delayed filing its 48 pages of detailed comments (with accompanying exhibits) until 28 January.[1] Providing the United States eight days to comment from the date of the Panel's communication of the new deadline would preserve the procedural balance originally established by the Panel.

[1] The United States finds Brazil's eight-day delay in meeting the Panel's deadline particularly ironic in light of Brazil's letters, such as its letter of 23 December 2003, complaining about the time of US filings.

ANNEX K-45

LETTER FROM BRAZIL

2 February 2004

The Government of Brazil is in receipt of a letter from the United States dated 30 January 2004 requesting an additional eight days to respond to Brazil's 28 January 2004 *Comments and Requests Regarding Data Provided by the United States on 18/19 December 2003 and the US Refusal to Provide Non-Scrambled Data on 20 January 2004* ("*Brazil's Comments*"). Brazil would comment on the US request as follows:

First, the US 30 January 2004 letter suggests that Brazil was late in filing *Brazil's Comments*. This is incorrect. The US letter ignores the fact and the effect of the Panel's 12 January 2004 Communication, in which the Panel requested the United States to produce complete and unscrambled data concerning contract payment base and current plantings of upland cotton farms. This Communication necessarily mooted, at least temporarily, any comments by Brazil on the 18/19 December 2003 US "scrambled" data. It would have made little sense for Brazil to comment on the data deficiencies (and the implications thereof) on 20 January 2004, since Brazil trusted that the United States would have lived up to the Panel's repeated request and produced the data by 20 January 2004, as required by DSU Article 13.1. Only after the United States failed to produce the requested data was Brazil able to properly comment on the US data – and it did so on 28 January 2004 (in a much shorter time - 8 days - than originally foreseen by the Panel's 12 January 2004 deadline).

Second, the United States requests the opportunity to comment on Brazil's Comments and requests eight days to do so. Brazil is of the view that eight days from 28 January would be acceptable, which would make the US submission due on 5 February 2004. The United States already has had access to Brazil's Comments for five days (since 28 January 2004). The US request for what would amount to essentially two weeks to respond would further delay these proceedings. It would also violate Brazil's due process rights if the United States were given more time to comment on these documents than Brazil had to comment on the failure of the United States to produce the information on 20 January 2004.

Third, in order to preserve Brazil's due process rights, the Panel should limit the scope of the US "Comments" to responding to arguments that the United States has not yet had an opportunity to respond. For example, Sections 4, 5, 11 of *Brazil's Comments* simply respond to arguments and facts already presented in US letters of 18 December 2003 and 20 January 2004 in which the United States sought to justify the refusal to produce farm-specific data. The United States should not be given yet another opportunity to comment on Brazil's comments.

Fourth, the Panel should reject any attempt by the United States to present positive evidence in any comments without also giving Brazil an opportunity to respond. For example, the United States never presented the Panel with *any* application of its own proposed methodology for calculating and allocating the amount of contract payments to current upland cotton farmers. It would be manifestly unfair for the United States to present, in its last submission, positive evidence based on incomplete (non-farm specific data) in support of its defence when it has refused to provide any calculation, or even an estimate, for thirteen months – let alone produced the requested data that would permit Brazil or the Panel to do so.

Fifth, Brazil notes that the U.S. letter of 28 January 2004 provides Brazil and the panel with "revised" data files to correct for "certain errors" in the original data submitted forty days earlier on 18 December 2003. None of these "corrections" provide any useable farm-specific contract payment base and current planting data. Thus, the United States continues to violate the Panel's 8 December 2003 and 12 January 2004 requests for such information. Further, the 28 January 2004 revised data continues to suffer from the various aggregation problems identified in paragraphs 8-15, 22, 76-81, 90-98, of *Brazil's Comments*. Nor does the corrected data include complete information on market loss assistance payments (as identified in paragraphs 20, 22, 43, 82 and 95 as well as notes 40, 43, 75, 163, 164, 166, 195 and 197 of *Brazil's Comments*), or information on MY 2002 peanut base payments (as identified in paragraphs 21-23, 43 and 98 as well as notes 75, 132, 161, 166, 195 and 196 of *Brazil's Comments*). Thus, Brazil does not believe that this "revised" data, arriving *after* the 11th hour, is either timely or useful. If, however, the Panel believes that it would be useful for Brazil to provide revised calculations (based on the revised US summary data) replacing those set out in paragraphs 83 and 96 of *Brazil's Comments*, or comment in any other way on the revised US "scrambled" data, Brazil will be pleased to do so. Brazil recalls, however, that it provided the figures in those two paragraphs based on the flawed US summary data to demonstrate the existence of further support for its "$14/16^{th}$" methodology estimated figures.

ANNEX K-46

LETTER FROM THE UNITED STATES
3 February 2004

The United States is in receipt of a letter filed by Brazil on 2 February 2004, commenting on the US request for the Panel to establish a new deadline for the United States to file comments on Brazil's comments regarding data provided by the United States on 18 and 19 December 2003, and related matters.

My authorities have instructed me to inform the Panel that the United States welcomes Brazil's statement that it has no objection to the Panel establishing a new deadline for the United States to comment on Brazil's comments. Brazil, however, objects to the United States being given eight days from the Panel's communication establishing the new deadline, arguing that it would "violate Brazil's due process rights if the United States were given more time to comment on these documents than Brazil had to comment on the failure of the United States to provide the information on 20 January 2004". With respect, this fundamentally misstates the issue.

Brazil had access to the 18 and 19 December data for nearly *six weeks* before filing its comments, due on 20 January but submitted on 28 January, and evidently used that time in order to prepare quite lengthy and detailed comments (over 50 pages plus exhibits). Yet Brazil objects to the Panel providing the United States with notice that it has eight days to prepare its response. Brazil would have the Panel upset the balance of time set out in its communications for the preparation of the respective comments of Brazil and the United States.

We also note Brazil's argument that the Panel's 12 January letter "necessarily mooted, at least temporarily", the 20 January date for the filing of Brazil's comments. It is ironic, to say the least, that Brazil should have complained about delays (measured in minutes) in filing certain US documents and then unilaterally have decided that it was entitled to an additional *eight days* in filing its comments since, in Brazil's view, "[i]t would have made little sense" for Brazil to comply with the Panel's 20 January deadline. Brazil did not request the Panel to modify the deadlines as a result of the Panel's 12 January letter. Brazil simply decided not to abide by the deadlines established by the Panel. Indeed, Brazil should have filed its comments on the 18 and 19 December data on 20 January as scheduled and has provided no reason why it was unable to do so.

If Brazil wanted a further opportunity from the Panel to comment on any response to the Panel's 12 January letter, it could have so requested. Brazil did not do so. Instead it simply ignored the Panel's deadline and used a nearly six-week period to provide comments on the US data. Thus, Brazil's February 2 letter continues to evince its one-sided tactics on procedural issues, in which Brazil seeks (or simply provides to itself) substantial periods of time to prepare its filings but seeks to deny adequate time to the United States to prepare its responses.[1]

We note Brazil's request that the Panel *ex ante* "limit the scope of the US 'Comments' to arguments [to which] the United States has not yet had an opportunity to respond" and prevent the United States from "present[ing] positive evidence". However, the Panel had previously established that the United States "may submit any further comments on [Brazil's] comments" by 19 January, 2004[2], later revised to 28 January 2004.[3] Therefore, Brazil's request does not comport with the Panel's previous communication, would prejudge what comments the United States may provide (and perhaps preclude relevant comments on new information presented by Brazil), and would impose a limitation with respect to arguments and evidence on the United States that was not imposed on Brazil.

Finally, Brazil continues to mischaracterize the situation when it asserts that the United States should have breached US law regarding the protection of individual privacy in order to produce additional data relating to planting and contract payment information on a farm-by-farm basis. We have previously explained in our letters of 20 January 2004, and 18 December, 2003 why under US law we are unable to provide the data requested. In part, this results from Brazil's refusal at the second panel meeting to allow *any* deviation from the request set out in Exhibit BRA-369, which specifically requested that the data be provided by farm with its associated FSA farm number. The United States responded to that request to the maximum extent permissible under US law.

In sum, the Panel had intended for the United States to provide comments and have 8 days from the 20 January deadline for Brazil's comments to do so. However, Brazil seeks to impose limitations that were not applied to its own comments, and which would significantly impair the information available to the Panel in evaluating the material before it and US rights of defence. We request that the Panel reject Brazil's unbalanced suggestions and suggest that the US comments be due eight days from the Panel's confirmation of the new deadline for filing those comments.

---

1 For example, the United States recalls that at the panel organizational meeting, Brazil objected to the United States having more than two weeks to prepare its first submission while at the same arguing that Brazil would need a full two weeks to prepare the executive summary of its own first submission. (Brazil did not volunteer that it had already drafted a first submission that would ultimately turn out to be more than 135 pages in length, with over 100 exhibits.) As the United States noted at the time, it seemed implausible that the United States could prepare a *substantive response* to a submission in two weeks if Brazil was unable to prepare a *summary* of that submission in less than that time.

2 Panel Communication of 8 December 2003.

3 Panel Communication of 24 December 2003.

ANNEX K-47

LETTER FROM THE UNITED STATES
11 February 2004

Attached please find answers of the United States to 29 additional questions from the Panel following the second substantive meeting in the dispute *United States – Subsidies on Upland Cotton* (DS267) and the comments of the United States on Brazil's 28 January 2004 comments and new arguments on the extensive data provided by the United States.

The United States wishes to inform the Panel that it continues to work on preparing information requested by the Panel in its supplementary request for information pursuant to Article 13 of the DSU as well as certain information requested under the Panel's additional questions. Unfortunately, the very extensive nature of those requests for information have rendered it impossible for the United States to prepare and provide that information within the eight days requested by the Panel.

- For example, the Panel has requested that the United States provide "such of the information requested on 12 January 2004 in the format requested, as regards payment recipients who do not have interests protected under the Privacy Act [of] 1974, if any".[1] More than 250,000 farms fell within the farm criteria set out in Brazil's request in Exhibit BRA-369[2], to which the Panel's January 12 request referred. While it would not be possible to examine singly the records relating to each of these 250,000 farms, the United States continues to seek some means by which the identities of payment recipients who may not have protectable privacy interests could be identified. Eight days has not been sufficient time to complete that effort.
- In addition, the Panel has asked for a very substantial amount of acreage information for "covered commodities" over four marketing years under four different programmes and for all commodities for which planting information is maintained in marketing year 2002. A significant amount of time was required to generate the data in response to the Panel's earlier requests. That effort and the programming errors encountered in that response demonstrate that the response to the supplemental request also requires more than eight days.

Thus, the United States continues to work on responses to item (a) and all the bulleted subparts of item (b) of the Panel's supplementary request for information, as well as to Question 264(b) of the Panel's additional questions. Based on the work completed to date, our current understanding of the scope of the

---

[1] Panel's Supplementary Request for Information Pursuant to Article 13 of the DSU, item (a) (3 February 2004).
[2] *See* US Letter to the Panel at 3 (December 18, 2003).

Panel's requests, and our experience completing (and revising) a similar, but smaller, computerized search for electronic files in December, the United States estimates that it would be able to provide the requested information by four weeks from the date the Panel provides the clarifications requested below. Of course, should the United States complete its preparation of the requested information prior to that date, we would make that information available to the Panel and Brazil at that time.

With respect to item (b) of the Panel's supplementary request for information, the United States would seek clarification of that request. First, the United States would ask the Panel to specify which commodities are "covered commodities" as that term is used in several of the bullet points and subbullets. Second, the United States would seek confirmation that, with respect to the information sought for marketing year 2002 "with respect to all crops on cropland covered by the acreage reports", the relevant portions of the "above questions" are those that ask for planted acreage information for each Category of farm. Clarifications of these points will assist the United States greatly in preparing data responsive to the Panel's request.

Finally, the United States notes that the Panel's communication of 3 February invites the parties "to submit, by Wednesday 18 February 2004, any comments on material submitted on 11 February by the other party". The United States understands this procedure to mean that, with respect to Brazil's 28 January comments on the data submitted by the United States on 18 and 19 December 2003, Brazil would be permitted to file comments on the US comments filed today. If this is not the case, the United States would appreciate the Panel providing clarification to the parties at its earliest convenience.

However, to the extent that the Panel has given Brazil the opportunity to file a reply on 18 February to the US comments filed today, and Brazil chooses to do so, the United States would request an opportunity to respond to Brazil's comments. The procedure set out by the Panel in its communications of 8 and 24 December 2003, originally set out one opportunity for Brazil to comment on the US data (on 20 January 2004) and one opportunity for the United States to respond to Brazil's comments (on 28 January 2004). As the responding party, the United States believes that it is important that it have the opportunity to respond to Brazil's arguments, particularly in this dispute where Brazil's arguments and legal positions have changed from submission to submission. To the extent that Brazil as complaining party is now being provided two opportunities to comment on the US data, the United States would feel bound to request a similar second opportunity to comment. We suggest that the deadline for the US reply could be set for Wednesday, 25 February.

ANNEX K-48

LETTER FROM BRAZIL

13 February 2004

The Government of Brazil is in receipt of a letter from the United States dated 11 February 2004 in which it informs the Panel that it is not providing the requested information by the 11 February 2004 deadline. Further, the letter requests (1) four additional weeks to provide data, and (2) the opportunity to respond to Brazil's 18 February 2004 comments on the "US data". Brazil asks the Panel to reject both of these requests.

In putting these requests into perspective, Brazil recalls that the entire contract payment exercise is to provide the Panel with sufficient data to determine and calculate (using whichever methodology the Panel deems appropriate) the amount of "support to" upland cotton for MY 1999-2002. The best way for the Panel to do this is if it has the actual data to calculate the amount of contract payments received by producers that planted cotton in MY 1999-2002. As the Panel knows, it does not yet have this actual data. Any objective assessment of the record indicates that Brazil has sought this contract payment information since November 2002, and that the Panel has sought it since it posed Question 67 *bis* to the United States in August 2003.

The immediate focus of this lengthy exercise is the Panel's 3 February 2004 "Supplementary request for information pursuant to Article 13 of the DSU and additional questions." ("3 February 2004 Request"). In part (a) of that request, the Panel asked for "such information requested on 12 January 2004 in the format requested, as regards payment recipients who do not have interests protected under the Privacy Act of 1974, if any". In a completely separate request (not conditioned on the Privacy Act), the Panel asked in part (b) for summary *aggregated* information that required the United States to compare farm-specific contract acreage data with farm-specific planting data. Data provided in response to part (b) could not possibly include any confidential information since it is aggregated.

The United States letter of 11 February 2004 states that it needs four additional weeks to complete the part (a) analysis. Brazil notes that because the United States apparently intends only to provide farm-specific information for far less than the total amount of farms (*i.e.*, those that are not held by "individuals") this information will be useless for calculating the exact amount of *total* contract payments. Therefore, Brazil does not believe that the United States should be given any additional time to produce this information. In this regard, it is important to stress that even if part of the farm-specific information were confidential under US law (which Brazil believes is not the case), the United States would still be required to produce the information requested by the Panel on 8 December 2003 and 12 January 2004 subject to WTO confidentiality procedures.

With respect to part (b) of the Panel's 3 February 2004 Request, the United States also claims it needs four additional weeks to complete this analysis. And it asks the Panel to "clarify" its request regarding what are "covered commodities" and "with respect to all crops on cropland covered by the acreage reports". The Panel's 3 February 2004 Request provided a chart which listed the "covered commodities". If the United States had any questions despite the clarity of this chart, then why did it wait 8 days to raise these questions? Further, the request for "crops on cropland covered by the acreage reports *not simply commodities covered by the programmes*" could not be clearer. Again, why did the United States wait 8 days to bring this to the Panel's attention if it was truly puzzled by this condition of the Panel's request?

With respect to the enormous amount of time the United States claims it will take to produce information in response to part (b) of the Panel's 3 February 2004 Request, Brazil notes that the format of the Panel's Request was very similar to the *rice* FOIA request that is set out in Exhibit Bra-368. The testimony of Mark Somers before the Panel on 3 December 2003 indicated that the rice FOIA documents showed that USDA took less than a week to process the data and respond to the rice FOIA request once USDA's statistical experts began work on the project (and the time from filing the request to issuance of the data was 15 days). Indeed, Brazil was easily able to calculate the aggregate rice farm-specific base and acreage information in just a few days as set forth in Christopher Campbell's statement in Exhibit Bra-368. With its access to a number of USDA statistical experts, not to mention the centralized database with all of the records already inputted, it is simply not credible for the United States to claim that it needs more than five weeks to respond to the Panel's request.

As the Panel knows from reviewing Exhibit Bra-368, the data delivered by USDA's Kansas City office permitted the ready tabulation of the exact number of rice farms holding contract acreage and the amount of their rice acreage. The Panel's request for contract and planted acreage information on farms planting cotton is not fundamentally different from the rice request in terms of the type of data files at issue. The raw data in the contract and planted acreage (for all planted commodities) files that the United States would use to respond to the Panel's 3 February 2003 request are the same raw data files that have been in the centralized Kansas City database throughout this dispute. If there were any doubt about this, the United States demonstrated that it examined all the farm-specific data in its 18/19 December 2003 responses (albeit producing them in a scrambled format). Thus, part (b) of the Panel's 3 February 2004 Request did not involve any new data files – simply the writing of a programme that would allow the production of the data in an aggregated, non-confidential summary form, as defined and requested by the Panel.

Brazil believes that the Panel should not provide the United States with any additional time to respond to part (b) of its 3 February 2004 Request. The United States stood by and waited while the deadline approached without making any effort to request additional time or to seek clarifications. Yet, the United States had no difficulty during the same 8-day period in making extensive comments on Brazil's 28 January 2004 Comments and Requests Regarding Data

Provided by the United States on 18/19 December 2003 and the US Refusal to Provide Non-Scrambled Data on 20 January 2004. ("Brazil's 28 January Data Comments"). The United States provides no legitimate explanation why it could not complete part (b) of the Panel's request within the Panel's deadline. Indeed, the United States – in a non-litigation context – demonstrated in the rice FOIA request just how easy and fast it is to provide this information.

The Panel is now only one month away from the one-year anniversary of its establishment, and almost two months *beyond* the nine-month deadline for completing its work set out in DSU Article 12.9. Brazil has not objected to the Panel's laudable attempts to coax the United States into producing the actual non-scrambled data that would permit calculation of the amount of support provided to upland cotton producers from the four different contract payments. Brazil was willing to go along with the delays that each of these requests necessitated because it, presumably like the Panel, wanted the Panel to make use of the most complete and accurate information available to decide these important issues. Starting with its Question 67 *bis,* the Panel has now asked for contract payment information data on *five* separate occasions (Question 125(9) and 8 December 2003, 12 January 2004 and 3 February 2004 Requests). The Panel now has before it a pattern of delay by the United States that is seriously impinging on Brazil's due process rights to receive a timely resolution of its claims in this dispute.

Therefore, Brazil strongly believes that the United States has been given more than sufficient time (seven months) and opportunities (five) to produce the requested contract payment information in one form or another. If the Panel believes, however, that the required balance between ensuring high-quality panel reports and not unduly delaying the panel process requires providing yet another opportunity to the United States to produce the data requested in part (b) of the Panel's 3 February 2004 Request, then Brazil has the following additional comments. If the United States provides the complete information requested in part (b) of the 3 February 2004 Request, then most of Brazil's 28 January Data Comments would be rendered moot. The purpose of those comments was to (a) demonstrate the inadequacy of the US data production, (b) request the drawing of adverse inferences, and (c) in the absence of the actual data, to apply the inadequate summary data. Because the US 11 February 2004 comments on Brazil's 28 January 2004 Data Comments are only relevant to these underlying Brazilian comments, the US 11 February 2004 Comments will also similarly be largely rendered moot *if* the United States provides the data requested in part (b). With the actual and complete data, the Panel would be in the position to apply any methodology it determines to be acceptable. Further, by producing the complete aggregated information, there would no longer be a need to draw adverse inferences. Nor, would there be any need for Brazil to comment on the US use of the incomplete and inadequate data in applying the US methodology.

Accordingly, if the Panel provides the United States with additional time to provide the data (which Brazil opposes), it should allow Brazil the opportunity to file comments, to the extent any are still relevant, to the United States 11 February 2004 Comments to Brazil's 28 January 2004 Data Comments until 8 days *after* the United States has provided the information responsive to part (b) of the Panel's 3 February 2004 Request. By using this modified procedure, Brazil hopes to alleviate some of the considerable legal costs it has incurred in this extraordinary process. It would deny Brazil's due process rights to incur such unnecessary expenses by filing a response which would not assist the Panel in resolving the relevant issues in this dispute, assuming the United States provides the complete data requested in part (b).

Brazil also opposes the unjustified attempt by the United States to further delay this proceeding by seeking yet another opportunity to comment on Brazil's 18 February 2004 Comments. Brazil notes that the United States 11 February 2004 Comments to Brazil's 28 January 2004 Data Comments go far beyond what are legitimate comments on Brazil's original 28 January 2004 Data Comments. In particularly, in a number of instances, the US 11 February 2004 Comments address issues raised in Brazil's 28 January 2004 Comments on US Answers to Questions Posed by the Panel Following the Second Substantive Meeting of the Panel.

Thus, the United States, having already abused the Panel's procedures, now seeks yet another opportunity to comment. The Panel's 3 February 2004 Communication made it clear that the deadline for the United States to comment would be 11 February 2004. The US request would only serve to further delay these proceedings, to the detriment of Brazil.

Finally, Brazil asks the Panel to reject the United States' unilateral decision to take additional time to respond to Question 264(b). There is absolutely no legitimate reason for the United States to have failed to respond to this question; nor has the United States indicated any such reasons. The Panel's question in no sense called for a complicated analysis, and a response could readily have been provided within the 8-day response period. After reviewing the US response, Brazil was able to set up a table comparing the US and Brazilian figures in less than an hour.

ANNEX K-49

LETTER FROM THE UNITED STATES
16 February 2004

The United States is in receipt of a letter from Brazil dated 13 February 2004, requesting the Panel not to afford the United States additional time to provide certain requested information and the opportunity to respond to Brazil's anticipated 18 February 2004, comments on certain data submitted by the United States. My authorities have instructed me to make the following reply to these issues.

The United States has communicated to the Panel that work continues in response to the Panel's supplemental request for information and that the United States expects to complete this work within four weeks from the date the Panel provides certain clarifications to its request. The United States provided this time estimate on the basis of its work completed to date and questions that arose with respect to the Panel's request (the subject of our request for clarifications).[1] We also noted that item (a) in the Panel's request presented the challenge of seeking some means by which to review the identities of payment recipients on approximately 250,000 farms within the scope of the request, a task which was impossible to complete within the eight days the Panel had requested. Finally, in producing this time estimate, United States reflected on its experience in producing data for this dispute in December 2003. That data was provided within 15 days of its request, and, on subsequent review, contained a number of inaccuracies that had to be cured by a subsequent filing.[2] In addition to explaining the reasons supporting our estimate, we also made clear that "should the United States complete its preparation of the requested information prior to that date, we would make that information available to the Panel and Brazil at that time".[3]

If anything, the data requested by the Panel on 3 February 2004, is more extensive than the information requested in December as it requests that additional data be sought and that different aggregations be provided. By way of example, for marketing year 2002, we understand that the Panel has requested planted acreage data for all "crops" for each Category of farm set out in the request.[4] The

---

[1] With respect to the first point of clarification sought by the United States, Brazil points to a table in the Panel's supplemental request for information. We note that two of the headings in that table, "soybeans" and "other oilseeds", are marked with an asterisk, which denotes "[w]here applicable". *See* Panel's Supplemental Request for Information, at 2 (3 February 2004). The United States has requested clarification of the Panel's supplemental request because, even with that table, the precise scope of the term "covered commodity" and where soybeans and other oilseeds are "applicable" are not clear.

[2] *See* US Letter to Panel of 28 January 2003 (transmitting CD-ROM with revised data files).

[3] *See* US Letter to Panel of 11 February 2004, at 2.

[4] Whether the data sought was planted acreage only for farms falling within each Category of farm was the second point of clarification raised by the United States. *See* US Letter to Panel of 11 February 2004, at 2. The United States was not asking for a list of "crops" covered by that request, a point

Panel will recall that in marketing year 2002, the "crops" for which crop insurance premium subsidies were available included:

> Almonds, apples, avocado, avocado trees, barley, blackberries, blueberries, burley tobacco, cabbage, canola, cherries, chile peppers, cigar binder tobacco, cigar filler tobacco, cigar wrapper tobacco, citrus (grapefruit, lemons, limes, mandarins, murcotts, navel orange dollar, oranges, tangelos, tangerines), citrus trees, corn, cotton, cotton extra long staple, crambe, cranberries, cultivated clams, cultivated wild rice, dark air tobacco, dry beans, dry peas, figs, fire-cured tobacco, flax, Florida fruit trees, carambola, flue-cured tobacco, forage production, forage seed, forage seeding, fresh apricots, fresh nectarines, fresh market beans, fresh market sweet corn, fresh market tomatoes, grain sorghum, grapes, green peas, hybrid corn seed, hybrid sorghum seed, macadamia nuts, macadamia trees, mango trees, Maryland tobacco, millet, mint, mustard, nursery, oats, onions, peaches, peanuts, pears, pecans, peppers, plums, popcorn, potatoes, processing apricots, processing beans, processing cucumbers, prunes, raisins, rangeland, rapeseed, raspberries, rice, rye, safflower, soybeans, stonefruit (processing apricots, processing cling peaches, processing freestone), strawberries, sugar beets, sugarcane, sunflowers, sweet corn, sweet potatoes, table grapes, tomatoes (canning and processing), walnuts, wheat, and winter squash.[5]

Thus, this one element of the Panel's supplemental request would seem to require the United States to gather and organize a substantial amount of information not previously provided.

We do note again that the Panel's request for aggregated acreage data does not involve privacy issues and thank the Panel for seeking the data in this format, which allows the United States both to provide data in a manner consistent with its domestic law and to do so in a way that may be of assistance to the Panel. Had Brazil requested data in a similar aggregated format or responded positively to the US request at the second panel meeting for alternatives that would allow farmer privacy interests to be protected, a brief delay would not be necessary while the United States seeks to provide the requested data. Brazil did not respond positively to that request, insisted on receiving the data in a format that would reveal farmer identities, and never requested the Panel to seek data from the United States in aggregated form – despite the fact that *only Brazil was aware of its invented methodology until it responded to the Panel's Question 258 on 20 January 2004*. Had Brazil included its methodology in its first submission on Peace Clause issues (on 24 June 2003), all the time now being devoted to

---

which Brazil evidently misunderstands. Brazil's Letter to the Panel of 13 February 2004, at 2 ("Further, the request for 'crops on cropland covered by the acreage reports *not simply commodities covered by the programmes'* could not be clearer.").

[5] Exhibit Bra-62 (US Department of Agriculture, Crops Covered Under the 2002 Crop Insurance Programme) (www.rma.usda.gov/policies/02croplist.html).

these topics could quite likely have been saved. Brazil's complaint that the United States is responsible for any perceived delays in the Panel's schedule would thus appear to be sorely misdirected.

We note Brazil's suggestion that, should the Panel accept the data the United States is preparing in response to item (b) of the Panel's supplemental request for information, "then most of Brazil's 28 January Data comments would be rendered moot".[6] We are not exactly sure what that statement means or how it relates to Brazil's objection to the United States requiring additional time to provide a response to the information that the Panel has requested. However, Brazil further states that "by producing the complete aggregated information, there would no longer be a need to draw adverse inferences".[7] The United States welcomes this belated recognition by Brazil that disclosure of farm-specific information of contract acreage and planted acreage is *not* necessary under Brazil's invented allocation methodology.

Brazil also questions the United States' comment that it will require additional time to respond to Question 264(b), saying that "Brazil was able to set up a table comparing the US and Brazilian figures in less than an hour." It does not appear to the United States that the Panel's question simply called for "set[ting] up a table" to compare the data referenced in that question. For example, Brazil asserted in paragraph 135 of its 28 January 2004, comments on US answers that "the difference between the chart provided by the United States in Exhibit US-128 and Brazil's chart in para. 165 of its 11 August Answers lies in the treatment of rescheduled debt". To provide a helpful answer would seem to require that the United States examine what goes into each of the figures that are represented in Brazil's chart. The United States was not able to complete that analysis within the eight days provided – but was able to generate and provide in its 11 February answers copious amounts of numbers and data in response to the 29 Panel questions. Rather than seek an extension with respect to *all* questions, we provided the data we could on 11 February and will provide any other data in response to Question 264(b) within the time indicated (and sooner if the data can be collected and examined in less time).

With respect to comments by the Parties on the materials that the United States is preparing, we would not object to the Panel granting Brazil an opportunity to comment on the data to be provided by the United States in response to item (b) of the Panel's supplemental request. However, we cannot understand nor accept Brazil's suggestion that the United States should not be afforded an opportunity to reply to Brazil's comments. Since Brazil is seeking another opportunity to comment (eight days after the United States has provided the information in response to item (b)), there would be no significant "further delay in these proceedings, to the detriment of Brazil" were the United States to file its reply to Brazil's comments within, say, one week of those comments. In this respect, we note that Brazil continues its one-sided approach to procedural issues by seeking to provide itself with an opportunity to comment but to deny the same to the Uni-

6 Brazil's Letter to Panel of 13 February 2004, at 5.

7 *Ibid.*

ted States. Since this would be the first time Brazil's comments on the item (b) data would be presented, the United States as responding party must be given an opportunity to respond.[8]

Finally, the United States regrets that Brazil has repeated its suggestion that the United States should provide data protected by the Privacy Act and that the United States should rely on WTO confidentiality provisions in doing so. Apart from the fact that the United States is not able under its domestic law simply to ignore US persons' Privacy Act interests on that basis, the growing number of press articles revealing non-public information about this dispute makes that suggestion even less tenable.[9]

---

[8] In this connection we would like to draw the Panel's attention to a previous proceeding in which Brazil's last-minute submission of evidence and legal argumentation raised difficulties for the other party involved. Report of the Arbitrator in *Canada – Export Credits and Loan Guarantees for Regional Aircraft*, Recourse to Arbitration by Canada, WT/DS222/ARB, paras. 2.14 and 2.16. We recall that in the present dispute, Brazil first failed to explain its invented allocation methodology until 20 January 2004 – eight months into this dispute – when compelled to do so by the Panel. Then, Brazil delayed submitting its comments on the US December data until 28 January 2004 – eight days after the deadline set by the Panel. Now, Brazil would seek to have an opportunity to comment on the item (b) data – despite the necessary "delay in the proceeding" that would entail – but simultaneously seeks to deprive the United States of its "right – as respondent – to speak last." In this dispute, it would be singularly inappropriate to allow Brazil the final chance to comment.

[9] The most recent example contains a reference to the statement in a Panel communication to the United States that a failure to provide certain requested information without adequate explanation could lead to adverse inferences being drawn. (Exhibit US-155.) As far as the United States is aware, any communication from the Panel to the parties are subject to the confidentiality rules of the proceeding.

ANNEX K-50

LETTER FROM THE UNITED STATES

23 February 2004

The United States thanks the Panel for its communication of 20 February 2004, in which the Panel extends to the United States the opportunity to respond to Brazil's 18 February submission relating to certain data provided by the United States on 18 and 19 December 2003. The United States would like to confirm that it does wish to comment on this Brazilian submission. The Panel has asked the United States to file any comments within five days, that is, by Wednesday, 25 February. In light of the extensive material submitted by Brazil and US efforts to respond simultaneously to the Panel's supplemental request for information, the United States would like to ask the Panel to extend the deadline to provide these comments, to Wednesday, 3 March, the same due date for the US response to the Panel's supplemental request for additional information.

This extension would greatly assist the United States in providing useful comments for the Panel on Brazil's lengthy 18 February comments, which totalled 79 pages. Of these 79 pages, 41 pages were devoted to setting forth results of numerous calculations. The personnel who would need to review these calculations are also involved in the ongoing US efforts to provide data in response to the Panel's supplemental request for additional information. The extension requested would permit these personnel to better advance US efforts to respond fully and accurately to the Panel's supplemental request while simultaneously reviewing and providing comments on Brazil's 18 February submission.

In addition, we note that the extension requested would not impact any other dates set by the Panel in this proceeding. Thus, the United States respectfully requests the Panel to extend the deadline to provide the US comments, to Wednesday, 3 March.

The United States is providing a copy of this letter directly to Brazil.

ANNEX L

COMMUNICATIONS FROM THE PANEL

Contents	Page
L-2. Communications to Third Parties[1]	

[1] Communications included as L-1.4, -1.7, -1.11, -1.12, -1.13 and -1.14 were also sent to 3rd parties.

ANNEX L-1.1

COMMUNICATION TO BRAZIL AND THE UNITED STATES

21 May 2003

I refer to the letter from the United States dated 21 May 2003and addressed to the Chair of the Panel. I understand this was also copied to your delegation. The Panel wishes to ask Brazil to communicate its views, if any, in writing in response to this letter.

The Panel would appreciate if Brazil's written response could be submitted before the close of business this Friday, 23 May 2003. This is in view of the fact that the Chairman of the Panel, Mr. Rosati, is proposing to convene an organizational meeting with the parties on Monday 26 May 2003 from 11:30 a.m. The venue will be communicated to you shortly.

ANNEX L-1.2

COMMUNICATION TO BRAZIL AND THE UNITED STATES

27 May 2003

The Panel takes note of the United States' comments with respect to the Panel's timetable and working procedures, dated 21 May 2003, and Brazil's communication dated 23 May 2003.

Attached you will find the Panel's proposed **working procedures and timetable**. The Panel intends to hold an **organizational meeting with the parties at 8 a.m. on Wednesday, 28 May** 2003 at room C in order to hear the parties' views on these proposals.

As indicated in the attached proposed timetable, prior to the submission by the parties of their first written submissions, the Panel intends to request the parties to address, in their initial briefs to the Panel, the following:

- whether Article 13 of the *Agreement on Agriculture* precludes the Panel from considering Brazil's claims under the *Agreement on Subsidies and Countervailing Measures* in these proceedings in the absence of a prior conclusion by the Panel that certain conditions of Article 13 remain unfulfilled. In particular, the Panel invites the parties to explain their interpretation of the words "exempt from actions" as used in Article 13 of the *Agreement on Agriculture*, as well as bringing to the Panel's attention any other relevant provisions of the covered agreements and any other relevant considerations which the parties consider should guide the Panel's consideration of this issue.

As also indicated in the attached timetable, the Panel will invite the parties to submit any written comments on each other's comments on this issue. The Panel currently wishes to signal its intention to clarify to the parties its view on these issues prior to the parties' submission of their first written submissions.

In the event that the Panel were to rule that Article 13 precludes the Panel from considering certain claims raised by Brazil prior to a conclusion that certain conditions of Article 13 remain unfulfilled, we may decide to adjust the timetable to permit the parties to make further submission(s) after the second substantive meeting and to schedule further substantive meeting(s), as necessary, with the parties.

With respect to the participation of third parties in these Panel proceedings, the Panel is aware of the provisions of Article 10.3 of the *DSU*, which states that third parties shall receive the submissions of the parties to the dispute to the first meeting of the Panel. Given the significant systemic issues in this Panel proceeding, and in exercise of our discretion to manage these Panel proceedings, we believe that it would be appropriate in this case for the third parties to have access to the parties' initial written comments (and any written comments the parties may make on each others' comments) as well as to have the ability to submit any written comments they themselves may have on the issue that we have identified above. We therefore intend to invite the parties to serve also on the third parties their initial briefs and any responding comments. At the organizational meeting, we will invite any comments you may have on this proposed approach to third party participation.

[Attachment omitted]

ANNEX L-1.3

COMMUNICATION TO BRAZIL AND THE UNITED STATES
28 May 2003

Attached you will find the timetable and working procedures adopted by the Panel for this dispute in accordance with Article 12.1 of the *Understanding on Rules and Procedures Governing the Settlement of Disputes* (the "*DSU*"). In adopting the timetable and working procedures, the Panel has carefully considered the parties' comments at this morning's organizational meeting.

As indicated in the attached timetable, prior to the submission by the parties of their first written submissions, the Panel requests the parties to address, in their initial briefs to the Panel (to be submitted on *5 June 2003*), the following:

- whether Article 13 of the *Agreement on Agriculture* precludes the Panel from considering Brazil's claims under the *Agreement on Subsidies and Countervailing Measures* in these proceedings in the absence of a prior conclusion by the Panel that certain conditions of Article 13 remain unfulfilled. In particular, the Panel invites the parties to explain their interpretation of the words "exempt from actions" as used in Article 13 of the *Agreement on Agriculture*, as well as bringing to the Panel's attention any other relevant provisions of the covered agreements and any other relevant considerations which the parties consider should guide the Panel's consideration of this issue. For greater clarity, the Panel invites the parties, during this initial stage of the proceedings, to focus on matters of legal interpretation, rather than upon the submission of any factual evidence that might be associated with the substantive elements of Article 13.

As also indicated in the attached timetable, the Panel will invite the parties to submit any written comments on each other's comments on this issue (i.e. on *13 June 2003*). The Panel intends to rule on these issues on *20 June 2003*, prior to the parties' submission of their first written submissions.

As has been indicated, the Panel recognizes that it may need to revisit certain aspects of its timetable and working procedures in light of developments during the course of the Panel procedures, including the nature of the Panel's ruling that is scheduled for 20 June 2003. In particular, in the event that the Panel were to rule that Article 13 precludes the Panel from considering certain claims raised by Brazil prior to a conclusion that certain conditions of Article 13 remain unfulfilled, we may decide to adjust the timetable to permit the parties to make further submission(s) after the second substantive meeting and to schedule further substantive meeting(s), as necessary, with the parties. Related amendments to the working procedures may also be made, if necessary.

With respect to the participation of third parties in these Panel proceedings, we have carefully considered the parties' comments at this morning's organizational meeting. In exercise of our discretion to manage these Panel proceedings, we continue to believe that it would be appropriate in this case for the third parties to have access to the parties' initial written comments (and any written comments the parties may make on each others' comments) as well as to have the ability to submit any written comments they themselves may have on the issue that we have identified above. The Panel considers that such third party participation in this initial stage of the Panel proceedings is appropriate for the following reasons.

The Panel is aware of the provisions of Article 10.3 of the *DSU*, which states that third parties shall receive the submissions of the parties to the dispute to the first meeting of the Panel. We would also observe that the factual circumstance that presents itself here is not itself specifically addressed by the *DSU*. In our view, the legal issue that the Panel has asked the parties to address in their initial briefs will necessarily have ramifications for the remainder of the Panel proceedings, including the scope of the first substantive meeting, at which third parties will participate.

We therefore invite the parties to serve also on the third parties their initial briefs and any responding comments. The Panel will also invite third parties to submit any written comments they might have concerning the initial phase of these proceedings. The deadline for any third party comments is *10 June 2003*. The parties' comments to be submitted on 13 June may, of course, also address comments made by third parties.

[Attachment omitted]

ANNEX L-1.4

COMMUNICATION TO BRAZIL AND THE UNITED STATES AND THIRD PARTIES

20 June 2003

1. In a communication to the Panel, dated 21 May 2003, prior to the Panel's adoption of its working procedures, the United States had "propose[d] that the Panel organize its procedures to deal with the threshold Peace Clause issue at the outset of this dispute". The United States asserted *inter alia* that "[b]ecause in this dispute Brazil has made claims under 17 different provisions of the WTO Multilateral Agreements with respect to numerous US programmes under at least 12 US statutes, we believe the Panel's consideration of the critical Peace Clause issue would be aided by briefing and argumentation focused on this threshold issue". Brazil submitted a communication in response, dated 23 May 2003, opposing the US proposal.

2. On 28 May 2003, after having heard the views of the parties, we adopted our timetable and working procedures in accordance with Article 12.1 of the *Understanding on Rules and Procedures Governing the Settlement of Disputes* (the "*DSU*").

3. At the same time, we indicated that we would consider giving a ruling on certain issues on 20 June 2003, prior to the submission by the parties of their first written submissions, in relation to the following question and we requested the parties and third parties to address us in relation to it:

> "whether Article 13 of the *Agreement on Agriculture* precludes the Panel from considering Brazil's claims under the *Agreement on Subsidies and Countervailing Measures* in these proceedings in the absence of a prior conclusion by the Panel that certain conditions of Article 13 remain unfulfilled. In particular, the Panel invites the parties to explain their interpretation of the words "exempt from actions" as used in Article 13 of the *Agreement on Agriculture*, as well as bringing to the Panel's attention any other relevant provisions of the covered agreements and any other relevant considerations which the parties consider should guide the Panel's consideration of this issue. For greater clarity, the Panel invites the parties, during this initial stage of the proceedings, to focus on matters of legal interpretation, rather than upon the submission of any factual evidence that might be associated with the substantive elements of Article 13."

4. The parties submitted their initial briefs on this question on 5 June 2003. On 10 June, the following six third parties submitted briefs: Argentina; Australia; European Communities; India, New Zealand and Paraguay. The parties submitted further comments on 13 June 2003.

5. Article 13(a)(ii) of the *Agreement on Agriculture* states that domestic support measures that conform fully to the provisions of Annex 2 of the *Agreement on Agriculture* shall be exempt from actions based on Article XVI of *GATT 1994* and Part III of the *Agreement on Subsidies and Countervailing Measures* (the "*SCM Agreement*"). Article 13(b)(ii) of the *Agreement on Agriculture* states that domestic support measures that conform fully to certain conditions shall be "exempt from actions based on paragraph 1 of Article XVI of GATT 1994 or Articles 5 and 6 of the Subsidies Agreement, provided that such measures do not grant support to a specific commodity in excess of that decided during the 1992 marketing year." Articles 5 and 6 of the *SCM Agreement* are each qualified by the proviso that "[t]his Article does not apply to subsidies maintained on agricultural products as provided in Article 13 of the Agreement on Agriculture". Article 13(c)(ii) of the *Agreement on Agriculture* provides that export subsidies that conform fully to the provisions of Part V of that Agreement, as reflected in each Member's Schedule, shall be "exempt from actions based on Article XVI of GATT 1994 or Articles 3, 5 and 6 of the Subsidies Agreement". Article 3.1 of the *SCM Agreement*, which prohibits export subsidies, is qualified by the proviso: "Except as provided in the *Agreement on Agriculture...*". These provisions of Article 13 afford a conditional exemption from certain obligations relating to certain actionable and prohibited subsidies under the provisions of the *SCM Agreement* and Article XVI of the *GATT 1994*. This conditionality requires, *inter alia*, a comparison of facts with the applicable exemption requirements.

6. Briefly, Brazil asserts that the Panel can simultaneously consider all of the arguments and evidence on the substance of its claims under the *SCM* and *Agriculture Agreements*, while the United States asserts that the Panel is precluded from examining the SCM claims concerning prohibited and actionable subsidies in the absence of a prior ruling that the conditions of Article 13 of the *Agreement on Agriculture* are not satisfied, and, even if not, the Panel should exercise its discretion to order its proceedings in this way. All of the six third parties that made submissions support the view that the Panel is not precluded from simultaneously considering all of the arguments and evidence on the substance of Brazil's claims under the *SCM* and *Agriculture Agreements*, or, putting this another way, that conclusions on the applicability of the Article 13 exemptions do not have to be made before consideration of SCM claims in relation to the measures concerned.

7. We are faced with two questions:

- *first*, whether we are *required* to defer any examination of certain of Brazil's claims based on Articles 3, 5 and 6 of the *SCM Agreement* and Article XVI of the *GATT 1994* until after making a ruling or expressing views on the issue of fulfilment of *Agreement on Agriculture* Article 13 conditions; and
- *second*, if not, then *how* we should exercise our discretion to best structure our examination of the matter before us.

8. These questions concern the manner in which we should or must treat the claims of Brazil based on Articles 3, 5 and 6 of the *SCM Agreement* and Article

XVI of the *GATT 1994* having regard to the provisions of Article 13 of the *Agreement on Agriculture*.

9. We therefore look first to the dispute settlement procedures governing disputes under the *SCM Agreement*. Article 30 of the *SCM Agreement* states: "The provisions of Articles XXII and XXIII of GATT 1994 as elaborated and applied by the Dispute Settlement Understanding shall apply to consultations and the settlement of disputes under this Agreement, except as otherwise specifically provided herein."

10. We thus turn next to the *Understanding on Rules and Procedures Governing the Settlement of Disputes* (the "*DSU*") and to the terms of the *SCM Agreement* itself (in order to see whether or not there is anything otherwise specifically provided therein). Article 1.1 of the *DSU* is entitled "Coverage and Application". It states that "[t]he rules and procedures of this Understanding shall apply to disputes brought pursuant to the consultation and dispute settlement provisions of the agreements listed in Appendix 1 to this Understanding (referred to in this Understanding as the "covered agreements")."

11. As the Appellate Body has observed, "[a]rticle 1.1 of the DSU establishes an integrated dispute settlement system which applies to all of the agreements listed in Appendix 1 to the *DSU* (the "covered agreements"). The DSU is a coherent system of rules and procedures for dispute settlement which applies to "disputes brought pursuant to the consultation and dispute settlement provisions of" the covered agreements."[1] The *SCM Agreement* and the *GATT 1994* are Multilateral Agreements on Trade in Goods in Annex 1A of the *WTO Agreement* and are therefore "covered agreements" listed in Appendix 1 of the *DSU*. The general *DSU* rules and procedures do not set forth any specific distinct way to deal with claims under the *SCM Agreement* and the *GATT 1994* having regard to the provisions of Article 13 of the *Agreement on Agriculture*.

12. Article 1.2 of the *DSU* provides, in relevant part, that the rules and procedures of the *DSU* shall apply subject to such special or additional rules and procedures on dispute settlement contained in the covered agreements as are identified in Appendix 2 to the *DSU*.

13. We therefore examine whether Appendix 2 to the *DSU* identifies any special or additional dispute settlement rules or procedures relating to the *SCM Agreement* or to Article XVI of the *GATT 1994*.

14. Appendix 2 of the *DSU* does not identify Article XVI of the *GATT 1994* as a special or additional rule. It does identify Articles 4.2-4.12 and Articles 7.2-7.10 of the *SCM Agreement* as "special or additional rules and procedures". These provisions contain special procedures and remedies for disputes involving prohibited and actionable subsidies governed by the *SCM Agreement*. However, none of these provisions purports to confer any sort of precedence or priority for considering SCM remedies in a dispute involving claims under the *Agreement on*

---

[1] Appellate Body Report, *Guatemala – Anti-Dumping Investigation Regarding Portland Cement from Mexico* ("*Guatemala – Cement I*"), WT/DS60/AB/R, adopted 25 November 1998, DSR 1998:IX, 3767, para. 64.

Agriculture. Furthermore, Article 7.1 of the *SCM Agreement*, which is not identified as a special or additional rule or procedure in Appendix 2 of the *DSU*, indicates that it applies: "Except as provided in Article 13 of the Agreement on Agriculture....". This clearly indicates to us that this provision must be read in the light of the provisions of Article 13 of the *Agreement on Agriculture*. Moreover, as noted in para. 5 above, the substantive provisions to which these remedial articles are linked – Articles 3, 5 and 6 – stipulate either that they apply "except as provided in the Agreement on Agriculture" (Article 3 relating to prohibited subsidies), or that they do "not apply to subsidies maintained on agricultural products as provided in Article 13 of the Agreement on Agriculture" (Articles 5 and 6.9 of the *SCM Agreement*, entitled "Adverse Effects" and "Serious Prejudice", respectively).

15. The cited provisions of the *SCM Agreement* refer, as just indicated, to the *Agreement on Agriculture*, and some specify more precisely Article 13 of the *Agreement on Agriculture*. We therefore examine the rules applicable to dispute settlement under the *Agreement on Agriculture*, which is also a Multilateral Agreement on Trade in Goods in Annex 1A of the *WTO Agreement* and is, therefore, a "covered agreement" listed in Appendix 1 of the *DSU*. Article 19 of the *Agreement on Agriculture* is entitled "Consultation and Dispute Settlement". It states that the provisions of Articles XXII and XXIII of *GATT 1994*, as elaborated and applied by the *DSU*, shall apply to consultations and the settlement of disputes under that Agreement.

16. Appendix 2 to the *DSU* does not identify any special or additional dispute settlement rules or procedures relating to Article 13 of the *Agreement on Agriculture*.

17. Consequently, consistent with our consideration of the relevant provisions, there is no special dispute settlement requirement foreseen in the covered agreements in respect of a panel's consideration of the fulfilment of Article 13 conditions. The issue of fulfilment of the conditions of Article 13 of the *Agreement on Agriculture* is to be resolved using generally applicable *DSU* rules and procedures. The fact that certain very specific provisions are included in Appendix 2 of the *DSU* as special or additional rules indicates that, when the drafters intended to make a particular provision

applicable as a special or additional dispute settlement rule, they did so explicitly. Therefore, their failure to include a reference to any provision of the *Agreement on Agriculture* in the text of Appendix 2 demonstrates that they did not intend to make any provision of that Agreement a special or additional dispute settlement rule. It is not necessary for us to look for any further interpretive guidance on this issue.

18. We next turn to the issue of how we should structure our procedures to consider the matter before us. As we have concluded above, this issue is subject to the *DSU* but not otherwise affected by the covered agreements. In this regard, within the overall parameters set by the *DSU* of prompt and efficient dispute

resolution[2], we must exercise our discretion as to how best to organize our procedures. Our discretion must be guided by the instructions given to us by the *DSU*. Pursuant to Article 12.1 of the *DSU*, "[p]anels shall follow the Working Procedures in Appendix 3 unless the panel decides otherwise after consulting the parties to the dispute". Moreover, Article 12.2 provides: "Panel procedures should provide sufficient flexibility so as to ensure high-quality panel reports, while not unduly delaying the panel process."

19. Article 11 of the *DSU*, entitled "Function of Panels" provides that the function of panels is to assist the DSB in discharging its responsibilities under the *DSU* and the covered agreements. Accordingly, a panel should make an objective assessment of the matter before it, including an objective assessment of the facts of the case and the applicability of and conformity with the relevant covered agreements, and make such other findings as will assist the DSB in making the recommendations or in giving the rulings provided for in the covered agreements. Article 11 contemplates that a panel must make an "objective assessment of the facts of the case and the applicability of and conformity with the relevant covered agreements." It does not require that a panel must conduct its proceedings in any particular way, provided that its requirements are fulfilled. It is within our discretion to manage our procedures so as to best fulfil the requirements of Article 11.

20. Given the potential complexity of the claims before us, the conditional nature of certain of these claims and the volume of evidence which may be introduced by the parties in support of their claims and arguments, and in order to organize our proceedings in an orderly, effective and efficient manner which serves to facilitate an objective assessment of the matter before us, and optimizes use of our resources, we have adopted the following modifications to our procedures (as indicated in the attached timetable):

- The Panel intends to express its views on whether measures raised in this dispute satisfy the conditions in Article 13 of the *Agreement on Agriculture*, to the extent that it is able to do so, by **1 September 2003**, and will defer its consideration of claims under Articles 3, 5 and 6 of the *SCM Agreement* and Article XVI of the *GATT 1994* as those provisions are referred to in Article 13 of the *Agreement on Agriculture* until after it has expressed those views. The Panel's views may be expressed in the form of rulings which could affect the Panel's further consideration of this dispute.
- In order that third parties may participate effectively at the first meeting at which the claims under Articles 3, 5 and 6 of the *SCM Agreement* and Article XVI of the *GATT 1994* as referred to in Article 13 of the *Agreement on Agriculture* are examined (as necessa-

---

2 Article 3.3 of the *DSU* provides: "The prompt settlement of situations in which a Member considers that any benefits accruing to it directly or indirectly under the covered agreements are being impaired by measures taken by another Member is essential to the effective functioning of the WTO and the maintenance of a proper balance between the rights and obligations of Members."

ry), the Panel intends to divide its first meeting into two sessions, each of which will include a third party session.

- Accordingly, for the purposes of the first session of the first substantive meeting on 22-24 July 2003, the Panel does not require the parties to address claims under Articles 3, 5 and 6 of the *SCM Agreement* and Article XVI of the *GATT 1994* as referred to in Article 13 of the *Agreement on Agriculture*. Having said this, the Panel notes that this does not preclude the parties from addressing such matters in their first submissions.
- All other claims of Brazil in relation to measures which Brazil maintains do not involve a consideration of Article 13 of the *Agreement on Agriculture* should also be addressed in first submissions, in order for the other party and third parties to have an opportunity to express their views on any such claims.
- For the purposes of allowing the Panel to express its views on the exemption conditions of Article 13 of the *Agreement on Agriculture* by 1 September 2003, in relation to those measures which may be affected by Article 13, full and complete submissions on factual and legal issues related to Article 13 in this dispute will need to be provided, at the latest, in the parties' rebuttal submissions (to be submitted on 22 August 2003).

21. We recognize that we may need to revisit certain aspects of our timetable and working procedures in light of developments during the course of the Panel procedures. Related amendments to the working procedures may also be made, if necessary. We have been mindful of due process considerations in revising our timetable and will continue to ensure that the parties have reasonable time to prepare for any subsequent stages of the dispute, as appropriate.

[Attachment omitted]

ANNEX L-1.5

COMMUNICATION TO BRAZIL AND THE UNITED STATES
25 July 2003

Please find attached a communication from the Panel on the following issues:

1. The Panel's view on the preliminary ruling requested by the United States.
2. Questions from the Panel to the parties.
3. A copy of the Panel's questions to third parties (sent for your reference)

The Panel's questions are intended to facilitate the work of the Panel, and do not in any way prejudge the Panel's findings on the matter before it. Nor does the fact that the Panel has placed these questions under certain headings prejudge the Panel's findings on the matter before it. Each party is free to respond to or comment on questions posed to the other party or third parties.

Please be reminded that as stated by the Chairman of the Panel in the meeting, parties are requested to submit answers by the close of business of 4 August 2003. Subsequently, parties can submit comments to each other's responses by the close of business 22 August, the same deadline applicable to the rebuttal submissions

Panels' views on the preliminary ruling requested by the United States

1. The United States requests a preliminary ruling that:

    (1) export credit guarantee measures relating to eligible US agricultural commodities other than upland cotton,

    (2) production flexibility contract payments and market loss assistance payments, and

    (3) the Agricultural Assistance Act of 2003

are not within the Panel's terms of reference.[1]

2. Brazil asserts that these items are properly within the Panel's terms of reference and asks the Panel to reject the United States' request.[2]

3. The Panel wishes to indicate to the parties how it intends to rule on items (1) and (2), in order to assist them in deciding what argumentation and evidence to submit in their answers to questions and rebuttals.

4. The DSB established the Panel at its meeting on 18 March 2003 with the following standard terms of reference:[3]

---

1 US First Written Submission, para. 218.

2 Brazil's Oral Statement at the First Substantive Meeting, paras. 90, 144 and 145.

3 WT/DSB/M/145 (para. 35)

> "To examine, in the light of the relevant provisions of the covered agreements cited by Brazil in document WT/DS267/7, the matter referred to the DSB by Brazil in that document and to make such findings as will assist the DSB in making the recommendations or in giving the rulings provided for in those agreements".

5. With respect to item (1), the Panel intends to rule in its report that "export credit guarantees ... to facilitate the export of US upland cotton, and other eligible agricultural commodities" as addressed in document WT/DS267/7, are within its terms of reference.

6. With respect to item (2), the Panel intends to rule in its report that production flexibility contract payments and market loss assistance payments as addressed in document WT/DS267/7 are within its terms of reference. This is without prejudice to the relevance, if any, of those payments under Article 13(b) of the *Agreement on Agriculture,* Articles 5, 6 and 7 of the *SCM Agreement* and Article XVI of *GATT 1994*.

7. The Panel has not yet decided upon its approach to item (3) and asks the parties not to exclude consideration of the Agricultural Assistance Act of 2003 in responding to the Panels' written questions and in rebuttal submissions.

Questions from the Panel to the parties –
First session of the first substantive Panel meeting

UPLAND COTTON

1. Please confirm that all information and data that you have provided to the Panel relating to "cotton" in fact relates to upland cotton only. **BRA, USA**

PRELIMINARY ISSUES

Note to parties: As indicated in the cover note, the Panel has expressed its views in respect of the three United States requests for preliminary rulings. The Panel's questions reflected in this compilation relating to the requested preliminary rulings on which the Panel has expressed its views are those that were posed in the course of the first session of the first Panel meeting. This is to give an opportunity for the parties to transpose into writing their oral responses.

Product scope of Panel's terms of reference relating to Brazil's export credit guarantee claims

2. Is Brazil's claim in relation to export credit guarantees against the measures said to constitute the GSM-102, GSM-103 and SCGP programmes in their entire application, or against the measures said to constitute the GSM-102, GSM-103 and SCGP programmes in their application to upland cotton, or both? **BRA**

3. If the request for consultations in this dispute omitted certain *products* in relation to export credit guarantees, on what basis is it argued that it failed to identify the *measures* at issue in accordance with Article 4.4 of the *DSU*? **USA**

4. Is it argued that the export credit guarantee programmes concerning upland cotton are each a separate or independent *measure*, in that they operate independently? **USA**

5. Is there a specification in any legislation or regulation (or any other official government document) which limit or restrict the export credit guarantee programmes at issue exclusively to upland cotton? **USA**

6. For the purposes of the Panel's examination of Brazil's claims relating to GSM-102, GSM-103 and SCGP under the *Agreement on Agriculture* and the *SCM Agreement*, is accurate data and information available with respect to these export credit guarantee programmes concerning upland cotton alone (e.g. with respect to "long-term operating costs and losses")? In this respect, the Panel also directs the parties' attention to the specific questions below relating to the programmes. **USA**

7. Are commitments with respect to export subsidies under the *Agreement on Agriculture* commodity-specific? How, if at all, is this relevant? **BRA, USA**

8. Does the United States confirm that the questions referred to by Brazil in paragraph 92 of Brazil's oral statement were posed to the United States in the consultations? **USA**

9. How does the United States respond to paragraph 94 of Brazil's oral statement? **USA**

10. What actual prejudice, if any, has the United States suffered as a result of the alleged omission of products other than upland cotton from the request for consultations? **USA**

11. Does the United States agree that Brazil's request for establishment of the Panel can be understood to indicate that Brazil's export credit guarantee claims relatesto products other than upland cotton? How, if at all, is this relevant? **USA**

12. Please address issues and submit evidence regarding the three export credit guarantee programmes concerned relating to upland cotton and other eligible agricultural commodities in your answers to questions and rebuttal submissions. **BRA, USA**

13. Please include any argumentation and evidence to support your statement during the Panel meeting that the inclusion of such other eligible agricultural commodities would create additional "work" for the Panel with respect to each of these commodities under Article 13 of the *Agreement on Agriculture*. **USA**

Expired measures

14. Please submit evidence regarding the programmes under the 1996 FAIR Act, in particular, production flexibility contract payments and market loss assistance payments, to the extent that they would be relevant to the Panel's determination under Article 13 of the *Agreement on Agriculture* in your answers to questions and rebuttal submission. **USA**

15. Do the parties agree that it is beyond a Panel's power to recommend a remedy for an expired measure? Could the Panel could be required to examine

"expired measures" in order to conduct its assessment of the matter before it? How, if at all, is Article 7.8 of the *SCM Agreement* relevant to these matters? **BRA, USA**

Agricultural Assistance Act of 2003

16. What, if any, prejudice in terms of the presentation of its case does the United States allege, should the Panel proceed to consider the measures constituting the cottonseed payments under the Agricultural Assistance Act of 2003? **USA**

17. (a) What is the relationship of the Agricultural Assistance Act of 2003 to other legislation in the request for establishment of the Panel? **BRA, USA**

(b) Do the legal instruments follow directly one after another, or are there temporal gaps? Are payments authorized under a broad legislative authority or are they specific to each legal instrument? **BRA, USA**

(c) Please provide any implementing regulations. Do these implementing regulations resemble those relating to previous programmes or payments? Are payments made retrospectively? How if at all is this relevant? **BRA, USA**

18. If the Panel is correct in understanding that cottonseed payments are divided between processors and producers, how is this reflected in Brazil's calculations? **BRA**

Measures at issue

19. The Panel notes that Brazil's panel request refers, *inter alia*, to alleged "subsidies" and "domestic support" "provided" in various contexts. Please specify the measures, in particular, the legislative and regulatory provisions, by number and letter, in respect of which Brazil seeks relief and indicate where each is referred to in the panel request. **BRA**

ARTICLE 13(B): DOMESTIC SUPPORT MEASURES

"exempt from actions"

20. In paragraph 8 of its initial brief (dated 5 June, 2003), the United States argued that the word "actions" as used in the phrase "exempt from actions" in Article 13 of the *Agreement on Agriculture* includes the "bringing of a case" and consultations. In paragraph 36 of its first written submission (dated 11 July, 2003), the United States stated as follows:

> "[P]rior to this point in the process, the *DSU* rules did not afford the United States any opportunity to prevent the dispute from proceeding through consultations and panel establishment automatically, regardless of the U.S. insistence that its measures conform to the Peace Clause."

Is it the United States' understanding that the drafters used the phrase "exempt from actions" knowing that under the *DSU* it would not be possible fully to exempt "actions", as the United States interprets that term? **USA**

21. In *US - FSC* and *US - FSC (21.5)* the Appellate Body made findings under the *SCM Agreement* relating to export subsidies in respect of agricultural products without making a finding in respect of Article 13 of the *Agreement on Agriculture.* How is this relevant to the United States' interpretation of the phrase "exempt from actions" as used in Article 13? **USA**

"such measures" and Annex 2 of the *Agreement on Agriculture*

22. Please explain the difference, if any, between the meaning of "defined" and the meaning of "fixed" in the phrase "a defined and fixed base period" in paragraph 6(a) of Annex 2 of the *Agreement on Agriculture*. **BRA, USA**

23. Please explain the meaning of "a" in "a defined and fixed base period" in paragraph 6(a) of Annex 2 of the *Agreement on Agriculture*, the meaning of "the" in "the base period" in paragraphs 6(b), (c) and (d), and the difference between these and the phrase "based on the years 1986-88" in Annex 3. **BRA, USA**

24. How often can a Member define and fix a base period in accordance with paragraph 6 of Annex 2 of the *Agreement on Agriculture*? **BRA, USA**

25. Does the United States consider that there is any ambiguity in the term "type of production" as used in paragraph 6(b) of Annex 2 of the *Agreement on Agriculture*? **USA**

26. Can the United States confirm Brazil's assertions in paragraph 174 of its first written submission that the implementing regulations for direct payments prohibit or limit payments if base acreage is used for the production of certain crops? If so, can the United States clarify the statement in paragraph 56 of its first written submission that direct payments are made regardless of what is currently produced on those acres? Can the United States confirm the same point in relation to production flexibility contracts? **USA**

27. Does Brazil argue that any United States measure that does not comply with the fundamental requirement of paragraph 1 of Annex 2 of the *Agreement on Agriculture* is actionable independently of any failure of that measure to comply with the basic or policy-specific criteria in Annex 2? **BRA**

28. Please explain the meaning of the word "criteria" in Articles 6.1 and 7.1. What effect, if any, does the use of the word "Accordingly" in paragraph 1 of Annex 2 of the *Agreement on Agriculture* have on the meaning of the preceding sentence? **BRA**

29. Please explain the meaning of the words "the fundamental requirement" as used in paragraph 1 of Annex 2 of the *Agreement on Agriculture.* **USA**

30. Do the parties consider that direct payments and production flexibility contract payments meet or met the basic criteria referred to in paragraph 1 of Annex 2 of the *Agreement on Agriculture*? **BRA, USA**

31. If the first sentence of paragraph 1 of Annex 2 is not a stand-alone obligation, then must new, non- or minimally trade-distorting measures that do not conform to the criteria listed in Annex 2 be classified as non-Green Box? **BRA, USA**

32. If the first sentence of paragraph 1 of Annex 2 expresses a general principle which informs the interpretation of the criteria in Annex 2, please explain how this affects the assessment of the direct payments programme's compliance with paragraph 6 of Annex 2. **USA**

"do not grant support to a specific commodity"

33. According to the United States' interpretation of the word "grant", when can a Member claim that a measure is not exempt from action under Article 13(b)? What if the measure is enacted annually? Can the Member obtain a remedy in respect of that measure under the *DSU*? **USA**

34. Does Brazil interpret the word "grant" as used in Article 13(b)(ii) of the *Agreement on Agriculture* to mean payment made *in* a specific year or payment made *in respect of* a specific year? **BRA**

35. Does a failure by a Member to comply in a given *year* with either the chapeau of Article 13(b) or the proviso in subparagraph (ii) of Article 13(b) impact its entitlement to benefit in an earlier or a later year from the exemption from action provided by Article 13(b)? **BRA, USA**

36. Does a failure by a Member to comply with Article 13(b) in respect of a *specific commodity* impact its entitlement to benefit in respect of other agricultural products from the exemption from action provided by Article 13(b)? **BRA, USA**

37. In the United States' view, why did the drafters not use the exact term "product-specific" in Article 13(b)(ii)? **USA**

38. Given the fact that subsidies available for more than one product could have various effects on production, how does the United States demarcate between product-specific support and non-product specific support ? **USA**

39. If "such measures" in Article 13(b)(ii) refers to all those in the chapeau of Article 13(b), why are they not all included in the potential comparisons with 1992? In what circumstances can measures which grant non-product specific support lose exemption from action under Articles 5 and 6 of the *SCM Agreement* and Article XVI of *GATT 1994*? **USA**

40. In relation to which other provisions in the *Agreement on Agriculture* is it relevant to disaggregate non-product specific support in terms of specific commodities? **BRA**

41. What is the position of Brazil with regard to certain other domestic support measures not cited by Brazil that were notified by the United States as non-product-specific (e.g. G/AG/N/USA/43), some of which presumably deliver support to upland cotton (e.g. state credit programmes, irrigation subsidies etc). Why have budgetary outlays for such measures related to upland cotton not been included in the comparison of support with 1992? **BRA**

42. If the word "specific" were deleted from Article 13(b)(ii), would this change the meaning of the subparagraph? **BRA**

43. What are the precise differences between deficiency payments and counter-cyclical payments that lead you to classify the former as product-specific and the latter as non-product specific? How do you classify market loss assistance payments? **USA**

44. Do you allege that counter-cyclical payments could be considered product-specific? **BRA**

45. If the Panel considered that Step 2 payments paid to exporters were an export subsidy, would the United States count them as domestic support measures for the purposes of Article 13(b)? Please verify Brazil's separate data for Step 2 export payments and Step 2 domestic payments in Exhibit BRA-69 or provide separate data. **BRA, USA**

46. What is the relevance, if any, of the concept of "specificity" in Article 2 of the *SCM* Agreement and references to "a product" or "subsidized product" in certain provisions of the *SCM Agreement* to the meaning of "support to a specific commodity" in Article 13(b)(ii) *Agreement on Agriculture*? **BRA, USA**

"in excess of that decided during the 1992 marketing year"

47. Where does Article 13(b)(ii) require a year-on-year comparison? **BRA, USA**

48. Does Article 13(b)(ii) require a comparison of support granted with support decided? How could such a comparison be made? **BRA, USA**

49. Brazil claims that the terms "grant" and "decided" in Article 13(b)(ii) have broadly the same meaning. If so, why did the drafters not use the same term? **BRA**

50. Please provide any written drafting history which could shed light on why the proviso was added to what is now Article 13(b)(ii) and, in particular, why both words "grant" and "decided" were used. **USA**

51. Could the United States please comment on the interpretation advanced by the EC, in paragraphs 16 and 18 of its oral statement, of the words "decided during the 1992 marketing year"? **USA**

52. Please comment on an interpretation of the words "decided during" in Article 13(b)(ii) that would read them as synonymous with the words "authorized during". **BRA, USA**

53. Assume, for arguments sake, that the only "decision" made in the United States in 1992 was the target price. How would Brazil make the comparison *vis-à-vis*, for example, the year 2001? **BRA**

54. Please identify all United States legal and regulatory and administrative instruments decided during the marketing year 1992, with the respective dates of decision, that decided support for upland cotton. **BRA, USA**

55. Please provide a copy of the instrument in which the rate of support for upland cotton during the marketing year 1992 was decided, indicating the date of the decision. **USA**

56. Could the United States please explain how support granted under legislation that dates back to 1990 can have been support "decided during the marketing year 1992"? **USA**

57. If the United States decided on a rate of support for MY1992, does that not mean that it decided on whatever budgetary outlay was required to meet that rate of support, even if the exact amount was not known at that time? **USA**

58. Please comment on the argument advanced by the EC, in paragraph 17 of its oral statement that: "Had WTO Members intended a limitation to the support provided or granted in 1992 the word 'for' would have been used in place of 'during'." **BRA**

59. Should the rate of support as indicated in Article 13(b)(ii) include the market price? If so, why is it appropriate to include it in the comparison under Article 13(b)(ii)? **BRA, USA**

60. Can you provide information on support decided in 1992 and the years with which you believe it should be compared, on a per support programme / per unit of production / per annum basis? If possible, please specify how, if at all, budget outlays may be transposed into units of production, and which units of production are best to use. **BRA, USA**

61. Does the United States consider that Article 13(b)(ii) permits a comparison on any basis other than a per pound basis? **USA**

62. According to Prof. Sumner's calculation, the per pound support increased by approximately 24% from 1992 to 2002. On the other hand, the Panel understands that the total budget outlay, according to Brazil, increased more than that. What, in Brazil's view, is the reason for this difference in the rate of increase? **BRA**

63. In relation to Prof. Sumner's presentation at the first session of the first substantive meeting, please elaborate on the reasons behind the increase in the figures (from 1992 to 2002) concerning Loan Support and Step 2 payments. **BRA**

64. Do the figures cited in Prof. Sumner's presentation at the first session of the first substantive meeting indicate amount available or amount spent? Can the Panel derive amount spent from these figures? If Article 13(b)(ii) requires a rate of support comparison, is the rate of support the "rate" of support available or the "rate" at which the support was spent? **BRA**

65. Does Brazil consider that adjustment for inflation is relevant in the context of the comparison under Article 13 (b)(ii) ? **BRA**

66. Could you please comment on the relative merits of each of the following calculation methods for the purposes of the comparison of support to upland cotton with 1992, irrespective of whether a particular measure should be included or excluded:

(a) Total budgetary outlays (Brazil's approach). **USA**

(b) Budgetary outlays per unit of upland cotton: Could you please calculate and provide an estimate for the marketing years 1992 and 1999-2002, respectively, and draw attention to any factors/qualifications that the Panel would need to be aware of. **BRA, USA**

(c) Per unit rate of support (United States approach): How should changes in acreage, eligibility and payment limitations per farm(s) (commodity certificate programs) be factored into this approach? **BRA**

(d) Per unit rate of support for upland cotton (Prof. Sumner's approach at the first session of the first substantive meeting). **USA**

67. The Panel requests the parties to calculate and submit estimates of the AMS for upland cotton for marketing years 1992, 1999, 2000, 2001 and 2002. For this purpose the parties are each requested to submit AMS calculations for upland cotton (using the budgetary-outlay/non-price gap methodology employed by the United States in respect of cotton in its DS Notifications (e.g., G/AG/N/USA/43) and using the formats and supporting tables in document G/AG/2) on the same basis as would be the case in calculating a product specific AMS for the purposes of the calculation of the "Total Current AMS" in any year in accordance with the relevant provisions, including as appropriate Article 1(a), (b) and (h), Article 6 and Annex 3 to the Agreement. **BRA, USA**

68. Could you please clarify the result of the calculations of, and the meaning of the title, in Appendix Table 1 "Estimated per unit Subsidy Rates by Program and Year" in Annex 2 to Exhibit BRA-105, page 12. Why are the numbers calculated for marketing loans considered to be subsidies? Could the Panel, for example, read the "total level of support" (bottom line of the table) as the effective support *price* for upland cotton or the maximum rate of support for upland cotton? **BRA, USA**

69. Can the United States confirm that the "marketing year" for upland cotton is 1 August to 31 July ? Can the United States confirm the Panel's understanding that USDA data for the "crop year" corresponds to the "marketing year"? **USA**

EXPORT CREDIT GUARANTEE PROGRAMMES

70. How does Brazil respond to the United States' assertion that Brazil is trying to realize through litigation what it could not achieve in past negotiations ? **BRA**

71. (a) Is an export credit guarantee a financial contribution in the form of a "potential direct transfer of funds or liabilities (e.g. loan guarantee)" within the meaning of Article 1.1(a)(1)(i) of the *SCM Agreement*? Why or why not? Does it confer a benefit within the meaning of Article 1.1(b)? Why or why not? If so, to whom? **USA**

(b) How, if at all, would these elements be relevant to the claims of Brazil, and the United States response thereto? **BRA, USA**

72. Could Brazil expand on why, as indicated in paragraph 118 of its oral statement, it does "not agree" with the United States arguments relating to the viability of an *a contrario* interpretation of item (j) of the Illustrative List of Export Subsidies in Annex 1 of the *SCM Agreement*? **BRA**

73. The Panel could arguably take the view that Articles 1 and 3 of the *SCM Agreement* were relevant in assessing the WTO-consistency of United States export credit guarantees. The United States has yet to submit any evidence or argumentation on this point, either as potential context for interpretation of the terms in Article 10 of the *Agreement on Agriculture* or in relation to Brazil's claims under the *SCM Agreement*. The Panel would therefore appreciate United States views in respect of this situation, and invites the United States to submit relevant argumentation and evidence. **USA**

74. If the Panel decides to refer to provisions of the *SCM Agreement* for contextual guidance in the interpretation of the terms in Article 10 of the *Agreement on Agriculture*, should the Panel refer to item (j) or Articles 1 and 3 of the *SCM Agreement* or both? **BRA, USA**

75. The Panel's attention has been drawn to Article 14(c) of the *SCM Agreement* (see e.g. written third party submission of Canada) and to the panel report in DS 222 *Canada- Export Credits and Loan Guarantees*. How and to what extent are Article 14(c) of the *SCM Agreement*, and the cited panel report, relevant to the issue of whether or not the United States export credit guarantee programmes confer a "benefit"? What would be the appropriate market benchmark to use for any comparison? Please cite any other relevant material. **BRA, USA**

76. How does the United States respond to Brazil's statement that : "...export credit guarantees for exports of agricultural exports [*sic*] are not available on the marketplace by commercial lenders."? **USA**

77. How does the United States interpretation of "long term operating costs and losses" in item (j) as claims paid give meaning to *both* "costs" and "losses"? Do claims paid represent "losses" or "costs" or both? If claims paid is represented by "losses", what would go into the "cost" element of item (j)? Could the United States expand on why it disagrees with the items which Brazil identifies for inclusion in the examination to be conducted under item (j)? **USA**

78. Can the United States provide supporting documentation for data used relating to "costs and losses" in paragraph 173? Could the United States confirm that the figures cited in paragraph 173 of its first written submission relate to the SCGP? Why did the United States cite these figures after stating that it is not possible to make any assessment of the long-term operating costs and losses of this programme? **USA**

79. In respect of what time periods does Article 13(c) require an assessment of conformity with Part V of the *Agreement on Agriculture*? How does this affect, if at all, your interpretation of Article 13(b)? **BRA, USA**

80. In Brazil's view, why did the drafters of the *Agreement on Agriculture* not include export credit guarantees in Article 9.1? **BRA**

81. How does the United States respond to the following in Brazil's oral statement: **USA**

(a) paragraph 122 (rescheduled guarantees)

(b) paragraph 123 (interest on debt to Treasury)

(c) paragraphs 125 ff. (guaranteed loan subsidy)

(d) paragraphs 127-129 (re-estimates, etc.)

(e) Exhibits BRA-125-127

(f) the chart on page 53 of Brazil's oral statement at the first session of the first Panel meeting relating to "Guaranteed Loan Subsidy and Administrative Expenses of US Export Credit Guarantee Programs GSM-102 GSM 103 and SCGP"?

(g) In respect of (a)-(f) above, how and to what extent do the information and data presented for the export guarantee programmes concerning "program" and "financing", "summary of loan levels", "subsidy budget authority", "outlay levels", etc., in particular in Exhibits BRA-125-127, reflect "actual costs and losses" of the GSM-102, GSM-102 and SCGP export credit guarantee programmes(see e.g. Brazil's closing oral statement at the first session of the first substantive meeting, paragraph 24)? **USA**

82. Please explain each of the following statements and any possible significance it may have in respect of Brazil's claims about GSM-102 and GSM-103 (7 CFR 1493.10(a)(2), Exhibit BRA-38): **BRA, USA**

(a) "The programs operate in cases where credit is necessary to increase or maintain U.S. exports to a foreign market and where U.S. financial institutions would be unwilling to provide financing without CCC's guarantee. (7 CFR 1493.10(a)(2) Exhibit BRA-38)

(b) "The programs are operated in a manner intended not to interfere with markets for cash sales. The programs are targeted toward those countries where the guarantee is necessary to secure financing of the exports but which have sufficient financial strength so that foreign exchange will be available for scheduled payments." (7 CFR 1493.10(a)(2) Exhibit BRA-38)

(c) "In providing this credit guarantee facility, CCC seeks to expand market opportunities for US agricultural exporters and assist long-term market development for US agricultural commodities." (7 CFR 1493.10(a)(2) Exhibit BRA-38)

83. Could Brazil explain how the procedure in Annex V of the *SCM Agreement* would be relevant to its claims concerning agricultural export subsidies, prohibited subsidies and agricultural domestic support? (e.g. note 301 in Brazil's first submission and paragraph 4 of Brazil's oral statement at the first session of the first substantive meeting). **BRA**

84. Is the Panel correct in understanding that, under the *GSM-102 and GSM-103 programmes*, the exporter pays a fee calculated on the dollar amount guaran-

teed, based on a schedule of rates applicable to different credit periods? How and on what basis are the fee rates fixed? Do the fee rates ever change? If so, how and for what reason? Would it be necessary to amend the legislation and/or regulations in order to adjust the fee rates? **USA**

85. Is the Panel correct in understanding that, under the *SCGP*, the exporter pays a fee for the guarantee calculated on the guaranteed portion of the value of the export sales? How and on what basis are the fee rates fixed? Do the fee rates ever change? If so, how and for what reason? Would it be necessary to amend the legislation and/or regulations in order to adjust the fee rates? Please explain any "risk" assessment involved in the programme. **USA**

86. Is there a risk categorization in relation to three export credit guarantee programmes (GSM-102, GSM-103 and SCGP)? Does this have any impact on premiums payable and the ability of the CCC to on-sell the guarantees ? **USA**

87. What proportion of CCC (export-related and total) long term operating costs and losses are represented by GSM-102, GSM-103 and SCGP programmes? **USA**

88. (a) Is the Panel correct in understanding that the United States' argument is that, at present, by virtue of Article 10.2 of the *Agreement on Agriculture*, there are ***no*** disciplines on agricultural export credit guarantees under the *Agreement on Agriculture* (or the *SCM Agreement)*? **USA**

(b) Does the United States agree with the following proposition: a WTO Member may therefore extend agricultural export credit guarantees without charging a premium, and for an indefinite period, in addition to any other terms and conditions it may wish? How would this reconcile with the title of Article 10 of the *Agreement on Agriculture* ("Prevention of Circumvention on Export Subsidy Commitments"), and with other commitments contained in the *Agreement on Agriculture*? Please cite any relevant material, including any past WTO dispute settlement cases. How would this reconcile with the United States' own statement, at paragraph 21 of its closing oral statement that "of course, the United States may not provide subsidies without any limit". **USA**

(c) If, as the United States argues, there are no disciplines on export credit guarantees in the *Agreement on Agriculture*, how could export credit guarantees "conform fully to the provisions of Part V" of the *Agreement on Agriculture* within the meaning of Article 13 (how can you assess "conformity" or non-conformity when there are allegedly no disciplines against which such an assessment could occur)? **USA**

(d) Is the United States advocating the view that its own export credit guarantee programmes, which pre-dated the Uruguay Round, are effectively "grandfathered" so as to benefit from some sort of exemption from the export subsidy disciplines of the *Agreement on Agriculture*? How, if at all, is it relevant that the SCGP did not, according to the United States, become relevant for upland cotton until the late 1990's (i.e. after the entry into force of the *WTO Agreement*)? **USA**

STEP 2 PAYMENTS

89. Does the United States confirm Brazil's statement in paragraph 331 of its first submission that "The conditions and requirements for Step 2 domestic payments remain unchanged with the passage of the 2002 FSRI Act"? What is the relevance of this, if any, to this dispute? **USA**

90. Does the United States confirm Brazil's statement in paragraph 235 of its first submission that the changes concerning Step 2 export payments from the 1996 FAIR Act to the 2002 FSRI Act are: increase in the amount of the subsidy by 1.25 cents per pound and the removal of any budgetary limits that applied under the 1996 FAIR Act? What is the relevance of this, if any, to this dispute? **USA**

91. What is the significance of the elimination of the 1.25 cent threshold payment in the 2002 FSRI Act pertaining to Step 2 payments? **USA**

92. Does the United States confirm that Exhibit BRA-65 represents a sample contract for exporters of eligible upland cotton to conclude with the CCC under the FSRI 2002, and that an application form (Exhibit BRA-66) needs to be filled out with data on weekly exports and submitted to the USDA FAS. Is Exhibit BRA-66 - Form CCC 1045-2 – also a valid example? If not, please identify any differences or distinctions. **USA**

93. Please elaborate why the United States deems that Step 2 payments upon submission of proof of export are not subsidies contingent upon export. Is it the US contention that, in order to be contingent on export, exportation must be the exclusive condition for receipt of the payment? **USA**

94. Is the Panel correct in understanding that Brazil alleges an inconsistency with Article 3.1(b) of the *SCM Agreement* only with respect to Step 2 *domestic* payments? **BRA**

95. Do the criteria in 7 CFR 1427.103(c)(2) (Exhibit BRA-37) that Step 2 "eligible upland cotton" must be "not imported cotton" apply to *both* domestic and export payments? **USA**

96. Is a domestic sale a "use" for the purposes of Step 2 payments? Is a sale for export, or export, considered a "use"? **USA**

97. How does the United States respond to Brazil's assertion, at paragraph 70 of Brazil's oral statement at the first session of the first substantive meeting, that "It is obvious that a single bale of cotton cannot be both exported and used domestically." Is this a relevant consideration? **USA**

98. How many Step 2 payments are received if a bale of upland cotton is exported, and then opened by a domestic user in the United States, or *vice versa*? **USA**

99. How does the United States respond to Brazil's arguments in paragraphs 71-75 of Brazil's oral statement at the first session of the first Panel meeting concerning the relevance of the Appellate Body Report in *US-FSC (21.5)*. **USA**

100. How does Brazil respond to the statement in note 119 of the United States' first written submission that "...to the extent a consumer that had intended to export instead opens the bale, then that consumer could still obtain the Step 2 payment upon submission of the requisite documentation". The Panel notes that Step 2 payments all involve upland cotton produced in the United States. What are the two distinct factual situations that Step 2 payments involve? Other than the panel report in *Canada-Dairy* and the findings of the Appellate Body in *US-FSC (21.5)*[4], do any other dispute settlement reports offer guidance on this issue? For example, how, if at all is the Appellate Body's report in *Canada-Aircraft* relevant here?[5] **BRA**

101. How does Brazil respond to the United States' assertion at paragraph 22 of its oral statement that the programme involves "eligible users" who constitute the "entire universe" of potential purchasers of upland cotton? **BRA**

102. How does Brazil respond to the United States' assertion at paragraph 129 of its first written submission, that "[t]he program is indifferent to whether recipients of the benefit of this programme are exporters or parties that open bales for the processing of manufacturing raw cotton into cotton products in the United States." **BRA**

103. Is the Step 2 programme fund a unified fund that is available for either domestic users or exporters, without a specific amount earmarked for either domestic users or exporters? Please substantiate your response, including by reference to any applicable statutory or regulatory provisions. **USA**

104. How does the United States respond to the data presented in Exhibit BRA-69? Is it accurate? Please substantiate. **USA**

---

4 "We recall that the ETI measure grants a tax exemption in two different sets of circumstances: (a) where property is produced *within* the United States and held for use *outside* the United States; and (b) where property is produced *outside* the United States and held for use outside the United States. Our conclusion that the ETI measure grants subsidies that are export contingent in the first set of circumstances is not affected by the fact that the subsidy can also be obtained in the second set of circumstances. The fact that the subsidies granted in the second set of circumstances *might* not be export contingent does not dissolve the export contingency arising in the first set of circumstances.[4] Conversely, the export contingency arising in these circumstances has no bearing on whether there is an export contingent subsidy in the second set of circumstances. Where a United States taxpayer is simultaneously producing property within and outside the United States, for direct use outside the United States, subsidies may be granted under the ETI measure in respect of both sets of property. The subsidy granted with respect to the property produced within the United States, and exported from there, is export contingent within the meaning of Article 3.1(a) of the *SCM Agreement*, irrespective of whether the subsidy given in respect of property produced outside the United States is also export contingent."

5 There, the Appellate Body stated that,

> "the fact that some of TPC's contributions, in some industry sectors, are *not* contingent upon export performance, does not necessarily mean that the same is true for all of TPC's contributions. It is enough to show that one or some of TPC's contributions do constitute subsidies "contingent ... in fact ... upon export performance".[5]

105. Why is the Step 2 programme separated into "domestic users" and "exporters"? Apart from differentiating between exporters and domestic users, with consequential differentiation as to the forms that must be filled out and certain other conditions that must be fulfilled, are the eligibility criteria for Step 2 payments identical? Are the form and rate of payment, as well as the actual payment made, identical? **USA**

106. With respect to paragraph 139 of the United States' first written submission, are Step 2 *export* payments included in the annual reduction commitments of the United States? If so, why? **USA**

107. Please comment on any relevance, to Brazil's *de jure* claims of inconsistency with the provisions of the *Agreement on Agriculture*, of Exhibit BRA-69, which shows Step 2 payments made to (i) domestic users and (ii) exporters. This Exhibit shows that, from FY 91/92 through 02, the Step 2 payments for exporters exceeded those for domestic users in FY 94; FY 95; FY 96 (in fact there were no domestic payments in FY 96); and FY 02. In the other years, the domestic payments are greater than export payments. **BRA, USA**

108. At paragraph 135 of its first written submission, the United States states : "[T]he *subsidy* is not contingent upon export performance..." (emphasis added). Again, in the course of the first Panel meeting, the United States admitted that the Step 2 payments were "subsidies". Does the United States thus concede that Step 2 payments constitute a "subsidy" within the meaning of the *WTO Agreement*? **USA**

109. How does the United States respond to Brazil's arguments concerning a mandatory/discretionary distinction and the allegation that certain United States measures (including s.1207(a) of the 2002 FSRI Act) are mandatory? (This is referred to, for example, in paragraph 28 of Brazil's first written submission). Does the United States agree with the assertion that (subject to the availability of funds) the payment by the Secretary of Step 2 payments is mandatory under section 1207(a) FSRI upon fulfilment by a domestic user or exporter of the conditions set out in the legislation and regulations? If not, then why not? To what extent is this relevant here? What determines the "availability of funds"? Please cite any other relevant measures or provisions which you consider should guide the Panel in respect of this issue. **USA**

110. Section 1207(a) of the 2002 FSRI Act provides that during the period beginning on the date of the enactment of the FSRI Act through 31 July 2008, " .. the Secretary shall issue marketing certificates or cash payments, at the option of the recipient, to domestic users and exporters for documented purchases by domestic users and sales for export by exporters...". The Panel notes that Brazil does not appear to distinguish between the treatment of (i) cash payments and (ii) marketing certificates in terms of the issue of whether or not a "subsidy" exists. The United States refers to "benefits" and "payments" and "programme" in asserting that Step 2 is not export contingent (paragraphs 127-135 of the United States' first written submission).

(a) Do the parties thus agree that there is no need to draw any distinction between the treatment of (i) cash payments and (ii) marketing certificates in terms of the issue of whether or not a "subsidy" exists for the purposes of the *Agreement on Agriculture*? **BRA, USA**

(b) Why would a domestic user or an exporter select to receive a marketing certificate over a cash payment? What is the proportion of cash payments vs. marketing certificates granted under the programme? **USA**

111. Does the United States maintain its argument that actions based on Article 3.1(b) of the *SCM Agreement* are conditionally "exempt from actions" due to the operation of Article 13 of the *Agreement on Agriculture*? **USA**

112. In the event that the Panel finds that Article 6.3 of the *Agreement on Agriculture* does not preclude an examination of Brazil's claims under Article 3.1 of the *SCM Agreement* and Article III:4 of *GATT 1994*, how does the United States respond to the merits of Brazil's claims relating to Step 2 payments under those provisions? **USA**

113. Is it necessary for measures directed at agricultural processors included in AMS to discriminate on the basis of the origin of goods? **USA**

114. With respect to the last sentence of paragraph 22 of Brazil's closing oral statement, could Brazil elaborate on the circumstances in which a local content subsidy would comply with Article 3.1(b) of the *SCM Agreement*? **BRA**

115. What is the meaning and relevance (if any) to Brazil's claims under Article 3 of the *SCM Agreement* and Article III:4 of *GATT 1994* of the phrase "measures directed at agricultural processors shall be included to the extent that such measures benefit the producers of the basic agricultural products" in the *Agreement on Agriculture*? **BRA, USA**

116. With respect to paragraph 32 of the oral statement of the EC, are subsidies contingent on the use of domestic goods consistent with the *Agreement on Agriculture*? Does the phrase "provide support in favour of domestic producers" in Article 3.2 of the *Agreement on Agriculture* refer to, and/or permit such subsidies? **BRA, USA**

117. What is the relationship between Step 2 payments to exporters and the marketing loan payments, both of which appear to compensate for the price differences relative to the Liverpool A-Index? For example, is there double compensation? Or is one of the explanations that these export-related price compensatory payments are paid to different operators (namely, the producer, on the one hand under the marketing loan arrangements, and the processor/users (Step 2 programme) arrangements on the other? **USA**

118. Can the United States confirm that it does not rely on Article III:8 of *GATT 1994*? **USA**

ETI ACT

119. How does the United States respond to Brazil's reference to the panel report in *India - Patents (EC)* (at paragraph 138 of its oral statement at the first

session of the first substantive meeting)?[6] How, if at all, should the Panel take this report into account in considering the issues raised by Brazil's claims relating to the ETI Act? **USA**

120. Concerning its claims on the ETI Act, Brazil relies on the *US – FSC* case. However, it appears that the United States did not raise the issue of the Peace Clause in that case, nor did the United States appear to invoke Article 6 of the *Agreement on Agriculture*. If the Panel's understanding is correct, how, if at all, are these differences relevant here? Could you direct the Panel to any relevant findings or conclusions by the panel or Appellate Body in that case? **BRA**

121. How do you respond to the reference in paragraph 43 of EC third party oral statement with respect to the relevance of Article 17.14 of the *DSU*, and, in particular, the phrase "a final resolution to *that* dispute" (emphasis added)? Please explain the use, and relevance (if any) of the term "disputes" in Articles 9.3 and 12 and Appendix 3 of the *DSU*, and please cite any other provisions you consider relevant. **USA, BRA**

[Attachment on questions to Third Parties omitted]

[6] That panel stated: "It can thus be concluded that panels are not *bound* by previous decisions of panels or the Appellate Body even if the subject-matter is the same. In examining dispute WT/DS79 we are not legally bound by the conclusions of the Panel in dispute WT/DS50 as modified by the Appellate Body report. However, in the course of "normal dispute settlement procedures" required under Article 10.4 of the *DSU*, we will take into account the conclusions and reasoning in the Panel and Appellate Body reports in WT/DS50. Moreover, in our examination, we believe that we should give significant weight to both Article 3.2 of the *DSU*, which stresses the role of the WTO dispute settlement system in providing security and predictability to the multilateral trading system, and to the need to avoid inconsistent rulings (which concern has been referred to by both parties). In our view, these considerations form the basis of the requirement of the referral to the "original panel" wherever possible under Article 10.4 of the *DSU*." (footnote omitted)

ANNEX L-1.6

COMMUNICATION TO BRAZIL AND THE UNITED STATES
30 July 2003

The Panel is in receipt of the communication from the United States, dated 29 July, requesting an extension of the deadline for the submission of the parties' responses to questions, as well as the response from Brazil, dated 30 July.

Taking these communications into account, the Panel has decided to extend the deadline for the submission of the parties' responses to questions from Monday 4 August to **Monday 11 August**. The Panel reminds the parties that paragraph 17(b) of the Panel's working procedures indicates that the responses should be submitted by **17:30** (Geneva time).

The Panel has also decided upon the following additional changes to its schedule:

Panel's views on certain issues:	5 September 2003
Further submission of Brazil:	9 September 2003
Further submission of the US:	23 September 2003
Further submission of the third parties (as necessary):	29 September 2003

For the time being, all other dates remain unchanged. This includes the deadline for the submission of the parties' comments on each other's responses, as well as the submission of the parties' rebuttal submissions (i.e. 22 August). It also includes the dates for the resumption of the first substantive meeting (as necessary) and the second substantive meeting (i.e. 7-9 October).

ANNEX L-1.7

COMMUNICATION TO BRAZIL AND THE UNITED STATES AND THE THIRD PARTIES

5 August 2003

1. The Panel has received a letter from the European Commission, dated 31 July 2003, in which the European Communities ("EC"):

- seeks clarification of the Panel's procedures for its expression of views on 5 September 2003 in relation to Article 13 of the *Agreement on Agriculture*; and
- makes two requests for additional third party rights.

2. The Panel sought the views of the parties to the dispute on these requests, which it received in letters dated 1 August 2003. Neither party objects to the Panel communicating its views to the third parties on 5 September 2003, but neither party agrees that the Panel should accept the EC's requests for additional third party rights. The EC responded to the parties' letters in a further letter dated 4 August 2003.

1. Panel's procedures for its expression of views on 5 September 2003 in relation to Article 13 of the *Agreement on Agriculture*

3. The Panel confirms that, in accordance with its communication dated 20 June 2003, as amended on 30 July 2003, it intends to express its views on whether measures raised in this dispute satisfy the conditions in Article 13 of the *Agreement on Agriculture*, to the extent that it is able to do so, by 5 September 2003. Those views will be communicated to third parties, as well as to the parties to the dispute, in order to enable them to participate, as necessary and appropriate, in any second session of the first substantive meeting in a full and meaningful fashion.

2. EC requests for additional third party rights

4. The EC requests the following additional third party rights: (a) access to the oral statements of the parties to the dispute at the first session of the first substantive meeting held on 22-24 July 2003, and (b) the opportunity to comment on their responses to the Panel's questions, or questions that they have posed to each other.[1]

5. Third parties have certain rights in panel proceedings under Article 10 of the DSU, which a panel may not deny. The grant of third party rights beyond those provided in the DSU lies within the discretion and authority of a panel. That discretion is limited by the requirements of due process.

Article 10.1, 10.2 and 10.3 of the DSU provides as follows:

---

[1] The Panel notes that the parties to the dispute have not posed any written questions to each other, and therefore does not need to address the request to allow third parties to comment upon the responses to such questions.

Third Parties

> "1. The interests of the parties to a dispute and those of other Members under a covered agreement at issue in the dispute shall be fully taken into account during the panel process.
>
> "2. Any Member having a substantial interest in a matter before a panel and having notified its interest to the DSB (referred to in this Understanding as a "third party") shall have an opportunity to be heard by the panel and to make written submissions to the panel. These submissions shall also be given to the parties to the dispute and shall be reflected in the panel report.
>
> "3. Third parties shall receive the submissions of the parties to the dispute to the first meeting of the panel."

6. In our view, written versions of the parties' oral statements and the parties' responses to the Panel's questions do not form part of "the submissions of the parties to the dispute to the first meeting of the Panel", as provided for in Article 10.3 of the DSU. Articles 10.2 and 12.6 and the working procedure in paragraph 3 of Appendix 3 use the terms "written submissions" and "submissions" interchangeably. Appendix 3 distinguishes between "written submissions" in paragraphs 3, 4 and 10 and "a written version of ... oral statements" in paragraph 9. Under the standard panel working procedures set out in Appendix 3 of the DSU, third parties may only attend the third party session and are not present during the rest of the panel's meetings. The granting of access by the Panel to written versions of the parties' oral statements would run counter to the standard practice under the DSU of holding the sessions at which those statements are made in the absence of the third parties.

7. As the Panel indicated in its communication dated 20 June 2003, the first meeting in this dispute is to be held in two separate sessions two months apart, as necessary. The issues under consideration at each session are distinct, so that the written versions of oral statements at the first session cannot be considered submissions to the second session. The Panel's working procedures currently envisage that third parties will receive the parties' written submissions to any second session of the first meeting, and will have an opportunity to present their views at any such session. Thus, with respect to the issues that form the subject of each session of the first meeting, each third party will receive the rights provided for in Article 10.2 and 10.3 of the DSU.

8. Therefore, in our view, third parties have no entitlement under the DSU to the additional rights requested by the EC, and we also note that there is no agreement between the parties that such additional rights should be granted. In any case, the EC indicates in its letter dated 4 August 2003 that this was not the thrust of its requests but, rather, it would be a "reasonable exercise of the Panel's discretion" to allow the third parties also to comment on the responses of the parties to the dispute to the Panel's questions.

9. The Panel must consider whether it should grant such additional rights as part of its duty to ensure due process of law for third parties, or within its discretion to grant or refuse the rights requested as it believes appropriate, keeping

firmly in mind the Panel's duty to ensure an objective assessment of the matter before it in accordance with Article 11 of the DSU, and the requirement that the interests of the parties to the dispute and those of other Members under a covered agreement at issue in the dispute shall be fully taken into account during the panel process, in accordance with Article 10.1.

10. The EC has argued that access to oral statements would permit third parties to respond to arguments made by the parties to the dispute where such a response would be of relevance in answering the Panel's questions to third parties, and that this would benefit the Panel since the third parties would be able to provide more complete responses to the Panel's questions. It also argues that the third parties' comments on each others' responses to questions will be more full and meaningful, and consequently more beneficial to the Panel, if it is also possible for them to comment on the responses of the parties to the dispute.

11. In addition to the issues raised by the EC, the Panel is keenly aware of the implications of this particular dispute for third parties, including the systemic importance of the interpretation of Article 13 of the *Agreement on Agriculture* and its trade policy impact.

12. In fact, the Panel has already taken into account, to a certain extent, the systemic implications of this dispute and the issues now raised by the EC. The Panel has posed a large number of questions to third parties, including 39 questions addressed specifically to the EC. Through the third parties' responses to these questions, the Panel hopes to receive their views on the merits and systemic considerations presently at issue in this dispute, which it will take into account in its assessment of the matter before it. The questions are detailed precisely to ensure that third parties' views are fully taken into account in what is a complex case. The Panel believes that, through the questions that it has posed to the parties to the dispute and to third parties, it has ensured that it will benefit from third parties' input and that nothing prevents them from participating in a full and meaningful fashion.

13. This is not the only opportunity for third parties to express their views in this dispute. The Panel specifically sought the views of third parties on the issue of whether Article 13 of the *Agreement on Agriculture* precludes the Panel from considering Brazil's claims under the Agreement on Subsidies and Countervailing Measures in these proceedings in the absence of a prior conclusion by the Panel that certain conditions of Article 13 remain unfulfilled. Six third parties, including the EC, made submissions to the Panel on that issue, which the Panel took into account.

14. Nothing precludes the Panel from posing further questions to the parties to the dispute or third parties as the Panel deems necessary or appropriate throughout the course of these proceedings. The Panel may also seek the views of third parties in further questions at any second session of the first meeting that may be held, by posing questions on the issues under consideration at that session.

15. The Panel notes that none of the third parties, including the EC, requested any additional rights prior to the first meeting, even after the Panel's communica-

tion of 20 June 2003, in which it announced that the first meeting would be held in two sessions, as necessary. The parties to the dispute therefore delivered their oral statements at that meeting in closed session without third parties present, as is the usual procedure under Article 12 and Appendix 3 of the DSU, on the basis that the confidentiality of those statements was within their own respective control. The Panel is therefore unwilling to direct the parties to grant access to written versions of those statements after the event.

16. The Panel notes that nothing in the DSU or the Panel's working procedures precludes a party to the dispute from disclosing statements of its own positions to the public, as foreseen in Article 18.2 and paragraph 3 of the working procedures, and that the United States has indicated that it makes its oral statements available on its website and has already provided a copy directly to the EC.

17. For the reasons set out above, the Panel denies both the EC's requests for additional third party rights. Nonetheless, in view of the phased nature of the first meeting, the Panel directs the parties to the dispute to make best efforts to ensure that their submissions to any second session of the first meeting are understandable either on their own or in conjunction with the submissions to the first session of the meeting. In particular, such submissions should not refer to any document to which the third parties do not have access without, at the very least, a summary, explanation or description of the contents of that document (or a citation indicating where that document may be found on the public record).

ANNEX L-1.8

COMMUNICATION TO BRAZIL AND THE UNITED STATES

19 August 2003

The Panel has received a communication from Brazil dated 14 August 2003 in which Brazil draws attention to the timing and format of service of the United States' responses to the Panel's questions, in light of paragraphs 17(b) and (d) of our Working Procedures, and in which it raises issues of procedural fairness.

The Panel has taken note of the matters raised in the communication from Brazil and draws them to the United States' attention. The Panel recalls that, at its meeting with the parties on 22 July 2003, it also drew the attention of the United States to these issues as raised by Brazil in connection with the filing of the United States' first written submission and comments on Brazil's initial brief.

In its communication dated 14 August 2003, Brazil also requested the right to comment on any new information, arguments or documents presented for the first time in the United States' rebuttal submission with respect to specific questions posed by the Panel. It raised considerations of due process and requested that the Panel provide it until 28 August 2003 to file any such comments without granting the United States any corresponding right.

The Panel has a duty to ensure the fairness of its proceedings, which requires that the parties receive sufficient opportunity to comment on information, argumentation and documents submitted. Due to the phasing of the first meeting, a party might lack sufficient opportunity to comment on such material presented for the first time in a rebuttal submission before the Panel expresses its views on certain issues in dispute. However, this will depend on what the rebuttal submissions actually contain.

Accordingly, when each party receives the other party's rebuttal submission, it is invited, without delay, to draw the Panel's attention to any specific material on which it has not had an opportunity to comment and to show cause why it needs such an opportunity. Upon a showing of good cause, the Panel will permit that party to comment in writing by 27 August 2003. The Panel is willing to grant such permission on Saturday, 23 August 2003, if necessary.

ANNEX L-1.9

COMMUNICATION TO BRAZIL AND THE UNITED STATES
23 August 2003

The Panel has received a communication from Brazil dated 23 August 2003 in which Brazil requests the opportunity to comment on specific paragraphs of the United States' rebuttal, and exhibits thereto, as the parties were invited to do by the Panel in its communication dated 19 August 2003.

The Panel considers that Brazil has not had sufficient opportunity to comment on new material specifically listed in its communication of 23 August 2003. The Panel notes that the argument raised in paragraph 123 of the United States' rebuttal is not new but was raised earlier in the United States' response to question 66(d) posed by the Panel and in section 2.3.2 of Brazil's rebuttal.

Accordingly, the Panel permits Brazil to comment in writing on such new material by 27 August 2003. The procedures regarding service of documents set out in paragraph 17 of the Panel's working procedures shall apply.

ANNEX L-1.10

COMMUNICATION TO BRAZIL AND THE UNITED STATES
25 August 2003

The Panel has received a communication from the United States dated 25 August 2003 in which the United States requests the opportunity to comment on specific paragraphs of Brazil's rebuttal, and comments on responses to questions, as the parties were invited to do by the Panel in its communication dated 19 August 2003. The Panel has also received a response to that communication from Brazil, also dated 25 August 2003, in which Brazil submits that the United States' request should be rejected.

The Panel considers that the United States has not had sufficient opportunity to comment on new material specifically listed in its communication of 25 August 2003, other than the alleged misstatements in paragraphs 88, 90-94 of Brazil's rebuttal which the Panel can check against the cross-referenced United States' responses and Panel report, if necessary.

Accordingly, the Panel permits the United States to comment in writing on such new material by 27 August 2003. The procedures regarding service of documents set out in paragraph 17 of the Panel's working procedures shall apply.

The Panel notes that the United States welcomes the opportunity to respond to any further questions that the Panel may have. Therefore, the Panel poses the following additional question to the United States and seeks a response by 27 August 2003:

> 67*bis*. Please state the annual amount granted by the US government in each of the 1999, 2000, 2001 and 2002 marketing years (as applicable) to US upland cotton producers, per pound and in total expenditures, under each of the following programs: production flexibility contract payments, market loss assistance payments, direct payments and counter-cyclical payments.

ANNEX L-1.11

COMMUNICATION TO BRAZIL AND THE UNITED STATES AND THIRD PARTIES

5 September 2003

1. On 20 June 2003, the Panel communicated to the parties and third parties that:

> "Given the potential complexity of the claims before us, the conditional nature of certain of these claims and the volume of evidence which may be introduced by the parties in support of their claims and arguments, and in order to organize our proceedings in an orderly, effective and efficient manner which serves to facilitate an objective assessment of the matter before us, and optimizes use of our resources, we have adopted the following modifications to our procedures ..."

2. The first modification to our procedures was as follows:

> "The Panel intends to express its views on whether measures raised in this dispute satisfy the conditions in Article 13 of the *Agreement on Agriculture*, to the extent that it is able to do so, by 1 September 2003, and will defer its consideration of claims under Articles 3, 5 and 6 of the *SCM Agreement* and Article XVI of the *GATT 1994* as those provisions are referred to in Article 13 of the *Agreement on Agriculture* until after it has expressed those views. The Panel's views may be expressed in the form of rulings which could affect the Panel's further consideration of this dispute."

3. In a fax dated 30 July 2003, the Panel decided to modify the date for expression of its views to 5 September 2003.

4. The Panel takes note of the correspondence from the parties dated 27, 28 and 29 August 2003 and declines to make findings at this stage as to whether measures raised in this dispute satisfy the conditions in Article 13 of the *Agreement on Agriculture*, for the reasons given in its communication dated 20 June 2003. The Panel's findings on that issue will be included in its interim report, on which the parties will have the right to comment in accordance with Article 15.2 of the *DSU*.

5. The Panel has now had the opportunity to consider the parties' and third parties' evidence and arguments to date. At this stage, the Panel cannot conclude its assessment of the matter before it on the basis that the measures raised in this dispute satisfy the conditions in Article 13 of the *Agreement on Agriculture*. The expression by the Panel of this view is without prejudice to the Panel's eventual findings, and is subject to paragraph 6 below. In this context, the Panel is of the view that consideration, as appropriate, of Brazil's claims under Articles 3, 5 and 6 of the *SCM Agreement* and Article XVI of the *GATT 1994*, as those provisions

are referred to in Article 13 of the *Agreement on Agriculture*, is warranted in order for the Panel properly to discharge its responsibilities under the *DSU* and the relevant covered agreements. Therefore, the Panel will consider those claims at a second session of the first substantive meeting.

6. The Panel also wishes to inform the parties that, on the basis of the evidence and arguments presented to date, it is unable to form any view on whether the ETI Act satisfies the relevant provisions of the *Agreement on Agriculture*.

7. Regarding the Panel's procedures:

(a) the Panel invites the parties to address in further submissions, due on 9 and 23 September respectively, the claims referred to in paragraph 5 above;

(b) the Panel also invites the parties to address further the issue whether the export credit guarantee programs at issue constitute export subsidies for the purposes of the *Agreement on Agriculture*;

(c) the Panel confirms that items (o), (p) and (q) of its timetable will be necessary, and confirms the following dates:

Further submissions of the third parties:	29 September 2003;
First substantive meeting with the parties (resumed second session): (as necessary)	7, 8 and 9 October 2003;
Third party session:	**8 October** 2003 [1];

(d) the Panel invites the third parties to address in their further submissions the claims referred to in paragraph 5 above;

(e) the Panel intends to postpone the second substantive meeting; and

(f) the Panel invites the parties to comment on the attached draft further revised timetable. Such comments should be submitted no later than close of business on Tuesday, 9 September 2003.

[Attachment omitted]

[1] The Panel wishes to inform parties and third parties that due to the availability of meeting rooms, the *third party session*, previously scheduled for 9 October, will now be held on *Wednesday, 8 October*. The Panel will continue its meeting with the parties after the third party session and also on 9 October, as necessary.

ANNEX L-1.12

COMMUNICATION TO BRAZIL AND THE UNITED STATES AND THIRD PARTIES

12 September 2003

Having carefully considered the parties' comments received on 9, 10 and 11 September, the Panel intends to follow the revised timetable, as attached.

In this connection, the Panel would like to inform the United States that the deadline for its "further submission" is **15h00 (i.e. 3 pm) Geneva time** on Monday, 29 September.

The Panel also wishes to draw the attention of **third parties** that the **deadline for their further submissions** has been changed to **3 October**.

In light of the US request for an opportunity to comment on the new dates of the second meeting, now rescheduled to be 2 and 3 December 2003, the Panel invites the US and Brazil to submit comments, if any, on these dates. Such comments, which should focus on the date of the second substantive meeting and other dates directly affected by this date, should be submitted no later than close of business on **Tuesday, 16 September**.

[Attachment omitted]

ANNEX L-1.13

COMMUNICATION TO BRAZIL AND THE UNITED STATES AND THIRD PARTIES

18 September 2003

The Panel has received letters from Brazil and the US dated 16 September and 17 September, in which they submit further comments on certain dates we indicated in our fax dated 12 September.

Having carefully considered the views of both parties, the Panel amends the dates indicated in the 12 September fax as follows:

- The deadline for the receipt of answers to Panel's questions (previously, 22 October) will be changed to **27 October**.
- The deadline for the receipt of further rebuttals of the parties (previously, 3 November) will be changed to **18 November.**

In respect of items (u) and (v), the Panel notes Brazil's preference for "the completion of the parties' main substantive work still in 2003". The Panel reminds the parties that, as indicated in the 12 September fax, items (u) and (v) are deadlines that would apply "as necessary". They may, therefore, depend upon various factors, including the number and nature of any questions the Panel may actually pose to one or both parties at that juncture. Therefore, at least for the time being, the Panel prefers to leave these dates as indicated (22 December and 19 January, respectively).

All other dates indicated in the fax of 12 September remain unchanged, and are now confirmed.

ANNEX L-1.14

COMMUNICATION TO BRAZIL AND THE UNITED STATES AND THIRD PARTIES

24 September 2003

The Panel has received a letter from the United States dated 23 September, in which it informs the Panel of delays in the preparation of its further submission caused by hurricane Isabel, as well as a response from Brazil, also dated 23 September. Having carefully considered the views of both parties, the Panel further amends the dates we indicated in our fax of 12 September as follows:

deadline for the US's further submission: **30 September, 2003 (by 17:30 Geneva time)**

All other dates and deadlines indicated in the fax of 12 September (and subsequently amended in the fax of 18 September) including the deadline for the "further submission from third parties" (3 October), **remain unchanged**.

The Panel notes that the time for the third parties to review the US's "further submission" before making their respective written submissions is limited. The Panel reminds third parties that they are free to present arguments in addition to those set out in their written submissions in their oral statements to be presented on 8 October.

ANNEX L-1.15

COMMUNICATION TO BRAZIL AND THE UNITED STATES

13 October 2003

1. Please find attached the Panel's questions to the parties following the resumed session of the first substantive Panel meeting. Parties are reminded that responses are due by **27 October 2003**.

2. The Panel's questions are intended to facilitate the work of the Panel, and do not in any way prejudge the Panel's findings on the matter before it. Nor does the fact that the Panel has placed these questions under certain headings prejudge the Panel's findings on the matter before it. Each party is free to respond to or comment on questions posed to the other parties or third parties.

3. The Panel takes note of Brazil's request in its letter dated 2 October 2003 regarding the late receipt of submissions, and the US response in its letter dated 6 October 2003. In accordance with paragraph 17(b) of the Panel's working procedures, the Panel sets the following time for the provision of submissions by the parties: 11:59 pm, Geneva time on the dates concerned. This time refers to *receipt* of submissions by the other party and the Secretariat and not to commencement of transmission. For greater clarity, this time for receipt of submissions also refers to the time of completion of receipt of any Exhibits and service of all Exhibits (if necessary, electronically) to the other party and to the Secretariat as envisaged in paragraphs 17(a)-(d) of the Panel's working procedures. All other provisions of the Working Procedures remain unchanged. The Panel confirms the dates in the revised timetable, as revised in its communication of 18 September 2003.

4. The Panel has set this time in light of the repeated service of submissions by the United States after 5.30 p.m. and in order to ensure due process and secure a balance between the two parties. The Panel stresses its expectation that the parties will respect all of the rules and procedures set out in the *DSU* and in the working procedures, including the new time set by the Panel above for the dates in question.

5. The Panel takes note of the United States' request in section II of its further submission for three preliminary rulings, regarding interest subsidies and storage payments; cottonseed payments; and export credit guarantees for products other than upland cotton. The Panel is not currently in a position to rule on these issues. The Panel will make rulings as necessary and appropriate in the course of this proceeding and hopes to be in a position to express its views, or give a ruling, on these requests, as appropriate, by 3 November (that is, shortly after the date of receipt of written responses to questions). Meanwhile, the Panel requests the parties not to exclude consideration of these issues in their responses to questions.

Questions from the Panel to the Parties – Resumed first session of the first substantive Panel meeting

A. REQUEST FOR PRELIMINARY RULINGS

122. Does Brazil allege that cottonseed payments, interest subsidies and storage payments are included in the subsidies that cause serious prejudice? Do they appear in the economic calculations? **BRA**

123. Does Brazil's request for the establishment of the Panel name the statute authorizing cottonseed payments for the 1999 crop? **BRA**

B. EXEMPTION FROM ACTIONS

124. According to its revised timetable, the Panel will issue its report to the parties after the end of the 2003 calendar year. Does this have any impact on "exempt[ion] from actions" under Article 13(b)(ii) and 13(c)(ii) of the *Agreement on Agriculture*? **BRA, US**

C. IDENTIFICATION OF THE SUBSIDIZED PRODUCT

125.

(1) In view of requirements in the FAIR Act of 1996 and the FSRI Act of 2002 that contract acreage remain in agricultural or conservation uses and which impose penalties if the producer grows fruits or vegetables, how likely is it that the producer with upland cotton base acreage will not use his or her land to produce programme crops or covered commodities? **US**

(2) Brazil has submitted that "The record suggests that *historic* producers are *current* producers." It points to factors including the specialization of upland cotton producers, the need to recoup expensive investments in cotton-specific equipment, and the geographic focus and climatic requirements of upland cotton production in the "cotton belt". (Brazil's rebuttal submission, footnote 98, on page 24)

(a) Regarding the specialization of upland cotton producers and the geographic focus of upland cotton production, how does Brazil take account of the fact that cotton is produced in 17 of the 50 states of the United States and that average cotton area is approximately 38% of a cotton farm's acres? (This information is taken from the US's response to question 67*bis*, footnote 35). **BRA**

(b) Regarding the geographic focus of upland cotton production, how many other crops can upland cotton producers viably grow in the cotton belt, other than fruits and vegetables? **US**

(c) Regarding the high cost of upland cotton production, can Brazil show that farms who planted upland cotton could only have covered their costs by receiving upland cotton, rice or peanut payments in every year from 1999 through 2002? **BRA**

(d) Regarding the need to recoup investments in cotton-specific equipment, is it important to planting decisions that upland cotton producers cannot run any other crop through their cotton-pickers? How does this affect the likelihood that they will grow other crops? **US**

(3) In calculating the amount of PFC, MLA, direct and counter-cyclical payments that went on upland cotton, Brazil made an adjustment for the ratio of current acreage to base acreage (see its answer to question 67, footnotes 2, 3, 4 and 5). Is this an appropriate adjustment for the particular factors referred to above? Why or why not? **BRA, US**

(4) Dr. Glauber has alleged that there are statistical problems in comparing planted acres to programme acres because of abandonment of crops and also because planted acres are only survey estimates, not reported figures (See Exhibit US-24, the first full paragraph in P2). Would it be more appropriate to divide harvested acreage by base acreage? What margin of error is there between the survey estimates and reported figures? **BRA, US**

(5) Do the acreage reports under section 1105(c) of the FSRI Act of 2002 indicate or assist in determining the number or proportion of acres of upland cotton planted on upland cotton base acres? Was there an acreage reporting requirement for upland cotton during MY1996 through 2002? **BRA, US**

(6) Please prepare a chart showing upland cotton base acreage, planted acreage and harvested acreage for MY1996 through 2002. Does the planted acreage fluctuate within a broad band? If not, does this indicate any stability in decisions to plant the same acres to upland cotton? **BRA, US**

(7) Brazil states that one third of all US farms with eligible acreage decided to update their base acreage under the direct payments and counter-cyclical payments programmes using their MY1998-2001 acreage. What is the proportion of the current base acreage for upland cotton resulting from such updating? Is the observed updating of base acreage consistent with Brazil's argument that it is only profitable to grow upland cotton on base acreage (and peanut and rice base acreage)? **BRA**

(8) How could one take account of upland cotton producers who receive PFC, MLA, direct and counter-cyclical payments for other covered commodity base acreage? **BRA, US**

(9) Assuming that Brazil's payment figures were to amount to a *prima facie* case, please answer the following questions: **US**

(a) How would the United States calculate or estimate the proportion of upland cotton producers

who receive subsidy payments for upland cotton base acreage?

(b) Should any adjustment estimates be made for any factors besides those listed by Brazil?

(c) What adjustment estimate would it be appropriate to make?

(d) How could one take account of upland cotton producers who receive decoupled payments for other programme crop base acreage?

(e) Could the US specifically indicate what, in its view, are the flaws in the approach summarized in paras. 6-7 of Brazil's closing oral statement[1] on 9 October (i.e. the use of the ration of 0.87 to adjust the amount of total upland cotton direct and CCPs for the MY to obtain the amount of subsidies received by upland cotton producers)? Can the US suggest an alternative approach that would yield reliable results in its view?

D. "LIKE PRODUCT"

126. Does the US agree that the product at issue is upland cotton lint and that Brazilian upland cotton lint is "like" US upland cotton lint within the meaning of Article 6.3(c) of the *SCM Agreement* in that it is a separate like product that is identical or has characteristics similar to the upland cotton lint from the United States? (e.g. Brazil's further submission, para. 81) **US**

E. "SUBSIDIES"

127. The Panel notes that the US contests that export credit guarantees constitute "subsidies". The Panel recalls that the US agrees that Step 2 payments are "subsidies" and wishes to have confirmation that it is correct in understanding that the US does not disagree that the following are "subsidies" for the purposes of Article 1 of the *SCM Agreement*: marketing loan/loan deficiency payments, PFC, direct payments, market loss assistance and CCP payments, crop insurance payments, cottonseed payments, storage payments and interest subsidy (without prejudice to the Panel's rulings on the US requests for preliminary rulings on the latter two payments). **US**

F. PROHIBITED SUBSIDIES

128. Could the US respond to Brazil's assertions relating to the meaning and effect of the introductory phrase of Article 3 ("Except as provided in the *Agreement on Agriculture....*")? Would the meaning/effect change if Article 13 of the *Agreement on Agriculture* did not exist? **BRA, US**

G. SPECIFICITY / CROP INSURANCE

129. In the event that the Panel does not consider that the alleged prohibited subsidies fall within the provisions of Article 3 and are therefore, pursuant to Article 2.3, "deemed to be specific", are there any other grounds on which Brazil would rely in order to support the view that such measures are "specific" within the meaning of Article 2 of the *SCM Agreement* (see, for example, fn 16 of Brazil's further submission)? **BRA**

130. Does Brazil agree that the US insurance premium subsidy is available in respect of all agricultural products? Please cite relevant portions of the record. **BRA**

[1] All of the paragraph numbers in relation to oral statements (opening statement and closing statement) cited in this document corresponds to the numbering made in the version available to the Panel on the date of the statement.

131. How should the concept of specificity – and, in particular, the concept of specificity to "an enterprise or industry or group of enterprises or industries" - in Article 2 of the *SCM Agreement* apply to subsidies in respect of agricultural commodities? Please answer the following questions, citing the principles in Article 2 of the *SCM Agreement*: **BRA, US**

(a) is a subsidy in respect of all agricultural, but not other, products specific?

(b) is a subsidy in respect of all agricultural crops (i.e. but not to other agricultural commodities, such as livestock) specific?

(c) is a subsidy in respect of certain identified agricultural products specific?

(d) is a subsidy in respect of upland cotton, but not other products, specific?

(e) is a subsidy in respect of a certain proportion of the value of total US commodities (or total US agricultural commodities) specific?

(f) is a subsidy in respect of a certain proportion of total US farmland specific?

132. Please state the amount and percentage of upland cotton acreage covered by each crop insurance programme and/or policy under the ARP Act of 2000. **US**

133. Concerning Brazil's arguments in its oral statement, para. 7, can the US indicate if any producers of livestock outside a pilot programme are covered by the crop insurance programme? **US**

134. Please state the annual amount of premiums paid or contributions made by US upland cotton farmers relating to each of the crop insurance programmes and/or policies supported by the US Risk Management Agency and the Federal Crop Insurance Corporation in each year from 1992 through 2002. **US**

135. Please state the annual amount of insurance indemnity payments made by the US government; or insurance companies participating in crop insurance programmes and/or policies under the ARP Act of 2000 to upland cotton farmers in each year from 1992 through 2002. **US**

136. Is the US arguing that crop insurance subsidies corresponding to "over 90 per cent of insured cotton area" (US 7 October oral statement, para. 46) in MY1999 through 2002 are consistent with paragraph 8(a) of Annex 2 of the *Agreement on Agriculture*? Is it correct that in the past these subsidies were nonetheless notified to the Committee on Agriculture as non-product specific AMS (see, for example, G/AG/N/USA/43 in Exhibit BRA-47)? **US**

H. EXPORT CREDIT GUARANTEES

137. Please elaborate the meaning of "net losses" as is used in paragraph 70 of Brazil's 7 October oral statement. **BRA**

138. Please comment on Brazil's views stated in paragraph 70 of its 7 October oral statement. **US**

139. In the context of export credit guarantees, is the Panel correct in understanding that Brazil's claims of inconsistency with the *Agriculture Agreement* involve GSM 102, GSM 103 and SCGP, but that it limits its "serious prejudice"

allegations in respect of export credit guarantee programmes to the GSM 102 programme, and does not challenge GSM 103 and SCGP in this respect? If so,

(a) could Brazil please explain why it did so, and confirm that all the data relied upon in its further submissions (e.g. in Table 13) relate to the GSM 102 programme rather than to GSM 102, GSM 103 and SCGP (and, if the data needs to be adjusted to take account of a narrower "serious prejudice" focus, supply GSM-102-relevant data)? **BRA**

(b) for the purposes of Article 13(c)(ii) of the *Agreement on Agriculture*, is it necessary for the Panel to examine only GSM 102 or should the Panel's examination include also GSM 103 and SCGP? Why or why not? **BRA**

140. Could Brazil explain how, if at all, it has treated export credit guarantees for the purpose of Table 1 of its further submission? **BRA**

141. The Panel notes the US argument, *inter alia* in its further submission, that the export credit guarantee programmes are "self-sustaining". Recalling that item (j) of the Illustrative List of Export Subsidies in Annex I of the *SCM Agreement* refers to "premium rates", could the US expand upon how it takes into account the premium rates for the export credit guarantee programmes in its analysis. **US**

142. The US has pointed out that there are many limitations on granting export credit guarantees and that there is no requirement to issue any particular guarantee (US further submission, paras 153-156). Can the Commodity Credit Corporation decline to grant an export credit guarantee even in cases where the programme conditions are met? **US**

143. Brazil agrees with National Cotton Council estimates of the effects of the GSM 102 programmes (Brazil's further submission, para. 190) but it also cites a different conclusion by Prof. Sumner (paragraph 192). Brazil cites other estimates by Prof. Sumner throughout its further submission. Does Brazil adopt Prof. Sumner's conclusions and estimates as part of its submission? **BRA**

I. STEP 2 PAYMENTS

144. Is the Panel correct in understanding that the US does not dispute that Step 2 (domestic) payments are contingent upon import substitution, and that it argues that such measures are permitted due to the operation of the provisions of the *Agreement on Agriculture*? How is that relevant to a claim under Articles 5 and 6 of the *SCM Agreement*? **US**

J. ACTIONABLE SUBSIDIES

145. The Panel notes that different remedies are available in respect of prohibited and actionable subsidies under Articles 4.7 and 7.8 of the *SCM Agreement*. If the Panel were to conclude that a subsidy was prohibited and were to make a recommendation under Article 4.7 of the *SCM Agreement* to withdraw the subsidy without delay, can the Panel:

(a) also conclude that the same subsidy had resulted in adverse effects to the interests of another Member? If so, what would be the value of such a conclusion in terms of the settlement of the matter before the Panel? **BRA, US**

(b) take into account the effects of the interaction of those prohibited subsidies with other, allegedly, actionable subsidies? If so, how is this relevant to the issue of causation under Article 5 of the *SCM Agreement*? **BRA, US**

146. Brazil acknowledges that there are some interaction effects that may increase or decrease the overall effects of the subsidies (Brazil's further submission, para. 225). How would your analysis under Articles 5(c) and 6.3 of the *SCM Agreement* and Article XVI of *GATT 1994* differ if it excluded, for example, crop insurance subsidies, PFC and/or direct payments? **BRA**

147. Does the US agree that subsidies provided under the marketing loan programme, counter-cyclical payments and market loss assistance are or were more than minimally trade-distorting? If so, please elaborate on the type of effects which are more than minimally trade-distorting within the meaning of Annex 2 of the *Agreement on Agriculture* but less than adverse effects within the meaning of Article 5 of the *SCM Agreement*. **US**

148. How should the significance of price suppression or depression be assessed under Article 6.3(c) of the *SCM Agreement*? In terms of a meaningful effect? Or another concept? **BRA, US**

149. What is the meaning of "may" in the chapeau of Article 6.3(c) in the context of Brazil's assertion that there is no need to conduct a distinct analysis of "serious prejudice" under Article 5(c) after having made a finding under 6.3(c) or (d)? (Brazil's further submission, paras 437 ff). How, if at all, are Articles 6.2 and 6.8 relevant in this context? What context should the Panel use for assessing serious prejudice under Article 5(c) of the *SCM Agreement* if the Panel takes the view that Article 6.3(c) and (d) are permissive conditions for a determination of serious prejudice? **US**

150. Is the list in Article 6.3 of the *SCM Agreement* exhaustive, or could serious prejudice arise in circumstances other than those listed in paragraphs (a) through (d)? **US**

151. Where in the text of Article 6.3(d) of the *SCM Agreement* is there a basis to take into account that 1998 may be a "misleading" year for the purposes of comparison? For example, unlike the text of Article XVI:3 of the GATT 1994, there does not seem to be a general reference to "special factors". **US**

152. If the US is correct in asserting that the Article 13(b)(ii) *Agreement on Agriculture* analysis is a year-by-year analysis, how would this affect the Panel's examination of Brazil's claims of serious prejudice, including the three year period and the trend period in Article 6.3(d) of the *SCM Agreement*? **US**

153. Would the conditions in Article 6.3(d) of the *SCM Agreement* be satisfied in respect of time periods other than the one specified? What relevance, if any, would this have for Brazil's claims? **BRA**

154. Does the US agree that upland cotton is a "primary product or commodity" within the meaning of Article 6.3(d) of the *SCM Agreement*? (ref. Brazil's

further submission, para. 262) and within the meaning of Article XVI:3 of the GATT 1994? **US**

155. Please respond to Brazil's identification of the seven-year period beginning with MY1996 (following the passage of the FAIR Act of 1996) as the "most representative period" for the purposes of Article 6.3(d)? (ref. Brazil further submission, para. 269) **US**

156. Does the US agree that "...footnote 17 [of the SCM Agreement] does not carve out upland cotton from the scope of Article 6.3(d) of the SCM Agreement"? (ref. Brazil further submission, para. 275). **US**

157. Does the reference to "trade" in footnote 17 of the *SCM Agreement* have any impact on the interpretation of "world market share" in Article 6.3(d)) If so, what is it? **US**

158. Please respond to Brazil's assertion that "...the absence of any payment, production or expenditure limitations in the US marketing loan programme is analogous to the EC sugar regime that was challenged in *EC – Sugar Exports II (Brazil)* and *EC – Sugar Exports I (Australia)*." (ref. Brazil further submission, para. 317) **US**

159. The EC, in its oral statement (paras 9 and 10), disagrees with the US interpretation of the terms "same market". Can the US comment on the EC's view? **US**

160. Without prejudice to the meaning of "world market share" as used in Article 6.3(d) of the *SCM Agreement*, can you confirm the world export share statistics provided in Exhibit BRA-206? **US**

161. Would a finding of serious prejudice under Article 5(c) of the *SCM Agreement* be determinative for a finding under Article XVI:1 of the GATT 1994? Why or why not? What, if any, is the role of footnote 13 of the *SCM Agreement* in this context? **BRA, US**

162. Can the US confirm that marketing loan/LDP, step 2 and counter-cyclical payments are mandatory if the price conditions are fulfilled? **US**

163. Are US cotton producers able to cover the fixed and variable costs without subsidies? Please provide substantiating evidence. Of what relevance is this, if any, to Brazil's actionable subsidy claims ? **US, BRA**

K. CAUSATION

164. When the US points, in its oral statement of 7 October, to the alleged "bias" of Prof. Sumner's model, is it arguing that US subsidies are irrelevant to the movement in prices and production (acreage) of upland cotton? **US**

165. Please comment (and submit substantiating evidence) on the US assertion that the FAPRI model has been designed and developed for prospective analysis, and is not suitable for retrospective counterfactual analysis. What is the reliability of past FAPRI-produced analyses when compared with actual data for the period covered by them? Is there any other instrument that can be used to try to identify the effect of subsidies already granted, or of their removal? **BRA, US**

166. The US states that "futures prices demonstrate that market participants predict increasing upland prices over the course of the marketing year" (US 7 October oral statement, para. 62). Please elaborate on this argument including citing specific futures prices. **US**

167. How does Brazil react to Exhibit US-44? **BRA**

168. Please confirm that the production figures cited in Exhibit US-47 are for upland cotton only and do not include textiles. **US**

169. Can the US confirm the accuracy of the facts and figures cited in the four bullet points in paragraph 12 of Brazil's 7 October oral statement? **US**

170. Brazil quotes a report that states that a 10% increase in soybean prices reduces upland cotton acreage by only 0.25% (Brazil's 7 October oral statement, para. 27). Could Brazil indicate if this analysis is done on a short-run basis or a long-run basis? **BRA**

171. In paragraphs 22 and 23 of its further submission, we understand that the US is, in short, claiming that increased total supply (i.e. including polyester) drove prices down. On the other hand, we note that, according to the figures in the chart in paragraph 22 of the same submission, the world production of cotton during this period has basically been steady. Do all polyester fibres as represented by these figures compete directly with cotton? That is to say, do these figures for polyester fibres include, for example, those that are used for textiles that technically cannot be substituted by cotton? **US**

172. Please estimate the price effect, in cents per pound, of the growth in the US retail market which it is said has directly contributed to strengthening world cotton prices. **US**

173. The US asserts that "burgeoning US textile imports … shifted the disposition of US cotton production from domestic mills to export markets" (US further submission, para. 20). A similar description appears in paragraph 33, together with the explanation that "the share of world cotton consumption supplied by US cotton has been roughly the same since 1991/92". Why have sales of US cotton for export increased and sales of cotton imported into the US increased? **US**

174. How, if at all, did the Asian financial crisis affect the United States' world market share? Did it disproportionately affect the US as compared to other exporters? **US**

175. With reference to paragraphs 57-58 and the related table on page 21 of the US further submission, could you please clarify the arguments regarding the ratio of the soybean futures to the cotton futures prices since in the table the inverse ratio is used? **US**

176. With reference to Figure 4 of Brazil's Further Submission, how does Brazil explain the apparent decrease in prices in 2001 and the increase of the A-Index in recent months, despite the continued use of US subsidies on upland cotton? **BRA**

177. Could the United States further elaborate on paragraph 50 of its 7 October oral statement? **US**

178. The Panel notes Exhibit US-63. Could the US please provide a conceptually analogous graph concerning US export sales during the same period? **US**

179. Could Brazil comment on the argument that decoupled payments and other subsidies to upland cotton are largely being capitalized into land values and that removing these subsidies would reduce the cost of production of upland cotton producers (US 7 October oral statement, para. 48). What would be the net effect of these adjustments? **BRA**

180. Please describe the precise formula as to how USDA determines the "adjusted world price" using the Liverpool A-Index, the NY futures price and any other relevant price indicators. Please submit substantiating evidence. **BRA, US**

181. Please provide a side-by-side chart of the weekly US adjusted world price, the Liverpool A-Index, the NY futures price, and spot market prices from 1996-present. What, if anything, does this reveal? **BRA, US**

182. Please explain why the US can be taken to be price *leaders*, or price *setters*, (and not just takers) when US producers receive large subsidy payment to support the difference between *world prices* and their own costs? **BRA**

L. ARTICLE XVI OF GATT 1994

183. Why does Brazil believe that the appropriate "previous representative period" is the term of the previous Farm Bill, MY1996-2002? (Brazil's further submission, para. 282) **BRA**

184. Why does Brazil believe that an "equitable share" is one which factors out all subsidies? To the extent that domestic support and export subsidies are permitted by the *Agreement on Agriculture*, why should they not be accepted as being normal conditions in analyzing an equitable market share? (See Brazil's further submission, paras 288-289) **BRA**

185. Please respond to the following questions concerning the relationship between Article XVI:3 of the GATT 1994, the disciplines on export subsidies and domestic support in the *Agreement on Agriculture* and the disciplines on prohibited export subsidies and actionable subsidies in Articles 3, 5(c) and 6.3(d) of the *SCM Agreement*. **BRA, US**

(a) Are agricultural domestic support programmes challengeable under Article XVI:3 of the GATT 1994? How, if at all, is the title of Section B of Article XVI ("Additional provisions on *export subsidies*" (emphasis added)) relevant? How, if at all, are Articles 13 and 21.1, or any other provisions of the *Agreement on Agriculture,* relevant?

(b) Are the requirements of Article XVI:3 of the GATT 1994 reflected in, developed by or subsumed by the requirements in Article 6.3(d) of the *SCM Agreement*, or in any other provisions of the covered agreements? Of what relevance, if any, is the Appellate Body Report in *US-FSC*, para. 117[2] here?

---

2 WT/DS108/AB/R, para 117:

(c) Of what relevance, if any, is the fact that the definition of "subsidy" in Article 1 of the *SCM Agreement* and the prohibition on subsidies contingent upon export in Article 3.1(a) were introduced in the Uruguay Round, but did not exist at the time that the GATT 1947 was negotiated?

186. Could the United States please expand upon its statement that "[t]hese are the types of considerations that led to the negotiation of the Subsidies Agreement...." (US further submission, para. 109)? Is there any relevant material, including, for example, drafting history that might support this statement? **US**

M. THREAT CLAIMS

187. Please provide USDA's projections of marketing loan/LDP payments, direct payments and counter-cyclical payments to be made during MY2003 through 2007 based on the most recent USDA baseline projection. **US**

188. Can the United States comment on the FAPRI projections for cotton provided in Exhibit BRA-202? **US**

N. CLARIFICATIONS

189. Please indicate whether the correct figure in paragraph 37 of Brazil's 7 October oral statement is 38.1% or 38.3%? **BRA**

"... the provisions of the *SCM Agreement* do not provide explicit assistance as to the relationship between the export subsidy provisions of the *SCM Agreement* and Article XVI:4 of the GATT 1994. In the absence of any such specific textual guidance, we must determine the relationship between Articles 1.1(a)(1) and 3.1(a) of the *SCM Agreement* and Article XVI:4 of the GATT 1994 on the basis of the texts of the relevant provisions as a whole. It is clear from even a cursory examination of Article XVI:4 of the GATT 1994 that it differs very substantially from the subsidy provisions of the *SCM Agreement*, and, in particular, from the export subsidy provisions of both the *SCM Agreement* and the *Agreement on Agriculture*. First of all, the *SCM Agreement* contains an express definition of the term "subsidy" which is not contained in Article XVI:4. In fact, as we have observed previously, the *SCM Agreement* contains a broad package of new export subsidy disciplines that "go well beyond merely applying and interpreting Articles VI, XVI and XXIII of the GATT 1947". Next, Article XVI:4 prohibits export subsidies only when they result in the export sale of a product at a price lower than the "comparable price charged for the like product to buyers in the domestic market." In contrast, the *SCM Agreement* establishes a much broader prohibition against *any* subsidy which is "contingent upon export performance". To say the least, the rule contained in Article 3.1(a) of the *SCM Agreement* that all subsidies which are "contingent upon export performance" are prohibited is significantly different from a rule that prohibits only those subsidies which result in a lower price for the exported product than the comparable price for that product when sold in the domestic market. Thus, whether or not a measure is an export subsidy under Article XVI:4 of the GATT 1947 provides no guidance in determining whether that measure is a prohibited export subsidy under Article 3.1(a) of the *SCM Agreement*. Also, and significantly, Article XVI:4 of the GATT 1994 does not apply to "primary products", which include agricultural products. Unquestionably, the explicit export subsidy disciplines, relating to agricultural products, contained in Articles 3, 8, 9 and 10 of the *Agreement on Agriculture* must clearly take precedence over the *exemption* of primary products from export subsidy disciplines in Article XVI:4 of the GATT 1994."

190. Please confirm that the figure "17.5" in paragraph 43 of Brazil's 7 October oral statement, is "percentage point". **BRA**

191. Brazil clarify its statement in para. 12 of its 9 September further submission: "Alternatively crop insurance is **not specific** because the 2000 ARP Act denies benefits to commodities representing more than half of the value of US agriculture. Further US crops represent only 0.8 per cent of total US GDP." (emphasis added) **BRA**

ANNEX L-1.16

COMMUNICATION TO BRAZIL AND THE UNITED STATES
3 November 2003

1. The Panel recalls that paragraph 5 of its 13 October 2003 communication reads as follows:

> "The Panel takes note of the United States' request in section II of its further submission for three preliminary rulings, regarding interest subsidies and storage payments; cottonseed payments; and export credit guarantees for products other than upland cotton. The Panel is not currently in a position to rule on these issues. The Panel will make rulings as necessary and appropriate in the course of this proceeding and hopes to be in a position to express its views, or give a ruling, on these requests, as appropriate, by 3 November (that is, shortly after the date of receipt of written responses to questions). Meanwhile, the Panel requests the parties not to exclude consideration of these issues in their responses to questions."

2. Accordingly, please find attached a communication from the Panel.

Panel's views on the preliminary ruling requested by the United States in its further written submission of 30 September 2003

1. In its further written submission of 30 September 2003, the United States requests a preliminary ruling that:

> (1) Brazil may not advance claims under either Article 4 or Article 7 of the *SCM Agreement* with respect to export credit guarantee measures relating to eligible US agricultural commodities other than upland cotton, because it did not include a statement of available evidence with respect to these measures as required by Articles 4.2 and 7.2 of the *SCM Agreement*;
>
> (2) cottonseed payments made for the 1999 and 2000 crops are not within the Panel's terms of reference; and
>
> (3) storage payments and interest subsidies referred to as "other payments" for upland cotton are not within the Panel's terms of reference.[1]

2. Brazil asks the Panel to reject the United States' request. In respect of item (1), Brazil asserts that the US request is not new and is untimely, groundless and "mooted by" the Panel's 25 July communication indicating that the Panel intended to rule that export credit guarantees to facilitate the export of US upland cotton and other eligible agricultural commodities are within the Panel's terms of

[1] US Further Written Submission, Sections II and XIII.

reference.[2] Brazil asserts that items (2) and (3) are properly within the Panel's terms of reference.[3]

3. The Panel wishes to indicate to the parties how it intends to rule on items (1) and (2), in order to assist them in deciding what argumentation and evidence to submit in their further rebuttal submissions.

4. With respect to item (1), assuming *arguendo* that the US request was timely,[4] the Panel intends to rule in its report that Brazil provided a statement of available evidence with respect to export credit guarantee measures relating to eligible US agricultural commodities other than upland cotton, as required by Articles 4.2 and 7.2 of the *SCM Agreement.* As previously indicated in the Panel's communication of 25 July 2003, the Panel also intends to rule that "export credit guarantees ... to facilitate the export of US upland cotton, and other eligible agricultural commodities" as addressed in document WT/DS267/7, are within its terms of reference.

5. With respect to item (2), the Panel intends to rule that cottonseed payments made under Public Laws 106-224 and 107-25 (in respect of the 2000 crop) are within its terms of reference, but that cottonseed payments made under Public Law 106-113 (in respect of the 1999 crop) are not within its terms of reference. This is without prejudice to the relevance, if any, of the cottonseed payments in respect of the 1999 crop to the conditions set out in Article 13(b) of the *Agreement on Agriculture.*

6. The Panel has not yet decided upon its approach to item (3) and asks the parties not to exclude consideration of these other payments in their further rebuttal submissions.

2 Brazil's Oral Statement at the Resumed First Substantive Meeting, paras. 73-78.

3 Brazil's Oral Statement at the Resumed First Substantive Meeting, paras. 79-81.

4 The Panel recalls paragraph 12 of its working procedures but, in light of its intended ruling, does not need to address the issue of timeliness here.

ANNEX L-1.17

COMMUNICATION TO BRAZIL AND THE UNITED STATES

14 November 2003

1. The Panel takes note of the United States' written request of 14 October 2003 for certain information relating to the quantitative simulation model used by Dr. Sumner in his analysis presented in Annex I to Brazil's 9 September 2003 further written submission. The Panel also takes note of the parties' related communications dated 5, 11, 12 and 13 November 2003, and the submissions by Brazil on 12 and 13 November 2003.

2. The Panel confirms the dates in its existing timetable, subject to the following.

3. The Panel does not require the parties' 18 November further rebuttal submissions, nor their oral statements during the second Panel meeting, to address the methodology, equations or parameters underlying the quantitative modelling simulation in Annex I to Brazil's further written submission which are directly linked to the information requested by the United States on 14 October 2003 and the submissions by Brazil on 12-13 November 2003. Having said this, the parties are not precluded from doing so.

4. Mindful of the requirements of Article 12.4 of the *Understanding on Rules and Procedures Governing the Settlement of Disputes* and in keeping with its duty to conduct an objective assessment of the matter before it, the Panel invites the United States to submit, on 22 December, in conjunction with its responses to any questions following the second Panel meeting, any comments that it may have on Brazil's submissions of 12-13 November 2003. Brazil may submit any comments on any such US comments by 12 January 2004, and the United States may submit any further comments by 19 January 2004. If necessary, at the discretion of the Panel, a further Panel meeting with the parties may be held to address this specific material.

5. This decision is without prejudice to the relevance and significance which the Panel may ascribe to the quantitative simulation model and related evidence and argumentation in its report.

6. Finally, the Panel wishes to ask the United States to respond, by 22 December, to the following:

> Is the Panel correct in understanding that the US government (including the United States Department of Agriculture) does not have a license or any other form of permission (standing or otherwise; free of charge or otherwise) to run, electronically, the FAPRI/CARD model and/or Professor Sumner's adaptations thereto?

ANNEX L-1.18

COMMUNICATION TO BRAZIL AND THE UNITED STATES
8 December 2003

1. Please find attached:

- a communication from the Panel concerning its views on one of the preliminary ruling requests from the United States.
- a communication from the Panel concerning the FAPRI model, the essence of which was communicated to the parties by the Chairman of the Panel on 3 December 2003. As indicated therein, any US comments are due by **22 December**. Brazil will be given until **12 January 2004**, to comment on the US comments.
- the questions from the Panel. As was indicated earlier, responses to these questions are to be submitted by **22 December**.

2. As stated by the Chairman on 3 December, the United States will be given until **18 December** to respond to Brazil's request made in Exhibit BRA-369. Brazil will be given until **12 January 2004**, to comment on the US response.

3. The parties may submit any further comments on each other's comments by **19 January 2004**.

Panels' views on the preliminary ruling requested by the United States regarding the Agricultural Assistance Act of 2003

7. The United States requests a preliminary ruling that any measure under the Agricultural Assistance Act of 2003, including a cottonseed payment under that Act, is not within the Panel's terms of reference.[1]

8. Brazil asserts that that Act is properly within the Panel's terms of reference and asks the Panel to reject the United States' request.[2]

9. The Panel wishes to indicate to the parties how it intends to rule on this item in order to assist them in deciding what argumentation and evidence to submit in their answers to questions.

10. The Panel intends to rule that cottonseed payments made under the Agricultural Assistance Act of 2003 are not within its terms of reference. This is without prejudice to the relevance, if any, of those cottonseed payments to the conditions set out in Article 13(b) of the *Agreement on Agriculture*.

11. The Panel notes that it has not expressed a view concerning the United States' request for a preliminary ruling that storage payments and interest subsidies referred to as "other payments" for upland cotton are not within the Panel's

[1] US First Written Submission, paras 217, 218; US Further Submission, para. 8.

[2] Brazil's Oral Statement at the first session of the First Substantive Meeting, para. 145; Brazil's Response to Panel Question No. 17 and comments on US Response to Panel Question No. 17.

terms of reference.[3] The Panel has not yet decided upon its approach to this item and asks the parties to respond to its written questions relevant to these payments, and not to exclude consideration of these payments in their answers to other questions.

Panels' communication concerning the FAPRI model

1. The Panel has been advised by Brazil that, to the best of Brazil's knowledge and belief, all of the information used by FAPRI to generate the various results presented in Brazil's submissions concerning the effects of the subsidies, and their removal, has been provided to the US in an electronic format. Conceptually speaking, the information is in two parts: (a) the model used as the basis for generating the results ("the FAPRI model"), and (b) adaptations to the model and other specific pieces of information which effect the calculations made by the model ("the Brazil information"). FAPRI has possession of the FAPRI model and the Brazil information. Brazil only has possession of the Brazil information. Brazil instructed FAPRI as to the use of the Brazil information that FAPRI then used to generate the various results presented by Brazil to the Panel.

2. We say that the US has all of the information (ie both the FAPRI model and Brazil's information) "to the best of Brazil's knowledge and belief" because Brazil itself has never had access to all of the data comprising the FAPRI model, which is voluminous. FAPRI considers the model to be its own work product. At the request of Brazil, FAPRI has made all of the information available to the US. Why it has done this in the case of the US, but not Brazil, relates to the relationship (commercial or otherwise) between FAPRI (which receives US funding for its work) and the US Government. FAPRI has provided all of the information to the US on the express stipulation that the model not be provided to the Panel or Brazil ("the FAPRI stipulation").

3. At para 74 of its Opening Statement at the Second Panel Meeting, the US asks this of the Panel:

> "[W]hether it intends the United States to comment on this new model, documentation, and results by the original 22 December deadline to file comments on the methodology underlying the Annex I model."

4. During the Second Panel Meeting, Brazil advised the Panel that it had no objection, then, to the US looking at the information provided to it by FAPRI, notwithstanding the FAPRI stipulation. The Panel acknowledges this, but also notes that it would be open to Brazil to reconsider its position depending on anything that the US may wish to present to the Panel about the FAPRI model.

5. The Panel's view in these circumstances is that the US should comment on the FAPRI model, if it believes that it needs to do so in the interests of presenting its case to the Panel, by **22 December**. The FAPRI stipulation does not, in the Panel's view, affect the Panel's ability to make an objective assessment of

[3] US Further Written Submission, Sections II and XIII.

the matter before it in the terms of Article 11 of the DSU. The Panel will assess the reliability and relevance of the FAPRI model on the basis of the evidence presented to it by the parties.

6. Brazil will be given until **12 January 2004**, to comment on the above US comments.

Questions from the Panel to the Parties –
second substantive Panel meeting

A. TERMS OF REFERENCE

192. Regarding the interest subsidies and storage payments listed by the United States in its response to the Panel's Question No. 67:

(a) Please provide a copy of the regulations under which they are currently provided and under which they were provided during the marketing years 1996-2002;

(b) Please indicate whether there are any such payments which are not provided to implement the repayment rate for upland cotton within the marketing loan programme. **USA**

193. Are interest subsidies and storage payments already included in the amounts shown in your submissions to date for payments under the marketing loan programme? Has there been any double-counting? **BRA**

194. Does the United States maintain its position stated in response to the Panel's Question No. 67 that "it would not be appropriate for the Panel to examine payments made after the date of panel establishment"? If so, please explain why. Can Brazil comment on this statement? **BRA, USA**

B. ECONOMIC DATA

195. Does the United States wish to revise its response to the Panel's Question No. 67*bis,* in particular, its statement that "the United States ... does not maintain information on the amount of expenditures made under the cited programmes to US upland cotton producers"? Did the United States make enquiries of the FSA in the course of preparing its original answer? **USA**

196. Please provide the latest data for the 2002 marketing year on payments under the marketing loan, direct payments, counter-cyclical payments, user marketing certificate (step 2) programmes and export credit guarantee programmes. **BRA, USA**

197. Please provide actual data for 2002/2003 for US exports, US consumption and per cent of world consumption to replace the projected data in Exhibit US-47. If available, please provide projected data for 2003/2004 to replace the forecast data. **USA**

198. Please comment on the respective merits of the price-gap calculations of MY1992 deficiency payments in US comments of 27 August, footnote 14 ($867 million), and Brazil's response to the Panel's Question No. 67 ($812 million). **BRA, USA**

199. What is the composition of the A-Index? We do note footnote 19 and, for example, Exhibit BRA-11, but please explain more in detail how this index is calculated. **BRA**

200. Concerning the chart on page 37 of Brazil's further rebuttal submission, why did Brazil use a futures price at planting time? Is this a relevant measure for assessing acreage response? **BRA**

201. Is data available to show the proportion of US upland cotton production sold under futures contracts, and the prices under those contracts, at different times during the marketing year? If so, please provide summarized versions to the Panel. How does a futures sale impact the producer's entitlement to marketing loan programme payments? **BRA, USA**

202. Concerning paragraph 7 of the US oral statement, are the expected cash prices shown for February only? Can the US provide the prices for January and March of each year as well? **USA**

203. Please provide information concerning the organization, mandate, credentials and standing of FAPRI. **BRA**

204. Which support to upland cotton is not captured in the EWG data referred to in Brazil's 18 November further rebuttal submission? **BRA**

205. Does the United States accept or agree with the EWG data submitted by Brazil? If not, please explain your reasons. **USA**

206. Please explain how the graph in paragraph 40 of the US further rebuttal submission was derived. In so doing, please clarify whether the figures are on a cents per pound basis or some other basis. What averaging method was used? Can you prepare individual charts showing average US and Brazilian cotton prices for each of those third country markets? **USA**

207. Please indicate whether any of the measures challenged in this dispute *obliges* cotton farmers to harvest their crop in order to receive the benefit of the programme (subsidy). **USA**

208. Please provide data for the marketing years 1992 and 1999-2002 of the "quantity of production to receive the applied administered price" (*Agreement on Agriculture*, Annex 3, paragraph 8) for purposes of a price-gap calculation of support through the marketing loan programme. **USA**

209. It is understood that the data in the graph in paragraph 5 of the US oral statement are as at harvest time, while the data in the graph in paragraph 39 of Brazil's oral statement are as at planting time. Please explain why the trend of US acreage increase/decrease differs between these two graphs. **BRA, USA**

210. Are worldwide planted acreage figures available? **BRA, USA**

211. Brazil presents a graph in paragraph 59 of its further rebuttal submission indicating the increasing cumulative loss incurred by cotton producers. Please comment on the argument that US cotton producers could not continue operating without subsidies. In particular:

(a) to what extent does the use of 1997 survey technological coefficients with annually updated values affect the results?

(b) to what extent do producers base planting decisions on their ability to cover operating costs but not whole farm costs? **USA**

212. Brazil states in paragraph 37 of its oral statement that studies of Westcott and Price found that the effect of the programme on cotton is to add an additional 1 to 1.5 million acres during marketing years 1999-2001 and to suppress US prices by 5 cents per pound. Does the US reject these findings? Why or why not? **USA**

213. What differences, if any, can be observed in the results of econometric models in the literature which use lagged prices and those which use futures prices to analyse the effect of prices on planting decisions? **BRA, USA**

C. DOMESTIC SUPPORT

214. Please provide a copy of regulations regarding the marketing loan programme and loan deficiency payments published at 58 Federal Register 15755, dated 24 March 1993. What does this regulation indicate about the target price? **USA**

215. Please expand or comment on the statement at paragraph 91 of the US further rebuttal submission that the counter-cyclical target price ceases to be paid when the farm price rises above 65.73 cents per pound. In this scenario, should the Panel disregard Direct Payments? **BRA, USA**

216. How many times have upland cotton producers been able to update their base acres since 1984? How do upland cotton producers come to note the possibility of future updating? Please provide examples of relevant material. **BRA, USA**

217. What is the reason for reducing payments under the PFC and direct payments programmes for planting and harvesting fruit, vegetables and wild rice on certain base acreage? Please comment on the statements by the European Communities that "the reduction in payment for fruit and vegetables, if the EC understands correctly, is in fact designed to avoid unfair competition within the subsidising Member." (EC oral statement at first session, first substantive meeting, paragraph 29) and "To find otherwise would not permit a WTO Member wishing to introduce decoupled payments to take account of important elements of internal competition (...)" (EC response to Panel third party Question No. 5). **USA**

218. Please comment on the testimony of USDA Chief Economist Keith Collins cited in paragraph 36 of Brazil's oral statement regarding the trade-distorting and production-distorting nature of the marketing loan payments. **USA**

D. EXPORT CREDIT GUARANTEES

219. Under the *Agreement on Agriculture* the general position is that the use of export subsidies, both those listed in Article 9.1 as well as those within the scope of Article 1(e) which are not so listed, may only be used within the limits of the product specific reduction commitments specified in Part IV of Members' Schedules. One might therefore have expected that Article 3.3 of the *Agreement on Agriculture* would have prohibited the use of both listed and non-listed export

subsidies in excess of reduction commitment levels in the case of scheduled products and, in the case of non-scheduled products, would have simply prohibited the use of any export subsidy. Instead, the Article 3.3 prohibition is limited in both cases to export subsidies listed in Article 9.1. What significance, if any, does this contextual aspect have for how Article 10.2 might be interpreted having regard, *inter alia*, to:

(a) the fact that export performance-related tax incentives, which like subsidised export credit facilities were considered as a possible candidate for listing as an Article 9.1 export subsidy in the pre-December 1991 Draft Final Act negotiations, have been held (for example, in *United States – Tax Treatment for Foreign Sales Corporations*, WT/DS108) to be subject to the anti-circumvention provisions of Article 10.1; and

(b) the treatment of international food aid and non-commercial transactions under Article 10? **USA**

220. What will be the relevance of Articles 9 and 10.1 of the *Agreement of Agriculture* to export credit guarantees when disciplines are internationally agreed? **BRA**

221. In respect of the table in paragraph 161 of the US August 22 rebuttal submission (concerning the cohort specific treatment of export credit guarantees), the Panel notes the subsequent US agreement (footnotes 82 and 96 in US further submission of 30 September 2003; footnote 160 in US 18 November further rebuttal submission) to Brazil's assertion (footnote 67 in Brazil's 27 August 2003 comments on US rebuttal submission) that the total figure net of re-estimates should be $230,127,023 instead of the figure which originally appeared ($381,345,059).

(a) Please submit a corrected table reflecting all of the necessary information to produce this result, to the extent this is possible for the reasons indicated in footnote 96 in US further submission of 30 September 2003.

(b) Please clarify whether and how the Panel should treat the figures in Exhibit BRA-182 for the net lifetime re-estimates for each respective cohort.

(c) The Panel notes that the CCC 2002 financial statement in Exhibit BRA-158 refers to annual "administrative" expenses of $4 million, and that the US has also referred to this figure in its submissions (e.g. US first written submission, paragraph 175). Please confirm whether the figures in the table in paragraph 161 of the US August 22 rebuttal submission (or a corrected version thereof) includes "administrative expenses", of approximately $4 million per year over the period 1992-2002, and explain why (or why not) this affects the substantive result.

(d) Please identify what is considered an "administrative expense" for this purpose.

(e) The Panel notes the US statement in paragraph 160 of its answers to Panel questions following the first meeting that all cohorts are still open although the 1994 and 1995 cohorts will close this year. Is this still an accurate statement? If not, please indicate whether any cohorts have since "closed" for the period 1992-2002.

(f) The Panel notes the current "high" figures for 1997 and 1998 indicated in the original US chart. Pending their confirmation and/or updating by the US, why does the US assert that a cohort will *necessarily* reach a "profitable" result (for example, the 1994 cohort, which has almost closed still indicates an outstanding amount)? Do "re-estimates" reflect also expectations about a cohort's future performance?

(g) Why should the Panel "eliminate" the 2001 and 2002 cohorts from its examination, as suggested in paragraph 198 of the US further rebuttal submission?

(h) Why should the Panel "eliminate", in addition, the 2000 cohort, as also suggested in paragraph 198 of the US further rebuttal submission for which information is presumably more "complete"?

(i) Under the US approach, at what point in time could a Panel ever make an assessment of the programme, if it had to wait for each cohort to be completed before it could be "properly" assessed? Why is it inappropriate for the Panel to include these "most recent years" in its evaluation, as the US suggests in paragraph 199 of its 18 November further rebuttal submission? **USA**

222. For GSM 102, 103 and SCGP, please provide year-by-year amounts from 1992 to 2003 with respect to: (i) cumulative outstanding guarantees; (ii) claims paid; (iii) recoveries made; (iv) revenue from premiums; (v) other current revenue, including interest earned; (vi) interest charges paid; and (vii) administrative costs of running the programmes. Please indicate any allocation methodologies used to calculate administrative costs. **USA**

223. Are the premium rates applicable to GSM 102, 103 and SCGP subject to regular review as to their adequacy in enabling the operating costs and losses associated with these programmes? If so, what criteria or benchmarks are taken into consideration for this purpose? Secondly, how do the premium rates applied compare with the implicit cost of forfaiting transactions and with premiums for export credit insurance? **USA**

224. Please indicate how the CCC's cost of borrowing was treated in the 2002 financial statement of the CCC, in Exhibit BRA 158. **USA**

225. Please indicate whether there was any instance where the CCC "wrote off" debt and, if so, please indicate the accounting regulation or principle used. If a "written off" debt is subsequently recovered, do the CCC's accounts reflect both the interest cost and interest received in relation to the debt during the time it was "written off"? **USA**

226. If a debt was "written off" more than ten years ago, does it still create a cost to the programme? If so, how is this reflected in the 2002 financial statement of the CCC, in Exhibit BRA 158 (or any other material)? **USA**

227. The United States has indicated that Brazil continues to "mischaracterize" the amount of $411 million in the 2002 financial statement of the CCC, in Exhibit BRA 158, pp. 18 & 19. Can the United States please indicate how it believes this amount – referred to on p. 19 of the Exhibit as "Credit Guarantee Liability-End of Fiscal Year" - should be properly characterized? How, if at all, does it represent CCC operating costs or losses? **USA**

228. What accounting principles should the Panel use in assessing the long-term operating costs and losses of these three programmes? For example, if internal US Government regulations require costs to be treated differently to generally accepted accounting principles, is it incumbent on the Panel to conduct its analysis in accordance with that treatment? **BRA, USA**

E. SERIOUS PREJUDICE

229. What is the meaning of the words "may arise in any case where *one or several* of the following apply" (emphasis added) in Article 6.3 of the *SCM Agreement*? Please comment on the possibility that these words indicate that one of the Article 6 subparagraphs may not be sufficient to establish serious prejudice and that serious prejudice should be considered an additional or overriding criterion to the factors specified in the subparagraphs. **BRA**

230. Please comment on Brazil's views on Article 6.3 of the *SCM Agreement* as stated in paragraphs 92-94 of its further submission. **USA**

231. Do you believe that the now-expired Article 6.1 and/or Annex IV of the *SCM Agreement* are relevant context for the Panel's interpretation of Article 6.3? **USA**

232. How, if at all, should the Panel take into account the effects of other factors in its analysis of the effects of US subsidies under Article 6.3? If the Panel should compare the effects of other factors to establish the relative significance of one compared to others, how would this be done? What would be relevant "factors" for this purpose? **BRA**

233. In Brazil's view, what is or are the "same market(s)" for the purposes of Article 6.3(c)? Does Brazil's view of "world market" imply that regardless of which domestic (or other) "market" is examined, price suppression will be identifiable? **BRA**

234. Does "significant" price suppression under Article 6.3(c) necessarily amount to "serious" prejudice within the meaning of Article 5(c)? Could the level of "significance" of any price suppression under Article 6.3(c) determine whether any prejudice under Article 5(c) rises to the level of "serious prejudice"? **USA, BRA**

235. Please comment on paragraphs 8, 9 and 10 of the US 2 December oral statement, in particular, why the average Brazilian price is shown as lower than the average US price. **BRA**

236. The Panel notes Exhibit US-47 (and the chart in paragraph 13 of the US 2 December oral statement). Please provide a conceptually analogous chart to Exhibit US-63 with respect to data relating to the US interpretation of "world market share". **USA**

237. Could a phenomenon that remains at approximately the same level over a given period of time be considered a "consistent trend" within the meaning of Article 6.3(d)? Do parties have any suggestions as to how to determine a "consistent trend", statistically or otherwise? **BRA, USA**

238. According to the US interpretation of the term "world market share":

(a) should the domestic consumption of closed markets be added into the denominator?

(b) if US production and consumption increased by the same percentage, whilst the rest of the world's production and consumption remained steady, would this imply an increase in the US "world market share" by a different percentage?

(c) does Saudi Arabia have a small world market share for oil? **USA**

239. How does the US respond to Brazil's assertions that, under the US interpretation of the term "world market share":

(a) there would be no WTO disciplines on production-enhancing subsidies that increase a Member's world market share of exports? (see paragraph 64 of Brazil's 2 December oral statement);

(b) a Member's exports would have to be disregarded in calculating their "world market share" in terms of "world consumption"? (see e.g. paragraph 65 of Brazil's 2 December oral statement) **USA**

240. Does Article XVI:3 of GATT 1994 provide context in interpreting Article 6.3(d) of the *SCM Agreement*? Do these provisions apply separately? If not, could it indicate that "world market share" is intended to mean the same as "share of world export trade"? **USA**

241. How does the US reconcile its data on consumption for 2002 in US Exhibit 40, Table 1 with the "consumption" data it refers to in its 30 September submission, paragraph 34, Exhibit US-47 or US-71? **USA**

242. How much of the benefits of PFC, MLA, CCP and Direct Payments go to land owners? If not all of the benefits go to land owners, what proportion goes to producers? **USA**

243. Can the Panel assume that any support at all, even marketing loan programme payments, benefits upland cotton if an upland cotton producer has other agricultural production besides upland cotton? **USA**

244. What proportion of the 2000 cottonseed payments benefited *producers of upland cotton*, given that payments were made to *first handlers*, who were only obliged to share them with the producer to the extent that the revenue from sale of the cottonseed was shared with the producer? (see 7 CFR §1427.1104(c) in Exhibit US-15). **BRA**

245. Can a panel take Green Box subsidies into account in considering the effects of non-Green Box subsidies in an action based on Articles 5 and 6 of the *SCM Agreement*? **BRA, USA**

246. Can a panel take prohibited subsidies into account in considering the effects of subsidies in an action based on Articles 5 and 6 of the *SCM Agreement*? **BRA, USA**

247. Can the Panel take into account trends and volatility in market and futures prices of upland cotton after the date of establishment of the Panel? If so, how do they affect the analysis of Brazil's claim of a threat of serious prejudice? **BRA, USA**

F. STEP 2

248. In respect of the level of Step 2 payments in certain time periods, the Panel notes, *inter alia*, footnote 129 in the US first written submission; footnote 33 in the US 18 November further rebuttal submission; and Exhibit BRA-350. Have Step 2 payments ever been zero since the elimination of the 1.25 cent per pound threshold in the FSRI Act of 2002? In what circumstances could a Step 2 payment be zero? How does the elimination of the 1.25 cent per pound threshold in the FSRI Act of 2002 affect your response? **BRA, USA**

249. The Panel notes that the definition of eligible "exporter" in 7 CFR 1427.104(a)(2) includes "a producer":

(a) How does this reconcile with Brazil's argument that Step 2 "export payments" do not directly benefit the producer?[4] How, if at all, would this be relevant for an analysis of the issue of export contingency under the *Agreement on Agriculture* or the *SCM Agreement*? **BRA**

(b) How does this reconcile with Dr. Glauber's statement in Exhibit US-24, p. 3 (referring to "the 1990 Farm Bill and subsequent legislation") that Step 2 payments do *not* go directly to the producer? **USA**

(c) What proportion of Step 2 "export payments" go to producers? Please supply supporting evidence. **USA**

G. REMEDIES

250. Does Brazil seek relief under Article XVI of *GATT 1994* in respect of expired measures? What type of recommendation would the Panel be authorized to make? (Brazil further submission, paragraph 471 (iii)) **BRA**

251. In light, *inter alia*, of Article 7.8 of the *SCM Agreement*, if the Panel were to find that any subsidies have resulted in adverse effects to the interests of another Member within the meaning of Article 5 of the *SCM Agreement*, should it make any recommendation other than the one set out in the first sentence of Article 19.1 of the DSU? **BRA**

[4] For example, Brazil's response to Panel Question 125, para. 14.

252. Without prejudice to any findings by the Panel, if the Panel were to find that any of the challenged measures constitute prohibited subsidies within the meaning of Article 3 of the *SCM Agreement*, what are the considerations that should guide the Panel in making a recommendation under Article 4.7 of the *SCM Agreement* relating to the time period "within which the measure must be withdrawn"? What should that time period be? **BRA**

H. MISCELLANEOUS

253. Regarding the adjustment authority related to Uruguay Round compliance in s.1601(e) of the FSRI Act of 2002 (the so-called "circuit-breaker provision"):

(a) Does it relate to export credit guarantees, crop insurance and cottonseed payments?

(b) Does it relate only to compliance with AMS commitments?

(c) Is the authority discretionary? If so, can its exercise be limited by the legislative branch of government?

(d) How would the Secretary exercise her authority to prevent serious prejudice to the interests of another Member? How would she exercise her authority to prevent a threat of serious prejudice to the interests of another Member? At what time and on the basis of what type of information would she exercise her authority?

(e) What does "to the maximum extent practicable" mean? In what circumstances would it not be practicable for the Secretary to exercise her adjustment authority? **USA**

254. Would payments made after the date of panel establishment be *mandatory* under the marketing loan, direct payments, counter-cyclical payments and user marketing certificate (step 2) programmes, but for the circuit-breaker provision? **USA**

255. How does Brazil respond to US assertions concerning the circuit-breaker provision? (see US 2 December oral statement, paragraph 82). Does this mean that US subsidies cannot be "mandatory" for the purposes of WTO dispute settlement? **BRA**

256. The United States submits that the Panel cannot make rulings without allocating precise amounts of payments to upland cotton production. However, to the extent that such precise data is not on the Panel record, to what extent can the Panel rely on less precise data, and on reasonable assumptions, in fulfilling its duty under Article 11 of the *DSU* in this case? **USA**

ANNEX L-1.19

COMMUNICATION TO BRAZIL AND THE UNITED STATES
23 December 2003

Please find attached additional questions from the Panel.

We would ask the parties to provide their responses by **12 January 2004.** The parties may submit any comments on each other's responses by **19 January 2004**.

Additional Questions from the Panel to the parties – following the second substantive Panel meeting

257. The Panel takes note of the Appellate Body Report in *United States – Sunset Review of Anti-Dumping Duties on Corrosion-Resistant Carbon Steel Flat Products from Japan* (DS244), which was circulated to WTO Members on 15 December 2003. The Panel is aware that this report has yet to be adopted by the Dispute Settlement Body. Nevertheless, the Panel asks the parties to respond to the following related questions.

(a) In that report, the Appellate Body cautioned against the "mechanistic" application of the so-called "mandatory/discretionary distinction" and stated that the import of this distinction may vary from case to case (para. 93). For the Appellate Body, the question of whether a measure is mandatory or not is relevant "if at all" only as part of the assessment of whether the measure is, as such, inconsistent with particular obligations. How, if at all, are these statements and the related findings concerning the mandatory/discretionary distinction in that Appellate Body Report relevant to:

(i) the legal standard and elements Brazil sets out to establish its export and prohibited subsidy claims under the provisions of the *Agreement on Agriculture* and Articles 3.1(a) and (b) of the *SCM Agreement*, concerning: **BRA**

- Step 2 payments (see, *e.g.* paras. 244-245 & 250 Brazil's first written submission; Panel Question 109 and parties' responses/comments thereon); and
- export credit guarantee programmes: GSM-102, GSM-103 and SCGP (see, *e.g.*, para. 90 Brazil's oral statement at second Panel meeting).

(ii) the legal standard and elements Brazil sets out to establish its serious prejudice and "threat of serious prejudice" claims, and in particular, its designation of marketing loan; crop insurance; countercyclical payments; direct payments and Step 2 as "mandatory"? **BRA**

(iii) the legal standard and elements Brazil sets out to establish its "*per se*" "serious prejudice" claims (*e.g.* Brazil's 9 September further submission, para. 417 *ff*; US oral statement at second Panel meeting, para. 86 *ff.*)? **BRA**

(b) How and to what extent are the legal and regulatory provisions cited in paras. 415 and 423 of Brazil's 9 September further submission "normative" in nature and treated as binding within the US legal system (see, *e.g.*, para. 99 of the Appellate Body Report)? Does your response differ depending on whether the payments are dependent upon market price conditions? **BRA**

(c) Does Brazil challenge as "mandatory" the "subsidies" themselves, the subsidy programmes or the legal/regulatory provisions for the grant or maintenance of those subsidies, or something else? **BRA**

(d) Does the "requirement" upon the CCC to make available "not less than" $5.5 billion annually in guarantees have a normative character and operation? (see, e.g. Brazil's response to Panel Question 142; Exhibit BRA-297, 7 USC 5641(b)(1); 7 USC 5622(a) & (b); paragraph 201 of US 18 November further rebuttal submissions). Is this requirement "mandatory"? If so, how does the CCC have "discretion" not to make this amount of guarantees available in a given year? **USA**

(e) Does the US agree that, under the Budget Enforcement Act of 1990, the Office of Management and Budget classifies the export credit guarantee programs as "mandatory" (see Brazil's response to Panel Question 142, para. 89)? Does this exempt the programmes from the requirement to receive new Congressional budget authority before it undertakes new guarantee commitments (*e.g.* Exhibit BRA-117 (2 USC 661(c)(2))? **USA**

ANNEX L-1.20

COMMUNICATION TO BRAZIL AND THE UNITED STATES

24 December 2003

The Panel has received a letter from Brazil dated 23 December (numbered 760), in which it requests extension of certain deadlines. The Panel has also received a response from the US, dated 23 December. Having carefully considered the views of both parties, the Panel notifies the parties that it would amend the four immediate deadlines and schedules as follows:

(1) all submissions originally due 12 January 2004 would now be due **Tuesday, 20 January 2004**

(2) all submissions originally due 19 January 2004 would now be due **Wednesday, 28 January 2004**.

(3) issuance of descriptive part of the report to parties (currently scheduled for 26 January) would be rescheduled to **Wednesday, 4 February 2004**.

(4) receipt of comments by parties on the descriptive part of the report (currently scheduled for 19 February) would be rescheduled to **Monday, 1 March 2004**.

All subsequent dates remain unchanged. However, please be reminded that such dates may be changed in light of further developments.

ANNEX L-1.21

COMMUNICATION TO BRAZIL AND THE UNITED STATES

12 January 2004

The Panel takes note that, as stated in its letters dated 18 and 22 December 2003, the United States provided certain data requested by Brazil, but deleted from farm-level planted acreage data any fields that could identify individual farms. Brazil commented on this in its answer to Panel Question No. 196. The United States stated in its letter dated 18 December 2003 that "the release of planted acreage information associated with a particular farm, county and state number is confidential information that cannot be released under US domestic law, in particular the Privacy Act of 1974."

The Panel has reviewed the material submitted in support in Exhibits US-102 through 107, and makes the following observations:

- in the sample Freedom of Information Act ("FOIA") determination submitted to the Panel, the FSA appears to have relied on the fact that the acreage requested concerned a single producer only and that there was no public interest in disclosure of records which did not directly reveal the operations or activities of the US Federal Government;
- in that sample FOIA determination, the FSA applied the relevant US domestic law and expressly acknowledged that disclosure of individual data on commodity programme recipients can be released where the recipients' privacy interests in that information are outweighed by the public interest in disclosure;
- the information which the US asserts that it cannot disclose is relatively generic, concerning planted acreage, and does not relate to one individual but to tens of thousands of business people, and can be protected under the DSU and our working procedures;
- farm-specific information on contract payments is already available free of charge on the internet on the EWG database, having been disclosed under the FOIA; and
- comprehensive farm-specific information concerning rice, including planted acreage data associated with particular farm, county and state numbers, was provided on request under the FOIA to a member of the public who was assisting Professor Sumner in the presentation of Brazil's case to the Panel. A sample of this data is set out in Exhibit BRA-369.

Article 13.1 of the DSU relevantly provides as follows:

"A Member should respond promptly and fully to any request by a panel for such information as the panel considers necessary and appropriate. Confidential information which is provided shall not be revealed without formal authorization from the individual, body, or authorities of the Member providing the information."

Pursuant to Article 13 of the DSU, the Panel requests the United States to provide the same data that it agreed to provide in its letters dated 18 and 22 December 2003 but in a format which permits matching of farm-specific information on contract payments with farm-specific information on plantings. The Panel considers it both necessary and appropriate to seek this information in a suitable format in order to undertake its mandate to assist the DSB in discharging its responsibilities under the DSU and the covered agreements. Disclosure is sought to permit an assessment of the total expenditures of PFC, MLA, CCP and direct payments by the US Federal Government to upland cotton producers in the relevant marketing years.

The United States may again designate the data as confidential in accordance with paragraph 3 of the Panel's working procedures. Disclosure can be limited to Brazil's delegation, the Panel and Secretariat staff assisting the Panel. The United States may also protect the identity of individual producers by, for example, using substitute farm numbers which still permit data-matching.

A refusal by the United States to provide the information as requested without an adequate explanation may lead to adverse inferences being drawn.

The Panel reminds Brazil that it may not disclose the above information outside its delegation in this proceeding if it is designated by the United States as confidential.

The Panel also wishes to pose the following additional question to Brazil:

> 258. Please submit a detailed explanation of the method by which one could calculate total expenditures to producers of upland cotton under the four relevant programmes on the basis of the data which it seeks.

The Panel asks the parties to provide the respective information requested by 20 January 2004.

ANNEX L-1.22

COMMUNICATION TO BRAZIL AND THE UNITED STATES

3 February 2004

Please find attached the Panel's supplementary request to the United States for information pursuant to Article 13 of the DSU, as well as additional questions to both parties. The Panel would like to ask the parties to provide the information requested and responses to the additional questions by **Wednesday 11 February 2004**. The Parties are invited to submit, by **Wednesday 18 February 2004,** any comments on material submitted on 11 February by the other party.

In light of the above development, the Panel intends to postpone the issuance of the descriptive part until **Friday 20 February 2004**. The remainder of the Panel's schedule remains unchanged for the time being.

The Panel recalls that it indicated, in its communication dated 14 November, that "[i]f necessary, at the discretion of the Panel, a further Panel meeting with the parties may be held" to address the issue of econometric models. The Panel would like to indicate that, at this stage, it does not see the need to hold such a meeting.

The Panel has noted the US letter dated 30 January, Brazil's response dated 2 February, and a further letter from the US dated 3 February 2004. Keeping in mind the dictates of due process and relevant provisions of the covered agreements - including Article 12.2 of the DSU which requires Panel procedures to provide sufficient flexibility so as to ensure high-quality panel reports while not unduly delaying the panel process - the Panel is of the view that the above revisions to the timetable provide the United States and Brazil sufficient opportunity to comment on each other's comments. Accordingly, the US is free to submit its comments on Brazil's above mentioned submission by 11 February (**but no later**).

This is without prejudice to any definitive view of the Panel on the characterization of any of the above communications by the parties and, in particular, of the document submitted by Brazil entitled "Brazil's Comments and Requests Regarding Data Provided by the United States on 18/19 December 2003 and the US Refusal to Provide Non-scrambled Data on 20 January 2004".

PANEL'S SUPPLEMENTARY REQUEST FOR INFORMATION PURSUANT TO ARTICLE 13 OF THE DSU AND ADDITIONAL QUESTIONS

The Panel has reviewed the United States' letters dated 18 December 2003 and 20 January 2004, and the material submitted in support in Exhibits US-102 through 107, and Brazil's response to Question No. 258.

Pursuant to Article 13 of the DSU, the Panel requests the United States to provide:

(a) such of the information requested on 12 January 2004 in the format requested, as regards payment recipients who do not have interests protected under the Privacy Act 1974, if any; and

(b) the following information for each of the PFC, MLA, CCP and direct payments programmes for each of the 1999, 2000, 2001 and 2002 marketing years, showing as many of the underlying calculations as possible:

- How many farms had fewer upland cotton planted acres than upland cotton base acres, or equal numbers of each? We refer to these as "Category A" farms. What was the total of their upland cotton base acreage? What was the total of their upland cotton planted acreage?
    - How many Category A farms did not plant any other covered commodities? What was the total of their upland cotton base acreage? What was the total of their upland cotton planted acreage?
- How many farms had more upland cotton planted acres than upland cotton base acres? We refer to these as "Category B" farms. What was the total of their base acreage for each covered commodity, including upland cotton? What was the total of their planted acreage for each covered commodity, including upland cotton? Please also provide the following information concerning these farms:
    - How many Category B farms had equal numbers of acres planted to all covered commodities and base acres for all covered commodities? We refer to these as "Category B-1" farms. What was the total of the base acreage of Category B-1 farms for each covered commodity, including upland cotton? What was the total of the planted acreage of Category B-1 farms for each covered commodity, including upland cotton?
    - How many Category B farms had fewer acres planted to all covered commodities than base acres for all covered commodities? We refer to these as "Category B-2" farms. How much was the total acreage of Category B-2 farms planted to all covered commodities less than their base acreage for all covered commodities? What was the total of the base acreage of Category B-2 farms for each covered commodity, including upland cotton? What was the total of the planted acreage of Category B-2 farms for each covered commodity, including upland cotton?
    - How many Category B farms had more acres planted to all covered commodities than base acres for all covered commodities? We refer to these as "Category B-3" farms. How much did the total acreage of Category B-3 farms planted to

all covered commodities exceed their base acreage for all covered commodities? What was the total of the base acreage of Category B-3 farms for each covered commodity, including upland cotton? What was the total of the planted acreage of Category B-3 farms for each covered commodity, including upland cotton?

- How many farms had upland cotton planted acres but no upland cotton base acres? We refer to these as "Category C" farms. What was the total of the base acreage of Category C farms for each covered commodity? What was the total of the planted acreage of Category C farms for each covered commodity, including upland cotton?
- In addition, for the marketing year 2002, please reply to the above questions with respect to all crops on cropland covered by the acreage reports, not simply commodities covered by the programmes.
- In addition, please provide all of the above information on a state-by-state basis.

You may wish to present your responses regarding acreage for each covered commodity in a table as follows:

TABLE

Programme:
Marketing year:
Category of Farm:

	Covered commodities								
	Upland Cotton	Barley	Corn	Oats	Rice	Sorghum	Wheat	Soybeans*	Other Oilseeds*
Base acres									
Planted acres									

* Where applicable.

The Panel considers it both necessary and appropriate to seek this information to undertake its mandate to assist the DSB in discharging its responsibilities under the DSU and the covered agreements. However, the Panel reserves its views as to the extent to which any methodology might be appropriate to determine support provided to upland cotton in the circumstances of this case.

A refusal by the United States to provide the information as requested without an adequate explanation may lead to adverse inferences being drawn.

The Panel also wishes to pose the following additional questions to the United States (Nos. 259 – 275) and to Brazil (No. 276):

259. With respect to the Privacy Act of 1974, 5 U.S.C. 552a:

(a) Whose interests are protected under section 552a(b) in light of the definition of "individual" in section 552a(a)(2)? Do all payment recipients, including corporations and organizations, have Privacy Act rights? If not, is the United States prevented by its domestic law from releasing such of the information requested on 12 January 2004 as relates to payment recipients without Privacy Act rights? Please explain with references to case law.

(b) The Panel notes that data concerning the four relevant programmes, in particular, payment amounts, identified by specific farms, is freely available on the internet. Please explain why that data can be disclosed but the requested planted acreage data cannot. Do individual recipients have Privacy Act rights with respect to their entrepreneurial activity? Please explain with references to case law.

(c) Please provide any further available evidence of the USDA's longstanding policy that planted acreage information will not be released.

260. On 27 August 2003, in its response to Question No. 67 *bis*, the United States indicated that "it does not maintain information on the amount of expenditures made under the cited programmes to US upland cotton producers". On 12 January 2004, the Panel requested the United States to provide information "to permit an assessment of the total expenditures of PFC, MLA, CCP and direct payments by the US Federal Government to upland cotton producers in the relevant marketing years". On 20 January 2004, the United States informed the Panel that "the data already provided by the United States to Brazil and the Panel would permit an assessment of total expenditures of decoupled payments to farms planting upland cotton." Is the latest statement responsive to the Panel's request? If so, how can it be reconciled with the first statement?

261. Please confirm that each record in the actual planting database relates to a specific farm (Filenames: rPFCplac and rDCPplac in Exhibits US-111 and US-112). For example, in the data from rDCPplac:

First line:
Field9;Field16;Field22;Field28;Field34;Field40;Field46;Field52;Field58;
Field64;Field70;Field76;Field82;Field88;Field94;Field100

Second line:
237.10;23059.80;5566.20;0.00;0.00;0.00;0.00;0.00;0.00;0.00;0.00;0.00;0.
00;0.00;0.00;0.00

Does the second line represent data on plantings by the same farm?

262. The Panel has noted the two CD-ROMs delivered by the US in the evening of 23 December 2003. They are marked "US-111" and "US-112" respectively, but the contents actually do not correspond to the indication. The Panel also takes note of the US letter dated 28 January 2004 and the CD-ROM delivered together with it. For the record, please clarify the cor-

rect CD-ROMs and provide corresponding descriptions of their contents with exhibit numbers.

263. The Panel has noted that the United States' response to Question No. 214 refers to Exhibits US-117 and US-118. Are these the correct documents to which the United States intended to refer in that response? If not, please provide a copy of regulations regarding the marketing loan programme and loan deficiency payments published at 58 Federal Register 15755, dated 24 March 1993.

264. The Panel asks the United States to clarify certain aspects of Exhibit US-128:

(a) Is the Panel correct in understanding that - as Brazil asserts in footnotes 290 and 291 of Brazil's 28 January 2004 comments on US responses to questions - Exhibit US-128, all data are presented on a cohort-specific basis? If so, please also present the information originally requested by the Panel in another chart containing *programme* (as opposed to cohort-specific) activity by fiscal year.

(b) Does the US agree with the statement in paragraph 135 of Brazil's 28 January 2004 comments on US responses to questions that the difference between the $1,148 billion in the chart at para. 165 of Brazil's 11 August answers to questions and the $666 million amount in Exhibit US-128 ($1.75 billion) closely corresponds to the total "Claims rescheduled" figure reported by the US in Exhibit US-128 (column F)?

(c) Does the US agree that from the formula in column G (that is: (Column (D) minus (E) minus (F)), it follows that a rescheduled claim no longer constitutes an outstanding claim at the moment the terms of the rescheduling are agreed and that a rescheduling is treated as 100 per cent recovered, as Brazil states in footnote 292 of Brazil's 28 January 2004 comments on US responses to questions?

(d) Is the Panel correct in understanding that the amount of $888,984,792.04 in column F in Exhibit US-128 under "ALL" for 1992 represents the total continuing amount of unrecovered claims for the 1992 cohort, and that the amount of 387,692,219.39 represents the total continuing amount of unrecovered claims for the 1993 cohort, etc? Please indicate and substantiate how much principal and/or interest has actually been paid/recovered/rescheduled *annually* 1992-2003 in respect of each of the amounts shown in Columns D, E & F in the table.

265. In connection with the US response to Question No. 225, please also provide amounts actually "written off" and "forgiven" annually for each *post*-1992 cohort, with annual details of country and amount (principal/interest).

266. What are the precise terms, conditions and duration of each rescheduling reflected in column F in Exhibit US-128?

267. Is the Panel correct in understanding that "interest collected on reschedulings" in Column M in Exhibit US-128 refers not to amounts that

have been actually collected by the CCC but rather to interest capitalized in conjunction with the rescheduling? If so, what are the terms, conditions and duration of the arrangements pertaining to these amounts?

268. Concerning Column N in Exhibit US-128, please elaborate upon "Interest earned from US Treasury on uninvested funds". What is the source and authority for these funds and for the interest thereon to be part of the CCC total revenues? What are the terms, conditions and duration of the arrangements pertaining to these amounts?

269. The Panel notes the table submitted by the US in its answer to Question No. 224 (CCC Financing Account Payments of Interest on Borrowings from Treasury and Interest Earned on Uninvested Funds). Is the Panel correct in understanding that the figures in this table correspond to the "ALL" figures in Columns I and N of Exhibit US-128?

270. With respect to Column I in Exhibit US-128, ("Interest paid on borrowing from US Treasury") and Note 8, p. 25 of Exhibit US-129:

(i) please provide the total annual amounts (interest bearing and non-interest bearing) borrowed by the CCC from the US Treasury (annually since 1992), as well as the terms, conditions, interest rate (where applicable) and duration of such borrowing. Please provide details of any other amount borrowed by the CCC from the US Treasury during this period that may not have formed part of the regular annual borrowings.

(ii) Please explain the nature of "CCC's permanent indefinite borrowing authority from Treasury" referred to in Note 8, p. 25 of Exhibit US-129.

(iii) What determines the level of CCC export credit guarantee borrowing (interest-bearing and non-interest-bearing)? Is the interest-free borrowing up to the amount of unreimbursed realized losses?

(iv) Why are repayments applied to non-interest bearing notes first, as indicated at Note 8, p. 25 of Exhibit US-129?

271. Note 8, p. 25 of Exhibit US-129 states that "In fiscal year 2003, CCC was fully reimbursed for its prior year net realized losses." Please indicate the amounts of prior year net realized losses (annually, since 1992) for which the CCC has been fully reimbursed.

272. With respect to the US response to Question No. 226, is the Panel correct in understanding that the reflection of write-offs as part of the operating loss of the CCC which in turn was replenished through the annual appropriations process ended with the entry into force of the FCRA in fiscal year 1992? If not, what amounts have been replenished through this process annually since fiscal year 1992?

273. With respect to the US response to Question No. 225, what criteria does the CCC apply to "independently determine" that a debt is uncollectible? For post-1992 cohorts, what are these uncollectible amounts (an-

nually) and how, if at all, are such "uncollectible amounts" shown in Exhibit US-128?

274. The Panel notes the US statement in the US response to Question No. 81 that "All rescheduled claims are currently performing " and that "all payments due up to this point under [rescheduling] agreements have been received". However, the Panel also notes Exhibit US-129 (in particular, Note 5 on p. 22) and Brazil's reference thereto in Brazil's 28 January comments on the US response to Question No. 222. In this connection:

(a) How does the US respond to Brazil's statement in Brazil's 28 January comments that Exhibit US-129 confirms that rescheduling of export credit guarantee receivables cover both principal and interest, thereby confirming that not all of the rescheduled debt performs and that additional interest charges were also rescheduled?

(b) In Note 5 on p. 22 of Exhibit US-129, what is the definition of "non-performing"? What is the meaning of "delinquent"? What is the current principal balance and amount of interest of the three CCC export credit guarantee programme "receivables" in a non-performing status (individually and together, for GSM 102, GSM 103 and SCGP))? What is the amount of interest on non-reporting "receivables"?

(c) The Panel notes the US reference to the "Paris Club" in US response to Question No. 225. What is the P.L. 480 programme referred to in Note 5 on p. 22 of Exhibit US-129 (including the Paris Club debt reduction process and the HIPC Initiative) ? To what extent is the P.L. 480 programme and Paris Club process relevant to the export credit guarantee programmes at issue in this dispute? Please identify and give the amounts of all CCC export credit guarantee debt subject to the P.L. 480 debt reduction (or other similar) process since 1992.

(d) Can the US explain the process referred to in the second column of Note 5 on p. 22 ("CCC is awaiting an apportionment from the Office of Management and Budget before the transaction can be completed. Until such time, however, there is a 100% subsidy allowance established against the relevant debt as of September 30, 2003.") Please provide details of all such "apportionments" relating to the three export credit guarantee programmes in fiscal years 1992-2003.

275. Please provide evidence (or cite relevant portions of the record) that the premium rates for the export credit guarantee programmes are "reviewed annually" as stated in US 28 January comments on response to Question No. 223 (see also US 22 December response to Question No. 107; Brazil's 28 January 2004 comments on responses to Question No. 223.).

The Panel wishes to pose the following additional question to Brazil:

276. The Panel notes the parties' responses and comments relating to Question No. 252 concerning the time period within which any prohibited

measure must be withdrawn within the meaning of Article 4.7 of the *SCM Agreement*. Please supplement your original response, taking into account the particular nature of each alleged prohibited subsidy measure (i.e. "Step 2" payments under Section 1207(a) of the 2002 FSRI Act, export credit guarantee programmes and the ETI Act) and the functioning of the US legal and regulatory system in respect of these measures.

ANNEX L-1.23

COMMUNICATION TO BRAZIL AND THE UNITED STATES

16 February 2004

1. The Panel is in receipt of the letter from the U.S. dated 11 February, the response from Brazil dated 13 February and another US letter dated 16 February.

2. On page 2 of the United States letter of 11 February, with respect to item (b) of the Panel's supplementary request for information, the United States asks the Panel to specify which commodities are "covered commodities". We would like to clarify that "covered commodities" and "commodities covered", as used in the bullet points and sub-bullets, refer to wheat, corn, grain sorghum, barley, oats, upland cotton, rice, soybeans, "other oilseeds" as defined in Section 1001(9) of the FSRI Act of 2002, and peanuts, except that soybeans do not apply to PFC payments and "other oilseeds" and peanuts do not apply to PFC or MLA payments.

3. The Panel also confirms that the additional information sought for marketing year 2002 "with respect to all crops on cropland covered by the acreage reports" refers to the reports filed under Section 1105(c) of the FSRI Act of 2002. The relevant portions of the "above questions" are those that ask for planted acreage information for each Category of farms. All crops other than "covered commodities" as defined in Section 1001(4) of the FSRI Act of 2002 and peanuts may be aggregated as "other crops".

4. In relation to the third point the US raises in its letter dated 11 February, the Panel informs the parties as follows:

(a) Without prejudice to whether any further comments are necessary, we would consider the US request for another opportunity to comment if Brazil submits any such comments on the US submission entitled "Comments of the United States of America on the Comments of Brazil to US data Submitted on 18 and 19 December 2003" (submitted 11 February).

(b) The US would be granted until **Tuesday 3 March**, at the latest, to submit all remaining data that was requested by the Panel in its communication dated 3 February.

(c) The issuance of the descriptive part would be changed to **Friday 5 March**.

(d) The remainder of the Panel's schedule remains unchanged for the time being.

5. The Panel notes that the data submitted by the United States, as described in Exhibit US-145, does not include data on MLA and CCP payments. The Panel asks the United States to address these payments and include this information in its response to the supplementary request for information.

6. The Panel also notes that the US response to Panel Question No. 263 refers to Exhibit US-263. Could the United States please confirm that this should refer to Exhibit US-146.

7. The Panel further notes Brazil's request for an opportunity to comment after the United States has submitted the data referred to in paragraph 4(b) above. The Panel will consider this request after it has had the opportunity to review data submitted by the United States.

ANNEX L-1.24

COMMUNICATION TO BRAZIL AND THE UNITED STATES
20 February 2004

1. The Panel refers to its communication dated 16 February. Item 4 (a) of this communication deals with the request made by the United States (in its letter dated 11 February) that it be provided another opportunity to comment on a certain submission from Brazil. The Panel has informed parties in the same 4 (a) that it would consider this request if Brazil submits any such comments. The Panel has received on 18 February a submission entitled "Brazil's Comments on United States 11 February Comments on Brazil's 28 January 'Comments and Requests Regarding Data Provided by the United States on 18/19 December 2003 and the US Refusal to Provide Non-scrambled Data on 20 January 2004'". The Panel understands that this submission corresponds to what the United States was requesting to be given another opportunity to comment on. The Panel would now allow the United States to submit, if it so wishes, comments on this specific submission from Brazil by **Wednesday 25 February**. The Panel informs parties that it does not see, at this time, the need to have further opportunities to comment on this submission (if any) from the United States.

2. The Panel also takes note of Brazil's observation in paragraph 33 of its 18 February "Comments on US 11 February 2004 Answers to Additional Questions from the Panel Following the Second Meeting of the Panel with the Parties" that "...the Panel did not respond to Brazil's request that it deny the United States' efforts to decide at what pace it wishes to offer responses to the Panel's questions". The Panel also recalls the United States' original statement in connection with Question 264(b) that it "expects to be able to provide an answer within the same time period as its response to the Panel's supplemental request for information." In this connection, we wish to draw the parties' attention to our statement in item 4(b) of the 16 February communication, and to clarify that that statement also pertains to the United States response to Question 264(b). Thus, the United States has until **3 March**, at the latest, to submit its response. We further note that Brazil states in the same paragraph 33 that it "reserves the right to comment" on the United States response to Question 264(b). In line with what we mentioned in paragraph 7 of our communication dated 16 February, we would decide whether it is appropriate to give Brazil the opportunity, *after* we have had the opportunity to review the response from the United States.

ANNEX L-1.25

COMMUNICATION TO BRAZIL AND THE UNITED STATES
24 February 2004

The Panel is in receipt of the letter from the United States dated 23 February 2004.

After carefully considering the views of the United States, we now change the date by which the United States is expected to submit its comment from the date originally designated as 25 February in our communication dated 20 February, to **3 March 2004**.

All other statements in our communication dated 20 February remain unchanged.

ANNEX L-1.26

COMMUNICATION TO BRAZIL AND THE UNITED STATES

4 March 2003

The Panel is in receipt of the submissions from the United States dated 3 March. The Panel reminds parties of our communications dated 16, 20 and 24 February 2004, especially in relation to our intention to consider whether or not to allow Brazil to comment on certain US submissions. After carefully examining yesterday's submission from the United States, the Panel informs parties of the following amendment to the current timetable.

1. Brazil is granted until **10 March 2004** to submit comments, if any, on (a) the data supplied by the United States, dated 3 March, in the form of a CD-ROM (i.e. 8 data files therein) and (b) the submission entitled "Answers of the United States of America to Questions 264(b) Dated 3 February 2004, from the Panel to the Parties following the Second Panel Meeting". The Panel does not see the need to grant Brazil the opportunity to comment on any other submission from the United States.

2. The United States is granted until **15 March 2004** to submit comments, if any, on the submission from Brazil to be received by 10 March 2004.

3. The descriptive part will be issued on **16 March 2004**.

4. Comments on the descriptive part is to be received by **30 March 2004**.

5. The rest of the timetable remains unchanged for now.

ANNEX L-1.27

COMMUNICATION TO BRAZIL AND THE UNITED STATES

7 April 2004

The Panel informs the parties of the following change in the timetable for this dispute. As indicated, the Panel now intends to issue the interim report to the parties on Monday 26 April 2004.

Issuance of the interim report, including the findings and conclusions, to the parties:	26 April 2004
Deadline for parties to request review of part(s) of report:	10 May 2004
Interim review meeting with the parties, if requested. If interim review meeting not requested, the deadline for comments on each others' comment.	3 June 2004 (if a review meeting is to be held, **4 June** as well as 3 June, as necessary.)
Issuance of final report to the parties:	18 June 2004
Circulation of the final report to Members:	[after translation]

ANNEX L-2.1

COMMUNICATION TO THIRD PARTIES

28 May 2003

Your delegation has reserved its rights to participate as a third party in the Panel *United States - Subsidies on Upland Cotton (DS267)*- Complaint by Brazil - established by the DSB on 18 March 2003. The Panel has now started its work.

Attached you will find the timetable and working procedures adopted by the Panel for this dispute in accordance with Article 12.1 of the *Understanding on Rules and Procedures Governing the Settlement of Disputes* (the "*DSU*").

As indicated in the attached timetable, prior to the submission by the parties of their first written submissions in these proceedings, the Panel has requested the parties to address, in their initial briefs to the Panel (to be submitted on *5 June 2003*), the following:

- whether Article 13 of the *Agreement on Agriculture* precludes the Panel from considering Brazil's claims under the *Agreement on Subsidies and Countervailing Measures* in these proceedings in the absence of a prior conclusion by the Panel that certain conditions of Article 13 remain unfulfilled. In particular, the Panel invites the parties to explain their interpretation of the words "exempt from actions" as used in Article 13 of the *Agreement on Agriculture*, as well as bringing to the Panel's attention any other relevant provisions of the covered agreements and any other relevant considerations which the parties consider should guide the Panel's consideration of this issue. For greater clarity, the Panel invites the parties, during this initial stage of the proceedings, to focus on matters of legal interpretation, rather than upon the submission of any factual evidence that might be associated with the substantive elements of Article 13.

As also indicated in the attached timetable, the Panel will invite the parties to submit any written comments on each other's comments on this issue (i.e. on *13 June 2003*). The Panel intends to rule on these issues on *20 June 2003*, prior to the parties' submission of their first written submissions.

We have invited the parties to serve also on the third parties their initial briefs and any responding comments. The Panel also invites third parties to submit any written comments they might have concerning the initial phase of these proceedings. **The deadline for any initial third party comments on the specific issue identified above is *10 June 2003*.**

Moreover, as also indicated in the attached timetable, the Panel invites your delegation to present its views at a meeting with the parties to the dispute and other third parties, which is scheduled for *24 July 2003*. The exact time and venue will be communicated to you in due time.

The Panel would appreciate it if your delegation could provide the Panel with your written submission by 5.30 p.m. on *15 July 2003*. If you so wish, this written statement may take the place of an oral presentation to the Panel. The Panel would appreciate the submission being kept as short as possible. I would appreciate it if you would advise the Panel before *1 July 2003* through me as Secretary to the Panel (telephone 022/739 6419) whether your delegation will be represented at the meeting and whether your delegation will require interpretation services into and out of English.

[Attachment omitted]

ANNEX L-2.2

COMMUNICATION TO THIRD PARTIES

25 July 2003

Please find attached a communication from the Panel on the following issues:

1. The Panel's view on the preliminary ruling requested by the United States.
2. Panel's questions to third parties.

The Panel's questions are intended to facilitate the work of the Panel, and do not in any way prejudge the Panel's findings on the matter before it. Nor does the fact that the Panel has placed these questions under certain headings prejudge the Panel's findings on the matter before it. Each third party is free to respond to or comment on questions posed to the other third parties.

Please be reminded that you are requested to submit answers by the close of business of 4 August 2003. Subsequently, third parties can submit comments to other's responses by the close of business 22 August.

[1st attachment omitted]

Questions from the Panel to the third parties – First session of the first substantive Panel meeting

ARTICLE 13 OF THE AGREEMENT ON AGRICULTURE

1. Australia has argued that Article 13 of the *Agreement on Agriculture* is an affirmative defence. How do you reconcile this with your view that the conditions in Article 13 are a "prerequisite" to the availability of a right or privilege? **Australia** Would other third parties have any comments on Australia's assertion? **3RD parties, in particular Argentina, Benin, China, Chinese Taipei**

ARTICLE 13(B) OF THE *AGREEMENT ON AGRICULTURE*: DOMESTIC SUPPORT MEASURES

2. Please explain the difference, if any, between the meaning of "defined" and the meaning of "fixed" in the phrase "a defined and fixed base period" in paragraph 6(a) of Annex 2 of the *Agreement on Agriculture* . **3rd parties, in particular Australia, Argentina, Canada, EC, NZ**

3. Please explain the meaning of "a" in "a defined and fixed base period" in paragraph 6(a) of Annex 2 of the *Agreement on Agriculture*, the meaning of "the" in "the base period" in paragraphs 6(b), (c) and (d), and the difference between these and the phrase "based on the years 1986-88" in Annex 3. **3rd parties, in particular Australia, Argentina, Canada, EC, NZ**

4. How often can a Member define and fix a base period in accordance with paragraph 6 of Annex 2 of the *Agreement on Agriculture*? **3rd parties, in particular Australia, Argentina, Canada, China, EC, NZ**

5. Do you agree that a payment penalty based on crops produced is "related to type of production"? **EC**

6. Please explain the meaning of the word "criteria" in Article 6.1 and 7.1. What effect, if any, does the use of the word "Accordingly" in paragraph 1 of Annex 2 of the *Agreement on Agriculture* have on the meaning of the preceding sentence? **3rd parties, in particular Australia, Argentina, Canada, EC, NZ**

7. Please explain the meaning of the words "the fundamental requirement" as used in paragraph 1 of Annex 2 of the *Agreement on Agriculture.* **3rd parties, in particular Australia, Argentina, Canada, EC, NZ**

8. In your oral statement, you emphasize the use of the word "criteria" in other parts of the *Agreement on Agriculture*, as distinct from the reference to "fundamental requirement" in the first sentence of paragraph 1 of Annex 2. Is it the case that sub-paragraphs (a) and (b) of paragraph 1 of Annex 2 are also "criteria"? **EC**

9. If the first sentence of paragraph 1 of Annex 2 is a stand-alone obligation, does this allow effects-based claims of non-compliance with Annex 2? If so, how does this affect the purpose of Article 13(b)? **3rd parties ' in particular Australia, Argentina, Canada, EC, NZ**

10. If the first sentence of paragraph 1 of Annex 2 is not a stand-alone obligation, then must new, non- or minimally trade-distorting measures that do not conform to the criteria listed in Annex 2 be classified as non-Green Box? **3rd parties, in particular Australia, Argentina, Canada, EC, NZ**

11. If the first sentence of paragraph 1 of Annex 2 expresses a general principle which informs the interpretation of the criteria in Annex 2, please explain how this affects the assessment of the direct payments programme's compliance with paragraph 6 of Annex 2. **3rd parties, in particular, Australia, Argentina, Canada, EC, NZ**

12. Where does Article 13(b) require a year-on-year comparison? **3RD parties, in particular Australia, Argentina, Canada, China, EC, NZ**

13. Does a failure by a Member to comply in a given *year* with either the chapeau of Article 13(b) or the proviso in subparagraph (ii) of Article 13(b) impact its entitlement to benefit in an earlier or a later year from the exemption from action provided by Article 13(b)? **3RD parties, in particular Australia, Argentina, Canada, China, EC, NZ**

14. Does a failure of a Member to comply with Article 13(b) in respect of a *specific commodity* impact its entitlement to benefit in respect of other agricultural products from the exemption from action provided by Article 13(b)? **3RD parties, in particular Australia, Argentina, Canada, China, EC, NZ**

15. Is there any basis on which counter-cyclical payments could be considered product-specific? **3RD parties, in particular Australia, Argentina, Canada, China, EC, NZ**

16. If the word "specific" were deleted from Article 13(b)(ii), would this change the meaning of the subparagraph? **3RD parties, in particular Australia, Argentina, Benin Canada, China, EC, NZ**

17. What is the relevance, if any, of the concept of "specificity" in Article 2 of the *SCM Agreement* and references to "a product" or "subsidized product" in certain provisions of the *SCM Agreement* to the meaning of "support to a specific commodity" in Article 13(b)(ii) *Agreement on Agriculture*? **3RD parties, in particular Australia, Argentina, Canada, China, EC, NZ**

18. Benin's oral statement considers the phrase "support to a specific commodity" in Article 13(b)(ii) of the *Agreement on Agriculture*. How does Benin believe that phrase is best interpreted. Please substantiate your response, commenting on other submissions by parties and third parties as you believe appropriate. **Benin**

19. Where does Article 13(b)(ii) require a year-on-year comparison? **3rd parties, in particular Australia, Argentina, Canada, EC, NZ**

20. Does Article 13(b)(ii) require a comparison of support granted with support decided? How could such a comparison be made?

21. Please comment on Brazil's assertion that the terms "grant" and "decided" in Article 13(b)(ii) have broadly the same meaning. If so, why did the drafters not use the same term? **3rd parties, in particular, Australia, Argentina, Canada, China, EC, NZ**

22. What is the meaning of "support" in *Agreement on Agriculture* 13(b)(ii) ? Why would it be used differently from Annex 3, where it refers to total outlays? **3rd parties, in particular, Australia, Argentina, Canada, China, EC, NZ**

23. Should support be compared under Article 13(b)(ii) in terms of unit of production or total volume of support or both? **3rd parties, in particular, Australia, Argentina, Canada, China, EC, NZ**

24. Please provide any written drafting history which could shed light on why the proviso was added to what is now Article 13(b)(ii) of the *Agreement on Agriculture* and, in particular, why the words "grant" and "decided" were used. **EC**

25. Please comment on an interpretation of the words "decided during" in Article 13(b)(ii) that would read them as synonymous with the words "authorized during". **3rd parties, in particular Australia, Argentina, Canada, China, EC, NZ**

26. Under Article 13(b)(ii), a comparison is required between support at different times. One of the issues which is contested between the parties is whether the only later period that the Panel can consider is the present one (i.e. the period underway at the time of the request for establishment of the Panel). This argument is based on the present tense of the words "do not grant" in the English text. The Panel asks whether there is any difference in the verb tense as used in the Spanish-language text, or any other difference which might aid the Panel in interpreting these words? **Argentina, EC, Paraguay, Venezuela**

27. If the 1992 "decision" led to or was the funding source for the money provided in 1992 and later years, is it the full amount of all that funding that

constitutes the "support" decided in 1992? If the answer to this question is that it is the full amount of all the support provided pursuant to the "decision" that must be taken into account, must this be compared with the total amount of support that will or might flow from the decision made in the more recent period for the purposes of the comparison required under Article 13(b)(ii)? If a Member did not make a "decision" (however that may be interpreted) in 1992 about "support", is it the case that the Member has a zero base for the purposes of the comparison required under Article 13(b)(ii)? **EC**

28. In paragraph 13 of Australia's oral statement, you state that a "question" is: "could conditions of price competition for the purposes of a non-violation or impairment claim be assessed solely on the basis of budgetary outlay figures, as argued by Brazil, or on the basis of a rate of payment, as argued by the United States? In Australia's view, both factors put forward by Brazil and the United States would properly form a part of that assessment, but not the whole." Could you please clarify this statement (indicating other elements which would complete the "whole" and explain its relevance for the purposes of our consideration of Article 13 of the *Agreement on Agriculture*? **Australia, EC**

EXPORT CREDIT GUARANTEE PROGRAMMES

29. (a) Is an export credit guarantee a financial contribution in the form of a "potential direct transfer of funds or liabilities (e.g. loan guarantee)" within the meaning of Article 1.1(a)(1)(i) of the *SCM Agreement*? Why or why not? **3rd parties, in particular, Argentina, Canada, EC, NZ**

(b) How, if at all, would this be relevant to the claims of Brazil? **3rd parties, in particular, Argentina, Canada, EC, NZ**

30. The Panel could arguably take the view that Articles 1 and 3 of the *SCM Agreement* were relevant in assessing the WTO-consistency of United States export credit guarantees. The Panel would therefore appreciate third party views on this situation, including with respect to the viability of an *a contrario* interpretation of item (j) of the Illustrative List (as addressed in paragraphs 180-183 of the United States' first written submission). **3rd parties, in particular, Argentina, Canada, EC, NZ**

31. If the Panel decides to refer to provisions of the *SCM Agreement* for contextual guidance in the interpretation of the terms in Article 10 *Agreement on Agriculture*, should the Panel refer to item (j) or Articles 1 and 3 of the *SCM Agreement* or both? . **3rd parties, in particular, Argentina, Canada, EC, NZ**

32. The Panel's attention has been drawn to Article 14(c) of the *SCM Agreement* (see third party submission of Canada) and to the panel report in DS 222 *Canada- Export Credits and Loan Guarantees*. How and to what extent are Article 14(c) of the *SCM Agreement*, and the cited panel report, relevant to the issue of whether or not the United States export credit guarantee programmes confer a "benefit"? What would the appropriate market benchmark be to use for any comparison? Please cite any other relevant material. . **3rd parties, in particular, Argentina, Canada, EC, NZ**

33. What is the relevance (if any) of Brazil's statement that : "...export credit guarantees for exports of agricultural exports [sic] are not available on the marketplace by commercial lenders." . **3rd parties, in particular, Argentina, Canada, EC, NZ**

34. Comment on the United States' view of the meaning of "long term operating costs and losses" in item (j) of the Illustrative List of Export Subsidies in Annex I of the *SCM Agreement* as meaning "claims paid" under the export credit guarantee programmes. Does the United States' interpretation give meaning to both "costs" and "losses"? Do claims paid represent "losses"? **3rd parties, in particular, Argentina, Canada, EC, NZ**

35. Did the drafters of the *Agreement on Agriculture* include export credit guarantees in Article 9.1 of the *Agreement on Agriculture*? Why or why not? **3rd parties, in particular, Argentina, Canada, EC, NZ**

36. Please explain any possible significance the following statements may have in respect of Brazil's claims about GSM102 and 103 (7 CFR 1493.10(a)(2), Exhibit BRA-38) **3rd parties, in particular, Argentina, Canada, EC, NZ**

(a) "The programmes operate in cases where credit is necessary to increase or maintain US exports to a foreign market and where US financial institutions would be unwilling to provide financing without CCC's guarantee. (7 CFR 1493.10(a)(2) Exhibit BRA-38)

(b) "The programmes are operated in a manner intended not to interfere with markets for cash sales. The programmes are targeted toward those countries where the guarantee is necessary to secure financing of the exports but which have sufficient financial strength so that foreign exchange will be available for scheduled payments." (7 CFR 1493.10(a)(2) Exhibit BRA-38)

(c) "In providing this credit guarantee facility, CCC seeks to expand market opportunities for US agricultural exporters and assist long-term market development for US agricultural commodities." (7 CFR 1493.10(a)(2) Exhibit BRA-38)

37. The United States seems to argue that, at present, by virtue of Article 10.2 of the *Agreement on Agriculture*, there are **no** disciplines on agricultural export credit guarantees under the *Agreement on Agriculture* (or the *SCM Agreement*).

(a) Comment on the following proposition: a WTO Member may therefore extend agricultural export credit guarantees without charging a premium, and for an indefinite period, in addition to any other terms and conditions it may wish? How would this reconcile with the title of Article 10 of the *Agreement on Agriculture* ("Prevention of Circumvention on Export Subsidy Commitments"), and with other commitments contained in the *Agreement on Agriculture*? Please cite any relevant material, including any past WTO dispute settlement cases. **3rd parties, in particular, Argentina, Canada, EC, NZ**

(b) If, as the United States argues, there are no disciplines on export credit guarantees in the *Agreement on Agriculture*, how could export credit guarantees "conform fully to the provisions of Part V" of the *Agreement on Agriculture* within the meaning of Article 13 (how can you assess "conformity" or non-conformity with non-existent disciplines)? **3rd parties, in particular, Argentina, Canada, EC, NZ**

STEP 2 PAYMENTS

38. Please comment on the statement in note 119 of the United States' first written submission that "...to the extent a consumer that had intended to export instead opens the bale, then that consumer could still obtain the Step 2 payment upon submission of the requisite documentation". The Panel notes that Step 2 payments all involve upland cotton produced in the United States. What are the two distinct factual situations that Step 2 payments involve? Other than the panel report in *Canada-Dairy* and the findings of the Appellate Body in *US-FSC* (21.5)[1], do any other dispute settlement reports offer guidance on this issue? For example, how, if at all is the Appellate Body's report in *Canada-Aircraft* relevant here?[2] . **3rd parties, in particular, Australia, Argentina, NZ, Paraguay**

39. Please comment on the United States assertions at paragraph 129 of its first written submission, that "[t]he programme is indifferent to whether recipients of the benefit of this programme are exporters or parties that open bales for the processing of manufacturing raw cotton into cotton products in the United States." . **3rd parties, in particular, Australia, Argentina, NZ, Paraguay**

40. With respect to paragraph 32 of the oral statement of the EC, are subsidies contingent on the use of domestic goods consistent with the *AoA*? Does the phrase "provide support in favour of domestic producers" refer to, and/or permit such subsidies? What is the meaning and relevance of this (if any) to Brazil's

---

1 "We recall that the ETI measure grants a tax exemption in two different sets of circumstances: (a) where property is produced *within* the United States and held for use *outside* the United States; and (b) where property is produced *outside* the United States and held for use outside the United States. Our conclusion that the ETI measure grants subsidies that are export contingent in the first set of circumstances is not affected by the fact that the subsidy can also be obtained in the second set of circumstances. The fact that the subsidies granted in the second set of circumstances *might* not be export contingent does not dissolve the export contingency arising in the first set of circumstances.[1] Conversely, the export contingency arising in these circumstances has no bearing on whether there is an export contingent subsidy in the second set of circumstances. Where a United States taxpayer is simultaneously producing property within and outside the United States, for direct use outside the United States, subsidies may be granted under the ETI measure in respect of both sets of property. The subsidy granted with respect to the property produced within the United States, and exported from there, is export contingent within the meaning of Article 3.1(a) of the *SCM Agreement*, irrespective of whether the subsidy given in respect of property produced outside the United States is also export contingent."

2 There, the Appellate Body stated that,

> "the fact that some of TPC's contributions, in some industry sectors, are *not* contingent upon export performance, does not necessarily mean that the same is true for all of TPC's contributions. It is enough to show that one or some of TPC's contributions do constitute subsidies "contingent ... in fact ... upon export performance".[2]

claims under Article 3 of the *SCM Agreement* and Article III:4 of the GATT 1994.. **3rd parties, in particular, Australia, Argentina, EC, NZ, Paraguay**

ETI ACT

41. Concerning its claims on the ETI Act, Brazil relies on the *US – FSC* case. However, it appears that the United States did not raise the issue of the Peace Clause in that case, nor did the US appear to invoke Article 6 of the *Agreement on Agriculture*. If the Panel's understanding is correct, how, if at all, are these differences relevant here? **Argentina, China, EC, NZ**

42. How do you view the reference in paragraph 43 of the EC's third party oral statement with respect to the relevance of Article 17.14 of the DSU, and, in particular, the phrase "a final resolution to *that* dispute" (emphasis added)? Please explain the use, and relevance (if any) of the term "disputes" in Articles 9.3 and 12 and Appendix 3 of the DSU, and please cite any other provisions you consider relevant. **Argentina, China, EC, NZ**

ANNEX L-2.3

COMMUNICATION TO THIRD PARTIES

30 July 2003

Taking into account a 29 July 2003 communication received from the United States, and Brazil's 30 July response, the Panel has decided to extend the deadline for the submission of the parties' and third parties' responses to questions from Monday 4 August to **Monday 11 August** (**17h30** (Geneva time)).

The Panel has also decided upon the following additional changes to its schedule:

Panel's views on certain issues:	5 September 2003
Further submission of Brazil:	9 September 2003
Further submission of the US:	23 September 2003
Further submission of the third parties (as necessary):	29 September 2003

For the time being, all other dates remain unchanged. This includes the deadline for the submission of the parties' and third parties' comments on responses. It also includes the dates for the resumption of the first substantive meeting and the third party session (as necessary) and the second substantive meeting (i.e. 7-9 October).

ANNEX L-2.4

COMMUNICATION TO THIRD PARTIES

13 October 2003

Please find attached the Panel's questions to third parties following the resumed first session of the first substantive Panel meeting.

The Panel's questions are intended to facilitate the work of the Panel, and do not in any way prejudge the Panel's findings on the matter before it. Nor does the fact that the Panel has placed these questions under certain headings prejudge the Panel's findings on the matter before it. Each third party is free to respond to or comment on questions posed to the other third parties.

You are requested to submit answers by close of business on **27 October 2003**. All provisions of the existing working procedures, including the time specified in paragraph 17(b) of the Panel's existing working procedures for service of submissions by third parties, are confirmed.

Questions from the Panel to the third parties – resumed first session of the first substantive Panel meeting

A. QUESTIONS TO INDIVIDUAL THIRD PARTIES

43. Please elaborate, citing figures, on your statement that polyester fibre prices actually follow cotton prices. Argentina

44. Please explain how Articles 5 and 6 of the *SCM Agreement* and Article XVI of the GATT 1994 would permit or require the Panel to take account of any effects of the subsidies in question on the interests of Members other than the complaining party. **Benin and Chad**

45. In relation to the term "same market" in Article 6.3(c) of the *SCM Agreement*, the EC states in paragraph 10 of its oral statement that a "world market" cannot exist if there are significant trade barriers between Members. On the other hand, the Panel notes that in relation to cotton, the EC takes the position in paragraph 14 of its further submission that the term "same market" in Article 6.3(c) should be read to include the domestic market of the subsidising Member. In light of the fact that many domestic cotton markets, possibly including that of China, have significant trade barriers, how can the EC reconcile these two positions? **EC**

46. Should the Panel prefer a concept of allocation of the benefit of subsidies to later years, to a concept of fully expensing subsidies to the year in which the benefit was provided? **EC**

47. In the EC further submission, it is said that significantly different conditions of competition in regional markets may prevent the Panel from arriving at the conclusion that there is a world market. Is the payment of a subsidy a "condi-

tion of competition" and, if so, how should that impact upon the Panel's analysis? **EC**

48. In the further submission of India, it is stated that "there is "no obligation under the *SCM Agreement* to demonstrate serious prejudice separately after establishing that one of the effects of a subsidy listed under Article 6.3 applies, as the effects listed in Article 6.3 themselves equate to serious prejudice". How does this view relate to Article 6.3(d), which appears to contain no element of degree? **India**

B. QUESTIONS TO ALL THIRD PARTIES

49. What is the meaning and effect of the introductory phrase of Article 3 of the *SCM Agreement* ("Except as provided in the *Agreement on Agriculture*...")? **All third parties**

50. According to its revised timetable, the Panel will issue its report to the parties after the end of the 2003 calendar year. Does this have any impact on "exempt[ion] from actions" under Article 13(b)(ii) and 13(c)(ii) of the *Agreement on Agriculture*? **All third parties**

51. How should the concept of specificity – and, in particular, the concept of specificity to "an enterprise or industry or group of enterprises or industries" - in Article 2 of the *SCM Agreement* apply to subsidies in respect of agricultural commodities? Please answer the following questions, citing the principles in Article 2 of the *SCM Agreement*: **All third parties**

(a) is a subsidy in respect of all agricultural, but not other, products specific?

(b) is a subsidy in respect of all agricultural crops (i.e. but not to other agricultural commodities, such as livestock) specific?

(c) is a subsidy in respect of certain identified agricultural products specific?

(d) is a subsidy in respect of upland cotton, but not other products, specific?

(e) is a subsidy in respect of a certain proportion of the value of total US commodities (or total US agricultural commodities) specific?

(f) is a subsidy in respect of a certain proportion of total US farmland specific?

52. The Panel notes that different remedies are available in respect of prohibited and actionable subsidies under Article 4.7 and 7.8 of the *SCM Agreement*. If the Panel were to conclude that a subsidy was prohibited and were to make a recommendation under Article 4.7 of the *SCM Agreement* to withdraw the subsidy without delay, can the Panel:

(a) also conclude that the same subsidy had resulted in adverse effects to the interests of another Member? If so, what would be the value of such a conclusion in terms of the settlement of the matter before the Panel? **All third parties**

(b) take into account the effects of the interaction of those prohibited subsidies with other, allegedly, actionable subsidies? If so, how is this relevant to the issue of causation under Article 5 of the *SCM Agreement*? **All third parties**

53. Would a finding of serious prejudice under Article 5(c) of the *SCM Agreement* be determinative for a finding under Article XVI:1 of the GATT 1994? Why or why not? What, if any, is the role of footnote 13 of the *SCM Agreement* in this context? **All third parties**

54. Are US cotton producers able to cover the fixed and variable costs without subsidies? Please provide substantiating evidence. Of what relevance is this, if any, to Brazil's actionable subsidy claims ? **All third parties**

55. In light of the fact that certain third parties have provided submissions about the price effect of claimed US subsidies, which Member or Members is, or are, the "other party" under Article 6.3(c) ("*another Member*") for the purposes of these proceedings? **All third parties**

56. Please respond to the following questions concerning the relationship between Article XVI:3 of the GATT 1994, the disciplines on export subsidies and domestic support in the *Agreement on Agriculture* and the disciplines on prohibited export subsidies and actionable subsidies in Articles 3, 5(c) and 6.3(d) of the *SCM Agreement*. **All third parties**

(a) Are agricultural domestic support programmes challengeable under Article XVI:3 of the GATT 1994? How, if at all, is the title of Section B of Article XVI ("Additional provisions on *export subsidies*" (emphasis added)) relevant? How, if at all, are Articles 13 and 21.1, or any other provisions, of the *Agreement on Agriculture,* relevant?

(b) Are the requirements of Article XVI:3 of the GATT 1994 reflected in, developed by or subsumed by the requirements in Article 6.3(d) of the *SCM Agreement*, or in any other provisions of the covered agreements? Of what relevance, if any, is the Appellate Body Report in *US-FSC*, para. 117[1] here?

---

1 WT/DS108/AB/R, para 117:

"... the provisions of the *SCM Agreement* do not provide explicit assistance as to the relationship between the export subsidy provisions of the *SCM Agreement* and Article XVI:4 of the GATT 1994. In the absence of any such specific textual guidance, we must determine the relationship between Articles 1.1(a)(1) and 3.1(a) of the *SCM Agreement* and Article XVI:4 of the GATT 1994 on the basis of the texts of the relevant provisions as a whole. It is clear from even a cursory examination of Article XVI:4 of the GATT 1994 that it differs very substantially from the subsidy provisions of the *SCM Agreement*, and, in particular, from the export subsidy provisions of both the *SCM Agreement* and the *Agreement on Agriculture*. First of all, the *SCM Agreement* contains an express definition of the term "subsidy" which is not contained in Article XVI:4. In fact, as we have observed previously, the *SCM Agreement* contains a broad package of new export subsidy disciplines that "go well beyond merely applying and interpreting Articles VI, XVI and XXIII of the GATT 1947". Next, Article XVI:4 prohibits export subsidies only when they

(c) Of what relevance, if any, is the fact that the definition of "subsidy" in Article 1 of the *SCM Agreement* and the prohibition on subsidies contingent upon export in Article 3.1(a) were introduced in the Uruguay Round, but did not exist at the time that the GATT 1947 was negotiated?

---

result in the export sale of a product at a price lower than the "comparable price charged for the like product to buyers in the domestic market." In contrast, the *SCM Agreement* establishes a much broader prohibition against *any* subsidy which is "contingent upon export performance". To say the least, the rule contained in Article 3.1(a) of the *SCM Agreement* that all subsidies which are "contingent upon export performance" are prohibited is significantly different from a rule that prohibits only those subsidies which result in a lower price for the exported product than the comparable price for that product when sold in the domestic market. Thus, whether or not a measure is an export subsidy under Article XVI:4 of the GATT 1947 provides no guidance in determining whether that measure is a prohibited export subsidy under Article 3.1(a) of the *SCM Agreement.* Also, and significantly, Article XVI:4 of the GATT 1994 does not apply to "primary products", which include agricultural products. Unquestionably, the explicit export subsidy disciplines, relating to agricultural products, contained in Articles 3, 8, 9 and 10 of the *Agreement on Agriculture* must clearly take precedence over the *exemption* of primary products from export subsidy disciplines in Article XVI:4 of the GATT 1994."

ANNEX M

WORKING PROCEDURES AND TIMETABLE OF THE PANEL

Contents	Page

ANNEX M-1

WORKING PROCEDURES FOR THE PANEL

1. In its proceedings the Panel shall follow the relevant provisions of the Dispute Settlement Understanding (DSU). In addition, the following working procedures shall apply.

2. The Panel shall meet in closed session. The parties to the dispute, and interested third parties, shall be present at the meetings only when invited by the Panel to appear before it.

3. The deliberations of the Panel and the documents submitted to it shall be kept confidential. Nothing in the DSU shall preclude a party to a dispute from disclosing statements of its own positions to the public. Members shall treat as confidential information submitted by another Member to the Panel which that Member has designated as confidential. Where a party to a dispute submits a confidential version of its written submissions to the Panel, it shall also, upon request of a Member, provide a non-confidential summary of the information contained in its submissions that could be disclosed to the public.[1]

4. Before the first substantive meeting of the Panel with the parties, the parties to the dispute shall transmit to the Panel written submissions in which they present the facts of the case, their arguments and their counter-arguments, respectively. Third parties may transmit to the Panel written submissions after the first written submissions of the parties have been submitted.

5. At its first substantive meeting with the parties, the Panel shall ask Brazil to present its case. Subsequently, and at the same meeting, the United States will be asked to present its point of view. Third parties will be asked to present their views thereafter at the separate session of the same meeting set aside for that purpose. The parties will then be allowed an opportunity for final statements, with Brazil presenting its statement first.

6. All third parties which have notified their interest in the dispute to the Dispute Settlement Body shall be invited in writing to present their views during a

[1] The Panel notes that parties have agreed between themselves as to applicable deadlines for the submission of non-confidential summaries: 14 days after the submission of the confidential version.

session of the substantive meeting of the Panel set aside for that purpose. All such third parties may be present during the entirety of this session.

7. Formal rebuttals shall be made at a second substantive meeting of the Panel. The United States shall have the right to take the floor first, to be followed by Brazil. The parties shall submit, prior to that meeting, written rebuttals to the Panel.

8. The Panel may at any time put questions to the parties and to the third parties and ask them for explanations either in the course of the substantive meeting or in writing. Answers to questions shall be submitted in writing by the date(s) specified by the Panel. Answers to questions after the first meeting shall be submitted in writing at the same time as the written rebuttals, unless the Panel specifies a different deadline.

9. The parties to the dispute and any third party invited to present its views shall make available to the Panel and the other party or parties a written version of their oral statements, preferably at the end of the meeting, and in any event not later than the day following the meeting. Parties and third parties are encouraged to provide the Panel and other participants in the meeting with a provisional written version of their oral statements at the time the oral statement is presented.

10. In the interest of full transparency, the presentations, rebuttals and statements shall be made in the presence of the parties. Moreover, each party's written submissions, including responses to questions put by the Panel, shall be made available to the other party.

11. The parties shall provide the Secretariat with an executive summary of the claims and arguments contained in their written submissions, oral presentations, and, if necessary, answers to questions. These executive summaries will be used by the Secretariat only for the purpose of assisting the Secretariat in drafting a concise arguments section of the Panel report so as to facilitate timely translation and circulation of the Panel report to the Members. They shall not serve in any way as a substitute for the submissions of the parties. The summaries of the first written submission and rebuttal written submission shall be limited to ten (10) pages each, and the summaries of the oral statements at the meetings will be limited to five (5) pages each. The Panel will determine the page limit for executive summaries of parties' responses to questions, if necessary and as appropriate. Third parties are requested to provide the Panel with executive summaries of their written submissions and oral presentations, of no more than 5 pages each. The executive summaries shall be submitted to the Secretariat within ten days of the original submission, presentation or, if necessary, written replies, concerned. Paragraph 17 shall apply to the service of executive summaries.

12. A party shall submit any request for preliminary ruling not later than its first submission to the Panel. If the complaining party requests such a ruling, the respondent shall submit its response to the request in its first submission. If the respondent requests such a ruling, the complaining party shall submit its response to the request prior to the first substantive meeting of the Panel, at a time to be determined by the Panel in light of the request. Exceptions to this procedure will be granted upon a showing of good cause.

13. Parties shall submit all factual evidence to the Panel no later than during the first substantive meeting, except with respect to evidence necessary for purposes of rebuttals or answers to questions. Exceptions to this procedure will be granted upon a showing of good cause. The other party shall be accorded a period of time for comment, as appropriate, on any new factual evidence submitted after the first substantive meeting.

14. The parties to the dispute have the right to determine the composition of their own delegations. The parties shall have the responsibility for all members of their delegations and shall ensure that all members of the delegation act in accordance with the rules of the DSU and the Working Procedures of this Panel, particularly in regard to confidentiality of the proceedings. The parties as well as third parties shall provide a list of their delegation before each meeting to Mr. Hiromi Yano (office 3036 ; e-mail hiromi.yano@wto.org).

15. To facilitate the maintenance of the record of the dispute, and to maximize the clarity of submissions, in particular the references to exhibits submitted by parties, parties shall sequentially number their exhibits throughout the course of the dispute. For example, exhibits submitted by Brazil could be numbered BRA-1, BRA-2, etc. If the last exhibit in connection with the first submission was numbered BRA-5, the first exhibit of the next submission thus would be numbered BRA-6.

16. Following issuance of the interim report, the parties shall have two weeks to submit written requests to review precise aspects of the interim report and to request a further meeting with the Panel. The right to request such a meeting must be exercised no later than at that time. Following receipt of any written requests for review, if no further meeting with the Panel is requested, the parties shall have the opportunity, within a time-period specified by the Panel, to submit written comments on the other party's written requests for review. Such comments shall be strictly limited to responding to the other party's written request for review.

17. The following procedures regarding service of documents shall apply:

(a) Each party and third party shall serve all of its written submissions, executive summaries and written versions of oral statements, directly on all other parties, and on third parties as appropriate, and confirm that it has done so at the time it provides those submissions to the Secretariat.

(b) The parties and third parties should provide their submissions to the Secretariat by 5:30 p.m. on the deadlines established by the Panel, unless a different time is set by the Panel.

(c) The parties and third parties shall provide the Secretariat with nine paper copies of each of their written submissions. Seven of these copies should be filed with Mr. Ferdinand Ferranco (Office 3154). Two copies should be filed with the Secretary to the Panel. The final written versions of the parties' and third parties' oral statements shall be provided not later than noon of the day following the date of the presentation.

(d) The parties and third parties shall provide electronic copies of all submissions to the Secretariat at the time they provide their submissions, if possible in a format compatible with that used by the Secretariat. If the electronic version is provided by e-mail, it should be addressed to DSRegistry@wto.org, and cc'd to susan.hainsworth@wto.org, matthew.kennedy@wto.org, *paul.shanahan@wto.org*, thomas.friedheim@wto.org and hiromi.yano@wto.org. If a diskette is provided, it should be delivered to Mr. Ferdinand Ferranco.

(e) The Panel will endeavour to provide the parties with an electronic version of the descriptive part, the interim report and the final report, as well as of other documents as appropriate. When the Panel transmits to the parties or third parties both paper and electronic versions of a document, the paper version shall constitute the official version for the purposes of the record of the dispute.

ANNEX M-2

TIMETABLE

UNITED STATES – SUBSIDIES ON UPLAND COTTON (wt/ds267)

Timetable for Panel Proceedings[1]

1.	Establishment of the Panel:	18 March 2003
2.	Constitution of the Panel:	19 May 2003
3.	The following dates apply:	
(a)	Organizational meeting:	28 May 2003
(b)	Parties' comments on certain issues as indicated in the cover letter	5 June 2003
(c)	Third parties' comments on certain issues	10 June 2003
(d)	Parties' comments on each others' and third parties' comments submitted	13 June 2003
(e)	Issuance of Panel ruling on certain issues	20 June 2003
(f)	First submission of Brazil (complaining party)	24 June 2003
(g)	First submission of the US (party complained against)	11 July 2003
(h)	Submissions from third parties:	15 July 2003
(i)	First substantive meeting with the parties [2]:	22, 23 July 2003 24 July 2003
(j)	Third party session:	
(k)	Receipt of written rebuttals of the parties:	29 August 2003 [3]
(l)	Second substantive meeting with the parties:	17,18 September 2003[4]

[1] As was presented to parties and third parties on 28 May 2003. Subsequent changes are indicated in footnotes. Original footnote omitted.

[2] In a communication delivered on 20 June 2003 in accordance with item (e) of the timetable above, the Panel changed this meeting (including the third party session) to the "**first session of the first substantive meeting**" . The same communication also established the following dates: (a) the **Panel's view on certain issues** (i.e. issues relating to the "Peace Clause") to be issued on 1 September 2003, (b) **second session of the first substantive meeting** to be held on 7- 9 October 2003 (third party session held on 8 October), and (c) deadlines to submit further submissions for this second session: 4 September (from Brazil), 18 September (from the US) and 22 September (from the third parties). These dates were further changed by the Panel's communication dated 30 July to : (a) the Panel's view on "certain issues" on 5 September and (b) deadline to submit further submissions from Brazil by 9 September, from the US by 23 September (changed further to 29 September by the Panel's communication dated 12 September and changed again to 30 September by the Panel's communication dated 24 September), and from third parties by 29 September (changed further to 3 October by the Panel's communication dated 12 September). The 12 September communication from the Panel established a deadline for parties to submit, before the second session of the second substantive meeting, "**further rebuttals**" by 3 November 2003. This date was further changed to 18 November by the Panel's communication dated 18 September.

[3] Changed to 22 August 2003 by the Panel's communication dated 20 June.

[4] Changed to 7, 8 October 2003 by the Panel's communication dated 20 June. These dates were subsequently changed to 2, 3 December by the Panel's communication dated 12 September. Apart from responses to Panel's questions, the Panel has established several deadlines after the second substantive meeting for parties to submit various documents. (See Panel's communications dated 14 November 2003, 8 December 2003, 24 December 2003, 12 January 2004, 3 February 2004, 16 February 2004, 20 February 2004, 24 February 2004 and 4 March 2004.)

(m)	Issuance of descriptive part of the report to the parties:	1 October 2003 [5]
(n)	Receipt of comments by the parties on the descriptive part of the report:	15 October 2003
(o)	Issuance of the interim report, including the findings and conclusions, to the parties:	4 November 2003[6]
(p)	Deadline for parties to request review of part(s) of report:	18 November 2003
(q)	Interim review meeting with the parties, if requested. If interim review meeting not requested, the deadline for comments on each others' comment.	24 November 2003
(r)	Issuance of final report to the parties:	10 December 2003
(s)	Circulation of the final report to Members:	[after translation]

[5] The dates for items (m) and (n) were delayed several times and were ultimately set to be 16 March and 30 March 2004, respectively, by the Panel's communication of 4 March 2004.

[6] The dates for items (o) - (r) were delayed several times and were ultimately set to be as follows, respectively, by the Panel's communication of 7 April, 2004: 26 April, 10 May, 3 June and 18 June 2004.

ANNEX N

REQUEST FOR CONSULTATIONS AND REQUEST FOR THE ESTABLISHMENT OF A PANEL

ANNEX N-1

WORLD TRADE ORGANIZATION

WT/DS267/1G/L/571
G/SCM/D49/1
G/AG/GEN/54
3 October 2002
(02-5314)

Original: English

UNITED STATES – SUBSIDIES ON UPLAND COTTON

Request for Consultations by Brazil

The following communication, dated 27 September 2002, from the Permanent Mission of Brazil to the Permanent Mission of the United States and to the Chairman of the Dispute Settlement Body, is circulated in accordance with Article 4.4 of the DSU.

Upon instruction from my authorities, the Government of Brazil hereby requests consultations with the Government of the United States pursuant to Articles 4.1, 7.1 and 30 of the Agreement on Subsidies and Countervailing Measures (SCM Agreement), Article 19 of the Agreement on Agriculture, Article XXII of GATT 1994 and Article 4 of the Understanding on Rules and Procedures Governing the Settlement of Disputes (DSU).

The measures that are the subject of this request are prohibited and actionable subsidies provided to US producers, users and/or exporters of upland cotton[1], as well as legislation, regulations, statutory instruments and amendments thereto providing such subsidies (including export credits), grants, and any other assistance to the US producers, users and exporters of upland cotton ("US upland cotton industry"). The measures include the following:

- Domestic support subsidies provided to the US upland cotton industry during marketing years 1999-2002;[2]
- Export subsidies provided to the US upland cotton industry during marketing years 1999-2002;[3]
- Subsidies provided contingent upon the use of US upland cotton;
- Subsidies and domestic support provided under the Farm Security and Rural Investment Act of 2002 (FSRIA), including the regulations, administrative procedures and other measures implementing FSRIA related to marketing loans, loan deficiency payments (LDPs), commodity certificates, direct payments, counter-cyclical payments, conservation payments (to the extent they exceed the costs of complying with such programs), Step 2 certificate program payments, export credit guarantees, and any other provisions of FSRIA that provide direct or indirect support to the US upland cotton industry;
- Subsidies and domestic support provided under the Agricultural Risk Protection Act of 2000 and any other measures that provide subsidies relating to crop, disaster or other types of insurance to the US upland cotton industry;
- Subsidies and domestic support provided under the Federal Agricultural Improvement and Reform Act (FAIR Act) of 1996, and programs under the FAIR Act or amendments thereto relating to marketing loans, loan deficiency payments, commodity certificates, production flexibility contract payments, conservation payments, Step 2 certificate program payments, export credit guarantees, and any other FAIR Act provisions providing direct or indirect support to the US upland cotton industry;
- Export subsidies, exporter assistance, export credit guarantees, export and market access enhancement to facilitate the export of US upland cotton provided under the Agricultural Trade Act of 1978, as amended, and other measures such as the GSM-102, GSM-103, and SCGP programs, and the Step 1 and Step 2 certificate programs, among others;
- Subsidies provided to the US upland cotton industry under the Agricultural Act of 1949 as amended;

1 Except with respect to export credit guarantee programs as explained below.

2 The "marketing" year for upland cotton runs from 1 August through 31 July. For example, marketing year 2001 started on 1 August 2001 and ended on 31 July 2002. Brazil, as does the United States in its official USDA documents, treats "marketing year" to mean the same thing as "crop year".

3 The adverse effects and serious prejudice and threat thereof created by the measures in the marketing years 1999-2007 also exists for the corresponding (somewhat overlapping) US fiscal years 2000-2008. The US government fiscal year runs from 1 October to 30 September. For example, the fiscal year for 2001 started on 1 October 2000 and ended on 30 September 2001.

- Export subsidies provided to exporters of US upland cotton under the FSC Repeal and Extraterritorial Income Exclusion Act of 2000 ("ETI Act");
- Subsidies provided under the Agriculture, Rural Development, Food and Drug Administration and Related Agencies Appropriation Act of 2002 (November 2001), the Crop Year 2001 Agricultural Economic Assistance Act (August 2001), the Agriculture, Rural Development, Food and Drug Administration, and Related Agencies Appropriations Act of 2001 (October 2000), the Agriculture, Rural Development, Food and Drug Administration, and Related Agencies Appropriations Act of 2000 (October 1999), and the Agriculture, Rural Development, Food and Drug Administration, and Related Agencies Appropriations Act of 1999 (October 1998);
- All subsidies or support measures benefiting upland cotton that have trade-distorting effects or effects on production by the US upland cotton industry, or that have an effect of providing price support for upland cotton, or that are otherwise not exempt from the reduction commitments of the United States, as described in Annex 2 of the Agreement on Agriculture, because they do not meet the policy-specific criteria and conditions set out in paragraphs 2-13 of Annex II of the Agreement on Agriculture (*i.e.* they are not so-called green box subsidies);
- Export subsidies, domestic support, and other subsidies provided under regulations, administrative procedures, administrative practices and any other present measures, amendments thereto, or future measures implementing any of the measures listed above, that provide for or facilitate the payment of domestic support, export subsidies, and other subsidies for the production, use and/or export of US upland cotton and upland cotton products.

The Government of Brazil considers that these measures are inconsistent with the obligations of the United States under the following provisions:

1. Article 5(c) of the SCM Agreement;
2. Article 6.3(b), (c) and (d) of the SCM Agreement;
3. Article 3.1(a) of the SCM Agreement including item (j) of the Illustrative List of Export Subsidies in Annex I thereto;
4. Article 3.1(b) of the SCM Agreement;
5. Article 3.2 of the SCM Agreement;
6. Article 3.3 of the Agreement on Agriculture;
7. Article 7.1 of the Agreement on Agriculture;
8. Article 8 of the Agreement on Agriculture;
9. Article 9.1 of the Agreement on Agriculture;
10. Article 10.1 of the Agreement on Agriculture; and
11. Article III:4 of GATT 1994.

Brazil is of the view that the US statutes, regulations, and administrative procedures listed above are inconsistent with these provisions as such and as applied.

The United States has no basis to assert a defense under Article 13(b)(ii) of the Agreement on Agriculture that the domestic support measures listed above are exempt from action based on Articles 5 and 6 of the SCM Agreement, because these measures provide support to upland cotton in marketing years 1999-2002 in excess of the support decided by the United States in the 1992 marketing year. Similarly, the United States has no basis to assert a defense under Article 13(c)(ii) of the Agreement on Agriculture that the export subsidies listed above are exempt from action based on Article 3, 5 and 6 of the SCM Agreement, because these export subsidies do not conform fully to the provisions of Part V of the Agreement on Agriculture, as reflected in the Schedule of the United States.

The measures listed above are subsidies because in each instance there is a financial contribution by the US government, or an income or price support in the sense of Article XVI of GATT 1994, and a benefit is thereby conferred within the meaning of Article 1.1(a) and (b) of the SCM Agreement. Each of the listed subsidies is specific to US producers of primary agricultural products and/or to the upland cotton industry within the meaning of Articles 2.1 and 2.3 of the SCM Agreement.

The use of these measures causes adverse effects, *i.e.* serious prejudice to the interests of Brazil:

- The effect of the measures is significant price depression and price suppression in the markets for upland cotton in Brazil and elsewhere during marketing years 1999-2002 in violation of SCM Articles 5(c) and 6.3(c).
- The effect of the measures is to displace or impede exports of Brazilian upland cotton in third country markets during marketing years 1999-2002, in violation of Articles 5(c) and 6.3(b) of the SCM Agreement.
- The effect of the measures is to increase the world market share of the United States for upland cotton in marketing year 2001 as compared to the average share of the United States between marketing years between 1998-2000, and by increasing its world market share for the production of upland cotton in the period from marketing year 1985 (the first year in which LDP and marketing loan payments were made for upland cotton) to marketing year 2001 from 16.7 to 20.6 percent in violation of Articles 5(c) and 6.3(d) of the SCM Agreement.

The statutes, regulations, and administrative measures listed above and the subsidies they mandate threaten – as such and as applied – to cause serious prejudice to the interests of Brazil as follows:

- By mandating conditions that will result in continued depressed and suppressed upland cotton prices for marketing years 2002 through 2007 through the guaranteed payment of subsidies to the US upland cotton industry, which artificially increases and/or maintains high-cost US upland cotton production in violation of SCM Articles 5(c) and 6.3(c); and

– By mandating conditions that will result in over-production of high-cost US upland cotton, which will continue to displace and impede Brazil's export market share in the world market and specific national markets for upland cotton, in violation of SCM Articles 5(c) and 6.3(b).

With respect to the Step 2 program, Brazil believes that the program as such and as applied to provide payments to exporters of US upland cotton is inconsistent with Articles 3.3, 8, 9.1, and 10.1 of the Agreement on Agriculture, and with Articles 3.1(a) and 3.2 of the SCM Agreement. Brazil further believes that the program, as such and as applied to provide payments to US domestic mill users of US upland cotton, are inconsistent with Article 3.1(b) of the SCM Agreement, and Article III:4 of GATT 1994. Step 2 payments are actionable subsidies for the purpose of Brazil's claims under Articles 5 and 6.3 of the SCM Agreement.

Regarding export credit guarantees, export and market access enhancement provided under the Agricultural Trade Act of 1978, as amended, and other measures such as the GSM-102, GSM-103, and SCGP programs, Brazil is of the view that these programs, as applied and as such, violate Articles 3.3, 8, 9.1, and 10.1 of the Agreement on Agriculture and are prohibited export subsidies under Article 3.1(a) and item (j) of the Illustrative List of Export Subsidies included as Annex I to the SCM Agreement. Subsidies provided under these programs are also actionable subsidies for the purpose of Brazil's claims under Article 6.3 of the SCM Agreement.

Articles 4.2 and 7.2 of the SCM Agreement together require that this request for consultations include a statement of available evidence (1) with regard to the existence and nature of the subsidies in question and (2) the adverse effects and serious prejudice to the interests of Brazil. This letter identifies the existence and nature of the subsidies, and further evidence is provided in the annex to this letter.

The Government of Brazil reserves the right to request the United States to produce information and documents regarding the measures in question and thir effect on the interests of Brazil, during the consultation process. The Government of Brazil also reserves the right to address additional measures and claims under other WTO provisions during the course of the consultations.

My authorities look forward to receiving in due course a reply from the United States to this request. Brazil is ready to consider with the United States mutually convenient dates to hold consultations in Geneva.

ANNEX

Statement of Available Evidence With Regard to the Existence and Nature of the Subsidies in Question and the Serious Prejudice Caused to the Interest of Brazil

1. Brazil's request for consultations dated 27 September 2002 identifies the prohibited and actionable subsidies that are the subject of this request for consultations.

2. The evidence set out below is evidence available to Brazil at this time regarding the existence and nature of those subsidies, and the adverse effects caused by them to the interests of Brazil. It reflects the presently available evidence regarding the claims reflected in Brazil's request for consultations and is supported by documents that are described and set out in United States Department of Agriculture (USDA) and non-governmental internet locations set out in paragraph 4 below. Brazil reserves the right to supplement or alter this list in the future, as required.

3. The evidence presently available to Brazil includes the following:

- US producers of upland cotton received domestic support in excess of 100 percent of the US crop value in marketing year 2001;
- US domestic and export support subsidies to upland cotton in marketing year 2001 exceeded $4 billion – far greater than the value of total US production;
- Compared with marketing year 1992, US Government subsidies to US producers of upland cotton have increased significantly, particularly for the 1999 and 2001 marketing year;
- The provisions of the 2002 Farm Bill mandate the payment of subsidies considerably in excess of those provided in the 1996 FAIR Act, including a new counter-cyclical payment program providing for more than $1 billion for marketing year 2002 at current market prices for upland cotton. The 2002 Farm Bill provides similar (although increased) payments as the FAIR act in the form of a "direct payment" program (a successor to production flexibility payments) and continues largely unchanged the loan deficiency payments, marketing loans payments, crop insurance payments, and the Step 2 program and other export subsidy programs that provided support to the US upland cotton industry prior to passage of the 2002 Farm Bill;
- For a significant number of US producers of upland cotton, total cost of production in 2001 (and from 1991 through 2000) was well *above* the US market price of upland cotton;
- Thus, without the benefit of US domestic and export subsidies, many US producers would not be able to produce upland cotton without sustaining a significant loss; current price projections for marketing years 2003-2007

indicate that US upland cotton prices are expected to remain well below the US cost of production;

- With upland cotton prices declining over the 4-year period from 1998 through 2001, US production increased from 14 million tons in marketing year 1998 to a record 20.3 million metric tons in marketing year 2001;
- In marketing year 2001 the United States was the world's largest exporter of upland cotton, with a 38 percent share. It is expected that the United States will remain by far the world's largest exporter of upland cotton in marketing year 2002;
- The volume of US exports of US upland cotton increased significantly from 946.000 metric tons in marketing year 1998 to 1.829.000 metric tons in marketing year 2001, with 1.960.000 metric tons expected to be exported in marketing year 2002;
- The effect of the US subsidies over the period of marketing years 1999-2001 was an increase in production of US upland cotton, an increase in US exports, and a corresponding significant decrease in Brazilian, world, and US prices of upland cotton;
- US year-end surplus stocks of upland cotton in marketing year 2001 increased steadily between marketing years 1999-2001 with the additional surplus creating a depressing and suppressing effect on US and world prices;
- Brazilian upland cotton is like or has characteristics closely resembling US upland cotton, is used interchangeably by customers in third country markets with US upland cotton and competes in the same markets for the same customers. Thus, the overproduction of US upland cotton suppresses and depresses the price that Brazilian producers can obtain for their upland cotton on the world and Brazilian market;
- Prices for upland cotton in Brazil follow trends created in the US and Northern European markets and experienced significant declines between marketing years 1999-2002;
- Brazilian production of upland cotton decreased between marketing year 2000 and 2001 from 939.000 to 718.000 metric tons;
- Prices for upland cotton in the Brazilian, worldwide, and other regional and third country markets were significantly depressed and suppressed over the period of marketing years 1999-2002 as a result of the effect of US subsidies;
- Prices for upland cotton in the Brazilian, worldwide, and other regional and third country markets continue to be suppressed in marketing year 2002 as a result of US subsidies;
- The world market share of the United States for upland cotton in marketing year 2001 increased over the average share of the United States between marketing years 1998-2000. In addition, the United States increased its world market share for the production of upland cotton in the period from marketing year 1985 (the first year in which LDP and marketing

loan payments were made for upland cotton) to marketing year 2001 from 16.7 to 20.6 percent;

- The United States' notifications of subsidies to the WTO Committee on Agriculture provide information indicating that the loan deficiency payments (LDP), marketing loan gains, crop insurance programs, marketing loss payments, and Step 2 certificate payments made in connection with upland cotton are not "green" box payments;
- USDA econometric analyses demonstrate the actual or potential production enhancing effects for particular crops in the United States of LDP, marketing loan payments, crop insurance subsidies, and even production flexibility payments. Certain of these studies demonstrate the production enhancing effects of such subsidies on US production of upland cotton;
- Econometric studies by the International Cotton Advisory Committee, the World Bank, and the International Monetary Fund demonstrate that many of the US subsidies at issue in the consultation request have a price suppressive and depressive effect on prices of upland cotton and other crops;
- The US Step 1 and Step 2 programs, since their origin and up to the present, enhance the export competitiveness of US-produced upland cotton - an effect consistent with the expressed purpose of such programs;
- US export credit guarantee programs have caused serious prejudice to Brazilian upland cotton producers by providing below-market financing benefits for the export of competing US upland cotton;
- US export credit guarantee programs, since their origin in 1980 and up the present, provide premium rates that are inadequate to cover the long-term operating costs and losses of the programs; in particular there were losses caused by large-scale defaults totalling billions of dollars that have not been reflected in increased premiums to cover such losses;
- The volume of production and export of lower-cost Brazilian upland cotton have been impeded by US subsidies that have built and maintained excess US production by higher-cost US producers;
- The estimated losses suffered by Brazil due to price suppressed or depressed by US subsidies to the US upland cotton industry are well in excess of $ 600 million for marketing year 2001 alone including lost revenue, lost production, losses of related services, lost federal and state revenue, higher unemployment and losses in Brazil's trade balance.

4. The statistics, data and analytic documents supporting the summary of evidence above can be found in the following documents published by among others the US Department of Agriculture, the International Cotton Advisory Committee and the Food and Agriculture Policy Research Institute, University of Missouri as well as others:

US Department of Agriculture, Economic Research Service:

http://www.ers.usda.gov

- Comparison and Summary of 1996 and 2002 farm bills
  http://www.ers.usda.gov/Features/farmbill/titles/titleIcommodities.htm#c
- Briefing on Cotton
  http://www.ers.usda.gov/briefing/cotton/
- Cotton and Wool Outlook: Various Editions
  http://www.ers.usda.gov/publications/so/view.asp?f=field/cws-bb/
- Factors Affecting the US Farm Price for Upland Cotton, Cotton and Wool Situation and Outlook, April 1998
- Cotton and Wool Outlook: Latest Statistical Information
  http://www.ers.usda.gov/briefing/cotton/Data/data.htm
- Statistical Information of the Cotton and Wool Yearbook
  http://www.ers.usda.gov/data/sdp/view.asp?f=crops/89004/
- 1996 FAIR Act Frames Farm Policy for 7 Years
  http://www.ers.usda.gov/publications/agoutlook/aosupp.pdf
- US Farm Program Benefits: Links to Planting Decisions & Agricultural Markets
  http://www.ers.usda.gov/publications/agoutlook/oct2000/ao275e.pdf
- Production and Price Impacts of US Crop Insurance Subsidies: Some Preliminary Results
  http://www.ers.usda.gov/briefing/FarmPolicy/ffc_insurrance.pdf
- Commodity Cost and Returns
  http://www.ers.usda.gov/data/costsandreturns/
- Characteristics and Production Costs of US Cotton Farms
  http://www.ers.usda.gov/publications/sb974-2/
- Analysis of the US Commodity Loan Program with Marketing Loan Provisions
  http://www.ers.usda.gov/publications/aer801/aer801fm.pdf
- Agricultural Outlook December 1999: Ag Policy: Marketing Loan Benefits Supplement Market Revenues for Farmers
  http://www.ers.usda.gov/publications/agoutlook/dec1999/ao267b.pdf
- Farm and Commodity Policy: 1996-2001 Program Provisions
  http://www.ers.usda.gov/briefing/FarmPolicy/1996malp.htm
- Farm and Commodity Policy: Questions and Answers
  http://www.ers.usda.gov/briefing/FarmPolicy/questions/index.htm
- Farm and Commodity Policy: Crop Insurance
  http://www.ers.usda.gov/briefing/FarmPolicy/cropInsurance.htm

– Cotton: Background Issues for Farm Legislation
  http://www.ers.usda.gov/publications/CWS-0601-01/
– Cotton Policy: Special Program Provisions for Upland Cotton
  http://www.ers.usda.gov/briefing/cotton/specialprovisions.htm
– List of Studies Analyzing Market Effects of US Agricultural Policy
  http://www.ers.usda.gov/publications/tb1888/tb1888ref.pdf
– Major Agricultural and Trade Legislation, 1933–1996
  http://www.ers.usda.gov/publications/aib729/aib729a3.pdf

US Department of Agriculture, Farm Service Agency:

http://www.fsa.usda.gov

– Statistics on Price Support Loans and Loan Deficiency Payments
  http://www.fsa.usda.gov/pscad/:
– FSA Fact Sheets:
  http://www.fsa.usda.gov/pas/publications/facts/pubfacts.htm
– Fact Sheet: Upland Cotton: Locking the Adjusted World Price (AWP) by Loan Deficiency Payments on Upland Seed Cotton
  http://www.fsa.usda.gov/pas/publications/facts/html/upcotlock00.htm
– Price Support Programs
  http://www.fsa.usda.gov/dafp/psd/default.htm
– Loan Deficiency Payment and Price Support Cumulative Activity
  http://www.fsa.usda.gov/pscad/answer82rnat.asp

Congressional Budget Office Current Budget Projection:

http://www.cbo.gov/showdoc.cfm?index=1944&sequence=0

Food and Agriculture Policy Research Institute, University of Missouri:

http://www.fapri.missouri.edu/FAPRI_Publications.htm

International Cotton Advisory Committee:

http://www.icac.org/icac/english.html

– Cotton: Review of the World Situation August 2002
  http://www.icac.org/icac/CottonInfo/Publications/Reviews/english.html
– Production and Trade Policies Affecting the Cotton Industry, November 2000
– Production and Trade Policies Affecting the Cotton Industry, September 2001
– Production and Trade Policies Affecting the Cotton Industry, July 2002
  http://web.worldbank.org/WBSITE/EXTERNAL/NEWS/0,,contentMDK:20053593~menuPK:34463~pagePK:34370~piPK:34424~theSitePK:4607,00.html

– Cotton: World Statistics

  http://www.icac.org/icac/CottonInfo/Publications/Statistics/statsws/english.html

– Report from Brazil on Injury From Low Cotton Prices

– Survey of Cost of Production of Raw Cotton

World Trade Organization:

– US notification on Domestic Support for Marketing Year 1998 - G/AG/N/USA/36

International Monetary Fund:

– World Economic Outlook September 2002

  http://www.imf.org/external/pubs/ft/weo/2002/02/pdf/chapter2.pdf

World Bank:

– Cotton Producers Face Losses Because of Rich Country Subsidies

  http://web.worldbank.org/WBSITE/EXTERNAL/NEWS/0,,contentMDK:20053593~menuPK:34463~pagePK:34370~piPK:34424~theSitePK:4607,00.html

ANNEX N-2

WORLD TRADE ORGANIZATION

WT/DS267/7
7 February 2003

(03-0838)

Original: English

UNITED STATES – SUBSIDIES ON UPLAND COTTON

Request for the Establishment of a Panel by Brazil

The following communication, dated 6 February 2003, from the Permanent Mission of Brazil to the Chairman of the Dispute Settlement Body, is circulated pursuant to Article 6.2 of the DSU.

On 27 September, the Government of Brazil requested consultations with the Government of the United States pursuant to Articles 4.1, 7.1 and 30 of the Agreement on Subsidies and Countervailing Measures (SCM Agreement), Article 19 of the Agreement on Agriculture, Article XXII of GATT 1994 and Article 4 of the Understanding on Rules and Procedures Governing the Settlement of Disputes (DSU). This request was circulated to the WTO Members on 3 October 2002 as document WT/DS267/1, "United States – Subsidies on Upland Cotton". Consultations were held on 3, 4 and 19 December 2002 and on 17 January 2003 with a view to reaching a mutually satisfactory solution. Unfortunately, these consultations failed to settle the dispute.

The Government of Brazil therefore hereby requests that a panel be established pursuant to Articles 6 of the DSU, Article XXIII:2 of GATT 1994, Article 19 of the Agreement on Agriculture, and Articles 4.4, 7.4 and 30 of the SCM Agreement (to the extent that Article 30 incorporates by reference Article XXIII of GATT 1994).

The Government of Brazil further requests that the DSB initiate the procedures provided in Annex V of the SCM Agreement pursuant to paragraph 2 of that Annex. The Government of Brazil intends to put forward suggestions as to the information that should be sought under this procedure once the panel is established.

The measures that are the subject of this request are prohibited and actionable subsidies provided to US producers, users and/or exporters of upland cotton[1], as well as legislation, regulations and statutory instruments and amendments thereto providing such subsidies (including export credit guarantees), grants, and any other assistance to the US producers, users and exporters of upland cotton ("US upland cotton industry"). The measures include the following:

Domestic support subsidies provided to the US upland cotton industry during marketing years 1999-2001[2];

Domestic support subsidies that are mandated to be provided to the US upland cotton industry during marketing years 2002-2007;

Export subsidies provided to the US upland cotton industry during marketing years 1999-2001;

Export subsides that are mandated to be provided to the US upland cotton industry during marketing years 2002-2007;

Subsidies provided contingent upon the use of US over imported upland cotton in marketing years 1999-2001 and that are mandated to be provided to the US upland cotton industry during marketing years 2002-2007;

Subsidies and domestic support provided under the Farm Security and Rural Investment Act of 2002 (FSRIA), including the regulations, administrative procedures and other measures implementing FSRIA related to marketing loans, loan deficiency payments (LDPs), commodity certificates, direct payments, counter-cyclical payments, conservation payments (to the extent they exceed the costs of complying with such programs), Step 2 certificate programme payments, export credit guarantees, crop insurance, and any other provisions of FSRIA that provide direct or indirect support to the US upland cotton industry;

Subsidies and domestic support provided under the Agricultural Risk Protection Act of 2000 and any other measures that provide subsidies relating to crop, disaster or other types of insurance to the US upland cotton industry;

Subsidies and domestic support provided under the Federal Agricultural Improvement and Reform Act (FAIR Act) of 1996, and programs under the FAIR Act or amendments thereto relating to marketing loans, loan deficiency payments, commodity certificates, production flexibility contract payments, conservation payments, Step 2 certificate programme payments, export credit guarantees, crop insurance, and any other FAIR

---

1 The term "upland cotton" means raw upland cotton as well as the primary processed forms of such cotton including upland cotton lint and cottonseed. The focus of Brazil's claims relate to upland cotton with the exception of the US export credit guarantee programs as explained below.

2 The "marketing" year for upland cotton runs from 1 August through 31 July. For example, marketing year 2001 started on 1 August 2001 and ended on 31 July 2002. Brazil, as does the United States in its official USDA documents, treats "marketing year" to mean the same as "crop year."

Act provisions providing direct or indirect support to the US upland cotton industry;

Export subsidies, exporter assistance, export credit guarantees, export and market access enhancement to facilitate the export of US upland cotton, and other eligible agricultural commodities as addressed herein, provided under the Agricultural Trade Act of 1978, as amended, and other measures such as the GSM-102, GSM-103, and SCGP programs, and the Step 1 and Step 2 certificate programs, among others;

Subsidies provided to the US upland cotton industry under the Agricultural Act of 1949 as amended;

Export subsidies provided to exporters of US upland cotton under the FSC Repeal and Extraterritorial Income Exclusion Act of 2000 ("ETI Act");

Subsidies provided under the Agricultural Assistance Act of 2003; Subsidies provided under the Agriculture, Rural Development, Food and Drug Administration and Related Agencies Appropriation Act of 2002 (November 2001), the Crop Year 2001 Agricultural Economic Assistance Act (August 2001), the Agriculture, Rural Development, Food and Drug Administration, and Related Agencies Appropriations Act of 2001 (October 2000), the Agriculture, Rural Development, Food and Drug Administration, and Related Agencies Appropriations Act of 2000 (October 1999), and the Rural Development, Food and Drug Administration, and Related Agencies Appropriations Act of 1999 (October 1998);

All subsidies or support measures benefiting upland cotton that have trade-distorting effects or effects on production by the US upland cotton industry, or that have an effect of providing price support for upland cotton, or that are otherwise not exempt from the reduction commitments of the United States, as described in Annex 2 of the Agreement on Agriculture, because they do not meet the policy-specific criteria and conditions set out in paragraphs 2-13 of Annex II of the Agreement on Agriculture (*i.e.* they are not so-called "green box" subsidies);

Export subsidies, domestic support, and other subsidies provided under regulations, administrative procedures, administrative practices and any other present measures or future measures implementing or amending any of the measures listed above, that provide for or facilitate the payment of domestic support, export subsidies, and other subsidies for the production, use and/or export of US upland cotton and upland cotton products.

The measures, and any amendments to these measures, are inconsistent with the obligations of the United States under the following provisions:

1. Article 5(a) of the SCM Agreement;
2. Article 5(c) of the SCM Agreement;
3. Article 6.3(b), (c) and (d) of the SCM Agreement;
4. Article 3.1(a) of the SCM Agreement including item (j) of the Illustrative List of Export Subsidies in Annex I thereto;

5. Article 3.1(b) of the SCM Agreement;
6. Article 3.2 of the SCM Agreement;
7. Article 3.3 of the Agreement on Agriculture;
8. Article 7.1 of the Agreement on Agriculture;
9. Article 8 of the Agreement on Agriculture;
10. Article 9.1 of the Agreement on Agriculture;
11. Article 10.1 of the Agreement on Agriculture; and
12. Article III:4 of GATT 1994
13. Article XVI.1 and Article XVI.3 of GATT 1994

The US statutes, regulations and administrative procedures and any amendments thereto listed above are inconsistent with these provisions as such and as applied.

The United States has no basis to assert a defense under Article 13(b)(ii) of the Agreement on Agriculture that the domestic support measures listed above are exempt from action based on Articles 5 and 6 of the SCM Agreement, because these measures provide support to upland cotton in marketing years 1999-2001 in excess of the support decided by the United States in the 1992 marketing year. Similarly, the United States has no basis to assert a defense under Article 13(c)(ii) of the Agreement on Agriculture that the export subsidies listed above are exempt from action based on Article 3, 5 and 6 of the SCM Agreement, because these export subsidies do not conform fully to the provisions of Part V of the Agreement on Agriculture, as reflected in the Schedule of the United States.

The measures listed above are subsidies because in each instance there is a financial contribution by the US government, or an income or price support in the sense of Article XVI of GATT 1994, and a benefit is thereby conferred within the meaning of Article 1.1(a) and (b) of the SCM Agreement. Each of the listed subsidies is specific to US producers of primary agricultural products and/or to the upland cotton industry within the meaning of Articles 2.1 and 2.3 of the SCM Agreement.

The use of measures provided to the US upland cotton industry causes adverse effects including material injury to the Brazilian upland cotton industry under SCM Article 5(a), and serious prejudice to the interests of Brazil under SCM Article 5(c) including:[3]

> The effect of the measures is significant price depression and price suppression in the markets for upland cotton in Brazil, the United States, other third country markets, and the world market during marketing years 1999-2002 in violation of SCM Articles 5(c) and 6.3(c).

---

[3] The adverse effects and serious prejudice and threat thereof created by the measures in the marketing years 1999-2007 also exists for the corresponding (somewhat overlapping) US fiscal years 2000 - 2008. The US government fiscal year runs from 1 October to 30 September. For example, the fiscal year for 2001 started on 1 October 2000 and ended on 30 September 2001.

The effect of the measures is to displace or impede exports of Brazilian upland cotton in third country markets during marketing years 1999-2002, in violation of Articles 5(c) and 6.3(b) of the SCM Agreement.

The effect of the measures is to increase the world export market share of the United States for upland cotton in marketing year 2001 as compared to the average share of the United States between marketing years 1998-2000, and by increasing its world export market share for the production of upland cotton in the period beginning with the FAIR Act in marketing year 1996 from 24 percent to 37 percent in marketing year 2001 in violation of Articles 5(c) and 6.3(d) of the SCM Agreement.

The effect of the measures during marketing years 1999-2002 is to increase and maintain high levels of exports of upland cotton from the United States and to provide the United States with an inequitable share of world export trade in upland cotton in violation of Article XVI.1 and 3 of GATT 1994.

The statutes, regulations, and administrative measures and any amendments thereto listed above and the actionable subsidies they mandate threaten, as such and as applied, to cause material injury to the Brazilian upland cotton industry, and serious prejudice to the interests of Brazil including:

By mandating conditions that are having and will continue to result in significant suppression and depression of upland cotton prices for marketing years 2002 through 2007 through the guaranteed payment of amounts of subsidies to the US upland cotton industry, which artificially increases and/or maintains high-cost US upland cotton production in violation of SCM Articles 5(c) and 6.3(c); and

By mandating conditions that will result in over-production of high-cost US upland cotton, which will continue to displace and impede Brazil's export market share in the third country markets for upland cotton, in violation of SCM Articles 5(c) and 6.3(b).

By mandating conditions that will result in over-production of high-cost US upland cotton, which will increase or continue to maintain high levels of exports of upland cotton from the United States in violation of SCM Articles 5(c) and 6.3(d) and continue to result in the United States having an inequitable share of world upland cotton export trade in violation of Article XVI.1 and 3 of GATT 1994.

With respect to subsidies provided under the so-called "Step 2" programmes, one type of subsidy under the programme provides payments to exporters contingent upon the export of US upland cotton and is inconsistent with Articles 3.3, 8, 9.1, and 10.1 of the Agreement on Agriculture, and with Articles 3.1(a) and 3.2 of the SCM Agreement. Another type of subsidy under the Step-2 programme provides payments to US domestic mill users contingent upon the use of US upland cotton and is inconsistent with Article 3.1(b) and 3.2 of the SCM Agreement, and Article III:4 of GATT 1994. Brazil challenges these two types of subsidies under the Step 2 programme as such and as applied. These two Step

2 subsidies are actionable for the purpose of Brazil's claims under Articles 5 and 6.3 of the SCM Agreement.

Regarding export credit guarantees and export and market access enhancement provided under the Agricultural Trade Act of 1978, as amended, and export credit guarantee measures relating to eligible US agricultural commodities, such as the GSM-102, GSM-103, and SCGP programmes, these programs violate, as applied and as such, Articles 3.3, 8, 9.1, and 10.1 of the Agreement on Agriculture and are prohibited export subsidies under Articles 3.1(a), 3.2 and item (j) of the Illustrated List of Export Subsidies included as Annex I to the SCM Agreement. Subsidies provided under these programs are also actionable subsidies for the purpose of Brazil's claims under Articles 5 and 6.3 of the SCM Agreement.

Brazil requests that a Panel be established with standard terms of reference, in accordance with Article 7 of the DSU.

Brazil asks that this request for the establishment of a Panel be placed on the agenda for the next meeting of the Dispute Settlement Body, which is scheduled to take place on 19 February 2003.

ANNEX O

LIST OF EXHIBITS

ANNEX O-1

TABLE OF EXHIBITS OF BRAZIL

Exhibit BRA-1	Draft Understanding on Rules and Procedures Governing the Settlement of Disputes, 15 June 1992
Exhibit BRA-2	Draft Understanding on Rules and Procedures Governing the Settlement of Disputes, 15 November 1993
Exhibit BRA-3	Roger Thurow and Scott Kilman, "US Subsidies Create Cotton Glut That Hurts Foreign Cotton Farms", The Wall Street Journal, 26 June 2002
Exhibit BRA-4	"Fact Sheet: Upland Cotton", USDA, January 2003.
Exhibit BRA-5	"Agricultural Policies in OECD Countries – Monitoring and Evaluation 2003," OECD, 2003
Exhibit BRA-6	CCC Marketing Loan Write – Offs (Gains) – FY 1994-2002
Exhibit BRA-7	ERS Data: Commodity Costs and Returns
Exhibit BRA-8	Cotton and Wool Situation and Outlook Yearbook 2002, USDA, November 2002
Exhibit BRA-9	"Cotton: World Statistics", ICAC, September 2002.
Exhibit BRA-10	Cotton and Wool Outlook, 12 June 2003
Exhibit BRA-11	Cotton Outlook, 30 November 2001 and 5 April 2002
Exhibit BRA-12	"Cotton: Background for 1995 Farm Legislation", USDA, April 1995
Exhibit BRA-13	ERS Briefing Room Cotton: Background
Exhibit BRA-14	"Survey of Cost of Production", ICAC, September 2001
Exhibit BRA-15	"Cultivating Poverty: The Impact of US Cotton Subsidies on Africa", Oxfam Briefing Paper 30, 27 September 2002

Exhibit BRA-16	"Characteristics and Production Costs of US Cotton Farms", USDA, October 2001
Exhibit BRA-17	Yearly A – Index Prices
Exhibit BRA-18	"Prospective Plantings", USDA, 31 March 2003
Exhibit BRA-19	"Cotton this Month", ICAC, 1 April 2003
Exhibit BRA-20	Cotton and Wool Outlook, USDA, 11 April 2003
Exhibit BRA-21	"Cotton: World Markets and Trade", USDA Foreign Agricultural Service, January 2003 Edition
Exhibit BRA-22	"Cotton Marketing Weekly" dated 25 April 2003
Exhibit BRA-23	"Cotton: Total Accumulated Exports of Cotton by Country", USDA
Exhibit BRA-24	"Provisions of the Agricultural Improvement and Reform Act of 1996, Appendix III: Major Agricultural and Trade Legislation, 1933-96", USDA
Exhibit BRA-25	"1996 FAIR Act Frames Policy For 7 Years", Agricultural Outlook Supplement, April 1996
Exhibit BRA-26	7 CFR 1413, Deficiency Payment Program, 1993 Edition
Exhibit BRA-27	Side by Side Comparison of the 1996 and 2002 Farm Act, USDA
Exhibit BRA-28	1996 Federal Agriculture Improvement and Reform Act
Exhibit BRA-29	2002 Farm Security and Rural Investment Act
Exhibit BRA-30	Federal Crop Insurance Act
Exhibit BRA-31	7 CFR 1412: Production Flexibility Contracts for Wheat, Feed Grains, Rice, and Upland Cotton, 2002 Edition.
Exhibit BRA-32	7 CFR 1427.1100 at seq.: Cottonseed Payment Program, 2002 Edition
Exhibit BRA-33	7 CFR 1400: Payment Limitation and Payment Eligibility, 2003 Edition
Exhibit BRA-34	7 CFR 1401: Commodity Certificates, in Kind Payments, and Other Forms of Payment, 2003 Edition
Exhibit BRA-35	7 CFR 1412: Direct and Counter-Cyclical Program and Peanut Quota Buyout Program, 2003 Edition
Exhibit BRA-36	7 CFR 1427.1 at seq.: Nonrecourse Cotton Loans and Loan Deficiency Payments, 2003 Edition
Exhibit BRA-37	7 CFR 1427.100 at seq.: Upland Cotton User Marketing Certificates, 2003 Edition
Exhibit BRA-38	7 CFR 1493: CCC Export Credit Guarantee Programs, 2003 Edition
Exhibit BRA-39	7 CFR 400 Excerpts: Federal Crop Insurance Corporation, 2003 Edition

Exhibit BRA-40	ERS Briefing Room Cotton: Policy
Exhibit BRA-41	Congressional Hearing, "The Future of Federal Farm Commodity Programs (Cotton)", House of Representatives, 15 February 2001
Exhibit BRA-42	"The 2002 Farm Act, Provisions and Implications for Commodity Markets", USDA, November 2002
Exhibit BRA-43	67 Federal Register, N° 203, 21 October 2002
Exhibit BRA-44	"Direct Payment and CCP Enrolment Report", USDA, 19 June 2003
Exhibit BRA-45	"Fact Sheet: Upland Cotton", USDA, June 2001
Exhibit BRA-46	"Cotton: Background and Issues for Farm Legislation", USDA, July 2001
Exhibit BRA-47	G/AG/N/USA/43
Exhibit BRA-48	"Counter-Cyclical Payments under the 2002 Farm Bill", National Cotton Council, June 2003
Exhibit BRA-49	Brazil's Questions for the purposes of Annex V Procedure, March 2003
Exhibit BRA-50	"Farm Services Agency Background Information: Non-recourse Marketing Assistance Loans and Loan Deficiency Payments", USDA, March 1998
Exhibit BRA-51	Cotton Outlook, 1 February 2002: US Price Mechanism
Exhibit BRA-52	"Fact Sheet: Commodity Certificates", USDA, July 2000
Exhibit BRA-53	"NCC Delegates Focus on Farm Program Specifics", National Cotton Council, 31 January 2001
Exhibit BRA-54	"Farm Subsidy Limit Loophole Cost taxpayer Billions in Payments to Biggest Farmers", Environmental Working Group, 1 May 2002
Exhibit BRA-55	Loan Deficiency Payment and Price Support Cumulative Activity as of 6/11/2003, USDA, 13 June 2003.
Exhibit BRA-56	Bruce Gardner, "American Agriculture in the Twentieth Century", Cambridge: Harvard University Press, 2002
Exhibit BRA-57	"Crop Year Statistics", Federal Crop Insurance Corporation
Exhibit BRA-58	"US Crop Insurance: Premiums, Subsidies & Participation", USDA, Agricultural Outlook, December 2001
Exhibit BRA-59	"Briefing Room: Farm and Commodity Policy: Crop Yield and Revenue Insurance", USDA
Exhibit BRA-60	RMA Online, Crop Policies, 23 March 2003
Exhibit BRA-61	"NCC Summary of Key Provisions of Crop Insurance Reform Legislation", NCC.

Exhibit BRA-62	RMA Online – Crops Covered under the 2002 Crop insurance Program
Exhibit BRA-63	"Production and Price Impacts of US Crop insurance Subsidies: Some Preliminary Results"
Exhibit BRA-64	"Weak Demand Dampens Outlook for US Cotton", USDA Agricultural Outlook, November 1999
Exhibit BRA-65	Upland Cotton Domestic User/Exporter Agreement
Exhibit BRA-66	Sample Format Weekly Consumption/Application For Payment Report
Exhibit BRA-67	Cotton Outlook
Exhibit BRA-68	"Weekly Step 2 Certificate Values". EconCentral, National Cotton Council of America, 13 June 2003
Exhibit BRA-69	Step 2 Domestic and Export payments by US Fiscal Year
Exhibit BRA-70	"Export News and Opportunities", USDA Foreign Agricultural Service
Exhibit BRA-71	"Fact Sheet: CCC Export Credit Guarantee Programs (GSM-102/103"
Exhibit BRA-72	"Fact Sheet: CCC Supplier Credit Guarantee Program"
Exhibit BRA-73	Summary of Export Credit Gurantee Programs, FY 1999-2003
Exhibit BRA-74	Farm Service Agency News Room, Release N° 1532.03, 25 April 2003
Exhibit BRA-75	Stewart, Terrence, The GATT Uruguay Round, A Negotiating History, Vol. IV, p. 24-25
Exhibit BRA-76	CCC Loan Deficiency Payments – FY 1994-2002
Exhibit BRA-77	"Fact Sheet: Agricultural Assistance Act of 2003", February 2003.
Exhibit BRA-78	G/AG/N/USA/17
Exhibit BRA-79	"US Farm Program Benefits: Links to Planting Decisions & Agricultural Markets", Agricultural Outlook, October 2000
Exhibit BRA-80	"How Decoupled Is US Agricultural Support for Major Crop", American Journal of Agricultural Economy 82, August 2000
Exhibit BRA-81	Ivan Roberts and Frank Jotzo, "2002 US Farm Bill: An Australian Perspective on its Impact", ABARE, Australian Commodities, Vol. 9, N° 2 June Quarter 2002
Exhibit BRA-82	"USDA Baseline Projections", USDA, February 2003
Exhibit BRA-83	Schedule XX of the United States of America, part IV, Section II entitled Export Subsidies: Budgetary Outlays and Quantitative Reduction Commitments

Exhibit BRA-84	G/AG/W/56
Exhibit BRA-85	"FATUS Export Aggregations"
Exhibit BRA-86	"FAS Agricultural Export Commodity Aggregations"
Exhibit BRA-87	Testimony of August Schumacher Jr., Under Secretary, Farm and Foreign Agricultural Service, USDA, before the Subcommitte on General Farm Commodities, Hearing on the Asian Financial Crisis, 4 88February 1998
Exhibit BRA-88	US Budget for Fiscal Year 2003
Exhibit BRA-89	US Budget for Fiscal Year 2002
Exhibit BRA-90	US Budget for Fiscal Year 2001
Exhibit BRA-91	US Budget for Fiscal Year 2000
Exhibit BRA-92	US Budget for Fiscal Year 1999
Exhibit BRA-93	US Budget for Fiscal Year 1998
Exhibit BRA-94	US Budget for Fiscal Year 1997
Exhibit BRA-95	US Budget for Fiscal Year 1996
Exhibit BRA-96	"Iraqgate: Saddam Hussein, US Policy and the Prelude to the Persian Gulf War, 1980-1994"
Exhibit BRA-97	"Agricultural Export and Food Aid Programs", Congressional Research Service: Issue Brief to Congress, 14 June 2002
Exhibit BRA-98	"Guarantee Fee Rate Schedule Under GSM 102 and GSM 103"
Exhibit BRA-99	G/AG/N/USA/39
Exhibit BRA-100	"US Cotton and the Appreciation of the Dollar", USDA, Agricultural Outlook, April 2002
Exhibit BRA-101	Brazil's Questions for the Purposes of the Consultations, 22 November 2002
Exhibit BRA-102	Statement of Administrative Action
Exhibit BRA-103	"1993 Cotton Management Economic Notes", University of Arizona, 27 July 1993.
Exhibit BRA-104	CV and Selected Publications of Professor Daniel Sumner
Exhibit BRA-105	Statement by Professor Daniel Sumner at the First Meeting of the Panel.
Exhibit BRA-106	"United States State Fact Sheet", ERS, USDA Data, 15 July 2003.
Exhibit BRA-107	"US and State Farm Income Data, Farm Cash Receipts, 1924-2001," ERS, USDA, June 2003.
Exhibit BRA-108	"United For Profits", National Cotton Council Organizational Chart and Membership.

Exhibit BRA-109	Testimony (Full) of Robert McLendon, Chairman, NCC Executive Committee, Before the House Agricultural Committee. National Cotton Council (NCC)
Exhibit BRA-110	"Cotton Briefing Room: Farm Commodity Policy, Updating Base Acres and Payment Yields", USDA, 30 June 2003
Exhibit BRA–111	"The Six Year World Outlook for Cotton and Peanuts: Implications for Production and Prices." Bob McLendon, National Cotton Council
Exhibit BRA–112	"Expected Payment Rates to Upland Cotton Producers for Calendar Years 2002 and 2003", prepared by the National Cotton Council, October 2002.
Exhibit BRA–113	"Farm Bill: Fundamental Change in Farm Policy", Delta Farm Express.
Exhibit BRA-114	"US Debt Reduction Activities, FY 1990 through FY 1999," US Treasury Department, Public Report to Congress, February 2000.
Exhibit BRA-115	US General Accounting Office, Report to the Chairman, Subcommittee on Criminal Justice, US House of Representatives Committee on the Judiciary, "Loan Guarantees: Export Credit Guarantee Programs' Long Run Costs are High," GAO/NSIAD-91-180, 19 April 1991.
Exhibit BRA-116	"OMB Circular A-11"
Exhibit BRA-117	2 U.S.C § 661 *et seq.*
Exhibit BRA-118	Federal Accounting Standards Advisory Board, "Statement of Federal Financial Accounting Standards N° 19, Technical Amendments to Accounting Standards for Direct Loans and Loan Gurantees" in STATEMENT OF FEDERAL FINANCIAL ACCOUNTING STANDARDS N° 2, March 2001.
Exhibit BRA-119	US Federal Reform Act of 1990, adopted as Public Law 101-508, 5 November 1990
Exhibit BRA-120	GAO, Report to the Director, Office of Management and Budget, "Credit Reform: Review of OMB's Credit Subsidy Model," GAO/AIMD-97-145, August 1997.
Exhibit BRA-121	US General Accounting Office, Report to Congressional Committees, "Credit Reform: US Needs Better Method for Estimating Cost of Foreign Loans and Guarantees," GAO/NSIAD/GGD-95-31, December 1994.

Exhibit BRA-122	Federal Accounting Standards Advisory Board, Statement of Federal Financial Accounting Standards N° 18, "Amendments to Accounting Standards for Direct Loans and Loan Guarantees" in STATEMENT OF FEDERAL FINANCIAL ACCOUNTING STANDARDS N°2, May 2000.
Exhibit BRA-123	Congressional Budget Office, "Budgeting for Administrative Costs under Credit Reform." January 1992.
Exhibit BRA-124	Ashoka Mody and Dilip K. Patro, "Valuing and Accounting for Loan Guarantees," 11 WORLD BANK RESEARCH OBSERVER, February 1996.
Exhibit BRA-125	US Budget for FY 1994
Exhibit BRA-126	US Budget for FY 1995
Exhibit BRA-127	US Budget for FY 2004
Exhibit BRA-128	*www.europa.eu.int*, http://mkaccdb.eu.int/miti/dsu
Exhibit BRA-129	"USDA Issues $ 50 Million in Payments for 2002 Crop Cottonseed Program", USDA News Release, 5 June 2003.
Exhibit BRA-130	"Farm Program Payments and the Economic Viability of Production Agriculture," A Report to the US Congress, August 2002, ERS, USDA.
Exhibit BRA-131	"The Effects of the 1996 Farm Bill on Feed and Food Grains", Vincent H. Smith/ Joseph W. Glauber, Trade Research Center, Policy Issues paper N° 3.
Exhibit BRA-132	Fruits, Nuts and Vegetables Share of Total Farm Income
Exhibit BRA-133	Guaranteed Loan Subsidy and Administrative Cost Chart
Exhibit BRA-134	Brazil's Questions to the United States Concerning the support to upland cotton decided in MY 1992
Exhibit BRA-135	Agricultural Assistance Act of 2003, in P.L. 108-7
Exhibit BRA-136	P.L. 106-113
Exhibit BRA-137	P.L. 106-224
Exhibit BRA-138	P.L. 107-25
Exhibit BRA-139	68 Federal Register 20331, 20331-20332
Exhibit BRA-140	Pindyck, Robert S. and Rubinfeld, Daniel L., Microeconomics, 5 Edition (2002), Prentice hall, New Jersey
Exhibit BRA-141	7 U.S.C. 5622
Exhibit BRA-142	Agricultural Outlook, USDA, May 2002
Exhibit BRA-143	Agricultural Statistics 2003, USDA
Exhibit BRA-144	G/AG/R/31

Exhibit BRA-145	US and State Farm Income Data, (United States and States 1997-2001), USDA
Exhibit BRA-146	Acreage, NASS, 28 June 2002
Exhibit BRA-147	Estimate of Support Granted by Commodity via Counter-Cyclical Payments. Agricultural Prices
Exhibit BRA-148	Statement of Administrative Action
Exhibit BRA-149	Agricultural Outlook, USDA, August 2002
Exhibit BRA-150	G/AG/N/USA/10
Exhibit BRA-151	"US Export Credit Guarantee Programs: What Every Importer Should Know About the GSM-102 and GSM-103 Programs", USDA, November 1996.
Exhibit BRA-152	GAO, Statement of Allan I. Mendelowitz, Director, Trade, Energy and Finance Issues, National security and International Affairs Division, before the Task Force on Urgent Fiscal Issues of the Committee on Budget of the US House of Representatives, "Status Report on GAO's Reviews of the Targeted Export Assistance Program, the Export Enhancement Program, and the GSM 102/103 Export Credit Guarantee Programs," GAO/T-NSIAD-90-53, 28 June 1990.
Exhibit BRA-153	US Department of Agriculture Office of Inspector General Financial and IT Operations Audit Report of the Commodity Credit Corporation's Financial Statements for Fiscal Year 2000, Audit Report N° 06401-14-FM, June 2001
Exhibit BRA-154	US Department of Agriculture Office of Inspector General Great Plains Region Audit Report of the Commodity Credit Corporation's Financial Statements for Fiscal Year 2001, Audit Report N° 06401-4-KC, February 2002.
Exhibit BRA-155	US Department of Agriculture Foreign Agricultural Service, "Notice to GSM – 102 and GSM – 103 Program Participants", 24 September 2002
Exhibit BRA-156	US Export-Import Bank, "Comparison of Major Features of Programs Offered by Ex-Im Bank and Commodity Credit Corporation for Support of Bulk Agricultural Commodities"
Exhibit BRA-157	US General Accounting Office, Report to the Chairman, Task Force on Urgent Fiscal Issues, Committee on the Budget, House of Representatives, "International Trade: Iraq's Participation in US Agricultural Export Programs", GAO/NSIAD-91-76, November 1990

Exhibit BRA-158	US Department of Agriculture, Office of Inspector General, Financial and IT Operations Audit Report, "Commodity Credit Corporation's Financial Statement for Fiscal Year 2002", Audit Report N° 06401-15-FM, December 2002
Exhibit BRA-159	US General Accounting Office, Report to Congressional Requesters, "Loan Guarantees: Export Credit Guarantees Programs' Costs are High", GAO/GGD-93-45, December 1992
Exhibit BRA-160	US Department of Agriculture, Office of the Chief Financial Officer, Credit, Travel, and Accounting Division, "Agriculture Financial Standards Manual (May 2003)
Exhibit BRA-161	US Federal Accounting Standards Advisory Board, Federal Financial Accounting and Auditing Technical Release 3, "Preparing and Auditing Direct Loan and Loan Guarantee Subsidies under the Federal Credit Reform Act", 31 July 1999.
Exhibit BRA-162	Government – Wide Audited Financial Statements Task Force on Credit Reform, "Issue Paper, Model Credit Program Methods and Documentation for Estimating Subsidy Rates and the Model Information Store", 96-CR-7, 1 May 1996
Exhibit BRA-163	Office of Management and Budget Annual Training, Introduction to Federal Credit Budgeting, 24 June 2002
Exhibit BRA-164	US Department of Agriculture, Foreign Agricultural Service, "Revised FY 2001 and FY 2002 Annual Performance Plan".
Exhibit BRA-165	US Department of Agriculture, Foreign Agricultural Service, "Revised FY 2000 and FY 2001 Annual Performance Plan".
Exhibit BRA-166	US Department of Agriculture Foreign Agricultural Service, News Releases regarding extension of GSM 102 and GSM 103 guarantees to Dominican Republic, Morocco, Ghana, South Korea, Vietnam and Algeria
Exhibit BRA-167	12 Steps to Participating in the USDA Supplier Credit Guarantee Program, Step 5.
Exhibit BRA-168	US Department of Agriculture Foreign Agricultural Service, News Releases regarding extension of SCGP guarantees to Tunisia, Azerbaijan, Vietnam, South Korea, Japan and Nigeria
Exhibit BRA-169	Market Revenue and US Government Payments to US Upland Cotton Producers

Exhibit BRA-170	PFC, MLA, DP and CCP Payments per Base Acre of Covered Crops
Exhibit BRA-171	"Counter-Cyclical Payments under the 2002 Farm Bill," NCC, August 2003
Exhibit BRA-172	Rice Outlook, USDA, 13 August 2003, Table 1
Exhibit BRA-173	Revised Estimate of Support Granted by Commodity via Countercyclical Payments.
Exhibit BRA-174	"Income Protection – Cotton Crop Provisions," USDA Federal Crop Insurance Corporation, 2000-321
Exhibit BRA-175	"Cotton Crop Provisions," USDA Federal Crop Insurance Corporation, 99-021
Exhibit BRA-176	"Course Grain Crop Provisions," USDA Federal Crop Insurance Corporation, 98-041
Exhibit BRA-177	"ERS Briefing Room: Farm Income and Costs: Farm Income Forecasts"
Exhibit BRA-178	"Facts About Texas and Agriculture," Texas Cooperative Extension, The Texas A&M University System
Exhibit BRA-179	JunJie Wu, "Crop Insurance, Acreage Decisions, and Nonpoint-Source Pollution," American Journal of Agricultural Economics 81, May 1999
Exhibit BRA-180	Keith J. Collins and Joseph W. Glauber "Will Policy Changes Usher in a New Era of Increased Agricultural Market Variability?," Second Quarter 1998.
Exhibit BRA-181	US General Accounting Office, Report to the Ranking Minority Member, Committee on Agriculture, Nutrition and Forestry, US Senate, *Former Soviet Union: Creditworthiness of Successor States and US Export Credit Guarantees*, GAO/GGD-95-60 (February 1995)
Exhibit BRA-182	2004 US Budget, Federal Credit Supplement, Table 8
Exhibit BRA-183	US Budget for FY 1992
Exhibit BRA-184	US Budget for FY 1993
Exhibit BRA-185	Congressional Budget Office Staff Memorandum, *An Explanation of the Budgetary Changes Under Credit Reform*, April 1991
Exhibit BRA-186	Congressional Research Service Issue Brief for Congress, *Agriculture and the Budget*, IB95031, (16 February 1996)
Exhibit BRA-187	O.A. Cleveland Newsletter, 25 April 2003; O.A. Cleveland Newsletter, 8 August 2003

Exhibit BRA-188	Testimony of James Echols, Chairman of the National Cotton Council before the Committee on Agriculture, Nutrition and Forestry of the US Senate, 17 July 2001
Exhibit BRA-189	Cotton and Wool Outlook, USDA, 13 August 2003
Exhibit BRA-190	Affidavit of Marcelo Pinheiro Franco
Exhibit BRA-191	G/AG/AGST/USA
Exhibit BRA-192	Reestimated Guaranteed Loan Subsidy based on Original Budget Year Estimate.
Exhibit BRA-193	Net Lifetime Reestimates of Guaranteed Loan Subsidy by Cohort.
Exhibit BRA-194	US Department of Agriculture Office of Inspector General Great Plains Region Audit Report, Commodity Credit Corporation's Financial Statements for Fiscal Year 2001, Audit Report N° 06401-4-KC, February 2002
Exhibit BRA-195	US Department of Agriculture Office of Inspector General Financial and IT Operations Audit Report, Audit Report N° 06401-14-FM, Commodity Credit Corporation's Financial Statements for Fiscal Year 2000, June 2001
Exhibit BRA-196	US Department of Agriculture Office of Inspector General Financial and IT Operations Audit Report, US Department of Agriculture Consolidated Financial Statements for Fiscal Year 1999, Report N° 50401-35-FM, February 2000
Exhibit BRA-197	http://www.nedcor.co.uk/forfait-website/forfaiting.htm
Exhibit BRA-198	Vincent Whittaker, "The Quick Buck, International Finance and Forfaiting," 23 *Thomas Jefferson Law Review* (Spring 2001)
Exhibit BRA-199	Trade and Forfaiting Review, *"Argentina Trade Finance to the Rescue"* Volume 6, Issue 9 July/August 2003
Exhibit BRA-200	Congressional Record 107 Congress
Exhibit BRA-201	Newspaper Articles on the Impact of Cotton Subsidies to African Countries
Exhibit BRA-202	Agricultural Outlook Tables, USDA, August 2003
Exhibit BRA-203	"US and World Agricultural Outlook," FAPRI, January 2003
Exhibit BRA-204	"USDA's Cotton Classification Overview"
Exhibit BRA-205	Cost and Revenues of US Upland Cotton Producers
Exhibit BRA-206	Data on Article 6.3(d) Claim
Exhibit BRA-207	Cotton Lint: International Prices & Brazilian Prices
Exhibit BRA-208	"Cotton: World Statistics," ICAC, September 2003
Exhibit BRA-209	Yearly A-Index Prices

Exhibit BRA-210	"Production and Trade Policies Affecting the Cotton Industry," ICAC, July 2002.
Exhibit BRA-211	"The Current State of the Farm Economy and the Economic Impact of Federal Policy on Agriculture," Hearing before the House of Representatives Committee on Agriculture, 14 February 2001.
Exhibit BRA-212	"United States Dumping on Agricultural Markets," Institute for Agriculture and Trade Policy
Exhibit BRA-213	"The Impact of Exchange Rates on the US Cotton Industry," National Cotton Council, 10 September 2001.
Exhibit BRA-214	"Exchange Rate Indexes & US Ag. Trade," USDA Agricultural Outlook, January-February 2001.
Exhibit BRA-215	Cotton Outlook, 29 August 2003
Exhibit BRA-216	US Exports of Cotton, USDA, 5 September 2003
Exhibit BRA-217	Brazilian Exports in Calendar Year 2002
Exhibit BRA-218	"Cotton's Three Step Competitiveness Plan," National Cotton Council, 10 September 2001
Exhibit BRA-219	Cotton Outlook, 4 June 1999
Exhibit BRA-220	Cotton Outlook, (26 January 2001, 8 March 2002, 21 February 2003)
Exhibit BRA-221	Calcot Cotton Capsules, 26 April 2002
Exhibit BRA-222	"Analysis of the US Commodity Loan Program with Marketing Loan Provisions," USDA, AER 801
Exhibit BRA-223	"The US Commodity Loan Program," Paul C. Westcott, Economic Research Service, USDA/ A.L. (Roy) Frederick (University of Nebraska)
Exhibit BRA-224	"Factors Affecting the US Farm Price of Upland Cotton," USDA, Cotton and Wool Situation Outlook, Special Edition, November 1998
Exhibit BRA-225	Statement of Bruce Gardner before the US House of Representatives Committee on Agriculture, 14 February 2001
Exhibit BRA-226	Price Effect of the US Marketing Loan Program (Gardner)
Exhibit BRA-227	"The House and Senate Farm Bills: A Comparative Study," Food and Agriculture Policy Research Institute, March 2002
Exhibit BRA-228	FAPRI Analysis of Stricter Payment Limitations, FAPRI, 17 June 2003; FAPRI Analysis of Stricter Payment Limitations, FAPRI, 24 June 2003

Exhibit BRA-229	"Agricultural Insurance Programs: Challenges and Lessons Learned," Jerry R. Skees, May 2000
Exhibit BRA-230	"Weekly Step 2 Certificates Values," National Cotton Council, 29 August 2003
Exhibit BRA-231	"Elimination of Cotton's Step 2 Threshold," National Cotton Council, 10 September 2001
Exhibit BRA-232	Summary of Export Credit Guarantee Program Activity, FY 2003, GSM 102 Summary, 1 August 2003
Exhibit BRA-233	"Production and Trade Policies Affecting the Cotton Industry," ICAC, September 2001
Exhibit BRA-234	"Rethinking US Agricultural Policy: Changing Course to Secure Farmer Livelihoods Worldwide," Daryll E. Ray, Daniel G. De La Torre Ugarte, Kelly J. Tiller, Agricultural Policy Analysis Center, The University of Tennessee
Exhibit BRA-235	"What is the Impact of Removing Agricultural Support," IMF World Economic Outlook 2002," Chapter II
Exhibit BRA-236	"Market Access for Developing Country Exports – Selected Issues," IMF and the World Bank, 26 September 2002
Exhibit BRA-237	"Rich Countries Should Show the Way to Trade: World Bank Urges Action to Further Open Markets to Developing Countries," World Bank, press release 2003/094/S, 27 September 2002.
Exhibit BRA-238	"Trade Distortions and Cotton Markets: Implications for Australian Cotton Producers," Cotton Research and Development Corporation, April 2001
Exhibit BRA-239	Brazilian Cotton Import Tariff
Exhibit BRA-240	International, US and Brazilian Prices
Exhibit BRA-241	Brazilian and NY Futures Prices
Exhibit BRA-242	A and B-Index Quotes from Major Producers
Exhibit BRA-243	Brazilian Export Prices
Exhibit BRA-244	"Impact of Global Cotton Markets on Rural Poverty in Benin," Nicholas Minot and Lisa Daniels, 25 April 2003
Exhibit BRA-245	World Agricultural Supply and Demand Statistics, USDA, 12 August 2003
Exhibit BRA-246	International Agreement on Olive Oil and Table Olives," Official Journal of the European Communities L214 of 4 August 1987
Exhibit BRA-247	International Commodity Agreements
Exhibit BRA-248	International Sugar Agreement of 1977
Exhibit BRA-249	Share of the World Exports Market

Exhibit BRA-250	Total Cost and Return in Various Countries
Exhibit BRA-251	Market Reports
Exhibit BRA-252	"Counter-Cyclical Payments under the 2002 Farm Bill," National Cotton Council, September 2003
Exhibit BRA-253	Cotton and Wool Outlook USDA, 9 February 2001
Exhibit BRA-254	Monthly US Spot Market Prices
Exhibit BRA-255	"Farm Commodity Programs: A Short Primer," Congressional Research Service
Exhibit BRA-256	"Agriculture Policy and Farm Bill Briefing Book," Congressional Research Service
Exhibit BRA-257	"Cost of Farm Production Up in 2003," USDA, 6 May 2003
Exhibit BRA-258	"Loan Deficiency Payments and Price Support Cumulative Activity As of 8/27/2003," USDA, 1 September2003.
Exhibit BRA-259	Newspaper Articles
Exhibit BRA-260	"2002 US Farm Bill: An Australian Perspective on Its Impact," ABARE, Australian Commodities, Vol.9 N°2, June 2002
Exhibit BRA-261	"Lower US Cotton Consumption May Undermine Cotton Subsidies," 2002 Ag Perspectives, John Baize, 23 January 2003.
Exhibit BRA-262	"The Future of Brazil's Agricultural Sector," USDA, Agricultural Outlook, May 1998
Exhibit BRA-263	"Argentina & Brazil Sharpen Their Competitive Edge," USDA, Agricultural Outlook, September 2001
Exhibit BRA-264	"Prejudice Caused by Industrialized Countries Subsidies to Cotton Sectors in Western and Central Africa," Louis Goreux
Exhibit BRA-265	"Cotton Sector Strategies in West and Central Africa," World Bank Policy Research Working Paper 2867, July 2002.
Exhibit BRA-266	TN/AG/GEN/4
Exhibit BRA-267	TN/AG/GEN/6
Exhibit BRA-268	WT/GC/W/511
Exhibit BRA-269	"Gross Domestic Product by Industry for 1999-2001," Robert J. McCahill and Brian C. Moyer; November 2002
Exhibit BRA-270	Statement to Commission on the Application of Payment Limits to Agriculture, Mark Lange, National Cotton Council, 17 June 2003

Exhibit BRA-271	Analysis of the Market Value of Livestock in Adjusted Gross Revenue Insurance Pilot States and Counties.
Exhibit BRA-272	Fact Sheet: Adjusted Gross Revenue, Risk Management Agency, USDA, February 2003
Exhibit BRA-273	Data on US Price vs Planted Acreage
Exhibit BRA-274	Data on World Price, Production & Consumption
Exhibit BRA-275	"US Cotton Supply Response under the 2002 Farm Act," Paul Westcott and Leslie Meyer, USDA, 21 February 2003
Exhibit BRA-276	Report of the Commission on the Application of Payment Limitations for Agriculture, August 2003.
Exhibit BRA-277	World Market Share Documents
Exhibit BRA-278	O.A. Cleveland's Newsletter, 26 September 2003
Exhibit BRA-279	Statement by Professor Daniel Sumner
Exhibit BRA-280	"Brief Review of Empirical Assessments of Production Impacts of US Upland Cotton Subsidies" by Professor Daniel Sumner.
Exhibit BRA-281	Statement by Andrew Macdonald
Exhibit BRA-282	"About the Liverpool Cotton Association," The Liverpool Cotton Association Ltd.
Exhibit BRA-283	Statement by Christopher Ward
Exhibit BRA-284	"Production and Trade Policies Affecting the Cotton Industry," ICAC, September 2003
Exhibit BRA-285	"Agriculture Fact Book 2001-2002," Chapter 3 – American Farms.
Exhibit BRA-286	Direct and Counter-Cyclical Program Contract, Form CCC-509, USDA, Commodity Credit Corporation
Exhibit BRA-287	Market Revenue and US Government Payments to US Upland Cotton Producers.
Exhibit BRA-288	"NASS to Update Acreage If Necessary," National Agricultural Statistics Service, USDA, 29 September 2003.
Exhibit BRA-289	7 CFR 1412.606; 7 CFR 718.102, 2003 Edition
Exhibit BRA-290	"Farmers Must File Acreage to Receive 2002 Payments," Kansan Online Ag Briefs; AFBIS Inc. Crop Watch, June 2003
Exhibit BRA-291	"Direct and Counter-Cyclical Payment Program," Farm Service Agency, USDA, April 2003.
Exhibit BRA-292	7 CFR 718.102, 2002 Edition
Exhibit BRA-293	Data for Acreage Chart
Exhibit BRA-294	"The World Fact Book – Benin," CIA.

Exhibit BRA-295	2004 US Budget, Federal Credit Supplement, Introduction and Table 2
Exhibit BRA-296	"USDA Announces $2.8 Billion in Export Credit Guarantees," FAS Press Release, 30 September 2003
Exhibit BRA-297	7 U.S.C § 5641(b)(1); 7 U.S.C. § 5622(a), (b)
Exhibit BRA-298	"USDA Amends Commodity Eligibility under Credit Guarantee Programs," FAS Press Release, 24 September 2002.
Exhibit BRA-299	"Summary of FY 2003 Export Credit Guarantee Program Activity," USDA, Covering GSM-102, GSM 103 and SCGP
Exhibit BRA-300	Calculation on US Rice Exports Benefiting from GSM-102, GSM-103 and SCGP.
Exhibit BRA-301	Additional Results from Professor Sumner's Model.
Exhibit BRA-302	Revised and Extended Data on Article 6.3(d) Claim.
Exhibit BRA-303	John C. Beghin and Holger Matthey. "Modelling World Peanut Product Markets: A Tool for Agricultural Trade Policy Analysis." Center for Agricultural and Rural Development (CARD), May 2003.
Exhibit BRA-304	John C. Beghin, Barbara El Osta, Jay R. Cherlow, and Samarendu Mohanty. "The Cost of the US Sugar Program Revisited," Center for Agricultural and Rural Development (CARD), March 2001.
Exhibit BRA-305	Larry Salathe, J. Michael Price and David Banker. "An Analysis of the Farmer Owned Reserve Program 1977-82. American Journal of Agricultural Economics, February 1984.
Exhibit BRA-306	"Supply Response under the 1996 Farm Act and Implications for the US Field Crops Sector," Lin et al., USDA, July 2000.
Exhibit BRA-307	Change in US and World Exports in Percent.
Exhibit BRA-308	"Decoupled Payments: Household Income Transfers in Contemporary US Agriculture," ERS, Agriculture Economic Report N° 822.
Exhibit BRA-309	Barnard C., Nehring, R., Ryan, J., Collender, R. "Higher Cropland Values from Farm Program Payments: Who Gains?" Economic Research Service. USDA, Agricultural Outlook November 2001.
Exhibit BRA-310	"The Incidence of Government Payments on Agricultural Land Rents: The Challenges of Identification," Roberts, Kirwan and Hopkins, August 2003, American Journal of Agricultural Economics.

Exhibit BRA-311	Side by Side Chart of the Weekly US Adjusted World Price, the A-Index, the nearby New York Futures Price, the Average US Spot Market Price and Prices Received by US Producers from January 1996 to the present.
Exhibit BRA-312	Cotton Outlook Reports dated 7 June 2002, 27 September 2002 and 4 October 2002.
Exhibit BRA-313	Analysis of Counterfactual Retrospective Scenarios and Prospective Scenarios of Elimination of Upland Cotton Subsidies in the United States using an elaboration of the FAPRI/CARD Modeling Framework
Exhibit BRA-314	Summary of Equations in the FAPRI/CARD Modeling System as Used for the Analysis of US Cotton Subsidies
Exhibit BRA-315	Documentation for the CARD International Cotton Model.
Exhibit BRA-316	Statement of Christopher Campbell- Environmental Working Group.
Exhibit BRA-317	EWG Database: Tables of Results
Exhibit BRA-318	Discussions Held With FSA Contacts in County and State Offices.
Exhibit BRA-319	FSA-578 Manual: Report of Acreage
Exhibit BRA-320	CCC-478 Production Flexibility Contract. USDA, Commodity Credit Corporation.
Exhibit BRA-321	"Veneman Reminds Farmers to Complete DCP Sign-Up by June 2." Office of Communications News Room 460-A. USDA, 29 May 2003
Exhibit BRA-322	"Kansas City Administrative Office." Farm Service Agency, USDA.
Exhibit BRA-323	Costs and Returns of US Upland Cotton Farmers MY 1997-2002
Exhibit BRA-324	NCC Chairman's Report by Kenneth B. Hood, 24 July 2002
Exhibit BRA-325	Results of Professor Sumner's Modified Model Based on the January 2003 FAPRI Baseline
Exhibit BRA-326	Results of Professor Sumner's Modified Model
Exhibit BRA-327	Cotton Marketing Weekly, O.A. Cleveland, 7 November 2003
Exhibit BRA-328	Cotton and Wool Outlook, USDA, 14 October 2003
Exhibit BRA-329	Cotton and Wool Situation and Outlook Yearbook, Table 16, USDA, November 2002.
Exhibit BRA-330	Agricultural Exchange Rate Data Set, ERS, USDA

Exhibit BRA-331	"Description of Methodology Comparing the Analysis of US Upland Cotton Subsidies Under the January 2003 Baseline to Analysis under the November 2002 FAPRI Baseline," Daniel A. Sumner, November 2003.
Exhibit BRA-332	Newspaper Articles on the Step 2 Program
Exhibit BRA-333	Cotton: World Markets and Trade, USDA, October 2003
Exhibit BRA-334	"Additionality of Credit Guarantees for US Wheat Exports," M. Diersen et al., Agricultural Economics Report N° 377-S, July 1997
Exhibit BRA-335	Canada, Gross Domestic Product by Industry 1997-2001
Exhibit BRA-336	Section 523(b)(10), Federal Crop Insurance Act.
Exhibit BRA-337	"Crop Year Statistics," Federal Crop Insurance Corporation, As of 11 November 2003.
Exhibit BRA-338	"Adjusted Gross Revenue-Lite (AGR-Lite)," A Risk Management Agency Fact Sheet, USDA, February 2003.
Exhibit BRA-339	"Livestock Gross Margin Insurance Policy Questions and Answers," 03-LGM-Question and Answers, RMA/USDA
Exhibit BRA-340	"USDA Announces First Partial 2003-Crop Counter-Cyclical Payments," USDA Press Release, 17 October 2003
Exhibit BRA-341	"Riceland's Bell Urges Maximum Rice CCP," Delta Farm Press, 16 September 2003.
Exhibit BRA-342	Statement of Professor Daniel Sumner – 2 December 2003
Exhibit BRA-343	Response to US Statements about Access to Background Information about my US Cotton Policy Simulation Results
Exhibit BRA-344	Discussion of the US Critique of Third Party Studies of the Economic Effects of US Cotton Subsidies
Exhibit BRA-345	Response to Further US Criticisms of the Annex I Model of the Effect of US Cotton Subsidies
Exhibit BRA-346	Email Exchange between Professor Bruce Babcock and Dr. Joseph Glauber, 26 November 2003
Exhibit BRA-347	Brazilian Exports, MY 1999-2002
Exhibit BRA-348	BICO Export Commodity Aggregations (Quantities), USDA, FSA dated 27 November 2003
Exhibit BRA-349	Comparison of US and Brazilian Exports, MY 1999-2002
Exhibit BRA-350	Weekly Step 2 Certificate Values, National Cotton Council, 28 November 2003

Exhibit BRA-351	BICO Export Commodity Aggregations (Values), USDA, FSA dated 21 November 2003
Exhibit BRA-352	Value of US. Upland Cotton Exports under GSM 102 by Country and Year
Exhibit BRA-353	Cumulative Loss from Upland Cotton Production MY 1997-2002 Without US Contract Payments
Exhibit BRA-354	"Brazilian Soybeans – Can Iowa Farmers Compete?" Iowa State University, December 2000
Exhibit BRA-355	US Acreage Response to Futures Prices at Planting Time
Exhibit BRA-356	January – March Quotes of the December Futures Contract, Expected and Actual AWP and Cash Price
Exhibit BRA-357	Expected and Actual Adjusted World Price and Corresponding December Futures Price
Exhibit BRA-358	Expected Adjusted World Price and Marketing Loan Payments
Exhibit BRA-359	30 October and 25 November Cotton Futures Quotes
Exhibit BRA-360	Adjusted World Price v Nearby Futures Price (1996-present)
Exhibit BRA-361	Cotton Pricing Guide, July 2001
Exhibit BRA-362	Suspension of Anti-Dumping Duty Investigation: Cold-Rolled Flat Rolled Carbon-Quality Steel Products from the Russian Federation, Department of Commerce, 4 February 2000
Exhibit BRA-363	Global Steel Trade, Chapter 7: Avoiding Future Crises, Department of Commerce
Exhibit BRA-364	2003 US Budget, Federal Credit Supplement, Table 8
Exhibit BRA-365	2002 US Budget, Federal Credit Supplement, Table 8
Exhibit BRA-366	7 U.S.C. § 5622
Exhibit BRA-367	Section 3203 of the 2002 FSRI Act
Exhibit BRA-368	Second Statement of Christopher Campbell – Environmental Working Group, 1 December 2003
Exhibit BRA-369	Brazil's Request to the United States for Farm – Specific Planting and Base Acreage Data, 3 December 2003
Exhibit BRA-370	The Difference between the Average World Price and the Nearby December Futures Contract Price
Exhibit BRA-371	Simple Example of the Calculations of Marketing Lon Benefits (Probability Distribution)
Exhibit BRA-372	Negotiating History of Articles 6.3(c) and 6.5 of the SCM Agreement

Exhibit BRA-373	Loan Deficiency Payment and Price Support Activity as of 12/3/2003
Exhibit BRA-374	"Crop Year Statistics MY 2002" – Federal Crop Insurance Corporation
Exhibit BRA-375	Information Provided by Gerald Estur, ICAC.
Exhibit BRA-376	"About FAPRI," Center for Agricultural and Rural Development, Iowa State University
Exhibit BRA-377	"About FAPRI," Food and Agricultural Policy Research Institute at the University of Missouri.
Exhibit BRA-378	"About FAPRI," Food and Agricultural Policy Research Institute.
Exhibit BRA-379	CARD Report, 40 Anniversary Commemorative Issue
Exhibit BRA-380	"Food and Agriculture Policy Research Institute Receives USDA's Highest Honor," CARD Press Release, 9 July 2002.
Exhibit BRA-381	Jeffrey D. McDonald and Daniel A. Sumner. "The Influence of Commodity Programs on Acreage Responses to Market Price: With and Illustration concerning Rice Policy in the United States." American Journal of Agricultural Economics, (85) 4 November 2003.
Exhibit BRA-382	Cotton and Wool Outlook, USDA, 12 December 2003.
Exhibit BRA-383	Brazil and US Export Data on Export Quantities and Values by Country
Exhibit BRA-384	Import Prices from Various Countries
Exhibit BRA-385	Domestic Prices from Various Countries
Exhibit BRA-386	Brazil and US Export Prices by Country
Exhibit BRA-387	Brazil Export Prices v A-Index Prices by Country
Exhibit BRA-388	US Export Prices v A-Index Prices by Country
Exhibit BRA-389	Brazilian Domestic Price Data
Exhibit BRA-390	"Glickman Proposes Cottonseed Payment Program," USDA News Release, 29 February 2000.
Exhibit BRA-391	Cost of Ginning and Value of Cottonseed per pound of Cotton Lint
Exhibit BRA-392	"William Duvanant Says: Overproduction Thwarts Cotton price Upturn," Western Farm Press.
Exhibit BRA-393	Futures Prices as of 19 December 2003
Exhibit BRA-394	Agricultural Outlook Tables, USDA, November 2003, Table 19

Exhibit BRA-395	"Trade Issues Facing the US Cotton Industry," Speech by Dr. Mark Lange, President and CEO, National Cotton Council, 6 January 2004.
Exhibit BRA-396	"Farm Groups Shocked at UC Economist's Testimony in WTO Dispute," Western Farm Press, 2 September 2003.
Exhibit BRA-397	"Report of the Commission on the Application of Payment Limitations for Agriculture," August 2003.
Exhibit BRA-398	Western Farm Press, 7 January 2003
Exhibit BRA-399	Acreage Discrepancies.xls
Exhibit BRA-400	List of Publications of Professors Babcock and Beghin
Exhibit BRA-401	Second Declaration of Andrew Macdonald, 27 January 2004.
Exhibit BRA-402	"Genetically Engineered Cotton Suffering from Production Problems," Organic Consumers Organization, 11 January 2002.
Exhibit BRA-403	"NCC will Intensify Emphasis for Quality, Yield Answers," Western Farm Press, 3 March 2001.
Exhibit BRA-404	"Benefits - BT Cotton," Monsanto Imagine.
Exhibit BRA-405	"Sample Costs to Produce Cotton Transgenic Herbicide-Resistant Acala Variety," San Joaquin Valley, University of California Cooperative Extension, 2003.
Exhibit BRA-406	"Cotton Cost-Return Budget in Southwest Kansas," Kansas State University Agricultural Experiment Station and Cooperative Extensive Service, October 2003.
Exhibit BRA-407	Documents on Cost of Production Insurance Plan for Cotton.
Exhibit BRA-408	Export – Import Bank of the United States, Standard Repayment Terms.
Exhibit BRA-409	Ex-Im Bank Fee Schedule.
Exhibit BRA-410	Export Insurance Services.
Exhibit BRA-411	"The Federal Scoop: US Government Financing for Service Exports," Export America, May 2003.
Exhibit BRA-412	Cotton and Wool Situation Outlook and Outlook Yearbook, USDA, November 2003, Table 16.
Exhibit BRA-413	"Agricultural Cash Rents," USDA, NASS, July 1999.
Exhibit BRA-414	"Agricultural Land Values and Cash Rents," USDA, NASS, August 2003.
Exhibit BRA-415	"Agricultural Land Values," USDA, NASS, April 1999.
Exhibit BRA-416	"What is a Farm Bill?," Congressional Research Service, Report for Congress, 5 May 2001.

Exhibit BRA-417	"Commodity Program Entitlements: Deficiency Payments," USDA, May 1993.
Exhibit BRA-418	Washington Post v. United States Department of Agriculture, 943 F. Supp. 31 (D.D.C. 1996).
Exhibit BRA-419	Allocation Calculations Based on Brazil's Methodology and US Summary Data.
Exhibit BRA-420	Agricultural Outlook Tables, November 2003, Table 17.
Exhibit BRA-421	ERS Briefing Room: Farm Income and Costs: US Farm Sector Cash Receipts from Sales of Agricultural Commodities, USDA.
Exhibit BRA-422	Fruits and Tree Nuts Yearbook, USDA, October 2003, Table A-2.
Exhibit BRA-423	Vegetables and Melons Yearbook, USDA, July 2003, Table 3.
Exhibit BRA-424	Allocation Calculations Based on US Methodology and US Summary Data.
Exhibit BRA-425	Dresser Industries v United States, 596 F.2d 1231 (5th Cir. 1979)
Exhibit BRA-426	Center for Auto Safety v National Highway Traffic Safety Administration, 244 F.3d 144 (DC Cir 2001)
Exhibit BRA-427	CNA Financial Corporation v Donovan, 830 F.2d 1132 (DC Cir 1987)
Exhibit BRA-428	United States Department of Justice at al. v Reporters Committee for the Freedom of the Press et al., 489 US 749 (1989)
Exhibit BRA-429	Metadure Croporation v United States, 490 F. Supp. 1368 (S.D.N.Y. 1990)
Exhibit BRA-430	Campaign for Family Farms v Glickman, 200 F.3d 1180 (8th Cir. 2000)
Exhibit BRA-431	Comparison of US and Brazil's Cash-Basis Accounting Methodologies for Purposes of the Item (j) Analysis
Exhibit BRA-432	Congressional Budget Office, Fact Sheet, row titled "Export Credit Guarantee Program, Subsidy Account"
Exhibit BRA-433	Calculations Acreage Based Methodologies.xls' provided in electronic format
Exhibit BRA-434	Calculations Value Based Methodologies.xls' provided in electronic format

ANNEX O-2

LIST OF EXHIBITS OF THE UNITED STATES

US-1	2002 Farm Security and Rural Investment Act, Public Law 107-171, 116 Stat. 134 (13 May 2002) (Title I)
US-2	57 *Federal Register* 14,326 (20 April 1992)
US-3	7 C.F.R. Part 1413 (1 January 1993)
US-4	7 C.F.R. 1413.6 (1991 ed.)
US-5	7 U.S.C. § 1444-2 (1992 supp.)
US-6	7 C.F.R. Part 1493 (2003) (excerpts)
US-7	Organization for Economic Co-operation and Development, *The Chairman's Revised Proposal for a Sector Understanding on Export Credits for Agricultural Products*, TD/CONSENSUS(2000)25/REV4 (9 July 2002)
US-8	Cairns Group, *Negotiating Proposal on Export Competition,* JOB(02)/186 (20 November 2002)
US-9	*Negotiations on Agriculture: First Draft of Modalities for the Further Commitments*, TN/AG/W/1/Rev.1 (18 March 2003)
US-10	MERCOSUR *et al.*, *Export Credits for Agricultural Products,* G/AG/NG/W/139, G/AG/W/50 (21 March 2001)
US-11	2 U.S.C. §§ 661 *et seq.* (2003)
US-12	Examples of export credit guarantee program announcements issued pursuant to applicable program regulations (7 C.F.R. §§ 1493.10(d), 1493.400(d))
US-13	Schedule XX – United States of America, Part IV, Section II: Export subsidy reduction commitments
US-14	2002 Crop Cottonseed Regulations, 68 *Federal Register* 20,331 (25 April 2003)
US-15	Regulations to disburse the 2000 crop cottonseed payment, 65 *Federal Register* 65,718 (2 November 2000)
US-16	1999 Crop Cottonseed Program Regulations, 65 *Federal Register* 36,563 (8 June 2000)
US-17	US Department of Agriculture, Upland Cotton Fact Sheet (September 1992)
US-18	USDA budget data (MY1999 & MY2000 marketing loan payments) (*www.fsa.usda.gov/dam/BUD/estimatesbook.htm*)
US-19	Marketing Year 2002 Loan Deficiency Payment and Price Support Cumulative Activity As of 3/12/2003

US-20	Schedule of current fees paid by an exporter participating in either the GSM-102 or GSM-103 program
US-21	Recently updated program documents for the Step 2 program
US-22	The Agricultural Market Transition Act, Title I of the Federal Agriculture Improvement Act of 1996, Public Law No. 104-127 (4 April 1996)
US-23	The Production Effects of Decoupled Payments, by Dr. Joseph W. Glauber, Deputy Chief Economist, US Department of Agriculture
US-24	Calculating the Per-Unit Rate of Support, by Dr. Joseph W. Glauber, Deputy Chief Economist, US Department of Agriculture (22 August 2003)
US-25	MTN.GNG/NG5/W/170 (11 July 1990)
US-26	MTN.GNG/AG/W/1 (24 June 1991)
US-27	MTN.GNG/AG/W/1/Add.1 to Add.11 (2 August 1991)
US-28	Uruguay Round Agriculture Negotiations, Discussion Paper, Draft Text on Agriculture (12 December 1991)
US-29	Agriculture text of the Draft Final Act, MTN.TNC/W/FA (20 December 1991)
US-30	Articles 1 - 3 and the Illustrative List of Export Subsidies within the Draft SCM Agreement of the Draft Final Act, MTN.TNC/W/FA
US-31	Budget Summary GSM-102, 103 and Supplier Credit; Subsidy Estimates and Reestimates by Fiscal Year; Fiscal Years 1992 through 2004
US-32	United States Department of Agriculture, Advice of Allotment, Allotment Numbers 01-CCC-47; 02-CCC-28; 02-CCC-27; 03-CCC-26
US-33	Status of Reschedulings for CCC Export Credit Guarantee Program activity for fiscal years 1992-2002
US-34	World Trade (December 1998)
US-35	"Financial Know-How Pays Off," Journal of Commerce (14 June 1995)
US-36	Financial Times (27 January 1994)
US-37	Latin Finance, 1 June 1999, "Brazil Bounces Back," pg. S16; Trade Finance, 1 October 2002. "Forfaiters Seek Eastern Promise," No. 8, vol. 5, pg. SS7
US-38	US Department of Agriculture, Fiscal Year Actual Budgetary Expenditures by Crop Year (http://www.fsa.usda.gov/dam/BUD/bud1.htm)
US-39	US Department of Agriculture, Compliance Report for 1992 Acreage Reduction Program

US-40	US Department of Agriculture, Understanding Factors Driving World Cotton Markets is Crucial for Explaining What Affected World Cotton Prices and US Production and Exports between 1995-2002 (2003)
US-41	Foreign Agricultural Service, US Department of Agriculture, Export Credits Sales Registration Data
US-42	OMB Circular No. A-11, sections 20.5(a); 20.5(f), pages 20-19, 20-22 (July 2003)
US-43	OMB Circular No. A-11, Part 4, Instructions on Budget Execution, Section 120.1, page 120-2 (July 2003)
US-44	Marketing loan rate and A-Index prices, MY 1996-2002 (graph and data)
US-45	Harvest season futures prices at planting and US loan rate, MY1996-2002 (graph and data)
US-46	Low US Northern Europe quote and A-Index, 1999-2003 (graph and data)
US-47	US world market share, MY1995-2003 (graph and data)
US-48	Muth, J.F. "Rational Expectations and the Theory of Price Movements," Econometrica 29(1961): 315-335.
US-49	Gardner, B.L. "Futures Prices in Supply Analysis," American Journal of Agricultural Economics 58(1976):81-84.
US-50	Chavas, J.P., R.D. Pope, and R.S. Kao. "An Analysis of the Role of Futures Prices, Cash Prices and Government Programs in Acreage Response," Western Journal of Agricultural Economics 8(1983): 27-33.
US-51	Morzuch, B.J., R.D. Weaver, and P.G. Helmberger. "Wheat Acreage Supply Response Under Changing Farm Programs," American Journal of Agricultural Economics 62(1980):29-37.
US-52	Food and Agricultural Policy Research Institute. "FAPRI 2003 US Baseline Briefing Book." FAPRI-UMC Technical Data Report 04-03 (March 2003).
US-53	USDA, ERS, Decoupled Payments: Household Income Transfers in Contemporary US Agriculture, M.E. Burfisher and J. Hopkins, Eds. USDA ERS AER Number 822 (February 2003).
US-54	Anderson, C.G. "Consider 'Hedging' Strategies to Enhance Income Beyond Farm Program Payments." Texas A&M University, Extension Economics, October 2002.
US-55	Anderson, J.D., K. Coble, and C. Miller. "Protecting the Counter-Cyclical Payment on Cotton." Agricultural Economic and Policy Perspectives, Vol. 1, No. 6 (November 2002), Mississippi State University, Department of Agricultural Economics, pp. 3-4.

US-56	Sumner, D.A. "Implications of the US Farm Bill of 2002 for Agricultural Trade Negotiations," Australian Journal of Agricultural and Resource Economics 47(2003): 99-123, at 114.
US-57	Young, C.E., M.. Vandeveer, and R. Schnepf. "Production and Price Impacts of US Crop Insurance Programs," American Journal of Agricultural Economics 83(2001): 1196-1203.
US-58	Smith, V. and B. Goodwin. "Crop Insurance, Moral Hazard and Agricultural Chemical Use," American Journal of Agricultural Economics 78(1996):428-38.
US-59	Babcock, B. and D. Hennessy. "Input Demand Under Yield and Revenue Insurance," American Journal of Agricultural Economics 78(1996):416-27.
US-60	Goodwin, B. and V. Smith. "An Ex Post Evaluation of the Conservation Reserve, Federal Crop Insurance, and other Government Programs: Program Participation and Soil Erosion," Journal of Agriculture and Resource Economics 28(2003):201-216.
US-61	Food and Agricultural Policy Research Institute, Step 2 Analysis Presented to US Senate Committee on Agriculture, Nutrition and Forestry (1999).
US-62	Tokarick, S. "Measuring the Impact of Distortions in Agricultural Trade in Partial and General Equilibrium," IMF Working Paper, WP/03/110 (May 2003).
US-63	MY1996-2002 Upland Cotton Harvested Area, US and Rest of World (percent change from previous marketing year).
US-64	Lin, W., et al.. Supply Response Under the 1996 Farm Act and Implications for the US Field Crops Sector. US Department of Agriculture, Economic Research Service, Technical Bulletin No. 1888, Appendix table 21
US-65	Amount and percentage of upland cotton acreage coverage by crop insurance policy
US-66	Premiums paid by upland cotton producers
US-67	Insurance indemnity payments to upland cotton producers
US-68	New York Cotton Futures, Average Daily Closing Prices for December 2003 Contract (chart and data)
US-69	US Department of Agriculture, Economic Research Service, Cost of Production Estimates; Commodity-Weighted Exchange Rate Estimates
US-70	US and Rest of World Exports of Upland Cotton, Year-Over-Year Percent Change, 1996-2002
US-71	US Exports and Domestic Consumption of Upland Cotton, 1996-2002

US-72	US Department of Agriculture, Press Release on Adjusted World Price (18 October 2003)
US-73	Weekly Price Movements: Adjusted World Price, Liverpool A-Index, New York cotton futures, spot market price, January 1996 to present
US-74	National Agricultural Statistics Service, Planted Acreage of Selected Crops by Region and State
US-75	Chart and Table of US and Brazilian Unit Value Prices to Various Third-Country Markets
US-76	Dr. Joseph W. Glauber, US Department of Agriculture, Estimating Cotton Price Volatility
US-77	Hennessy, D. "The Production Effects of Agricultural Income Support Policies Under Uncertainty." American Journal of Agricultural Economics 80(1998):46-57.
US-78	Burfisher, M. and J. Hopkins. "Farm Payments: Decoupled Payments Increase Households' Well-Being, Not Production." Amber Waves, Vol. 1, Issue 1 (February 2003): 38-45.
US-79	Ryan, J., C. Barnard, and R. Collender. "Government Payments to Farmers Contribute to Rising Land Values." Agricultural Outlook, June-July 2001:22-26.
US-80	Barnard, C., R. Nehring, R. Ryan, and R. Collender. "Higher Cropland Value from Farm Program Payments: Who Gains?" Agricultural Outlook, November 2001:26-30.
US-81	US Department of Agriculture, National Agricultural Statistics Service: Acreage (June 1999)
US-82	Westcott, P.C. and C. E. Young. "US Farm Program Benefits: Links to Planting Decisions and Agricultural Markets," Agricultural Outlook, AGO-275, October 2000:10-14.
US-83	Young, C.E. and P.C. Westcott. "How Decoupled is US Agricultural Support for Major Crops?" American Journal of Agricultural Economics 82 (2000):762-767.
US-84	McBride, W. "Production Costs Critical to Farming Decisions." Amber Waves, Vol. 1, Issue 4 (September 2003):38-45.
US-85	Cornejo-Fernandez, Jorge and William D. McBride. "Adoption of Bioengineered Crops." Economic Research Service, US Department of Agriculture. AER-810. May 2002.
US-86	US Department of Agriculture, National Agricultural Statistics Service: Acreage (June 2003):1-3, 18, 25.
US-87	Price, G., W. Lin, J.B. Falck-Zepeda, and J. Fernandez-Cornejo. "Size and Distribution of Market Benefits from Adopting Biotech Crops." US Department of Agriculture, Economic Research Service. Technical Bulletin No. 1906, November 2003.

US-88	International Cotton Advisory Committee, "Cost of Production of Raw Cotton," M. Raffiq Chaudhry. Presented at the III Brazilian Cotton Congress, Brazil, 31 August 2001.
US-89	US Department of Agriculture, National Agricultural Statistics Service, "Usual Planting Dates and Harvesting Dates for US Field Crops." Agricultural Handbook Number 628. December 1997:1-2, 7-8.
US-90	US Department of Agriculture, Agricultural Marketing Service: Cotton Price Statistics (October 2003):18 (table 13)
US-91	Detailed Critique of Third-Party Economic Studies
US-92	Year-to-date MY2003 A-index prices, daily
US-93	US Department of Agriculture, unofficial marketing year 2002 marketing loan payments for soybeans corn, and wheat
US-94	US Department of Agriculture, Farm Services Agency, summary of marketing year 2002 enrolled direct and counter-cyclical payment base acres, upland cotton farms
US-95	Comparison of MY2002 enrolled direct and counter-cyclical payment base acres for upland cotton to NASS upland cotton planted acres
US-96	Total US upland cotton planted acreage, MY2001-2003, by state
US-97	US MY2002 upland cotton exports to Argentina, Bolivia, and Paraguay
US-98	E-mail communication from S. Tokarick, International Monetary Fund
US-99	Preparatory Committee for the World Trade Organization, *Notification Requirements and Formats Under the WTO Agreement on Agriculture*, PC/IPL/12, circulated 2 December 1994
US-100	US Notification, G/AG/N/USA/47, circulated 6 June 2003
US-101	[This exhibit number was not used.]
US-102	Excerpts from Exhibit BRA-369
US-103	US Freedom of Information Act
US-104	US Department of Agriculture, Decision under FOIA (11 April 2002)
US-105	7 C.F.R. § 1.14
US- 106	US Department of Agriculture, Farm Services Agency, FOIA Handbook (excerpts)
US-107	5 U.S.C. § 552a(b)
US-108	Excerpt of BRA-316
US-109	Description of electronic file "Pfcby.txt."
US-110	Description of electronic file "Pfcplac.txt."

US-111	Description of electronic file "Dcpby.txt"
US-112	Description of electronic file "Dcpplac.txt"
US-113	Graphical representation of scope and disclosure of Brazil's modeling system
US-114	Letter from Dr. Bruce Babcock (10 December 2003)
US-115	Electronic version of spreadsheets referenced in US Comments Concerning Brazil's Econometric Model
US-116	Electronic version of spreadsheet referenced in US Comments Concerning Brazil's Econometric Model
US-117	7 CFR §§ 1427.13 and 1427.19 (2000 ed.)
US-118	7 CFR §§ 1427.13 and 1427.19 (2003 ed.)
US-119	USDA Office of the Chief Economist, *World Agricultural Supply and Demand Estimates* (11 December 2003)
US-120	USDA, Economic Research Service, Fibers Yearbook, Appendix Table 2, Upland Cotton Supply and Use
US-121	US General Accounting Office. *Agriculture in Transition: Farmers' Use of Risk Management Strategies*. GAO/RCED-99-90. April 1999.
US-122	Total open interest for all cotton futures contracts on the New York Board of Trade for 18 December 2003
US-123	Total open interest for all cotton options contracts on the New York Board of Trade for 18 December 2003
US-124	Daily December Futures Closing Prices ($/lb) (New York Board of Trade)
US-125	Statement of Federal Financial Accounting Standards No. 18: Amendments To Accounting Standards for Direct Loans and Loan Guarantees In Statement of Federal Financial Accounting Standards No. 2, Appendix B: Schedule B, entitled "Schedule for Reconciling Loan Guarantee Liability Balances."
US-126	Calculations of "additional marketing loan facilitated revenue" realized per pound of cotton, MY 1998-2003 (partial year)
US-127	Statement of Federal Financial Accounting Standards No. 2: Accounting for Direct Loans and Loan Guarantees, issued 23 August 1993, pp. 187-267
US-128	Chart of data from 1992 to 2003 (as of 30 November 2003) for GSM 102, 103 and SCGP with respect to: (i) cumulative outstanding guarantees; (ii) claims paid; (iii) recoveries made; (iv) revenue from premiums; (v) other current revenue, including interest earned; (vi) interest charges paid; and (vii) administrative costs of running the programmes
US-129	Commodity Credit Corporation Consolidated Statement of Net Cost (Note 13) for the Fiscal Year Ended 30 September 2002

US-130	Statement of Federal Financial Accounting Concepts and Standards (May 2002), Appendix E, pages 1140-1141
US-131	Inae Riveras, Brazil's Mato Grosso to triple winter cotton area (Reuters 2004-01-20)
US-132	Chart, US Crops Cotton supply and utilization, and Baseline
US-133	O.A. Cleveland, Cotton Market Weekly, 1/16/04
US-134	Charts of US and Brazilian Export Unit Values to 7 Destinations
US-135	Production, Yield, Trade, and Stocks Data, MY99-02
US-136	USDA/FAS US trade data, MY99-03
US-137	World Trade Atlas official Brazilian trade data, MY99-03
US-138	Statement of the United States at the Dispute Settlement Body (9 January 2004) on adoption of the reports in *United States – Sunset Review of Anti-Dumping Duties on Corrosion-Resistant Carbon Steel Flat Products for Japan*
US-139	USDA Weekly Cotton Market Review 1/9/04
US-140	USDA Weekly Cotton Market Review 1/23/04
US-141	Charts of Chinese (Domestic, Import, Export) Prices vs. A-Index
US-142	NY Board of Trade, NY Cotton Exchange, 27 January 2004 futures data
US-143	Memorandum from Larry Mitchell, USDA Farm Services Agency, to Various FSA Offices, Administrators, and Divisions on Release of Restricted Information under the Freedom of Information Act (18 September 1998)
US-144	USDA Farm Services Agency, Notice INFO-16: Releasing Lists of Names and Addresses in Response to Requests Under FOIA (1 December 1998)
US-145	Contents of four corrected data files submitted on 28 January 2004
US-146	USDA, Commodity Credit Corporation, 58 *Federal Register* 15755-15756 (24 March 1993).
US-147	Data in response to Panel Question 264(a): Exhibit US-128 on a Fiscal Year/ Cash Basis
US-148	Data in response to Panel Question 264(d): Claim Payments/ Recoveries/ Reschedulings on a Fiscal Year/ Cash Basis
US-149	United States Department of the Treasury Financial Manual I TFM 2-4600 (December 2003)
US-150	"Annual Review of Fees for USDA Credit Programs,"25 March 2003 and 8 April 2002.
US-151	United States Office of Management and Budget Circular No. A-129 (November 2000), Table of Contents, General Information, Appendix A, Sections I and II.